THE

MUSICIAN'S

BUSINESS

& LEGAL

GUIDE

REVISED 2nd EDITION

REVISED
2nd
EDITION

THE
MUSICIAN'S
BUSINESS
&LEGAL
GUIDE

COMPILED AND EDITED BY

MARK HALLORAN, ESQ.

A PRESENTATION OF

THE BEVERLY HILLS

BAR ASSOCIATION

COMMITTEE FOR THE ARTS

Library of Congress Cataloging-in-Publication Data

The musician's business and legal guide/compiled and edited by Mark Halloran; introduction by
Gregory T. Victoroff. — Rev. 2nd ed.

      p.   cm.

"A Jerome Headlands Press book."

Includes bibliographical references (p.   ) and index.

ISBN 0-13-237322-X

    1. Music trade—Law and legislation—United States. 2. Musicians—Legal status, laws,
etc.—United States. 3. Music—Economic aspects—United States. 4. Copyright—
Music—United States.

    I. Halloran, Mark E.

ML3790.M85 1996

780'.23'73—dc20

95-26842
CIP
MN

Prentice-Hall, Inc.
Simon & Schuster/A Viacom Company
Upper Saddle River, NJ 07458

Designed and Produced by:
Jerome Headlands Press, Inc.
Jerome, Arizona 86331

    Design by Sullivan Scully Design Group
    Special thanks to production manager P.J. Nidecker
    Cover and still life photography by Michael Thompson
    Copyeditor George Glassman
    Index by Rebecca R. Plunkett Indexing Services

Manufactured in the United States of America

10 9 8 7 6 5 4 3 2 1

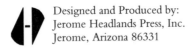

Prentice Hall International (UK) Limited, London
Prentice-Hall of Australia Pty. Limited, Sydney
Prentice-Hall Canada Inc., Toronto
Prentice-Hall Hispanoamericana, S.A., Mexico
Prentice-Hall of India Private Limited, New Delhi
Prentice-Hall of Japan, Inc., Tokyo
Simon & Schuster Asia Pte. Ltd., Singapore
Editora Prentice-Hall do Brasil, Ltda., Rio de Janeiro

Disclaimer of Liability

This publication is intended to provide accurate and authoritative information regarding the subject matter
covered. It is sold with the understanding that Jerome Headlands Press, Inc., Prentice-Hall, Inc. and the Committee for the Arts of the Beverly Hills Bar Association are not engaged in rendering legal, accounting or other
professional service. The information in this book is subject to change at any time without notice and should
not be relied upon as a substitute for professional legal advice. Neither the publisher, distributor nor the authors
make any guarantees or warranties concerning the information in this publication. If legal advice or other expert
assistance is required, the services of a competent, experienced professional person should be sought.

DEDICATION

The past five years have taken some important talent from the music world.

Musical innovators Kurt Cobain and Eric ("Easy-E") Wright were both at the forefront of important movements in popular music. Cobain's grunge rock and Easy-E's gangsta rap made bold and enlightening contributions which will endure. Both careers ended abruptly, yet deeply affected a broad spectrum of young people worldwide.

Rock and roll impresario Bill Graham was well known to many of the authors of the Guide including myself. Bill Graham was (and, with the renaming of the San Francisco Civic Auditorium, will always be), a San Francisco Bay Area institution. He was a great believer in empowering musicians, and did not hesitate to give the *Guide* his glowing endorsement.

Composer, guitarist and visionary, Frank Zappa had a profound effect on contemporary music. He transcended the musical classifications of rock, jazz, classical and avant-garde. Frank courageously acted and spoke out against corruption and hypocrisy in the music industry. He formed his own record label, exalted musical integrity, and protested and triumphed over commercialization and censorship of music.

Composer and guitarist Jerry Garcia has been described as the fulcrum behind the profound influence of the Grateful Dead. For over 25 years, his unique rock/jazz improvisations shaped the ever-changing, yet ever-constant musical caldron from which flowed the Dead's magic. Jerry Garcia provided us with a musical institution whose legend and lore will surely be celebrated for many generations to come.

It is my sincerest wish that in some small way this current edition of the Guide will help to foster the same qualities of honesty and imagination shared by Frank Zappa, East-E, Kurt Cobain, Bill Graham and Jerry Garcia. They will be with us always.

I once again thank and gratefully acknowledge all of the dedicated authors and contributors that have unselfishly donated their valuable time and expertise to the *Guide.*

Gregory T. Victoroff, Esq.
Committee for the Arts
Beverly Hills Bar Association

ACKNOWLEDGMENTS

This book was originally compiled from materials prepared for a Beverly Hills Bar Association Committee for the Arts Symposium for Musicians held in 1979. Since then, the book has been updated four times and now has a life of its own.

Initially, my thanks to Jordon Kerner and Norman Beil who started the Committee for the Arts and invited my participation.

I also wish to thank Gunnar Erickson and Ned Hearn with whom I cowrote *Musician's Guide to Copyright* for Bay Area Lawyers for the Arts in 1978. Gunnar and Ned have been terrific mentors in my career as a lawyer and as a writer.

Although I have contributed chapters and edited, this book is the sum total of the contributions of many authors. With this in mind, I thank the following authors that made contributions to prior editions: Wayne Coleman, William Dobishinski, Richard Flohil, and Marshall Gelfand.

It often takes more energy and effort to update a chapter than to write one from scratch. Thus, I offer kudos to the following authors that spent their precious time in revising their chapters for this edition: Stephen Bigger, Lawrence Blake, John Braheny, Robert Dudnik, Steven Gardner, Brad Gelfond, Ronald Gertz, Edward (Ned) Hearn, Neville Johnson, Evanne Levin, Linda Newmark, Peter Paterno, John Phillips, Diane Rapaport, Alfred Schlesinger, James Sedivy, Gregory Victoroff, and Thomas White.

The vitality of this book has been augmented by the following authors that contributed new chapters to this edition: Bartley Day, Todd Gelfand, Christopher Knab, Margaret Robley, Madeleine Seltzer, and Peter Spellman.

For their assistance with compiling and updating the Resource Directory and Selected Bibliography, I would like to thank the following individuals: Committee for the Arts volunteer, William Vu Tam Anh; Peter Spellman; Sue Tillman; and for their help on earlier versions—Marianne Borselle; Debra Graff; Harris Tulchin; and Gregory Victoroff.

Combining the styles of so many authors into one cohesive unit is always a challenge. I would like to thank our copyeditor George Glassman for his help in creating a clear and comprehensible book.

Thanks also to Julie Sullivan and P.J. Nidecker of the Sullivan Scully Design Group for designing the Guide's new, updated look.

Special thanks are due to the following people that provided assistance with sample agreements used in the book: Vincent Castellucci of the Harry Fox Agency, Inc.; Ron McGowan; and Suzy Vaughan.

This book would not exist in its current form without the help of Diane Rapaport and Sue Tillman of Jerome Headlands Press. In her role as publisher, Diane has solicited and edited the new chapters and coordinated all the revisions. Her contribution is incalculable.

Lastly, Prentice Hall has done a terrific job in distributing the book and my thanks to them.

Mark Halloran, Esq.
Editor

CONTENTS

MANAGERS AND AGENTS   263–316

RECORDING 317–413

PREFACE

by Mark Halloran, Esq.

Welcome to the revised second edition of this book. (There were also three prior editions published under the title *The Musician's Manual,* the first in 1979.) As the music business changes, we strive to keep each new edition current. We have updated the media chapters and have added six new ones: "Collaborator/Songwriter Agreements," "Contracts and Relationships Between Independent and Major Labels," "Mediation for Musicians," "Music and New Media," "Sampling: Legal Overview and Practical Guidelines," and "Using the Internet to Promote Your Music." However, the basic messages from the first edition remain constant. As a musician, at some point in your professional career, you will learn that there are legal questions implicit in almost everything you do. Whether you write, perform, or sell a song, your actions give rise to rights and obligations that you should consider. The time to learn is now.

The purpose of this book is to impart knowledge. To demystify the music business and the indecipherable body of law which shapes it. And to help you "make it" by explaining the industry and the laws that govern it.

This book is a collection of chapters written by people that work in the music industry. Many are lawyers, some are musicians. We have tried to make our information comprehensible to everyone, and have avoided presupposing a lot of knowledge on your part.

For the most part the book follows a loose chronological scheme that parallels the typical development of a musician's career. It should be noted at the outset that the particular problems of musicians working in the fine arts—symphony orchestras, ballet, and opera to name a few—are not treated here.

At this point we must present a few warnings. First, there is no substitute for obtaining competent help as you build your career. Talent agents, personal managers, lawyers and business managers are trained to guide you. Their expertise costs money, but you must think of these expenses as an investment in your career. Also, the chapters written by lawyers are designed to identify problems, not to give specific solutions. If you have a legal problem, do not rely on the information contained in this book, *see an attorney.* The chapters in this book are not the law, but merely describe legal applications, in general terms, for the music industry. Additionally, do not photocopy our forms for submittal, as many organizations require you to fill out their original forms. One final note. Although this book should be a useful tool, musicians should write music, not contracts. Unless you devote your time and energy to developing and exploiting your talent, this book doesn't matter. Make it matter.

INTRODUCTION

Eighteen years ago, a handful of idealistic and ambitious young lawyers and musicians compiled and published the first edition of *The Musician's Manual,* a product of the Committee for the Arts (CFTA) of the Barristers (young lawyers division) of the Beverly Hills Bar Association.

Today, CFTA has the same objectives: to produce an educational and informative publication relating to music and law, of lasting value to both music professionals and lawyers, and to assist in the delivery of high quality legal services to musicians, singers, songwriters, arrangers, producers and others, at a nominal cost.

Many of the original volunteer authors, now heads of movie studios, record companies and respected law firms have revised their chapters, reaffirming their dedication to the CFTA mission. New chapters have been contributed by new volunteers that are maintaining CFTA's tradition of helping to "make music" by clarifying the maze of legal formalities.

Exciting technological advances such as compact discs, direct satellite transmissions, music videos, MIDI, DAT and sampling have brought forth many new trends in music styles. Digitization and the electronic transmission of music over the Internet offer new avenues for performing and distributing music, as well as new ways to illegally exploit and pirate musical property. In such a volatile, rapidly changing industry, there is something reassuring in the publication of this new edition. This restatement of the laws that protect Americans' rights to perform their music echoes the wisdom of the founding fathers that is embodied in the U.S. Constitution, where the first American laws respecting the arts, including music, were promulgated.

In one way or another, music benefits everyone in our society. From birthdays, graduations and weddings, to inaugurations and revolutions, music helps define who we are. Yet few people ever appreciate how difficult it is for a musician, singer or songwriter to make a living working at their craft. Little attention is given to the years of study and practice, the enormous expense of musical instruments and equipment, the problems and paradoxes of auditions, showcasing and recording demo tapes, and continual rejection by music buyers.

Musicians' awareness of their legal rights helps to protect the free expression of political and social ideas as well as the musicians themselves. Many of the legal rights described in this book were not created and guaranteed out of friendship. Musicians and lawyers organized and fought for these laws. By enforcing their rights, musicians and songwriters exercise a degree of control over their individual careers and music's place in our culture.

The public interest is well served by fostering an awareness of laws governing musical endeavors. Moreover, by providing access to affordable legal information we hope to reinforce musicians' constitutional rights and protect us all from self-serving politicians that would muzzle this lyrical form of social commentary.

> *"All art constantly aspires towards the condition of music."*
> —Walter Pater (1873)

Gregory T. Victoroff
Committee for the Arts
Beverly Hills Bar Association

COMMITTEE FOR THE ARTS

From left to right: James Sedivy, Greg Victoroff, William Vu Tam Anh, Robert Dudnik, Mark Halloran, Gloria Ruiz, Matt Burrows, Ben McLean, Paul Supnik

GETTING STARTED: MUSIC AS A BUSINESS

Group Breakups

**Entertainment Group Names:
Selection And Protection**

Business Entities

How To Set Up A Money Deal

Music Attorneys

Mediation For Musicians

GROUP BREAKUPS

by Peter T. Paterno

As with a marriage, the best time to plan for a group breakup is at the outset of the relationship. Practically speaking, however, very few people are concerned with planning a breakup when things are going well. This chapter will discuss the problems that arise at the time of a breakup (or, more commonly, at the time a member of the group chooses to leave), and will describe some planning devices that can help avoid these problems.

MEET THE RUMMIES

The Rummies are a successful recording group on the White Noise label. The Rummies consist of the following four individuals:

Richie, the drummer, a former butcher who wouldn't know one chord from another, but is tough on the backbeat.

John, the bass player, a former session player with the creativity and stage presence of a cadaver.

David, a flashy lead guitarist who writes about half of the group's material.

Fred, the lead singer and occasional rhythm guitar player who writes the rest of the group's material.

THE INITIAL BREAKUP

John, the bass player decides to leave the group to become a Moonie (the religious organization, not the rock group). At this point, the group is required to notify White Noise that John has decided to leave the group (Section 2.01.2(a)(i) of Exhibit 1, Group Artist Rider).

The remaining members of the group decide to find a new bass player. After a quick search, they settle upon Floydine, a bass player for a local punk rock group. White Noise, quite concerned that this new bass player will affect the Rummies bubblegum sound, refuses to allow Floydine to join the group. The group is outraged, and wants to know what right White Noise has to keep them from letting whomever they choose join their group. Unfortunately, the Rummies have not read their contract. The contract essentially provides that White Noise has a right to veto any replacement members selected by the group (Section 2.01.2(a)(i) of Exhibit 1, Group Artist Rider). While White Noise may have been willing to give up this right in initial negotiations, the Rummies' lawyer never raised the point, and the Rummies are now paying the price.

In fact, under the provisions of the Group Artist Rider, the record company retains the right to split up the group in the event of a leaving member situation and may thereafter treat each member of the group as a leaving member (Section 2.01.2(a)(ii) of Exhibit 1, Group Artist Rider). Provisions such as these give the record company considerable leverage in a leaving member situation. They permit the record company to threaten to break up the group and keep certain members. (It should be pointed out that it is unlikely that a record company would actually try to assert this right.) In any event, some foresight by the group's lawyers would probably have resulted in the tempering of much of this language.

White Noise and the Rummies eventually agree on a replacement bass player named Craig. Craig will become bound to the terms of the Rummies' recording contract with White Noise (Section 2.01.2(a)(i) of Exhibit 1, Group Artist Rider). Although White Noise has the right to retain John's services as a solo recording artist (Section 2.01.2(b) of Exhibit 1, Group Artist Rider), it is quite satisfied, given John's distinct lack of creative talents, to let John sign with the Moonies.

CRAIG SIGNS ON

With the departure of John and the addition of Craig, the Rummies have some fairly complicated financial problems to think about. John is entitled to receive his share of the group's royalties on all albums on which he participated. In general, however, a record company will keep all royalties earned by a recording artist until such time as the artist has "paid back" all advances made to him, including any recording costs incurred by the artist in making records. Until those advances are paid back, the artist is "unrecouped." The advances are not actually returnable— i.e., the artist has no general obligation to pay them back—but the record company has the right to recoup them from any royalties earned by the artist. As a result, an artist can have significant record sales and still not receive any royalties from those sales. It might be that advances to the group and recording costs, both incurred after John's departure, will place the group in an unrecouped position with White Noise. If subsequent earnings are not ample enough to recoup these advances, the group may not have sufficient funds to pay John his share of royalties for the records on which he participated.

Craig faces the opposite side of this problem. It may be that when Craig joins the group, the Rummies' royalty account is in a seriously unrecouped position. Craig may prove to be the catalyst the band needs to obtain massive commercial success, which will lead to large royalties. Craig may feel, however, that his share of the royalties should not be used to recoup advances and recording costs in which he did not share.

The best way to handle the problems outlined above is for the group to enter into a formal partnership agreement or to incorporate. This should be done as early in the group's career as is financially possible. The partnership agreement, or, in the case of an incorporation, the bylaws or shareholders' agreement, should contain buy out and buy in provisions that provide an adequate vehicle for dealing with the legal and financial ramifications of a leaving member situation. These are sophisticated agreements, which require considerable legal expertise to prepare, and a discussion of their specific terms is beyond the scope of this article. References below to a partnership agreement will apply with equal force to a shareholders' agreement—the choice of entity (*i.e.,* partnership or corporation) will not affect the basic terms that should be in these agreements. Consult your attorney to determine which will work best for your group.

TREATMENT OF THE LEAVING MEMBER

After receiving a large advance, the Rummies spend six months in the studio recording their next album. The album is an incredible stiff. Fred believes the group is not a proper forum for exhibiting his talent and decides to leave. Once again the group notifies White Noise of the leaving member situation (Section 2.01.2(a)(i) of Exhibit 1, Group Artist Rider).

White Noise is interested in keeping Fred as a solo recording artist. It therefore exercises the leaving member option to which it is entitled under its recording contract with the Rummies (Section 2.01.2(b) of Exhibit 1, Group Artist Rider). By exercising its rights under the leaving member clause of its contract with the Rummies, White Noise will now have the exclusive right to Fred's services as a solo recording artist. Unfortunately, the terms of Fred's contract with White Noise are not very favorable to Fred. Generally, the terms of a leaving member contract will be the standard terms contained in the record company's form contract (Section 2.01.2(b) of Exhibit 1, Group Artist Rider). The number of renewal terms of that contract will usually be the number of renewal terms remaining at the time the member becomes a leaving member (Section 2.01.2(b)(1) of Exhibit 1, Group Artist Rider), no advances will be provided, the royalty rate will be significantly lower than the group's royalty rate (Section 2.01.2(b)(3) of Exhibit 1, Group Artist Rider), the recording commitment may be lower (Section 2.01.2(b)(2) of Exhibit 1, Group Artist Rider), and most deal points negotiated in the group's contract will be deleted from the leaving member's contract. Fred, who considers himself a major talent and a superstar but for White Noise's lack of support, is not pleased with this state of affairs. There are, however, several reasons for having leaving member provisions which are worse than the provisions of the group's recording contract.

Initially, the record company does not want to provide an incentive for a member to leave the group. For instance, if, instead of splitting advances and royalties three or four ways, a member could receive the same advances or royalties as the group does and keep them entirely for himself, he might be more inclined to leave the group. In addition, when a record company retains a leaving member, it often has no idea how that member will fare as a solo artist. Accordingly, it will not wish to risk as much money on or commit to record as many records with the leaving member. At the time a member leaves the group, the record company will want as few obstacles as possible standing in the way of its decision as to whether or not to retain that person, since it is taking a risk on whether the leaving member will be able to generate the same quality and chemistry with a new band as he did with the old.

Knowing these justifications does not make Fred feel any better, however. Having just left the group, he is staring at a contract that he does not feel is fit for an artist of his stature. Often, if the record company is interested enough in an artist to exercise its leaving member option, it will be interested enough to renegotiate the contract. Just incidentally, this willingness to renegotiate will arise to some extent from the record company's lack of certainty as to its rights under the leaving member clause. The effectiveness of a leaving member clause has never been tested in the courts. Also, because the clause operates by reference to a contract which was drafted to deal with a group, the clause typically suffers from ambiguities and lacunae. Moreover, the record company is desirous of coercing additional product out of the artist. The leaving member will invariably leave at a time when there are less than the customary seven or eight option LPs left for the record company to exercise. By exercising its option to retain Fred, White Noise is committing itself to Fred's new career. If White Noise is going to spend the time and money necessary to develop Fred as a solo artist, it will want to be assured of receiving the maximum amount of product in return for its commitment. In any event, White Noise will probably elect to renegotiate. However, since the terms of the leaving member contract are so onerous, Fred will likely be renegotiating from a position of weakness, unless the amount of product he owes White Noise at the time of his departure is quite small (e.g., if there are only one or two LPs left in the Rummies' contract).

Another problem Fred faces arises from the fact that, because of the group's disastrous last album, the Rummies are, when Fred leaves, in a seriously unrecouped position. White Noise may try to recoup the Rummies' deficit position from Fred's earnings as a solo artist. Thus, if Fred is quite successful, and the Rummies fade, Fred's initial platinum album may go entirely towards paying off the Rummies' unrecouped royalty account.

If White Noise retains the right to recoup the Rummies' deficit from Fred's royalties as a solo artist (this is known in the record industry as cross-collateralization), Fred would have been much better off if White Noise had dropped him and let him sign with another record company. White Noise would then have had no right of recoupment against Fred's subsequent royalties (since the royalties would have been earned with another record company) and would have been left solely with the Rummies' earnings to recoup the Rummies' deficit balance. At best, Fred should be treated by White Noise as a new artist who has signed a new contract and should be given a fresh start and a fresh, zero-balance royalty account. At worst, Fred should be responsible for no more than his pro rata share of any deficit incurred by the Rummies. To the extent that Fred's earnings are used to

---

SUMMARY OF CRITICAL LEAVING MEMBER ISSUES TO BE SETTLED BY AGREEMENT

The method of orderly withdrawal of old members from and addition of new members to a group should be spelled out.

The equitable division of advances and royalties among old and new members, with an eye towards the recoupment problems discussed above, must be delineated.

Who owns the group name?

What happens at the complete breakup and dissolution of the group?

Language that may provide the record company with an absolute veto power in the selection of replacement members should be avoided, if possible.

Provisions that may provide the record company the unfettered right, in a leaving member situation, to break up the group and treat all the members as leaving members should be avoided, if possible.

Provisions that may allow the record company to cross-collateralize advances and charges under the particular recording contract against charges and advances under other agreements between the record company and the group or its members can (hopefully) be written more favorably for the group.

Unfavorable provisions (e.g., lower royalty rates, smaller advances and reduced recording commitment) in the leaving member's contract must be discussed.

pay the Rummies' deficit balance, Fred should later be credited with any royalties the Rummies do manage to accumulate. It should be noted, however, that the group has an interest in whether or not Fred's earnings can be used to recoup their deficit. Since Fred received his share of the group's advances and recording costs, the group might be justified in requesting some recoupment out of Fred's earnings.

There is a familiar solution to the problems a leaving member will face in his contractual relations with the record company that retains his services as a recording artist—proper planning by the group and its lawyer. In many record contract negotiations, the leaving member provisions of the contract are given short shrift. More attention should be paid to these provisions, and to the extent that the group is able, it should attempt to make the leaving member provisions as favorable to the group as possible. Not only will this provide a leaving member with better contract terms if he is forced to perform under the leaving member clause, but it will also provide the leaving member with a stronger bargaining position in the event of a renegotiation.

The financial problems of a leaving member situation can be minimized through preplanning. The cross-collateralization problem discussed above can probably be satisfactorily resolved in initial negotiations for the group's record contract. Intragroup problems of recoupment should be dealt with in the group's partnership agreement.

UP FROM THE ASHES

The Rummies, sans Fred, decide to continue on as a power trio. A little later, Richie is reading the trades when he notices that a group called "John and the Rummies" is playing revival meetings throughout the Midwest. After a little research, the group discovers that John has gone back to playing music and is actively seeking a recording contract. The group is disturbed by this development since John is doing a lot of their old hits and the public believes that John and the Rummies is the same group as the Rummies. White Noise is also quite concerned, since it does not want a group on a competing label using the Rummies' name and possibly hurting the Rummies' sales. Many record companies have provisions in their contracts preventing leaving members from using the group name as long as any members of the group are still under contract to the record company. Unfortunately, the same lawyer who negotiated the Rummies' contract with White Noise originally drafted the White Noise recording agreement form, and did not cover this point.

White Noise and the Rummies file suit against John to keep him from using the Rummies' name, but, given the absence of any clearly defined rights regarding the group name, the lawsuit will be over at about the same time the Electric Prunes have their next hit. The entire problem could have been avoided, however, if the group had included provisions dealing with the ownership of the group name in their partnership agreement.

DOWN FOR THE COUNT

David discovers that his dog loves Richie more than it loves him. He cannot stand the competition and decides to leave the group. White Noise Records exercises its leaving member option and keeps David as a recording artist (Section 2.01.2(b) of Exhibit 1, Group Artist Rider). However, White Noise decides that its mail room staff has more talent than the remaining members of the Rummies, and it decides to drop the group (Section 2.01.2(a)(ii) of Exhibit 1, Group Artist Rider). Richie and Craig realize they have no future as rock and roll stars and decide to join the A&R department at White

Noise Records. However, the group has pending litigation against John, payments to make on the group bus, a lawsuit from a Bakersfield promoter on a concert for which they did not show, and a large quantity of equipment which Richie, David and Craig all think they own. David consults his lawyer at Pig, Pork, Swine & Razorback regarding the impending lawsuit over these items and asks how he can avoid some of these problems in his new group. After discussing David's situation, the lawyer sits down and prepares a draft of a partnership agreement which resolves the critical issues. Now, with all his bases covered, David lies in bed, safe and secure. He reads his partnership agreement and the leaving member clause of his contract with White Noise, and dreams of the day when his new group can break up.

GROUP ARTIST RIDER

Author's note: This "rider" is commonly appended to recording contracts or incorporated into the contract. See contract provision 15 in the chapter "Analysis of a Recording Contract."

GROUP ARTIST RIDER annexed to and made part of the agreement dated _____ between _____ (name of record company) and the _____ (name of Artist or group).

The provisions of this Rider shall be deemed to be part of the aforesaid (recording) agreement. To the extent that anything in said agreement is inconsistent with any provisions of this Rider, the latter shall govern. Numerical designations in this rider refer to the related provisions of the aforesaid agreement.

2.01.1 (a) The Artist's obligations under this agreement are joint and several and all references herein to the "Artist" shall include all members of the group inclusively and each member of the group individually, unless otherwise specified.
(b) Notwithstanding any change in the membership of the group, _____ (name of record company) shall continue to have the right to remit all payments under this agreement in the name of the (name of Artist/group).

2.01.2 (a) If any member of the Artist shall cease to perform as a member of the group:
(i) You shall promptly notify _____ (name of record company) thereof and such leaving member shall be replaced by a new member, if you and _____ (name of record company) so agree. Such new member shall thereafter be deemed substituted as a party to this agreement in the place of such leaving member and, by performing hereunder, shall automatically be bound by all the terms and conditions of this agreement. Upon _____ (name of record company)'s request, you will cause any such new member to execute and deliver to _____ (name of record company) such documents as _____ (name of record company), in its judgment, may deem necessary or advisable to effectuate the foregoing sentence. Thereafter, you shall have no further obligation to furnish the services of the leaving member for performances hereunder, but you (and such leaving member individually) shall continue to be bound by the other provisions of this agreement, including, without limitation, subparagraph 2.01.2(b) below.
(ii) Notwithstanding anything to the contrary contained herein, _____ (name of record company) shall have the right to terminate the term of this agreement with respect to the remaining members of the Artist by written notice given to you at any time prior to the expiration of ninety (90) days after _____ (name of record company)'s receipt of your said notice to _____ (name of record company). In the event of such termination, all members of the Artist shall be deemed leaving members as of the date of such termination notice, and paragraph 2.01.2(b) hereof shall be applicable to all of them, collectively or individually, as _____ (name of record company) shall elect.

(b) _____ (Name of record company) shall have, and you and the Artist hereby grant to _____ (name of record company), an option to engage the exclusive services of such leaving member as a recording artist ("Leaving Member Option"). Such Leaving Member Option may be exercised by _____ (name of record company) by notice to such leaving member at any time prior to the expiration of ninety (90) days after the date of: (1) _____ (name of record company)'s receipt of your notice provided for in section 2.01.2(a)(i), or (2) _____ (name of record company)'s termination notice pursuant to section 2.01.2(a)(ii), as the case may be. If _____ (name of record company) exercises such Option, the leaving member concerned shall be deemed to have executed _____ (name of record company)'s then current standard form of term recording agreement for the services of an individual artist containing the following provisions:

(i) A term consisting of an initial period of one year commencing on the date of _____ (name of record company)'s exercise of such Leaving Member Option, which term may be extended by _____ (name of record company), at its election exercisable in the manner provided in paragraph 1.01, for the same number of additional periods as the number of option periods, if any, remaining pursuant to paragraph 1.02 at the time of _____ (name of record company)'s exercise of the Leaving Member Option;

(ii) A Minimum Recording Commitment, for each Contract Period of such term, of *two (2)* satisfactory Sides, or their equivalent; and

(iii) A basic royalty at the rate of *five percent (5%)* in respect of phonograph records embodying performances recorded during such term.

_____

(NAME OF RECORD COMPANY), A DIVISION OF

_____

(NAME OF RECORD COMPANY), INC.

_____

BY

_____

(NAME OF ARTIST OR GROUP)

_____

BY

ENTERTAINMENT GROUP NAMES: SELECTION AND PROTECTION

by Stephen Bigger

The first rule in selecting a name for an entertainment group is a simple one: *Be original*. It can, however, be quite difficult to put this rule into practice, since the field is very crowded. A brief check of a trade reference such as the *Billboard International Talent & Touring Directory* shows, for example, that there are two different groups called Blur; as well as different groups called The Dixie Cups and The Dixie Kups, and Full Circle and Full Circle Band.

One reason why it is important to create an entirely original name is to avoid being sued for infringing someone else's name. Rights in a group name or a trademark usually derive from priority of use. This means that a prior group, even a small one, can successfully stop a new and more successful group from using the same name, at least in the area of the prior group's reputation. Another good reason for being original is that it will be easier to protect the name if you are the first one to use it. If you know that there is already a group called The Sledgehammers, it would be a poor choice to call your group something like The Sledgehammer Band.

SERVICE MARKS

A group name used for entertainment services is legally known as a service mark. What is the difference between a service mark and a trademark? A trademark is a brand name used for a product. A trademark can be a word, a logo design, or both together. A service mark is also a brand name, but is used for services rather than for physical goods. Can a service mark also be used as a trademark? Yes. For example, a group name can be used as a trademark for such things as T-shirts, toys, games or other merchandising items. However, use of a group name as a service mark for entertainment services will not necessarily entitle you to use the same mark as a trademark for goods. Again, in the United States, trademark and service mark rights are usually created by use and therefore, in order to create rights in a trademark for a product, it is usually necessary to use the mark by actually selling the product bearing the trademark to the public.

Although the owner of a trademark for a particular product or service generally cannot stop someone else from using the same or similar name on a completely different type of product or service, there is an exception for famous names and trademarks. It would not be a good idea to call your new group something like Pepsi-Cola, since to do so would be inviting a lawsuit from the owners of this famous name. No one would confuse a bottle of rum with a diamond ring, but the owners of the famous

Bacardi name were able to stop someone else from using that name on jewelry. Yes, there are exceptions. For example, a group called The Cadillacs is listed in the *Billboard Directory*. Still, it is not a good idea to court lawsuits by trading on someone else's famous name.

A trademark for a record label can usually coexist with the same or similar name for an entertainment group, publishing company, talent agency and so forth without problems. There is a Genesis record label and also a group by that name. It would be best, however, for a group to find a completely original name so that no confusion could exist with a record or publishing company of the same name. And, there is that famous trademark exception: if someone were to adopt the name RCA or EMI or MCA for the name of their group, you can be sure that they would quickly find themselves on the wrong end of a lawsuit brought by the owner of the famous trademark.

Likewise, the title of a song or record album can usually coexist with the same or similar name of an entertainment group, especially if the words are commonplace and the group name is not famous. Recently, for the first time, a federal court ruled on just such an issue in a case where a little-known rock band named Pump, composed of a group of singing body-builders, sued the famous Aerosmith entertainment group, trying to stop their sale of an album of the same name. At the time the lawsuit was filed, Aerosmith had already sold over one million copies of their *Pump* album in the U.S. and 600,000 copies abroad. Although the band had a federal registration for the word Pump combined with a barbell design covering entertainment services, and had played at a few local high school concerts in the New England area, the court held that the *Bigfoot* case (see below) did not apply, since no likelihood of confusion had been established between the group and the Aerosmith record album title. The attorneys for the Aerosmith group presented a number of examples where group names had peacefully coexisted, without confusion, with similar album or song titles. A song and album named *The Kiss* coexisted with the Kiss group name and the album *Rumors* (by Fleetwood Mac) coexisted with The Rumors group name. Does this mean that the little-known group named Pump could, by the same token, issue a record album titled *Aerosmith* and get away with it? Absolutely not! The extensive fame and reputation of the Aerosmith group name precludes it. In cases of this kind, where it is *not* a question of group name versus group name, but rather group name versus something else, the relative fame of the group name is an important and probably crucial factor.

Special problems may arise when a group name is going to be used with the name of a star performer. Some thought should be given as to whether the star should have any rights in the group name or should that name belong separately to the group, whether or not it continues to perform with the star. (See also the chapter "Group Breakups.")

Until recently, it was not possible to obtain a federal service mark registration (granted by the U.S. Patent and Trademark Office) for the name of an individual performer. That was changed a few years ago when Johnny Carson was able to convince the Patent Office that he was entitled to register his name, but only upon proving that the name was used together with the words "in concert" in connection with entertainment services.

A common question is whether anyone can use his or her own name as a performer, even if it may conflict with the name of someone famous. The answer is, not necessarily. If your name happens to be Neil Diamond, you would have a difficult time convincing a court that you were entitled to use that name, as a singer, in view of the likelihood of confusion with the famous Neil Diamond.

RESEARCHING THE NAME

As soon as you have selected a name for the group, and before it is used, a search should be conducted to see whether the proposed name conflicts with any prior name. As mentioned above, rights in a group name or trademark usually derive from priority of use. Therefore, if a prior group has used the same or a similar name, it is entitled to object to your use of that name, at least in the area of its reputation.

Trade references that are easily checked include the *Billboard International Talent & Touring Directory* (which has a section on performing artists), and the *Phonolog Reports*, a phonograph record directory, which is published triweekly and includes a section on pop artists.

The *Billboard Directory* is a fairly good listing of active performing groups, but it only includes those that request to be listed (by responding to an annual questionnaire) and is not necessarily complete. The *Phonolog Reports* (available at some larger record stores) lists performing artists whose records are currently being sold.

In addition, a search should be conducted through a professional searching bureau to see whether the name has been registered as a trademark or service mark with either the U.S. Patent and Trademark Office in Washington, D.C. (federal registration) or with the Secretary of State in any of the 50 states (state registration). A comprehensive search by a professional searching bureau will cover the federal trademark register, all of the state trademark registers, and common law rights (that is, trademarks and names in use but not necessarily registered) reflected in trade directories, etc. It is advisable to have the results of such a search reviewed by an attorney who is experienced in trademark law to give you some sense of the relative importance of the various references turned up in the search.

CREATING RIGHTS IN THE NAME

In the United States, rights in a group name, trademark or service mark are usually created by use and *not* by registration or any other kind of filing or claim. So, can you "reserve" a name before you use it? Yes, by filing a federal "intent to use" trademark or service mark application (see the section titled *U.S. Trademark Registration*).

Reserving a name for incorporation with the Secretary of State of your particular state, or filing a fictitious business name statement will not create any rights in the name that you can enforce against the first commercial user of the same or a similar name.

The United States is a common law jurisdiction where you acquire trademark rights by using the mark, quite apart from any statutory registration procedure. In several European and Latin American countries, however, trademark rights are created solely by registration. The U.S. system is designed to protect the person who has created some reputation in a name by using it even if he or she cannot afford to register the name. This positive aspect, whereby prior users cannot lose their rights as long as they continue to use the name, despite any subsequent user who may be bigger or more famous, also includes a definite element of uncertainty. Even if you conduct an extensive search, you cannot be absolutely certain that you are not infringing on the rights of some prior group that may be performing in some backwater. There is nothing you can do to dislodge the rights of such a group, provided that they continue to use the name and maintain some kind of public reputation.

If you search the name you wish to use and find another group with the same or a similar name you have two choices: (l) use a different name or (2) try to buy out the rights to the name from the prior group. Do not ignore the rights of the prior group, even if you are about to sign a big recording contract and they have never recorded their music. To try to "roll over" a prior, relatively unknown, group because you are bigger, more famous, or better financed, could be a fatal mistake.

What if you discover that there was a prior group of the same or similar name, but they are no longer performing? Do they still have any rights in the name? That depends on the circumstances. If the prior group still has some kind of "residual reputation," even though they are not currently performing, it could be very dangerous to go ahead and use the name without coming to terms with them, either by obtaining their permission to use the name or (preferably) an assignment of their rights. Rights in a group name, like other property rights, can be sold or transferred to someone else, even though such rights are not physical property.

In a recent case involving the group name The Buckinghams, the residual reputation of a group that had been disbanded for five years was protected by the court. Although the group had not performed for that period of time, the members had no intention to abandon the name, and they continued to collect royalties from their records that were currently being sold. The Buckinghams were, therefore, entitled to stop another group from using the name, even though they had stopped performing and making records.

Territoriality

Another basic concept in trademark and service mark law is that of "territoriality." In the entertainment area, this means that it is possible for two groups to operate under the same name in different parts of the country and for each of them to own the name in its own territory. Of course, everyone wants to own his or her own group name for the entire country, if not the entire world. However, if two groups, each without knowledge of the other, independently adopt the same name, then both are entitled to use it in their respective territories. It is even possible for each of the parties to obtain a separate federal registration, with an appropriate limitation as to the area of the group's reputation. If, however, you are aware of a group in another part of the country that has the name you wish to use, then you cannot, without risking a lawsuit, use the name in the other group's territory, either by performing there, distributing records, or engaging in advertising or promotional activities for your group. Since every group hopes to be successful nationwide, and to perform and distribute records on a national basis, it makes no sense to pick a name used by another group even if it is purely local, unrecorded, and in a different part of the country. Further, if it can be shown that you were aware of the other group's name before you began use of that name, your adoption of the name was not "innocent," and a court may rule against your right to use the name even in your own territory.

Ownership of the Name

After selecting the name and searching it, the next important step in protecting the name is to decide who is going to own it and to put this decision in writing. Even if you cannot afford a lawyer, confirm your agreement in writing. This can be as simple as a signed and dated statement that says that if Tom, Dick, or Harry leaves the group, then the departing member will have no right to use the group name, which shall continue to be owned by the remaining members of the group. A simple agreement along these lines can help avoid complicated hassles and problems in the future.

Doesn't the person who thought up the name own it? No. Remember, the group name is like a brand name for a product. It identifies to the public the services provided by the group. Rights in the name are only created when it is used to create a public reputation. (With the single exception of a federal "intent to use" trademark or service mark application that must be validated by actual commercial use of the name before registration is granted.) If one member of the group thinks up the group name, that person does not, individually, own the name. Ordinarily, the entity that actually uses the name owns it, subject to some agreement to the contrary. It would be possible, although not usual, for some other party to own the group name, such as the manager of the group, the record company, or the financial backer. However, any such unusual ownership arrangement should be confirmed by a written agreement. If there is nothing in writing to the contrary, the general assumption is that the members of the group, as a whole, own the group name and any member or members leaving the group would have no further rights in the use of the name.

There are some interesting decisions in this area. In the *Rare Earth* case, a federal district court held that in the event of a group breakup, where the group was organized as a corporation, the faction having working corporate control would prevail in a dispute over the right to use the name. In a Michigan state court decision involving The Dramatics name, the court held that upon dissolution, where a partnership made no advanced disposition of the group name, the group name became "the property of the partners in common and belongs to each of them with a right to use it in common, but not the exclusion of the other partners." In other words, after the breakup of the group, you could have three or four different individuals calling themselves The Dramatics. Such a result seems in the interests of no one and underlines the advisability of having a written agreement, at the outset, as to the ownership of the group name.

Typically, a group starts out as a partnership and the members own the group name in common. In other words, they have the right to use the group name together, but not separately. The question of ownership can be simplified to some degree by having the members of the group form a corporation that will own the name. Then, if a federal registration is obtained in the name of the corporation, the departure of one or more members will not affect the title to the registration.

A situation that can become complicated is when a solo performer works with a group and the performer and the group use separate names. The solo performer may believe, if there is no agreement to the contrary, that he or she has some rights to the ownership of the group name. Imagine that a solo performer named Lucky Starr and a backup group called The Sledgehammers perform together. They sign their first contract with a record company, and the record company designs a composite logo for the entire performing unit including the words Lucky Starr & the Sledgehammers. Together, the solo performer and the group obtain a federal registration for the composite mark (including both names and the logo design). If the parties have a falling-out, you can imagine how difficult it will be to answer the question of who owns what. (See the chapter "Group Breakups.")

On the question of ownership of the copyright in a logo design prepared, for example, by an artist hired by the record company, it would be advisable to have an agreement with the artist and the record company confirming that the ownership in the copyright for the logo design belongs to the group, or at least that the record company makes no claim to the words that are included in the logo design. Otherwise, if there is a dis-agreement between the record company and the group, the record company may claim that it owns the logo design. Generally though, the fact that the record company's artist designed the logo would not give it any ownership rights in the name, since the group owns the name in whatever form it is depicted.

U.S. TRADEMARK REGISTRATION

Although U.S. trademark rights are usually created and must be maintained by use rather than by registration, it is advisable to register a trademark. State trademark registrations are obtained from the local Secretary of State and a federal registration may be obtained at the U.S. Patent and Trademark Office in Washington, D.C. The rights conferred by federal registration are so much wider than those afforded by a state registration that normally a federal registration, which covers the entire country, would be the only registration of the group name that you would want and need.

Since the amendment of the U.S. Federal Trademark Law in 1989, it is possible to reserve a name in advance of any actual commercial use by filing an intent to use trademark or service mark application for federal registration—so long as there is a bona fide intention to use the mark on the specific goods or services covered by the application. The simple filing of such an application will create superior rights in the name, even if some other party begins later use of the same or a similar name before the applicant begins commercial use. For this reason, it is now *very* important to *search* a group name to see whether a federal application for registration might have been filed for the same or a similar name (even in the absence of any public use by the applicant), which may bar the use of a new group name. The intent to use trademark or service mark application must be validated by filing evidence of actual commercial use of the name before the registration is granted. If such evidence is not filed within four years, the application will be declared invalid.

A federal trademark or service mark registration provides very important rights in court, including the right to sue for trademark infringement in federal district court. It provides an arsenal of procedural weapons that can be used against an infringer, including extensive discovery procedures that allow you to discover the evidence and information available to the other side. Significantly, a federal registration also provides "constructive notice," so that any subsequent user of the same or a similar name is deemed to have knowledge of your rights. Someone with constructive notice cannot claim that he or she innocently adopted the name and is entitled to use it notwith-standing your prior registration. Only a federal registration entitles the owner to use the ® symbol denoting a federally registered mark.

The ™ symbol is unofficial and without any legal meaning or definition under federal or state statutes. It has been used on an optional basis to indicate a claim to trademark ownership for an unregistered trademark. Sometimes the ™ symbol is used to indicate a service mark. It is not essential to use either symbol and, in fact, their use is not especially popular in the entertainment world, except on merchandising items. However, it is advisable to use the ® symbol if you have a federally registered mark since it puts other parties on actual notice of your federal registration and may affect the question of damages (i.e., whether the damages should be counted from the beginning of the infringement or from when the infringer was notified in writing by you or your lawyer).

Registration Procedure

The procedure for obtaining a federal trademark or service mark registration begins with the filing of an application for registration with the U.S. Patent and Trademark Office in Washington, D.C. Before that application can be filed, it is necessary to have used the mark in interstate commerce (that is, commerce across state lines)—or to base the application on a bona fide intent to use the mark on the goods or services specified in the application. This requirement of use in interstate commerce for a federal application is met if there is a public performance by the group under the group name in a place that attracts an interstate clientele or where the group performance is advertised in a newspaper or publication that crosses state lines. When based on preapplication use, a federal application requires the submission of specimens showing the use of the name. Usually, this would be in the form of advertisements or promotional materials for the public performance of the group. The Patent Office *does not* accept album covers bearing the group name as specimens of use for entertainment services. This seems a very narrow view, but it has been established practice at the Patent Office for some time. (I hope, someday someone will challenge this practice by an appeal to the Trademark Trial and Appeal Board or to the courts, and win.)

If no special problems are encountered, it takes about one year to obtain a federal registration after filing the application. The application procedure has two stages. The first involves an official examination by the Patent Office for both registrability of the mark and any prior registrations for similar marks, which may be cited against the new application as barring registration. The second stage is the opposition period, during which the application is published in the *U.S. Official Gazette* (Trademark Section) and may be opposed by any party wishing to do so within 30 days following the publication date. *The U.S. Official Gazette* is issued weekly and may be ordered by writing to the Superintendent of Documents, Government Printing Office, Washington, D.C. 20402.

The cost of obtaining a federal registration (excluding special problems), is several hundred dollars, which includes official filing fees and legal fees. If an application is opposed by a determined adversary, the defense of the application is tantamount to fighting a lawsuit in federal court. This could cost several thousand dollars. The applicant, of course, has the option of defending against the opposition or withdrawing the application without incurring any additional expense.

After a federal registration is obtained, it is necessary to continue use of the name in order to preserve the validity of the registration. A federal registration may be canceled for abandonment of the name. The statute provides (effective 1996) that three years' nonuse constitutes prima facie (that is, a legally sufficient case on its face) abandonment. Further, after the fifth anniversary of the registration, it is necessary to file (within one year) an affidavit that confirms that the use of the name has been continued. An affidavit of incontestability should be filed at the same time, provided that the name has been used continuously for the past five years. This will make the registration incontestable (it cannot be canceled by someone else based on a prior registration or on a claim of prior use). Renewal of the registration is required every ten years.

Foreign Registration

Generally, you will want foreign registration for only those countries where you have, or believe you will have, some real commercial interest. Frequently, new groups will search their chosen name in the United States and Canada at the same time, and if the name is clear, file in both countries.

The United States is a member country of the Paris Convention, the Magna Carta of the international patent and trademark field. It is possible, under this convention, to file foreign applications within a six-month term following the filing of a U.S. application, claiming the priority date of the U.S. application. This can be very helpful for a group that becomes famous overnight, and is faced with infringements in other countries where others try to register the name before the group has had the opportunity to get applications on file. There are approximately 175 trademark jurisdictions in the world. The cost of registering a name as a trademark or service mark in all of these jurisdictions, without any special problems, would cost about $200,000. If there are Patent Office or third-party objections, the cost could escalate to over $300,000. Approximately 125 countries provide for the registration of service marks, which is what you really want, rather than a trademark registration. Some jurisdictions, including Ireland and India, have no provisions for the registration of service marks. However, it is expected that in the near future legislation will be approved providing for service mark registration in these countries as well.

The Latin American countries and a number of countries in Europe (France, Germany, Italy and Spain) are "first to file" countries, where trademark and service mark rights derive from registration rather than from use. In other words, the first to register the name is the one who owns it. There are exceptions for famous names (if they can be proven by evidence of local reputation), which are, under the Paris Convention, entitled to special protection even in the absence of registration.

If someone has filed for your group name, prior to you, in a first-to-file country such as France, and you try to perform or sell records in that country, the owner of the registration would be entitled to stop you from performing in France under that name, *and,* chances are, stop you from selling records bearing that group name.

Prior use is not required for filing trademark or service mark applications in most foreign countries. In Australia, Canada, and the United States, an application can be filed on the basis of either prior use or proposed use. You may reserve a name in foreign countries by filing a trademark or service mark application, even before you use the name. However, many of these countries have user requirements after registration, so that if you do not use the name within a certain period of time, your registration may be canceled for nonuse.

MINIMUM PROTECTION: DOING IT YOURSELF

Even if your group is starting out on a shoestring budget and you cannot afford a lawyer, you can still take some of the most important steps in selecting and protecting the group name.

First, you can engage in some minimal searching, which will entail little or no expense, including checking the pop artists section in the *Phonolog Reports,* which you may be able to find in a local record store. You can also check the *Billboard Directory* to see if there are names listed that are the same or similar to yours. Further, you can check *The Trademark Register,* which lists all federal registrations, by class, that are currently in force. You should check International Class 41, which covers entertainment services. *The Trademark Register* may be ordered by writing to that publication at the National Press Building, Suite 1297, Washington, D.C. 20045. Some libraries carry it as a reference work.

You can make an informal survey of people you know in entertainment to see whether they have heard of any name that is the same or similar to the one you propose to use. You could order a search report from a professional searching bureau at a cost of approximately $300 for a comprehensive search covering federal and state registrations and common law rights. It is advisable to have a trademark lawyer review such a search. Professional searching bureaus are listed in the telephone yellow pages under "Trademark Agents" or "Trademark Consultants."

After you have satisfied yourself as best you can that the use of the proposed name will not infringe on the rights of some other group, the most important thing you can do is to go ahead and use the name publicly so that you create rights in the name. Keep a careful record of the performance places, dates and publicity, so that you can, if necessary, prove that you used the name, in what territory and for how long. It is also helpful in protecting the name to use it consistently and with some continuity. If the name is unused for a period of time and you no longer have a public reputation in the name, you have lost your rights in that name.

THE LITTLE GUY PREVAILS

In the landmark *Bigfoot* case, a large tire company knew of a smaller company on the West Coast that had been using the trademark Bigfoot. They very effectively wiped out the reputation of the smaller company by blitzing the media on a nationwide basis, so that by the time they were through, Bigfoot meant only one thing to the public and that was the tire sold by the larger company. When the case came before the court, it resulted in the largest award ever given in a U.S. trademark case: over $19,000,000 in damages, in view of the deliberate infringement, by the larger company, of the smaller company's trademark rights. (In the trial court, there was a punitive damage award by the jury of $16,800,000 and an actual damage award of $2,800,000, both of which were upheld on post trial motions. However, on appeal, the higher court reduced the awards to something over $4,000,000 for punitive damages and $600,000 for actual damages.)

In a more recent decision, which cited the *Bigfoot* case, a court awarded $250,000 in damages to a little-known group called The Rubberband, which had prior use and a federal registration and had objected to a later use of the name by the well-known group, Bootsy's Rubber Band. The court noted that the later group's fame had effectively wiped out any reputation that the earlier group had, and held that the little-known group was entitled to receive all of the profits earned by the willful infringement of their name, although the newcomer was allowed to keep its name.

Another pertinent case concerned the right to use the group name Flash. A California group by that name had performed in the San Francisco Bay Area but had never recorded an album. There was also an English group called Flash, which had recorded with a major company. When the records bearing their group name were distributed in the San Francisco area, the unrecorded Bay Area group was able to stop distribution of them based on their prior use and reputation for that territory.

Finally, you can stand up for your rights once you have used the name, notwithstanding any "big" group that comes along later and tries to bluff you into discontinuing the name because they are famous and you are not. Remember the *Bigfoot* case and the *Flash* decision mentioned earlier. Do not let your group be pushed around if, in fact, you are the prior user. As the prior user, you have superior rights, at least for the area of your reputation, and you can enforce them against any subsequent user no matter how big or famous.

MAXIMUM PROTECTION

If you have just become famous and have signed a big recording contract, you will want to decide how extensively you should protect the group name by way of registration. You should focus on those foreign jurisdictions where service marks can be registered for entertainment services. The most important are Australia, the Benelux area, Brazil, Canada, Denmark, Finland, France, Germany, Great Britain, Italy, Japan, Mexico, Norway, South Africa, Spain, Sweden and Switzerland.

You can get trademark registrations in jurisdictions (such as Ireland and India), where service mark registrations are not available, to cover merchandising items like T-shirts, toys, games or whatever. Generally, however, it is not worthwhile to spend the money on trademark registrations for merchandising items unless you have a real commercial interest in merchandising the name in those jurisdictions. Many of these countries have user requirements, so that a registration is subject to cancellation after five years of nonuse (or some lesser period).

If you do intend to actively merchandise the group name, it is highly advisable to obtain trademark registrations for the merchandising items, especially in those jurisdictions where trademark rights derive from registration rather than from use. Without a trademark registration for the goods concerned, you have nothing to license to another party for manufacturing the goods and selling them in the local jurisdiction. The chapter "Merchandising Agreements" discusses this issue more fully.

You may also want to consider "defensive merchandising," registering the mark for merchandising items, simply to prevent someone else from doing so. For example, a famous performer may not wish to merchandise his or her name in order to sell T-shirts or whatever, but may be plagued by unscrupulous persons that capitalize on the name by emblazoning it on T-shirts anyway. The famous performer has two choices in these cases, ignore the infringements or try to stop them.

The most effective way of stopping infringements of this kind is to register the name for merchandising items and then license the name on a selective basis to create trademark rights in the area of most active infringements. A case in point is that of the unauthorized sale, in Great Britain, of T-shirts bearing the group name Abba. In that case, the merchandising company representing the famous Swedish group was not able to stop the sale of the T-shirts, since they were being sold by the first user, despite the fact that there was no connection with or authorization from the famous group. The English court indicated (in 1976) that the fame of the Abba name for entertainment services in Great Britain (where service marks were not yet registrable) was not enough to entitle the group or its merchandising company to prevent use of the name on T-shirts by the unauthorized party, who was the first user of the name on the goods in the jurisdiction.

Since the amendment of the U.K. Trademark Law in 1994, the registration of an entertainment group name provides a basis for stopping the unauthorized use of the name on the same kind of goods or services covered by the registration. There is also a provision in the new law that protects registered marks, which are well-known in the U.K., against use of the same name on dissimilar goods or services if such use would take unfair advantage of, or be detrimental to, the character of the well-known mark. In order to take advantage of this expanded protection, however, it is crucial to obtain a U.K. registration of the name for the goods or services for which the name has become well-known.

There is some question, by the way, whether the use of a group name on only the front (or back) of a T-shirt is, in fact, trademark use. It is better, from the standpoint of trademark protection, if the group name also appears on the neck label, indicating that it is the brand name for the shirt itself. Otherwise an infringer may be able to claim that the use of the group name on only the front of the shirt is an ornamental use (open to anyone) and not a trademark, which only the trademark owner is entitled to use or authorize. Also, adding the ™ symbol to the name on the front of the shirt (or the ® symbol if the name is federally registered as a trademark for shirts) helps to show that trademark rights are being claimed.

Finally, a maximum approach to protection of a group name should include a system to watch for infringements. There are trademark surveillance services that survey trademark journals, where applications are published for opposition purposes, which are available in something like 150 countries. Costs average $300 per year for surveillance on an international basis. In this way, you will be informed if someone in Peru or France or Sweden files to appropriate your group's name for entertainment services, merchandising items or whatever and you will have the opportunity to oppose the applications or obtain cancellation of the resulting registration before it can be used to damage or block your rights in the name in that country.

BUSINESS ENTITIES

by Edward R. Hearn

There are mainly three forms of business that can be used to organize your music business affairs. These are (1) sole proprietorship (a single self-employed individual running the business); (2) partnership (two or more self-employed people running the business); and (3) corporation (which can be owned by one or more individuals and is organized under specific state laws). Each of these forms has special features that should be examined when making a decision about how to organize your business. These features include, among others, expenses, personal liability, and taxes. You should seek professional advice to determine the best form for your particular situation before investing too much time and money in your enterprise. The cost of planning to minimize problems is *much less* than the cost of trying to cure those problems after they have materialized.

SOLE PROPRIETORSHIP

A sole proprietorship is a business conducted by one individual who is the sole owner. If you have your own business for the purpose of making money, whether by making or selling records, writing and publishing songs, operating a recording studio or performing solo, you have a proprietorship business, and this material applies to you.

A proprietorship is the simplest form of business to start because it generally requires no contracts (contracts require at least two people) and only a few special papers have to be prepared. These papers include a fictitious business name statement, commonly called a DBA ("doing business as"), which identifies you as the owner by your name and address and the name under which the proprietor is doing business. Note, however, that a DBA need only be filed if you use a name other than your own to do business. That statement must be filed with the county recorder located in your local county courthouse. After filing with the county recorder, you must publish a legal notice statement of your doing business. You can inquire at your county recorder's office to find out which local newspapers publish the notices and have the least expensive legal notice rates. Certain local governments may require the proprietor to obtain a separate business license or that license may be covered by the fictitious business name filing. Your county recorder's office can fill you in on this.

If you resell goods, you will need a resale permit issued by the appropriate tax authority. This is discussed later in this chapter in the section titled *General Obligations as a Business.*

You, as the sole proprietor, are the only one who makes decisions on how the business should operate and what its focus should be. With a proprietorship, you enjoy all the profits, but must absorb all the losses. Employees do not participate in the ownership. A proprietor who has employees must withhold income and social security taxes, unemployment, and other insurances required by state and federal law and must submit the withheld sums to the appropriate government agencies. While a proprietorship usually has fewer regulatory and record-keeping requirements than a partnership or corporation, the ones on which you *must* focus are the reports to be filed with the local, state, and federal taxing authorities. If you are going to start your own proprietorship and hire employees, be certain to contact each of those authorities to obtain the required forms and instructional booklets that tell you what to do. A good bookkeeper or accountant will be able to assist you with that part of your business. These requirements are discussed in more detail later in this chapter.

As a proprietorship, you are responsible for your acts and, in general, the acts of your employees. If, for example, you or one of your employees should injure someone in a car accident while promoting your record to radio stations, you would be responsible for compensating the injured party. A judgment against you would enable the judgment creditor (the person who won the suit and to whom you owe the money) to look to all your assets, both business and personal, to recover on the judgment.

The entire income of a proprietor, assuming there is no loss, is taxable income, while business expenses and losses are deductible from income. Proprietors, as self-employed, must file quarterly estimated income tax returns and make prepayment of anticipated taxes with the Internal Revenue Service and their state tax authorities. The estimated tax is based on a projection of expected income during your first year of business and thereafter on your prior years taxes. You should consult an accountant who has a tax orientation to assist you in these matters.

PARTNERSHIPS

Assuming that your band of one, or your one-person record or publishing company has grown to two or more people that share the profits and losses, and you plan to stay in business for a while, you now have a partnership. A partnership is defined as an association of two or more persons conducting a business on a continuing a basis as co-owners for profit. Usually, the relationship among the partners is governed by a written partnership agreement that details the rights and responsibilities of each partner. Although you do not need a written contract to be considered a partnership, obtaining a written partnership agreement is recommended. If there is no written partnership agreement, then state statutes control the relations of the partners with each other. The partners can be individuals, other partnerships, corporations, or a combination of any. Each partner contributes property, services, and/or money to the business of the partnership. Partners also may loan property, money, or services to the partnership.

General Partnership

In a partnership, each of the partners has an undivided interest in all of the partnership property. Essentially, each partner owns the assets in common with the other partners and has a duty to each of the other partners to take care of that property and not to dispose of it without the consent of the other partners.

WHEN THERE ARE NO WRITTEN PARTNERSHIP AGREEMENTS

A frequently raised issue is how to structure the business arrangements among the members of a band. Whenever two or more musicians form a band, they have formed a general partnership. While it is important to have a written agreement at some point, most struggling bands cannot afford to hire a lawyer to prepare one for them. If this is the case, it is important for the members of the band to work out answers among themselves. Communicate with each other. Seek professional help. Don't be afraid to follow your instincts on what seems fair and reasonable to you. A good issue on which to focus is to determine at what point your band should make an effort to have a written agreement. It is far less expensive to plan your business properly in the beginning than it is to resolve problems after the fact, especially if the resolution takes the form of expensive litigation. If you cannot reach an agreement, maybe that is a sign you should not be in business together.

Legal Presumptions

If the members of a band have formed a partnership by working together but do not have a written agreement, state statutes presume that certain conditions apply to the band's arrangements. These conditions are that each partner; (a) has an equal vote in the affairs of the partnership and a majority vote determines the decision of the partners; (b) owns an equal share in the assets of the partnership, which include equipment purchased by the band, the name of the band, and income; (c) shares equally in the profits and losses of the partnership; and (d) is responsible for the acts of all of the other partners performed in pursuing the partnership business. If a partner, for example, delivers the band's independently produced recording to record stores for sale and in the course of making a delivery has a car accident, then all of the partners are liable for any damages.

Leaving Members

When there is no written agreement and a partner leaves the partnership, whether willingly or at the demand of the other partners, then the band's partnership terminates automatically. The band has a responsibility to pay all of the debts of the partnership and, if necessary, sell the partnership's assets to do so. If thereafter, the remaining members of the partnership wish to continue performing as a band they may, but in effect they form a new partnership and start over again. If the band's creditors cooperate, you may be able to avoid having to liquidate the band's assets so long as the remaining band members continue paying the creditors. You need to work out with the departing members their continuing responsibility to make payments owed or to receive payments due.

Taxes

The partnership does not pay taxes on income earned by the band. Instead, the band files an informational tax return on Federal Partnership Return of Income Form 1065, wherein each partner states his or her distributive share of income or loss. Then each partner lists and adds or subtracts that share of income or loss on his or her individual tax return.

PARTNERSHIPS: CRITICAL WRITTEN AGREEMENT DECISIONS

Acquired Property

When a band acquires expensive property, such as a sound or lighting system, each of its members assumes a share of that system's cost. The partners should be aware of their payment responsibilities and what happens if somebody leaves the band. For example, will the departing member have to continue to make payment? Do the remaining members of the band have any obligation to pay the departing member for the equipment based on its market value or the money paid by the departing member, if the band is going to keep that equipment?

Name

If the band becomes well-known and its name is recognizable to a large audience, who will have the rights in the name if the band breaks up, or individual members leave the band? Partnership agreements generally state that the group, as a whole, owns the name. A provision should be included in the agreement stating that if any member leaves the group, whether voluntarily or otherwise, that member surrenders the right to use the band name, which will stay with the remaining members of the group. Any incoming member would have to acknowledge in writing that the name of the band does belong to the partnership and the new member does not own any rights in the band's name greater than the partners' interests.

The partnership agreement could provide that none of the band members may use the name if the group should completely disband, or that any one of the members could buy from the others the right to use the name at a value to be established by binding arbitration with expert testimony concerning the valuation of the band's name, for example, if the members cannot agree among themselves.

Leaving Members

Prior to signing long-term contracts such as recording or publishing agreements, the band should determine how to resolve the issues regarding the rights of departing and new band members concerning services already performed or commitments that have to be met under those agreements.

Song Rights

Can the departing member take his or her songs when they leave the group? If the songs were cowritten with remaining band members, the band can continue to use the songs and record them, as can the departing member, but each will have to report to the other that share of income earned from such usages. If the departing member is the sole author of certain compositions, that could prevent the band from recording them if they had not already been released on commercially distributed phonorecords, and from performing them if they had not been licensed to a performing rights society like BMI or ASCAP. Sometimes bands form a publishing company as part of the assets of the partnership, which will control what happens when a writer member leaves the band. Usually the band will continue to be able to use the songs as will the departing member.

Each person who is a partner may act on behalf of the partnership and that act binds all of the partners in the partnership. Each person in the partnership is liable for the business obligations of the partnership incurred by any of the partners. In other words, if your partner signs a business commitment to pay for advertising for the business, you as a partner are responsible with the other partners for making payment. On contract actions, the creditor can sue all of the partners, but cannot single out any one partner to sue exclusive of the others. A tort claim (inflicting harm on another person or property) for injuries is different. If, for example, a partner runs a car through a record store display window while delivering records in the normal course of partnership business, each partner is severally (individually) liable and the store owner could sue any individual partner or all the partners in the partnership.

The personal assets of the partners can be taken by the creditors of the business, but only after all of the partnership assets have been taken and the personal creditors of the individual partners have satisfied their claims out of the partners' personal assets. For example, the business creditors must exhaust all of the property and money of the partnership before they can look to your car, stereo, or instrument, and the person you still owe for the car, stereo, or instrument has to be paid before the business creditor can claim any of these prized items. Some states' laws will allow certain "necessary" property of the debtor to be exempt from creditors' claims, such as food and clothing.

Death or withdrawal of a partner (or some other specified event set out in a partnership agreement) will dissolve the partnership. By written agreement, however, the partners can provide that the partnership will continue despite a partner's death or withdrawal. In that case the agreement establishes distribution rules to determine how the departing partner is to be compensated (this is called a buy out) and how the partnership is to continue without the deceased or withdrawn partner.

As with a proprietorship, a partnership must file a fictitious business name statement (if all the partners' surnames are not in the partnership name) and publish a doing-business statement in a local county newspaper. You also must file a form SS-4 with the Internal Revenue Service to obtain an employer identification tax number *even if you do not employ anybody.* These forms can be obtained by calling, faxing or writing to your regional Internal Revenue Service center. The performing rights organizations, ASCAP, BMI and SESAC, ask publisher members to include their employer identification tax numbers on their membership applications. You must also secure any required local licenses and permits.

In a general partnership, all of the partners participate in the control of the business. Partners may agree among themselves to assign specific duties according to ability. Voting on business decisions may be equal, or may be weighted according to capital contribution (money and property contributed to making the partnership work), or on some other basis.

The profits, losses, and risks are shared equally among the partners unless they agree, in writing, to a different division.

At income tax time, the partnership files an informational tax return, describing losses or profits, but the partnership itself pays no taxes. Rather, the losses or profits are passed through to the individual partners for reporting on their individual tax returns (thus, a partnership is often described as a tax conduit) and again, unless the agreement provides otherwise, losses or profits are shared equally. As with a proprietorship, the partners must file quarterly returns and personal income tax prepayments.

On dissolution of the partnership, the assets of the partnership are liquidated (turned into cash) and the creditors of the partnership are paid first. The balance of the liquidated assets, if any, is distributed to the partners, first to repay loans by any of the partners to the partnership, secondly to return any money or assets contributed by the partners, and finally to the partners according to how they share profits.

Joint Venture

A joint venture is a form of business relationship consisting of an association of two or more persons, partnerships, corporations or some combination thereof, for the purpose of accomplishing a single or limited series of business transactions for profit rather than carrying on a continuous business. A venture is a partnership with respect to all the applicable rules discussed above and the terms of the relationship should be governed by a written agreement. Examples of a musical joint venture include recording a single album, producing one video, or promoting a concert.

Limited Partnership

A limited partnership functions as a financing vehicle to raise capital to fund identified business goals. It consists of a least two people, corporations, partnerships, or some combination thereof. A limited partnership requires at least one general partner, whether a person, another partnership, or a corporation, and one or more limited partners as investors. The limited partners contribute capital but take no part in the management of the business and have no liability beyond the amount of money that each contributed to the partnership. Should a limited partner become involved in the management of the business then he or she would lose this limited liability status. Generally, a limited partnership is for an established duration and must be set out in a written limited partnership agreement. State and federal securities laws that regulate investments apply to limited partnerships and a discussion of these laws is found in the chapter entitled "How to Set Up a Money Deal."

CORPORATIONS

At some point in your career, you may decide that it is time to incorporate, either because you have reached a high income level, or because you wish to protect your personal assets from the claims of your business creditors. Frequently, successful entertainers form what in the business is known as a "loan-out" corporation. In other words, you have yourself incorporated and that corporation agrees to make your services available to other parties (for example, record companies) in any particular deal.

What does it mean to be a corporation? Corporations differ substantially from proprietorships and partnerships. A corporation is an artificial, separate, legal entity recognized by state law, the formation of which is regulated by procedures established by state law. Ownership of a corporation is obtained by buying shares of stock for value. A corporation can be owned by one or more persons (including a partnership) or other corporations. A corporation can be owned privately (the stock is not traded on the stock market) or publicly (the corporation's stock is sold on the stock market and is held by the public at large).

The corporation is a separate legal entity with a life apart from the persons that own and operate it. Corporations raise capital by selling shares. The issuance of shares in the corporation is a security subject to state and, under some circumstance, federal securities laws. Like an individual or a partnership, a corporation can own, buy, or sell property in its own name, enter into contracts, borrow money, raise capital, and do the various kinds of activities that a proprietorship and partnership can do.

The corporation is governed by a board of directors elected by the shareholders. In turn, the corporation is managed by officers (such as a president and treasurer) that are employees of the corporation hired by the board of directors. In loan-out corporations, the officers and directors usually are the individuals that form the corporation and are the shareholders. If the corporation was formed by one person, then that person usually holds all of the officer positions and is the sole director.

Risks of the business are borne by the corporation. The shareholders' liabilities are limited to the amounts invested in the corporation and their share of the profits. The investments are usually evidenced by issued shares (stock).

The corporation must file annual tax returns and pay taxes on profits. After taxes, profits can be retained for operating capital or distributed to shareholders as dividends, which are taxable as income. Profits are shared among shareholders in proportion to their ownership participation. Unlike partnerships, there is no passing of profits and losses from a corporation to the individual owners of shares except in a Chapter S corporation.

With a Chapter S corporation, the shareholders get the benefits of a partnership by having profits and losses passed through to them for tax purposes, while they retain the benefit of the corporation's limited liability status. Losses passed through to the shareholders cannot exceed the amounts invested by the shareholders.

A corporation is brought into existence by filing a document known as the articles of incorporation (or charter or articles of association in some states), the filing of which, for example costs approximately $100 in California, plus a prepayment of an annual minimum franchise tax payment, currently $800. Forming a corporation, however, will cost more than this because of attorneys' fees to organize the corporation and prepare shareholder and buy/sell agreements concerning the stock issued to the shareholders. In addition, there may be local fees for permits and business licenses.

Shares of publicly held companies are generally transferable from one owner to a subsequent owner on the open market. With nonpublic corporations, there is no ready market for the shares and the shareholders have to seek out specific buyers. Also, the law often restricts the sale of shares, and requires that certain procedures, established by state and federal statutes, be followed before they can be sold. This is a complex area that requires professional counsel on securities, tax, and accounting issues and is too involved a topic to examine in this chapter. You should be aware that these are considerations that require some attention and you will need professional advice when it comes time to focus on them.

The rules that govern the operation of the corporation are known as the bylaws and these are adopted at the beginning of the life of the corporation. Generally, the officers of the corporation are empowered to operate the daily affairs of the corporation, subject to approval or disapproval by the board of directors, that in turn answers to the shareholders. The board of directors will hold periodic meetings to review the acts of the officers. The shareholders will hold periodic meetings to review the board of directors.

Voting among shareholders is based on the number of shares owned—generally one vote per share. Shareholders are sometimes divided into different classes. Some classes of shares may be nonvoting. Some corporations' bylaws provide for "cumulative" voting for the directors of the board. In other words, a shareholder can multiply the number of his or her shares (e.g. 100 out of 500) by the number of board positions (e.g. 3) and apply all of the total (300) to one candidate on the board, and thereby increase that shareholder's assurance of placing a representative on the board.

The corporation's existence is perpetual unless the shareholders vote to terminate the corporation or the corporation cannot continue financially. On dissolution, creditors, such as banks, trade creditors, employees and taxing bodies are paid first. Then shareholders receive a return of capital (that is, they get back what they paid for their shares if the dissolved corporation has sufficient funds), and finally, a distribution of profits, if any.

LIMITED LIABILITY COMPANIES (LLCS)

Over the past 20 years, a new form of business has been evolving, which has come into its own in only the past few years. It is called a "limited liability company" (LLC) and has elements of both a partnership and a corporation. This chapter provides a brief summary of LLCs, which can be advantageous for entertainers that work in a group, such as a performing and recording band. Discuss with your attorney the pros and cons of structuring your business as an LLC, instead of as a partnership or regular corporation (usually a Chapter S).

An LLC is an organization in which the owners (members) have an interest in the LLC and are parties to a contract, known as the operating agreement, which details the rights and duties of the members and acts as the guiding rules for the LLC. Some state statutes require that the operating agreement be in writing, but this can vary from state to state. Generally, a written agreement better serves the interests and needs of the members regardless of statutes.

THE CASE OF DEEP PURPLE

An example of the issues involved when a group disbands but its product still sells involved the group "Deep Purple," which had not been performing as a band for many years. Its records, however, still sold. One of the original members of that band formed a new group. None of the other members of that new group had been members of the original "Deep Purple."

This new group began to perform under the name "Deep Purple." The corporation, owned by the original members of "Deep Purple" and their management, still owned the rights to the name "Deep Purple." They sued the new "Deep Purple" to stop them from performing under that name and were awarded damages of $672,000; compensatory damages (actual damages suffered by the corporation) were $168,000 and $504,000 was for punitive damages.

Since then, the authorized "Deep Purple" has reformed, and resumed performing and recording.

There are two types of LLCs, member-managed, in which members, by statute, have the agency and authority to make management decisions; and manager-managed, in which the members are not the agents of the LLC and have the authority to make only major decisions, leaving the authority to exercise day-to-day management decisions to the managers. For the most part, bands that organize as an LLC should be member-managed.

LLCs provide limited liability (as do corporations) and the freedom to establish ownership and management relationships based on the contract of the members as in partnerships. They are treated as partnerships for tax purposes. While there are still a number of issues concerning the application of partnership tax considerations as the prevailing norm for LLCs, the overriding trend among the state and federal taxing authorities supports that approach. These elements may cause LLCs to be increasingly preferred for performing and recording groups.

The members of the LLC are not individually liable for the obligations and liabilities of the organization. This also extends to the relationships among members. While general partners, in a partnership, have an obligation to contribute to the partnership and indemnify other partners for losses and obligations incurred in carrying on the business, no such individual obligations exist for members in an LLC. Generally, the LLC will be required to indemnify a member for obligations incurred by the members in carrying on the business of the LLC. But, if the LLC does not have sufficient assets to fully indemnify the member, the member may not look to the individual assets of other members for contribution, as may a partner in a general partnership.

Under most LLC statutes, members have the right to withdraw at any time and demand payment for their interest. This right to return an interest to the LLC is similar to the rule that applies to partnerships. Some state statutes limit members' rights to withdraw or to demand that the LLC purchase their interests, unless the members have agreed otherwise. Consequently, like a partnership (or like shareholder agreements with a corporation), the operating agreement among the members of the LLC should specify the conditions under which the LLC is obligated to purchase the interests of a leaving member. The disassociation from the LLC, by a member, due to death, bankruptcy, dissolution, or some other event will cause the dissolution of the LLC unless the remaining members consent to continue the business. Structuring the operating agreement so that an LLC does not dissolve upon the disassociation by a member is especially helpful when the organization holds title to property, like advances and royalty payments under a recording agreement, which might be adversely affected by the dissolution and reformation that technically accompanies the withdrawal of a member.

It will take some years for the unanswered issues concerning LLCs to be resolved. In the interim, unless a recording and performing group has sufficient funds to deal with the cost of experimenting with the still unanswered issues regarding LLCs, most are likely to follow the more time-tested structures of partnership agreements or corporations with an eye on the possibility of converting to an LLC as more information becomes known.

The need to get professional counsel when you begin your own business cannot be stressed too strongly. Your lawyer or accountant will help you determine which form will be best for your situation and will, thereafter, monitor the operation of your business to decide whether you should switch to another form as your needs change.

LEGAL OBLIGATIONS OF EMPLOYERS AND BUSINESS

As an individual involved in the music business, you may find it necessary to hire others to work for you. If you hire employees you must satisfy certain obligations imposed on employers by state and federal laws. This section briefly identifies those obligations and others of which you should be aware. If you start your own business and hire employees, consult with an attorney or accountant, or at least with the appropriate government officials to make certain that the federal and state laws regarding wages, benefits, hours, compensation, insurance, taxes, licenses, and other matters are satisfied.

Employers' Tax Obligations

Becoming an employer imposes a host of form-filling and form-filing obligations. One of the first things an employer must do is obtain an employer identification number from the Internal Revenue Service. This number must be shown on all federal tax returns, statements, and other documents. Application for this number is made on form SS-4, which may be obtained from and filed with your local IRS office.

Generally, employers must withhold federal income and social security taxes as well as state income taxes and other state taxes from the wages they pay to their employees. Contact your nearest IRS office and the local office of your state taxing bureau to obtain the necessary information on the procedures for withholding such taxes.

The employer must have all employees complete the employee withholding allowance certificate (form W-4). If the employee had no federal income tax liability for the preceding year and anticipates no liability for the current year, the employee withholding exemption certificate form W-4E should be completed. These forms should be returned to your local IRS office. Based on the information contained in the W-4 forms and in tax tables (which should be included in the information you receive from the federal and state taxing authorities) you will be able to determine the amount of income and social security taxes to be withheld from each wage payment and the amount of the employer's matching contributions for social security taxes.

The withheld income and social security taxes are deposited along with federal tax deposit form 501 at an authorized commercial bank depository or the federal reserve bank in your area. The deposits are required on a monthly, semimonthly, or quarterly basis, depending on the amount of the tax involved. Form 941, which describes the amounts withheld, must be filed on a quarterly basis.

The employer must furnish to each employee two copies of the annual wage and tax statement form W-2 for the calendar year no later than January 31 following the end of the calendar tax year. If the service of the employee is terminated before the end of the year the W-2 form must be submitted to the employee not later than thirty days after the last payment of wages to that employee. This W-2 form is an informational one for the purpose of advising the employee how much tax money was withheld and it may be combined with state and city withholding statements. It must be used by the employee in filing annual income tax returns.

It is important to remember that if you are the person responsible for withholding taxes on behalf of employees (yourself or others), you may become personally liable for a 100% penalty on the amount that should have been withheld if you fail to comply with these obligations.

Note also that the employer may be subject to federal and state unemployment taxes and to withholding on state disability insurance taxes. You should consult your accountant or the local office of the IRS, the state unemployment compensation bureau, and the state disability insurance office to find out the details on unemployment taxes and disability insurance. Generally, the procedures for withholding money for these programs are similar to those for withholding federal and state income taxes and social security taxes.

If you hire independent contractors that will be responsible for making their own tax payments, it should be clear that they are operating their own businesses, have been retained by you to perform services, are not under your control or direction, and will be performing the same or similar services for others. Also, you should file a 1099 form with the IRS by February 28th of each year identifying the independent contractors and the amounts paid for the services. Examples of independent contractors include; someone to set up and engineer the sound for a showcase concert; a producer to oversee and produce a recording of the masters for your albums; an arranger to arrange your original compositions for your album. The IRS is particularly interested in independent contractors you retain, that perhaps should have been treated as employees, so be sure to review with your accountant the current rules and regulations that distinguish employees from independent contractors.

Other Employer Obligations

Most employers are subject to state workers' compensation laws. These laws impose liability on the employer for industrial accidents sustained by employees regardless of the employer's negligence. They provide a schedule of benefits to be paid to the employees for injuries or to their heirs if the employees are killed in an accident. It is important that you obtain sufficient workers' compensation liability insurance from an authorized insurer or a certificate of consent from your state's director of industrial relations if you are going to self-insure. Generally, insurance coverage can be obtained through the local office of your state's compensation insurance fund or through a private licensed workers' compensation carrier.

Both state and federal laws impose minimum obligations on the employer concerning wages, hours, and working conditions. You can obtain detailed information by contacting the Department of Labor, Department of Industrial Welfare or Department of Industrial Relations in your state as well as the U.S. Department of Labor. Both state and federal laws impose obligations on the employer to refrain from discrimination in hiring and in the conditions of employment. You must be careful to comply with these laws.

GENERAL BUSINESS OBLIGATIONS

As a business you have certain additional obligations. We will not go into detail here, but will simply identify problem areas with the advice that you become aware of them either by consulting with your local, state, and federal authorities or with an attorney.

If you engage in retail sales to consumers you must comply with state sales and use taxes. Generally, this tax is imposed on the consumer but the seller is obligated to collect the tax. On the seller's failure to collect, he or she will be obligated to pay the sums to the state that should have been collected from the consumer. Also, as a seller of retail goods, you must obtain a seller's permit from the local office of your state taxing authority. If you sell your product to a distributor who will in turn sell to retailers or if you sell directly to a retailer, then you need to obtain a resale tax exemption certificate from the state.

Note that businesses in most states must pay personal property tax on certain items of personal property that the business owns or possesses at a certain point in each calendar year. You must file a property statement with the county assessor within the period of time required by state law. You should check with your accountant or state's business property tax department to obtain the necessary information to enable you to comply with the state's laws on such taxes.

It is advisable to obtain casualty and public liability insurance and you should consult with local insurance agents to give you advice on this matter.

Many trades, occupations, and businesses are required to obtain state and sometimes local business licenses. Again, consult with your local and state authorities to determine what your obligations are.

It should be clear from the items discussed here that starting a business involves numerous filings and much record keeping. These requirements are unquestionably a burden, particularly for a small business. Nonetheless, they are unavoidable. While it may be possible to ignore them and "fly below radar" for awhile, the odds are against doing it for long. The more successful the enterprise, the sooner it will become visible.

The recommended approach is to comply from the outset. If the requirements seem confusing or you do not have sufficient business experience to feel confident that you have undertaken all the proper steps, have an accountant, business person or lawyer look over what you have done and advise you. Once your bookkeeping and reporting systems are established, they are not difficult to maintain.

HOW TO SET UP A MONEY DEAL

by Edward R. Hearn

This chapter explores some of the alternative forms of financing that may be available to you and shows how to analyze and structure a financial package to obtain the money for your dream project. The suggestions made below apply whether you are tomorrow's rock star, the next Hemingway, or a budding filmmaker hoping to follow in the footsteps of George Lucas. The examples used will draw on common experiences in the music industry, but the concepts and ways of structuring deals apply whether you are a musician, writer, actor, or, for that matter, if you want to establish your own instrument manufacturing company.

DEVELOPING THE BUSINESS PLAN

A business plan tells potential investors who you are. It describes your professional goals, what you plan to do to achieve those goals, and how that achievement can generate income to pay back the investor and further finance your career. An outline of the general headings of a business plan is at the end of this article.

Identifying Your Goals

The first and most important thing to be done is to clearly identify the reasons you need to raise money. To establish a clear focus, you must identify your career goals, your immediate project goals, and your strengths and weaknesses. Identifying your goals, such as securing a recording contract or getting a name artist to record your songs, will assist you in determining a feasible project to undertake to achieve that end. The project might be producing an independent record so you can market it and demonstrate that there is an audience for your product or it could be preparing a publishing demo to shop your songs.

In identifying your goals, you need to analyze your strengths and weaknesses. What is your best selling point? Identifying your strongest talents will assist in determining the project that would be most appropriate to achieve your goals. If your best skill is songwriting, perhaps you should raise funds to do a publishing demo of some of your songs to send to publishers and to performers who record material written by others. If your best talent is performance skill, perhaps you should develop a video package that will show the style you use to slay your audience. Money can be raised for other projects as well, such as producing a master sound recording, backing a tour for promotional or showcase purposes, buying equipment to enhance your stage show, or hiring a publicist to orchestrate a media blitz before you storm into Los Angeles.

Reaching a final decision on your goals and the projects designed to achieve them is a precondition to figuring out how much money you must raise and what kind of information to include in the business plan you will present to prospective investors.

Preparing the Budget

Once you have decided on the project, your next step is to determine its costs. You must develop a budget that shows the amount of money you need and how it will be spent. To do this, you must determine the cost of the various elements of your project. If you plan to record your own album, you must budget the cost of studio time, tape, musicians, arrangers, producer and engineer, mixing, mastering, pressing, cover art, design, packaging, distribution, advertising and marketing. Each project has its own cost items. It is your responsibility to develop a clear and accurate picture of what those costs will be. The section entitled *Identifying and Evaluating Sources of Income,* discusses analyzing future sources of income to be used in scheduling pay back arrangements with investors.

Preparing the Proposal

Having identified your goals, the project, and the amount of money you will need, you must reduce all that information to a proposal or business plan that you can submit to individuals that may have an interest in funding your project. The proposal should itemize the elements we have just explored, explain what the end product will be, how your business operates, how marketing the product or implementing the service will assist you in developing your career, and how money will be earned to repay the investors. The proposal should also contain information on your background and the current status of your career, and a clear statement of your goals. There is no better way to force yourself to develop a clear focus than having to articulate it to others, especially if you are asking them for money.

RAISING CAPITAL

Your project, most likely, will be financed by one of three methods: self-financing, borrowing or profit sharing. This section will discuss these methods and the advantages and drawbacks inherent in each.

Self-financing

The best way to retain full control of your project is to use your own money. It is the only technique that allows you to be free of financial obligations to lenders and gives you maximum artistic and financial control. Although it means that you must bear all the risk of the project, it also means that you will enjoy all the benefits.

Self-financing also minimizes the paperwork, record keeping, and other business complications involved in other ways of raising money. It is advisable to keep your record keeping to a minimum until you are able to devote full time to managing the business.

Borrowing

If you are not in a position to self-finance, borrowing is the second basic technique for raising funds. Borrowing means accepting a loan for a fixed sum and agreeing to repay that sum plus a specified percentage of interest by a certain time. Arrangements where the return to the lender depends on the success of the project will be discussed under the section on profit sharing.

Loans are, usually, absolute obligations that must be repaid whether or not the project is successful. If the rate of interest is high, you will have to earn a substantial amount of money from the project before you make any profit. For example, on a loan of $10,000 at 18% annual interest payable in two years, your interest obligation would be more than $3,600. To pay back the principal and interest on a self-produced album that sells for $5 (average wholesale price), you would have to sell about 2,720 albums, plus an additional number to cover your cost of sales. Only then would you be able to sell for a profit. As costs climb, of course, the number of records you must sell to break even also rises.

Loan Sources

There are several possible sources of loans. The first are commercial sources. They include banks, finance companies, savings and loan associations, and credit cards with cash advance provisions.

Interest on commercial loans, secured by such collateral as a home, auto, recording or performing equipment or even the cosignature of a person in whom the bank has confidence will usually be lower than interest on unsecured loans. The reason is obvious: the risk is lower. Loans backed up with collateral or the cosignature of a credit worthy individual are also easier to secure.

In deciding whether or not to give you a personal loan, a bank will look at your credit rating and at whether you own property that can be used as collateral for the loan. Unfortunately, musicians' credit ratings aren't always good, because of the fluctuating conditions of their employment. But if you have a credit card or two and have lived in the same place for a couple of years without having trouble paying the rent, you may be able to convince a bank to loan you a modest amount of money—e.g. $5,000. Some banks, however, state that they will sometimes loan more than this amount if the borrower's credit rating is good. Banks may want to see your income tax returns for the last couple of years.

Some banks refuse to make a personal loan of more than $5,000 unless the loan is secured by collateral, which generally means a house that you are buying. If you're looking for a loan to buy new keyboard equipment, you'll find that banks generally will not consider securing the equipment itself as collateral for the loan. Some banks will let you use an automobile as collateral, however, provided you have title to it.

In the event you don't qualify for a personal loan yourself, you can ask a relative or a friend to act as a cosigner for the loan, which means that they promise to make the payments if you are unable to. The bank will be more concerned with their credit rating than with yours, but will still want to make sure that you actually have the ability to make the payments.

In addition to personal loans, banks regularly make commercial loans to businesses. You may feel that since music is your business, you belong in this category, but you'll find that commercial loans have their own rules and regulations. If you have a solidly established band with established income, a commercial loan might be your best option. But if what you have in mind is borrowing money to start a project, you'll probably have to go with a personal loan. When you become more established, some banks, especially those with operating offices in Los Angeles, will lend money secured by the copyrights in your songs, master recordings, and other intellectual property.

A commercial loan package usually contains your business plan, the profit and loss statements of your business, tax returns for the last two or three years, and a personal financial statement. Banks will check your credit history. They need to know you have a sound financial plan and that you are financially responsible. They will generally insist that you put up as much as 50% of the money for improving the business out of your own pocket, with the loan supplying the balance.

Since commercial lenders make money lending money, you should shop for the best deal.

A second source for loans is family and friends. Usually, they will lend money at a rate lower than that of a commercial lender. The important thing to consider when borrowing from friends is that strong pressure for timely repayment may result, which often is more burdensome (because of the personal nature of the debt) than the legal obligation to repay.

When you borrow from friends, the usury laws of most states come into play. These statutes limit the amount of interest a private lender can charge a borrower. Banks and other commercial lenders are generally exempt from the usury limits and can charge higher rates.

Whether you borrow from friends or from commercial lenders, you will want to structure a written repayment plan that states the amount lent, the rate of interest, and the method of repayment.

This can be a simple written promissory note: "On or before June 15, 1997, John Debtor promises to pay Sally Lender the sum of $2,500 plus 9% interest from January 1, 1996, (signed) John Debtor."

The note from a commercial lender is more complex, but it will contain similar elements. Sometimes commercial loans are structured so that you pay a smaller monthly amount the first two years and a larger one the next two to three years. Once again, you should shop for the most favorable terms, interest and monthly pay back amounts.

INVESTMENTS

Another source of money is investment from a financial backer. The arrangement can take several forms, depending on whether the investor is "active" or "passive."

Active Investors

Active investors are individuals that put up money to finance a project for another person and become involved in the project (or fail to take adequate action to insulate themselves from responsibility). They assume all of the risks of the business, including financial liability for all losses, even if the losses go beyond the amount invested. Generally, such persons are responsible for the obligations of the business even if they have not given their approval or have not been involved in incurring business debts.

The forms of businesses in which the financing participants are active include general partnerships, joint ventures and corporations. The profits or losses of such businesses are shared among the participants according to the nature of their agreement. This is discussed more fully in the chapter titled "Business Entities."

A general partnership is co-ownership of an ongoing enterprise in which the partners share both control and profits. A joint venture is a general partnership that either has a very short term or a limited purpose. For example, the production of a single record by a group of people could be termed a joint venture.

The general partners and the joint venturers are each personally liable for all the debts of the enterprise. The liability is not limited to the amount that they invested nor to the debts that were incurred with their approval. All of the personal assets of each of the general partners or joint venturers are liable for repayment of the debts incurred by the enterprise.

If a corporation is formed, then even if the project is a total failure, only the assets of the corporation are vulnerable to the business creditors. A corporation is a separate entity formed under state laws. Its ownership is divided among its shareholders. A corporate structure provides limited liability to the shareholders. If you are thinking about setting up a corporation, you'll need some sound legal advice.

Passive Investors

A more complex category of investments is that in which backers provide money for the project but take no role in the management and affairs of the project. Such backers are passive investors whose return is based on the success of the project.

The primary advantage of profit sharing arrangements, from the point of view of the person getting the money, is that the downside risks are shared. If a project fails to recoup the money invested, you are not obligated to repay the investors. Offsetting this advantage are several problems that make profit sharing the most complicated form of financing a project.

The foremost problem is security law requirements. Any time one enters into an agreement in which someone gives money for a project with the understanding that part of the profits are to be shared with them and the investors do not actively participate in the management of the funds or the operation of the business, a "security" has been sold. A security can be a promissory note, stock, points or any other form of participation in a profit sharing arrangement, either written or oral, where the investor's role in the business is passive. Because general partners and joint venturers are actively involved in the business, their participation is generally not considered a security.

Limited partnerships, promissory notes structured with profit sharing, corporate stock and contracts providing for points participation are all securities, and state and federal securities statutes must be satisfied when these types of funding are used. Failure to comply may have serious civil and, in extreme circumstances, even criminal consequences.

What does this legal talk mean to you? Why should you have to worry about it if all you want to do is raise some money to record some music or finance a performance tour? The securities laws were enacted to protect investors from being harmed by the fraud of others or by their own lack of sophistication or even their inability to afford to lose the money they invest in the project. The legal burden falls on the one seeking to raise the money to make certain the investor is getting a fair deal and fully understands the risks involved. "Let the seller beware," is the rule that operates.

If you want someone to invest money without allowing them a hand in controlling the project, then you should be willing to accept some responsibility to them. Willing or not, state and federal statutes place responsibility on you.

Investment Loans Conditional on the Success of the Venture

In these types of loans, the debt is evidenced by a promissory note and repayment is conditional on the success of the funded project. The note should set out the terms of repayment, including interest rates and payment schedules.

A common form of this kind of loan is a "point" arrangement in which a percentage (points) of sales from the funded project are shared with an investor who puts in only time or with some other investor who puts in only money. Another form is a percent interest in the income (or losses) generated by the business. This arrangement can be provided in a written contract rather than in the form of a conditional promissory note.

Limited Partnerships

Like a general partnership, a limited partnership has co-ownership and shared profits, but only some of the participants are entitled to control or manage the enterprise. Those persons are termed the general partners. The other investors are called limited partners and their only involvement is the passive one of putting funds into the project.

A partner receives that percentage of the business profits or losses set out in the agreement between the partners, for example, 10% of the net profits up to $10,000 and 5% of the net profits after the first $10,000. The term of the partnership is often limited to a specified period. If the project has not earned the hoped for return by the end of the term, the investor has to absorb the loss.

There are rules in the federal law and in several states that apply to limited partnerships and other security investments that are structured as private offerings (i.e., to only a small number of people), which are easier to qualify under than the laws regarding public offerings (i.e., to the general public).

Corporate Shares

A third way to raise investment capital is through the sale of shares in a corporation. Corporate shares are securities that are usually sold for a stated number of dollars per share. That money is used to operate the business or pay for a specific project. Shareholders own whatever percentage of the corporation their shares represent in relation to the total number of shares sold.

Shareholders participate in the profits of the corporation when they are distributed as dividends and vote on shareholder issues according to their percentage of ownership.

Whatever method of financing you use, it is wise to check with your lawyer and set up a good financial record keeping system with your bookkeeper.

COMPLYING WITH LEGAL STATUTES

After deciding on the legal structure to use in raising the money for your project, you must make certain that your efforts comply with state and federal law. California statutes require that (unless an exemption applies), the party raising and accepting investment capital must file documents with the Commissioner of Corporations explaining, in part, the proposed investment project, how the money will be used, all of the risks in the venture, the financial ability of the investors, and the background of the persons seeking the funding. The commissioner must conclude that the proposed offer and sale is "fair, just and equitable." On an affirmative finding, the commissioner will issue a permit authorizing the sale. A negative conclusion will bar the sale. Most states have statutes imposing similar requirements.

Fundamental in any offering of a security (whether public or nonpublic), is the disclosure, to potential investors, of all the risks involved in the project, including the risk that the project may fail, that no profit may be made, and that the investors may never have their investment returned. In seeking investment money, you must disclose in writing, the risks, the background of the principals (the people starting and running the business), the nature of the proposed business, the manner in which the money will be used, and the way that the investor will share in any profits (or losses). Also, the offer and sale of securities that involves an interstate transaction may require registration of those securities with the Securities and Exchange Commission (SEC) in Washington, D.C. Knowledgeable legal counsel should be obtained before seeking to offer any securities.

State Law Exemptions

Under the securities statutes and regulations of most states, there are certain exemptions from the requirement to obtain a permit. These exemptions occur only in very specific situations. Three common exemptions are the nonpublic partnership interest, the limited number of shareholder exemptions for corporations, and the nonpublic debt security (note for a loan). In California, a limited partnership interest or other security will be presumed to be a nonpublic offering not requiring a permit from the commissioner provided that (1) there is no advertising of the investment; (2) there are no more than 35 investors contributing to the project; (3) the investor represents that he or she is purchasing the interest for his or her own account and not with the intent to distribute the interest to others; and (4) either the persons investing the money have a preexisting business or personal relationship with you, or their professional financial advisor can reasonably be presumed to have the ability to protect their interests because of the advisor's business experience. Also, a notice detailing information about the investment must be filed with the Commissioner's Office, which office establishes the kind of information that must be presented.

If the financing arrangement is to be in the form of a debt that is secured by a note with payment to the investor to come from the proceeds, if any, of the venture, then the requirements just described must be met to qualify the arrangement as an exempt nonpublic debt offering under California law. However, the investments may not be taken from more than 10 persons. This description is overly simplified and is not intended to be a full explanation of all the nuances and requirements of the security statutes and regulations. Its purpose is merely to give you a sense of how the laws operate.

IDENTIFYING AND EVALUATING SOURCES OF INCOME

If you lack your own money for your project, and do not have the credit necessary to borrow money, then you must face the reality of raising investment capital and complying with the appropriate securities statutes discussed above. Probably the most frustrating aspect of this will be your quest to identify the angel who will give you the money you need. Frequently, investors are attracted by the idea of putting money into entertainment projects because of the mistaken impression that it is a glamorous business and they desire to be associated with the glamour, or they have read that the entertainment industry can generate a substantial amount of money and wish to gamble that they will earn a great return if your project is successful.

For the most part, the money usually comes from family, friends, or interested persons that have seen your talents and wish to be involved in developing your potential. If the money does come from family and friends, however, it is critical that you act in a business-like manner to help preserve your personal relationships.

Unfortunately, there is no magic source of money. It will be up to you to identify who has enough faith in your talents and future to make their money available to you. Other possible sources of money are investment counselors and accountants that are searching for reasonable business opportunities for their clients. In reviewing proposals for investments, financial advisors analyze the possibilities of eventual return on the investment and the tax benefits, if any, that may be made available to the investors.

Educating Investors About Risk

Once you have identified individuals that are willing to put money into your project, it is very important that you examine their expectations and compare them with your own perspective. It is crucial for you to educate your investors about the risks, the rewards, and all the problems and variables that can arise over which you may have little or no control. Investors need to know how much money is required for your project in order to evaluate whether they can afford it. If they have any reservations, you should uncover them. If the reservations cannot be resolved, you should not accept money from them. Spend time talking with them and make certain that you really understand each other and that they are people to whom you want to be committed.

Fair Return

In discussing pay back with the investor, you need to identify and explore three specific areas. What will be the share of the investor's participation? For how long will the investor participate? And from what sources of income will the investor be repaid? The argument that the investor can make, and it's a good one, is that he or she is taking a substantial risk in putting money into your project that could be invested in other ways for a more certain return. As a consequence, the investor will insist on a very healthy return. This is not unreasonable, provided that it leaves you with enough of a share to continue your life and career.

Measuring a fair return is a function of how badly you need the money and how eager the investor is to put money into your project. This will frequently determine how much each side is willing to offer. Investors generally have alternative places to put their money for a good return, and if you have no other source of income for a project, you may not be in a position to do a lot of arguing. If you have to give up an amount that you feel will hurt your business or your ability to fund your career, then you should not accept the money; go look for another investor.

A more constructive way of measuring a reasonable return is to look at the amount of risk assumed by the investor in relation to the amount of money invested; the smaller the number of dollars and the smaller the risk of failure, the smaller the return. For example, if your project cost $2,000 it would be hard to justify returning 10% of your income for life to an investor. If however, the investor put $200,000 into your project, it is easy to justify committing a reasonable percentage of your income to the investor for a substantial period of time.

You can determine the proper percentage to offer to an investor by looking at how much you can afford to give up. Remember, there are only so many slices in the money pie, and if you give up too many slices there will be little for you to eat. Consequently, you should identify all of your existing commitments, such as those to managers, attorneys, other investors, partners, and the like. After you pay those people, you will still need money to run your business and support your private needs. You must carefully analyze your income potential and anticipated expenses.

You must identify the sources of income from which the investor will be repaid. Will the money be coming from the revenue generated by the project itself or will it be coming from other sources such as record sales, live performances, music publishing, or merchandising? These points must be clearly and carefully thought out before you commit to a participation with an investor.

CONCLUSION

There are no simple answers. Deals can be structured in many ways. Your decisions depend on a business analysis of your funding sources, the urgency of your need, the risks the investors are taking, their alternative investment possibilities, and your other money commitments. Do your homework and be very careful about the commitments you make. When in doubt, seek advice. If the deal doesn't make sense or doesn't feel good to you, trust your instincts and walk away from it. Don't be pressured into a commitment that may later hinder your career. In any event, be honest with yourself, identify your goals, your value system and what you are willing and not willing to give up. Only by taking all these factors into account can you arrive at a financial package that will work for you. Once you set up such a package, however, you may be able to accomplish career objectives otherwise beyond your reach.

BUSINESS PLAN OUTLINE

Here are the topics usually covered in business plans. Even if you are not using a business plan to find financing for your project, it will help identify your goals, outline the strengths and weaknesses of your project, and help determine when your project will make a profit. In short, a business plan is the map that shows how to get from an idea stage to project completion and profit.

When you want to obtain investment money, the business plan is a vital sales tool that can impress prospective investors with your planning ability and general competence as a manager.

1. Summary of your project, including the money you need to successfully launch it and reach your market.

2. Company description (history, background and management).

3. Description of your background.

4. Description of industry you are operating in.

5. Project description and planning schedule.

6. Description of the market for your project.

   A. Market size

   B. Market trends

   C. Competition

7. Marketing plan.

   A. Estimated sales and market share

   B. Strategy

   C. Pricing

   D. Sales and distribution

   E. Publicity and advertising

8. Operations (If project is a "product" i.e., a compact disc or new software, describe how it will be manufactured).

9. Project time line.

10. Critical risks and problems.

11. Financial information.

    A. Financing required

    B. Current financial statements

    C. Financial projection (three-year profit and loss, cash flow and balance sheet projections).

MUSIC ATTORNEYS

by Mark Halloran

Musicians face myriad legal problems throughout their careers. Only a competent attorney, knowledgeable in the music business, can help a musician effectively solve these problems. The following will discuss music attorneys—who they are, what they do, what they cost, and what their obligations are to you.

An attorney or lawyer is a professional with legal training who is licensed to practice law in a particular state or states. Typically, an attorney must be a college and law school graduate. Full-time law schools have broad-based curriculums that last three years. After graduation, the student must pass a state's "bar exam" before being admitted to practice law. The "bar" is a state sponsored monopoly—only attorneys can practice law. The traditional professional activities of lawyers fall into roughly four categories: consulting with clients; drafting and negotiating legal documents; representing clients before the courts; and insuring compliance, by clients, with local, state and national laws and contracts (such as union agreements), which govern the client's business activities. For musicians, the most important of these four functions is the lawyer's drafting and negotiating legal agreements.

SPECIALIZATION

Most attorneys specialize in particular fields of practice. The primary reason for specialization is the complexity of the problems that confront the professional and the sophistication and training necessary to apply the correct problem-solving tools. The law is far too complex for a lawyer to have adequate competence in all areas. Specialists, at least in theory, can do a better job for their clients because of their acquired experience in particular areas.

Due to the growth and complexity of the entertainment field, a legal specialty, called entertainment law, has arisen. Music lawyers are entertainment lawyers that specialize in the legal and business aspects of the music business.

A recent trend is the certification of lawyers that practice a specialty. In California, for example, there are five certified specialties: criminal law, workers' compensation, taxation, patent law, and family law. Entertainment law is not one of the certified specialties. Thus, at this time, there are no state certified music lawyers in California (or elsewhere). This does not mean lawyers can't specialize in representing music industry clients. They can and do. What distinguishes a music attorney, then, is not certification, but that he or she has more experience in solving the problems musicians encounter. It is not necessary for an attorney to specialize exclusively in music to have enough expertise to help you. In fact, only a handful of lawyers (mostly in Los Angeles,

New York and Nashville) are exclusively music attorneys. Many entertainment lawyers concentrate on film and TV as well.

MUSIC ATTORNEY FUNCTIONS

Recording and publishing agreements can be incredibly complex, and proper negotiating and drafting require superior legal skills and a thorough knowledge of music business practice.

In addition to negotiating and drafting a wide variety of agreements for songwriters, recording artists, record companies, music publishers, record producers, personal managers and music investors, some music attorneys solicit deals for their clients by "shopping" (distributing) demo tapes. Over time they develop relationships with people and companies in the industry, and their recommendation of a music client is sometimes influential in obtaining a contract. Most music attorneys, however, do not find deals for their clients. That task is left to the musicians and their managers. The attorney's foremost functions are structuring, negotiating and documenting deals to maximize their benefits to the client.

Another important function of the music attorney is to act as a business hub, coordinating the activities of your agent, personal manager and business manager. Because music attorneys deal with these representatives, they develop a working knowledge of their functions in the music industry and help to insure that they act in your best interests.

Music attorneys are sometimes empowered to be attorneys-in-fact for their clients. In this regard, they collect and receive all monies due you or your companies from all sources relating to your agreements with them. They deposit, into a client trust account, all checks and monies payable to you and your companies and deduct any fees for attorney compensation before remitting the remainder to you or your companies.

A music attorney may also provide general career advice, such as you would expect from a personal manager. This can be crucial in the early stages of your career, as it is often difficult to attract competent, experienced personal managers until you are signed to a major label.

FINDING A MUSIC ATTORNEY

Music attorneys may work alone ("sole practitioner"), or as part of a law firm. Law firms can range in size from two to as many as several hundred lawyers. Entertainment divisions of large firms are often divided into two departments: TV/film and music. Generally, the more experienced lawyers (often partners, that is, owners of the firm), negotiate the big deals, while the nonpartners (associates) negotiate the small ones. Associates usually do the lion's share of drafting agreements.

In recent years, the large firms have lost much of their business to smaller "boutique" entertainment law firms, which typically have 10 to 20 lawyers. These firms usually handle only entertainment clients. Many boutique entertainment firms charge either a flat amount or 5% of the dollar value of the deal negotiated, rather than on an hourly basis. Although percentage arrangements may be advantageous when you are unable to afford hourly rates, you may end up paying more than the hourly rate on large dollar deals. Remember that your income is also diminished by your personal manager (10% to 25%), agent (10%) and your business manager (5%).

Few music lawyers will take clients "on the come" (work free until the client is successful). Simple economics justify this policy. Attorneys must cover their overhead and the music industry is overcrowded and fiercely competitive. The odds are a music lawyer will never collect delayed fees from an aspiring client.

You should interview a number of lawyers before retaining one. Lawyers have various personalities, legal skills, music business experience and contacts. It is important to retain an attorney who specializes in entertainment law and knows how the industry works. A working knowledge of the standard (and nonstandard) contracts is mandatory—attorneys that don't have this knowledge will spend a lot of your money researching or buying time from another entertainment attorney, or even steering you wrong. Do not be afraid to interview a lawyer, but be sure to make your intention clear when making the appointment, and confirm you will not be charged for the time. Be prepared to ask pointed questions about the lawyer's music business experience. Don't try to use the interview as a ruse for getting free legal help—that's not fair and will put off the attorney. It is best to talk to successful musicians and managers that can recommend lawyers that have done good work for them. When you call to set up an appointment, the fact that you know someone who has an ongoing relationship with the attorney should help you get in the door. It is also helpful if your lawyer likes your music—he or she will be more motivated to work for you.

There are various ways to find a music attorney. Some well-known practitioners, such as John Branch (Michael Jackson), Don Passman (Janet Jackson), Lee Phillips (Barbra Streisand) and Alan Grubman (Madonna), command coverage in the music industry press.

Another way to meet music lawyers is to attend music conferences. Prominent music attorneys are often invited to appear at music symposia, and some business relationships are started as a result of meeting at such functions. However, it may not be advisable to retain an attorney who is far beyond your status in the industry, because high-powered music lawyers will first serve their successful clients—if it's your telephone call or Michael Jackson's, their choice is clear!

Lawyer Referral Services

Many lawyer referral services have been established that will discuss problems and refer the caller to an attorney on the service's referral panel. This attorney will interview the referred client for a moderate fee. After the first interview, fee arrangements and the legal services to be rendered are left up to the lawyer and client. Sometimes, fees are split between the referral panel and the lawyer. In California the best known referral service is California Lawyers for the Arts (CLA). This nonprofit organization, based in San Francisco, is devoted exclusively to the arts. CLA has been authorized by the California State Bar Association to refer clients statewide.

In Los Angeles, you can call the Lawyer Referral Service of the Los Angeles County Bar Association for recommendations. The Beverly Hills Bar Association Committee for the Arts Lawyer Referral and Information Service offers lawyer referrals to those with entertainment-related legal problems. These referral panels only provide you with the name of an attorney, registered with them, who claims to have some experience in your area of concern. The panels do not rate lawyers or guarantee that the attorney will have the skills and experience you need. It should also be noted that the "heavy weights," usually, are not on these panels.

Another source of music attorneys is the National Academy of Songwriters (NAS). For its members, NAS makes referrals to music attorneys that have agreed to charge reduced fees. Any one-hour consultation on a new matter is $75, the next two hours are also $75 each, and additional hours are at the lawyer's normal rate.

If you live outside California, check with your state or local bar association for lawyer referral services.

WHEN TO SEE A MUSIC ATTORNEY

The cardinal rule in seeking legal representation is—see a lawyer *before you sign* anything except autographs. In essence, when you sign a contract, you are setting up your own law (with the other party) that will govern your relationship with that party. Even though in some instances a lawyer may not be able to negotiate more favorable contract terms for you, at the very least he or she can explain the agreement so you know what you are getting into. Most likely, however, your lawyer can help by negotiating terms more favorable to you. These terms might include higher advances and royalty rates (in recording contracts), partial ownership of your copyright and a participation in the "publisher's share" of revenue (in publishing contracts), and a way to get you released from a contract if it doesn't work out. You should consult with an attorney when establishing contracts with your other advisors, such as your talent agent, your business manager and especially your personal manager. Don't sign a contract *assuming* you can get out of it.

Be wary of people who give you form or standard contracts to sign, saying that "everybody accepts these terms." Although standard contracts exist, they are drafted by attorneys that are out to protect their clients' interests, not yours. Odds are that your attorney also has a standard contract—but it's much more favorable to you. The negotiating process consists of each side making specific demands and seeing if the other side will agree. If you retain a lawyer, the other side may give in to at least some of your demands. Together, the opposing lawyers can identify issues and potential problems. The result is a contract that is different from the form contract and more favorable to you.

First Meeting

Your first meeting with an attorney will probably be arranged over the phone. You should be prepared to talk about two things at that meeting: your specific legal needs and your fee arrangement with the attorney.

Fees

Lawyers cost money. Many lawyers cost a lot. Fees can exceed $300 an hour. Non-superstar music attorneys normally charge $100 to $200 per hour. The legal fee for negotiating an agreement with a major record company, even by a relatively low priced attorney, will be at least $2,000 to $4,000.

Lawyers sell *services*. They must cover their overhead (rent, employee salaries, insurance, taxes, etc.) and make a decent profit. Overhead often exceeds 50% of the billing rate, so don't get the impression that all the money goes into their pockets. It's not, especially if their bill is unpaid.

You should realize that in retaining a lawyer you are making a contract, even if your agreement is not written. In return for a fee, your lawyer promises to render legal services on your behalf and both parties should do their best to fulfill their obligations.

It is preferable for the fee agreement to be written. In California, if the bill will likely exceed $1,000, the fee arrangement *must* be written.

Not all lawyers charge on a per hour basis. Some will charge a set fee, such as $500, to negotiate or draft a contract. Others will set their charge as a percentage of the money you receive under contracts they negotiate. This fee generally runs 5% of the deal, although the percentages and structures of these types of arrangements vary greatly. You should check around to see if the fee arrangement proposed by the lawyer is competitive, although price (whether low or high) is not necessarily an accurate indication of the value or quality of the attorney's work. Cautious lawyers will remind you that you have the right to seek the advice of another lawyer as to the propriety of the fee arrangement. Many lawyers will represent you on a percentage basis for negotiating only a specific contract. Additional services, such as tax advice, formation of corporations, etc., will have separate and additional charges.

Lawyers generally ask reimbursement for their out-of-pocket costs, which may include long-distance telephone calls, photocopies, word processing, postage, messenger service, fax, etc. These expenses are *not* considered part of the hourly fee, which only covers the lawyer's services.

Fee Payment

The quickest way to sour your attorney-client relationship is not pay your bill. Lawyers that bill on an hourly basis will render a monthly statement that sets out the services rendered, date of services, costs, and the total bill. If you can't pay the bill, at least call to say you can't and arrange some payment schedule. Some music attorneys will accept partial payment and continue to work for you.

In the good old days lawyers rarely sued their clients for nonpayment. Now they are doing so with increasing regularity. In California, you have the right to a fee arbitration if the lawyer's claim exceeds $1,500 (the small claims court limit). The lawyer will send a notice to you, advising you of your right to arbitrate. You must respond within 30 days or lose your arbitration right.

Retainers

Many lawyers require a retainer (initial payment). Most retainers are credited against your bill, but make sure that is your agreement. Thus, if you retain an attorney with $500 it is usual for that $500 to be credited to your account. These funds are held "in trust" for you until your lawyer renders sufficient legal services to earn them. For example, in the first month your attorney negotiates a publishing contract and spends six hours at $100 an hour doing it. You will get a bill showing $500 received and $600 due for services rendered. Thus, you owe $100 at that point. Some attorneys require that you keep replenishing the retainer. In the foregoing example, you would be billed $600 so the retainer would be brought back up to $500. Keep a record of all legal bills so you can try to deduct them as business expenses. You should also keep copies of all documents and correspondence.

Conflicts of Interest

In return for the monopoly on practicing law, lawyers are constrained by very special ethical obligations. Like all agents, lawyers have a "fiduciary" obligation to their "principal"—you. The heart of this obligation is that they must act with your best interests as the goal in all situations.

As part of this obligation lawyers have an ethical duty to avoid so-called conflicts of interest. If you think your attorney may be representing conflicting interests you should seriously contemplate retaining a different lawyer. Closely scrutinize the conflict, especially in recording contract situations. The most prevalent conflict of interest occurs when a lawyer concurrently represents multiple clients with potentially adverse interests. For example, assume your attorney represents XYZ Records and XYZ Records wants to sign you to a recording contract. XYZ wants to give you as little as they can; you want as much as you can get. This is a conflict of interest, as your interest and XYZ's interest are opposed to one another, or "adverse."

Under the California Rules of Professional Conduct (3-310), if a conflict arises, the lawyer must disclose his relationship with the adverse party and obtain the client's *written* consent to dual representation. A lawyer cannot represent both parties except with the written consent of all parties concerned. Lawyers violating this rule are subject to discipline by the state bar, as well as malpractice claims by clients whose interests are damaged by the lawyer with the conflict. Similar legal controls are in effect in other states.

A lawyer *may* represent multiple clients with adverse interests if (l) it is obvious that he can adequately represent the interests of each; *and* (2) each client consents to the representation after full disclosure of the possible effect of such representation on the exercise of the lawyer's independent professional judgment on behalf of each. The conflict of interest situation extends to all members of a law firm. Under the American Bar Association's Code of Professional Responsibility, a lawyer cannot avoid a conflict by referring you to someone else in the firm.

In our previous hypothetical situation, it may be that the attorney for XYZ Records can adequately represent you in your negotiations with XYZ. After discussing the conflict, he may present you with what is known as a "conflict" letter. This letter will say (l) the lawyer informed you of the conflict; (2) it is suggested you seek independent counsel; (3) the agreement is fair to you; (4) you consent to your lawyer's representation of the other party; and (5) you will not claim in the future that your lawyer breached his fiduciary duty (trust) to you in regard to the conflict. This letter, at least in theory, protects the attorney from your future claim that you were not fairly represented. The ethical lawyer will act in accordance with the terms of the conflict letter, which you will be asked to sign. You should feel free to have another lawyer look at it.

If the conflict cannot be overcome, you have to get another lawyer. The lawyer with the conflict may suggest specific counsel, or, preferably, provide you with a list of

---

TIPS FOR DEVELOPING A GOOD WORKING RELATIONSHIP WITH YOUR LAWYER

- Remember your lawyer's time is money. If you are organized in your legal and business affairs, it makes your lawyer's job easier and cheaper for you.

- Keep accurate records and communicate in *writing*. People read faster than they talk and written communications provide records.

- Always be honest with your lawyer. They operate more efficiently on facts than on lies.

- Pay your bills on time.

- Keep your lawyer informed. An ounce of prevention is worth a pound of cure in music business legal affairs.

- Prepare for meetings with your lawyer. Bring all documents that might be useful, such as letters and your calendar.

- Don't sign anything until your lawyer has reviewed it.

competent lawyers and leave the choice to you. The fact you are referred to another lawyer does not mean the lawyer with the conflict cannot subsequently represent you. He or she just can't represent you with regard to the conflict situation.

Confidentiality

Your lawyer is under a duty to keep your communications confidential. Frequently, negotiations are secret and it is in your best interest to keep them that way. News can get out, though, as when the trades note that a particular record company is negotiating with a specific act. Conceivably, this can help you if more than one company is interested in you. Your lawyer can play them one against the other. However, in order to "leak" information, your lawyer needs your consent.

Changing Lawyers

Although many attorney-client relationships are long-lasting, you may find that you want to change attorneys. If you do, you should inform your new attorney of your previous relationship. Your new lawyer cannot simultaneously represent you in a matter that is being handled by another lawyer.

The technical description used by the bar is that you "discharge" your lawyer. By law, a client has an absolute right to discharge an attorney at any time, regardless of the reason. This does not mean, however, that you don't have to pay the discharged lawyer for the reasonable value of the services already provided to you. As an initial step, your new lawyer will want to obtain your previous files. Your former lawyer has an ethical duty to let the successor counsel inspect and copy the documents in the file. Because much of the information in the files is confidential, you must authorize that the files be copied. The fact you owe your old lawyer money is irrelevant as far as turning over the files is concerned. Your previous lawyer still has a duty to represent your best interests, which includes turning over the files and cooperating with your new lawyer.

You should note that your attorney can also sever this relationship (except in litigation), but must avoid prejudicing your rights by giving you notice and time to hire another lawyer. And all your papers and any unearned retainer must be delivered to you.

CONCLUSION

Developing an effective lawyer-musician relationship can be a valuable step in your career. Your decision in selecting an attorney is crucial—it should be an informed decision and should be done as early in your career as possible.

ATTORNEY/CLIENT FEE LETTER AGREEMENT
HOURLY ARRANGEMENT

Dear Client:

It is a pleasure to undertake your representation in connection with the above referenced matter.

We are writing this letter to set forth the basis under which our firm will represent you, your related entities and any other persons or entities that you request us to represent with respect to this matter.

Our fees on all matters will be based on the guidelines set forth in the Rules of Professional Conduct of the State Bar of California. Our hourly rates range between $45 and $175 per hour, depending on which attorney or paralegal performed the work. Fees for services will be charged on a minimum quarter-hourly basis and, when services are rendered outside our office, you will be charged on a portal-to-portal basis. We will be sending you itemized monthly statements, which will be due upon receipt and will include our costs advanced in connection with your representation. Such cost charges include, but are not limited to, messenger service, shipping, postage, copying expenses and telephone charges.

An initial retainer fee in the sum of $_____ is due at the commencement of our representation. ★ The retainer will be applied to fees and costs as they are incurred. You will not receive any interest on the retainer, and upon completion of our work, any remaining balance will be either refunded to you or applied toward future legal services rendered by our firm on your behalf. At this time, the services contemplated will encompass representing you in connection with:

(Specific contract or project is outlined here.)

It is the policy of our firm to look to clients jointly and severally regarding any fees incurred either on their behalf or at their direction on behalf of any person, firm or entity for which our clients request we render services. This firm reserves the right to withdraw from this matter at any time should fees and costs not be paid as agreed. In the event it becomes necessary for this firm to take legal action for the collection of fees and costs due, the prevailing party in such action shall be entitled to collect attorneys' fees from the other party.

If the foregoing agrees with your understanding, please execute the enclosed copy of this letter and return it in the envelope provided, together with your check in the sum of $_____ as our retainer, as explained above.

If you have any questions concerning this agreement, please do not hesitate to contact me. Additionally, if at any time you have questions regarding anything relating to our services or fees charged, we encourage you to bring such matters to our attention so that we may discuss and resolve them at once.

We look forward to the opportunity of working with you on this matter.

Yours truly,

★ Optional—We acknowledge receipt of the sum of $_____ and will proceed on your behalf at once.

PERCENTAGE FEE LETTER AGREEMENT

Dear Client:

This letter will confirm our agreement with you whereby we agree to render our services as your attorneys in connection with your professional career.

You engage us during the period of this agreement as your attorneys and will cause any companies connected with your professional career in which you have any controlling interest to engage us as their attorneys in connection with all legal matters pertaining to your professional career in the entertainment industry. The term of this agreement shall commence on the date hereof, and shall continue until terminated by either of us by written notice, which shall be personally delivered or mailed by certified or registered mail, postage prepaid, to the respective address set forth on this page (or to such other address as either of us may notify the other of). No termination shall affect our right to be paid our percentage fee described below.

For our services to be rendered during the term of this agreement you and each of your companies (but not both regarding the same gross consideration) will pay us as and when received by you or such companies, respectively, beginning as of the date hereof, five percent (5%) of all gross consideration (including salaries, bonuses, percentages, commissions, royalties, profit shares, stock interests, and all other forms of compensation of any nature and from any source), prior to any withholding or deductions, earned, accrued, paid or payable (directly or indirectly) to you or your companies from and after the date hereof, for your services or the services of such companies in connection with any facet of your professional career in the entertainment industry rendered during the term hereof, or for such services rendered by you or such companies pursuant to any agreement (oral or written) (and any extensions, renewals, substitutions, or resumptions thereof) substantially negotiated or entered into during the term hereof (irrespective of when such services under such agreement were or are to be rendered), whether such gross consideration is received by you or your companies (or any third party on your or their behalf) during or after the term hereof.

Notwithstanding anything in the preceding paragraph to the contrary, the aforesaid percentage shall be ten percent (10%) [not five percent (5%)] with respect to gross consideration as defined above that is not subject to being commissioned by a licensed artist's manager (commonly referred to as an "agent"). Our additional compensation with respect to such uncommissioned gross consideration arises out of situations where no licensed artist's manager is involved, resulting in greater responsibility on our part in connection with the negotiations in connection therewith. There shall be no inference from this increase that we in any way agree to seek personal employment for you.

The services that we shall be expected to render in return for the above compensation shall include reviewing, drafting, modifying, negotiating and otherwise assisting you in connection with all agreements, contracts or other legal matters in connection with your professional career in the entertainment industry, and consulting with you and advising you regarding all other legal aspects of your professional career in the entertainment industry; but the services we shall be expected to render in return for the above compensation shall not include matters that involve litigation, arbitration or other contested proceedings, planning or the preparation of tax returns, preparation or administration of pension or profit sharing plans, or matters pertaining to your personal life or other businesses as opposed to your professional career.

You understand, of course, if we represent you in any such matter involving litigation, arbitration or other contested proceedings, the preparation or administration of profit sharing plans, or matters pertaining to your personal life or other businesses, as opposed to your professional career, we shall be paid an additional reasonable fee for such services, to be agreed upon between us, and costs reasonably incurred in connection therewith.

You are hereby authorizing us and empower us, and appoint us as your attorneys-in-fact and as attorneys-in-fact for your companies to collect and receive all monies due you or your companies from all sources relating to this agreement, to negotiate and endorse your (or your companies') name(s) upon and deposit into our clients' trust account all checks and other monies payable to you or your companies, to deduct therefrom our compensation as set forth above, together with any costs advanced by us and to remit the remainder to you or your companies as the case may be.

The terms "you" and "your," as used herein, shall refer to you or any firm, partnership, corporation or other entity owned or controlled by you.

If the foregoing meets with your approval, please sign and return the original and one copy of this letter; the other copy is for your files.

Inasmuch as this letter constitutes an agreement between us, we cannot, of course, advise you concerning it, and we suggest that you retain outside counsel to advise you concerning this agreement.

Yours truly,

ATTORNEY CONFLICT OF INTEREST
WAIVER LETTER

Dear Attorney:

We understand that you have been representing and continue to represent each of us in connection with a variety of matters. We also understand that you have and may in the future represent one of us in matters involving the other and in which the other has been or will be represented by his own counsel.

We would like your firm to represent us in connection with the following matters: (Description of project/contract, etc.)

In connection with the above, you have advised us of the following terms of the provisions of Section 3-310 of the California State Rules of Professional Conduct: ★

"(A) If a member has or had a relationship with another party interested in the representation, or has an interest in its subject matter, the member shall not accept or continue such representation without all affected clients' informed written consent."

"(B) A member shall not concurrently represent clients whose interests conflict, except with their informed written consent."

You have also advised us of the following provisions of California Evidence Code Section 962 relating to the attorney-client privilege: ★

"Where two or more clients have retained or consulted a lawyer upon a matter of common interest, none of them, nor the successor in interest of any of them, may claim a privilege under this article as to a communication made in the course of that relationship when such communication is offered in a civil proceeding between one of such clients (or his successor in interest) and another of such clients (or his successor in interest)."

Notwithstanding such joint representation and any actual or potential conflict of interest, we hereby request that you represent both of us in connection with the aforesaid matters and consent to such representation. Furthermore, we acknowledge and agree that at no time will your representation of us be construed, claimed or deemed to be a breach of a fiduciary relationship, a conflict of interest or a violation of any other obligation to either of us. We each agree that at no time shall we claim or contend that you should be or are disqualified from representing either of us in connection with said matter or any other matter, related or unrelated.

Yours truly,

★ These are similar to other states' rules of professional conduct.

MEDIATION FOR MUSICIANS

by Madeleine E. Seltzer

Inherent in any agreement is the possibility of disagreement. When the relationship between a musician or composer and his or her manager, agent, record company, producer, etc., breaks down, or a dispute arises, it may be advisable to consider mediation as a means of resolving the problem. Mediation is usually superior to the traditional manner of settling disputes in our society—litigation in the courts—for a variety of reasons. It is particularly well-suited for resolving disputes involving musicians and composers because of its unique characteristics and should be considered before other options are pursued.

GENERAL PRINCIPLES

Mediation is a form of alternative dispute resolution (resolving disagreements outside of the court system). It differs from other alternative dispute resolution methods in that the parties themselves craft their own settlement. Ideally, mediation removes the adversary structure of the conflict in which only one party comes out the winner. Instead of a judge or arbitrator imposing a decision, a neutral third party, the mediator, assists them in the process of determining solutions. Because the parties deal directly with each other, set their own agenda, and work out their own resolution, mediation allows them to explore their relationship and the difficulties that led to their conflicts and helps them to reach creative solutions.

Mediation has other attractive features. First, it is low risk because it is voluntary and nonbinding. If it does not result in a mutually agreeable settlement of the dispute, the parties are free to pursue other courses of action, including litigation. Second, it is flexible, adaptable and applicable to almost any kind of dispute; it can be utilized at any stage of a conflict; and the parties can choose any available mediator. Third, it is informal—there are few structural or substantive rules such as rules of evidence or procedure or legal precedents that must be followed. Finally, it is cost-effective—legal fees are minimized, and mediation takes much less time to conclude than other methods of dispute resolution. Also, the nonadversarial and cooperative nature of mediation helps avoid the costs associated with the damage or destruction of the business relationship, enabling it to continue profitably. In addition, the emotional costs of litigation are avoided; agreements arrived at through mediation are usually quite durable, thereby minimizing the possibility of future disputes.

HOW MEDIATION WORKS

Mediation may involve two individuals, several individuals, or even groups, and one mediator or two comediators. Mediators try to facilitate discussion among the parties and create an environment that allows them to communicate effectively, express their grievances and discover their own road to settlement of their conflict. The mediator may also help by articulating a potential agreement that the parties are close to reaching: that is, the mediator may help to draft an agreement that fairly, fully and specifically incorporates the parties' intentions.

The mediation process is quite simple. It usually begins with each party giving his or her account of the situation that led to the mediation. Then, with the help of the mediator, the parties set an agenda as to how they want the mediation to proceed. Issues are narrowed and, with the use of various devices employed by the mediator, such as private meetings with the individual parties (caucusing), the resolution process begins. The goal is to reach a written agreement as to some, if not all, of the matters in dispute. Such agreements are usually enforceable as contracts in courts of law.

In order to encourage free and uninhibited dialogue among the parties, it is imperative that all oral and written information presented in a mediation be treated as confidential. Therefore, the parties are encouraged to enter into a confidentiality agreement before the commencement of the mediation to ensure that the information provided will not be used in a subsequent legal proceeding. Some states, such as California, Colorado and Virginia have enacted legislation ensuring confidentiality. For example, according to California Code, "…evidence of anything said or of any admission made in the course of the mediation is not admissible in evidence or subject

ARTS ARBITRATION AND MEDIATION SERVICES: A MODEL PROGRAM

The California Lawyers for the Arts (CLA), a nonprofit organization that has served and promoted the interests of artists, including musicians and composers, in California for many years, established Arts Arbitration and Mediation Services (AAMS) in 1980. Since then, more than 400 cases have been resolved. There is a panel of specially trained volunteer mediators and arbitrators whose backgrounds include the arts, music industry, law and business.

It was the first program in the country to offer alternative dispute resolution services to artists, musicians and composers and it has served as a model for similar services in Texas, Washington, and Washington, D.C. According to the director of the Southern California office of CLA, many of the disputes that are handled in the program involve musicians and composers and include such issues as copyright, royalties, personality conflicts, and negotiating collaborations, contracts and payment for work. The rate of success in resolving these matters is about 75%.

to discovery, and disclosure of this evidence shall not be compelled, in any action or proceeding in which, pursuant to law, testimony can be compelled to be given." This rule also applies to documents. In addition, the statute pronounces that, "When persons agree to conduct or participate in mediation for the sole purpose of compromising, settling, or resolving a dispute…all communications, negotiations, or settlement discussions by and between participants or mediators in the mediation shall remain confidential."

Because of all of the advantages of mediation described here, it is advisable that mediation clauses be included in standard agreements. By so doing, the parties will be required to employ mediation before other methods of dispute resolution are used.

MEDIATION: A PROCESS OF BEST RESORT

There is often an emotional undercurrent in disputes that involve musicians and composers, particularly when their work is at issue. These issues may include the content of the work; credit for work performed; and the factors that contributed to the production of the work. Mediation allows for the airing of feelings and enables the intangible and even irrational elements of a situation to be given as much weight as the tangible and rational. Rules of law and other external standards such as the market value of the services or work produced need not control the result in a mediation. The parties create their own rules to fashion their own particular resolution. The musician or composer retains the power that he or she may have historically relinquished to other representatives or lawyers. This gives them dignity and a sense of control that they may not otherwise have. Unlike judges and arbitrators whose function is to impose their will and decide the matter, the mediator is there to facilitate the process. If the parties have not entered into a written contract it makes the enforcement of their rights and obligations very difficult using traditional means and the relatively inexpensive cost of mediation makes it an extremely attractive alternative to litigation. Finally, since mediation tends to preserve rather than destroy relationships, it is preferable to other forms of dispute resolution.

PROTECTING YOUR COMPOSITIONS

**Copyrights:
The Law And You**

Copyright Infringement

**Sampling: Legal Overview
And Practical Guidelines**

Music And New Media

Collaborator/Songwriter Agreements

COPYRIGHTS:
THE LAW AND YOU

by Mark Halloran

A copyright is a property right, comprised of a set of legally enforceable privileges, granted by law to creators of artistic works such as songs and recordings. These privileges ("exclusive rights") vary depending on the type of creation. The most important is the exclusive right to make and sell copies of the creation, and (especially in the case of music), the exclusive right to publicly perform it. Copyright owners make money by selling or licensing these rights to others, or by exploiting the rights themselves.

Although the copyright law recognizes that artistic creations ("works") other than music are copyrightable, the most important artistic creation for a musician is what the law terms a "musical work," that is, a musical composition such as a song or instrumental piece. For simplicity's sake, we will refer to a musical work as a "song."

Two prerequisites must be met before a song can be protected by copyright. The song must be original to the author and fixed in a tangible medium of expression. "Original" means that you yourself created the work (rather than copied it). "Fixed in a tangible medium of expression" means you put your song on paper, tape, or any other medium from which it can be perceived for more than a very short period of time. Singing a song in a club does not fix that song for you to have a copyright in it. Once you have recorded a demo or written a lead sheet, the song is fixed. Copyright law terms you the "author" of the song.

The recording of a song is called a "sound recording." Sound recordings have separate copyrights from songs, as discussed below.

Arrangements of copyrighted material may be copyrighted only when made by the owner(s) of the copyright or with their consent.

> ## THE BUNDLE OF COPYRIGHTS
>
> The U.S. Copyright Act gives copyright owners the right to control the use of their compositions in the following ways:
>
> - Reproduction of the work in copies or phonorecords
>
> - Distribution of the work for sale to the public
>
> - Public performance of the work
>
> - The creation of derivative works based upon the copyrighted work
>
> - Display of the work in printed form, such as sheet music.

Ideas are not copyrightable. The originators of rap could not copyright one rap song and then say that everyone is forbidden to write rap songs. Only the expression of the idea, that is, what has been put on paper or tape, is protected. Thus you are free to write a rap song even if you did not originate the rap mode. You cannot, however, steal a previous rap song note for note and word for word.

Song titles are not copyrightable, as they do not possess sufficient expressive content. However, this does not mean you could write a new song and entitle it "Like a Rolling Stone" with total impunity. The owners of "Like a Rolling Stone" have legal recourse, but this recourse is under laws other than copyright law.

PUBLIC DOMAIN SONGS

Not all songs are copyrighted. Songs whose copyright renewal periods have lapsed and songs that were not re-registered after their 28th year of copyright protection fall into the "public domain"; they are owned by the public. You are free to use a song in the public domain in any way you choose. Many new songs take material liberally from the public domain.

New material added to public domain songs makes these compositions eligible for copyright to the extent new material is added and the public domain portion is not resurrected. New material includes editorial revisions of old lyrics, new lyrics, changes in melodies, arrangements, and compilations of versions of the same song. In the copyright form PA, line 5, "Previous Registration" and line 6, "Derivative Work or Compilation" ask you to furnish pertinent information regarding public domain work.

New copyrights based on public domain material, make it possible for writers and publishers to receive performance monies, and mechanical license fees from record companies.

If you are unsure as to whether a song is public domain, you can have the Copyright Office or a private search service check the copyright status. The Copyright Office charges $20 per hour and normally takes six weeks to do a search. Private services, such as Copyright Data Management, charge on a sliding scale, but are quicker than the Copyright Office and usually have more complete and current information.

For information on copyright searches you can call the Reference & Bibliography Section of the Copyright Office.

You should be aware that even if a song or recording is in the public domain in the United States, it may still be protected by copyright overseas. To be used without permission, a public domain song must be cleared worldwide.

You can call ASCAP or BMI to determine the publisher of a song. CD labels typically list songwriters and publishers, as well as the record company that owns the recording.

COPYRIGHTS, PATENTS AND TRADEMARKS

Copyright protects works that are artistic in nature, such as songs and sound recordings. Patents protect new and useful inventions, such as new processes and machines. Trademarks are words or symbols used in association with products or services, which distinguish the goods or services in the marketplace. A registered trademark's notice is ®. Don't confuse it with the copyright notices, which include the symbols © and ℗.

Copyrights, patents and trademarks make up the bulk of what is known as "intellectual property law." This body of law recognizes that the products of people's minds that are in tangible form have a value that should be protected.

Generally, in the music field, you can get a copyright for two types of creations: musical works and sound recordings. Although dramatic works (such as a musical play, e.g., *Phantom of the Opera*) may include accompanying music, they are beyond the scope of this discussion.

Interestingly, the copyright law does not define "musical works." However, what most people consider a song is a musical work. Both the music and the lyrics (or each of them separately) can constitute a musical work.

A sound recording is a work comprised of a series of recorded sounds. Thus, the sounds recorded on an album, cassette or compact disc constitute a sound recording. You must distinguish between the musical work and the sound recording. Linda Ronstadt's version of Roy Orbison's song "Blue Bayou," which you hear when her album is played, is a sound recording. However, "Blue Bayou" the musical work, is distinct from Ronstadt's performance as embodied in the sound recording.

This distinction is important when it comes to public performance income (i.e., fees paid for the public performance of copyrighted material by users such as television broadcasters and radio stations). In the United States there is no exclusive right to publicly perform a sound recording, even if you own it, but there is as to a musical work. Accordingly, public performance royalties (distributed by ASCAP, BMI and SESAC) are paid to the writer and publisher of the musical work, not the performer or owner of the sound recording. Thus, the public performance income generated by Ronstadt's version of "Blue Bayou" is paid to the writer and publisher of the song, not to Ronstadt or her record company.

Congress has considered, but not passed, bills that would create public performance right in sound recordings. Systems similar to those of ASCAP and BMI could be used to compute frequency of performances, and the money would be distributed by the licensing agency among record companies, producers and performers. It should be noted that public performance income from the exploitation of sound recordings is currently paid in some countries outside the United States but it is not yet a significant source of revenue to record companies and recording artists.

Many provisions of the Copyright Act refer to "phonorecords." A phonorecord is the physical object (tape, cassette, record, compact disc or other device) that embodies the sounds of a sound recording. When you buy a compact disc, you have purchased a phonorecord that embodies a sound recording. However, although you own the compact disc, you do not own the sound recording—the copyright owner has only parted with the physical embodiment of the copyrighted work, not ownership in the sound recording.

COPYRIGHT REGISTRATION

Some people are under the misapprehension that you send to Washington, D.C. to get a copyright. What you send for is not a "copyright"—which you get as soon as you fix the work in a tangible medium of expression—but a copyright registration, a very valuable piece of paper that is not only evidence of your claim to copyright, but also makes it easier for you to sue if someone infringes your copyright. In general, failure to register does not invalidate the copyright, and as of March 1, 1989, you are no longer legally required to put a copyright notice on published copies.

For free copyright registration forms write to the Library of Congress, Washington, D.C. 20559, or call the Copyright Office at (202) 707-3000 (if you're not sure which form you need), or (202) 707-9100 (if you know the specific form you want). Allow at least two to four weeks for delivery. This time does vary, however, so ask the person at the Copyright Office how long you will have to wait. The Copyright Office is very helpful with any questions regarding registration. Sample forms are duplicated at the end of this chapter. You should keep at least one original form on file so you can photocopy it. You may also order Copyright Office circulars, which are written in plain English and are very helpful.

What to Submit

To register a copyright in a song, you submit the appropriate form plus one lead sheet or cassette if the work is not published. The cassette need only contain words, basic melody and rhythm; it doesn't have to be a fully arranged and beautifully produced demo. You must submit two lead sheets or cassettes if the work is published (i.e., copies have been distributed to the public). The appropriate forms for registering a song are form PA (performing arts) or SR (sound recording). When you are the copyright owner of all the songs on the sound recording, form SR covers both the copyright of the songs and the copyright in the sound recording. Please note that the Copyright Office keeps the materials you submit, and stores them as a national artistic treasure of the Library of Congress.

Registering Collections

You may register many songs for a single fee by putting them on a tape and registering them as a collection by using form PA. The biggest drawback to this method is that since the songs are clumped together as one work under one title it is difficult to identify just one of the songs. If you want to pull out one of the songs you can do so by filing form CA (correction and amplification) or by registering a separate form PA for the song.

Alternative Registration

At the outset it must be emphasized that *no* alternative means of registration will protect your songs to the extent that formal registration with the Copyright Office does. Because of the high cost of copyright registration

> ### REGISTERING COLLECTIONS
>
> A group of unpublished songs may be registered as a collection under the following conditions:
>
> - The elements of the collection are assembled in an orderly form.
> - The combined elements bear a single title identifying the collection as a whole.
> - The copyright claimant in all the elements and in the collection as a whole is the same.
> - All of the elements are by the same author, or, if they are by different authors, at least one of the authors has contributed copyrightable authorship to each element.
>
> (From Circular 1 "Copyright Basics," available at no charge from the U.S. Copyright Office.)

(currently $20 per song), and the technical requirements of the copyright office, alternative forms of registration have arisen. The primary reason for using an alternative registration method is to provide proof of the date of creation (fixation) of a song, which is crucial in determining who first created copyright in the song.

So-called poor man's copyright consists of enclosing a copy of your song in an envelope, sending it by registered mail to yourself, and not opening the envelope. The postmark serves as proof as to the date of creation of the song. Some variations of the poor man's copyright theme include having a notary public notarize a lead sheet with their signature and date, placing lead sheets or tapes of the song in a safe deposit box, and having people listen to a song so that they can testify that the song had been created as of a certain date.

The National Academy of Songwriters (NAS) in Hollywood, California provides a registration service called SongBank, and for a very modest fee keeps a record of your song on file. This is similar to script deposits kept by the Writers' Guild of America for screenplay writers. NAS's SongBank is designed as an interim measure to use before you register your song with the Copyright Office.

PROPER COPYRIGHT NOTICE

Proper notice of a claim to copyright in a song or sound recording is an important step in protecting your rights, since it puts people on notice that you claim the copyright. Failure to attach proper notice to published copies, however, no longer invalidates your copyright. There are separate symbols for notice of copyright in songs (sheet music, written lyrics) © and in sound recordings (CDs, cassettes, etc.) ℗. The copyright notices for songs and sound recordings must include three elements: the symbol © or ℗, the year of publication, and the name of the copyright owner. The word "Copyright," or the abbreviation "Copr.," may be used instead of the symbol ©. Proper notices are illustrated below.

A copyright notice for a song fixed on sheet music should look something like this:
© 1995 Sally Songwriter.
All Rights Reserved.

Notices that vary from this form are common. A popular one is "Copyright © 1995 Sally Songwriter," or "© Copr. Sally Songwriter 1995." All the law requires is that these three symbols "give reasonable notice of the claim of copyright."

The words "All Rights Reserved" are not suggested by U.S. copyright law, but they are recommended because they provide additional copyright protection in certain South American countries.

The copyright notice for sound recordings fixed in tapes, records or CDs looks something like this:
℗ 1995 XYZ Records.
All Rights Reserved.
This notice may be put on the surface, label or container of the phonorecord.

Omission of Notice

Under the pre–1978 U.S. Copyright Law, omission of a copyright notice on published copies was fatal to a claim of copyright. This is not true under the present law. However, if you omitted the notice between January 1, 1978 and February 28, 1989, the law allows you to take certain corrective actions. These curative provisions may be invoked if the notice was omitted from a small number of copies, if the song was registered within five years of publication and a reasonable effort is made to add the notice to the copies of phonorecords already distributed to the public, or if the notice had been omitted in violation of a written requirement that published copies bear the required notice. There are also curative provisions if your song is published with inaccurate information (for example, the wrong publication date).

Copyright Notice on Demos

Legally you don't have to put any copyright notice on unpublished lead sheets, demonstration tapes, or demonstration 45s, etc. However, the prudent thing to do is to put the appropriate notice on every one of your songs or tapes.

Put a © notice on every lead sheet or lyric sheet as soon as you write it down. Put a ℗ notice on every tape or record you submit or loan. This puts people on notice that you are claiming copyright in your songs and recordings and that you take your craft seriously.

PUBLICATION

A song is published when it is distributed to the public by sale or by some other means. The most common way songs are first published is through the distribution of records containing them. Be sure the appropriate copyright notice is affixed to the record, tape, sheet music or other physical embodiment of the work.

RECORDING A COPYRIGHTED SONG

The copyright law gives the owner of a copyrighted song the exclusive right to make the first sound recording of the song. However, once the song has been recorded and distributed to the public, others are entitled to make their own recordings of that work.

If you want to record a song, you have two alternatives: you may negotiate a "mechanical license" from the copyright owner; or you may use the "compulsory mechanical license" provision of the copyright law, which does not require that you gain permission of the copyright holder, but does require you to account to the copyright holder and to pay fixed rates per song for each record manufactured and sold. In practice, however, the vast majority of mechanical licenses are negotiated primarily through The Harry Fox Agency in New York. Mechanical license fees are paid to that agency, which deducts its administration fee, and remits the balance to the copyright holder (usually a publisher) on a quarterly basis.

DURATION OF COPYRIGHTS

Copyright protection begins on the date of creation (i.e., fixation in a tangible medium of expression) and, in most cases, lasts for the lifetime of the author plus 50 years. Thus, if you write a song in 1995, and die in the year 2010, the copyright lasts until 2060. If there is a coauthor or authors, then the 50 years are measured from the last surviving author's death.

"Works made for hire" (discussed below) are protected for 75 years from the date of publication, or for 100 years from the date of creation (fixation), whichever is shorter.

TRANSFER OF COPYRIGHTS

Copyrights can be divided and bought and sold. When you license ASCAP to collect public performance royalties you have, in effect, transferred part of your copyright to ASCAP. You still own the rest of the copyright, however. Also, in typical music publishing and record deals, you transfer your copyright to the label or publisher, in return for their promise to pay you royalties.

You can also give permission to someone to exploit your copyright without transferring ownership. This is called a "license." For example, someone may record your song under a mechanical license—but you still own the song.

If you transfer your copyright, or any exclusive right under copyright, the transfer of ownership must be in writing and be signed by the copyright owner (you). The transfer should be recorded in the Copyright Office. Recording is important to the person to whom the copyright is transferred, as it is a prerequisite for bringing a copyright infringement suit. Also, conflicts may emerge between persons that claim the same copyright. In such cases, the first to record the transfer will prevail in a lawsuit arising from a dispute over copyright ownership. Failure to register the transfer, however, does not invalidate the transfer.

Reacquiring Copyright

The present law provides that an author or author's heirs may reacquire a copyright between the 35th and 40th year after transfer by serving a written notice on the person who, at that time, holds the copyright. They then regain ownership of the copyright for the rest of its duration. This does not apply to works made for hire as your employer or the person commissioning the song is deemed the author of the song.

Obviously, for you or your heir to take advantage of this provision you must keep good records and a prospective calendar.

WORKS FOR HIRE

Songwriters are frequently hired to write songs. In such cases, they are described as "employees for hire" or "writers for hire," in songwriting contracts. The significance of this is that the employer (person who hired the writer) is deemed to be the author of the song, and owns the song unless the contract states otherwise. If a song is not produced by an employee in the course of his or her employment, it will be considered a work made for hire only if there is a written agreement to consider it such and the song falls into the specific list of "specially ordered or commissioned works" found in the Copyright Act. Remember, in the work-made-for-hire situation, you do not have copyright in the song as your employer is the author of the song. The Copyright Act lists the following uses as specially ordered or commissioned works—a contribution to a collective work; a part of a motion picture or other audiovisual work; a translation; a supplementary work; a compilation; an instructional text; a test; answer material for a test; or an atlas.

COPYRIGHT INFRINGEMENT

A work is infringed when any of the exclusive rights in a copyright are violated. Persons that infringe copyrights are subject to both civil and criminal penalties. Here are some examples:

You write a song, and the sheet music is sold in a store. An infringer purchases the sheet music, duplicates it and sells it. This is an infringement of your right to reproduce the work and of your exclusive right to distribute copies of the work to the public.

You record an album containing your songs, and an infringer dubs hundreds of cassettes and sells them. This violates your exclusive reproduction and distribution rights and also infringes your rights in both the songs and the sound recording fixed in the album. Consequently, you and your record company can sue for infringement.

George Harrison was found to have infringed the Chiffons' 1962 classic "He's So Fine" with his 1970 hit "My Sweet Lord." The court found the music of the two songs to be identical. Even though the lyrics and concepts of his song were different, and Harrison only subconsciously took from "He's So Fine," it was still an infringement.

Statute of Limitations

The copyright law has a statute of limitations. In cases of infringement you have three years from the initial date of infringement to bring suit. Any delay, however, can harm you. See a lawyer as soon as you learn of an unauthorized use of your song.

Doing a Cover

As long as you have permission to rerecord a song (whether from the copyright owner or by filing the compulsory mechanical license), you can try to make it sound like the original. As discussed above, you get permission to record the song by getting a compulsory license through complying with copyright law formalities, or by obtaining a negotiated license from the owner of the copyright in the song. You don't have to have the permission of the original performer unless that performer happens to have the rights to the song. If you record "Born in the U.S.A." you can try to sound like Bruce Springsteen, but you must have permission to record the song.

You should be careful, however, if an advertising agency hires you to imitate the sound of a well-known performer. Recent cases involving Bette Midler and Tom Waits have led to substantial judgments against advertising agencies that deliberately had singers imitate their voices.

Infringement Remedies

The remedies provided by law in an infringement suit include both injunctions and money damages. If you prove infringement at a preliminary stage of the suit the court will make the infringer stop.

This is a form of injunction—that is, a court order against the infringer. The court can also order the impoundment of the allegedly infringing copies or phonorecords as well as the machinery that produced them.

Since proving money damages is difficult the law sets "statutory damages," which generally run from $500 to $20,000 for a single act of copyright infringement.

If you win your infringement suit you may elect to receive either the actual damages you suffered plus the profits the infringer earned from the infringement, or statutory damages. In certain instances the court will also award court costs and attorneys' fees. *Remember, statutory damages and attorneys' fees will be awarded only if you make timely registration of your copyright with the Copyright Office.*

The copyright law also provides for criminal penalties.

Digital Audio Recording Technology (DART) Act

On October 7, 1992, the U.S. Congress passed the Digital Audio Recording Technology (DART) Act. The act requires manufacturers and importers of digital audio recording devices and media that distribute the products in the United States to pay a set percentage royalty of the transfer price to the Licensing Division of the Copyright Office which invests the fees in U.S. Treasury securities until royalties are distributed. The Copyright Arbitration Royalty Panel (CARP), administered by the Librarian of Congress, adjusts copyright royalty rates and distributes royalties to eligible claimants that file proper and timely claims.

The law also requires manufacturers of digital audio equipment to install serial copy-prevention systems that permit copies to be made from original recordings, but not from copies, thereby preventing unauthorized mass duplication.

DART is an attempt to balance the concerns of copyright owners and music publishers about unlawful infringement (unauthorized tape duplication and distribution) with the public's demand for DAT technology. The act includes a special provision which protects the consumer against an infringement action when the consumer uses the technology to create a digital copy for private noncommercial use.

The royalty fees are deposited into two funds, a Sound Recordings Fund and a Musical Works Fund. The money in the Sound Recordings Fund is allocated to copyright owners of sound recordings (not copyright owners of the musical compositions), featured artists, nonfeatured musicians and nonfeatured artists. The Musical Works Fund is distributed to music publishers and songwriters.

The total royalty pool is allocated by the following percentages:

Record companies	38.41%
Featured artists	25.60%
Songwriters	16.66%
Music publishers	16.66%
Musicians	1.75%
Background vocalists	0.92%

Under DART, the copyright owners of the sound recording and the American Federation of Musicians jointly appoint an independent administrator for the Nonfeatured Musicians Subfund; and the copyright owners of the sound recording and the American Federation of Television and Radio Artists jointly appoint an independent administrator for the Nonfeatured Vocalists Subfund. Although there could be two independent administrators, a single person has administered both funds to date.

The rest of the royalty pool is distributed among copyright owners that have filed claims and whose musical works or sound recordings have been: (1) embodied in a digital or analog musical recording lawfully made; and (2) distributed in the form of digital or analog musical recordings or disseminated to the public by video or audio transmissions.

Claimants should send CARP an original and two copies of a letter stating the basis for the claim during January or February following the year for which royalties are sought. The Copyright Office does not provide special claim forms. In their letter, the claimant must provide (1) the full legal name of the person or entity claiming royalty payments; (2) the telephone number, facsimile number, if any, and the full address, including a specific street name and number or rural route, of the place of business of the person or entity; (3) a statement as to how the claimant fits the definition of interested copyright party; (4) a statement indicating the fund (and fund segment, e.g. nonfeatured vocalist) the claim is for; and (5) identification of at least one musical work or sound recording establishing the basis for the claim. All claims must be signed by the claimant or the claimant's representative. Claims filed for more than one subfund must be filed separately. Joint claims must include a statement of authorization and the name of each claimant to the joint claim.

In March, CARP writes the claimants, telling them what other claimants have filed. It is then up to the claimants to negotiate in good faith with each other to reach a settlement on how to distribute the funds for which they are applying. Once this is done, the Librarian of Congress places a notice in the Federal Register asking whether there are any controversies among the claimants as to the distribution of royalties. If there are no controversies, the Copyright Office distributes the royalties.

If the claimants can't reach an agreement, the Librarian designates the CARP panel to arbitrate a distribution settlement among claimants. In this case, the claimants will bear the entire cost of the arbitration proceeding in proportion to their share of the distribution.

Claims and statements should be sent by certified mail, return receipt requested, to: Copyright Arbitration Royalty Panel, PO Box 70977, Southwest Station, Washington, D.C. 20024.

For more information, call CARP, (202) 707-8380.

Fair Use

Generally, a person who wishes to use copyrighted material must seek permission of the copyright holder. However, the law recognizes certain limited uses of copyrighted material without permission as "fair use." In broad terms, the doctrine of fair use means that in some circumstances, where the use is reasonable and not harmful to the copyright owner's rights, copyrighted material may be used, to a limited extent, without permission of the copyright owner. Under this doctrine, critics have been held to be free to publish short extracts or quotations for purposes of illustration or comment, and record reviewers may quote from songs. Also, in a recent famous case, Two Live Crew was found not to have infringed a song by doing a parody of it.

The line between fair use and infringement is unclear and not easily defined. There is no specific number of words, lines, or notes that can be safely taken without permission. Acknowledging the source of the copyrighted material does not avoid infringement. The safe course is to get permission before using copyrighted material. The Copyright Office cannot give this permission. It will, as discussed previously, supply information regarding copyright ownership as disclosed by a search of its records.

Use of copyrighted material without permission (even in a parody), should be avoided unless it is clear that the doctrine of fair use would apply to the situation. If there is any doubt or question, consult an attorney.

We all know that new songs frequently incorporate parts of old ones. A pervasive myth is that you can graft four bars from a copyrighted song without subjecting yourself to a lawsuit by the copyright owner, as taking four bars is a fair use. In fact, there is no such provision in the law. The test is whether the amount taken from the old song was substantial. This rather loose standard is applied by a judge or jury when they listen to your song. Remember, there is no standard measure of how much music, or how many lyrics can be incorporated in a new song without infringing the old.

CONCLUSION

As a performing musician or songwriter you should have a basic understanding of copyright law. When you write or record a song you have certain valuable rights in that song that you can exploit. By knowing your rights you can protect them; when you have a specific problem, you should consult an attorney for guidance.

SUMMARY OF NOTICES
THAT APPEAR ON RECORDINGS

ITEM	LOCATION	PURPOSE
℗, year, owner	Typically on label and packaging	Gives notices of owner of sound recording.
©, year, owner	Label, packaging	Provides notice of ownership of the art and text on the label and packaging when the owner of the sound recording is the same.
©, year, owner	Beside specific text or art on packaging	Identifies ownership of specific text or art when they are owned by another.
© year, owner	At end of written lyric	Provides notice of ownership of songs.
All Rights Reserved	After each © notice	Provides notice required for copyright protection in certain foreign countries.
Used by permission	After certain © notices	Typically used when permission to use another's copyrighted work has been granted.
Unauthorized reproduction prohibited, etc.	Packaging	Optional warning designed to deter infringement; can take various forms*
Songwriters' names	Adjacent to song titles	Not required by copyright law, but customarily added as a matter of courtesy or as required by contract to facilitate payment of songwriter royalties.
BMI/ASCAP/SESAC	Next to song title	Not part of the copyright notice, but identifies the performing rights society that licenses the song for public performances and collects royalties on behalf of the songwriter and publisher.
Playing time	Next to song title	Not part of the copyright notice but convenient for disc jockeys.

*(i.e., "WARNING: Unauthorized reproduction of this recording is prohibited by federal law and is subject to criminal prosecution" or "Unauthorized duplication is a violation of applicable laws").

FORM PA

UNITED STATES COPYRIGHT OFFICE

REGISTRATION NUMBER

_____

PA   PAU

EFFECTIVE DATE OF REGISTRATION

_____

Month	Day	Year

DO NOT WRITE ABOVE THIS LINE. IF YOU NEED MORE SPACE, USE A SEPARATE CONTINUATION SHEET.

1

TITLE OF THIS WORK ▼

PREVIOUS OR ALTERNATIVE TITLES ▼

NATURE OF THIS WORK ▼ See instructions

2

a

NAME OF AUTHOR ▼

DATES OF BIRTH AND DEATH
Year Born ▼   Year Died ▼

Was this contribution to the work a "work made for hire"?
☐ Yes
☐ No

AUTHOR'S NATIONALITY OR DOMICILE
Name of Country
OR { Citizen of ▶ _____
Domiciled in ▶ _____

WAS THIS AUTHOR'S CONTRIBUTION TO THE WORK
Anonymous? ☐ Yes ☐ No
Pseudonymous? ☐ Yes ☐ No

If the answer to either of these questions is "Yes," see detailed instructions

NATURE OF AUTHORSHIP Briefly describe nature of the material created by this author in which copyright is claimed. ▼

NOTE

Under the law, the "author" of a "work made for hire" is generally the employer, not the employee (see instructions). For any part of this work that was "made for hire" check "Yes" in the space provided, give the employer (or other person for whom the work was prepared) as "Author" of that part, and leave the space for dates of birth and death blank

b

NAME OF AUTHOR ▼

DATES OF BIRTH AND DEATH
Year Born ▼   Year Died ▼

Was this contribution to the work a "work made for hire"?
☐ Yes
☐ No

AUTHOR'S NATIONALITY OR DOMICILE
Name of country
OR { Citizen of ▶ _____
Domiciled in ▶ _____

WAS THIS AUTHOR'S CONTRIBUTION TO THE WORK
Anonymous? ☐ Yes ☐ No
Pseudonymous? ☐ Yes ☐ No

If the answer to either of these questions is "Yes," see detailed instructions

NATURE OF AUTHORSHIP Briefly describe nature of the material created by this author in which copyright is claimed. ▼

c

NAME OF AUTHOR ▼

DATES OF BIRTH AND DEATH
Year Born ▼   Year Died ▼

Was this contribution to the work a "work made for hire"?
☐ Yes
☐ No

AUTHOR'S NATIONALITY OR DOMICILE
Name of Country
OR { Citizen of ▶ _____
Domiciled in ▶ _____

WAS THIS AUTHOR'S CONTRIBUTION TO THE WORK
Anonymous? ☐ Yes ☐ No
Pseudonymous? ☐ Yes ☐ No

If the answer to either of these questions is "Yes," see detailed instructions

NATURE OF AUTHORSHIP Briefly describe nature of the material created by this author in which copyright is claimed. ▼

3

a **YEAR IN WHICH CREATION OF THIS WORK WAS COMPLETED** This information must be given in all cases.
◀ Year

b **DATE AND NATION OF FIRST PUBLICATION OF THIS PARTICULAR WORK**
Complete this information ONLY if this work has been published.
Month ▶ _____ Day ▶ _____ Year ▶ _____ ◀ Nation

4

See instructions before completing this space

COPYRIGHT CLAIMANT(S) Name and address must be given even if the claimant is the same as the author given in space 2.▼

DO NOT WRITE HERE OFFICE USE ONLY

APPLICATION RECEIVED

ONE DEPOSIT RECEIVED

TWO DEPOSITS RECEIVED

REMITTANCE NUMBER AND DATE

TRANSFER If the claimant(s) named here in space 4 are different from the author(s) named in space 2, give a brief statement of how the claimant(s) obtained ownership of the copyright.▼

MORE ON BACK ▶
• Complete all applicable spaces (numbers 5-9) on the reverse side of this page
• See detailed instructions.
• Sign the form at line 8.

DO NOT WRITE HERE

Page 1 of _____ pages

EXAMINED BY	FORM PA

CHECKED BY

☐ CORRESPONDENCE
Yes

FOR
COPYRIGHT
OFFICE
USE
ONLY

DO NOT WRITE ABOVE THIS LINE. IF YOU NEED MORE SPACE, USE A SEPARATE CONTINUATION SHEET.

PREVIOUS REGISTRATION Has registration for this work, or for an earlier version of this work, already been made in the Copyright Office?

☐ **Yes** ☐ **No** If your answer is "Yes," why is another registration being sought? (Check appropriate box) ▼

a. ☐ This is the first published edition of a work previously registered in unpublished form.

b. ☐ This is the first application submitted by this author as copyright claimant.

c. ☐ This is a changed version of the work, as shown by space 6 on this application.

If your answer is "Yes," give: **Previous Registration Number ▼**   **Year of Registration ▼**

5

DERIVATIVE WORK OR COMPILATION Complete both space 6a & 6b for a derivative work; complete only 6b for a compilation.

a. Preexisting Material Identify any preexisting work or works that this work is based on or incorporates. ▼

b. Material Added to This Work Give a brief, general statement of the material that has been added to this work and in which copyright is claimed. ▼

6

See instructions
before completing
this space

DEPOSIT ACCOUNT If the registration fee is to be charged to a Deposit Account established in the Copyright Office, give name and number of Account.
Name ▼   **Account Number ▼**

7

CORRESPONDENCE Give name and address to which correspondence about this application should be sent.   Name/Address/Apt/City/State/Zip ▼

Area Code & Telephone Number ▶

Be sure to
give your
daytime phone
◀ number

CERTIFICATION* I, the undersigned, hereby certify that I am the

Check only one ▼

☐ author

☐ other copyright claimant

☐ owner of exclusive right(s)

☐ authorized agent of _____
Name of author or other copyright claimant, or owner of exclusive right(s) ▲

8

of the work identified in this application and that the statements made
by me in this application are correct to the best of my knowledge.

Typed or printed name and date ▼ If this application gives a date of publication in space 3, do not sign and submit it before that date.

_____ date ▶ _____

Handwritten signature (X) ▼

**MAIL
CERTIFI-
CATE TO**

**Certificate
will be
mailed in
window
envelope**

Name ▼

Number/Street/Apartment Number ▼

City/State/ZIP ▼

YOU MUST:
• Complete all necessary spaces
• Sign your application in space 8
SEND ALL 3 ELEMENTS
IN THE SAME PACKAGE:
1. Application form
2. Nonrefundable $20 filing fee
   in check or money order
   payable to Register of Copyrights
3. Deposit material
MAIL TO:
Register of Copyrights
Library of Congress
Washington, D.C. 20559

9

February 1991—200,000   ☆U.S. GOVERNMENT PRINTING OFFICE: 1991—282-170/20,014

FORM SR

UNITED STATES COPYRIGHT OFFICE

REGISTRATION NUMBER

_____

SR   SRU

EFFECTIVE DATE OF REGISTRATION

Month   Day   Year

DO NOT WRITE ABOVE THIS LINE. IF YOU NEED MORE SPACE, USE A SEPARATE CONTINUATION SHEET.

1

TITLE OF THIS WORK ▼

PREVIOUS OR ALTERNATIVE TITLES ▼

NATURE OF MATERIAL RECORDED ▼ See instructions.
☐ Musical   ☐ Musical-Dramatic
☐ Dramatic   ☐ Literary
☐ Other _____

2

a

NAME OF AUTHOR ▼

DATES OF BIRTH AND DEATH
Year Born ▼   Year Died ▼

Was this contribution to the work a "work made for hire"?
☐ Yes
☐ No

AUTHOR'S NATIONALITY OR DOMICILE
Name of Country
OR { Citizen of ▶_____
Domiciled in ▶_____

WAS THIS AUTHOR'S CONTRIBUTION TO THE WORK
Anonymous? ☐ Yes ☐ No
Pseudonymous? ☐ Yes ☐ No
If the answer to either of these questions is "Yes," see detailed instructions

NATURE OF AUTHORSHIP Briefly describe nature of the material created by this author in which copyright is claimed. ▼

NOTE
Under the law, the "author" of a "work made for hire" is generally the employer, not the employee (see instructions). For any part of this work that was "made for hire" check "Yes" in the space provided, give the employer (or other person for whom the work was prepared) as "Author" of that part, and leave the space for dates of birth and death blank.

b

NAME OF AUTHOR ▼

DATES OF BIRTH AND DEATH
Year Born ▼   Year Died ▼

Was this contribution to the work a "work made for hire"?
☐ Yes
☐ No

AUTHOR'S NATIONALITY OR DOMICILE
Name of Country
OR { Citizen of ▶_____
Domiciled in ▶_____

WAS THIS AUTHOR'S CONTRIBUTION TO THE WORK
Anonymous? ☐ Yes ☐ No
Pseudonymous? ☐ Yes ☐ No
If the answer to either of these questions is "Yes," see detailed instructions

NATURE OF AUTHORSHIP Briefly describe nature of the material created by this author in which copyright is claimed. ▼

c

NAME OF AUTHOR ▼

DATES OF BIRTH AND DEATH
Year Born ▼   Year Died ▼

Was this contribution to the work a "work made for hire"?
☐ Yes
☐ No

AUTHOR'S NATIONALITY OR DOMICILE
Name of Country
OR { Citizen of ▶_____
Domiciled in ▶_____

WAS THIS AUTHOR'S CONTRIBUTION TO THE WORK
Anonymous? ☐ Yes ☐ No
Pseudonymous? ☐ Yes ☐ No
If the answer to either of these questions is "Yes," see detailed instructions

NATURE OF AUTHORSHIP Briefly describe nature of the material created by this author in which copyright is claimed. ▼

3

a **YEAR IN WHICH CREATION OF THIS WORK WAS COMPLETED** This information must be given in all cases.
_____ ◀ Year

b **DATE AND NATION OF FIRST PUBLICATION OF THIS PARTICULAR WORK** Complete this information ONLY if this work has been published.
Month ▶_____ Day ▶_____ Year ▶_____ ◀ Nation

4

See instructions before completing this space.

COPYRIGHT CLAIMANT(S) Name and address must be given even if the claimant is the same as the author given in space 2.▼

TRANSFER If the claimant(s) named here in space 4 are different from the author(s) named in space 2, give a brief statement of how the claimant(s) obtained ownership of the copyright.▼

DO NOT WRITE HERE OFFICE USE ONLY
APPLICATION RECEIVED
ONE DEPOSIT RECEIVED
TWO DEPOSITS RECEIVED
REMITTANCE NUMBER AND DATE

MORE ON BACK ▶ • Complete all applicable spaces (numbers 5-9) on the reverse side of this page
• See detailed instructions • Sign the form at line 8

DO NOT WRITE HERE
Page 1 of_____ pages

EXAMINED BY	**FORM SR**
CHECKED BY	

☐ CORRESPONDENCE
Yes

☐ DEPOSIT ACCOUNT
FUNDS USED

FOR
COPYRIGHT
OFFICE
USE
ONLY

DO NOT WRITE ABOVE THIS LINE. IF YOU NEED MORE SPACE, USE A SEPARATE CONTINUATION SHEET.

PREVIOUS REGISTRATION   Has registration for this work, or for an earlier version of this work, already been made in the Copyright Office?
☐ **Yes** ☐ **No**   If your answer is "Yes," why is another registration being sought? (Check appropriate box) ▼

☐ This is the first published edition of a work previously registered in unpublished form.

☐ This is the first application submitted by this author as copyright claimant.

☐ This is a changed version of the work, as shown by space 6 on this application.

If your answer is "Yes," give: **Previous Registration Number** ▼   **Year of Registration** ▼

5

DERIVATIVE WORK OR COMPILATION   Complete both space 6a & 6b for a derivative work; complete only 6b for a compilation.
a.   Preexisting Material   Identify any preexisting work or works that this work is based on or incorporates. ▼

b.   Material Added to This Work   Give a brief, general statement of the material that has been added to this work and in which copyright is claimed.▼

6

See instructions
before completing
this space.

DEPOSIT ACCOUNT   If the registration fee is to be charged to a Deposit Account established in the Copyright Office, give name and number of Account.
Name ▼   **Account Number** ▼

7

CORRESPONDENCE   Give name and address to which correspondence about this application should be sent.   Name/Address/Apt/City/State/Zip ▼

Area Code & Telephone Number ▶

Be sure to
give your
daytime phone
◀ number.

CERTIFICATION*   I, the undersigned, hereby certify that I am the
Check one ▼

☐ author

☐ other copyright claimant

☐ owner of exclusive right(s)

☐ authorized agent of
Name of author or other copyright claimant, or owner of exclusive right(s) ▲

8

of the work identified in this application and that the statements made
by me in this application are correct to the best of my knowledge.

Typed or printed name and date ▼ If this application gives a date of publication in space 3, do not sign and submit it before that date.

_____ date ▶ _____

☞   Handwritten signature (X) ▼

**MAIL
CERTIFI-
CATE TO**

**Certificate
will be
mailed in
window
envelope**

Name ▼

Number/Street/Apartment Number ▼

City/State/ZIP ▼

YOU MUST
• Complete all necessary spaces
• Sign your application in space 8
SEND ALL 3 ELEMENTS
IN THE SAME PACKAGE
1. Application form
2. Nonrefundable $20 filing fee
   in check or money order
   payable to *Register of Copyrights*
3. Deposit material
MAIL TO
Register of Copyrights
Library of Congress
Washington, D.C. 20559

9

* 17 U.S.C. § 506(e): Any person who knowingly makes a false representation of a material fact in the application for copyright registration provided for by section 409 or in any written statement filed in connection with the application, shall be fined not more than $2,500.

December 1990—100,000

☆U.S. GOVERNMENT PRINTING OFFICE: 1990—282-170/20,006

COPYRIGHT INFRINGEMENT

by Robert M. Dudnik

To establish a claim of copyright infringement, the plaintiff (person who files the lawsuit) must first demonstrate either ownership of the copyright of the song that was supposedly copied, or ownership of a copyright interest in that song, such as an exclusive license. The plaintiff must then demonstrate that the composer of defendant's song in fact copied from plaintiff's song and that the material that was copied results in a finding of copyright infringement. Once infringement is established, then the question becomes what remedies are available to the plaintiff.

ESTABLISHING OWNERSHIP

Copyright of a song is established when the work is first fixed in a tangible form—for example, notated on paper or recorded on tape. Registration of the song with the Copyright Office is not a prerequisite to the song being protected by copyright. However, before an infringement case may be filed in court, the owner of the copyright must, as a general rule, register the song with the Copyright Office.

Typically, the copyright owner will be either the composer of the song, the employer of the composer (if the composer wrote the song during the course and scope of employment as a work for hire) or a person or company to whom the original owner of the song transferred a copyright interest in the song.

Proof of ownership may become complicated where the plaintiff is not the composer of the song but, instead, claims ownership either as the employer of the composer or by virtue of a transfer in ownership. Further, the fact that the plaintiff has registered the song with the Copyright Office and has claimed ownership of the song on the registration certificate does not conclusively establish that the plaintiff is, in fact, the true owner of the copyright in the song.

ESTABLISHING COPYING

A composer who is charged with copyright infringement rarely admits copying from the plaintiff's song. And it is very unusual for there to be what the law calls "direct" evidence of copying, such as testimony by a witness who observed the composer listening to the plaintiff's song while writing the defendant's.

Since admissions of plagiarism as well as other forms of direct evidence of copying are hard to come by, the law permits a copyright plaintiff to prove copying through "circumstantial" evidence—by showing that the composer of defendant's song had "access" to plaintiff's song and that the two songs in issue are "substantially similar."

Access

Access means that there is a "reasonable possibility" that the composer of defendant's song heard plaintiff's song or saw a print version of it before writing defendant's song. If the plaintiff can establish only that there is a "bare possibility" that the composer of defendant's song heard or viewed a printed version of the song before defendant's song was written, then plaintiff has not established access and, with one exception discussed below, plaintiff's case will be dismissed from court.

A plaintiff can establish access under this reasonable possibility test by showing that the composer of defendant's song, as a member of the general public, had a reasonable opportunity to have been exposed to plaintiff's song. For example, where plaintiff's song was a major hit before defendant's song was written, access would ordinarily be established. This is true even if the composer of defendant's song denies having heard plaintiff's song since, in the eyes of the law, there was a reasonable possibility that the defendant would have heard plaintiff's song on the radio or on television. If, on the other hand, plaintiff's song received only limited airplay in one region of the country and little other exposure, and the composer of defendant's song could show that he never visited that region while plaintiff's song was being played, access would, ordinarily, not be established. As another example, if plaintiff's song was played during only a few club dates, access would ordinarily not be established unless it could be shown that the composer of defendant's song frequented one or more of the clubs where plaintiff's song was performed.

There is a second way of establishing access. If the plaintiff can establish that plaintiff's song was auditioned for or submitted to the composer of defendant's song before defendant's song was written, then access would be established. Access might also be established where plaintiff's song was auditioned for or submitted to a business associate or close friend of the composer of defendant's song. More difficult questions arise where plaintiff's song was auditioned for or submitted to a large company, such as a major record label, with which the composer of defendant's song has a business relationship.

In the end, the question of whether access is established is usually one of degree, which raises interesting and difficult issues for lawyers and judges. However, it is clear that the stronger the showing of access, the greater the chance plaintiff will have of proving copying by circumstantial evidence.

Substantial Similarity

As mentioned above, to prove copying by circumstantial evidence, the plaintiff must, ordinarily, show not only access, but also that there are elements in the two songs in issue that are substantially similar.

There is no precise definition of substantially similar. Clearly, it means something less than identical and something more than a little bit alike. Probably the best way of defining substantially similar is "so similar that an ordinary listener to music would believe that there was a strong possibility that one song, or at least an important part of it, was copied from the other."

As discussed above, even where the two songs in issue are substantially similar, the plaintiff's case will ordinarily be dismissed from court if the plaintiff cannot also present evidence of access. There is, however, one exception to the general rule that both access and substantial similarity must be proved to establish copying by circumstantial evidence. Where an expert witness will testify that the similarity between plaintiff's song and defendant's song is so overwhelming that there is no explanation for the similarity between them other than that one was copied from the other, access will be "inferred" from the similarity and the plaintiff will not be required to present any other evidence showing access, so long as there is some evidence that plaintiff's song was written before defendant's. It should, however, be pointed out that it is a rare case where this exception—known as the "striking similarity doctrine"—to the general rule would be applicable.

ESTABLISHING INDEPENDENT CREATION

It is important to keep in mind that the plaintiff does not conclusively establish copying just by presenting evidence showing both access and substantial similarity. Presentation of this evidence merely means that the issue of copying will be presented to the jury. Even if the plaintiff proves both access and substantial similarity, the defendant can win by convincing the jury that defendant's song was created independently of plaintiff's song. Regardless of how similar the songs in issue are, if the defendant did not in fact copy from the plaintiff's song, there can be no finding of copyright infringement. This is true even if the songs are identical—without copying there cannot be infringement. This is the law's way of recognizing that two composers could conceivably compose the very same song without either having heard the other's composition.

To establish independent creation (lack of copying), defendant will attempt to show a number of things. First, defendant will try to prove that the composer of defendant's song had solid musical training and a substantial background in music. This supports the conclusion that there was no need to copy from anything to write a good song.

Second, defendant will attempt to show that the composer of defendant's song wrote several hit songs before writing defendant's song. This supports the conclusion that the composer is skilled and successful and had no motivation or need to copy.

Third, and of great importance in persuading a jury that the similarity between the songs in issue did not result from copying, defendant will try to present music researchers and expert witnesses who can testify, using examples, that several songs or other musical works, written prior to plaintiff's and defendant's songs, are similar to both of them. This evidence is used to show that the musical elements causing the aural similarity between the two songs are elements commonly used by composers of popular music. This increases the likelihood that the similarities between the songs are coincidental and, thus, decreases the likelihood that defendant's song was copied from plaintiff's.

The law has long recognized that there are limits on the abilities of songwriters to combine notes, chords and rhythms so as to make music that will be relatively easy for most musicians to play, as well as both pleasing and accessible to the musically-untrained. Because of these limits, courts recognize that simple musical phrases are likely to recur in popular songs spontaneously—not as the result of one composer copying from another. Consequently, defendant will attempt to prove (using expert witnesses), that the musical elements of defendant's song, upon which the plaintiff's claim of copying is based, are simple musical elements that are pleasing to the musically-unsophisticated audience for contemporary popular music and are relatively easy for most musicians to perform.

Finally, defendant will attempt to show that the composer of defendant's song previously wrote one or more songs that also contained the musical elements supposedly copied from plaintiff's song. If defendant had used these same elements in songs written before there was a possibility of hearing plaintiff's song, it would be unlikely that defendant's song was copied from plaintiff's. It is, after all, ordinarily permissible to use material from one's own compositions, and composers of contemporary music often write songs that, in terms of the music, are very much like their earlier songs. If, however, a composer uses material from one of his or her songs that is now owned by someone else, a problem may arise.

In the final analysis, assuming that plaintiff puts on evidence sufficient to make a showing of access and substantial similarity, and defendant then puts on evidence of independent creation, it will be for the jury to determine whether the composer of defendant's song in fact copied from plaintiff's.

ESTABLISHING INFRINGEMENT

Even if the plaintiff establishes ownership of plaintiff's song and that the composer of defendant's song copied from it, still more must be shown to establish infringement.

The plaintiff must show that more than a minimal amount of material contained in defendant's song was copied from plaintiff's. However, contrary to what many musicians believe, there is no legal rule stating that a composer may freely borrow four bars, or six notes, or any other set amount of material from a copyrighted work without being found liable for infringement. Indeed, the copying of a very brief musical passage from plaintiff's song may result in a finding of infringement if that passage is *qualitatively* important to both songs in issue. For example, the copying of a brief melodic "hook" might well result in infringement if that hook is the centerpiece of plaintiff's song and is important in defendant's.

Defendant will not avoid liability for infringement by showing that there is much material in defendant's song that is not in any way similar to, and thus not copied from, plaintiff's song. For example, if the basis of plaintiff's claim is a strong musical similarity between the choruses of the two songs, defendant cannot avoid a finding of infringement by showing that the verses and bridges of the songs are totally dissimilar and there is no similarity in lyrics.

Copyright law does not protect ideas, only their expression. Accordingly, to establish infringement, plaintiff must demonstrate that the composer of defendant's song copied both the musical ideas and the manner in which the composer of plaintiff's song expressed those ideas. The distinction between a musical idea and the manner in which it is expressed is quite puzzling to musicians, lawyers and judges. Nevertheless, it is a distinction that is central to United States copyright law.

For there to be infringement, the material that was copied from the plaintiff's song must have been "original" to its composer. That is so because the copyright in a song protects only those musical elements, and combinations of musical elements, that are original to its composer. If certain elements of a copyrighted song were original and others were copied from an earlier song, the copyright in the song is valid, but protection in the song extends only to those elements that were original to its composer. It must, however, be understood that original does not mean novel or unique. For example, if a composer writes a theme that is similar (or identical) to an earlier one without copying from it, then, under copyright law, that composer's theme is considered his original theme.

The fair use doctrine may provide a defense even where the composer of defendant's song is found to have copied from plaintiff's song. However, this defense—which involves the weighing of several factors—is rarely useful in music infringement cases except where the defendant's song is a musical parody.

Finally, plaintiff is not required to show that the composer of defendant's song deliberately infringed the copyright in plaintiff's song. In fact, plaintiff need not even establish that the copying was a conscious act. Subconscious copying will result in a finding of infringement.

Significantly, if defendant's song is found by the jury to be an infringing copy of plaintiff's song, everyone who commercially exploits defendant's song will be liable for infringement, regardless of whether they had any reason to suspect that defendant's song infringed plaintiff's. Thus, a record company that innocently puts out a record containing a performance of defendant's song is liable for copyright infringement even if it has no possible way of knowing that the song is infringing, and even if the person or company supplying the recording represented and warranted that the song did not infringe any other musical work. The same is true with respect to a motion picture company that innocently includes defendant's song in the soundtrack of one of its films, and a manufacturer that innocently employs defendant's song in a television commercial.

The fact that companies in this position are treated as infringers, despite their lack of knowledge, is of great consequence, since the remedies available to a winning plaintiff apply to these companies.

REMEDIES

It is important to note that, after being charged with infringement, a losing defendant cannot avoid the remedies discussed below by expressing a willingness either to negotiate a "fair" license to use plaintiff's song or to pay plaintiff the prevailing "statutory rate" for a compulsory mechanical license, assuming the defendant could have avoided liability in the first place by paying plaintiff the statutory rate.

The four most important remedies available to a winning plaintiff are (1) injunctive relief, (2) statutory damages, (3) actual damages, and (4) the profits of each of the infringing defendants that is attributable to their use of infringing musical material (often perceived as the pot of gold at the end of the rainbow).

Injunctive Relief

Injunctive relief is a court order enjoining (*i.e.*, prohibiting) each of the defendants from further distributing and selling works, such as records, which contain material that infringes plaintiff's song. For example, if one of the defendants is a record company that has released an album containing a song that is found to infringe plaintiff's song, the record company may be enjoined from further distributing and selling the album until the infringing song is removed. Similarly, if one of the defendants is a motion picture company that has released a film containing infringing music, the company may be ordered to discontinue distribution and exhibition of the film unless the infringing music is removed from the soundtrack. If, however, the amount of infringing material in a work is insignificant when compared to that which is contained in the rest of the work, it is unlikely that the court would issue an injunction order unless it would be relatively easy to delete the infringing material.

Where a plaintiff is able to obtain an order enjoining a defendant from commercially exploiting a work—such as a successful album or film—which is producing substantial revenues for that defendant, plaintiff will have enormous economic leverage, permitting plaintiff to dictate the terms of a monetary settlement with that defendant.

Statutory Damages

Statutory damages are a form of damages provided for in the Copyright Act. They are calculated by multiplying a set amount of money times the number of infringements. This calculation can, however, become very complicated. Ordinarily, statutory damages are not nearly as meaningful to a plaintiff as any of the other remedies. Nevertheless, if an infringement action is contemplated or pursued, the option of statutory damages should be examined carefully.

Actual Damage

Actual damages are those damages actually suffered by the plaintiff as the result of the infringement of plaintiff's song. For example, if defendant's song was comprised of music copied from plaintiff's song, coupled with obscene or distasteful lyrics, plaintiff might find it difficult to thereafter commercially exploit the song. Or if a song that infringed plaintiff's song was included on the soundtrack of a successful film, plaintiff might well find it difficult to license the song to a motion picture company. In sum, any use of an infringing song that tends either to make plaintiff's song "old news" or to tarnish it is damaging to the plaintiff, and the plaintiff (generally through the use of expert witnesses) will attempt to prove the monetary extent of those damages.

Award of Profits

Often the most significant remedy available to a prevailing plaintiff is an award of the profits of each of the defendants that are attributable to the use of the infringing material. Profits, simply put, means revenues minus properly deductible costs and expenses, including, in some cases, income taxes. The issues that relate to the calculation of an award of profits are among the most challenging faced by lawyers involved in copyright cases.

In establishing the profits of an infringing defendant, the plaintiff is only required to present proof of the gross revenues realized by the defendant from its exploitation of the infringing song or, where the infringing song is embodied in a larger work, such as a motion picture or an album containing a number of other songs, from defendant's exploitation of that larger work. Defendant is then required to prove its properly deductible costs and expenses, which gives rise to a series of complicated accounting questions that are too complex to be treated in this chapter.

Since a prevailing plaintiff is entitled only to the profits attributable to the use of infringing material, two separate issues frequently arise. First, a determination must be made as to what extent the commercial success of the infringing song is attributable to its inclusion of infringing material, as distinguished from other factors, such as, for example, its use of noninfringing material and/or the talent of the performer who sings it. This question will often be the subject of expert testimony, with the plaintiff trying to prove that the infringing material was crucial to the popularity of the infringing song, and the defendant trying to prove that the infringing material played an insignificant role in the infringing song's success.

Second, where the infringing song is embodied in a work (such as an album or a motion picture) that includes other material that has no connection with plaintiff's song, another question becomes how much of the profits realized from the exploitation of that work is attributable to the infringing song and how much to the other material? For example, where the infringing song is one of 10 cuts on an album, more than 10% of the profits realized by the record company from its sales of the album would be attributable to the infringing song if it was the hit, or one of the hits, that drove up the sales of the album, and less than 10% if it was not one of the hits and therefore received little airplay.

Where an infringing song is used on the soundtrack of a motion picture, how much of the motion picture studio's profits from its distribution of the film were attributable to the song's presence on the soundtrack? If the infringing song's inclusion on the soundtrack constituted an incidental or minor use, only a minuscule percentage of the film's profits would be attributable to its inclusion. If, on the other hand, the song was the film's title song, which was released on a record that was successfully used to promote the film and keep the radio-listening public reminded that the film was in theaters, the plaintiff's case for profits would be much better.

A very difficult question arises where an infringing song is used in a commercial for a product, such as a beer. The question then becomes how much of the company's profits from beer sales were attributable to the use of the song in the commercial?

In dealing with the difficult questions regarding attribution of profits discussed above, both plaintiff and defendant will rely upon statistics, sales figures and expert testimony in their attempts to maximize (in the case of the plaintiff) or minimize (in the defendant's case) the significance of the song in "selling" the album, the film or the beer.

Punitive Damages/Attorneys' Fees

Finally, there is the question of whether punitive damages and/or attorneys' fees are available as remedies. The Copyright Act does not provide for punitive damages and the prevailing view is that punitive damages are not a remedy available to a successful plaintiff. Unlike most cases filed in U.S. courts, the prevailing (winning) party in an infringement case may be entitled to an award of his, her or its attorneys' fees. The courts are presently grappling with the issue of under what circumstances the prevailing party will receive an award of fees.

CONCLUSION

While no statistics are kept regarding the number of music infringement cases that are filed, it seems that the number has increased over the past 10 years and the costs involved in prosecuting and defending these types of cases tend to be substantial. And, while the majority of these cases are settled out of court, a surprisingly high percentage have actually gone to trial.

SAMPLING: LEGAL OVERVIEW AND PRACTICAL GUIDELINES

by Gregory T. Victoroff

A dwarf standing on the shoulders of a giant sees farther than the giant does. When a musician, record producer or recording engineer "samples" and adds portions of preexisting musical compositions or recordings to new recordings, it can be compared to "standing on the shoulders of a giant"—using the musical achievements of others to create a new musical composition.

The phenomenon is not new. In the 19th century, Rachmaninoff, Brahms and Liszt "borrowed" portions of contemporary Niccolò Paganini's "Caprice" for use in their own compositions.

At its best, sampling benefits society by creating a valuable new contribution to modern music literature. At its worst, sampling is vandalism and stealing, chopping up the songs and recordings of other artists without permission or payment; fraudulently passing off the joint work as the work of a single artist, without giving credit to the sampled work or the unwilling collaborators.

With the advent of digital technology, MIDI, electronic tone generators and computers, sampling sounds and manipulating them is relatively easy. As a result, sampling has opened a Pandora's box of old and new sound combinations, and with that, the necessity for new interpretations of issues like copyright infringement, privacy rights and unfair competition.

COPYRIGHT INFRINGEMENT

One of the many rights included in copyright is the right to copy a copyrighted work. Unauthorized sampling violates this right by copying a portion of a copyrighted work for a new recording.

The music publisher by itself or together with the songwriter usually owns the copyright in the song. The recording company usually owns the copyright in the sound recording. These copyright owners are most directly affected by sampling and have the right to sue unauthorized samplers in federal court for copyright infringement. (See also the chapters "Copyrights: The Law and You" and "Copyright Infringement.")

BREACH OF CONTRACT
Warranties

Copyright infringement from illegal sampling may also breach warranty provisions in recording contracts. Provisions called "Warranties," "Representations" and "Indemnifications" are almost always found in contracts between musicians and record companies, musicians and producers, producers and record companies, music publishers and record companies, songwriters and music publishers, record companies and distributors, and between distributors and record stores. According to these clauses, the person providing the product (e.g., the songs, recordings, publishing rights, records, tapes or CDs) promises the person buying or licensing the product (the record company or record store), that the recordings will not infringe anyone's copyrights or other rights.

If a lawsuit for illegal sampling is filed, it could result in lawsuits for "breach of warranty" between each person selling the illegally sampled product. Claims apply from person to person along the chain of the record-making process, creating a duty of indemnification for each person along the chain. Final legal responsibility may lie with the recording artist. The indemnification rights existing between each person or company in the record-making process trigger one another like a chain reaction. This can result in hundreds of thousand of dollars in liability to the artist at the end of the chain who has no one but him or herself to blame for the illegal sampling.

Indemnification provisions require the record distributor to pay the record store's damages and attorneys' fees, the record company is required to pay the distributor's fees and damages, the producer pays the record company's fees and damages and the artist may be technically liable for everyone's attorneys' fees and damages.

Unsatisfactory Masters

Another potential contract problem for musicians that sample is that most recording contracts give the record company the right to reject masters that are unsatisfactory. Masters that infringe copyrights of other sound recordings or musical compositions can be rejected as unsatisfactory.

The artist will be required to obtain copyright licenses or "clearances" from the owners of the sampled material or to deliver substitute masters, which do not contain samples, to satisfy contract obligations to the record company.

Failure to comply with the record company's master delivery requirements could result in the artist having to repay recording fund advances and possibly defending legal claims for breach of contract.

Fair Use Defense

The defense of fair use permits reasonable unauthorized copying from a copyrighted work, when the copying does not substantially impair present or potential value of the original work, and in some way advances the public benefit.

One rationale for the so-called fair use defense to copyright infringement is that only a small portion of the copyright work is copied. For many years there was a popular myth among musicians and producers that up to eight bars of a song was fair use and could be copied without constituting copyright infringement. Of course this is not true. The rules controlling which uses are fair uses, and not copyright infringement are not clear or simple, and the fair use standard for sound recordings is generally stricter than for fair uses of musical compositions.

The reason for this difference is that U.S. copyright law only protects the expression of ideas, not the idea itself. Since there are a limited number of musical notes, copyright law treats single notes like ideas, and does not protect them. For this reason, it is safe to say that borrowing one note from a song will usually be a fair use of the copyright in the song, and not an actionable infringement. Borrowing more than one note, however, could be trouble. Lawsuits have involved copying as few as four notes from "I Love New York" and three words from "I Got Rhythm."

By selecting and arranging several notes in a particular sequence, composers create copyrightable musical compositions, or songs. Songs are the expression of the composer's creativity and are protected by copyright.

But different fair use standards apply to sound recordings. Since there is virtually an unlimited number of sounds that can be recorded, sound recordings are, by definition, comprised of pure, copyrightable expression.

For musicians, engineers and producers, the practical effect of the two different fair use standards is that sampling a small portion of a musical composition may sometimes be fair use because copying a small portion may borrow uncopyrightable single notes like uncopyrightable ideas. But sampling even a fraction of a second of a sound recording is copying of pure, copyrightable expression and is more likely to be an unfair use, constituting copyright infringement.

One way some producers and engineers that sample attempt to reduce the chances of a successful copyright infringement lawsuit is by "camouflaging" or electronically processing portions of the sampled sounds beyond the point of their being easily recognizable. Filtering, synthesizing or distorting recorded sounds can help conceal the sampled material while still retaining the essence of an instrumental lick or vocal phrase embodied in a few seconds of sound. Adding newly created sounds to the underlying sampling further dilutes the material. This is an attempt to change the sampled materials so that even though material was illegally *copied*, there is no substantial similarity, thus avoiding a suit for copyright infringement.

UNFAIR COMPETITION

State and federal unfair competition laws apply when the record buying public is misled as to the source or true origin of recordings that contain sampled material. The Lanham Act is a federal law that punishes deceptive trade practices that mislead consumers about what they are buying or who made the product.

If a customer in a record store is confused by hearing a recording containing sampled vocal tracks of James Brown, or sampled guitar licks by Eddie Van Halen, and mistakenly buys the record only to discover that he or she has bought a recording by a different artist, the customer has been deceived by the sampling. Such confusion and deception is a form of unfair competition, giving rise to legal claims for Lanham Act violations that can be brought in federal court, or unfair competition claims that may be brought in state court. All of the previous warnings about the costs of litigation apply here as well.

RIGHTS OF PRIVACY VIOLATIONS

When sampled material incorporates a person's voice, statutory and common law rights of privacy (also called "rights of publicity") may be violated. In California, Civil Code section 3344 establishes civil liability for the unauthorized commercial use of any living person's voice. Such a use would include sampling.

Although current federal moral rights legislation does not protect sound recordings or voices, such protection may be available in the near future. Meanwhile, many state laws make unauthorized sampling of voices a violation of state right of publicity laws. Further, if the sampled voice was originally recorded without the vocalist's permission, sampling such an unauthorized recording may violate other state privacy laws as well.

FEDERAL ANTIBOOTLEGGING STATUTES

Effective December 8, 1994 the Uruguay Round Agreements Act amended U.S. law by adding both civil and criminal penalties for the unauthorized recording or video-taping of live musical performances.

Any person who recorded or sampled in the past, or records or samples in the future, any part of any live musical performance without the performer's consent, can now be sued under the new federal law for the same statutory damages, actual damages and attorneys' fees that are available in a traditional copyright infringement suit.

Previously, unauthorized recording of live performances was prohibited only under certain state laws.

Now, section 1101 *et seq.* of the federal copyright law (17 U.S.C. §1101 *et seq.*) can be used to prosecute so-called bootleggers that secretly record or sample live musical performances, or copy such illegal recordings by including sampled portions in new recordings. This strict new law also prohibits selling or even transporting bootlegged recordings.

Remarkably, the law is retroactive, protecting even pre–1994 recordings if they are currently being sold or distributed, and has no statute of limitations, so that suit can be brought against bootleggers and sellers of bootlegged recordings 10, 20, even 100 years after the unauthorized recording was made, if the unauthorized recordings are sold or distributed after the effective date of the Act. Unlike copyrights which usually only last for the life of the author plus 50 years, the new federal musical performance rights are perpetual, lasting forever. Moreover, the defense of fair use may not apply to such unauthorized recordings.

Of even greater concern are newly enacted criminal penalties (18 U.S.C. §2319A) of forfeiture, seizure, destruction and up to ten years imprisonment for knowingly, for profit, making or distributing copies of the illegally recorded performances, transmitting an illegally recorded performance, or distributing, selling, renting or even transporting illegally recorded performances, even if the performance occurred outside the United States!

The serious implications of this new law for outlaw samplers should be obvious. Sampling any part of a live performance, or any part of an unauthorized recording of a live musical performance triggers a minefield of federal civil and criminal penalties. Great care should be taken to avoid using such bootlegged recordings in any way.

LANDMARK LAWSUITS

In one of the most publicized sampling cases, the publisher of songwriter Gilbert O'Sullivan's song "Alone Again (Naturally)" successfully sued rap artist Biz Markie, Warner Brothers Records and others for sampling three words and a small portion of music from O'Sullivan's song without permission on Markie's rap tune "Alone Again."

A lawsuit involving the unauthorized use of drumbeats sought strict enforcement of copyright laws against sampling. Tuff City Records sued Sony Music and Def Jam Records claiming that two singles by rap artist L.L. Cool J ("Around the Way Girl" and "Six Minutes of Pleasure") contained drum track samples from "Impeach the Presidents," a 1973 song by the Honeydrippers and that another Def Jam Record, "Give the People" included vocal samples from the same Honeydrippers song.

The case is important because the common practice of sampling drumbeats is often overlooked as a minor use, too insignificant to bother clearing. If successful, this lawsuit will reinforce the rule that any sampling of a sound recording may lead to a lawsuit for copyright infringement.

A lawsuit testing the limits of the fair use defense was brought by the Ireland-based rock group U2. The band, its recording company, Island Records, and music publisher Warner–Chappell Music sued the group Negativland for sampling a part of the U2 song, "I Still Haven't Found What I'm Looking For" without the group's permission. While attorneys for U2 claimed that the sampling was consumer fraud, Negativland maintained that the use was parody, satire & cultural criticism, and was therefore protected under the fair use doctrine. The case was settled out of court, and Negativland agreed to recall the single and return copies to Island Records for destruction.

Jarvis v. A&M Records was a lawsuit over the taking of eight words ("Ooh ooh ooh ooh…move…free your body") and a keyboard line. The sampling party argued that the amount of material taken was too insignificant to constitute copyright infringement. The federal district court in New Jersey disagreed, and refused to dismiss the suit on that ground. Instead, the court dismissed the suit because the sampling party had obtained a copyright registration for the sampled sound recording, and the plaintiff had not disproved the validity of the registration.

PENALTIES

Attorneys are always expensive. Entertainment attorneys usually charge $100 to $400 per hour. Those that are experienced in federal court copyright litigation may charge even more. Court costs and one side's attorneys' fees in a copyright trial average about $150,000. If you lose the trial you will have to pay the judgment against you, which could be as high as $100,000 for a single willful infringement (or higher if there are substantial profits involved). An appeal of a judgment against you involves still more attorneys' fees and sometimes requires the posting of a bond.

In some cases a copyright infringer may have to pay the winning party's attorneys' fees. Copyright law also authorizes injunctions against the sale of CDs, tapes and records containing illegally sampled material, seizure and destruction of infringing matter, and other criminal penalties.

In short, defending a copyright infringement lawsuit is a substantial expense and a risky proposition, exposing you to the possibility of hundreds of thousands of dollars in legal fees and costs.

Even if your particular sampling does not constitute copyright infringement, and is a fair use, it must still avoid violation of state and federal unfair competition laws.

COPYRIGHT CLEARANCES

Obtaining advance "permission," "copyright licenses" or "clearances" from owners of both the musical composition and the sound recording you want to sample is the best way to avoid the problems and expenses that can result from illegal sampling.

Many factors affect whether and when musicians should request and pay for clearances for samples. Although copyright laws and general music industry practices do not give rise to a lawsuit in every sampling situation, the enormous expenses of any sampling dispute should be avoided whenever possible.

In many cases, it is wise to clear samples early in the recording process even if, eventually, they are not used, because when the record is finished and the sample must be cleared, the artist will have little leverage in negotiating the clearance fee.

In some cities, special music clearance firms routinely request, negotiate, prepare and process clearances for sampled material for a fee. Music clearance firms know reasonable rates for clearances and will prepare valid copyright licenses for less cost to the requesting party than will most music attorneys.

Clearance Costs/Royalties

The cost of clearances is a major consideration in deciding whether to sample. Generally, record companies will not pay an artist more than the full statutory mechanical license fee for permission to sell recordings of the artist's composition. The current statutory rate is 6.6 cents per unit, for up to five minutes of a recording. However, most clearance companies and others typically negotiate mechanical license fees of only 50% to 75% of the statutory rate to record an entire composition. Out of that mechanical license fee, the sampling artist must pay the owners of any sampled material. If the clearance fees for the sampled material are too high, none of the mechanical license fee will be left for the sampling artist, and sampling makes no economic sense.

Sampling royalty rates for musical compositions can range from approximately 10% to 25% of the statutory rate. Sampling royalty rates for sound recordings range from approximately .5 cents to 3 cents per unit sold.

Clearance costs double or triple when more than one sampled track is included in a recording. Imagine, for example, a composition containing Phil Collins' snare drum sound, Jimi Hendrix's guitar sound, Phil Lesh's bass and Little Richard's voice. In this case, combined sampling clearance fees would make the multitrack recording impossibly expensive.

Sample clearance practices vary widely throughout the music industry. The sampling license fee will be affected by both the quantity of material being sampled (a quarter second is a "minor use," five seconds is a "major use") and the quality of the sampled material (i.e., a highly recognizable lyric sung by a famous artist would be more expensive than an anonymous bass drum track). Certain artists demand exorbitant fees to discourage sampling. On the other hand, some music publishers offer compositions in their catalogs and actively encourage sampling. Prices are affected by the popularity and prestige of the sampling artist and the uniqueness and value of the sampled sounds.

CLEARANCE HOUSES

Here are a few businesses that specialize in obtaining clearances. Average charges are between $50 and $80 an hour.

Clearance 13'8"
26 West 76th Street
New York, NY 10023
(212) 580-4654

Copyright Data Management
405 Riverside Drive
Burbank, CA 91506
(818) 558-3480

Songwriter Services
21704 West Golden Triangle Road North, Suite 405
Santa Clarita, CA 91350
(805) 259-8300

Suzy Vaughan Associates, Inc.
2029 Century Park East, Suite 450
Los Angeles, CA 90067
(310) 556-1409

Clearance Costs/Buyouts and Co-ownership

A percentage of the mechanical license fee (royalty) is one type of clearance fee. Another, is a one-time flat-fee payment (buyout) for the use of sampled material. Buyout fees range from $250 to $10,000, depending on the demands of the copyright owners, with most under $1,000 for minor uses, and in the $2,000 range for major uses. Up to $50,000 may be charged for a major use of a famous artist's performance or song. An upper limit on the number of units embodying the sampled material that may be sold may be imposed by some licensors, requiring additional payment at a higher royalty rate or an entirely new license if the maximum is exceeded.

In some cases music publishers and record companies have requested to be co-owners of the new composition as a condition of granting permission to sample. The option of assigning a share of the publishing (i.e., the copyright) in the song containing the sampled material to a publisher or record company may be helpful to the sampling artist, particularly when a buyout of all rights is not possible. Assigning a portion of the copyright in lieu of a cash advance may be less of a financial burden on an artist, enabling a song to be released where the cost or availability of a license would otherwise preclude the record from being distributed legally. If you license the sample for a percentage of the statutory rate, and you later want to license your song with the sample in it for a film, the film producer must obtain separate permission from the publisher who has granted the license. That publisher must always be consulted in new licensing situations. On the other hand, if you negotiate a buyout, you are free from any continuing obligation to the publisher. Similarly, if you negotiate income participation, that is, sell a percentage of your song in return for permission to sample, the publisher becomes a part owner of your song, but in most cases will not have approval rights in future licensing of the new work. Percentage of income participation ranges from 5% for a minimal use within the song to as much as 75% if the sample has been utilized throughout the song and is an integral part of the work.

Soundtrack Sampling

Occasionally, artists sample things other than music, such as audio bytes from feature films, television shows or news footage. In these cases, permission must be obtained from the owner of the footage. Fees range from $1000 to $8000 per minute for buyouts. Sometimes, permission is granted for free, or for the Screen Actors Guild minimum scale payment of approximately $600. Much more is usually charged for permission to sample the voice of someone of the caliber of Marilyn Monroe. If a film or television program is used, payments may also be due to the writers and directors guilds or to the American Federation of Musicians.

CONCLUSION

Throughout history, every new development in music has been greeted with suspicion by the music establishment of the day. Polyphony (playing harmonies) was considered demonic in medieval times, and was punishable by burning at the stake. As modern musicians explore innovative chord progressions, syncopated rhythms, and new electronic instruments, we all learn more about the musical landscape around us. It remains to be seen whether the musicians and record producers that sample from the vast collective library of music and sound will be viewed as musical innovators or plagiarists.

SAMPLE USE AGREEMENTS

The Master Sample Use License Agreement and Mechanical License are short-form examples of licenses to incorporate or sample portions of a recording of a musical composition. Permission to sample the musical composition is granted by the music publisher(s) in the Mechanical License; permission to sample the *recording* of the musical composition is granted by the record company in the Master Sample Use License Agreement.

Fees for using the master and the musical composition are expressed as a one-time flat fee, or buyout, and perpetual, worldwide rights are granted. As discussed above, such extensive rights may not always be granted. Limits on the term, territory or number of units that may be sold, co-ownership of the recording and/or co-ownership of the musical composition embodying the sampled material, or statutory compulsory license fees on every copy sold, may be required by certain record companies or music publishers.

MASTER SAMPLE USE LICENSE AGREEMENT

In consideration of the sum of $_____ which covers _____\% of the copyright and full payment for the rights and license herein granted thereto, _____ (hereinafter referred to as "Licensor") hereby grants to _____ (hereinafter referred to as "Licensee") the non-exclusive, limited right, license, privilege and authority, but not the obligation, to use a portion of the Master Recording, defined below (hereinafter referred to as the "Master"), as embodied in the tape approved by Licensor, with no greater usage of the Master than is contained in the approved tape (the "Usage"), in the manufacture, distribution, and sale of any phonorecord (as that term in defined in Section 101 of the Copyright Act) entitled "_____" ("Album"), performed by _____ ("Artist") embodying the recording _____ (Master) as performed by _____ ("Sample Artist"), and produced by _____ ("Producer"). Licensor additionally grants to Licensee the right to exploit, advertise, publicize, and promote such Master, as embodied in the phonorecord, in all media, markets, and/or formats now known or hereafter devised.

1. The term of this agreement ("Term") will begin on the date hereof and shall continue in perpetuity.

2. The territory covered by this agreement is _____.

3. It is expressly understood and agreed that any compensation to be paid herein to Licensor is wholly contingent upon the embodiment of the Master within the phonorecord and that nothing herein shall obligate or require Licensee to commit to such usage. However, such compensation shall in no way be reduced by a lesser use of the Recording than the Usage provided for herein.

4. Licensor warrants only that it has the legal right to grant the aforesaid master recording use rights subject to the terms, conditions, limitations, restrictions and reservations herein contained, and that this license is given and accepted without any other warranty or recourse. In the event said warranty is breached, Licensor's total liability

shall not exceed the lesser of the actual damages incurred by Licensee or the total consideration paid hereunder to Licensor.

5. Licensor reserves unto itself all rights and uses of every kind and nature whatsoever in and to the Master other than the limited rights specifically licensed hereunder, including the sole right to exercise and to authorize others to exercise such rights at any and all times and places without limitation.

6. This license is binding upon and shall inure to the benefit of the respective successors and/or assigns of the parties hereto.

7. This contract is entered into in the State of California and its validity, construction, interpretation and legal effect shall be governed by the laws of the State of California applicable to contracts entered into and performed entirely therein.

8. This agreement contains the entire understanding of the parties relating to the subject matter herein contained.

IN WITNESS WHEREOF, the parties have caused the foregoing to be executed as of this _____ day of _____, 199__.

AGREED TO AND ACCEPTED:

_____   _____
LICENSOR   LICENSEE

_____   _____
BY   BY

_____   _____
NAME AND TITLE (AN AUTHORIZED SIGNATORY) NAME AND TITLE (AN AUTHORIZED SIGNATORY)

_____   _____
FEDERAL I.D. / SS#   FEDERAL I.D. / SS#

MECHANICAL LICENSE

In consideration of the sum of $_____ which covers _____% of the copyright and full payment for the rights and license herein granted thereto, _____ (referred to herein as "Licensor") hereby grants to _____ (referred to herein as "Licensee") the nonexclusive, right, license, privilege and authority to use, in whole or in part, the copyrighted musical composition known as _____ written by _____ and _____ (hereinafter referred to as the "Composition"):

1. In the recording, making and distribution of phonorecords (as that term is defined in Section 101 of the Copyright Act) to be made and distributed throughout the world in accordance with the provisions of Section 115 of the Copyright Act of the United States of America of October 19, 1976, as amended (the "Act"), except it is agreed that: (1) Licensee need not serve or file the notices required under the Act; (2) consideration for such license shall be in the form of a one-time flat-fee buyout; (3) Licensee shall have the unlimited right to utilize the Composition, or any portion thereof, as embodied in the phonorecord, in any and all media now known or hereafter devised for the purpose of promoting the sale of the phonorecord which is the subject of this agreement; and (4) this license shall be worldwide.

2. This license permits the use of the Composition or any portion thereof, in the particular recordings made in connection with the sound recording _____ ("Album") by _____ ("Artist"), and permits the use of such recording in any phonorecord in which the recording may be embodied in whatever form now known or hereafter devised. This license includes the privilege of making a musical arrangement of the Composition to the extent necessary to conform it to the style or manner of interpretation of the performance involved.

3. Licensor warrants and represents that it has the right to enter into this agreement and to grant to Licensee all of the rights granted herein, and that the exercise by Licensee of any and all of the rights granted to Licensee in this agreement will not violate or infringe upon any common law or statutory rights of any person, firm or corporation including, without limitation, contractual rights, copyrights and rights of privacy.

4. This license is binding upon and shall inure to the benefit of the respective successors, assigns and/or sublicensees of the parties hereto.

5. This agreement sets forth the entire understanding of the parties with respect to the subject matter hereof, and may not be modified or amended except by written agreement executed by the parties.

6. This license may not be terminated for any reason, is entered into in the State of California, and its validity, construction, interpretation and legal effect shall be governed by the laws of the State of California applicable to contracts entered into and performed entirely therein.

IN WITNESS WHEREOF, the parties have entered into this license agreement as of this
_____ day of _____, 199_.

AGREED TO AND ACCEPTED:

_____   _____
LICENSOR   LICENSEE

_____   _____
BY   BY

_____   _____
NAME AND TITLE (AN AUTHORIZED SIGNATORY)   NAME AND TITLE (AN AUTHORIZED SIGNATORY)

_____   _____
FEDERAL I.D. / SS#   FEDERAL I.D. / SS#

Special thanks to Suzy Vaughan, Esq. and Ron McGowan for their generous assistance in the preparation of these agreements.

MUSIC AND NEW MEDIA

by Mark Halloran and Thomas A. White

The new media of computer games, CD-ROMs and online computer services have raised numerous issues regarding the use and protection of musical works and sound recordings.

The onslaught of new technologies that utilize music will not be stopped and technology is always ahead of the law. Each new media causes musicians and those in the business of distributing music to deal with new business and legal practices.

Norms will evolve as the music business determines how each new use is similar to prior uses and how it is different.

The most recent "buzz" has been over so-called multimedia—the combination of film, graphics, music and other material on a disc, which can be manipulated by the user. The basic distinction in the use of music in multimedia is between being hired to create the music and licensing already created music to the multimedia producer.

If you are hired to write and record music for a multimedia project the negotiations are akin to those for a film or television composition. You will negotiate a fee for your services, the scope of the rights granted, what you will deliver, your credit and royalties, and creative control.

The most important of these, from a long term perspective, is the scope of the grant of rights. The multimedia producer will want to own all rights to the songs and recordings, with the unrestricted right to use them in the multimedia project itself and otherwise and be able to exploit the music without paying royalties.

Whether or not a proposed multimedia music deal is fair to the composer depends on a variety of factors. One useful analytical framework is to compare the composer deal with composer deals in television and film. In television, composers' fees for services are usually in the low thousands for single episodes; for movie of the weeks (MOWs) they can be in the $10,000 to $50,000 range. However, television composers can be assured that if the television program is broadcast that they will receive royalties from ASCAP, BMI or SESAC, which can equal or in many cases, exceed their fee.

In assessing whether a fee for a multimedia project is sufficient, a composer should keep in mind potential future income. In film and television a composer may make money from mechanical licenses from soundtrack album sales and public performance income from the performance of the score or songs on radio and television. Such sources of income do not exist for CD-ROMs and video games; at present, the initial fee is the only income.

Film composers' fees range to $500,000. In addition, they can receive monies from performing rights societies if their film is broadcast, or shown in theaters outside the United States. In both television and film, composers reserve the writer's share of music publishing income, and sometimes share in part or all of the publisher's share. They also participate in mechanical license income from soundtrack album royalties.

At present, music budgets for multimedia projects are much less than those for television and film and composers' fees are correspondingly lower.

As with film production companies, multimedia companies acquire copyrights from composers in one of three ways: (1) In the case of preexisting works, copyrights are conveyed by means of a written transfer; (2) where the composer is a legitimate employee of a multimedia company, the company owns the copyright from inception by operation of law; and (3) multimedia companies also own, from inception, specially ordered or commissioned works when created pursuant to a written agreement with a composer. The latter two categories are examples of works made for hire under the Copyright Act of 1976. (See the chapter "Copyrights: The Law and You.")

When composers negotiate the scope of the grant of rights it is a given that the music can be used in the "platform" for which it is being written (e.g., CD-ROM or video game), and for advertising and publicity. However, issues such as uses in different platforms in audio only soundtracks or in film or television can be negotiated. Obviously, composers should seek to reserve as many rights as possible. To the extent that rights cannot be reserved, composers should make sure they are paid royalties for those uses.

Video and arcade games based on movies are becoming popular. One such is *The Lion King* by Disney and though the film prominently featured the Academy Award winning songs of Elton John and Tim Rice, these songs, recorded by Elton John, do not appear in the game.

As the composer you should make sure that if you are being hired for a film and a game that you are paid for both.

> The White House Task Force on National Information Infrastructure, chaired by Bruce A. Lehman, Patent and Trademark Office Commissioner, has recommended changes to existing copyright law. According to Lehman, the changes will "allow owners and users of all types of materials, from movies to software, to realize the full potential of the information superhighway as a commercial marketplace." The task force says existing laws must be clarified to make it clear that any electronic transmission of material falls within the exclusive distribution rights of the copyright owner.

THE MUSIC IS LICENSED

Typically, when there are preexisting songs and recordings the multimedia producer will acquire a license for the use of the songs and recording. The Harry Fox Agency Multimedia Rights License is attached. It is essentially a hybridized mechanical and synchronization license (which are discussed below).

A mechanical license is the right to reproduce a song in a record and to distribute the records to the public.

A synchronization license is the right to reproduce a song in time relation to an audiovisual work, typically a film or TV program.

A public performance license is the right to publicly perform a song. These are issued by ASCAP, BMI and SESAC.

The Harry Fox Agency Multimedia License form makes it clear that it does not license public performance rights. Thus, if you write music for an arcade game, the video arcade where your music is performed should have ASCAP, BMI and SESAC licenses. To the extent that your performing rights society tracks arcade performances, you may receive public performance royalties from the performance of your song in an arcade. However, at present none of the performing rights societies have video arcade music performance tracking mechanisms.

If you own your song and recordings, it is up to you whether to grant a license to the producer of a multimedia project. However, if your song or recording is owned by a music publisher or record company, that entity has the right to grant multimedia licenses. Many music publishers and record companies, however, will tell you in advance if they plan to grant the license and give you an opportunity to voice your concerns. The money generated from such licenses is typically split fifty-fifty between you the writer or recording artist and the publisher or label.

Obviously there are different concerns when the interactive project is your own. Many major acts—The Rolling Stones and Sting for example—are creating multimedia projects. In such cases the act works in concert with the record label. As discussed in the chapter "Analysis of a Recording Contract," the label has the exclusive right to the act's recording services, so the label must approve the act's recording services for the interactive project.

CD-I

Just as CDs replaced vinyl discs, it appears inevitable that CDs will be replaced by CD-Is (CD Interactive), which will contain the audio and video of the recording act. Record companies have been taking the position that video games, multimedia and other computer software programs, which are sold for home use, e.g., on CD-ROM or CD-I are to be encompassed within the definition of records, and the companies are enforcing their rights of exclusivity with respect thereto.

PURCHASE OF RECORDS THROUGH INTERNET

As soon as credit card security systems become fully integrated and modem and Internet provider port speeds increase, and reduced data storage cost makes it practical, online ordering will deliver prerecorded product directly to consumers either on a pay-per-play basis or by downloading a copy of the product to the consumer's computer storage medium (e.g., a hard drive). This true "celestial jukebox" will put record companies in direct competition with their traditional retail outlets such as Blockbuster, Musicland, Tower Records, etc., with a far greater reach into consumers' homes than has ever been achieved.

A critical issue in the implementation of online purchasing capabilities is the evolution of laws to accommodate technological advancement while preserving the rights and enforcement mechanisms upon which that commerce is dependent. The consumer will receive the equivalent of a record without the song and sound recording being put into a phonorecord. Still, the songwriter and music publisher should share in a license fee, and the recording artist should receive a royalty since when the consumer downloads and copies, a sale is taking place.

COPYRIGHT REGISTRATION FOR MULTIMEDIA WORKS

The Copyright Office defines a multimedia work as one which "combines authorship in two or more media." The authorship may include text, artwork, sculpture, cinematography, photography, sounds, music or choreography. The media may include two or more of the following: printed matter (book, charts, posters, sheet music);

audiovisual material (filmstrip, slides, videotape, videodisc); phonorecord (audiodisc, audiotape); or a machine readable copy (computer-read disc, tape or chip). The appropriate application form to use for copyright registration depends on what elements make up the multimedia work.

A GUIDE TO WHICH APPLICATION FORM TO USE

(Taken from Copyright Office Circular 55, *Copyright Registration for Multimedia Works*.)

The following are examples of typical multimedia deposits showing the appropriate form and authorship statements for registration. The elements that make up a particular claim will determine the correct way to complete the form.

Form to Use	Nature of Deposit	Suggested Nature of Authorship Statement
PA	Slides and booklet	(1) Entire work *or* (2) Text and Photography
PA	Slides (or filmstrips), and booklet, and audiocassettes	(1) Entire work *or* (2) Text as printed and recorded; photography, and sounds
PA	Videocassettes, manual with text and pictorial illustrations	(1) Entire work *or* (2) Cinematography, text, and illustrations
PA	Filmstrip, pamphlets, poster, and music soundsheet	(1) Entire work *or* (2) Photography, text, artwork, lyrics, music, and sounds
PA	Manuals, container with artwork, and identifying materials (computer program listing, videotape) for machine-readable diskette which produces pictorial screen display	Printed text and artwork, text of computer program, and audiovisual work
PA	Manual, interactive compact disk, and identifying material for computer program on machine-readable diskette (or cassette)	Printed text, photographs, and text of computer program
SR	Audiocassettes and manual	**Do Not Use "Entire Work" on Form SR.** Text as printed and recorded, and sound recording
SR	Music soundsheets, booklets, and posters	Text, artwork, lyrics, music, and sound recording
SR	Audiocassettes, manual and identifying material for computer program on machine-readable diskette (or cassette)	Text of manual and computer program, recorded text, and sound recording
TX	Manuals and identifying material for computer program on machine-readable diskette (or cassette) which produces textual screen display	Text of manuals and computer program

MULTIMEDIA RIGHTS LICENSE (MMERL)

The Harry Fox Agency, Inc.
711 Third Avenue, 8th Floor
New York, New York 10017
License No.: _____
Date of Issuance:
The following provisions shall apply as indicated in the body of this License: _____
(A) Licensee: _____
(B) Musical Composition: _____
(C) Licensor(s) and percentage of ownership: _____
(D) License Date: _____
(E) Term: _____
(F) Advance: _____
(G) Units: _____
(H) Royalty Per Unit: "Two times the so-called statutory royalty rate (provided pursuant to Section 115 of the United States Copyright Act for the making and distribution of phonorecords) (17 U.S.C. 115)."
OR
(H) Royalty Per Unit: "_____ cents"
(I) Territory: _____
(J) Software Serial Number: _____

DEFINITIONS:
1. For the purposes hereof, the following terms shall have the following meanings:
   (a) "MULTIMEDIA" shall mean the medium in which a musical composition will be utilized in conjunction with, but not limited to, computer monitor visual displays.
   (b) "MULTIMEDIA DISC" which shall include, but not be limited to CD ROM or computer assisted laser discs, shall mean those MULTIMEDIA DISCS containing those musical recordings which is the subject of this license.
   (c) The term "MULTIMEDIA DISC MARKET" shall refer to the sale, lease, license, use or other distribution of MULTIMEDIA DISCS directly or indirectly to individuals for playback through, but not limited to, a personal computer, whether now in existence or hereafter developed.
   (d) "Copy" or "copies" shall mean all MULTIMEDIA DISC copies manufactured and distributed by Licensee.

Now it is therefore agreed as follows:

1. Licensee is hereby applying to Licensor for a MULTIMEDIA rights license to use the musical composition referred to in (B) (above) for the purposes of manufacturing, distributing and selling to the public throughout the territory (I), MULTIMEDIA, embodying the musical composition.

2. Licensor hereby grants to the Licensee the following nonexclusive rights with respect to MULTIMEDIA DISC, in all respects subject to the terms and conditions herein provided:

(a) To record and rerecord in digital, computer readable or other form consistent with the integral requirements of the MULTIMEDIA, the musical composition for use in whole or in part in connection with and with respect to MULTI-MEDIA DISC;

(b) To make and distribute copies of the MULTIMEDIA DISC program through the territory only (I).

(c) Licensee may make arrangements and orchestrations of the Composition for its recording purposes, however, this license does not include the right to alter the fundamental character of the Composition, to print sheet music or to make any other use of the Composition not expressly authorized hereunder, all rights to uses not expressly granted hereunder are hereby expressly reserved by the Licensor.

3. Licensee covenants that it shall place on the outside of all containers or, where possible, in every MULTIMEDIA DISC copy a conspicuous notice to clearly read as follows:

Title of Composition and Names of writers. Copyright © 19__ (owner of composition). International Rights Secured. Not for broadcast transmission. All rights reserved. DO NOT DUPLICATE. NOT FOR SEPARATE RENTAL.

WARNING: "It is a violation of Federal Copyright Law to synchronize this MULTI-MEDIA DISC with videotape or film, or to print this MULTIMEDIA DISC in the form of standard music notation without the express written permission of the copyright owner."

4. The musical composition recorded as a MULTIMEDIA DISC shall not exceed _____ minutes and _____ seconds.

5. The use of the musical composition hereunder shall be:

6. The term during which the rights licensed hereunder may be exercised shall be _____ (the number referred to in (E)) years from the License date (D).

7. (a) Licensee shall make the royalty payments hereunder, which shall be accompanied by a detailed accounting statement listing units distributed within forty-five (45) days after the end of each calendar quarter during which the MULTIMEDIA DISC copies are distributed, equal to _____ (the amount referred to in (H)) per MULTIMEDIA DISC copy of the work which is manufactured and distributed during each such respective calendar quarter. Within thirty (30) days after the execution of this license, Licensee shall make such payment and render such statement for all units distributed prior to the execution of this license.

(b) In the event that Licensee fails to account and pay royalties as herein provided, Licensor shall have the right to give written notice to Licensee that unless the default is remedied within thirty (30) days from the date of the notice, this license shall be deemed terminated. Such failure to pay and cure default in such thirty (30) day period shall render either the making or the distribution, or both, of all MULTIMEDIA DISC copies hereunder for which royalties have not been paid, actionable acts of infringement under, and fully subject to the remedies provided by the U.S. Copyright Act.

8. Upon ten (10) business days prior written notice, Licensor, by the Harry Fox Agency ("HFA"), shall have the right during reasonable business hours at Licensee's place of business and at HFA's sole expense to examine, and make copies and extracts from the books and records of Licensee relating to its production, making and distribution of MULTIMEDIA copies hereunder for the purpose of verifying the accuracy of statements and payments and the performance of Licensee's obligations hereunder. Licensee shall not be required to submit to such an examination more than once during any twelve (12) month period.

9. This license does not include the rights to:
   (a) Rent separately the musical composition included in the MULTIMEDIA copies or to permit purchasers or others to do so;
   (b) Use the story of the musical composition or dramatically depict the musical composition;
   (c) Parody the lyrics and/or music of the musical composition in any way;
   (d) Publicly perform, broadcast/cablecast or transmit the work in any manner;
   (e) Make, sell or distribute audio phonorecords of the musical composition;
   (f) Utilize a sound recording and/or audiovisual master(s) not owned or separately licensed by Licensee.

10. All rights of every kind and nature with respect to the composition which are not expressly granted to licensee hereunder are expressly reserved by Licensor.

11. Licensor warrants only that it has the right to grant this license, and this license is given and accepted without any other representation, warrant or recourse, express or implied, except for Licensor's agreement to repay the consideration paid for this license if the aforesaid warranty should be breached. In no event shall the total liability of the Licensor exceed the total amount of consideration received by it hereunder.

12. Upon the expiration of this license, all rights herein granted shall cease and terminate and the right to make or authorize any further use or distribution of any recordings made hereunder shall also cease and terminate subject to Licensee's right to sell of its inventory of MULTIMEDIA DISC for an additional period of one year subject to the continuing obligation to pay royalties therefor. No right to make, sell, or distribute MULTIMEDIA DISC programs or copies embodying the composition shall survive the termination of this license pursuant to Paragraph 7(b) hereof.

13. This license does not include a grant of performing rights. The public performance of the musical composition as part of the MULTIMEDIA DISC which is the subject of this license, is expressly conditioned upon such performers or places of performance thereof, having valid performing rights licenses from the respective copyright owners or their designated performing rights societies.

14. This license supersedes and renders null and void any prior agreements otherwise in effect respecting the Composition and those rights which are the subject of this license.

15. This license is being entered into on an experimental and nonprejudicial basis, shall apply for the term set forth herein only, and shall not be binding upon or prejudicial to

any position taken by Licensor or Licensee for any period subsequent to the period of this license.

16. This license sets forth the entire understanding of the parties hereto with respect to the subject matter thereof, may not be altered, amended or assigned without an express written instrument to such effect accepted by Licensor and shall be governed and construed by and under the laws of the State of New York applicable to contracts wholly to be performed therein.

_____   _____
BY: (LICENSEE)
BY: THE HARRY FOX AGENCY, INC. ON BEHALF OF:

_____   _____
BY: (LICENSOR)

COLLABORATOR/SONGWRITER AGREEMENTS

by Mark Halloran and Edward R. Hearn

If you cowrite a song with someone, both of you own the song as "joint owners" in what the copyright law calls a "joint work." This is irrespective of whether one of you writes the music and the other the lyrics, or you both write music and lyrics. Both of you have an "undivided" ownership in the song (i.e., you each own 50% of the whole song). There is not a separate copyright in the music and lyrics. There is one copyright in both.

The essence of cowriting is writing together to create a single song, regardless of who contributes what. This does not mean that you have to work together physically, or in tandem, or that your creative contribution be equal in quality or quantity. You also needn't have an express "collaboration agreement," although it is probably a good idea, given the myriad issues that can arise.

One of the most famous cowriting teams is Bernie Taupin and Elton John. Bernie, on his own, first writes the lyrics. John, on his own, then writes the music. Since both Bernie and Elton intend that their work be a united whole, the result is a joint work, which they co-own fifty-fifty.

PERCENTAGE OWNERSHIP

As joint owners you and your cowriter can divide your song ownership in whatever proportion you want. In the absence of an agreement you share equally, even if it is clear that your contributions are not equal. Thus, if there are two songwriters, you own the song fifty-fifty; three songwriters, one-third each; etc. Dividing the ownership ratably is also the most common way to divide ownership in a collaboration agreement.

One common benchmark in dividing ownership is that the lyrics are worth 50% and the music 50%. For example, if two people write the music and one person writes the lyrics, they may divide the ownership 25% each for the two music writers, with the lyricist retaining the remaining 50%. However, if there is no agreement, each would own one-third of the song.

GRANT OF RIGHTS

Now that we have determined who owns the song, who controls it? It is crucial to the exploitation of the song that there be a central place to license a work and collect money.

Coadministration of Licenses

It is usually more convenient for one music publisher to collect and divide all the income. Licensing can become complicated when a licensor has to seek the approval and document permission from multiple publishers. However, many cowriters prefer that there be separate administration among the various publishing companies. This has its advantages. You have control over to whom licenses are granted, how much is charged, how the money is collected, and what costs are incurred.

As joint owner (in the United States), you may exploit the song yourself and also grant nonexclusive licenses. Still, you must account to your cowriters for the money that is generated from the nonexclusive licenses.

A license is permission to use a work. It is not a transfer of copyright ownership, which requires the permission of all songwriters (see discussion below).

- Public Performances. Public performances agreements must be entered into with ASCAP, BMI or SESAC. Typically, they are done in the name of the songwriter's publishing company. If cowriters want to use one company, they may use that company and divide the income. Or, each of the separate publishing companies may enter a public performances agreement with ASCAP, BMI or SESAC.

- Mechanical Licenses. Since mechanical licenses are nonexclusive licenses, any cowriter can grant them, but must account to and pay the other cowriters.

- Print Rights. Since these agreements are usually exclusive, all cowriters must agree.

- Subpublishing Rights. Since foreign subpublishing deals are usually exclusive, all cowriters must agree. Additionally, most foreign jurisdictions require that all co-owners agree to licensing, so the subpublishers are going to want to have all cowriters sign.

DIVISION OF INCOME

Just as a contributing author is entitled to a ratable share of ownership, the coauthor is also entitled to a ratable share of income, absent an agreement to the contrary.

PURSUIT OF INFRINGEMENT

One obligation that cowriters have together is to protect the copyright. This includes pursuing infringers. Can you sue if your co-owner doesn't want to sue? The answer appears to be yes, at least with respect to your interest in the copyright. However, the court may require that you bring in your cowriter as a coplaintiff, so it's best that you decide to sue together.

What if you have to sue your co-owner, for example, for failure to account to and pay you? You may, but you need not, bring in all your other co-owners in order to sue.

COPYRIGHT DURATION

The basic rule is that the copyright of a song written after January 1, 1976 lasts for the life of the author plus 50 years. In the case of a joint work, the copyright lasts for the life of the last surviving author plus 50 years. Thus, if you cowrite a song with someone who dies in the year 2000 and you live to 2050, the copyright will last until the year 2100.

COPYRIGHT TRANSFERS

Each collaborator, independently of the other collaborators, has the right to transfer his or her copyright ownership to another party. That transfer may be for the full copyright share of the collaborator to a publisher, or a partial copyright transfer to a copublisher. A collaborator may also grant all administration and supervision rights of that collaborator's share to a third party as the publishing administrator, while still retaining ownership of the copyright.

If one collaborator transfers his or her copyright interests to a third party, but the second collaborator does not do the same, then the third party would co-own the copyright with the other collaborator. At the same time, the second collaborator has the option to transfer his or her copyright interest, in the whole or in part, or just the administration rights, to the same new owner as did the first collaborator or to a different party.

Unless either collaborator has granted to the other collaborator the administration rights in the copyright for the song, the new co-owner will have to share decision-making and the publisher's income share with the collaborator who did not transfer his or her interests. The accounting can become cumbersome if efforts are not made to coordinate income sharing and accounting procedures.

DIFFERENT PERFORMING RIGHTS SOCIETY AFFILIATIONS

It is also possible for each coauthor to belong to a different performing rights society, namely ASCAP, BMI, or SESAC. If that is the case, then a share of the performance income collection would be allocated to each collaborator's affiliated performing rights society. For example, if the song is performed as a part of a soundtrack to a television program, then, with the performance rights for that song being divided between two different performing rights groups, the performance fee also would be so divided. Each performing rights group would receive its allocated share and would report to the collaborator/member affiliated with it the latter's performance income share as songwriter and as copublisher. Since each of the performing rights societies use a different reporting mechanism, it is quite possible that one collaborator, being paid by a different performing rights society, would not receive the same level of writer and publisher performance income as the other.

SONGWRITERS AS MEMBERS OF DIFFERENT BANDS

In the event one of the collaborating songwriters is a member of a band and the other is not, the collaborator who is a member of the band will have the authority to allow the band to rehearse and perform the collaborated song in live concerts and to record the song for release on phonorecords. While, technically, it is best to have both writers approve and issue a combined use license, i.e., a mechanical license to reproduce the song on phonorecords, it is enough that one has the authority to do so, but he or she must account to the collaborator who is not a band member for their share of writer and publisher income. Most record labels will want to get both coauthors and copublishers to provide written authorization for the initial reproduction of that song on phonorecords. After the first release of the phonorecords, a compulsory mechanical license procedure may apply to any future recordings of that song, whether by that same or any other band.

CONTROLLED COMPOSITION CLAUSE

Of particular significance is the situation where one of the coauthors is a band member (while the other is not) and has a recording agreement with a record label that requires the writer/band member to agree to a controlled composition clause in the recording agreement. This clause authorizes the record company to pay a reduced mechanical royalty, usually 75% of the prevailing statutory mechanical rate, as the royalty fee for the right to reproduce the song on phonorecords that are sold to the public.

Generally, the recording artist/collaborating writer will be required by the record company to represent that he or she has obtained permission from the collaborating writer who is not the band member and not a signatory to the recording agreement to issue a mechanical license for the reduced rate. But often, the collaborator/recording artist cannot guarantee that, and most likely will not be able to provide the record label with written authorization from the collaborator accepting a reduced mechanical royalty rate. In those situations, the record company will have to pay the collaborating writer who is not a member of the band nor a signatory to the recording agreement that cowriter's share of mechanicals, both as writer and copublisher, at full statutory rate, while paying the collaborator, who is a signatory, the reduced rate. It is also possible that the rate will be reduced even further, given the need to pay the unsigned collaborator the higher amount, which will reduce the amount available to pay the collaborator who is a signatory to the agreement.

By way of illustration, assume that the maximum pool of mechanical royalties for all of the songs on the recording artist's album is 50¢, as distinct from the current statutory rate of 6.6¢ per song, which would earn 66¢ if 10 songs are on the album, or 79.2¢ if there are 12 songs. The payout to the collaborating coauthor who is not a signatory to the recording agreement will reduce the overall pool available for mechanical royalties, causing the amount payable to the collaborator/band member to be even less than the 75% fractional statutory rate.

COACCOUNTING

Any income that either collaborating writer receives from the commercial exploitation of the song, whether it is from their own use or from use by an authorized third party, must be accounted for and apportioned to the other collaborating songwriter. Such payments should be made in a timely manner, for example, no less than 30 days after receipt. Also, statements that accompany the payments to the first collaborator should be copied and forwarded with the payment to the other collaborator.

FUTURE GENERATIONS

The rights of each deceased coauthor will pass on to the benefit of the heir(s) and descendant(s) of that coauthor, either by way of a will (testate) or without a will (intestate). If there is no will, the distribution will be governed by state statutes, usually to surviving spouses and children, on a first priority basis, before other relatives. It then would be the heir or the executor of the estate of the deceased who will have the authority to grant and make decisions with respect to the use of a collaborated composition. By the same token, the surviving collaborator will have the authority to continue to exploit the song while having a reporting and payment sharing obligation to the deceased's descendants or executor. The estate of the deceased collaborator can exploit the song too, but, in turn, must account to the surviving coauthor.

MUSIC PUBLISHING

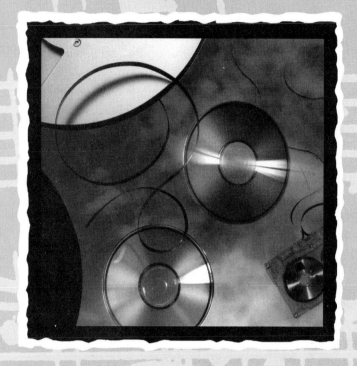

PERFORMING RIGHTS ORGANIZATIONS: AN OVERVIEW

by Mark Halloran

If a song you write is commercially recorded, you will want to join a performing rights organization so you can collect money for the public performance of your song. Which organization you join is one of the most important business decisions you will make in your career, so a basic understanding is crucial.

This chapter provides an overview of the three U.S. performing rights organizations—the American Society of Composers, Authors and Publishers (ASCAP), Broadcast Music Incorporated (BMI) and SESAC (formerly called the Society of European Stage Authors and Composers). The vast majority of U.S. copyrighted songs are in the repertory of either ASCAP (with a total of over 3,500,000 songs) or BMI (with more than 3,000,000 songs and compositions). We will discuss performing rights, the issue of nondramatic versus dramatic public performance rights, how television and blanket licenses work, the agreements you enter, collaboration, how money is generated and divided and grievance procedures.

COPYRIGHT LAW UNDERPINNING

To understand exactly how performing rights organization work, you must understand one fundamental tenet of copyright law: a copyright owner in a musical work (song) has the exclusive right to perform the work publicly. The concept "performance" includes live performances and the rendering of previous performances that are fixed in records, videotape, or film. Thus, when a radio station broadcasts a song, that song is being publicly performed, even though the recording artist is not performing live. Thus, the radio station must be licensed by the copyright owner to play the song. Radio stations normally obtain public performance licenses from ASCAP, BMI, or SESAC for a fee. The same is true for songs in television programs. When a television program is broadcast, the songs in the program are being publicly performed. The network or local station must be licensed to publicly perform those songs.

Radio and TV are not the only kinds of public performance. When you are dancing to "I'm Every Woman" by Whitney Houston in a nightclub, the playing of that song and recording by the disc jockey is a public performance. But at this point you should consider an absolutely crucial distinction. What performance does the performing rights organization license? The performance of the musical composition in the record is licensed, not the performance of the sound recording. (A sound recording is a series of sounds. Its copyright is separate from the copyright in the song.) If the disc jockey is playing "I'm Every Woman," then the song "I'm Every Woman," not Whitney Houston's recording, is licensed. In the United States there is no public performance right in a sound recording. To perform a song without violating copyright law, the nightclub must have a license to publicly perform this song. That is where ASCAP, BMI and SESAC step in. They negotiate licenses (permissions) with radio and TV stations, nightclubs, cabarets, discos and the like, enabling them to perform publicly the musical compositions contained in the performing rights organizations' catalogues.

The essence of the agreement between performing rights organizations and nightclubs is simple: the performing rights organizations grant the right to the nightclubs to use the songs (perform them publicly), and in return the performing rights organizations are paid fees by nightclubs. These fees are ultimately divided among the songwriters and publishers that create and publish the songs. The company that publishes "I'm Every Woman" and the song's writers must authorize ASCAP, BMI or SESAC to license the public performance. Whitney Houston, who performs the song, and her label, Arista, which owns the recording, do not license the public performance of the song. They are not the copyright holders of "I'm Every Woman," but merely the performer of the song and owner of the sound recording respectively. As such, they do not collect public performance royalties in the United States. In certain foreign territories, performing rights organizations also license public performances of sound recordings, but ASCAP, BMI and SESAC do not. However, this may change soon, as Congress is considering creating a public performance right in sound recordings.

There is an exception to this "blanket" license procedure. As a result of an antitrust case brought on behalf of theater owners, ASCAP, BMI and SESAC do not license the public performance of musical works in U.S. motion picture theaters. However, certain foreign performing rights organizations do so in their respective territories.

DRAMATIC VERSUS NONDRAMATIC RIGHTS

ASCAP, BMI and SESAC do not license dramatic performance rights. Dramatic performing rights ("grand rights") must be distinguished from nondramatic performance rights ("small rights"). The Copyright Act grants the exclusive right to perform publicly a dramatic work to the copyright owner. Dramatic works include, among other things, plays (both musicals and dramas), dramatic scripts for radio, television, ballets and operas. A musical composition (a song), in and of itself, is a nondramatic work.

Drawing the line between a dramatic and nondramatic performance is sometimes difficult, if not impossible. The standard ASCAP, BMI and SESAC contracts state they license only nondramatic performances of the compositions they administer. Thus radio and television licensees must be careful to make sure their blanket license covers their use of a song from a play or opera. The industry practice is that radio stations play unlimited numbers of instrumentals from cast albums, or will play a sequence of up to two vocals and an instrumental from the cast album. Some record companies and publishers, however, avoid this licensing problem by obtaining clearance from the copyright holder for unrestricted radio use of songs from cast albums, and notify broadcasters of such.

Dramatic performances are usually licensed directly from the writers of the music, lyrics, and book of the play, or from their agents. Writers usually reserve dramatic rights in their contracts with publishers. A sample illustration: if a theater company wants to stage *A Chorus Line,* they must seek permission directly from the writers of the play to perform the play and the accompanying music. On the other hand, if a radio wants to play only the song "At the Ballet" from the *A Chorus Line* cast album, this is not a dramatic performance, and ASCAP, BMI and SESAC license this sort of performance.

ASCAP

In 1914, Victor Herbert and a handful of other composers organized ASCAP because performances of copyrighted music for profit were so numerous and widespread, and most performances so fleeting, that as a practical matter it was impossible for individual copyright owners to negotiate with and license the music users and to detect unauthorized public performances of their songs. ASCAP was organized to serve as a clearinghouse for copyright owners and users and to solve those problems. Today ASCAP is a membership society which represents approximately 65,000 composers, lyricists and publishers. ASCAP collected $423,000,000 in 1994, and distributed over $230,000,000 to its members.

BMI

BMI is a not-for-profit corporation, organized in 1939, whose stock is owned by members of the broadcasting industry. BMI represents some 60,000 publishing companies and 110,000 songwriters and composers, and operates in much the same manner as ASCAP. In fiscal year 1994–1995, BMI collected more than $300,000,000 and distributed over $246,000,000 to its affiliates.

SESAC

SESAC, formed in 1930, is a privately held corporation. SESAC has approximately 5000 writer/publisher affiliates. Although traditionally known for its strength in country, gospel and band music, it is now moving into jazz, new age and pop, as evidenced by its recent signing of Bob Dylan and Neil Diamond. SESAC differs from ASCAP and BMI in that it is much smaller and consequently its service is efficient and personalized. Some of SESAC's services include catalog consultation and collaboration recommendations.

Television and Radio Licensing

The bulk of money paid to the performing rights organizations comes from radio and television broadcasters.

ASCAP, BMI and SESAC negotiate blanket licenses that cover all the works in their catalogues. Thus, television and radio stations do not have to clear the music before it is broadcast—stations can be confident the song being played is somewhere in the performing rights organizations catalogue. The granting of blanket licenses makes sense when you consider the vast number of songs in the performing rights organizations catalogues. If a broadcaster or nightclub individually negotiated with the copyright holder each time a song was played, chaos could result. Blanket licenses also benefit writers and publishers, as they do not have the means to enforce their exclusive right to public performance of their songs. The performing rights organizations will sue broadcasters, clubs and others who publicly perform songs without a license. Enforcing the copyright laws is one of their most important functions.

After a performing rights organization issues its blanket license, the license holder may use any of the works of any of the members of that organization as often as desired during the license term. The performing rights organizations use sampling techniques to figure out to whom the money should go, and compute the division of income based on the frequency and the kind of public performance of songs. The computation and payment of royalties is discussed more fully below.

Broadcast blanket licenses have been under fire by nonnetwork television stations in both the courts and in Congress. Although the legal and legislative attacks have so far been unsuccessful, nonnetwork television stations are increasingly negotiating for a "per program" use fee in lieu of blanket licenses.

Through its use of BDS (Broadcast Data Systems) Airplay Recognition Services, SESAC charges Spanish-language radio stations for actual airplay. SESAC currently uses blanket licenses for most other licensees.

ASCAP, BMI AND SESAC CONTRACTS WITH SONGWRITERS AND PUBLISHERS

Assuming you qualify for membership in ASCAP, BMI or SESAC you will then be asked to enter a contract with one of them. Basically, if you have a song which is published, recorded or publicly performed, you can join and in so doing you are giving that organization the right to license the public performance of songs that you write in return for their promise to pay you royalties for the reported performances of your songs.

Publishers can also join ASCAP, BMI or SESAC. Their contracts are much the same as for writers.

MEMBERSHIP

As performing rights organizations pay writers and publishers separately, both must join. Writers can only belong to one performing rights organization at a time. Even when writers are affiliated with publishing companies, they should join performing rights organizations so that they can directly receive any royalties that are due.

Publishers always have separate ASCAP, BMI and SESAC-affiliated legal entities (e.g., A Tunes [ASCAP], B Tunes [BMI] and C Tunes [SESAC]). Each organization has name clearance procedures to avoid name duplication or the confusion of similar names.

If you are an ASCAP writer and your song is administered by a publisher, it will be handled by the entity of the publisher that is affiliated with ASCAP.

ASCAP dues are $10 for writers; $50 for publishers. BMI has no dues, but charges a one-time publisher administration fee of $100. There is no fee to affiliate with SESAC for writers or publishers.

COLLABORATION

If an ASCAP writer collaborates with a BMI or SESAC writer, the song is licensed concurrently by both organizations. Thus, you will notice on some record albums that song listing for the performing rights organization will list ASCAP, BMI and/or SESAC.

COLLECTIONS

ASCAP, BMI and SESAC also collect money from affiliated foreign performing rights organizations. However, most income comes from the United States. For example, in 1994, ASCAP's U.S. receipts were $319,000,000 and foreign receipts $104,000,000. ASCAP, BMI and SESAC all charge a service fee for such collections. Many U.S. publishers, however, have subpublishers or agents overseas who collect and remit monies to American publishers directly.

REGISTRATION OF COMPOSITIONS

It is essential to collecting royalties that you or your publisher register your composition. Prior to choosing which performing rights organization to join, you should register your songs with the U.S. Copyright Office in order to establish authorship and ownership of your songs.

ASCAP requires a magnetic tape, floppy diskette or 8-1/2" x 11" paper form. If music is embodied in a television program, a music cue sheet should be filed for every song (cue).

BMI's registration (clearance) form must be completed for each song. BMI also requires cue sheets for television music.

SESAC provides index forms for the purpose of registering all musical works.

PAYING FOR PERFORMANCES

With minor exceptions, it is impractical for ASCAP, BMI and SESAC to monitor and pay for performances in bars or nightclubs. There are no significant royalties paid for nontelevision/radio performances. Royalties for radio and television performances come from licensing fees from radio, television and other licensees such as bars and nightclubs. The fees collected from bars and nightclubs are allocated to the same funding pool that pays songwriters and publishers for radio and television performances.

SESAC accepts performance information from its affiliates. Payments are made for performances in bars, nightclubs, etc., upon verification.

Radio

ASCAP annually samples some 60,000 hours of AM and FM radio per year in order to produce a model for the music broadcast on radio, sampling larger stations more heavily. Weighted multipliers are then applied to calculate radio royalties.

BMI annually samples some 500,000 hours of selected AM and FM radio programming to develop their model, with the information coming in the form of detailed logs.

SESAC's Radio Payment System is based on the premise that the charts in national music trade publications such as *Billboard, Gavin, College Music Journal (CMJ)* and *Radio & Records* are representative of radio airplay across the United States. The Radio Payment System, one part of SESAC's royalty distribution system, uses this data in order to compensate affiliates whose works are or have been active on radio. Under the Radio Payment System, radio performances are recognized in prechart payments (prior to a song's appearance on a national chart), chart payments (based on the highest chart position a song reaches in the *Billboard, Radio & Records, Gavin* or *CMJ* singles or tracks charts used in the SESAC system) and post chart payments (paid for three years [12 quarters] beginning in the quarter after the last chart payment is earned on songs that appear in the top 20 positions in *Gavin, Billboard* or *Radio & Records* singles or tracks charts).

In SESAC's Radio Payment System, a song begins earning royalties when it is released on a commercial phonorecord (record, cassette, CD, etc.). These prechart payments acknowledge performances of the recorded song even before it appears on national charts. When a record appears on any one of the charts used in the system, a chart payment is paid. Chart payments are determined by the position of a song or album on the particular musical format charts. Most songs that reach a top twenty or higher position on a singles (or tracks) chart are paid postchart payments. In subsequent years, works receive royalties based on then current performance information.

The independent statisticians that develop the radio broadcast models do not warn either the performing rights organizations or the stations as to which stations and periods will be surveyed. Although it surveys substantially fewer hours than BMI, ASCAP uses actual "off-the-air" audiotapes to avoid any potential alterations (as could occur with a log). BMI prefers to survey performances using lists (logs) furnished by the stations being sampled. They sample nearly eight times as many hours as ASCAP to provide for inclusion and identification of many more compositions (particularly non-hits). There is no consensus as to whether the ASCAP or BMI sampling system is more accurate.

The number of surveyed performances of the compositions, not the chart position, determines the amount of performance royalties paid. These royalties fluctuate depending on the music category (e.g., pop, country, rhythm and blues, religious, gospel, symphonic), and also whether the composition "crosses over" to other music charts or categories.

SESAC's payment fee depends on whether a song is a prechart, chart or postchart performance activity. For prechart songs, SESAC uses a new technology created by Broadcast Data Systems (a sister company of The Hollywood Reporter) to track actual SESAC songs that are played on any radio or TV outlet, charge those stations a licensing fee based specifically on airplay and pay their songwriter and publisher affiliates a specified royalty for exactly what is used. SESAC pays a slightly higher fee for prechart songs when they appear on popularity charts in national music trade publications, and a slightly higher fee for songs and albums that appear in the top 20 positions.

Network Television

To track network television performances, ASCAP, BMI and SESAC receive cue sheets submitted by the networks' program producers, which detail the seconds of music used in network programs and the types of use. ASCAP, BMI and SESAC also tape network shows to spot check information on the cue sheets.

Local Television

ASCAP uses cue sheets, a sample of regional TV Guides, audiotapes and inquiry letters to local television stations to sample 30,000 hours of local television. As with radio, this sampling is then multiplied using statistical models to calculate local television royalties. BMI and SESAC use similar techniques. They compile cue sheets and a complete computerized account of regional TV Guides and program listings from local television stations.

TELEVISION MUSIC

There are three main categories of television music—theme, background, and feature performances, and performing rights organizations pay different rates for each. They factor in the number of stations airing the performance, the type of station (e.g. broadcast, local, cable and public television), and the duration of the performance. Payments are also made for music used for promotional purposes or for jingles.

Theme music appears at the opening or closing of a television program and during segments within programs. Background music is played to enhance the program, but is not intended as the focus of the program. There is typically about 10 (although some animated programs often contain up to 20) minutes of background music in a 30-minute program. A feature performance is music that is the visual focus of the program. For example, a composition sung on camera is considered a feature performance. The following chart illustrates approximate ASCAP/BMI performance writer royalties payable for network and syndicated television programs. The rates specified below are estimates and fluctuate depending on many factors, including whether network or syndicated, time of day, and program type (e.g., series, soaps, quiz shows, movies). SESAC did not provide figures.

NETWORK TELEVISION RATES*

Theme—$250–$275
Background (1 minute)—$150–$200
Feature performance—$1,500–$2,000
*Average ASCAP/BMI Prime-time rates per 30-minute show.

LOCAL TELEVISION RATES **

Theme—$100–$260
Background (1 minute)—$60
Feature performance—$700
** ASCAP rates for local television, based on one surveyed performance.

SYNDICATED TELEVISION RATES***

Theme—$55
Background (1 minute)—$50
Feature performance—$165
*** BMI rates based on performance on 100 stations.

PAYMENT OF ROYALTIES

The amount of royalties paid varies between ASCAP, BMI and SESAC due to many factors, the most significant of which are differences in rates and survey methods. Generally, each organization divides and pays the revenues derived from licenses and fees 50% to publisher and 50% to writer. ASCAP and BMI assign varying credit values to publishers, factoring in the size and dollar value of their catalogs, but do not do so for writers.

ASCAP

ASCAP's method of paying royalties is to "follow the dollar" (e.g., television licensing fees are paid out only as television royalties). ASCAP calculates royalties on a quarterly basis. Songs that have generated high amounts of feature performances over time (e.g., 20,000 feature performances over a five-year survey period) are called "qualifying works" and are assigned higher credit values than performance royalties for background music.

BMI

BMI pays quarterly, seven to eight months after the end of the calendar quarter in which the performance occurs. Actual rates paid are typically larger than the minimums prescribed due to quarterly rate bonuses. Royalties are paid simultaneously to writer and publisher in equal lump sums. In the absence of a publisher, payment of the full amount of royalties may be made to the writer, or by agreement between the writer and publisher, payment may be split unequally, with the writer receiving the larger share (but not vice-versa).

BMI recognizes frequently performed works by awarding bonuses to both writers and publishers for songs reaching a high number of performances. Bonuses can range from one and one-half times the standard rate, to almost 17 times the standard rate.

To protect their writer members, neither ASCAP or BMI normally pay writer royalties to anyone other than the writer unless such royalties have been assigned by the writer to legitimate creditors as collateral.

SESAC

Distributions of domestic performance royalties are made to SESAC writer and publisher affiliates four times per year. Royalty distributions are made 90 days after the close of each quarter and are based on a quarterly review and analysis of each affiliate's catalog and its performance activity.

ADVANCES

Until the early 1980s, both ASCAP and BMI routinely paid advances (nonrefundable prepayments of estimated future royalties) to writers and publishers in an effort to stabilize their incomes and entice major musical stars to join their respective organizations. However, due to legal challenges to syndicated television blanket licenses and the resulting concern about future royalties, advances were discontinued and both organizations remain wary of them.

To replace advances, both ASCAP and BMI allow assignments of royalties as collateral against bank loans to composers and publishers. BMI and ASCAP also accept assignment of writer royalties against advances made to the writer by the writer's publisher. As the documentation for such assignments is complex, assignments are usually only cost-effective for composers and publishers with substantial projected royalties.

SESAC has begun to offer advances as part of their campaign to encourage ASCAP and BMI affiliates to switch or to sign promising unaffiliated writers and publishers.

FOREIGN COLLECTION

Foreign performing rights organizations (generally, only one performing rights organization exists in the majority of countries) monitor foreign performances of compositions in the ASCAP/BMI/SESAC domestic repertoires, and pay royalties for such performances to the U.S. writer and publisher through ASCAP, BMI and SESAC. The lag in payment of foreign royalties can range from concurrent to as long as five years.

One constant problem is that a U.S. writer's or publisher's foreign performing rights royalties may be diluted by the payment of royalties by the foreign performing rights organization to translators of popular American songs. Monies which are collected from U.S. songs, that are not distributed to ASCAP, BMI and SESAC, are generally forfeited to the foreign organization's general fund (the infamous so-called black box) for disbursement to the members of the foreign society. To avoid the black box and accelerate payments, most publishers prefer to have their foreign royalties collected "at the source" by their foreign publishers (i.e., subpublishers). Writer royalties, however, still flow from the foreign performing rights organizations to the domestic ones.

GRIEVANCE PROCEDURES

If you have a dispute with ASCAP or BMI (for example, you don't agree with your royalty statement), you have recourse through their grievance procedures. The ASCAP grievance procedure is set out in their articles of association. These articles are provided to you by ASCAP when you join. BMI grievances are submitted to the American Arbitration Association in New York City. SESAC has no formally established grievance procedure.

MUSIC PUBLISHING

by Neville L. Johnson

Songwriters should know the dynamics and economics of the exploitation of a song. This chapter explores the types of income that are generated in the music publishing industry and the kinds of deals that are commonly struck between publishers and songwriters. The attributes of a good publisher are summarized, suggestions for obtaining a publisher are made, and a typical music publishing agreement is examined.

Music publishing has been the major source of revenue for songwriters since the turn of this century when vaudeville was the primary vehicle for exploiting songs. Music publishers of that era worked to persuade entertainers to publicly perform musical compositions to stimulate the sale of printed editions and player piano rolls. Over the years, the technology for merchandising music has expanded with such inventions as the phonograph record, radio, motion pictures, television, videotape, compact discs, and now digital transmission of music looms large on the retail horizon. Songwriters and publishers have benefited from those new sources of income. As the complexity and size of the music publishing industry increased, so did the money that was capable of being earned within it. Today, one hit song can make someone a millionaire.

TYPES OF INCOME

There are four general categories of revenue in the music publishing industry: public performance income, mechanical rights income, sheet music income, and synchronization income.

Performance Income

The copyright laws in the United States and similar laws in virtually every other country of the world require that compensation be paid to copyright owners for the public performance of their music. Performing rights organizations exist because it is impractical for copyright owners to license the right to publicly perform their compositions to every music user, including radio and television stations, concert halls, nightclubs, and jukeboxes separately. Conversely, it would be impractical for music users to keep track of copyright owners and negotiate individual licenses to authorize the performance of each copyrighted work.

For these reasons, music users throughout the world make payments to performing rights organizations. After deducting their costs of administration, these organizations distribute their revenues to copyright owners and their publishers.

The United States has three performing rights organizations. ASCAP (American

Society of Composers, Authors and Publishers), BMI (Broadcast Music Incorporated) and SESAC (formerly Society of European Stage Authors and Composers). These organizations perform the difficult task of collecting public performance income and distributing it in proportion to the success of each composition they license.

These organizations also license public performance rights to sister performing rights organizations which exist in other territories of the world.

The performing rights organizations divide performance income so that 50% is paid directly to the composer (writer's share) and 50% is paid to the publisher (publisher's share).

You will need to join a performing rights organization when you get your first recording or placement in a film or video. It is the publisher's job to register your compositions with your society. See the chapter "Performing Rights Organizations: An Overview" for more information.

Mechanical Income

Mechanical income is earned from the manufacture and sale of sound recordings. The current rate, payable for each recording of a composition that is distributed, is 6.6 cents for songs of five minutes or less; and 1.2 cents per each minute or fraction thereof above that. (The rates are set by the Copyright Royalty Tribunal and will be increased in 1996 based on changes in the U.S. Consumer Price Index.) Thus, for a recording containing 10 compositions of five minutes or less, 66 cents is paid in mechanical income to the publisher(s) of the compositions. If 100,000 albums are sold, $66,000 is paid to the publisher(s) of the compositions on that album. In a typical publishing deal the songwriter will receive half this amount from the publisher.

In the United States, mechanical income is paid to the publisher of a composition by the record company that manufactures recordings of the composition pursuant to a contract between them called a mechanical license. Usually the record company is required to account to the publisher on a quarterly basis.

In most foreign countries, mechanical rights income is computed differently than in the United States. Instead of a flat rate per song, the royalty is computed on a basis that is usually 6% to 8% of the retail selling price of the recordings. Mechanical income is allocated evenly among the compositions on the record or tape. Usually, this income is collected and distributed by mechanical rights societies, which exist in most countries of the world.

The entity closest to a mechanical rights society, in the United States, is the Harry Fox Agency, Inc., headquartered in New York City. Although many American publishers issue their own mechanical licenses, others prefer to use this company, which, for a 3% fee, issues mechanical licenses to American record companies, and conducts audits of such companies to insure that proper payments are made.

Print Income

Sheet music can contribute substantial earnings to a songwriter. Today the industry is concentrated in a few companies that manufacture and distribute sheet music across the United States. A publisher who does not print and manufacture sheet music, but licenses such rights to another company, can be paid 50 to 75 cents or more per single edition sold, but the writer usually receives only eight to 12 cents per single edition. See discussion in the chapter "Analysis of a Single-song Agreement."

Synchronization Income

Synchronization income is the money paid by motion picture and television production companies for the right to use compositions in motion pictures or in dramatic presentations on television. The "synch right" for a composition, to be contained in a major motion picture, may cost $25,000 and the attendant exposure can stimulate the generation of additional revenue from those areas discussed above.

Foreign Income

The foregoing sources of income occur throughout the world. Domestic publishers enter into foreign licensing or subpublishing agreements with music publishers that operate outside the United States and Canada. Shrewd and successful commercial songwriters often retain foreign rights and make their own subpublishing deals, which often provide substantial income.

MUSIC PUBLISHING AGREEMENTS

There are three types of contracts pertaining to songwriters: standard agreements, copublishing agreements, and administration agreements.

Standard Agreements

These transactions come in two species—single-song agreements and long-term agreements. (See the chapters "Analysis of a Single-song Agreement" and "Analysis of an Exclusive Term Songwriter Agreement.") Under these agreements, the income is generally split as follows:

- Mechanical Income. Publisher collects all mechanical income and pays 50% to composer.

- Performance Income. Publisher receives and retains all of "publisher's share" of performance income. Composer is paid directly by the performing rights organization and retains all such "writer's share" of performance income.

- Print Income. Publisher collects all revenue and pays writer eight to 12 cents per printed edition.

- Synchronization Income. Publisher collects income and splits fifty-fifty with composer.

- Foreign Income. Net receipts (that amount received by or credited to publisher from subpublisher) are split fifty-fifty with composer.

In a single-song deal, the publisher owns the copyright in the composition for the term of its copyright, subject to the possibility of its reversion to its composer 35 years after its publication (its first commercial distribution) or 40 years after its assignment (transfer), whichever is earlier. Some long-term songwriter's agreements provide that compositions created pursuant to such agreements are works for hire for the publisher and, hence, incapable of being recaptured by the composer. Normally such agreements last for one year, with two to four one-year options being held by the publisher. All compositions created by the songwriter during the term are owned by the publisher. Under most such agreements, the writer is paid an advance on signing and with each option pickup, or a weekly salary ($18,000 to $25,000 per year is the average for a fledgling writer). Single-song agreements are entered into with or without advances paid to the songwriter: there is no common industry practice or standard.

Under both types of agreement, the publisher administers the compositions subject to them. That is, the publisher issues all documents and contracts affecting such compositions and collects all income, other than the writer's share of performance income, earned by the compositions.

Copublishing Agreements

Copublishing agreements differ in two material respects from standard agreements described above. Under copublishing agreements, as in standard agreements, the publisher administers the compositions subject to such agreements. However, the songwriter not only receives the writer's share of publishing income, or roughly 50% of the gross revenues (except print revenues) of the composition, but also shares in that portion of what traditionally was the publisher's share of music publishing income. Thus, under such agreements, the songwriter is ordinarily paid 75% of the mechanical income, print income, and synchronization income derived from the composition and, in addition to the writer's share of performance income, receives 50% of the publisher's share of performance income. Usually, copyrights to the compositions are owned jointly by the publisher and songwriter.

Copublishing agreements can encompass one song, a number of stated songs, or all compositions written over a period of years, as in a long-term songwriter's agreement.

Administration Agreements

The most advantageous arrangement for a songwriter is an administration agreement. Under this type of agreement, the administrative activities of a songwriter's company are conducted by another publisher, which issues mechanical licenses, registers compositions with performing rights organizations, and collects its income throughout the world. The administrator collects all income but remits at least as much as a copublisher's share, and often more, to the songwriter's administered company (10% to 15% of the gross revenues is the percentage normally retained by an administrator).

Such agreements extend for periods varying from three to five years, at the close of which all administrative rights to the compositions revert to the administered company. In practice, such agreements are difficult to obtain for songwriters who have no independent means of exploiting compositions that would be subject to such an arrangement. For singer-songwriters that have recording deals, or songwriters that can get their songs "covered" (recorded by others) such transactions are often the most beneficial and these are done frequently.

Points of Negotiation

Royalties are always negotiable, as are advances. A songwriter should always attempt to obtain a reversion of any composition subject to a single-song, long-term publishing, or copublishing agreement when any such composition has not been commercially exploited within a time period specified in any such contract. A composer should allow translations of or the addition of new lyrics to any composition only with his or her prior consent as in some countries a translator or lyricist may register and receive income from a translation which is never performed, sold, or even recorded.

Points in publishing contracts vary in importance among publishing companies. Similarly, songwriters differ on the priorities of the numerous issues involved in a songwriting agreement. Songwriters must become expert or have advisors, such as attorneys, personal managers, and business managers, to counsel them on the best methods of navigating the narrows of music publishing.

Self-publishing

Some composers are capable of creating and administering their catalogues. The music publishing industry is not so difficult that its mechanics would confound an attentive student. It is difficult, however, to obtain the commercial exploitation of compositions. For composers interested in and capable of properly administering and promoting the products of their artistry, self-publishing can be a viable alternative to the traditional arrangements with publishers, but in practice, few writers are successful going it alone.

When a record is released on an independent label, financed by the artist, self-publishing makes sense. Universal copyrights are valuable assets—don't transfer or lessen rights to them without a good reason.

FINDING A GOOD PUBLISHER

Music publishers play an important role in today's music industry. First, they have the best success at securing covers. Moreover, a songwriter usually needs a go-between, critic, cheerleader, and business manager. Good music publishers are enthusiastic and knowledgeable about their artists and their music; have good royalty departments and reputations for honesty; pay or advance money for demos; have aggressive professional managers that work to get songs to record producers and their artists; and are responsive to the needs, suggestions, and questions of their writers.

> **RESOURES FOR FINDING A GOOD PUBLISHER**
>
> National Academy of Songwriters (NAS)
> 6381 Hollywood Boulevard, Suite 780
> Hollywood, CA 90028
> (213) 463-7178
>
> Los Angeles Songwriter's Showcase (LASS)
> PO Box 93759
> Hollywood, CA 90093
> (213) 467-7823

Songwriters, with their advisors, should work out a strategy to find a good publisher and to enter an advantageous agreement with such. Some personal managers are capable of finding reputable publishers and subsequently obtaining agreements that are satisfactory. The songwriter's music attorney can often open doors to publishing companies. Representatives of ASCAP and BMI can be helpful, as can the recommendations of other songwriters.

Information and guidance is available at the National Academy of Songwriters (NAS) and the Los Angeles Songwriters Showcase (LASS), both nonprofit organizations.

Because music publishing agreements can be extremely technical, a music attorney should always be consulted to review most agreements a composer is requested to sign (in the case of single-song agreements, composers should master all salient points of negotiation and negotiate for themselves, or should obtain someone expert in the subject to advise them or liaise on their behalf.) Most importantly, composers should investigate carefully before choosing their advisors and business partners.

MECHANICAL LICENSE AGREEMENT

Date: _____

Composition Title: _____

Composer(s): _____

Gentlemen: _____

We own or control the mechanical recording rights in the copyrighted musical composition referred to above (hereinafter referred to as the "Composition"). You have advised us that you wish to use the Composition pursuant to the terms of the Compulsory License provisions of the United States Copyright Act (Title 17) relating to the making and distribution of phonorecords. We accede to such use, upon conditions specified below.

1. You shall pay royalties and shall render detailed accounting statements quarterly, within forty-five (45) days after each March 31, June 30, September 30, and December 31 for the calendar quarter year just concluded, whether or not royalties are due and payable for such period, for phonorecords made and distributed.

2. You shall pay us at the following rate for each part embodying the Composition manufactured by you, distributed and not returned (except for promotional copies distributed without charge to radio and television stations):

_____ for "single" recording;

_____ for "CD" or "cassette" recording.

3. This license is limited solely to the recorded performance of the Composition on the phonorecord which is identified as follows:

Record No.: _____

Artist: _____

Label: _____

This license shall not supersede or in any way affect any prior agreements now in effect with respect to recordings of the Composition.

4. In the event that you fail to account to us and pay royalties as herein provided, we may give you written notice that, unless the default is remedied within thirty (30) days from the date of this notice, this compulsory license will be automatically terminated. Such termination shall render either the making or the distribution, or both, of all phonorecords for which royalties have not been paid, actionable as acts of infringement under, and fully subject to the remedies provided by the Copyright Act.

5. You need not serve or file the notice of intention to obtain a compulsory license required by the Copyright Act.

6. This license is specifically limited to the use of the Composition, and the sale of the recording within the United States of America, unless we grant you written permission to the contrary.

7. On the label affixed to each part manufactured by you, you will include the title of the Composition, our name as Publisher, the name of the performing rights society with which we are affiliated (_____), and the last name of the composer and lyricist.

8. You will not use or authorize the use of the title of the Composition in any manner whatsoever on the label, cover, sleeve, jacket, or box in which the recording is sold, except in a list of musical compositions contained thereon and then only in print of size, type and prominence no greater than that used for the other musical compositions contained thereon.

Very truly yours,

By: _____

(RECORD COMPANY)

We acknowledge the receipt of a copy hereof and the accuracy of the terms contained herein:

By: _____

(PUBLISHER)

ANALYSIS OF A SINGLE-SONG AGREEMENT

by Neville L. Johnson

Single-song agreements are in wide use around the world. Such agreements allow publishers to pick and choose songs that they think they can get covered (recorded). I have negotiated several single-song agreements, where the songs went to number one on the pop charts, so it makes sense to pay close attention to what you are signing.

There are no standard forms for single-song agreements. There is no written agreement that cannot be modified before it is executed (signed)—be wary of printed forms, and be sure to understand what you are signing. The agreement below is representative and while it is not slanted in favor of the songwriter, it is not a total rip-off.

SINGLE-SONG AGREEMENT

AGREEMENT effective _____ day of _____
19 __, by and between _____
hereinafter referred to as "PUBLISHER," and _____
hereinafter (collectively) referred to as "WRITER."

1. ASSIGNMENT OF WORK

Writer hereby sells, assigns and delivers to Publisher, its successors and assigns, the original musical composition written and composed by Writer (hereinafter referred to as the "Composition" now entitled _____) including the title, words and music thereof, and all worldwide rights therein, and all copyrights and the rights to secure copyrights and any extensions and renewals of copyrights therein and in any arrangements and adaptations thereof, and any and all other rights that Writer now has or to which he may be entitled, whether now known or hereafter to become known.

The composition should revert to the songwriter at a stated time if the publisher cannot get the song covered. One to two years is fair.

2. USE OF COMPOSITION

Publisher shall have the free and unrestricted right to use the Composition in any way that Publisher may desire, and Writer hereby consents to such changes, adaptations, versions, dramatizations, transpositions, translations, foreign lyric substitutions, parody lyrics for commercial purposes, editing and arrangements of the Composition as Publisher deems desirable. In the event that the Composition is an instrumental composition, then Writer hereby irrevocably grants to Publisher the sole and exclusive right and privilege to cause lyrics to be written for the Composition by a lyricist or lyricists designated by Publisher, and in such event, one-half (1/2) of the royalties provided for herein shall be payable to Writer.

> *Advocates for songwriters attempt to limit this type of clause as much as possible. First, writers generally resist changes made to their music without their consent. Moreover, the songwriter may suffer a substantial decrease in his or her share of the revenue if another writer is added at the unilateral discretion of the publisher. Translations are a special problem, as songwriters frequently lose substantial portions of revenue to translators that write versions that are not successful commercially. Translations should not be registered with any foreign performing or mechanical rights society until a commercial recording of the translation has been released. All major changes and additions should be made with the consent of the songwriter.*

3. WARRANTIES AND REPRESENTATIONS

Writer hereby warrants and represents that the Composition is an original work, that neither the Composition nor any part thereof infringes upon the title, literacy or musical property of copyright or in any other work nor the statutory, common law or other rights (including rights of privacy) of any person, firm or corporation, that he is the sole writer and composer and the sole owner of the Composition and of all the rights therein, that he has not sold, assigned, transferred, hypothecated or mortgaged any right, title or interest in or to the Composition or any part thereof or any of the rights herein conveyed, that he has not made or entered into any contract with any other person, firm or corporation affecting the Composition or any right, title or interest therein or in copyright thereof, that no person, firm or corporation other than Writer has or has had claims or has claimed any right, title or interest in or to the Composition or any part thereof, or any use thereof or any copyright therein, that the composition has never been published, that where no copyright registration information has been given in paragraph 1 of this Agreement, the Composition has never been registered for copyright, and that the Writer has full right, power and authority to make this present instrument of sale and transfer.

> *This is typical boilerplate. Of course, the song must be noninfringing and not the property of someone else—this is the heart of the agreement. Virtually all publishing agreements contain language of the above nature. In any event, if the song is infringing or has been previously sold to a third party, the composer is liable.*

4. ROYALTIES

Publisher shall pay or cause to be paid to Writer the following sums with respect to the Composition:

(a) Five (5) cents per copy on all regular piano-vocal sheet music sold, paid for and not returned in the United States and Canada.

> *Songwriters have long received less than a fair share of print music income. Many publishing companies now split this revenue equally with the songwriter, rather than using a penny rate, and this is certainly the more enlightened view. A songwriter*

should receive a minimum of 25 cents per single edition, and the payment should increase with inflation. The increase can be tied to the Consumer Price Index. The publisher will usually make about 50 cents per sheet music sold with a retail selling price of $3.50.

There are six major print music companies in the United States: Warner Publications, Hal Leonard, Music Sales, Mel Bay, Alfred and Cherry Lane. As these companies are manufacturers and distributors, it is very difficult for them to agree to split profits, and usually only a penny rate can be negotiated if the deal is directly with them.

Further, in the case of "educational" markets, the royalty may be reduced to as little as 5% of the retail selling price if the choral arranger is a "big name."

(b) Ten (10) percent of the net wholesale selling price for each copy of all other editions sold, paid for and not returned in the United States and Canada.

"Net wholesale selling price" is ambiguous. What are the deductions from gross (which means all amounts received) to arrive at net? These deductions should be specified.

Most contracts, unlike this one, provide that the songwriter will be paid on the suggested retail selling price of the edition. The royalty commonly paid is 10% to 12-1/2% of any such selling price. Again, 50% of what the publisher receives is what the songwriter should ask.

(c) If the Composition is included in any song book, folio or similar publication issued by Publisher or its affiliates in the United States or Canada, a proportionate share of the royalty set forth in paragraph (b) above, which the number "one" bears to the total number of copyrighted musical compositions or arrangements of works on which royalties are payable included in such publications. If pursuant to a license granted by Publisher to an unaffiliated licensee, the Composition is included in any song book, folio or similar publication in the United States or Canada, the proportionate share of fifty percent (50%) of the net sums actually received by Publisher from said licensee, which the number "one" bears to the total number of Publisher's Compositions included in any such publication.

This is fair as the split is equal; 10% to 12-1/2% of the retail selling price is the going rate.

(d) Fifty percent (50%) of any and all sums actually received (less any costs for collection) by Publisher from mechanical rights, electrical transcription and reproducing rights, motion picture and television synchronization rights and all other rights therein (except as provided for in subparagraph (e) hereof), in the United States and Canada.

It should be specified that the songwriter be paid 50% of any advances paid to the publisher with respect to the composition. Costs of collection, such as Harry Fox Agency fees, should be charged against publisher's share. It is the publisher's job to administer.

(e) Writer shall have no claim whatsoever against Publisher for any royalties received by Publisher from any performing rights society or other similar organization which makes payment directly (or indirectly other than through Publisher) to writers, authors and composers.

The writer is paid performance income directly by ASCAP or BMI, not through the publisher.

(f) Fifty percent (50%) of any and all sums, after deduction of foreign taxes, actually received in the United States (less any costs for collection) by Publisher from sales and uses directly related to the Composition in countries outside of the United States and Canada (other than public performance royalties as hereinabove set forth in paragraph (e). This provision shall not apply to copies of printed music shipped from the United States to such countries, to which the rates set forth in subparagraphs (a), (b), and (c) above shall apply.

No subpublisher (licensee of original publisher) should be permitted to take a percentage greater than 25% to collect the income, or 50% of the income "at source" (i.e., where the revenue is earned) if he secures a cover record. The shrewd songwriter will limit any subpublishing fee to no more than 15% of the income collected at source. This is an important provision and can involve substantial income for the writer. Also, the writer should be paid when monies are credited to the subpublisher, not just received.

(g) No royalties are to be paid for professional copies, copies disposed of as new issues, or copies distributed for advertising purposes. No royalties are payable on consigned copies unless paid for, and not until such time as an accounting therefor can properly be made.

(h) Except as herein expressly provided, no other compensation, royalties or monies shall be paid to Writer.

This is a superfluous statement and should be deleted and replaced by a 50% catch-all provision. See Evanne L. Levin's commentary below.

Evanne L. Levin from "Analysis of an Exclusive Term Songwriter Agreement." Provision should be made for advances to be paid to the writer under any term songwriter agreement. The publisher is requiring the writer to write exclusively for it and in exchange is paying the writer only the royalties noted above, while retaining complete ownership of the songs and keeping 100% of the publisher's share of income. Nor is there any guarantee that the publisher will successfully exploit any of the writer's material, in which case the writer will see no income.

Advances are typically paid (1) in one lump sum on execution of the agreement and at the beginning of each succeeding year of the term, and/or (2) in regular installments over the term, like a weekly or semimonthly paycheck. $16,000 to $24,000 for the first year is not an unusual amount for a large publishing company to pay; small, independent publishers typically pay less but contend that more time will be devoted to promoting its staff writers since they have fewer staff. The amount of the advance typically escalates 10% to 20% for each succeeding year of the term, and may be boosted by additional advances triggered by a song's commercial success. This is commonly done by tying increases to Billboard Chart positions achieved or sales levels reached by previous albums. All advances are recoupable from both the writer's share and publisher's share of royalties otherwise payable to the writer (ASCAP/BMI royalties excluded).

A publisher who pays an advance to a writer will require the delivery of a specified minimum number of compositions written by the writer. Fifteen to 20 "Wholly Owned Compositions" is typical, with songs cowritten receiving partial credit. For example, if the writer writes a song with two other writers, the publisher will give the writer credit for 1/3 of a Wholly Owned Composition toward the minimum delivery requirement. If the writer fails to deliver the minimum number of songs required during any contract year, the publisher will have the right to extend the term without having to increase the advances beyond the agreed amount until a sufficient number of songs are delivered. The writer should object to any provision giving the publisher the right to suspend advances in addition to extending the term.

(i) Notwithstanding anything to the contrary herein contained in this Agreement, Publisher shall have the right to deduct ten percent (10%) of all sums received in the United States from all sources throughout the world as administration fees, before computing the compensation payable to Writer hereunder.

This clause is unfair and would reduce the writer's share by 5% of gross revenues. There is no justification for such a split—the publisher's job is to administer the composition, and he or she is well paid for it without this so-called administration fee.

5. ACCOUNTING

Royalty statements shall be rendered to Writer quarterly within forty-five (45) days following the close of each such quarterly period. Each statement shall be accompanied by a remittance of such amount as may be shown thereon to be due and payable. All royalty statements rendered by Publisher to Writer shall be binding upon Writer and not subject to any objection by Writer for any reason unless specific objection is made, in writing, stating the basis thereof, to Publisher within one (1) year from the date rendered. Writer shall have a reasonable right to audit those portions of the books and records of Publisher pertaining to the Composition.

Statements are rendered quarterly, which is nice, but the time should be stated more clearly (for example, within 90 days after each calendar quarter). Most agreements provide for semiannual accounting. The writer should have at least two and preferably three years to audit and object. The writer should, whenever possible, attempt to obtain the right to collect his or her share of income directly from any revenue generating source. Doing so could reduce delays in payment by six months to two years.

6. ASSIGNMENT OF COPYRIGHT

Writer hereby expressly grants and conveys to Publisher the copyright in the Composition, together with renewals and extensions thereof, and the right to secure any and all rights therein that Writer may at any time be entitled to. Writer agrees to sign any and all other papers which may be required to effectuate this Agreement, and hereby irrevocably authorizes and appoints Publisher, its successors or assigns, his attorneys and representatives in their names or in his name to take such actions and make, sign, execute, acknowledge and deliver all such documents as may from time to time be necessary to secure the renewals and extensions of the copyright in the Composition, and to assign to Publisher, its successors and assigns, said renewals and extensions of copyrights and all rights therein for the term of such renewals and extensions.

The first sentence is redundant: the songwriter assigned the copyright in paragraph 1. The rest of the paragraph is boilerplate and irrelevant now—copyrights are not capable of being renewed.

7. TRANSFER OF AGREEMENT

Writer agrees that he will not transfer nor assign this Agreement nor any interest therein nor any sums that may be or become due hereunder without the written consent of Publisher, and no purported assignment or transfer in violation of this restriction shall be valid to pass any interest to the assignee or transferee.

Prohibiting the assignment of income is unjustifiable and unlawful in those states which discourage agreements that prohibit assignment of monies.

8. ACTIONS AND INDEMNITIES

Writer hereby authorizes Publisher at its absolute discretion and at Writer's sole expense to employ attorneys and to institute or defend any action or proceeding and to take any other proper steps to protect the right, title and interest of Publisher in and to the Composition and every portion thereof acquired from Writer, pursuant to the terms hereof and in that connection to settle, compromise or in any other manner dispose of any matter, claim, action or proceeding and to satisfy any judgment that may be rendered and all of the expense so incurred and other sums so paid by Publisher. Writer hereby agrees to pay to Publisher on demand, further authorizing Publisher, whenever in its opinion its right, title or interest to any of Writer's compositions are questioned or there is a breach of any of the covenants, warranties or representations contained in this contract or in any other similar contract heretofore or hereafter entered into between Publisher and Writer, to withhold any and all royalties that may be or become due to Writer pursuant to all such contracts until such questions shall have been settled or such breach repaired, and to apply such royalties to the repayment of all sums due to Publisher with respect thereto.

This is a very tricky area. Too much control over litigation resides in the publisher. The publisher should be required to protect the copyright and to prevent and stop infringements, and should bear all costs of doing so. That is a risk of doing business.

When sued by third parties, the writer should have the right to have his or her own attorney and to consent to all settlements. Monies should not continue to be withheld unless a lawsuit is brought within six months after such monies are first withheld; any monies withheld should bear interest.

9. COLLABORATION

The term "Writer" shall be understood to include all the authors and composers of the Composition. If there be more than one, the covenants herein contained shall be deemed to be both joint and several on the part of all the authors and composers, and the royalties hereinabove specified to be paid to Writer shall, unless a different division of royalty be specified in paragraphs 2 and/or 14 hereof, be due to all the authors and composers collectively to be paid by Publisher in equal shares to each. This Agreement may be executed by the authors and composers in several counterparts.

If a lyricist and composer have written the song, their respective contributions should be delineated. The lyricist should not suffer if the music is infringing and vice versa with respect to the composer if the lyrics infringe. (I've represented writers where this has happened. The lyricist should not be liable for damages or costs if the music infringes.) Further, it is the lyricist, not the composer, who may suffer a loss in income from translations, which the composer may not wish to share. In the absence of a written agreement to the contrary, all creators are equal owners, irrespective of the amount of the contribution.

10. USE OF NAME

Writer hereby grants to Publisher the perpetual right to use and publish and to permit others to use and publish Writer's name (including any professional name heretofore or hereafter adopted by Writer), likeness and biographical material, or any reproduction or simulation thereof and the title of the Composition in connection with the printing, sale, advertising, distribution and exploitation of music, folios, recordings, performances, player rolls and otherwise concerning the Composition, and for any other purpose related to the business of Publisher, its associates, affiliates and subsidiaries, or to refrain therefrom.

The clause "any other purpose related to the business of Publisher, its associates, affiliates and subsidiaries," is too general and should be deleted. The artist should approve, or at least be consulted, anytime his image is used.

11. ASSIGNMENT

Publisher shall have the right to assign this Agreement and any of its rights hereunder and to delegate any of its obligations hereunder, in whole or in part, to any person, firm or corporation. Without limiting the generality of the foregoing, Publisher shall have the right to enter into subpublishing, collection, print or other agreements with respect to the Composition with any person, firm or corporation for any one or more countries of the world.

Publisher should be allowed to assign only to a person or entity acquiring all or substantially all of the assets of publisher. Writer should be allowed a "right of first refusal" to purchase the song at the same price at which it is sold to any third party (if it is part of a catalogue, an independent appraiser can be appointed), but few publishers will agree to this.

12. DISPUTES

This contract shall be deemed to have been made in the State of California, and its validity, construction and effect shall be governed by and construed under the laws and judicial decisions of the State of California applicable to agreements wholly performed therein.

In the event of a dispute, the prevailing party should be entitled to reasonable attorneys' fees and costs of suit. Oftentimes it costs as much to fight about the song as the amount at stake. If this provision is not in the contract, then, in most states, such fees are lost. Further, arbitration before the American Arbitration Association, which has offices across America, may be the most economical method of dispute resolution—it's generally less expensive and faster than the court system. See discussion in the chapter "Analysis of a Personal Management Agreement."

13. ENTIRE AGREEMENT

This Agreement contains the entire understanding between us, and all of its terms, conditions and covenants shall be binding upon and shall inure to the benefit of the respective parties and their heirs, successors and assigns. No modification or waiver hereunder shall be valid unless the same is in writing and is signed by the parties hereto.

14. ROYALTY DIVISIONS

Royalties payable to Writer hereunder shall be divided among the parties below in the proportions following if otherwise than provided for in paragraph 9 herein.

WRITER   PERCENTAGE

_____   _____

_____   _____

_____   _____

IN WITNESS WHEREOF, the parties hereto have executed this Agreement as of the day and year first above written.

AGREED TO AND ACCEPTED:

_____   _____
(WRITER)   (PUBLISHER)

_____   _____
ADDRESS   ADDRESS

_____   _____
FEDERAL I.D. / SS#   FEDERAL I.D. / SS#

ANALYSIS OF AN EXCLUSIVE TERM SONGWRITER AGREEMENT

by Evanne L. Levin

The agreement which follows is an example of an exclusive term songwriter agreement entered into between an unestablished songwriter (Writer) and a music publisher (Publisher). It provides that 100% of the ownership (Copyright) in the compositions written during a stated period of time will belong to the publisher. In many cases, an agreement of this type, either alone, or with a Copublishing Agreement (discussed later), is used to acquire the musical works of a writer who is also a recording or performing artist.

Although songwriters are required to relinquish part or all ownership in the musical compositions covered by this type of agreement, they seek term agreements for two basic reasons. First, the annual advance and/or weekly salary provides a financial foundation that enables the songwriter to dedicate more time and energy to writing and, with the assistance of the publisher's professional staff, develop the skills shared by successful songwriters. Second, the publisher will introduce the writer's material to a broad network of performers and record producers, increasing the likelihood of the songs being recorded. Negotiations for a term agreement typically take place only after a writer has had songs recorded by recording artists.

Like the single-song agreement analyzed earlier, there is no standard term agreement. Even a term agreement that is a particular publisher's standardized form is subject to modification by your legal representative. The term agreement is distinguished from the single-song agreement by the addition of provisions that may include—advances payable to the songwriter; a period of time the songwriter is employed to write and deliver original songs; the writer's exclusivity to the publisher; a guaranteed annual minimum compensation option; and the scope of the writer's earnings to be withheld for claims brought by others against the publisher. Many of the other provisions are essentially the same as those in the chapter titled "Analysis of a Single-song Agreement."

At the heart of the negotiation is the publisher's interest in acquiring the maximum rights and control in the maximum number of songs for the least amount of money, and the writer's interest in relinquishing the minimum of rights and control in fewer compositions for the maximum consideration.

Given the complexity of and variations in this type of agreement, it is recommended that a writer not sign a term agreement without first seeking the advice of an attorney familiar with the subject matter.

EXCLUSIVE TERM SONGWRITER AGREEMENT

AGREEMENT effective _____ day of _____19__ ,
by and between _____ hereinafter
referred to as "PUBLISHER" and _____
hereinafter (collectively) referred to as "WRITER."

WITNESSETH: in consideration of the mutual covenants and undertakings herein set
forth, the parties do hereby agree as follows:

1. SERVICES

Publisher hereby engages Writer to render his or her services as a songwriter and
composer and otherwise as may be hereinafter set forth. Writer hereby accepts such
engagement and agrees to render such services exclusively for Publisher during the
term hereof, upon the terms and conditions set forth herein.

> *Although the writer is not the publisher's employee, for the term of the agreement the
> writer is considered like an exclusive employee of the publisher, and as such, cannot
> write for anyone else.*

2. TERM

The term of this Agreement shall commence with the date hereof and shall continue
in force for a period coterminus with the term of that certain Exclusive Recording
Artist Agreement between Writer and Publisher, entered into concurrently with this
Agreement, as same is renewed, extended, amended or substituted.

> *Performers that record their own material often enter into term songwriter agreements
> with their record label's affiliated publishing company. In these instances, the writer
> should limit the term of the songwriter agreement to the length of the term of the record
> deal. Once the recording agreement is over the writer will want any new material to be
> available to negotiate a stronger agreement with the next record company, and by that
> time may be in a better position to keep some or all of the copyright in the new songs
> and a portion of the publisher's share of income. In instances where the songwriter
> agreement is not tied to a record deal, the term is usually three years with an initial
> term of one year and two one-year options, exercisable by the publisher. The songwriter
> may want to try to obtain some measure of performance by the publisher, such as
> obtaining a certain number of cover recordings, especially if little or no advances are
> paid, as a condition to the publisher's exercise of its option to extend the term. As a
> practical matter, the greater the advances, the less likely an option to extend the term
> will be exercised unless the publisher has been successful in exploiting the material.*
>
> *There are pros and cons to a performer-writer entering into a songwriting agree-
> ment with their record company's publishing affiliate. Since the publishing company
> knows that the writer's material will be recorded and released by its affiliated record
> company, it is not taking a great risk that it will not earn back advances paid. More-
> over, since the parent company will be earning money from two sources with each record
> sold (profits on the record and the publisher's share of mechanical royalties for the
> writer's compositions on the record), the writer should be able to negotiate a more favor-
> able advance in exchange for the publisher's share of the compositions. The writer may
> also insist that in exchange for signing with the affiliated publishing company, the*

record company must pay a full mechanical royalty rather than the usual 75% rate on the writer's compositions included on the record. The publishing company will also benefit to the extent it has acquired a copyright in the recorded songs. Finally, the affiliated companies have a double incentive to promote the writer and material.

Other considerations may suggest that the writer's best interests would be served by entering into a term songwriter agreement elsewhere. The record company's publishing arm may not be offering the best terms, or may not be the best publisher for that writer's material. Are the recording contract and term songwriter contract cross-collateralized in any way, so that advances or other costs incurred by one company under one contract can be recovered from the writer's income under the other contract? How do the different publishing companies measure up in various territories? The writer may be one whose material has tremendous foreign income potential in certain major markets where a different publisher would do a better job for the writer. The writer may wish to refrain from entering into any exclusive term songwriter agreement until the record is released, to be in a position to negotiate a better deal with competing suitors (if the record catches on).

Many times, however, the writer has cash flow problems and is anxious to receive the publisher's advance, and cannot or will not adopt the riskier but potentially more profitable, wait and see what happens posture.

3. GRANT OF RIGHTS

(a) Writer hereby irrevocably and absolutely assigns, transfers, sets over and grants to Publisher, its successors and assigns each and every and all rights and interests of every kind, nature and description in and to the results and proceeds of Writer's services hereunder, including but not limited to the titles, words and music of any and all original musical compositions in any and all forms and original arrangements of musical compositions in any and all forms, and all rights and interests existing under all agreements and licenses relating thereto, together with all worldwide copyrights (and any renewals or extensions thereof), which musical works have been written, composed, created or conceived, in whole or in part, by Writer alone or in collaboration with another or others, and which may hereafter, during the term hereof, be written, composed, created or conceived by Writer, in whole or in part, alone or in collaboration with another or others, and which are now owned or controlled and which may, during their term hereof, be acquired, owned or controlled, directly or indirectly, by Writer, alone or with others, or as the employer or transferee, directly or indirectly, of the writers or composers thereof, including the title, words and music of each such composition, and all worldwide copyrights (and renewals and extensions thereof), all of which Writer does hereby represent, are and shall at all times be Publisher's sole and exclusive property as the sole owner thereof, free from any adverse claims or rights therein by any other person, firm or corporation.

Note that the writer is assigning 100% of the compositions to the publisher even if cowritten or owned with others. The writer should be required to give the publisher only the writer's share, since the cowriter(s) or joint owner(s) will want the right to decide what to do with their share, and may even have their own term songwriter agreement with another publisher which contains an identical provision. Unless the other writers give you permission to give your publisher their share of the copyright, you may be in breach of your agreement with your publisher if you cannot grant 100% of the copyright in songs you cowrite. The prudent way to handle this common dilemma is to limit the publisher's ownership in the material to your share. It would also be acceptable to require you to use "reasonable efforts" to obtain the cowriter's copyright share. (For more information regarding cowritten compositions, see the chapter "Collaborator/Songwriter Agreements.")

Requiring the writer to also give the publisher ownership of all songs written before the term is unfair, unless the publisher is paying additional money for these. The writer should at least be entitled to have the copyright in these songs returned if the publisher fails to commercially exploit them within a reasonable period of time—one and one-half to two years would be fair. A similar reversion should also apply to songs written during the term if the advances are low. Advances refers to both money received by the writer at the beginning of each year of the contract and money paid out on a regular basis like a paycheck.

A concept having far-reaching effects on writers' future rights in their compositions is embedded in this provision. It is most significant that this provision, while assigning the writer's copyright in the compositions for the minimum copyright term, does not include specific language describing the writer as creating the compositions "within the scope of Publisher's employment of Writer's personal services" whereby the writer would be deemed the publisher's so-called employee for hire and the publisher would be "deemed the author of the Compositions initially created during the Term." When this language is used the compositions are deemed works made for hire under U.S. copyright laws and the publisher is considered the writer and original copyright owner of the compositions. This would preclude the writer from having any right to reclaim the copyright in these songs after 35 years, which writers can do if they have written the material prior to the term of the Exclusive Term Songwriter Agreement, or the language of the agreement provides for the writer to assign copyrights to the publisher without saying more about the publisher being considered the author from the outset or including the works-made-for-hire language. Even where employee/writer-for-hire language has been used, writers have succeeded in challenging the status of "author" claimed by their publishers by proving that the publisher was not in a position to actually control the development of the songs to be written. The control element is one factor considered by courts in characterizing whether a composition was written (1) independent of the publisher, or (2) under the direction of the publisher. The publisher might need to demonstrate that it was involved in the creation of the song by critiquing the material and instructing the writer to make changes, as well as giving the writer direction about the compositions it expects to be written. The opposite of this would be a writer delivering completed songs written without input from the publisher that were done on the writer's own time at a location other than the publisher's offices.

If the publisher agrees to allow the writer to keep a share of the copyright, or publisher's share of income (roughly fifty cents on each dollar generated from exploiting the composition) it is generally handled by the writer first assigning the entire copyright to the publisher and the publisher then assigning back to the writer a part of the copyright, or publisher's share of income if the publisher wants to maintain sole ownership and control of the copyright, but is willing to share part of the 50% income that comes to the copyright owner. This can be accomplished by adding a provision to the end of this agreement assigning back to the writer a percentage of the copyright and/or providing for payment of a percentage of the publisher's share of income to the writer. A separate agreement called a "Copublishing Agreement" often accompanies the Term Songwriter Agreement and spells out the writer's interest in the songs as a publisher, as distinguished from a writer. This represents an additional source of income from the songs but does not provide any additional control over if or how the copyrights will be used.

(b) Writer acknowledges that, included within the rights and interests herein-above referred to, but without limiting the generality of the foregoing, is Writer's irrevocable grant to Publisher, its successors, licensees, sublicensees and assigns, of the sole and exclusive right, license, privilege and authority throughout the entire world with respect to the said original musical compositions and original arrangements of compositions in the public domain, whether now in existence or hereafter created during the term hereof, as follows:

This is a more detailed version of paragraph 2 of the sample single-song agreement already commented on. The publisher should have to give the writer the first opportunity to make changes in the material.

(i) To perform said musical compositions publicly for profit by means of public and private performance, radio broadcasting, television or any and all other means, whether now known or which may hereafter come into existence;

(ii) To substitute a new title or titles for said compositions and to make any arrangement, adaptation, translation, dramatization and transposition of said compositions, in whole or in part, and in connection with any other musical, literary or dramatic material as Publisher may deem expedient or desirable;

The writer should seek to limit the changes that can be made without reasonable prior consent, at least title and lyric changes in English. Writer can also ask to be given the first opportunity to make the changes desired by the publisher.

(iii) To secure copyright registration and protection of said compositions in Publisher's name or otherwise as Publisher may desire, at Publisher's own cost and expense and at Publisher's election, including any and all renewals and extensions of copyright under any present or future laws throughout the world, and to have and to hold said copyrights, renewals, extensions and all rights of whatsoever nature thereunder existing, for and during the full term of all said copyrights and all renewals and extensions thereof;

Writers should attempt to require the publisher to secure valid copyright protection for the songs throughout the world wherever such protection is recognized. Although formal registration with the U.S. Copyright Office is no longer mandatory to claim ownership in a work, it establishes proof of ownership and is required in order to maintain a claim against another for infringement of the work. The $20 registration fee should not be a problem for the publisher. Since the United States recently joined the Berne Convention, registration in this country will be recognized by all other member countries. The specific requirements for establishing and maintaining a valid copyright are beyond the scope of this chapter but are covered in the chapter "Copyrights: The Law and You."

(iv) To make or cause to be made, master records, transcriptions, sound tracks, pressings, and any other mechanical, electrical or other reproductions of said compositions, in whole or in part, in such form or manner and as frequently as Publisher's sole and uncontrolled discretion shall determine, including the right to synchronize the same with sound motion pictures and the right to manufacture, advertise, license or sell such reproductions for any and all purposes, including, but not limited to, private performances and public performances, by broadcasting, television, sound motion pictures, wired radio, audio devices, and any and all other means or devices whether now known or hereafter conceived or developed;

Writers can protect the integrity of their music by requiring prior consent to its use in X-rated films or those taking an overt political, religious or moral stand. Writers may also seek to require their consent for the use of their music in commercials since the product or service advertised may be one that the writer feels is inappropriate and may diminish the value of the copyright by being associated with it.

(v) To print, publish and sell sheet music orchestration, arrangements and other editions of the said compositions in all forms, including the right to include any or all of said compositions in song folios or lyric magazines with or without music, and the right to license others to include any or all of said compositions in song folios or lyric magazines with or without music; and

The mandatory printing of sheet music or a folio can sometimes be tied to a song reaching a certain level on the Billboard sales charts, although this is not typically a significant source of income and is not equally suited to all types of music.

(vi) Any and all other rights of every and any nature now or hereafter existing under and by virtue of any common law rights and any copyrights (and renewals and extensions thereof) in any and all of such compositions.

Again, prior consent for the use of the song for merchandising purposes might be desired by the writer to prevent identification of the song with some ridiculous product or service. The publisher will want to limit such consent since it has a financial investment in the writer and will claim expertise as compared to the writer in determining the best use of the songs. A compromise can be reached by listing the types of goods or services that would reasonably require the writer's consent. These typically include alcoholic beverages, personal care products, firearms and tobacco products. In addition, writers may try to exclude what are called "grand" rights (the use of the musical material in combination with a dramatic rendition, such as a drama, play or opera).

(c) Writer grants to Publisher, without any compensation other than as specified herein, the perpetual right to use and publish and to permit another to use and publish Writer's name (including any professional name heretofore or hereafter adopted by Writer), likeness, voice and sound effects and biographical material, or any reproduction or simulation thereof and titles of all compositions hereunder in connection with the printing, sale, advertising, distribution and exploitation of music, folios, recordings, performances, player rolls and otherwise concerning any of the compositions hereunder, and for any other purpose related to the compositions hereunder, and for any other purpose related to the business of Publisher, its affiliated and related companies, or to refrain therefrom. This right shall be exclusive during the term hereof and nonexclusive thereafter. Writer will not authorize or permit the use of his name, likeness, biographical material concerning Writer, or the identification of Writer, or any reproduction or simulation thereof, for or in connection with any musical composition or works, in any manner or for any purpose, other than by or for Publisher. Writer further grants to Publisher the right to refer to Writer as "Publisher's Exclusive Songwriter and Composer" or other similar appropriate appellation.

The clause "any other purpose related to the business of Publisher, its associates, affiliates and subsidiaries," is too broad and should be deleted. The writer should be able to negotiate for reasonable approval of his pictures and biographical material. All uses of the writer's name and likeness, which are reasonably related to the compositions, have already been covered. In addition, the prohibition against writers allowing their names or information about them to be used in connection with any composition not covered by this agreement is overreaching and unfair since the agreement may not cover preexisting material or new material not accepted by the publisher. The designation "Publisher's Exclusive Songwriter and Composer" is merely descriptive of the writer's status and is standard in exclusive term agreements.

4. EXCLUSIVITY

From the date hereof and during the term of this Agreement, Writer will not write or compose, or furnish or dispose of, any musical compositions, titles, lyrics or music, or any rights or interests therein whatsoever, nor participate in any manner with regard to the same for any person, firm or corporation other than Publisher, nor permit the use of their name or likeness as the writer or cowriter of any musical composition by any person, firm or corporation other than Publisher.

This exclusivity provision should be qualified to state the writer retains ownership material written before the term of the agreement. In addition, the material written during the term should be evaluated by the publisher and either accepted or rejected as commercially viable within a reasonable period of time after delivery—30 to 60 days is fair. Rejected songs should be given back to the writer since the publisher does not believe in them and therefore will not promote them.

5. WARRANTIES AND REPRESENTATIONS

Writer hereby warrants and represents to Publisher that:

(a) Writer has the full right, power and authority to enter into and perform this Agreement and to grant to and vest in Publisher all the rights herein set forth, free and clear of any and all claims, rights and obligations whatsoever.

(b) All the results and proceeds of the services of Writer hereunder, including all of the titles, lyrics, music and musical compositions, and each and every part thereof, delivered and to be delivered by Writer hereunder are and shall be new and original and capable of copyright protection throughout the entire world.

(c) No part thereof shall be an imitation or copy of, or shall infringe any other original material.

(d) Writer has not and will not sell, assign, lease, license or in any other way dispose of or encumber the rights herein granted to Publisher.

This is essentially the same as the boiler plate language of paragraph 3 of a single-song agreement. The writer should try to limit the warranties to "the best of Writer's knowledge."

6. ATTORNEY IN FACT

Writer does hereby irrevocably constitute, authorize, empower and appoint Publisher, or any of its officers, Writer's true and lawful attorney (with full power of substitution and delegation) in Writer's name, and in Writer's place and stead, or in Publisher's name, to take and do such action, and to make, sign, execute, acknowledge and deliver any and all instruments or documents which Publisher, from time to time, may deem desirable or necessary to vest in Publisher, its successors, assigns and licensees, any of the rights or interests granted by Writer hereunder, including but not limited to such documents required to secure to Publisher the renewals and extensions of copyrights throughout the world of musical compositions written or composed by Writer and owner by Publisher, and also such documents necessary to assign to Publisher, its successors and assigns, such renewal copyrights, and all rights therein for the terms of such renewals and extensions for the use and benefit of Publisher, its successors and assigns.

This common boiler plate provision gives the publisher the authority to act on behalf of the writer to secure and protect the rights it has obtained from the writer. The power of attorney should be exercisable only if the writer fails to sign the requested documents within a reasonable period of time. Ten (10) business days is typical.

7. ADVANCES; ANNUAL GUARANTEES

Conditioned upon, and in consideration of, the full and faithful performance by Writer of all of the terms and provisions hereof, Publisher shall pay to Writer the following annual amounts, in equal monthly installments, all of which shall be recoupable by Publisher from any and all royalties payable to Writer under this or any other agreement between Writer and Publisher:

(a) (amount) ($___) during the initial term hereof.
(b) (amount) ($___) during the first renewal term hereof.
(c) (amount) ($___) during the second renewal term hereof.

The range of yearly advances for songwriter agreements of this type, where the songwriter is not already a recording artist, is anywhere from zero to $15,000 the first year.

A more experienced writer, depending on the level of prior success, should start at anywhere from $25,000 to $100,000, and would probably be able to insist on retaining part of the copyright in the songs by entering into a separate copublishing agreement. A new writer's advances in option years would likely increase EITHER a flat amount ($2,500 each year for years two and three), with a possible bonus of at least $5,000 for the first song each year that hits the top 20 on Billboard's record sale charts, OR an amount equal to 75% of the actual earnings in the prior year of the songs covered by the agreement, subject to some minimums and maximums, as follows:

YEAR	MINIMUM	MAXIMUM
(a) first renewal term	*$12,500*	*$25,000*
(b) second renewal term	*$15,000*	*$30,000*

*If the writer is also a recording artist, there will probably be no set advances as a song-
writer. Instead, advances will be contingent on delivery and release in the United States
by the record company of recordings of the writer's performance of the material, and will
cover a wide range of amounts, with $25,000 to $75,000 fairly typical for an
unknown group's first album.*

8. ROYALTIES

Provided that Writer shall faithfully and completely perform the terms, covenants and
conditions of this Agreement, Publisher hereby agrees to pay Writer for the services to
be rendered by Writer under this Agreement and for the rights acquired and to be
acquired hereunder, the following compensation based on the musical compositions
which are the subject hereof.

(a) Eight ($.08) cents per copy for each and every regular piano copy and for
each and every dance orchestration sold by Publisher and paid for, after deduction of each and every return, in the United States.

*This rate is far too low; 10 cents per single edition is reasonable, with increases tied to
the Consumer Price Index. In the alternative, and more beneficial to the songwriter,
many publishers now split their receipts from single editions with the songwriter.*

(b) Ten (10%) percent of the wholesale selling price upon each and every
printed copy of each and every other arrangement and edition thereof printed,
published and sold by Publisher and paid for, after deduction of each and every
return, in the United States, except that in the event that such composition shall
be used or caused to be used, in whole or in part, in conjunction with one or
more other musical compositions in a folio or album, Writer shall be entitled to
receive that proportion of said ten (10%) percent which the subject musical
composition shall bear to the total number of musical compositions contained in
such folio or album.

*The writer should try for 50% of what the publisher receives, but in any event at least
15% of the wholesale selling price, or its retail equivalent. Proration for use in folios
with material by other writers should be limited to copyrighted, royalty-bearing compositions. An additional 5% of wholesale to 5% of retail should be paid for use of the
writer's name and likeness in a personality folio.*

(c) Fifty (50%) percent of any and all net sums actually received (less any costs for
collection) by Publisher from mechanical rights, electrical transcription and
reproduction rights, motion picture synchronization and television rights and all
other rights (excepting public performing rights) therein, including the use
thereof in song lyric folios, magazines or any other editions whatsoever sold by
licensees of Publisher in the United States.

*While the equal split stated is fair, the agreement should also provide that the writer
receive 50% of any nonreturnable and earned advances the publisher receives with
respect to the composition(s). Also, since the publisher is the administrator of the compositions, collection costs should be charged against the publisher's share rather than the
writer's share, if possible. This comment applies wherever collection costs are referred to
in the agreement. The writer should see to it that he or she is paid on monies credited*

to the publisher wherever the agreement refers to the writer receiving a share of monies received by the publisher.

(d) Writer shall receive his public performance royalties throughout the world directly from his own affiliated performing rights society and shall have no claim whatsoever against Publisher for any royalties received by Publisher from any performing rights society which make payment directly (or indirectly other than through Publisher) to writers, authors and composers.

This is correct. The writer's performing rights society (usually ASCAP or BMI, but occasionally SESAC) pays the writer's share of public performance income directly to the writer.

(e) Fifty (50%) percent of any and all net sums, after deduction of foreign taxes, actually received (less any costs for collection) by Publisher from sales and uses directly related to subject musical compositions in countries outside of the United States (other than public performance royalties as hereinabove mentioned in paragraph 7(d).

Income generated through subpublishers (licensees of original publisher) or foreign affiliates of the publisher may far exceed United States income; it is important to establish ceilings that a subpublisher or affiliate of Publisher can charge. The collection fee charged by a subpublisher for obtaining a cover record (local version) of the writer's composition is usually greater than the fee charged for mechanical license and other income generated from the original recording in the territory involved. The fee should not exceed 30% to 40% (depending on the territory), of what the publisher would otherwise receive before paying the writer for income attributable to the cover recording, and 20% to 25% for original recording income. The split between the publisher and subpublisher (i.e., before the writer's share is computed) is often stated in songwriter agreements as "80/20," "75/25," etc., representing the publisher and subpublisher's shares of gross income from its origin.

(f) Publisher shall not be required to pay any royalties on professional or complimentary copies of any copies or mechanical derivatives which are distributed gratuitously to performing artists, orchestra leaders, disc jockeys or for advertising or exploitation purposes. Furthermore, no royalties shall be payable to Writer on consigned copies unless paid for, and not until such time as an accounting therefor can be properly made.

(g) Royalties as specified hereinabove shall be payable solely to Writer in instances where Writer is the sole author of the entire composition, including the words and music thereof. If this Agreement with Publisher is made and executed by more than one person in the capacity of Writer, the royalties as hereinabove specified shall be payable solely to the particular Writer or Writers who are the authors of the entire composition, including words and music thereof, and such royalties shall be divided equally among the particular Writers of such composition unless another division is agreed upon in writing between the Writers. However, in the event that one or more other songwriters are authors along with Writer on any composition, then the foregoing royalties shall be divided equally between Writer and the other songwriters of such composition unless another division of royalties is agreed upon in writing between the parties concerned.

(h) Except as herein expressly provided, no other royalties or moneys shall be paid to Writer.

Provision should be made for advances to be paid to the writer under any term songwriter agreement. The publisher is requiring the writer to write exclusively for it and in exchange is paying the writer only the royalties noted above, while retaining complete ownership of the songs and keeping 100% of the publisher's share of income. Nor is there any guarantee that the publisher will successfully exploit any of the writer's material, in which case the writer will see no income.

Advances are typically paid (1) in one lump sum on execution of the agreement and at the beginning of each succeeding year of the term, and/or (2) in regular installments over the term, like a weekly or semimonthly paycheck. ($16,000 to $24,000 for the first year is not an unusual amount for a large publishing company to pay; small, independent publishers typically pay less but contend that more time will be devoted to promoting its staff writers since they have fewer staff).

The amount of the advance typically escalates 10% to 20% for each succeeding year of the term, and may be boosted by additional advances triggered by a song's commercial success. This is commonly done by tying increases to Billboard chart positions achieved or sales levels reached by previous albums. All advances are recoupable from both the writer's share and publisher's share of royalties otherwise payable to the writer (ASCAP/BMI royalties excluded).

A publisher who pays an advance to a writer will require the delivery of specified minimum number of compositions written by the writer. Fifteen to 20 "Wholly Owned Compositions" is typical, with songs cowritten receiving partial credit. For example, if the writer writes a song with two other writers, the publisher will give the writer credit for one-third of a wholly owned composition toward the minimum delivery requirement. If the writer fails to deliver the minimum number of songs required during any contract year, the publisher will have the right to extend the term without having to increase the advances beyond the agreed amount until a sufficient number of songs are delivered. The writer should object to any provision giving the publisher the right to suspend advances in addition to extending the term.

In any event (h) is meaningless and should be deleted, since the rest of paragraph 7 provides for payment to the writer for all types of uses.

9. ACCOUNTING

Publisher will compute the royalties earned by Writer pursuant to this Agreement within ninety (90) days after the first day of January and the first day of July of each year for the preceding six (6) month period, and will remit to Writer the net amount of such royalties, if any, after deducting any and all unrecouped advances and chargeable costs under this Agreement, together with the detailed royalty statement, within such ninety (90) days. All royalty statements rendered by Publisher to Writer shall be binding upon Writer and not subject to any objection by Writer for any reason unless specific objection is made, in writing, stating the basis thereof, to Publisher within one (1) year from the date rendered. Writer shall have the right, upon the giving of at least thirty (30) days written notice to Publisher, to inspect the books and records of

Publisher, insofar as the same concerns Writer, at the expense of Writer, at reasonable times during normal business hours, for the purpose of verifying the accuracy of any royalty statement rendered to Writer hereunder.

> *Mechanical income should be paid on a quarterly basis since record companies usually account for mechanical income quarterly. Forty-five to 60 days after the close of an accounting period should be enough time for statements to be rendered. The writer should have at least two years from the time rendered to object to a statement.*

10. COLLABORATIONS

Whenever Writer shall collaborate with any other person in the creation of any musical composition, any such musical composition shall be subject to the terms and conditions of this Agreement and Writer warrants and represents that prior to the collaboration with any other person, such other person shall be advised prior to the collaboration of this exclusive agreement and that all such compositions must be published by Publisher in accordance with the terms and provisions hereunder. In the event of such collaboration with any other person, Writer shall notify Publisher of the extent that such other person may have in any such musical composition and Writer shall cause such other person to execute a separate songwriter's agreement with respect thereto, which agreement shall set forth the division of the songwriter's share of income between Writer and such other person, and Publisher shall make payment accordingly. If Publisher so desires, Publisher may request Writer to execute a separate agreement in Publisher's customary form with respect to each musical composition hereunder. Upon such request, Writer will promptly execute such agreement. Publisher shall have the right, pursuant to the terms and conditions hereof, to execute such agreement on behalf of Writer hereunder. Such agreement shall supplement and not supersede this Agreement. In the event of any conflict between the provisions of such agreement and this Agreement, the provisions of this Agreement shall govern.

> *This language is not consistent with the reality that writers do collaborate without regard to existing exclusive writer agreements, and is detrimental to the natural collaborate creative process. A better approach would be to require that the publisher be entitled to all of its own writer's ownership share of the song, and perhaps also the ownership share of any cowriter not similarly signed to a publisher. Moreover, it should state, "Writer shall use best efforts to cause such other person to execute a separate songwriter's agreement" with respect to cowritten compositions. Finally, writers should never authorize others to sign agreements in their name, except possibly to the extent necessary to allow the publisher to secure and protect the copyright share obtained from them, as discussed in paragraph 6 above. (For more information about collaborations, see the chapter, "Collaborator/Songwriter Agreements.")*

11. DEMOS

Writer will deliver a manuscript copy of each musical composition hereunder immediately upon the completion or acquisition of such musical composition. Publisher shall advance reasonable costs for the production of demonstration records and one-half (1/2) of such costs shall be deemed an advance which shall be deducted from royalties payable to Writer by Publisher under this Agreement. All recordings and reproductions made at demonstration recording sessions hereunder shall become the sole and exclusive property of Publisher, free of any claims whatsoever by Writer or any person deriving any rights from Writer.

It is unfair, but traditional, for publishers to recover one-half the demo costs from the writer's royalties. The writer should try to get this deleted, especially if they aren't also receiving part of the publisher's share of income. The writer should be able to keep copies of demos of songs that are rejected by the publisher and can offer to reimburse publisher the unrecouped share of demo costs of they are successful in exploiting the song on their own.

12. INJUNCTION

Writer acknowledges that the services rendered hereunder are of a special, unique, unusual, extraordinary and intellectual character which gives them a peculiar value, the loss of which cannot be reasonably or adequately compensated in damages in an action at law, and that a breach by Writer of any of the provisions of this Agreement will cause Publisher great and irreparable injury and damage. Writer expressly agrees that Publisher shall be entitled to remedies of injunction and other equitable relief to prevent a breach of this Agreement or any provision hereof, which relief shall be in addition to any other remedies, for damages or otherwise, which may be available to Publisher.

This standard provision allows the publisher to get a court order preventing the writer from writing for any other publisher if the writer becomes dissatisfied and wants to terminate the deal with the current publisher and write for someone else. It is doubtful, however, that a court would issue an injunction just because this clause is in the contract.

This provision should only allow the publisher to seek an injunction from the court so that the publisher would be required to prove that a money judgment would not be sufficient. In addition, this kind of relief should be available only if the writer's action or failure goes to the essence of the agreement, such as failing to deliver the songs required, or refusing to turn over the demos to the publisher.

It is also important to know that, for contracts governed by California law, the publisher cannot obtain an injunction against the writer unless it has agreed to pay certain annual minimums. The amounts for a three-year agreement are $6,000; $9,000; and $12,000, for years one through three, respectively. As all other advances, these are fully recoupable against writer's royalties.

13. REVERSION

If Publisher fails to secure a cover recording of the Compositions within the term of this Agreement, Writer may, during the fifteen (15) days following the expiration of said term, demand the return of the Compositions in writing and if Publisher receives such notice within said period, Publisher agrees to reassign the compositions and all Publisher's rights therein to Writer and to execute any documents necessary to effect such reconveyance. Notwithstanding the foregoing, Publisher shall not be obliged to reassign the Compositions to Writer until such time as Writer shall repay to Publisher any advances or unrecouped demonstration recording costs chargeable to Writer.

The maximum period of time possible should be negotiated for the writer to come up with the money to reacquire the compositions—two years is probably the most the publisher will allow. The writer should additionally have the right to recapture even those compositions that are covered but are not commercially released on a major label. Even better, but less likely to obtain unless the writer has a measure of bargaining power, is requiring that the recording be by a major artist and/or achieve a certain chart position. Top 50 is a reasonable target to request. In addition, the publisher may require at least a year following the term for exploitation of those songs delivered during the last year or two of the term so as to have at least two or three years to record them. A new writer may have to settle for reversion after four or five years after the term, but this still offers an opportunity to breathe new life into compositions that would otherwise languish in the publisher's archives and be lost to the world. Be sure that the reversion is at the writer's option if repayment of advances is tied to reversion; there is no point in being required to buy back those compositions that are not winners even in the writer's eyes. Finally, only unrecouped advances should be repaid.

14. ACTIONS; INDEMNITY

(a) Publisher may take such action as it deems necessary, either in Writer's name or in its own name, against any person to protect all rights and interest acquired by Publisher hereunder. Writer will at Publisher's request, cooperate fully with Publisher in any controversy which may arise or litigation which may be brought concerning Publisher's rights and interests obtained hereunder. Publisher shall have the right, in its absolute discretion, to employ attorneys and to institute or defend any action or proceeding and to take any other proper steps to protect the rights, title and interest of Publisher in and to each musical composition hereunder and every portion thereof and in that connection, to settle, compromise or in any other manner dispose of any matter, claim, action or proceeding and to satisfy any judgment that may be rendered, in any manner as Publisher in its sole discretion may determine. Any legal action brought by Publisher against any alleged infringer of any musical composition hereunder shall be initiated and prosecuted by Publisher, and if there is any recovery made by Publisher as a result thereof, after the deduction of the expense of litigation, including but not limited to attorneys' fees and court costs, a sum equal to fifty (50%) percent of such net proceeds shall be paid to Writer.

(b) If a claim is presented against Publisher in respect to any musical composition hereunder, and because thereof Publisher is jeopardized, Publisher shall have the right thereafter, until said claim has been finally adjudicated or settled, to withhold any and all royalties or other sums that may be or become due with respect to such compositions pending the final adjudication or settlement of such claim. Publisher, in addition, may withhold from any and all royalties or other sums that may be due and payable to Writer hereunder, an amount which Publisher deems sufficient to reimburse Publisher for any contemplated damages, including court costs and attorneys' fees and costs resulting therefrom. Upon the final adjudication or settlement of each and every claim hereunder, all moneys withheld shall then be disbursed in accordance with the final adjudication or settlement of said claim.

This version is more fair to the writer in several respects than the indemnity provision appearing in the single songwriter agreement in the previous chapter. It clarifies that the writer shares in any recovery obtained against infringers, limits the amount of money withheld from the writer to a sum related to the anticipated cost of the claim and continues payment to the writer for income from compositions not involved in the claim. Since many claims are made by third parties and are not pursued, the agreement should also provide that any monies withheld from the writer by the publisher when a claim is made against the publisher bear interest and be released to the writer if no formal lawsuit is filed within six months after the monies are first withheld. The writer should also have the right to be represented by his or her own attorney and to consent to at least those settlements in excess of a few thousand dollars. In addition, since the publisher has acquired the copyright and controls the compositions, the publisher should have not only the right but the obligation to protect the copyrights by taking action against infringers, and bearing all costs of defending or instituting claims.

15. NOTICES

Any written notice, statement, payment or matter required or desired to be given to Publisher or Writer pursuant to this Agreement shall be given by addressing the same to the addresses of the respective parties referred to herein, or to such other address as either party shall designate in writing, and such notice shall be deemed to have been given on the date when same shall be deposited, so addressed, postage prepaid, in the United States mail, or on the date when delivered, so addressed, toll prepaid, to a telegraph or cable company.

Be sure that the contract includes complete addresses for both parties. A copy of notices given by the publisher should also be sent to the writer's attorney so she or he can answer any questions that might arise from the notice. Notices exercising an option or claiming that a breach has occurred should be by certified mail with a return receipt.

16. ENTIRE AGREEMENT

This Agreement supersedes any and all prior negotiations, understandings and agreements between the parties hereto with respect to the subject matter hereof. Each of the parties acknowledges and agrees that neither party has made any representations or promises in connection with this Agreement or the subject matter hereof not contained herein.

17. MISCELLANEOUS

This Agreement may not be canceled, altered, modified, amended or waived, in whole or in part, in any way, except by an instrument in writing signed by both Publisher and Writer. The waiver by Publisher of any breach of this Agreement in any one or more instances, shall in no way be construed as a waiver of any subsequent breach (whether or not of a similar nature) of this Agreement by Writer. If any part of this Agreement shall be held to be void, invalid or unenforceable, it shall not affect the validity of the balance of this Agreement. This Agreement shall be governed by and construed under the law of the State of New York applicable to agreements executed in and to wholly performed therein.

These boiler plate provisions are like paragraphs 12 and 13 of the single-song agreement. If the writer and/or attorney reside in California it would be better for California law to apply since it is more familiar and may be more favorable to the artist inasmuch as this state's legislature and courts have adopted a role somewhat more protective of artists than other states.

18. BREACH; NOTICE

No breach of this Agreement on the part of Publisher shall be deemed material, unless Writer shall have given Publisher notice of such breach and Publisher shall fail to discontinue the practice complained of (if a practice of Publisher is the basis of the claim of breach) or otherwise cure such breach, within sixty (60) days after receipt of such notice, if such breach is reasonably capable of being fully cured within such sixty (60) day period, or, if such breach is not reasonably capable of being fully cured within such sixty (60) day period, if Publisher commences to cure such breach within such sixty (60) day period and proceeds with reasonable diligence to complete the curing of such breach.

The writer should be given the same opportunity to cure breaches.

19. ASSIGNMENT

This Agreement may not be assigned by Writer. Subject to the foregoing, this Agreement shall inure to the benefit of and be binding upon each of the parties hereto and their respective successors, assigns, heirs, executors, administrators and legal and personal representatives.

Publisher should be allowed to assign only to a person or entity acquiring all or substantially all of the assets of Publisher. Writer should be allowed to purchase the song at the same price at which it is sold to any third party (if it is part of a catalogue, an independent appraiser can be appointed), but few publishers will agree to this.

IN WITNESS WHEREOF, the parties hereto have executed this Agreement as of the day and year first above written.

AGREED TO AND ACCEPTED:

_____   _____
(WRITER)   (PUBLISHER)

_____   _____
NAME AND TITLE (AN AUTHORIZED SIGNATORY)   NAME AND TITLE (AN AUTHORIZED SIGNATORY)

_____   _____
FEDERAL I.D. / SS#   FEDERAL I.D. / SS#

MUSIC LICENSING FOR TELEVISION AND FILM: A PERSPECTIVE FOR SONGWRITERS

by Ronald H. Gertz

Television and film productions are important and accessible vehicles that can generate exposure for a writer's works and develop into immediate and long-term sources of revenue. This chapter will discuss how music is licensed by television and film producers.

Songwriters want to receive the greatest amount of income possible from the exploitation of their creations. One of the major sources is from the performance of works in feature films and in network, syndicated, cable and pay television programs. A significant portion of ASCAP, BMI and SESAC revenues are collected from television broadcasters and the royalties received from public performances of music in television and film soundtracks can far exceed the up-front money paid to composers for services in creating original songs or musical scores.

LICENSING THE RIGHTS

In general terms, copyright owners can usually prevent anyone who has not secured a license from using their songs. Under the copyright law, the owner is given the specific right to publish the composition, to reproduce and distribute copies of it; to perform the composition in public; to "display" the musical work as in a printed lyric sheet; and to make derivative works, such as different arrangements of the composition. Use of any of these rights requires the grant of a written license from the copyright owner to the user.

The producer who wishes to use *preexisting* music in a program must secure a license to do so from the owner of the song. (If the copyright owner has formed a publishing company or has signed a contract with an outside publishing company, then the publisher will negotiate and grant these licenses.) Such documents will usually require certain warranties and representations (guarantees)

> ## FOR THE SONGWRITER WHO IS JUST STARTING OUT
>
> If you are a songwriter or performer starting out in the business, you will be happy to know that there are television and film producers that actively look for new material for their projects in order to capture the latest sounds and styles. Some producers are looking for hot new talent, while others just want inexpensive music. Whatever the reason, the use of a song in a television or film program means exposure; the chance to be seen, heard and paid.

about the ownership of the material, because the producer must be sure to license the rights from the true owner of the song. This is not always a simple process because several writers can collaborate in creating a single song, and a copyright can be divided into separate parts with each part owned either individually or by several parties. The way a song is owned can cause complications because of the number of parties that can own it. If a song has been cowritten by several writers, each writer may legally own an undivided pro rata share of the copyright and each of the writers may have assigned all or a portion of their rights to various parties (or publishers) in different territories of the world. For more information on collaboration agreements, see the chapter "Collaborator/Songwriter Agreements."

These issues can make the licensing process a very lengthy one and can work against both new and established songwriters because music decisions are made very quickly in the television and film business. Songwriters are well-advised to make sure that a producer who wants the right to use the writer's song in a production can get the rights quickly and easily. All things being equal, the producer will usually license the song which is easiest and cheapest to use.

Since producers are ultimately liable if rights are not secured properly, they must be sure to deal with the true owner or publisher of the composition and make sure that the publisher has the legal right to grant the license, and that all rights are "cleared." The clearance process, in simplest terms, involves determining whether the copyright owner of the song will allow the producer to use the song in the way the producer intends, and negotiating the fee that the producer will have to pay for the right to use the song.

This music clearance process is important because producers, program distributors and broadcasters can be held liable for infringing copyrights if the music they use or broadcast has not been properly cleared. Producers have contractual obligations to a number of parties, including those that have paid for the program to be produced, and the companies that insure the program in the event its exhibition violates the rights of any third party. These contractual obligations require that the program be delivered for broadcast or other exhibition with all rights secured and be free of any restrictions which could limit the exploitation of the program.

THE PERFORMING RIGHTS ORGANIZATIONS

In the copyright law, one of the exclusive rights granted to the owner of a composition is the right to perform that composition publicly, subject to certain exceptions. In this context, "perform" is a term of art which means the singing, dancing to, playing, or broadcasting of a song. Broadcasters traditionally secure licenses, which allow them to broadcast programs containing music, from the performance rights organizations that represent songwriters and publishers: The American Society of Composers, Authors and Publishers (ASCAP), Broadcast Music, Inc. (BMI), and SESAC. It must be noted that there are differences in the working processes of each of these organizations, and a composer seeking affiliation with one of them should consult knowledgeable industry sources to help in making a choice. For a more complete discussion on these organizations, see the chapter titled "Performing Rights Organizations: An Overview."

The performing rights organizations make their entire catalogs of compositions available to broadcasters upon the payment of a fee, which gives them the right to perform all of the songs in the organization's catalog without having to contact each publisher directly. After deducting the costs of administration, those fees are divided between the writers and publishers based upon the number of performances logged by the performing rights organization.

SYNCHRONIZATION RIGHTS

Another major source of royalties for the songwriter comes from licensing the right to reproduce music in films. The right to reproduce (like the right to perform) is another exclusive right that the copyright law grants to the owner of the copyright in a song. A mechanical license, which refers to the right to mechanically reproduce music in the form of audio records and tapes, for distribution to the public, is an example of one type of reproduction. In the television and film business, music is reproduced when it is recorded on the soundtrack of a production. The industry has come to refer to the right to do this as a synchronization right, because the music is being reproduced on the soundtrack in synchronization with the pictures. Unlike performance royalties, which the performing rights organizations traditionally collect from broadcasters on a blanket basis, synchronization rights are a matter of individual negotiation for each composition used. Rights are secured by producers or their representatives directly from publishers or their agents.

In addition, there are organizations such as The Harry Fox Agency, Inc., and Finell-Brunow and Associates, which represent publishers in the negotiation and collection of synchronization fees.

Synchronization licenses are required in most situations where the composition is reproduced on film or videotape.

PER PROGRAM LICENSING

Another important performance rights issue is the per program license. The performing rights societies and the broadcasting and cable television industries have been negotiating and litigating new rate structures for free television and pay, cable and subscription television broadcasters. Recently, ASCAP and BMI have agreed to per program licenses in which local television broadcasters pay a society only for those programs which contain music from that society. This has resulted in a number of television stations opting for the per program license and securing performing rights for certain music directly from the copyright owners instead of through the performing rights societies. The net effect for certain music owners is a splitting of the revenue stream from performance rights. Thus, a composer can get paid through ASCAP or BMI for performances on television stations that utilize the blanket license and get additional monies directly from those television stations that utilize the per program license and negotiate directly with the copyright owner.

USE OF A SONG ON A TELEVISION PROGRAM

We are now going to follow, in general terms, what happens when a song is actually used on a television program. Let's assume that Fred Composer, Wilma Words and Lydia Lyric have cowritten a song called "Sing It High" which a young crooner would like to warble on the finals of the television series "You Too Can Hit It Big." Fred wrote the music while Wilma and Lydia wrote the words. Through their attorneys, an agreement was worked out which provided that they would divide all performance income equally, but because Fred owned the studio they produced the demo in, he would receive 50% of the publisher's share of income and Wilma and Lydia would each receive 25%. They also agreed that each would separately administer their own shares. Synchronization rights for Fred Composer Music Publishing are administered by The Harry Fox Agency, Wilma Words Music is administered by the law firm of Abdulla and Steinmetz, and the affairs of Lydia Lyric's publishing company Aidyl Time Music are handled by her manager. All of the above (for the sake of simplicity) are affiliated with BMI.

Let us first consider the public performance rights issues. The producer will make sure that "Sing it High," Fred, Wilma, Lydia and their respective publishing companies are registered and affiliated with a performing rights organization. If registered, the rights to publicly perform "Sing It High" will be covered under the terms of the blanket licenses secured by the broadcasters. A blanket license allows a broadcaster to broadcast any and all songs in the catalog of the performing rights organization.

The producer must also acquire a synchronization license from each of the publishers because each publisher controls its own share of the rights. The territories and term of distribution rights are a matter of negotiation between the parties, reflecting the producer's needs. However, synchronization licenses may run for a period of one, three or five years, and may cover only the territories in which the producer feels the program can be distributed. If a producer feels that the program will have a long life in syndication he may try to secure these rights for worldwide distribution of the program, in perpetuity (forever). A five-year worldwide television synchronization license allows the program on which a song is used to be broadcast an unlimited number of times throughout the world over a five-year period (assuming that the stations which broadcast the program are duly licensed by a performing rights organization).

The amount of money paid for the sync license depends upon the way the song is used. For example, a use with a singer on camera (visual vocal) or with a musician playing an instrument on camera (visual instrumental), may be more expensive than music that is used for background purposes only. Prices are also determined by the length of the song and whether the program is produced for network television, for syndication, or otherwise. Since a network program telecast in prime time may have a higher budget than a syndicated program, fees may be negotiated accordingly. ASCAP, BMI and SESAC also pay more money for performances in prime time, on the theory that more people are watching the programs.

Synchronization fees for television uses are traditionally modest, since publishers are usually willing to give producers a break on the price to have the song performed on television, thus generating performance revenue. Remember that public performance fees are paid by the broadcasters and have no affect on the production budget. However, synchronization fee payments are the responsibility of the producer and directly affect the producer's bottom line profit. Therefore, producers fight hard to limit expenditures for synchronization licenses, knowing that the songwriter and publisher stand to make a considerable amount of money and receive exposure from the television performances.

Since Fred Composer Music Publishing is represented by The Harry Fox Agency, the producer would negotiate with The Harry Fox Agency for a license covering Fred's 50% interest. The producer would also have to negotiate a deal with Wilma's law firm and with Lydia's manager for their respective interests. It is imperative that the producer be able to contact all of the representatives and negotiate acceptable license fees prior to taping the program.

USE OF A COMPOSITION IN A FEATURE FILM

Now let's suppose that "Sing it High" is proposed for use in a feature film. Many of the same rules apply with respect to clearing the use of the composition. However, the fees for use of music on theatrical films can be dramatically higher than those for television programs. This is for several reasons. A complete package of rights and media are involved and these rights are always secured for the duration of the copyright in the composition. Also, theatrical films are usually produced on a much higher budget than television programs. As a result, the producer requires a broad license with the right to exploit the film in all media in order to at least recoup the cost of the film.

First, the producer must secure a U.S. theatrical performing rights license. When a film with music on its soundtrack is exhibited in a movie theater, a public performance occurs for which the composers and their publishers are entitled to receive performing royalties. However, motion picture exhibitions in the United States do not generate royalties for the performing rights organizations. It is a violation of U.S. antitrust laws for ASCAP, BMI and SESAC to charge theater owners a license fee for the right to publicly perform the music included in the films. As a result, the film producer must go directly to the publishers to negotiate the fee for these rights.

The process is completely different outside the United States, where U.S. antitrust laws do not apply. Theater owners in many foreign countries are required to pay a percentage of box office receipts to the local performing rights organizations. Some portion of these monies eventually filter back to the composer and publisher through their domestic performing rights organizations by virtue of those societies agreements with the foreign performing rights organizations. These foreign performance royalties are a major source of publishing revenue, and can mean thousands of dollars to the songwriter and publisher.

The producer must also secure worldwide synchronization rights. As in television, these rights are obtained by dealing with the publishers, and are obtained for duration of copyright in the composition. As a practical matter, both the worldwide synchronization rights and the U.S. theatrical performing rights are negotiated as a package deal in one license agreement.

The film producer will also secure the "broad rights," which include the right to exhibit a program in essentially all possible media, including free television, cable, subscription, pay television, closed circuit television, and in film and video trailers and advertisements for the promotion of the film.

Producers also secure home video (videocassettes and discs) rights. The actual structure of home video rights negotiations may take several forms and an adequate discussion of such would go far beyond the scope of this chapter. However, most feature film producers have been adamant about securing a buyout of home video rights for a one-time flat-fee payment. For the most part they have been successful in securing buyouts and will generally not use a song which requires any form of continuing royalty. With television programs, or programs made specifically for the home video market, which use a substantial amount of music, it is likely that some kind of per unit royalty can be negotiated.

No producer will allow "Sing It High" to be used in a feature film without receiving nonexclusive rights to the music in all possible media of distribution of the film, with no restrictions or limitations. This is because a motion picture studio might not distribute a film if the right to do so could be enjoined (prohibited by court order) by a music publisher because all rights were not secured. The film companies have too much money at stake to allow a song to restrict their right to distribute.

In some situations the producer may require a hold back regarding future licensing of a song. For example, if "Sing It High" is expected to be a prominent song in the film, the producer may want to restrict other producers from using it for any purpose for a certain period of time to avoid competition. This may increase the cost of the license because the publisher will have to turn down other license requests during the hold back period. Hold backs occur typically where a song is written for a film, or is to be used in television commercials.

CONCLUSION

This brief explanation of television and film music licensing does not include all of the possible variations and nuances. The licensing process can become complicated in the extreme.

While producers are very serious about all of the legal ramifications mentioned here, they still have important creative needs. Their need for good music is an opportunity for both new and experienced songwriters to generate revenue and obtain the exposure that may lead to other successes.

DIGITAL PERFORMANCE RIGHT IN
SOUND RECORDINGS ACT

The Digital Performance Right in Sound Recordings Act (DPRSRA) provides an exclusive right (with specified limitations) to perform sound recordings publicly by means of digital transmissions and, in the case of a subscription transmission (radio or television subscription services to consumers that pay to receive digital transmissions), to be subject to statutory licensing.

DPRSRA authorizes copyright owners of sound recordings and any entities performing such recordings to negotiate and agree upon the terms and rates of royalty payments and the division of fees among owners and to designate common agents to negotiate, agree to, pay, or receive such payments.

It directs the Librarian of Congress to publish notice of the initiation of voluntary negotiation proceedings for purposes of determining reasonable terms and rates of royalty payments for activities involving subscription transmissions and requires such terms and rates to distinguish among the different types of digital transmission services then in operation. It permits copyright owners of affected sound recordings or entities performing such recordings to submit licenses covering such activities to the Librarian.

DPRSRA requires the Librarian, in the absence of negotiated license agreements, to convene a copyright arbitration royalty panel to be binding on such owners and entities and it directs the Librarian to establish requirements by which such owners may receive notice of the use of their sound recordings and under which records of use shall be kept by entities performing such recordings.

It directs persons wishing to perform a sound recording publicly by means of a subscription transmission to do so without infringing exclusive rights by complying with notice requirements of the Register of Copyrights and paying royalty fees.

It sets forth a formula for the allocation of proceeds from the licensing of such transmissions to recording artists.

It sets forth authorities of copyright owners with respect to licensing to affiliates.

It includes within the scope of a compulsory license to make and distribute phonorecords of nondramatic musical works the right of the phonorecord maker to distribute or authorize distribution of the sound recording by means of digital transmission which constitutes a digital phonorecord delivery and grants copyright owners of such works the right to receive royalty payments at the rate prescribed when the digital transmission constitutes such a delivery. It makes such transmission actionable by the owner as an act of infringement if a compulsory license has not been issued.

The act sets forth provisions regarding negotiation of rates of royalty payments for digital phonorecord deliveries which are reasonably expected to result from subscription transmissions.

DPRSRA was signed into law on November 1, 1995.

HOME VIDEO SYNCHRONIZATION LICENSE

In consideration of the fee(s) set forth below, Licensor hereby grants to Producer the nonexclusive right, license, privilege and authority to reproduce or fix the Composition listed below in synchronization or timed-relation with the below noted Production and to make and distribute Videogram copies of the Production for the Home Video Market, subject to the terms and conditions listed below.

PRODUCTION: _____

PRODUCER: _____

COMPOSITION:_____

COMPOSER(S): _____

PUBLISHER(S): _____

ADMINISTRATIVE SHARE: _____

USE: _____

TIMING: _____

LICENSE MEDIA: Manufacture of Videogram copies of the Production for the purpose of distribution in the Home Video Market. The "Home Video Market" shall refer to the sale, lease, license, use, rental or other distribution of Videograms to the public primarily for home use. "Videogram" shall mean videotape cassettes, videodiscs or any similar devices of a noninteractive nature which are presently in general commercial use and which are intended primarily for use in the Home Video Market.

LICENSE ROYALTY: _____

ADVANCE: _____

EXHIBITION TERRITORY: _____

LICENSE TERM: _____

COMMENCING: _____

ACCOUNTING PERIOD: _____

TERMS AND CONDITIONS:

1. Upon the expiration of this license, all rights herein granted shall cease and terminate and the right to make or authorize any further use or distribution of any recordings made hereunder shall also cease and terminate.

2. This license does not include the right to alter the fundamental character of the Composition, to use the title or subtitle of the Composition as the title of the Production, to use the story of the Composition, or to make any other use of the Composition not expressly authorized hereunder. Subject to the foregoing, Producer may make arrangements, orchestrations and adaptations of the Composition for its recording purposes.

3. For the purpose of this agreement, "Home Video Market" shall refer to the sale, lease, license, use, rental or other distribution of Videograms to the public primarily for home use. "Videogram" shall mean videotape cassettes, videodiscs or any similar devices, on which the Production may be duplicated for use in the Home Video Market.

4. Subject to the recoupment of any advance, and only with respect to Videogram units finally sold and not returned after the first commercial sale of a Videogram pursuant to this license, Producer shall account to Licensee within sixty (60) days after the close of the Accounting Period in any such Accounting Period in which Videogram copies are sold.

5. In the event that Producer fails to account and pay royalties as herein provided, if royalties have been earned, Licensor shall have the right to give written notice to Producer that unless the default is remedied within thirty (30) days from the date of the notice, this license shall terminate.

6. After reasonable written notice to Producer, for the purpose of verifying the accuracy of statements rendered, an authorized representative of Licensor may examine Producer's books and records pertaining to the sales of Videograms during normal business hours at the place where Producer maintains said books and records, however, no more than once per calendar year. Statements rendered shall become binding unless written objection is received by Producer within two (2) years after the rendering of such statement.

7. Licensor warrants only that it has the legal right to grant this license and that this license is given and accepted without other warranty or recourse. If said warranty shall be breached in whole or in part, Licensor shall either repay to Producer the consideration paid hereunder or hold Producer harmless to the extent of the consideration paid for this license.

8. This license shall run to Producer, its successors and assigns, provided that Producer remain liable for the performance of all the terms and conditions of this license on its part to be performed and provided further, that any disposition of the Production shall be subject to all the terms herein.

9. At the end of the License Term, Producer shall have the right to sell off its inventory of Videogram copies for an additional period of one year subject to the continuing obligation to pay royalties therefor.

10. This license is being entered into on an experimental and nonprejudicial basis and shall not be binding upon or prejudicial to any position taken by Licensor or Producer for any period subsequent to the term of this license.

11. Producer may exercise the option(s) listed in this agreement, if any, for the stated License Media, Territory, Term and Fee, by providing written notice to Licensor within the Option Period accompanied by payment of the specified fee and execution of any appropriate license agreement.

ADDITIONAL TERMS AND CONDITIONS:
1. This license grants permission to use the Composition for in-context trailers and promos for the Production.

2. This license further grants permission to reprint the lyrics of the Composition for the purpose of an insert to be included in each videocassette copy.

3. Nothing contained in this license shall be deemed to authorize the creation of a recording which deliberately imitates the featured and commercially exploited vocal performance of the Composition by any particular recording artist.

4. Paragraph 9 under TERMS AND CONDITIONS hereof is hereby amended to include the following:
"Producer shall not duplicate excessive quantities in anticipation of the sell-off period."

5. Paragraph 3 under TERMS AND CONDITIONS hereof is hereby deleted and replaced with the following:
Manufacture of Videogram copies of the Production for the purpose of distribution in the Home Video Market. The "Home Video Market" shall refer to the sale, lease, license, use, rental or other distribution of Videograms to the public primarily for home use. "Videogram" shall mean videotape cassettes, videodiscs or any similar devices of a noninteractive nature which are presently in general commercial use and which are intended primarily for use in the Home Video Market.

6. If, during the term hereof, you pay to another music publisher a fee in excess of the fee set out herein for the synchronization of a composition in the production, you shall pay to Licensor a corresponding amount equal to the difference between the fee set out herein and the fee paid to said other music publisher.

7. Options for additional rights:
License Media: Free television distribution and exhibition.
License Fee:_____
Exhibition Territory: World
License Term: _____
Option Term: _____
License Media: All forms of television distribution and exhibition including free, pay, cable and subscription television.
License Fee: _____
Exhibition Territory: World
License Term: _____
Option Term: To be exercised within twenty-four (24) months from date of first broadcast and exhibition.

AGREED AND ACCEPTED:

_____   _____
(PRODUCER)   (LICENSOR)

_____   _____
ADDRESS   ADDRESS

_____
LICENSE DATE

MOVIE MASTER USE RECORDING LICENSE

1. The sound recording ("Master") of the musical composition covered by this license: _____ performed by _____

2. The motion picture ("Motion Picture") covered by this license is tentatively entitled: " _____ "

3. The "territory" covered hereby is: _____

4. The type and number of uses of the Master to be recorded are:

_____

5. IN CONSIDERATION of the sum of _____ Dollars ($_____) receipt of which is hereby acknowledged, _____ (hereinafter referred to as "Licensor") hereby grants to _____ (hereinafter referred to as "Producer"), its successors and assigns the following rights:

    (a) the nonexclusive, limited right, license, privilege, and authority to record in any manner, medium, form or language, in each country of the territory the aforesaid type and use of the composition in synchronism or in timed-relation with the motion picture, but not otherwise, and to make copies of such recordings in the form of negatives and prints necessary for theatrical exhibition or broadcast on television as hereinafter provided for, and to import said recordings and/or copies thereof into any country throughout the territory all in accordance with the terms, conditions and limitations hereinafter set forth;

    (b) the nonexclusive, limited right and license to publicly perform for profit or nonprofit and authorize others so to perform the composition in the exhibition of the motion picture to audiences in motion picture theaters and other places of public entertainment where motion pictures are customarily exhibited throughout the world including the right to televise the motion picture into such theaters and other such public places;

    (c) the nonexclusive, limited right and license to publicly perform and authorize others so to perform in all form and media of distribution and exhibition of the Production for so-called Nonbroadcast (Nontheatrical) exhibition (including, without limitation, educational, institutional organizations, in-flight or in-transit distribution, corporate locations and U.S. military bases).

6. Licensee also grants to Producer the nonexclusive, limited right to reproduce the recording, as recorded in the motion picture in audiovisual devices, whether now known or hereafter devised, including, but not limited to, videocassettes and videodiscs, manufactured primarily for distribution for the purpose of "home use" ("Videograms") and to distribute them by sale or otherwise in each and every country of the territory for any and all purposes now or hereafter known, without Producer having to make any additional payments therefor.

7. The recording and performing rights hereinabove granted include such rights for air, screen, television and audiovisual trailers, promotions and advertisements for the promotion or exploitation of the motion picture in all media now known or hereafter devised.

8. The recording and performing rights hereinabove granted shall endure for the worldwide period of all copyrights in and to the composition and any and all renewals or extensions thereof without Producer having to pay any additional consideration therefor.

9. Licensee represents and warrants that it owns or controls the Master licensed hereunder and that it has the legal right to grant this license and that Producer shall not be required to pay any additional monies, except as provided in his license, with respect to the rights granted herein. Licensee shall indemnify, defend and hold harmless Producer, its successors, assigns and licenses from and against any and all loss, damages, liabilities, actions, suits or other claims arising out of any breach, in whole or in part, of the foregoing representations and warranties, and for reasonable attorneys' fees and costs incurred in connection therewith; provided, however, that such Licensee's total liability shall not exceed the consideration paid hereunder.

10. Licensee reserves all rights not expressly granted to Producer hereunder. All rights granted hereunder are granted on a nonexclusive basis.

11. This license is binding upon and shall inure to the benefit of the respective successors and/or assigns of the parties hereto.

12. This license shall be governed by and subject to the laws of the State of California applicable to agreements made and to be wholly performed within such State.

13. In the event of any breach of an provision of this agreement by Producer, Licensee's sole remedy will be an action at law for damages, if any, and in no event will Licensee be entitled to or seek to enjoin restrain, interfere with or inhibit the distribution, exhibition or exploitation of the motion picture. In no event shall Producer have less rights hereunder than a member of the public would have in the absence of this agreement.

14. No failure by Producer to perform any of its obligations hereunder shall constitute a breach hereof, unless Licensee gives Producer written notice of such nonperformance and Producer fails to cure such alleged nonperformance within sixty (60) days of its receipt of such notice.

15. All notices hereunder required to be given to the parties hereto and all payments to be made hereunder shall be sent to the parties at their addresses mentioned herein or to such other addresses as each party respectively may hereafter designate by notice in writing to the other.

IN WITNESS WHEREOF, the parties have caused the foregoing to be executed as of _____ on _____.

_____   _____
(LICENSOR)   (PRODUCER)

_____   _____
ADDRESS: ADDRESS:

MOVIE SYNCHRONIZATION AND PERFORMING RIGHTS LICENSE

1. The musical composition (hereafter referred to as "composition") covered by this license is: "_____"

2. The motion picture covered by this license is: "_____"

3. The type, maximum duration and number of uses of the composition to be recorded are: _____

4. Administrative share: _____

5. The territory covered hereby is:

_____

6. IN CONSIDERATION of the sum of _____ Dollars ($_____) receipt of which is hereby acknowledged, _____ ("Publisher") hereby grants to _____ ("Producer"), its successors and assigns the following rights:

    (a) the nonexclusive, limited right, license, privilege, and authority to record in any manner, medium, form or language, in each country of the territory the aforesaid type and use of the composition in synchronism or in timed-relation with the motion picture, but not otherwise, and to make copies of such recordings in the form of negatives and prints necessary for theatrical exhibition or broadcast on television as hereinafter provided for, and to import said recordings and/or copies thereof into any country throughout the territory all in accordance with the terms, conditions and limitations hereinafter set forth;

    (b) the nonexclusive, limited right and license to publicly perform for profit or nonprofit and authorize others so to perform the composition in the exhibition of the motion picture to audiences in motion picture theaters and other places of public entertainment where motion pictures are customarily exhibited throughout the world including the right to televise the motion picture into such theaters and other such public places;

    (c) the nonexclusive, limited right and license to publicly perform and authorize others so to perform in all form and media of distribution and exhibition of the Production for so-called Nonbroadcast (Nontheatrical) exhibition (including, without limitation, educational, institutional organizations, in-flight or in-transit distribution, corporate locations and U.S. military bases).

7. The exhibition of the motion picture in the United States by means of television (other than as described in subparagraph 6(b) herein above) including by means of "pay television," "subscription television," "CATV" and "closed circuit" into homes television, is subject to the following:

    (a) The motion picture may be exhibited by means of television by network, nonnetwork, local or syndicated broadcasts, "pay television," "subscription television," and "closed circuit" provided that such television stations have valid performance licenses therefor from the American Society of Composers, Authors and Publishers (ASCAP) or Broadcast Music, Inc. (BMI), from Publisher, or from a person, firm or corporation having the legal right to issue such license.

(b) It is agreed that public performance of the motion picture in such portion of the territory as is outside of the United States, will be in accordance with their customary practices and the payment of their customary fees.

8. Publisher also grants to Producer the nonexclusive, limited right to reproduce the composition, as recorded in the motion picture in audiovisual devices, whether now known or hereafter devised, including, but not limited to, videocassettes and videodiscs, manufactured primarily for distribution for the purpose of "home use" ("Videograms") and to distribute them by sale or otherwise in each and every country of the territory for any and all purposes now or hereafter known, without Producer having to make any additional payments therefor.

9. This license does not authorize or permit any use of the composition not expressly set forth herein and does not include the right to alter the fundamental character of the music of the composition, to use the title or subtitle of the composition as the title of any motion picture, to use the story of the composition, or to make any other use of the composition not expressly authorized hereunder.

10. The recording and performing rights hereinabove granted include such rights for air, screen, television and audiovisual trailers, promotions and advertisements for the promotion or exploitation of the motion picture in all media now known or hereafter devised.

11. The recording and performing rights hereinabove granted shall endure for the worldwide period of all copyrights in and to the composition and any and all renewals or extension thereof without Producer having to pay any additional consideration therefor.

12. Publisher represents and warrants that it owns or controls the aforesaid extent of interest of the composition licensed in the aforesaid Territory hereunder and that it has the legal right to grant this license and that Producer shall not be required to pay any additional monies, except as provided in this license, with respect to the rights granted herein. Publisher shall indemnify, defend and hold harmless Producer, its successors, assigns and licenses from and against any and all loss, damages, liabilities, actions, suits or other claims arising out of any breach, in whole or in part, of the foregoing representations and warranties, and for reasonable attorneys' fees and costs incurred in connection therewith; provided, however, that such Publisher's total liability shall not exceed the consideration paid hereunder.

13. Publisher reserves all rights not expressly granted to Producer hereunder. All rights granted hereunder are granted on a nonexclusive basis.

14. This license is binding upon and shall inure to the benefit of the respective successors and/or assigns of the parties hereto.

15. This license shall be governed by and subject to the laws of the State of California applicable to agreements made and to be wholly performed with such State.

16. In the event of any breach of any provision of this agreement by Producer, Publisher's sole remedy will be an action at law for damages, if any, and in no event will Publisher be entitled to or seek to enjoin restrain, interfere with or inhibit the distribution, exhibition or exploitation of the motion picture. In no event shall Producer have less rights hereunder than a member of the public would have in the absence of this agreement.

17. No failure by Producer to perform of any of its obligations hereunder shall constitute a breach hereof, unless Publisher gives Producer written notice of such nonperformance and Producer fails to cure such alleged nonperformance within sixty (60) days of its receipt of such notice.

18. All notices hereunder required to be given to the parties hereto and all payments to be made hereunder shall be sent to the parties at their addresses mentioned herein or to such other addresses as each party respectively may hereafter designate by notice in writing to the other.

IN WITNESS WHEREOF, the parties have caused the foregoing to be executed as of _____ on _____.

ON BEHALF OF _____

_____   _____
(PUBLISHER)   (PRODUCER)

_____   _____
ADDRESS: ADDRESS:

TELEVISION MASTER RECORDING LICENSE

In consideration of the below listed License Fee, receipt of which is hereby acknowledged, Licensor grants to Producer the nonexclusive and irrevocable right, license, privilege and authority to record, rerecord, perform, dub, edit and synchronize the Recording listed below into and with the soundtrack of the Production for distribution, exhibition and exploitation in the License Media and for the advertising and promotion thereof, subject to the terms and conditions listed below.

Production: _____

Producer: _____

Recording: _____

Artist: _____

Record Label: _____

Use: _____

Timing: _____

License Fee: _____

License Territory: _____

License Term: _____

Commencing: _____

License Media: _____

TERMS AND CONDITIONS:

1. RESERVATION OF RIGHTS

Upon the expiration of this license, all rights herein granted shall cease and terminate and the right to make or authorize any further use or distribution of the Recording shall also cease and terminate. Nothing contained herein shall obligate Producer to actually use the Recording in or in connection with the soundtrack of the Production. Licensor reserves exclusively to itself, its successors, licensees and assigns, all rights and uses in and to the Recording, except the limited uses expressly licensed hereunder. By way of illustration, and not in limitation thereof, the following rights are specifically reserved by Licensor for its own use and may not be exercised by Producer, unless otherwise provided for herein:

(a) All rights of reproduction or use of the Recording on phonograph records, tapes and other types of sound only reproduction, in all media, whether now or hereafter known or in existence. Without limiting the generality of the foregoing, Producer shall not have the right to include or authorize the use of the Recording, or any portion thereof, in any phonograph record of the soundtrack of the Program.

(b) The right to use the Recording in other motion pictures or television programs including uses similar to that authorized hereunder.

(c) The right to edit, alter, or otherwise modify the Recording in any way except with respect to duration.

(d) The right to reproduce the Recording by means of video Records (including, but not limited to, videocassettes, videotapes, and any other audiovisual devices intended primarily for "home use"), unless specifically provided for herein.

(e) The right to advertise, sticker and/or otherwise market and/or identify Records embodying the Recording as being contained in the Program.

2. CLEARANCE

Producer shall be responsible for obtaining appropriate synchronization licenses from the copyright proprietor(s) of the musical composition(s) embodied in the Recording and shall obtain all requisite consents and permissions, if any, including, without limitation, those of labor organizations, and agrees that it will pay all required reuse payments, fees and royalties, if any, required to be paid for such consents and permissions, under applicable collective bargaining agreements, or otherwise, in connection with Producer's use of the Recording. Licensor shall be responsible for the payment to all parties whose performances are embodied in the Recording including, but not limited to, the artist(s) and producer(s), under its various contractual agreements with such parties, out of License Fees paid hereunder, and shall hold Producer harmless from any claims therefor.

3. DUPLICATION FEES

Producer shall promptly pay, upon Licensor's request therefor, Licensor's actual duplication costs for master tape copies of the Recording, if any, furnished to Producer by Licensor.

4. CUE SHEET

Producer shall promptly provide Licensor with a complete and accurate music cue sheet for the Program, receipt of which is hereby acknowledged.

5. NAME AND LIKENESS

Producer shall have the right to use Artist's name and approved likeness and biography in connection with the exploitation and promotion of the Production. Upon request, Licensor will provide Producer with a reasonable number of approved photographs and an approved biography.

6. REPRESENTATIONS, WARRANTIES AND INDEMNIFICATION OF LICENSOR

Licensor warrants only that it has the full right, power and authority to grant the license specified herein. Licensor shall indemnify and hold Producer harmless from any and all claims, liabilities, losses, damages or expenses (including, but not limited to, reasonable attorneys' fees and legal expenses) actually incurred by Producer by reason of Licensor's breach of said warranty, but Licensor's aggregate liability to Producer shall be limited to the amount of the consideration actually paid by Producer to Licensor hereunder.

7. REPRESENTATIONS, WARRANTIES AND INDEMNIFICATION OF PRODUCER

Producer warrants that it has the full right, power and authority to enter into this agreement and to fully perform its obligations hereunder. Producer shall indemnify and hold Licensor harmless from any and all claims, liabilities, losses, damages and expenses (including, but not limited to, reasonable attorneys' fees and legal expenses) arising out of any breach of Producer's warranties, representations or covenants under this agreement, or in any way resulting from or connected with Producer's use of the Recording in a manner not authorized hereunder.

8. NOTICES

All notices hereunder required to be given to Producer (including notification of a change in ownership or administrative control) shall be sent to Producer at the address included herein. All notices, payments and/or royalties hereunder required to be made to Licensor shall be sent to Licensor at the address included herein or to such other address as Licensor may hereafter designate by notice in writing to Producer.

9. ASSIGNMENT

This license shall run to Producer, its successors and assigns, provided that Producer remain liable for the performance of all the terms and conditions of this license on its part to be performed and provided further, that any disposition of the Program shall be subject to all the terms hereof.

10. OPTIONS

Producer may exercise the option(s) listed in this agreement, if any, for the stated License Media, Territory, Term and Fee, by providing written notice to Licensor within the Option Period accompanied by payment of the specified fee.

AGREED AND ACCEPTED:

_____   _____
(PRODUCER)   (LICENSOR)

_____   _____
ADDRESS: ADDRESS:

_____
LICENSE DATE

TELEVISION SYNCHRONIZATION LICENSE

In consideration of the below listed License Fee, receipt of which is hereby acknowledged, Licensor grants to Producer the nonexclusive and irrevocable right, license, privilege and authority to record, reproduce or fix the Composition listed below in synchronization or timed-relation with the Production for distribution in the License Media, and for the advertising and promotion thereof, subject to the terms and conditions listed below.

Production: _____

Producer: _____

Composition: _____

Composer(s): _____

Publisher(s): _____

Administrative Share: _____

Use: _____

Timing: _____

License Fee: _____

Exhibition Territory: _____

License Term: _____

Commencing: Upon execution of this license or first airdate, whichever is earlier

License Media: Free television distribution and exhibition.

TERMS AND CONDITIONS:

1. EXPIRATION OF RIGHTS

Upon the expiration of this license, all rights herein granted shall cease and terminate and the right to make or authorize any further use or distribution of any recordings made hereunder shall also cease and terminate.

2. PERFORMANCE RIGHTS

Performance of the Composition in the exhibition of the Production is subject to the condition that each television station or other entity over which the Composition is so performed shall have a performance license issued by Licensor or from a person, firm, corporation, society, association or other entity having the legal right to issue such a performance license and it is understood that the public performance of the Production outside the United States is and shall be subject to clearance by performing rights societies in accordance with their customary practices and the payment of their customary fees.

3. RIGHTS NOT INCLUDED

This license does not include the right to alter the fundamental character of the Composition, to use the title or subtitle of the Composition as the title of the Production, to use the story of the Composition, or to make any other use of the Composition not expressly authorized hereunder. Notwithstanding the foregoing, Producer may make arrangements, orchestrations and adaptations of the Composition for its recording purposes hereunder.

> (a) The Production shall be for use solely as authorized hereunder, and may not be televised into theaters or other places where admission is charged. No sound records produced pursuant to this license are to be manufactured, sold and/or used separately or independently of the Production.

(b) Use of the Composition on videocassettes, videodiscs and/or any new technological methods of reproduction that are introduced into the entertainment industry for the purpose of sale and/or rental to the public for home use is specifically excluded from this license unless otherwise provided for herein.

4. WARRANTIES

Licensor warrants only that it has the legal right to grant this license and that this license is given and accepted without other warranty or recourse. If said warranty shall be breached in whole or in part, Licensor shall either repay to Producer the consideration paid hereunder or hold Producer harmless to the extent of the consideration paid for this license.

5. NOTICES

All notices hereunder required to be given to Producer (including notification of a change in ownership or administrative control) shall be sent to Producer at the address included herein. All notices, payments and/or royalties hereunder required to be made to Licensor shall be sent to Licensor at its current address or to such other address as Licensor may hereafter designate by notice in writing to Producer.

6. ASSIGNMENT

This license shall run to Producer, its successors and assigns, provided that Producer remain liable for the performance of all the terms and conditions of this license on its part to be performed and provided further, that any disposition of the Production shall be subject to all the terms herein.

7. EXERCISE OF OPTIONS

Producer may exercise the option(s) listed in this agreement, if any, for the stated License Media, Territory, Term and Fee, by providing written notice to Licensor within the Option Period accompanied by payment of the specified fee.

ADDITIONAL TERMS AND CONDITIONS:

1. If, during the term hereof, you pay to the copublisher a fee in excess of the fee set out herein for the synchronization of the Composition in the Production, you shall pay to Licensor a corresponding amount equal to the difference between the fee set out herein and the fee paid to said copublisher, on a pro rata basis.

2. OPTIONS FOR ADDITIONAL RIGHTS

License Media: All forms of television distribution and exhibition including, without limitation, free, pay, cable and subscription television.
License Fee: (Negotiated on Most Favored Nations basis with copublishers of the composition.)
Exhibition Territory: _____
License Term: _____
Option Term: _____

License Media: Manufacture and distribution of videogram copies of the production for the purpose of sale and/or rental to the public primarily for home use.

License Fee: One-time, flat-fee buyout

Exhibition Territory: _____

License Term: _____

Option Term: _____

AGREED AND ACCEPTED:

_____   _____
(PRODUCER)   (LICENSOR)

_____   _____
ADDRESS: ADDRESS:

_____
LICENSE DATE

POP MUSIC FOR SOUNDTRACKS

by Mark Halloran and Thomas A. White

In recent years, successful pop/rock songwriters and recording artists have moved, seemingly en masse, into motion picture soundtrack songwriting and performing. Some pop writers/performers such as Prince, Sting, Madonna and Mick Jagger have had star acting careers. However, these are exceptions. Typically, songwriters and recording artists are hired by film studios during or after the film is shot to write and record individual musical compositions specifically for the film. The songs are then synchronized with the picture and may be used in promotional trailers and television spots, included in a soundtrack album, and be released as singles and MTV promotional videos. This chapter examines relevant issues when nonacting writers/performers are commissioned to create new film music (such as Elton John for *The Lion King*). The primary focus is on practices at major Hollywood studios, although we also compare practices at the nonmajors as well. (When we say "major Hollywood studios" we mean 20th Century Fox, Warner Brothers, MCA/Universal, Columbia Pictures Entertainment [Columbia and Tri-Star], Paramount, and Disney.) You should be aware that much of the music used in films is preexisting. The songs are typically licensed from record companies for a fee. That fee is split with the recording artists. The licensing of music for film is discussed in more detail in the chapter "Music Licensing for Television and Film: A Perspective for Songwriters." The chapter does not cover composers that write orchestral scores or concert films. (MTV has seemingly killed concert films. Rock concert films have joined the ranks of documentaries, with very limited audience appeal.)

CURRENT PRACTICE IN WRITING AND RECORDING SOUNDTRACK MUSIC

Let's assume you are asked by a studio to write and record an original song for a motion picture. There are many fundamental business and legal concerns. How much money will you be paid initially? How will your music publisher and record label be involved in the deal? What controls concerning the use of the song and the recording will you have? How much money can you expect later from the exploitation of the song and the recording? First, let's look at the studio's viewpoint to better understand its motives.

The Creative Choices

The choice of songs and performing artists is usually made by the filmmaking team—the studio, the producer and the director—collectively trying to reach a creative and business consensus. Most major studios have music departments that are headed by creative music executives who, combined with the filmmaking team, represent the studio's music interests and are available to its producers for consultation referrals and other general music services. Absent a creative consensus, the amount of clout the individual members of the filmmaking team wield determines the choice of songs and performers. When dealing with high-powered, experienced, successful film producers and directors, the studio will often defer to their creative choice, but will still insist on consultation or approval of both the musical talent and their deal. Some directors have so-called final cut of the film, which may or may not include final determination of the musical talent and product in the film.

In some instances another team member is hired, the music supervisor, who reports to the director and producer and represents their interests. Music supervisors have gained prominence as filmmakers have recognized the affect successful records have in stimulating box office sales and have seen the necessity for a bridge between filmmakers, the music community, the studios, and the soundtrack record labels. Soundtrack singles are routinely released in advance of a picture so that its opening coincides with demand created by the record label's marketing efforts and the studio's film advertising, which, ideally, are coordinated to maximize public awareness of the film and its music. Music supervisors have varying degrees of involvement in the music that is commissioned or selected for films. The extent of their job is defined by how the filmmakers perceive their own abilities as music experts. Music supervisors are almost never delegated decision-making authority, but instead gather and present choices to the filmmakers.

Some supervisors offer only creative services (e.g., suggesting possible songs and artists or record producing). Others provide primarily business or sales services (e.g., publishing administration, music clearance, soundtrack placement, music production coordination). Business affairs (i.e., deal making) services are usually handled by the studio's music business affairs department or the filmmaker's music counsel. Although film music is a diverse and specialized field, virtually anyone who has ever worked in the music business may offer their services as a music supervisor. Consequently, competence varies greatly. Because the market has an excess of prospective music supervisors, most practitioners are not engaged in such services on an exclusive, full-time basis.

The main concern of the filmmaking team is whether the choice of a song and artist will enhance the dramatic and commercial impact of their picture. They in effect cast the songwriters and performers as they would theatrical talent by subjectively evaluating whether the writer or act's musical contribution will enhance the look, feel, and profit of their picture.

Budgets

In commissioning soundtrack songs, the established trend is for major studios to stick with top pop writers whose songs have sold millions of records and have had successful chart histories. The independent motion picture companies, however, have less financing available than do the majors and are prone to use less recognized writers and artists that have not had hit records. Accordingly, they pay less money.

Exhibit 1 compares the amount of money that is typically spent by the recognized independents, ministudios and major studios. The bottom line is that nonmajors pay less up-front money than the major studios. Major studios are frequently tied in with labels that own national branch distribution systems and they invest far greater sums than nonmajors in promoting their films and music. Back-end revenue potential is therefore usually higher at major studios.

Even studios that defer to the creative choices of filmmakers must approve the writer/performer deal because of the large studio investment. The studio intends to protect its multimillion-dollar investment, of which music is an important, but relatively minor, part. Average production budgets of major studios are around $28 million; exploitation budgets (principally ads) often approach $13 to $17 million. Although music budgets vary widely, they are usually 2% to 5% of the film budget.

Probably the most pervasive myth regarding songs that are written for soundtracks is that in some cases the studio makes more money from the music than from distribution of the film. Although it has been true in certain cases that an unsuccessful film has spawned a successful album, the authors are unaware of any case in which a film generated less money to a studio than did the film music. In contrast to this myth, there are some basic truths. One is that ultimately studios view film music, except in the rarest cases (perhaps *Flashdance*), as a less than integral part of the film and more of a promotional tool and ancillary market for the film. If a teenager has $6 to spend for entertainment and has a choice between seeing a film or buying the soundtrack album, the studio would much rather the money be spent on a theater ticket. The studio can expect to receive approximately half of the $6 spent at the theater, but is lucky if it nets 30 to 50 cents from the sale of each album.

The studio protects its investment by insisting that broad exploitation rights be obtained in the song and the recording. A studio's incentives for acquiring all rights to songs and recordings include (1) complete freedom of use and exploitation (including royalty-free use in other studio productions) without consultation, approval or further payment; (2) optimum duration of copyright ownership; (3) avoidance of third-party claims and controls; (4) actual profit from music revenues; (5) increased cash flow; and (6) the building of a publishing catalog as a perennial, liquid, and salable asset.

Limiting the Studio's Investment: Spec Writing Deals

Studios and filmmakers like to have the opportunity to choose songs that are not specifically commissioned and that require no guaranteed up-front payment. There is quite a lot of speculative songwriting for film soundtracks. By speculative we mean songs that are written or reworked for the film and submitted for consideration without the studio being committed to use or pay for the song. If the studio likes the song, a deal is negotiated. Some songwriters will not write spec songs since their time is valuable and they consider it an insult to their artistic integrity to be asked to write a song without a financial commitment. On the other hand, many songwriters are happy to have their song considered in this manner.

A variation of spec writing is the so-called songwriter's step or option deal. This means there will be an intermediate step after the song is written but before it is used in the film when the studio can decline to proceed further by not making further payment for the song. For example, in a step deal the studio may pay the songwriter $5,000 for a song to be written and demoed. If the studio approves the song and synchronizes it in the movie, the writer receives another $20,000.

Probably the most contentious point on step deals is whether or not the writer gets back rights to rejected songs, and under what conditions. Although the usual outcome is that the songwriter keeps the rights, studios may take the position that they will return the song provided it is subject to a lien for recovery of the amount the studio has invested. In the example above, if the studio were to reject the song and the song reverted to the songwriter, and it was subsequently exploited, the studio would receive the first $5,000. A variation of this is that the studio may retain a continuing financial participation in the publisher's share of music income, irrespective of recoupment of its investment. Alternatively, the writer may buy back the rights by reimbursing the studio for its out-of-pocket costs.

STUDIO/RECORD LABEL DEAL

The studio makes the basic arrangement for the production and distribution of the soundtrack with the label. Assuming a pop soundtrack rather than an orchestral one, the following delineates the basic issues.

Advances

Advances typically reflect record companies' perceptions of anticipated sales in the domestic territory, and can range from a nominal amount to, in extraordinary cases, $1 million. What makes the negotiations difficult is that soundtrack albums are usually one-shots, and the label cannot recover losses from subsequent product. Another difficulty is that typically, the final music choices have not yet been made. A graduated scale is created to remedy this, e.g., $150,000 with an additional $50,000 per platinum-certified artist and $25,000 per gold-certified artist, with a cap of $300,000.

Royalty Rate

Royalty rate negotiation is very similar to that for a normal recording artist. The range for a basic royalty is 10% to 19%. The studio hopes to maintain a minimum royalty override in the 4% to 6% range; thus, in a 16% of retail deal, 10% to 12% of royalty would be available to third parties.

Product

The record company is going to want to know what they are buying. Also, the record company would prefer a pop soundtrack with a potential single rather than an orchestral soundtrack, although in many cases the two are combined.

Promotion Fund

Oftentimes the record company will look to the studio to put up a matching fund for promotion under the theory that both the studio and the record company will profit.

Singles

The releasing label will always want singles rights. The singles are used as promotional tools to sell the LPs, which is where the real money is. If singles rights are not available, the record company will probably cut its advance.

Guaranteed Release

Studios will often insist that as long as the necessary materials are delivered on time, the record company will be required to release the LP no later than the theatrical release of the film, with singles preceding it by six weeks.

Ownership

The studio will continue to own the underlying musical compositions and the sound recording embodied in the film. The record company will want to assert ownership over the sound recording as embodied in records. The record company will want worldwide rights. Split territory deals with major labels are almost nonexistent.

ARTIST VIEWPOINT: PREEXISTING AGREEMENTS

The following are major concerns when you are approached by a studio to write and perform a soundtrack song. The threshold issue is whether you can grant the rights in the song and the recording that the studio requires.

Preexisting Term Songwriter's Agreement

If you are signed to a term songwriting deal, the publisher has the exclusive right to your songwriting services during the term and owns and administers the songs you compose or cowrite during the term, subject to paying the usually inviolate writer's share of music income. However, studios have music publishing holdings too. In these agreements, administration means the management of the copyright for purposes of collection and distribution of income. Like other music publishers, studios often insist on copyright ownership and administration of the song, and they normally retain all or part of the publisher's share of music income. Usually any conflict of rights between the songwriter's publisher and the studio is settled during initial discussions. In some cases, the studio's publishing arm and the songwriter's publisher will split the publisher's share of music income between the writer's publisher, the film production company, and the studio.

In order to avoid potential publisher/studio conflict and to freely shop their songs for soundtracks, a very few established writers have negotiated a fixed number of songs per year which are excluded from their exclusive term songwriting deal. If you are not signed to a term songwriting deal, have negotiated an exclusion, or have already reached the maximum number of songs required under the term songwriting deal, you are free to work out whatever arrangements you desire with the studio.

If you do not have a lot of clout, the studio will end up owning and administering the song, and you will be entitled to approximately 50% of the income generated from the song as the writer's share, plus whatever nonrecoupable creative fee is negotiated. (Note the studio will grant itself a free synchronization license in connection with the use of the song in the film and in-home video devices, so you will receive no further synchronization income from these sources.) Studios typically insist on free synchronization licenses for product based on the initial film, such as remakes, sequels, and television programs that they produce or distribute, and even for totally unrelated properties that they produce or distribute. However, the writer retains the writer's share of public performance rights.

Preexisting Recording Agreement

If you are signed to a term or multiple album recording contract, the label typically has the right to your exclusive recording services during the term for master recordings and phonograph records. Recording contracts usually define phonograph records as including "sight and sound devices," so unless you are the rare superstar artist who has a soundtrack exclusion (i.e., a provision excluding soundtrack recordings from the record deal) the label must grant a waiver of its services exclusivity for theatrical synchronization, home video, and phonograph records.

Record companies are understandably jealous of the services of their artists. Major record companies can invest $1 million or more to break in a new recording act. It is estimated that minimum sales of 300,000 LP units, or the equivalent in the current configuration mix of CDs and cassettes, are necessary for a major label to break even on a typical artist investment. Such costs include advances and royalties to artist, producer, and production companies; recording costs; manufacturing and distribution; marketing, including record promotion and advertising; mechanical licenses; video clip production; general overhead; legal expenses; salaries; taxes; product returns; and etc.

In order to receive a return on their investments, some record companies will insist on an "override" royalty (a royalty in addition to or to be deducted from the recording artist's royalty) from the studio as a condition to granting permission for the artist's soundtrack services. For example, if your deal with the studio is a basic album royalty of 10% of retail prorated, and you have two of ten cuts on a soundtrack album, the label may ask for a 1% override on your 2% of retail royalty. Your royalty will be about 18 cents per LP, and the label's royalty will be about 9 cents per LP.

Most studios, however, insist that the artist and the label work out the royalty arrangement between themselves. Some labels may require a 75% (artist)/25% (label) split of the prorated royalty for the sales of soundtrack records. The label retains its share and either credits the artist's royalty account or pays the 75% directly to the artist. For an illustration, see Exhibit 2. Also, just as major studios are music publishers, some major studios have record company divisions. MCA/Universal (MCA Records) and Time Warner (Warner Bros. Records) are the two leading examples.

In some cases, major labels insist that the entire royalty (and even part or all of the artist's up-front cash creative fee) be paid directly to them for their services exclusivity waiver, especially if the artist's royalty account is unrecouped. However, the artist more typically keeps the creative fee from the studio, which is deemed a fee for motion picture services rather than a recording advance.

RECORDING ARTIST AND STUDIO ISSUES

Assuming the artist and label make their arrangement, the next step is to sort out the soundtrack recording issues between the record company and its artist and the studio. These issues follow.

Marketing Fund

A guaranteed marketing fund to be spent by the studio (and perhaps a matching amount by the label) to promote the soundtrack album and/or singles, the aggregate of which can be $100,000 to $500,000 if on a fifty (studio)/fifty (label) matching basis.

Video Ownership

Regardless of the investment issue, both studios and labels compete for music video ownership. The studio wants to control the exploitation of the video, especially in conjunction with marketing the film, although promotion of the video is often a joint effort by the label and studio. Because of uncertainty about the impact of commercial exploitation under union agreements, studios rarely give record companies rights, other than for promotional use, if the video contains film clips and they try to limit the promotional use to the period when the film is in active distribution.

Singles Rights

The principal issue centers around prohibition of release of the recording as a single by any label other than the artist's label. Since the label distributing the soundtrack LP wants to use singles as a selling tool for the LP, retention of singles rights by the artist's nondistributing label can diminish the attractiveness of the LP to the distributing label. Additionally, the studio is anxious to use the single to promote the theatrical release of the film. One recent example of a master that the soundtrack distributing label did not have singles rights to was "I Want Your Sex" by George Michael, for *Beverly Hills Cop II*. CBS, not MCA Records (the soundtrack LP label), distributed the single. In rare cases, no singles rights are granted, as for the song "Say You, Say Me" by Lionel Richie on the *White Knights* soundtrack. This noncompetition restriction allows the artist and the label to reap full benefit by ensuring that a potential single used in a film is included on and stimulates the sale of the artist's own album, rather than a soundtrack album containing other artist's recordings which yields a prorated royalty to each.

Home Video Royalty

Home video device royalty overrides to the label by the studio are rarely, if ever, granted. Studios with unaffiliated home video distribution now typically receive 20% of the wholesale price as a royalty for cassettes. For an $89.95 cassette, the average wholesale price is about $50, so the studio receives $10 per cassette from the distributor, from which it must pay its costs and royalties. If, for example, the artist's label wanted a 10% home video override, the studio would have to pay approximately $5 per cassette to the label, i.e., 10% of $50.

THE ARTIST/STUDIO DEAL: MAJOR POINTS

The following is a list of the major deal issues which will be discussed between artist's counsel and the studio that commissions a song and record. Exhibit 1 provides a comparison on typical deals for major studios, mini-studios, and recognized independents.

Cash Creative Fee

Compensation for writing and recording can be structured either as a cash creative fee, not including recording costs, or an all-inclusive recording fund that includes writing, performing, producing, and recording costs. Writing fees per song range from a nominal amount for an unknown to $30,000 for a superstar's work. Recording fees are in the range of $10,000 per track for major performers.

If the deal is structured as a recording fund, the studio will pay a flat sum for delivery of the song and master, with the artist being responsible for all recording costs, keeping the balance as, in effect, the creative fee. The all-in fee per song for a top writer/performer ranges from $50,000 to $75,000, and for a midlevel writer/performer from $20,000 to $35,000. New acts may receive $7,500 to $15,000. The all-in structure is an inducement for the artist to limit recording costs, and also caps the studio's investment. However, the studio has no contractual assurance the money is being allocated judiciously. Problems sometimes arise when the studio is dissatisfied with the song or recording and asks the artist to rework it. Recording fund deals are particularly attractive to acts that own recording studios and/or computer-based music technology.

Song Royalties

The writer's share of royalties for songwriting services is negotiated the same as with a nonfilm song agreement, i.e., the writer basically receives 50% of the income, except for sheet music, which is typically about 8 to 12 cents per piano copy and 10% to 12-1/2% of wholesale for nonpiano copies. The writer may seek to guarantee a full statutory mechanical rate for the soundtrack LP or single (currently 6.6 cents per song or 1.25 cents per minute of playing time, whichever is greater). Most studios resist guaranteeing a full mechanical rate since the label will seek to limit the mechanical rate for LPs to 10 times 3/4 statutory (now 49.5 cents per LP, 4.95 cents per song) and for singles to 3/4 statutory for each side.

If you have a lot of clout or are signed exclusively to a publisher, you may be able to structure a copublishing agreement in which song ownership and administration may be shared, thus allowing the artist and/or the publisher to participate in a percentage of the publisher's share of music income. Independent motion picture companies—such as Crown International, Samuel Goldwyn Company and Trimark—which typically pay less up-front money and do not have affiliated music publishing arms are more likely than major studios to agree to grant a participation in the publisher's share. Assuming a fifty-fifty participation arrangement, the artist will receive approximately 75% of the total music income (the full writer's share and half of the publisher's share).

The split of copyright known as copublishing is considerably less common than financial participation in the publisher's share of income. In participation deals, the participant has little or no control over the use or exploitation of the copyright. Major writers/performers receive a participation in the publisher's share of income that ranges up to 50%.

Also, the publisher's share of income that is subject to participation is reducible if the studio or its music publishing arm charges an administration fee on income, if collected. For example, if there is a 15% administration fee, the publisher's net share would be reduced to about 42.5% of the total income derived from the song.

In extraordinary cases, superstars that both write and perform have been able to keep both copyright ownership (and administration) and all the publisher's share of music publishing income, subject always to a free synchronization license to the studio for use of the song in the film and home video devices.

Major writers/artists are much more likely to share in publishing revenue than writers that do not perform their own material, since successful artists are perceived to add great promotional value to the song and the film. However, to the extent the artist participates in the publisher's share of income, the up-front cash fee may decline correspondingly, because the studio is forgoing all or a portion of the publisher's share of income from which they hope to recover their investment and make some profit. However, for superstars, studios have a hard time reducing the cash creative fee, even if the publisher's share is relinquished or split.

Record Royalties

Record royalties, like music royalties, are negotiated much in the same manner as a normal recording agreement. However, there are a few points that are particularly important in soundtrack agreements.

Studios usually insist that the artist royalty be all-in, i.e., inclusive of all others that might be entitled to royalties with respect to the artist's recording, such as the record producer and the artist's label.

The royalty is usually subject to two forms of proration. First, it will be prorated for length, either by playing time or more typically by number of cuts. For example, if you have 2 out of the 10 cuts on the album, and receive a prorated 10% of retail royalty, your basic royalty will be .2 x 10%, or 2%. Second, the royalty is prorated by the number of artists on the cut. For example, if on the cuts the act performs together with a second recording act, the act's royalty will be cut in half (1/2 x .2 x 10% or 1%).

LP Override

Heavyweight artists ask for an album override, e.g., an additional 2% on the entire LP, regardless of proration. This may be fair when the soundtrack LP consists of filler that doesn't sell records or promote the film.

Royalty Allocation

Studios try to keep the aggregate artist royalties in check so they retain an appropriate net portion of the overall royalty from the soundtrack LP. For example, if the studio gets 16% of retail from the record company, they may allocate 10% to 12% to all royalty participants, retaining 4% to 6% for themselves. One way the studios try to contain royalties is to give the same royalty deal to every artist, e.g., 10% to 12% prorated.

Singles

The artists that anticipate release of their master as an A-side single may try to insulate themselves from royalty reduction for the B-side of the single to assure a full single record royalty. Singles royalties are not as heavily negotiated as LP royalties.

Recoupment

Smart artist representatives insist that the only recording costs the studio or label can recoup from the artist royalty account before royalties are paid are those paid solely in connection with the soundtrack LP, as opposed to the picture, since the studio pays recording costs whether or not there is a soundtrack LP. These nonpicture recording costs are called "soundtrack conversion costs" and usually include guild new use fees, and occasionally remixing. This point can have a major financial impact on the artist royalty. If not limited to nonpicture costs, the artist royalty account could be charged with film-related recording costs. For example, if the act's royalty is 10% of retail prorated on a cut, and they have one cut of 10, the royalty per LP sold would be .1 x 10%, or 1% of retail (about 7 cents/LP). If the label sells 100,000 LP units, the artist's royalty account would be credited with $7,000. To the extent the studio recoups soundtrack conversion costs, they are deducted from the royalty. Recoupment of recording creative fees from the artist's royalty account is negotiable. New acts often have their creative fee recouped from their royalties; established acts face this less often.

Song and Master Ownership

The studio's attitude is "we own what we pay for." The studio likely will insist on acquiring the song and master recording copyrights as works made for hire. As discussed above, superstars may occasionally succeed in sharing ownership and administration of the song and/or master recording. Artist ownership of master recordings may be allowed in rare cases when a superstar's recording services are furnished by their own production companies, e.g., Paul McCartney's MPL Communications, Ltd. or David Bowie's Main Man Productions, Inc.

Use of Master on Artist's Label

Some acts succeed in getting a license from the studio for use of the master recording on the acts' own records. The master might then be released both on the soundtrack album and on the artist's album. As a condition to granting the license, the studio may ask for an override royalty from the artist's label on records embodying the master. In any event, the studio will insist that any release of such master by the artist's label not compete with the studio's soundtrack records by conditioning the licensing grant on a holdback from release. This mostly applies from four to twelve months after release of the soundtrack album, so that the record-buying public associates the soundtrack song and master with the film and is motivated to buy the soundtrack LP. Studios are finding it more difficult, at least with major acts, to negotiate a holdback on the release of the master on the artist's home label.

Approval of Record Producer

Many established acts produce themselves or insist on using a record producer they approve. Studios rarely try to interfere with the artist's producer selection or the artist/producer creative relationship, especially if the deal is the typical recording fund deal, which makes the artist responsible for the producer's compensation. However, if the studio pays the producer's cash advance or royalty separately, they insist on approving the producer deal.

Credits

As long as the song is used in the film, most studios will agree to give an "end title" screen credit in the form of "[Song Title], written by [Artist], performed by [Artist]." Sometimes credit in the form of, "courtesy of [Label]" is accorded the artist's record company. Only rarely does an artist receive main title credit (where the writer, director, producer, and other major creative elements get credit). However, Huey Lewis and the News received main title credit in *Back to the Future* for their song "Power of Love." This may be desired by superstar artists.

Paid ad credits that promote the film, e.g., credits in newspapers, magazines, and the like, are usually not granted to writers/performers by major studios, except for main title songs such as to Lionel Richie for "Say You, Say Me" in *White Nights*, or when the prestige of the soundtrack artist is considered a significant marketing benefit. Independents tend to grant paid ad credits to writers/performers more frequently than major studios.

Record jacket credit is a different matter. Studios rarely refuse to give the recording act credit on the jackets of soundtrack LPs or CDs and on the jacket of singles since these are selling tools. Sometimes, if there are multiple recording artists, all the acts get credit in alphabetical order. In contrast to the normal competition among actors, directors, and producers for large and prominent credit, the act and label may try to keep the credit small so the soundtrack LP does not look like it is the act's own LP, which might compete with and thereby diminish sales of the act's own records. This makes sense because the act receives the entire royalty on their own LPs (subject to recoupment of recording costs by the label) and, if they write, they receive the mechanical royalties on the entire LP (always the writer's share and sometimes a portion of the publisher's share).

Additional Artist/Studio Deal Points

One issue to consider is that the studio will also insist on a provision whereby they are not obligated to use the song or the recording (whether in the film, soundtrack LP, or as a single), although they may have to pay whether or not they use the song. From the studio perspective, the filmmaking team must be allowed the freedom to add and subtract songs and recordings during the editing process. In some instances the artist will be paid whether or not their work is actually used.

Also, since music videos are an important selling tool, studios normally insist that the act provide music video services, usually at no additional cost or at minimum union scale. MTV prefers concept videos (such as Billy Ocean's *When the Tough Get Going* from *Jewel of the Nile*) to film-clip-only videos (such as Madonna's *Into the Groove* from *Desperately Seeking Susan*).

Finally, songwriters and soundtrack performers that do not perform onscreen are never granted a participation in the nonmusic receipts of a film. These participations are usually divided between the actors, director, producers and the studio. However, music artists have a distinct advantage as to the payment of royalties—they do not have to wait until the studio earns back its investment before songwriter royalties are paid. The same is true for artist royalties from the soundtrack LP. Usually only relatively minimal nonpicture soundtrack conversion costs are recouped before the artist is paid for record sales.

INCOME

Let's assume you make a deal at Paramount, you are a writer/performer/producer who writes a title song and records a title song master. You are paid $25,000 for the song and $25,000 to record. You retain the writer's share but Paramount retains the publisher's share. You receive a 12% retail U.S. record royalty, prorated, on LPs, and 9% on singles. Your master is three minutes long. The picture is a blockbuster; your single sells 1,000,000 copies in the United States, 750,000 foreign, and hits number one on *Billboard's* Hot 100 Pop Chart. The soundtrack LP, on which you have one of the 10 cuts, sells 500,000 copies in the United States and 375,000 copies overseas. Exhibit 3 gives you a rough idea of what your earnings might be.

CONCLUSION

The writing and recording of songs for films involves complex financial and business arrangements with studios, record labels, and music publishers. The advantages to both new and established songwriters and recording acts in participating in soundtracks are numerous. The song and its recording may be exposed to millions of people, it may be included in the soundtrack album, and, in the best case, be released as a single and MTV video. The down side is that the artist has very little, if any, input as to how the song is used in the film. You may write and record a beautiful four-minute ballad which is blared from a radio for only a few seconds, but that's the risk you take.

The most important advice to a new writer or recording act, however, is to not play prima donna if approached by a studio to work on a soundtrack. Only major acts have this luxury. Your goal should be to get the song considered and accepted. Non-established writers/performers should not expect the same sort of terms that Paul McCartney gets. Don't blow the deal. Once you get your foot in the door and make a positive contribution to a soundtrack, you may well have taken a substantial step in both your film and nonfilm writing and performing careers.

EXHIBIT I
Typical Music Acquisition Practices For Each Commissioned Song

	Major * Studios	Ministudios	Recognized Independents
Songwriter's fee	up to $25,000	up to $15,000	$500 to $5,000
Participation in publisher's share of income	zero to 50%	zero to 50%	zero to 100%
Writer/Artist recognition level	Major label (recently signed) to superstar	Unsigned to recognized label artists	Mostly unsigned
Artist's fee (off-camera)	Not less than $10,000	Zero to $15,000	$200 to $500 or scale
Recording budget	$15,000 to $50,000+	$5,000 to $10,000	$500 to $2,000
Copyright proprietor (occasionally writer)	Major studio	Ministudio	Independent
Artist's & producer's soundtrack royalty (subject to proration)	12% to 14% (foreign reduced to 1/2 or 3/4)	6% to 12% (foreign reduced to 1/2 or 3/4)	6% to 8% (if any, with foreign reduced to 1/2)
Copyright administrator	Major studio	Ministudio or its licensee	Outside publisher
Music producer's fee (if negotiated separately)	$4,000 to $10,000	Somewhat lower than major studios	None (usually artist or supervisor produced)

* *A major studio is defined as one with branch distribution systems; a ministudio is one without branch distribution systems; and an independent is one whose films are released through independent distributors.*

EXHIBIT 2
ARTIST'S ROYALTY STATEMENT

Sales for original soundtrack of "Century City Blues" cat. no. 14899

Statement Date:	September 30, 199_
Country of Sale:	United States
Period of Sales:	Second-Half 199_
Release Date:	April 5, 199_
Distributing Label:	Megabite Records, Inc.
Film Company	Behemoth Studios, Inc.

Prorata Per Unit

Configuration	Pkg. Deduct.	SRLP	Royalty	Share	Royalty	Sales	Earnings
Cassette single	20%	3.98	8%	2 on 2	.25472	5,000	$1274
CD singles	25%	4.98	8%	4 on 4	.29880	2,500	$747
Cassette album	20%	9.98	10%	2 on 10	.15968	450,000	$71,856
CD album	25%	15.98	10%	2 on 10	.23970	1,000,000	$239,700

Gross Earnings This Period	$313,577
Less Soundtrack Conversion	($6,000)
Total Payable This Period	**$307,577**

$230,683 remittance to artist (75%) enclosed
$76,894 remittance to artist's label (25%)

EXHIBIT 3
ROUGH INCOME SUMMARY

The following rough income summary is designed to alert you to sources of income rather than to provide exact figures (although we have done our best to be accurate).

A. Writer

1. Writing Fee (nonrecoupable)	$25,000
2. Song Synch License For Film	0
3. Performance Income (worldwide)	
(a) From Film In Theatres	
(i) United States	0
(ii) Foreign	$20,000
(b) Radio Performances	$100,000
(c) Home Video	0
(d) Pay TV	★
(e) Free TV	
(i) U.S. Network TV (two runs)	$3,000
(ii) U.S. Syndicated TV (two runs 150 stations)	$600
(iii) Foreign	$5,000
4. Sheet Music (40,000 copies @ 10 cents/copy)	$4,000
5. Mechanicals	
(a) United States (3/4 statutory)	
(i) Single (A-side only) (1,000,000 x 2.475 cents)	$24,750
(ii) LP (500,000 x 2.475 cents)	$12,375
(b) Foreign	
(i) Single (750,000 x 2.75 cents)	$20,625
(ii) LP (375,000 x 2.75 cents)	<u>$10,312</u>
Total	**$225,662**

B. Recording Artist

1. Recording Fee (nonrecoupable)	$25,000
2. Master License For Film	0
3. United States Record Sales	
(a) Singles (A-side only) (1,000,000 copies)	$76,500
(b) LPs (500,000 copies)	$49,401
4. Foreign Record Sales	
(a) Singles (750,000 copies)	$47,812
(b) LPs (375,000 copies)	$27,225
Less Soundtrack Conversion Costs	<u>($3,000)</u>
Total	**$222,938**

★ *Figures presently unavailable.*

PERFORMING AND MARKETING

Club Contracts

Showcasing

Publicity: How To Get It

Using The Internet To Promote Your Music

Music Unions

Merchandising Agreements

CLUB CONTRACTS

by Edward R. Hearn

Many bands get their start playing in clubs. There are several types—draw clubs, clubs with walk-in trades and lounge act clubs. A club or hotel room that has been booked by a private party for a special occasion, such as a wedding, anniversary, or industrial convention, etc., is called a "casual."

The draw clubs book acts with recognizable names to attract an audience. This could be a national recording act or a local act that has a following. Sometimes these clubs hire an opening act to reinforce the lead act's draw and help ensure a full house.

The walk-in trade club depends on a regular crowd that frequents the club. It normally hires "club bands" that play Top 40 and maybe some original material. Lounge act clubs focus on groups that do highly polished performances of popular music (also called "copy music"). They are prevalent in major cities' hotels, casinos, and in resort areas.

As some clubs are signatories of agreements with the American Federation of Musicians (AFM) you must find out if you need to be a member of the AFM before a club can book you.

Sometimes bands or their managers book their acts into clubs for showcase purposes, that is to "show" the group's talents to industry people that have promised to attend. Showcases are also used to generate enthusiasm for a group. For example, members of a Midwest group that has a huge regional following book themselves into a Los Angeles club for almost no pay to showcase for record companies, publishers or even prospective managers. Or a record company may fill (paper) a club, when a new record is released, to generate enthusiasm for the particular group being pushed by the record company, or the club may be filled by a group's personal manager or talent agency to influence record companies into developing an interest in the group.

APPROACHING THE CLUB

You should study the various kinds of clubs where you could perform and decide which best suit your act. Make presentations to clubs that most fit your style of music. It is important that you understand the reputation of the club and the makeup of the audience that is likely to enjoy your performance.

Club owners want bands that are professional and pleasing to their audiences. They want to know that the artists will work as promised, show up on time, and make money for their clubs.

The more clubs you perform in and the more reliable a track record you develop, the easier the bookings should become, particularly if you show a consistent (and growing) draw.

Most club owners also expect you to have publicity materials that they can use to help promote the performance. The chapter "Publicity: How to Get It" discusses publicity issues in detail.

CLUB CONTRACTS

When dealing with clubs, you should understand that even a casual agreement to show up and play for free, to see what happens, is a contract. This section focuses on the various points you should review with the club owner in order to arrive at a performing contract. These same points are relevant for standard AFM contracts that are used when bands are booked into clubs that are affiliated with the AFM.

Remember that the contractual relationship with a club is only as good as the relationship between the club owner and the group. You should determine whether the owners of a club are people with whom you really wish to deal. Counterbalancing that, if they are not people with whom you wish to deal, but playing their club is an important milestone in the development of your band and its credibility to the music industry, then that point has to be given consideration.

The contract with a club can be either oral or written. However, with an oral contract, in the event of a dispute, it is difficult to prove what terms were agreed to by the club owner and the band. If the contract is written, then the agreed-to points are documented. Rather than treating the written contract as an awesome legal document, consider it a checklist of important points that should be covered by the club owner and the group. Look at the contract as a way of clarifying the relationship between the club and you by bringing to light all of the issues that are important to both parties. This way, everyone will focus on those issues at the very beginning, hopefully eliminating any later surprises. Contract discussions are an indication of your professionalism to a club owner.

A Checklist of the Important Items in a Club Contract

- Identity of the performer and club owner.

- Dates and times of the performance.

- Number of sets to be performed and the length of those sets.

- Duration of the breaks between the sets.

- Special arrangements that need to be made in terms of equipment, stage settings, space for performance, and lighting.

- Refreshments (the house policy on drinks and food/snacks).

- Setup time and the time for sound checking.

- Whether any recording or broadcasting is to take place, and who controls the by-product of that effort.

- The advertising image of the group to be displayed by the club.

- What happens if the gig does not take place?

- What is your compensation?

Compensation

Your compensation could come in a number of forms. It could be from door receipts, in which case you should determine, with the club owner, the number of tickets to be sold, the prices of those tickets, and the number of freebies for the owner and the performers. With that information, you will have some idea how much to expect based on the percentage of the door receipts you have agreed to accept. Your compensation could be a flat sum, in which case the door receipts are not a problem. Reach an agreement on the form of compensation (i.e., cash or cashier's check). The norm is cash, but insist on at least a cashier's check. Part of the money should be paid, if not at the beginning, then at least part way through the performance with the balance due, if any, immediately at the conclusion of the performance.

Sound and Lights

An audience's perception of how good a performance is often depends on the quality of sound and lights. Make sure that the club has equipment that is adequate for your needs and that the club owner understands what those needs are.

If you (or the club) wishes to supplement the club's system with your own (or rented) equipment, work out the additional expense as part of your contract and arrange for a load-in time. If you are using an acoustic piano, your contract should state that it be tuned prior to performance. A simple performance contract is printed at the end of this chapter. Even if you don't use the contract, it is a good check list that can be used during contract negotiations with the club owner.

If the club has a resident sound engineer whose job is setting up and operating the house sound reinforcement system, establish a harmonious relationship by providing a plot plan of how the stage looks when your equipment is set up. Communicate your priorities regarding sound and provide the sound person with a set list. Ask whether your sound person can sit with the club sound engineer and provide direction about the mix.

AFM UNION CONTRACTS

Certain clubs have signed collective bargaining agreements with the AFM that establish the scale and working conditions that the club must pay and provide union musicians that perform at that club, based on the amount of time they play and the number of sets they perform. Union contracts are most prevalent with hotels, pit orchestras, house bands, and major clubs in large cities.

The musician members of the AFM also sign a contract with the AFM that requires its members to deal only with clubs that meet the AFM contract requirements. Technically, a musician member of the AFM should not play in nonunion clubs for less than union scales, since to do so is a violation of the contract.

It is not uncommon for clubs that have signed with the AFM to file, with the union local, what is known as a "dummy" contract between the performer and the club by which the club commits to pay at AFM scale, but the musician and the club owner agree (verbally) that the musician will perform at a lower price. This is done so that the AFM will not bother the club or the musician and the musician can get the work. The net effect is, the musician gets the short end.

Another common problem is that union clubs are barred by the AFM contract from hiring nonunion musicians. There is a provision in the AFM booking contract that says, "All employees covered by this agreement must be members in good standing of the Federation." Musicians that are engaged by the club and are not members of the union must become members of the union no later than the 30th day following the beginning of their employment or the effective date of the agreement, whichever of the two is later. Consequently, if you are not a union member when you start performing with a union club, you may find yourself in a situation where you must become a member of the union if you are going to continue to play in the club over a period of time—depending on the extent to which the AFM or the particular club enforce this provision.

Many of the points raised in the following checklist can be made a part of the AFM contract with the club.

Many smaller clubs do not sign contracts with the union and have no obligation to pay union scale. Union musicians, however, often perform in nonunion clubs on the q.t. or they file a dummy contract so that the AFM can get its cut.

When a club has no contract with the AFM the only leverage a union musician has is to refuse to perform in that club unless union scale is paid. The economic realities of the business, however, are such that the musician frequently has no bargaining power to force the club to pay union scale. Generally, the musician is glad to get any kind of work regardless of pay scale.

WHO SIGNS THE CONTRACT?

As a practical matter, one of the members of the group should be given authority to sign on behalf of all of the members of the group. Performing groups are, for all practical purposes, partnerships and one partner has the power to bind the other partners. Sometimes, a manager will be authorized to sign contracts on behalf of a group, although managers are better advised not to sign performance contracts if the state in which the band or manager is based requires talent agents to be licensed, as is the case

OTHER POINTS THAT SHOULD BE CONSIDERED IN YOUR RELATIONSHIP WITH A CLUB THAT USES THE AFM CONTRACT:

• The wage should be at least union minimum scale. Consider the costs that have to be paid from that wage, such as sound system, special instruments, and lighting.

• The customary union procedure is to pay half of the agreed-to wages in advance of the engagement and the remaining amount prior to the performance on the evening of the engagement. The AFM may demand that the entire amount be paid in advance or that a bond be posted.

• The union contract gives the club owner complete control, supervision, and direction over the musicians, including the manner, means, and details of the performance. This is more often than not a matter of bargaining power and the more popular the group, the less power the owner has over the group. As a practical matter, most club owners prefer not to be involved in decisions about a group's performance or the kind of materials to be performed. Presumably, if you have properly identified your style, the club owner has decided that you are the kind of act desired, and is expecting that kind of performance.

• Any disputes between the club owner and the musician under a union contract are, usually, resolved by an AFM arbitration proceeding and the results can be enforced by a court.

• If the performance is to be recorded or broadcast, the contract requires AFM approval. The AFM may demand additional compensation for the musician in that event. At the same time, the club owner may insist on additional compensation for use of the club if the performance is to be recorded by a record company or broadcast over a radio station. These are points that should be negotiated in advance.

in California. (See the chapter "Talent Agencies.") The extent of that authority depends on the agreements reached between the manager and the group and is another point to be considered carefully.

TAXES

Remember your tax obligations on your compensation. Generally, club owners will treat you as an independent contractor and you will be responsible for your own federal income tax and social security payment as well as any state, unemployment, or workman's compensation insurance that must be paid. The IRS may impose the responsibility on the club owner for withholding if it determines that there was an employer-employee relationship, but you should take responsibility for setting aside a portion of your payment so that you can pay the IRS when the time comes.

WHEN THE CLUB DOESN'T PAY YOU

If you are owed money by the club owner and the owner refuses to pay, you have recourse to the courts (and to your AFM local if it's a union club). Going to court, however, can be an expensive proposition, and is not one to be pursued lightly. California law provides that if the claim is no more than $5000 or if you are willing to limit your claim to that amount, you can bring your own action in the small claims court in the county where you reside or where the club is located. The small claims court procedure requires you to go to the county clerk for your local court system and pay a small fee for filing, stamping, and serving the complaint. The sheriff then serves the complaint on the defendant, which sets forth a date, time, and place for a hearing. The defendant can file a counterclaim within 48 hours of the hearing, but it has to be verified, or sworn to. (Your complaint does not have to be sworn to.) At the appointed date, time, and place, both parties must appear at the court and explain their stories to the judge. The judge can then order the club to pay you. If the judge does rule in your favor, the club owner can appeal to a higher level court. If you lose, you cannot appeal, and that is the end of the case. Similar small claims procedures are in effect in most states.

CONCLUSION

Making arrangements for performing in clubs deserves special consideration and planning. You should keep in mind that your ability to get gigs will be enhanced by getting your business act together.

PERFORMANCE AGREEMENT

Agreement made as of _____ , 19__ , between the parties identified below. In consideration for the following covenants, conditions, and promises, the Purchaser agrees to hire the Artist to perform an engagement and the Artist agrees to provide such performance services, under the following terms and conditions:

1. Artist _____

2. Purchaser _____

3. Place of engagement

NAME _____

STREET ADDRESS _____

CITY, STATE, ZIP _____

TELEPHONE _____

4. The dates, time, duration of show, and sound check time are as follows:

Dates _____ Time _____AM/PM
Number of Sets _____ Duration of Each Set _____
Sound Check Time _____

5. The consideration to be paid shall be
  (a) Guaranteed Fee of $ _____
  (b) Percentage _____ (gross/net of door)
  (c) Workshop Fee of $ _____
  (d) Meals/Lodging _____
  (e) Transportation _____
      (i) Air _____
      (ii) Ground _____
  (f) Materials _____
  (g) Total _____
  (h) Advance Payment of $ _____ due on _____ (Date)
  (i) Balance of Payment of $ _____ due on _____ (Date)

6. Further consideration to Artist by Purchaser is provided in the Rider of Additional Terms attached to this Agreement.

7. Sound and/or lighting equipment to be provided by Purchaser shall be as described in the separate Sound Reinforcement and Lighting Agreement.

8. This Agreement and the attached Sound Reinforcement and Lighting Agreement, which by this reference are incorporated into and made a part of this Agreement, constitute the entire agreement between the parties and supersedes all prior and contemporaneous agreements, understandings, negotiations, and discussions, whether oral or written. There are no warranties, representations, and/or agreements among the

parties in connection with the subject matter of this Agreement, except as specifically set forth and referenced in this Agreement and the attached Riders. This Agreement shall be governed by California law; is binding and valid only when signed by the parties below; and may be modified only in a writing signed by the parties. If Artist has not received the deposit in the amount and at the time specified in subsection 5(h), then Artist thereafter at anytime shall have the option to terminate this Agreement.

9. The persons signing this Agreement on behalf of Artist and Purchaser each have the authority to bind their respective principals.

10. If you have any questions, please contact our home office at _____

AGREED TO AND ACCEPTED

_____	_____
PURCHASER	ARTIST
_____	_____
BY DATE	BY DATE
_____	_____
NAME AND TITLE (AN AUTHORIZED SIGNATORY)	NAME AND TITLE (AN AUTHORIZED SIGNATORY)
_____	_____
FEDERAL I.D. / SS#	FEDERAL I.D. / SS#

PERFORMANCE AGREEMENT RIDER *

1. BILLING
Artist shall receive one hundred percent (100%) sole exclusive billing in any and all advertising and publicity when appearing as the sole act. When Artist is accompanied by other musicians, Artist shall receive prominent billing, and shall close the show at each performance during the engagement unless specifically provided otherwise. When headlining, Artist shall have the right of approval of any and all other acts in the show, their set times, and set lengths.

2. PAYMENT
All payments provided hereunder shall be made by Money Order, Cash, Cashier's, Certified, or School Check, made out to _____unless otherwise notified.

When a percentage figure is made a part of this Agreement, the Purchaser agrees to have on hand at the end of the engagement the ticket manifest and all unsold tickets for verification by Artist or Artist's representative.

(a) If the Artist is paid according to a percentage of the gross admissions, the following applies:

---

* *Riders to performance agreements specify additional requirements and working conditions that are essential and necessary for a quality performance. They can be extremely elaborate.*

(i) Purchaser must have all tickets printed by a bonded printer.

(ii) All tickets must be consecutively numbered.

(iii) Each set of tickets for a given price, and, if more than one performance is contemplated, each set of tickets for each performance must be printed on a ticket stock of contrasting color.

(iv) A bonded printer's manifest showing number, color and price of all tickets printed for the performance must be available for inspection by Artist's representative on afternoon of concert.

(v) All gross admission receipts shall be computed on the actual full admission price provided on each ticket, and, in the absence of prior written agreement by Artist, no tickets shall be offered or sold at a discount or a premium.

(vi) A representative of the Artist shall have the right to be present in the box office prior to and during the performance and intermission periods and such representative shall be given full access to all box office sales and shall otherwise be permitted to reasonably satisfy himself as to the gross receipts (and expenditures if required) at each performance hereunder.

(b) Purchaser warrants that tickets for the engagement will be scaled in the following prices:

_____ TICKETS AT _____ DOLLARS.

_____ TICKETS AT _____ DOLLARS.

_____ TICKETS AT _____ DOLLARS.

If the scale of prices shall be varied in any respect, the percentage compensation payable to Artist shall be based upon whichever of the following is more favorable to Artist: the scale of prices as set forth above, or the actual scale of prices in effect for the engagement.

(c) In the event that compensation payable to Artist hereunder is measured in whole or in part by a percentage of receipts, Artist shall have the right to set a limit on the number of free admissions authorized by Purchaser.

3. WITHHOLDING

If Purchaser is required by state or local law to make any withholding or deduction from the Artist fee specified in the attached contract, the Purchaser shall furnish to Artist a copy of the pertinent law governing said deduction when returning the Agreement to Artist or Artist's agent.

4. LIMITATIONS ON RECORDING

No performance during the engagement shall be recorded, copied, reproduced, transmitted, or disseminated in or from the premises in any manner or by any means now known or later developed, including audio and video, without the prior written permission of Artist.

5. PUBLICITY PHOTOGRAPHS

Only photographs sent to the Purchaser by Artist or Artist's representative shall be used in publicizing the engagement.

6. DRESSING ROOM

Purchaser shall provide one (1) clean, lockable dressing room. Purchaser agrees to be solely responsible for the security of all items in the dressing room area, and shall keep unauthorized people from entering said area.

7. ARTIST'S PROPERTY

Purchaser shall be responsible for any theft or damage to the equipment of Artist that may occur during the time that the equipment is located on Purchaser's premises.

8. SECURITY

Purchaser will make a diligent effort during the performance to maintain a quiet listening audience. Audience shall be seated prior to the performance. Purchaser is responsible for the conduct of its audience and shall provide adequate supervision of minors attending the performance. Any damage resulting from activities of the audience shall be the responsibility of Purchaser.

9. COMPLIMENTARY TICKETS

Purchaser agrees to make (_____) complimentary tickets available to Artist or Artist's representative, the unused portion of which may be placed on sale the day of performance with the permission of Artist or Artist's representative.

10. BACKSTAGE ACCESS

Purchaser shall provide (_____) backstage passes for Artist on Artist's arrival at venue.

11. MERCHANDISING

Artist shall have the option to sell albums, videos, books, and/or merchandising material at the performance and shall retain the proceeds of such sales.

> (a) Artist has sole right to merchandise any and all products pertaining to Artist at no expense to the Artist, excluding normal hall and vending fees agreed upon in advance by Artist in writing. Purchaser will not, nor will Purchaser allow, any other party to sell or distribute merchandise bearing name, likeness, or logo of Artist, before, during, or after concert date.
>
> (b) Purchaser will provide at its expense, (_____) persons to sell Artist's products.
>
> (c) Purchaser will provide the following equipment for merchandising:
>> (i) One (1) cash box with fifty dollars ($50.00) starting change (ones and fives).
>> (ii) Six-foot (6') table (to hold records and other Artist products).
>> (iii) Two (2) chairs (for the persons selling the products).
>
> (d) Merchandise shall be displayed in a prominent area of the foyer or lounge leading from the facility entrance to the performance area.
>
> (e) Person who is to vend Artist's products shall be available from time of stage call to receive product and set up merchandise area. Artist or Artist's representative will conduct and set up merchandise area with Purchaser's designated sellers. Artist or Artist's representative will conduct inventory of merchandise prior to start of sale.
>
> (f) After close of show (all audience will have left the facility) the vendor will close the merchandising booth and return all unsold product and receipts from sale to Artist or Artist's representative for final accounting.
>
> (g) Purchaser is responsible for all product and monies from sales as signed for by

the Purchaser's merchandising representative. Fifty dollars ($50.00) starting change is to be deducted from total receipts.

12. GROUND TRANSPORTATION

Unless otherwise indicated, Purchaser, at its expense, shall provide ground transportation to and from place of engagement, airport, and hotel. Artist requires large station wagon or van. Please send directions to concert site from the airport, or, if mode of travel is arranged other than by automobile, please send directions (and time tables) from airport, train station (etc.) to hotel, then from hotel to concert site. Copies of highlighted street maps are very much appreciated.

13. FOOD

Food and beverages appropriate for time of day for (_____) people shall be provided by Purchaser.

14. LODGING

If Purchaser is to provide lodging, it shall be at a hotel of Holiday Inn quality or better, four (4) quiet, nonsmoking rooms, in the vicinity of the venue, away from highway noise, with king-size beds in each room.

15. OUTDOOR VENUE

In the event the engagement is outdoors, there must be a covering over the stage area that will protect the Artist and equipment from the elements.

16. SEATING

House lights should be dimmed starting ten (10) minutes before the start of the concert to facilitate audience being seated on time.

17. BACKGROUND MUSIC

No background music, taped or otherwise, is to be played before the start of or after the concert without the approval of the Artist, unless the music is from Artist's albums.

18. STAGE

Stage must be accessible to performers in a manner other than through the audience. Stage and curtains must be in clean, good condition. Whenever possible, stage should be no further than fifteen feet (15') from the audience.

19. PROMOTION

Purchaser agrees to promote the scheduled performance(s) on television, radio, newspapers, and other print media, and will use its best efforts to obtain calendar listings, feature articles, interviews of the Artist, reviews of the performance and Artist's records in local major and alternative newspapers, radio, and television programs. Purchaser shall be responsible for all matters pertaining to the promotion and production of the scheduled engagement, including but not limited to venue rentals, security, and advertising.

20. CLIPPINGS

As a special request, Artist asks that Purchaser please forward clippings, reviews, advertising, and posters to Artist at _____. If there are any questions or suggestions, please direct them to _____.

21. FORCE MAJEURE

This agreement of Artist is subject to the unavailability of Artist because of sickness, accidents, riots, strikes, acts of God, or other conditions beyond Artist's control.

22. CANCELLATION

In the event Purchaser cancels the performance for any reason less than five (5) weeks before the date of such performance, Purchaser will pay Artist, as liquidated damages, one-half (1/2) of the guaranteed fee agreed to be paid for such performance in subsection 5(a). In the event Purchaser cancels the performance for any reason less than two (2) weeks before the date of such performance, Purchaser will pay Artist, as liquidated damages, the full guaranteed fee agreed to be paid for such performance, unless Artist subsequently agrees in writing to waive all or any part of that payment.

23. ATTORNEYS' FEES

In the event of any dispute arising under this Agreement that results in litigation or arbitration, the prevailing party shall be paid its reasonable attorneys' fees and costs by the losing party.

24. INSURANCE

Purchaser agrees to obtain any and all necessary personal injury and property damage liability insurance with respect to the activities of Artist on the premises of Purchaser or at such other location where Purchaser directs Artist to perform. Purchaser agrees to indemnify and hold Artist harmless from any and all claims, liabilities, damages, and expenses for injury, damages, or death to any person, persons, or property, including attorneys' fees, demands, suits, or costs of whatever nature, arising from any action, activity, or omission of Purchaser or third parties, except for claims arising from Artist's willful misconduct or gross negligence. At least ten (10) days prior to the date of performance, Purchaser shall provide to Artist a copy of Purchaser's policy of insurance indicating coverage in the sum of at least _____ dollars for personal injury and property damage, naming Artist as an additional insured for the date of the performance.

SOUND REINFORCEMENT RIDER

This rider for sound reinforcement services is entered into as of _____, 19 __, between the parties identified below.

1. NAME OF PURCHASER _____

_____
PURCHASER ADDRESS
_____
CITY/STATE/ZIP
_____
PHONE

2. NAME OF ARTIST _____

3. PLACE OF ENGAGEMENT _____

4. DATE OF EVENT _____

5. NUMBER OF SETS AND DURATION _____

6. TYPE OF EVENT _____

7. MAXIMUM AUDIENCE EXPECTED _____

8. LOAD-IN
Hall is available for load-in and set up at (date) _____ (time) _____

   (a) Purchaser agrees to provide a safe and proper 20-foot "A" type ladder (with wheels), at time of load-in and until all of Artist's equipment has been removed from venue.
   (b) Purchaser agrees to provide (_____) number of drum risers at a height of (_____) above the stage floor.
   (c) Ladder and drum risers are to be in place at time of load-in.

9. SOUND CHECK
Hall is available for sound check at (date) _____ (time) _____
   (a) Artist requires a (_____) hour sound check and technical setup period. Purchaser shall not allow the audience to enter the place of performance until such time as sound check and technical setup has been completed. Artist shall complete the setup and sound check (_____) hour(s) prior to the time of performance, provided that Purchaser makes the place of performance available for said setup at least (_____) hours prior to time of performance.

10. SOUND SYSTEM
Purchaser agrees to provide a complete sound system consisting of:

(____) Number of amplifiers at (____) kilowatts of power
(____) Number of main house speakers
(____) Number of monitor speakers
A main mixing board with (____) number of input channels
A monitor mixing board with (____) number in input channels
(____) Number of microphones and stands
Other special equipment _____
Any alterations or deviations from the above items involving extra cost of equipment or labor, or substitutions of equipment, are subject to written agreement.

11. PERSONNEL
Purchaser agrees to provide the following personnel to operate the equipment:

_____
_____

12. POWER
Purchaser agrees to provide at least _____ amps single phase and _____ volts of power.

13. SPEAKER SPACE

Purchaser agrees to provide adequate space for placement of loud speakers. The space needed for the speakers will be _____ feet by _____ feet. This area must be capable of supporting the weight (_____ lbs.) of the speakers safely.

14. MIXING PLATFORM

Purchaser agrees to provide a safe platform or space in the audience within 50 to 100 feet of the stage in order to set up mixers to mix the sound for the show. Platform or area should be _____ feet by _____ feet.

15. SECURITY

Purchaser agrees to hire adequate security for stage area and accepts full liability for any stolen articles and/or destruction of Artist's equipment.

SAMPLE OF SPECIFICATIONS FOR SOUND REQUIREMENTS
(SOUND REINFORCEMENT RIDER, CLAUSE 10).

(a) Purchaser shall provide a minimum of ten (10) high quality monitor speakers. These monitor speakers shall be capable of providing at least 120 dB of clear, undistorted sound between 100 and 10,000 cycles per second (plus or minus 4 dB) at a distance of ten (10) feet. The monitor speakers shall be placed as follows:

    3—stage center
    1—down stage left
    1—up stage right
    2—monitors behind drummer
    1—monitor behind keyboards
    2—side fill monitors

(b) There shall be a minimum of ten (10) boom stands, six (6) short stands, two (2) gooseneck-type attachments, and ten (10) regular stands for the microphones.

(c) If the performance area of the engagement is outdoors or semi-outdoors, all microphones shall be covered with filter windscreens.

(d) Purchaser further agrees to provide a six (6) station intercom hook-up between the following—

    stage right or left
    both spot lights
    sound console
    monitor mixer console
    dimmer board
    house lights and curtain

All intercoms are to be headphone type with microphone and two earpieces.

SHOWCASING

by John Braheny

Performing in live showcases is a great way for you to get feedback from an audience; network with other songwriters and find collaborators; and audition for record companies or other industry people (producers, managers, publishers, booking agents and club owners). You can make new friends and become part of a mutual support group; find out about resources, organizations and services that can further your career; and get the gossip about local movers and shakers, recording sessions and other projects that need material. You will get inspired and motivated by being around other creative people and the more people you meet, the more possibilities can open up for you.

Pick a showcase that wants the kind of music you enjoy playing. If the audience doesn't like you the gig will get old very fast. The attitude "we'll make them love what we do" is admirably ambitious but often self-defeating.

AUDITION NIGHTS

In the major music centers, "writers nights" or "open mike nights" are often held in local clubs. These are either fairly loose, informal gatherings where you just show up and play or they can be prescheduled, organized events that you may have to audition for in advance. Talk to whomever's in charge of organizing the talent and get the real story so you don't sign up late and end up showcasing for two drunks and a bartender at 3 a.m. For these types of showcases you rarely, if ever, get paid. Occasionally a club owner will split part of the gate with the performers, but don't count on it. The deciding factor is the degree of benefit you get out of playing. If you do it just for fun and performing experience, that may be enough. If you're a working band and you have to showcase without pay, you're going to want some assurance that someone who can help your career will be listening.

PAY TO PLAY

There has been some controversy, particularly in the L.A. club scene over "pay to play," a system in which the act is required to purchase and resell a specific amount of tickets in order to play the club. Generally, it means paying the sound and light people. It was instituted by some club owners that felt they were taking a loss on bands that had no following and did nothing to promote themselves. On the other hand, many music industry people feel that clubs should book acts for their talent and help them build audiences rather than book them on their ability to pay for tickets. Before you agree to pay to play check out the clubs that don't have that policy.

CLUB BUYOUTS

Another way to approach showcasing is a club buyout. You rent the club exclusively for the whole night, book your own opening act, hire sound and lighting operators, send invitations to music industry people and do your own publicity.

ESTABLISHED SHOWCASES

Established, well publicized showcases in major music centers that regularly draw industry people are always worth playing at (and attending regularly, even if you don't play). These showcases are sponsored by local clubs or by musician or songwriter organizations and are publicized in the events sections of local newspapers and in musician newspapers and newsletters. ASCAP and BMI have their own showcases.

OPTIMIZING YOUR SHOWCASE OR GIG

1. Make sure your appearance is listed on the club's mailer and see if the club has a place to display your photos.

2. Check with the people who run the showcase for any tips that will help you come off well in their club. Remember, they've seen lots of acts win or lose in their place and that perspective can be very valuable to you.

3. Make sure the stage is big enough to accommodate your instruments, amps etc. and has enough room for whatever movement you need to show yourself off to best advantage. If there isn't enough room, look for another club.

4. If there is an adequate house P.A. system and you have a sound person you work with regularly (who knows your music), it's better for him or her to work with the club's sound person who is used to getting the best sound out of the room. If the club's sound system isn't adequate, and you bring in your own, the procedure is riskier. Your sound person will have to tailor the sound output to the acoustic properties of the room and be willing to accept advice from the club's sound person. I've seen some good groups empty the house because they wouldn't listen to advice and played too loudly for the room. If you're doing a record company showcase, clean vocals are important, so start there and mix around them. Make sure you have a sound check to work out all the problems and to set your instrument levels.

5. Show up on time for sound checks and performances.

6. Make sure the lighting is adequate and write down any lighting cues you might need for the person who runs them.

7. Know exactly how much time you can have for your set and stick to it. Plan your set(s) carefully, consider their length, pacing, and where to place your strongest material. If you have a potential hit single, or other very commercial material, begin and end with it. If you're the last act, put it at the beginning of your performance. Record people frequently have other places to go and may be anxious to leave.

8. Be cooperative with everyone at the club, including the waitresses. It may make the difference between your coming back to the club or not and having the employees tell people to come and see you or telling them you're losers.

9. Talk with the owner about guest lists and guest policies beforehand to prevent bad scenes with your guests, whom you want to be in a receptive state of mind toward your group.

10. Dress with some thought about how you look as a group and no matter what you decide to wear, don't look like you just got off work as a mechanic and didn't bring along a change.

11. Make sure that all information concerning the showcase is conveyed to your whole group.

12. If you're auditioning for record companies, it's imperative that you perform primarily original material. A & R people are not interested in the way you play the hits. If you're working a Top 40 gig, make sure to check with the owner to see if you can throw in a set of originals when the company reps are there. Invite the appropriate music industry people on your mailing list. (The development of industry mailing lists is covered in the chapter titled "Publicity: How to Get It.") Make sure your letter and press releases inform them of the time you'll be doing your original set.

13. Try and fill the house with fans that appreciate your music. Get flyers printed and send them to your fan mailing list. If you're working a regular gig at a club, try to get the owner to kick in some money for the flyers. After all, the owner has a vested interested in showing off the club. You distribute the flyers at your expense, and make sure they are seen in the right places.

PUBLICITY: HOW TO GET IT

by Diane Rapaport

Playing to an empty house is every musician's nightmare. It means their act didn't draw.

Draw is a band's ability to fill a club, concert hall or arena with paying customers. A band's draw determines the pay scale it can demand, and club owners and concert producers can make or lose fortunes based on their ability to accurately predict what a band will draw on a particular day at a given price.

No matter what a band's potential draw is, one thing is certain—if no one knows about a gig, no one will attend. The purpose of publicity is to let people know where and when a gig is happening and persuade them to attend. Publicity can be as simple as calling up fans or, as in the case of a major tour by a top recording artist, a national media campaign that includes print, radio and television.

Well-executed publicity persuades people, whose opinions are respected, to share information and enthusiasm with others. This stimulates interest and, since it's not presented as advertising, adds credibility to the idea that they really believe in the music, band, etc.

Free publicity seldom happens by chance. In fact, millions of dollars are spent yearly by public relations firms and publicists to guarantee that publicity happens. These people understand that newspaper reporters, radio and television news directors, reviewers and critics often wait for news to be brought to them. They expect to be courted, cajoled and pleaded with to talk or write about an event or to play a recording.

Fortunately, you don't have to spend a fortune on public relations firms to help you get publicity. If you know the techniques and tools involved, it can be obtained by anyone who is willing to spend time, energy and a little money.

Success depends on how well the following are accomplished: assembling effective publicity materials; researching publicity outlets; and planning and carrying out a campaign.

Once you understand the basics of a successful publicity campaign, you can apply the techniques to publicizing any venture.

PUBLICITY RESPONSIBILITY

In an ideal situation, publicity is a shared effort. Six to eight weeks prior to a performance a representative from the band will sit down with the club owner or promoter and figure out who's doing what. The band provides photos, press releases and flyers; the club owner or promoter sends them to the media, following many of the steps described in this article. Some concert promoters reinforce their publicity efforts with colorful posters, which they pay for and distribute.

The band usually takes responsibility for mailings to fans and to music professionals they would like to impress, such as record executives and other club owners and promoters.

Unfortunately, this ideal situation doesn't always occur. Many club owners aren't very knowledgeable about courting the media, nor desirous of putting out the effort and money it takes. In order to save money, club owners and promoters often bunch several gigs into one press release and your band can get lost in the shuffle.

Unless you are working with a club owner or promoter who has a glorious reputation for publicity, do your own. Even if they do some publicity, your efforts will enhance theirs. What really matters is that the club or concert hall is full.

Doing your own publicity is mandatory when you are a second or third band in a concert lineup. Most of the promoter's publicity will be directed towards the main draw. Your interests are best served by using the main draw as a springboard for your efforts to gain publicity and attention for your band.

Even if you are signed to a record label (large or small), the record company may not always be interested in providing publicity for your performances, particularly when they are not accompanied by a new record release. They may, however, be willing to tag record advertisements with news about the performance. This is something you or your manager should ask for.

PUBLICITY MATERIALS

Publicity materials and demo tapes are your ambassadors. They deliver information, stimulate excitement, and imprint your name and image in people's minds. They create a draw for your performances and help to sell your recordings.

The basics are a year's supply of letterhead stationery and envelopes; black-and-white photographs of the band; bios; flyers and posters; and postcards.

Letterhead Stationery

Letterhead stationery helps establish your band as a business and makes communication with the media and other businesses more professional. Your symbol (logo) and the lettering style and colors you use have a great deal to say about your image.

Ideally, they will be created by a skilled graphic designer.

Mediocre work creates bad impressions that are hard to erase. If your publicity materials are amateurish, you create the impression that your music is amateurish—even if it isn't. Well-executed visual materials can induce people to come to your performances or listen to your music.

Photographs

Glossy black-and-white photographs are important promotional tools. They must show who you are and indicate what kind of music you do.

If you have a record, it is a good idea to have black-and-white photographs of the cover as well.

Most of the photographs that you see reproduced in magazines and newspapers have been provided by bands (or their management). Only after a band has become a major headliner will a newspaper or magazine bother to send a photographer to a performance.

Photographs should be no larger than 8" x 10" and no smaller than 5" x 7". They must be easy to crop to fit narrow newspaper columns. This means tight groupings of people and instruments. For good reproduction, photos must be in sharp focus and should be shot against an uncluttered background that doesn't compete with the musicians (plain white or very light grey backgrounds are best). Good, sharp black-and-white tones are mandatory.

Hire a professional photographer. The position of the musicians and their instruments, and the lighting and camera angle are very important. A good photographer will be able to relax the band members so they don't feel and look self-conscious.

A good photograph can be used to create flyers, posters, postcards, and record, cassette and CD covers.

Photographers can be found by reading the credits for photos in local music magazines and requesting photographers' phone numbers from those magazines. Record and CD jackets are good places to look for names of photographers and graphic designers. You can check the yellow pages, but make sure that the graphic designer or photographer is experienced in working with musicians.

Graphic designers and professional photographers are expensive to hire. Fortunately, the success rate of good publicity materials is so high that the initial costs are worth it. These materials will help you get better gigs at better pay; airplay for your music; and increased record sales. Frankly, if you have to choose between putting out money for a competent graphic designer or photographer and upgrading your amplifier, I advise that you spend the money on getting great publicity materials.

Bios

Another important publicity tool is a well-written bio that contains information about the music and the musicians.

It should describe the music, indicate who plays what instrument and discuss the band's experience (what gigs; what records; how long has the band been performing and/or recording)? It should also contain one or two complimentary quotes (if you have them) from reviews. Information about the birthplaces of musicians or the high school they attended is irrelevant. Try to keep bios to one page, double-spaced.

Many musicians have difficulty describing their music. Those who can, have a huge advantage over those who categorize their material with such ambiguities as "unique" or "it's a blend of many styles." Vague descriptions arouse resistance, not curiosity.

One way to be specific is to name the genre (e.g., classical, jazz, country, rock, rap) of your music and then describe what makes your music different in this genre. The more innovative your music is, the more important it is to give people a handle on what it's about.

If you're really at a loss for words, hire a professional writer to help you.

Flyers, Posters and Postcards

Once your image is created and the photographs are taken, they can be used to create flyers, posters and postcards to help you publicize your gigs and recordings. The cost of reproduction is low, 1000 sheets of letterhead stationery and envelopes, or flyers, for under $100; one hundred black-and-white reproductions of a photograph for under $40.

THE INTERNET

The Internet opens up new opportunities for creating publicity materials, communicating with fans and media resources, and making information about your band available. For a monthly fee, most of the publicity materials mentioned above can be shown on an Internet site, your own or someone else's. The site will be located on an Internet server, such as World Wide Web, America Online, Prodigy, etc.

Each site has a name and an Internet address. The site name can be the same as your business name. If it is different than your business name, it must be unique within the industry you are serving.

A site's Internet address is called a Universal Resource Locator (URL), which uses the standardized address format "http://". This format is commonly followed by one or all of the following: a unique abbreviation of the name of a server (such as World Wide Web or "www"), followed by an abbreviation of your site or the site where you are located, followed by the abbreviation of a domain (a domain is a category of network or a specific network name). Common domain suffixes are "com" (commercial organizations), "edu" (education), "gov" (government), and "net" (network). For example, Racer Records, an independent San Francisco based record label, uses the URL address: http://www.racer records.com. The address shows that Racer Records has its own site on the World Wide Web. On the other hand, the address for Millennium, a large arts organization located in Boston, Massachusetts, is "http://www.arts-online.com/millen."

(The URL is different from your e-mail address which uses an abbreviation of your name or your business name followed by "@" and the abbreviation of your Internet server. You can have an e-mail address without having a site or home page.)

The home page (sometimes referred to as a "web page") is the first page of a web site. It contains the site's name and a directory of its contents.

Your home page welcomes people visiting your site and introduces you. It tells them what they can expect to find on other pages and how to quickly access them. Here, you can provide your gig calendar, soundbyte samples of your songs, color posters, newsletters, special merchandise offerings and so forth. This information can be downloaded and/or printed by anyone accessing your home pages.

You can create home pages at your own Internet site, as many bands and recording labels have done, and/or rent space on other sites. In addition to home pages, the Internet has newsgroups, a collection of topic-specific discussion groups where you can talk about your music and there are music-related mailing lists. More detailed information is provided in the chapter "Using the Internet to Promote Your Music."

RESEARCHING PUBLICITY OUTLETS
Fan Mailing Lists

Fans should be the first to know where and when a gig is happening and first to receive news about other important events, such as a new record deal or the release of a record. They're the ones that have followed you from gig to gig and dragged their friends to hear you. They're the people that have talked up your band and played your recordings. Their loyalty should be repaid with care and regard.

Fans are a major source of support. Ask the Grateful Dead, whose list of "Dead-heads" now numbers well into the hundreds of thousands. The Deadheads were responsible for the Dead's ability to fill concert halls long before they had any hit records. This list has also allowed the Dead to set up their own in-house (and very successful) merchandising company.

When your band releases a record, your fan list will be an important source of mail-order sales.

Start a fan list with these established methods: Place an attractive card that has room for names and addresses on every table in each nightclub and bar you work. You might also ask people to list the magazines or newspapers they read most regularly and which radio stations they listen to most. Leave a guest book in a prominent place everywhere you perform. Pass around a guest book between sets.

During every performance, mention that you are assembling a fan mailing list so that you can let people know when and where you are playing.

Once you have a substantial mailing list, you can offer to exchange it with other bands that also keep fan lists. Combined mailing lists will help bands draw greater followings—especially if their music appeals to similar audiences.

Media Lists

Next, research how word about musical events in your community gets around. The most common outlets are newspapers, magazines, newsletters, community bulletin boards, storefront windows, and radio and television.

You'll need names, addresses and phone numbers of the people that are responsible for listings, reviews, interviews, stories, airplay, etc. Once assembled, this list is called a press list.

Research sources by spending a few afternoons at the local library reading magazines and newspapers and by visiting book and record stores that stock them. Listen to local radio stations and watch TV news and talk shows. You should be aware that many media resources provide online access to their magazines, newspapers and radio stations and also provide e-mail addresses.

Most major city newspapers and local magazines have a number of people writing about music: One may review only the big shows; another may concentrate on club performances; still another may specialize in interviews and feature stories; several might write columns. Spend time reading their work. You'll discover that all writers have special biases—and the ones that are biased towards your particular kind of music will be the ones you should spend time cultivating. By reading their work, you'll also be able to personalize your approach. Just as you like to know that a critic hears and likes your music, they enjoy knowing that you read and pay attention to their words.

Editorial information, addresses and phone numbers of magazines are listed in the magazine's masthead, which is usually located within a few pages of the table of contents. It is useful to obtain "media kits" from newspapers', magazines' and radio stations' advertising sales departments. Media kits contain important information about the readership, listening audience, advertisers and so on.

One person's name may appear in several different magazines and newspapers, which identifies him or her as a freelance writer. Like musicians competing for club gigs, freelancers compete for space (and pay) in newspapers and magazines by coming up with good ideas and performing them well. They are good people to know since they are always on the lookout for scoops, interesting events, side issues, and special news.

Many newspapers, magazines, radio stations, and television news programs feature special events as a community service. Listings are almost always free. The only rule is to get your information to the right people on time (lead time). When you notice a newspaper or magazine listing, call and ask for the name of the person to whom you should send information and what the lead time is. For monthly publications, lead time is generally four to eight weeks in advance of publication; for Sunday papers, 10 to 14 days.

Next, research the names and addresses of local organizations that send newsletters to or provide information on the Internet to their membership. These may be as obvious as organizations catering to a particular genre of music (i.e., folk or jazz clubs) or simply a membership of people that seems similar to those attending your performance. This might be anything from religious organizations to political groups, historical societies or specialty clubs.

Finally, if you are thinking of putting out a record, be sure to get the names of program directors that might consent to add your music to their playlists. Include the names of DJs that have the latitude to slip in cuts of music that are not normally on their playlists (late-night shows and special programs are good bets).

Research carefully. Find out the preferred format at each station. Airplay is difficult to obtain for bands that do not record for major labels. College radio stations and public broadcast stations with special music programs are the most open to new music. However, even radio stations playing only major label music may have event listings, which are open to any band that gets information to them on time.

The names of producers of special television programming may be obtained by calling the television station and asking. Also, ask for the names of the assignment editors that are responsible for scheduling news programming.

Organizing Your List

This research should net over 100 names. Split the list into these categories: (1) events reviewers; (2) record reviewers; (3) freelance writers; (4) feature writers; (5) program directors; (6) television talk show producers; (7) events listings people; and (8) Internet resources. Note the people you feel will be most sympathetic; they're the ones you will concentrate your publicity efforts on.

There is one more list to research: the names, addresses and phone numbers of people who might help further your career. These include club owners, concert promoters, booking agents, managers, entertainment lawyers, and record company executives. This list won't help your draw, but after six months or a year of sending information about your band to these people, they'll be a lot easier to court. You might call this your blue-ribbon list.

I put these lists on computer so that I can easily update them. You should update your lists every three months. You'll be surprised at how many changes there will be.

PLANNING AND CARRYING OUT A CAMPAIGN

Now that you have your basic tools—mailings lists and publicity materials—here's how to use them.

Send postcard invitations to gigs to your fans, or send a whole month's worth of performance listings. Send announcements about items you have for sale, such as records, T-shirts, posters and so forth. Save postage by sending the same information to fans through their e-mail addresses. If you have a home page on the Internet, highlight its location in every mailing you send.

Send your press and blue-ribbon mailing lists announcements of important gigs and events, such as the signing of a record contract or the release of a new record.

Press Releases

Announcements to media and other professionals are almost always sent in the form of a press release.

Press releases capsulize information. They are factual ministories that tell who, what, where, when and how, directly and simply. Good press releases anticipate basic questions and answer them. They are organized so that the most important information comes first and the least important last. Hype should be omitted—with this exception—you can use one or two quotes from favorable reviews or articles.

The press release should be double-spaced on your letterhead stationery. Double-spacing makes it easy to edit copy and make changes. At the upper right, type the words "For Immediate Release" and directly underneath that, put a date. On the upper left, type "Contact Person" and his or her name and phone number so that if further information is needed, people will know whom to call.

The title should be centered and keyed to what the release is about. "New Record Released by The KiX" or "KiX to Perform at Central Stadium." The body of the release should be factual and informative. Plainly written press releases work best.

This format works for almost any kind of announcement. I have used them for announcing a new scientific instrument, the opening of a new business, a record release and so forth.

Press releases usually get sent as part of a larger package, which should include a personal letter, photo and bio, and any other graphic that you use, such as a poster. Include copies of favorable reviews and list the radio stations where your music has been played. All this information is placed into a folder that can be plain or imprinted with your logo. The resulting package is called a press kit.

These same press kits can also be sent to the e-mail addresses of key media people. Your e-mail note should add a personal touch. (The e-mail note takes the place of the personal letter that would be enclosed with a press kit sent in the mail.)

Mailings to press people are vitally important. The most common misconception bands (and many new managers) have regarding being reviewed or written about is that newspaper, magazine and radio people are on the prowl, searching for the next superstar. The truth is, media people are deluged with information and don't have to go out at all.

You should recognize that newspapers and magazines cover bands that are, in the eyes of their readers, famous or notorious. When Metallica, The Boston Pops, Pink Floyd or the Rolling Stones come to town, that's where you'll find your media people.

If you want critics, writers and other media people to come to your performances, either get yourself booked with a name band that these people are likely to see anyway, or ask them to come to your performance on a weekend night at a reasonable hour.

Newspapers and magazines devote space to community news, new bands, old local bands with new players, or new records. They publish information about gigs in advance (thus helping to publicize them) and sometimes their writers show up and review acts (this gives you ammunition to court other critics, writers, club owners and record people). However, the time writers have to attend the performances of groups that are just starting out is often no more than one night a week.

The choice of what to write about, publicize, or review is often based on press releases, invitations, records, and cover letters, etc. Hot tips, fed by long-time business contacts (other managers, promoters, secretaries and friends), also influence the choices.

Mailings (including e-mail communications) to people on your blue-ribbon list should always be followed with a telephone call to make sure they received the material, and to establish personal contacts to whom you can pitch your cause. It's the perfect time to introduce yourself and your work and ask if you can provide any additional information. Spend no more than a minute or two on each contact. Phone calls are also the way to correct misinformation or make changes (such as a different starting time for the performance). Professionalism demands that you be polite—and stay polite, even if well-intentioned promises to show up are not fulfilled. Media people are not ogres, just overworked (and often underpaid) people in demand. In the long run, a friendly attitude and cooperative manner will help you gain support.

When you get reviews, reprint them on your letterhead stationery and include them in mailings. Hype breeds hype. When media people see favorable reviews and articles about your band, they may be stimulated to join the bandwagon. Use favorable quotes in posters, flyers and on recording materials.

Do these steps for every gig and you will get results. Perseverance and repetition work. The eighth time a club owner or record company executive sees a press release about your band, they will realize that you are consistently performing. The fifth time a critic is invited to a gig, he or she may actually show up. The tenth time you send out a press release announcing a gig, you may be surprised to open the newspaper and see it printed word for word.

This process familiarizes people with your name, lets them know you are in the public eye, helps keep them up to date on your progress, and shows your professionalism. A professional approach, accompanied by good manners and perseverance, will earn you success.

Remember, there is no such thing as too much publicity!!

TIMING A PUBLICITY CAMPAIGN

3–4 Weeks Prior to Performance

- Mail (and/or e-mail) a press release and bio to everyone on your media and blue-ribbon lists. Follow this mailing with phone calls, two to three days after you think your materials have been received.
- Put up posters and flyers.
- If you have a record send it, along with a press release and bio, to the radio stations that are likely to play it. Include a personal invitation to the gig. When you make your follow-up phone call, ask if the station would be interested in interviewing someone in your band.
- If you use the Internet, make sure you post gig information on appropriate Internet sites, on your own home page and to any appropriate newsgroups or special mailing lists.

2–3 Weeks Prior to Performance

- Send out the same release (or one with more information) and a photograph of your band, captioned with time, place, date and price of the performance, along with your other graphic materials. Include a personal letter of invitation. Keep it short. This is also the time to request an interview or feature story.
- Send postcards to your fans.
- Send a personal letter to club owners, record company executives and other music business people inviting them to the performance. Include your press release and other publicity materials with the invitation.
- Follow up with phone calls.
- Check the places where you put flyers and posters to make sure that they are still there. Repeat if necessary.

Day of Performance

- Make sure that people who are invited are on the guest list at the entrance to the bar or club or at the gate or ticket booth. I've seen quite a few embarrassing situations where important people showed up only to find that the band had forgotten to place their names on the list.

USING THE INTERNET TO PROMOTE YOUR MUSIC

by Peter Spellman

Back in December 1993 *Musician* magazine published a rather prophetic article by Fred Goodman titled "Future Shocks: The End of the Music Business As We Know it." Goodman opened with a peek into the future:

> *Fifteen years from now, you are sitting at home on a cold, rainy Thursday night. You're mindlessly flipping through the 427 cable channels (and, of course, there still isn't much to watch), when you notice one of the music channels showing a video for a tune off the new duet album by Evan Springsteen and Neil Young. Wow, Neil's really starting to look kinda old…but that last album of his was all right. Y'know—the one that was sort of a follow-up to Trans. It wasn't bad. Neither is this. In fact, it's pretty damn good and you'd like to buy the album. But who wants to go out on a night like this? Luckily, you don't have to. Instead, you dial up a shopping number through your TV's computer modem and pick the title off a menu of new album releases. The digital recording is immediately transmitted to your computer, where it is downloaded onto a blank compact disc. You load a sheet of laminated, precreased cardboard into your laser printer, and out comes the printed sleeve, complete with credits, lyrics, and thank-yous. The price of the album is automatically charged to your American Express card.*

Online distribution—actually delivering that album order not through the mail but as digital bits down telephone or cable wires—is still pretty much in the "wouldn't it be neat?" stages. Red-flag issues such as rights and royalties still need to be addressed, as do the technical hurdles of improving data compression and means of end-user download.

But the fact remains that the entire history of recorded music will soon be available for instant downloading. The technology to do this *already* exists though availability to the public is still a few years away. But what *is* available today for both record label and artist is the Internet—the closest thing we have to an information superhighway and, most certainly, a hint of things to come.

DIGITAL DEMOCRACY

The Internet (Net) is the fastest-growing communications pipeline on the planet. What makes it especially suited to the music community is the relatively new navigational tool known as the World Wide Web. Some have called the Web "the Internet on steroids." Why? While the traditional Net (say from 1969 to 1992) was primarily a black and white *text*-based system, the Web opened the door to full-color graphics,

CD-quality sound and real-time video. The Web turns every owner of a computer, a modem, and a telephone line into a publisher, a radio station, and soon enough, a television studio.

In essence the Net collapses distance. From my desktop in Boston I can connect with a guitarist in Zaire, a promoter in Australia and a fan in Poland simultaneously. For musicians, these developments bring tools to their cause that allow an extended reach on a playing field that is growing increasingly more level and accessible. On the Internet you can appear side-by-side with multimillion dollar companies. Both Warner Bros. Records and any single artist or small music business are on equal footing in the electronic environment. But before we flesh out the finer features of the Internet for music marketing, let's first debunk some myths.

UNMASKING CYBERLORE

Misinformation and myths about the vast Internet abound. They obscure the basic functions of the Net and undervalue its potential. Let's get a few of these out of the way first.

Myth #1—The Internet is a commercial service like AOL, CompuServ and Prodigy. Not so. Commercial online services are proprietary computer networks of select informational databases. They're centralized, monitored, and metered. The Net, on the other hand, is a patchwork of commercial, educational, government, and public and private networks, all cooperating to achieve an open, interconnected communications system based on trust and goodwill. It's decentralized, relatively unregulated and unmetered. But that doesn't mean...

Myth #2—The Internet is free. Don't believe it for a moment. For people who receive Internet access as part of their employment or student status, the Internet may *seem* free. However, organizations pay for the infrastructure, equipment, and connections to gateways (exchange points for trading Internet traffic), and hire commercial providers to supply their connections to the Internet itself. Plus, being the child of the Department of Defense, your tax dollars paid for it in the first place and, until recently, maintained it.

Myth #3—The Internet is chaotic. There's simply no way to find anything. While no Internet information-collection or resource-searching tool is flawless, there *are* landmark collections and tools (e.g., Yahoo! and Lycos) on the Internet that you can use to find what you want with little, if any, hassle.

Myth #4—The Internet is hostile to newcomers. Not many beginner tennis players would even consider running onto the court at Wimbledon and joining a match in progress. Instead, a new player typically seeks out information and support—by taking a class, learning from a teacher, watching tennis videos, or reading books about playing. Newcomers to the Net should spend some time learning its behavioral standards ("netiquette"), not just its technical necessities. The Internet has any number of different cultures. The liveliness of the Net derives from the people that take part in it, and different communities of people have different social norms.

SO WHAT ABOUT MUSIC AND THE NET?

The Net offers a banquet of opportunities, resources and services for musicians and fans. There are currently over 6000 music-related newsgroups, mailing lists and Web sites on the Net. Online there's a lot more conversation about music than actual music. One day cyberspace may come in Sensurround. Right now, though, most of what you do is read and type (except for the point-and-click Web which we'll get to later). There are two basic styles of computer communication: real-time chatting (like being on a party line) and bulletin-board posting (where a conversation on a topic, or "thread," can span months). Who are you talking to? You can never be sure. But since computers aren't cheap, and computer literacy isn't evenly spread among the population yet, Net music culture remains predominantly white and male. The Internet's massive bulletin-board system is referred to as Usenet. Usenet is often called "news," but it shouldn't be confused with a wire-service feed, such as the Associated Press or UPI. A newsgroup can best be pictured as a discussion group where participants post "articles" to the shared newsgroup "space" for all to see and respond to. Given the scope

and speed of the Net, it is possible to carry on discussions on any subject with participants around the world. Looking for a review of Burning Spear's latest release? Try the rec.music.reggae newsgroup. Have questions about Coltrane's improvisational technique? Chances are somebody reading or posting to alt.music.bluenote can help you. Hoping to locate the lyrics of an obscure Montana folk song? Then check out the rec.music.folk newsgroup. Curious about what's hot in Hawaii, Australia, or Vancouver? re.music.info will definitely have the charts you are seeking, straight off the press. There are newsgroups for afro-latin, a cappella, celtic, funk, bagpipe, industrial, hardcore, ska, trance, karaoke, even "filk" (fantasy-related folk music)! In other words, seek and ye shall find. There are three important points to make about Usenet: Make sure your access provider receives a full news feed, that it provides a decent means of viewing the news, and that it allows you to "post" to the server. If you can't post your own contributions to Usenet, you'll be limited to being an observer, not an active participant. In addition to newsgroups, you can locate over 400

INTERNET FACTS

- The Internet currently has about 40 million users in over 170 countries, and is growing at a rate of about 10% to 15% per month.
- The World Wide Web (the multimedia interface of the Net) grew over 1500% last year (1994) and is expected to grow by over 3000% in 1995. It's primarily the Web that's making so much noise in the press lately.
- In 1994, a study by Dataquest found that for the first time, PCs outsold TVs in the United States. Most of these machines are multimedia—and network-ready.
- The Wall Street Journal reported (September 1, 1995) that another study shows that people with Internet access watch 20% less television than those without access.
- According to a study reported in InfoWeek (May 8, 1995), the two products most Internet users intend to buy online are software applications and music CDs and cassettes.

music-related and subject-specific "mailing lists" on the Net. Mailing lists are different than newsgroups in that you can participate in discussions via e-mail only if you actually "subscribe" (for free, of course) to a given list. The range and scope varies from list to list, and there are many artist- or genre-specific lists on the Net. For example, lists for fans of bands and artists ranging from Morphine, Miles Davis and Primus to Elton John and R.E.M. are available for subscription. Mailing lists, like newsgroups, allow participants, no matter how distant geographically, to exchange concert and record reviews, tour schedules, discographies and gossip, among other things. To get the most current list of all e-mail music lists, e-mail to the Musical List of Lists: mlol@lariat.org. Both newsgroups and mailing lists are very sensitive about blatant self-promotion. The quickest way to make a bad name for yourself is to send obnoxious e-mail or news. This is called "spamming" the Net and it usually results in the sender being "flamed" (sent nasty or insulting messages for violation of cybermanners). So mind your netiquette. Here are some good ways to do this:

- Know the difference between the address you use to get on or off a mailing list and the address you use to send messages to the list itself. Read a mailing list or newsgroup for at least a week before you try to send anything to it so that you understand and grasp what topics it covers and the level of the discussion.
- Most lists and groups have an introductory message, and most newsgroups periodically post FAQ (frequently asked questions) messages that introduce the topic and answer the most common questions. Before sending in your question, make sure it's not already answered for you.
- When responding to a message, if you include a copy of the original message, trim it down to the minimum needed. No sense wasting bandwidth (the amount of "space" required to transmit a file over the Internet using a modem; a large graphics or sound file requires much more bandwidth than a simple text message).

ONLINE OPPORTUNITIES

E-mail, mailing lists and newsgroups are among the most popular tools for individual users on the Net. Consider these examples:

- Artists and managers regularly use the Internet to announce new releases and tour itineraries. And when a gig is added or canceled at the last minute, the Net makes it possible to get the word out quickly.
- DJs are posting playlists to share with each other and record companies, getting ideas for shows from each other and discovering artists and recordings they wouldn't otherwise know about.
- Songwriters are collaborating by e-mail by exchanging Midi song and sound files.

Most of superhighway traffic today is still just e-mail or in text form and the many frustrations of the UNIX operating system have so far kept many people away from the Internet. (The UNIX operating system was developed by Bell Labs to enable Internet communication. It is a "command-line interface," meaning you have to understand the UNIX language to operate it. In contrast, the Web is accessed in a point-and-click [or mouse-driven] environment not a command- or keyboard-driven one.) Other Net tools (e.g., ftp or file transfer protocol) allow users to browse and search distant public and private databases in order to download text, graphics and audio files. The one new Internet tool that's opening up unprecedented possibilities for artist promotion and music marketing is the World Wide Web (WWW), which integrates text, full-color graphics, movies and CD-quality sound into multimedia documents. Thanks to an intuitive interface and the widespread availability of "browsers" like Netscape and Mosaic for the Mac and PC, the WWW is growing faster than any other Internet service. Users typically come away from their first Web experience awestruck.

A number of commercial services have grown up lately that serve as "sites" from which musicians and others can promote their wares. Here are a few that stand out.

One of the first on the scene was IUMA, the Internet Underground Music Archive, started by two computer science students from the University of California, Santa Cruz. The two view their enterprise as a means for up-and-coming acts to find an audience among the estimated 40 million worldwide Net users. If the idea catches on, they believe IUMA can become a full-fledged alternative distribution system, offering entire albums at minimal costs to users. One can browse the IUMA site for free (http://www.iuma.com) but musicians are charged a $120 "donation" to place a song in the Archive. Internet users can download the music for free using a PC, a modem, Internet access, a sound card, and some software—which is available free on the Internet—to decompress the sound files. IUMA also offers fulfillment for record and merchandise ordering. For further information on IUMA call (408) 426-4862.

On the East Coast alternative music projects will find a ready home in New York's SonicNet. SonicNet is a multifunction system geared to serve the needs of both the business and consumer ends of the indie music spectrum. There are, for instance, maps to several hundred clubs that a band booked for its first gig in an unfamiliar town can access; there are also online discussion forums that fans can tap into. A forum, called "Demo Universe," offers unsigned bands a chance to put their demo tapes on line for review. Subscribers can order tickets to see those bands over the computer network. Admission to the whole raft of SonicNet services costs a mere $10 per month, which includes unlimited access and a free Internet address. SonicNet can be reached at (212) 941-5912 or check out their site at http://www.sonicnet.com.

Some sites have developed beyond music to become more comprehensive "cybervenues" for the arts. This is where you'll find both Kaleidospace and Millennium Productions, two of the first complete multimedia systems to allow artists to buy and sell their products over the Internet. Both sites are multiarts, allowing dancers, film makers, visual artists, writers, etc. as well as musicians, an opportunity to develop an Internet strategy and presence. Kaleidospace is described by cofounder Jeannie Novak as "a Multimedia Online Marketplace" (MOM), a virtual shopping mall and electronic bazaar on the Net. You can check out their Web site at http://kspace.com.

Cosponsored by *Musician* magazine, Millennium Productions' Music House, is even more ambitious, offering its services in sixteen languages and giving artists and businesses options in CD-ROM and software development as well. A key purpose of the Music House is to be an artist and small business development site for the music community. Besides a rich database of contact information you'll also find a variety of useful resources and links to other informational sites on the Web. The Music House can be accessed on the Web at http://www.arts-online.com.

With all of the above services musicians and songwriters are able to showcase their CDs through 15- or 30-second soundbytes. Additional promotional information, such as bios and video footage may also be displayed. Users interested in the products can fill out electronic order forms and send them over the Net. Orders are also accepted by phone, fax or U.S. mail. This way anyone who sees and hears your songs and wants to buy your CD or cassette can place an order directly with you, the artist. Some services also offer order fulfillment for the artist who doesn't want to be bothered with the mechanics of the selling process. Another cool service all the above companies provide are "statistical reports" which tell you how many people browsed your site and from whence they came, a feature traditional advertising can never deliver. This service is an option and costs extra.

Musicians are charged a nominal fee (anywhere from $200 to $400 per year) to promote their music this way. Artists retain full rights to their work and pay a periodic fee, rather than losing a major percentage of their unit sales to a large company. It's comparable to placing magazine ads, or commercials on television, except much cheaper. Plus your work gets to be seen and heard in a way not currently possible in those traditional types of media. Kaleidospace (jeannie@kspace.com) can be phoned in L.A. at (310) 399-4349. Millennium Productions' Music House (music@arts-online.com) in Cambridge MA, can be reached at (617) 577-8585.

These are just a few (albeit the original) of the many music-related sites spinning their way onto the World Wide Web. All major labels either have or are about to debut their own Web sites. Indies like Mammoth, Windham Hill, Higher Octave, Curve of the Earth, and Rykodisc all have cyber equivalents. Performance rights societies BMI and ASCAP have theirs, as do record chains Tower Records and the recently debuted Newbury Comics (titled "Newbury Comics Interactive"). Radio shows and networks are joining the action fast and furious, especially with the advent of "RealAudio" which allows AM quality sound transmission in real time over the Internet. Some smart music entrepreneurs are specializing in niches based on their own particular expertise. For example, Berklee College of Music faculty member Rob Jaczko brings his recording studio background to his "On-Site Entertainment," a Web site that showcases entertainment industry production services (studios, equipment manufacturers, etc.). The URLs (uniform resource locators) for all of the above sites can be found in the resource box accompanying this article.

DO-IT-YOURSELF WEB PAGE DESIGN

The benefits of going with a commercial music site provider are many: you get a built-in music-loving audience, Web design expertise, in-house familiarity with the online music market, and relatively inexpensive disc storage space for your data. But say you wanted to go it alone and design your own Web pages. What would you need? Your Web page construction should cost no more than $100 and about a week's time, depending on the information included, the complexity of the design and how long it takes you to learn HTML. Here is a list of things you'll need to create your own Web page:

- A computer and a modem. For best results, use a 486, Pentium or PowerMac with at least a 14.4 Kbps (kilobytes per second) modem. Anything less powerful can make cruising the Web feel more like creeping in rush-hour traffic.
- An HTML editor. A top-notch HTML (hypertext markup language) editor will give personality to the text of your Web page. HTML is essentially plain ASCII text (straight text without any formatting codes; available in most word-processing programs as a "save as" option) with embedded codes that enable you to create links, fill-in forms and clickable images—all elements of a great Web page.
- A Web Browser. Almost any browser will do—Netscape, Mosaic, Air Mosaic—even the ones built into the commercial online services, such as CompuServe. The only requirement is that the browser include an option that allows you to view files stored on your computer's hard drive before you add them to your Web pages.
- Graphics software. If you want your Web page to get noticed, it has to have cool graphics. You'll either have to create them yourself or find a good clip art program. You'll also need a graphic converter program, such as HiJaak Pro, to convert images you've created into GIF and JPEG formats that Web browsers use.
- A PPP or SLIP connection. This is your connection to the Internet's World Wide Web. You can obtain a SLIP or PPP connection through an Internet

service provider, such as Netcom, PSI or Holonet (see resource box). This is the most expensive part of setting up your Web page, so shop around.

There is a lot of help out there for amateur web page designers. Shareware (free) programs can be downloaded from:

http://www.oamag.com/online/access.html.

Keeping updated on the cool tips and tricks requires a little more effort, but you can learn a lot by seeing what other Web masters are doing on their pages.

SEVEN TIPS FOR CREATING A GREAT WEB PAGE

1) Get organized. Start visualizing your Web page before you ever turn on the computer. Think about what you want to put on your home page, what you want the reader to get out of it, how the information will relate and how you want everything to look. Some Web experts recommend creating a storyboard—small sketches of each page in outline form—before you start writing.

2) Give people a reason to visit. Don't waste people's time with a page that provides only a list of links to other Web sites. For example, if you're an avid blues lover and want to create a Web page on the subject, tell visitors where the best blues clubs are in your area and provide directions. Pull people in with useful information.

3) Keep it simple. The home page is to the rest of your Web site as a book's cover is to its contents. The design should be bold and understandable at a glance. Don't clutter it up with unnecessary details or overcomplicated layouts.

4) Get visual. Use imaginative layouts and good-looking typography to give your Web pages a unique and identifiable look. Graphical content should be of some practical value. Avoid empty window dressing. To save time, many users set their browsers to ignore graphics; all they see is text. It's essential that any important messages or links contained in graphics be duplicated in textual form. Test-drive your page in text-only mode to make sure it works.

5) Make it easy to navigate. One of the home page's primary roles is as a navigational tool, pointing people to information stored on your Web site or elsewhere. Make this function as effortless as possible. Also, don't bury information too deep in the page hierarchy. Sometimes to get to the thing you want to view on the Web you have to wade through "teaser" pages containing abbreviated information—it's a drag and time consuming. Stepping through five or more links can get pretty tedious.

6) Include the essentials. Here are a few things most every home page should have: a header that identifies your Web site clearly and unmistakably, an e-mail address for reporting problems, copyright information as it applies to online content, and contact information, such as mailing address and phone number.

7) Keep it fresh. Users get jaded if your Web site never changes. Encourage return visits by giving them something new to look forward to. Include your Web site in your established publicity program, so that new information (such as press releases), appears concurrently on your Web pages.

Getting involved in newsgroups and mailing lists or utilizing the resources mentioned in the Yahoo! directory will also go a long way toward keeping you abreast of the developments in HTML authoring. Books like Laura Lemay's *Teach Yourself Web Publishing with HTML in a Week* (SAMS Publishing) and Ian Graham's *HTML Sourcebook* (John Wiley & Sons, Inc.) will answer most of the do-it-yourselfer's questions about building a Web page. Yahoo! is a searchable, browsable hierarchical index of the Internet featuring over 13,000 entries located at:

http//www.yahoo.com/Computers/World_Wide_Web/Authoring/
Once you've finished your masterpiece, you'll need to transfer the files you created to your Internet access provider's Web server. This usually means that your access provider opens an account on its file server for you. Then you use the Internet ftp (file transfer protocol) function to upload your home page files to the Internet provider's computer. Voila. Your home page lives. One final note: In order to let people know that you've got a Web page up and running, you may consider registering it with a personal home page listing service, such as Who's Who on the Internet (http://web.city.ac.uk/citylive/pages.html).

MARKETING MUSIC ON THE NET

When it comes to marketing, the Net is a "soft sell" medium. Unlike traditional media (television, radio, magazines, etc.) which push information at us, the Internet pulls us in through the added dimension of interactivity. While traditional media is unidirectional, the Net is bidirectional and, as such, is revolutionary.

You sell on the Net by providing useful information to people. For example, say you're a rock band from Boston. Instead of just promoting yourself and your CD, you can also have some cool, hard-to-find information about Boston at your site (e.g., a list of your favorite live music clubs with reasons why). Don't forget, people will be checking you out from all over the world and some inside information about Boston's music scene will be much appreciated by the out-of-towner.

Record labels, retailers, manufacturers and talent agencies can also use the Net to increase their customer base and market their wares. The Web, in particular, offers a powerful forum to dispense product and service information, raise awareness, and generate brand loyalty in a global environment. Online marketing offers some significant advantages over traditional ads and catalogs:

- You are not limited by the price of printing and postage, which makes online selling extremely economical.
- You can change your content quickly, easily and at virtually no cost.
- An online catalog is easily searchable. All shoppers have to do is type in a key word or two to get the information they want.
- Technology allows you to offer audio and video clips with product demonstrations for deeper marketing.
- You can provide your customers with an essentially infinite amount of product information.
- The cost per exposure/per month is extremely reasonable compared to full-page print ads.

The Net is also a great medium for offering customer service, dispensing company information and even soliciting employees and interns. Any business with a mail-order component is especially well-positioned for online success. If it will sell in a mail-order catalog, it will work on the Internet.

HOW TO GET STARTED

So how does a band or music entrepreneur get started with this new medium? First, total up everything you've spent this past year on promotion and marketing—paper, copying, postage, gas, phone, etc., etc. What did you come up with? $500? $1000? $2000? Now realize that a small piece of this can get you a presence on a medium that's always turned on and that reaches millions around the globe. Here are some simple steps to help you get acquainted with the Net as a new promotional tool:

1. See the Net firsthand. The first and best thing to do is play on the Internet yourself. This will give you a sense of the possibilities. For newbies (beginners) the Web is probably the easiest entry point. There are a lot of other areas to explore on the Net but they can wait. Either set up your own hardware for an Internet connection (see the Getting Wired box below) or go check it out at a friend's house or office that's connected. You can also visit one of the many "cyber cafes" where, for a few bucks, you can explore the Web while sipping your mocha latte. Remember, this is an *emerging* technology. There are few rules and those that do exist grow more flexible every day. You yourself can contribute to the Net's overall makeup and development as you apply your imagination to the medium's vast possibilities.

2. Decide what you want to do on the Net. Are you interested in posting notice of some high-profile gig you're involved in or just generally promoting your band? Do you want to communicate via e-mail with your customers or is a "snail-mail" (U.S. mail) address sufficient? How about actually selling your tape or CD over the Net? Most artists choose to post their electronic press kit: bio, gig schedule, photo, album art, press reviews, soundbyte and video clip (if available). Including all contact information enables people to contact you if they like what they see and hear (and sometimes if they don't!) Remember, the Net is worldwide. At Millennium's Music House, artists have received e-mail all the way from Spain, New Zealand, Russia, Bombay and the Caribbean.

Also, think about how Internet marketing fits in with your traditional marketing mix of advertising, mailers, performances, press and airplay. The Net shouldn't *replace* these ongoing efforts but *enhance* them.

3. Choose an IPP (Internet Presence Provider) and a site location for your home page *carefully*. A presence provider (different from an *access* provider which helps you get connected) acts like a design house for your site. It can digitize your music and video, scan your graphics and translate your bio and everything else into hypertext markup language (HTML) so it's readable on the Web. HTML is relatively easy to learn which has resulted in a sudden explosion of people willing to "do your home page." But watch out. There's a lot more to effective Web design than mere HTMLing. Layout, color, tone, backgrounds, ease of navigation, clarity and uniqueness are other components that make a Web site shine rather than merely exist. And with thousands of new web sites coming online every month, it's more and more important to really shine.

Once your Page is designed you'll need a server to store it on so it can be seen. Most IPPs also have a server and a Web site where you can post your home page. For example, IUMA and Millennium Productions provide both Web design and site presence.

THE MUSICIAN'S BUSINESS AND LEGAL GUIDE

Some model themselves after stores or malls. Others choose a magazine format. Still others seek to create the atmosphere of a club.

The key thing to look for in a site is traffic. After all, why be sitting on a site no one visits? Fortunately, with the Internet you can know exactly how many times your page is seen. These viewings are called "hits" in Net parlance and a web site's traffic is measured by how many hits it gets in a given day or week. But this can be deceiving. Some equate hits with people whereas in actuality a hit is a "click," the action of clicking on an image or "link" on a web page. Since most people average seven clicks per visit, the overall hits should be divided by at least this number to obtain a realistic measure of site traffic.

Look for extra values when choosing a site—contests, promotional opportunities, cyberpublicity, order fulfillment, statistical reporting, helpful information, special programs, etc. For example, Kaleidospace sponsors an Artist-in-Residence program where, once a month, a high-profile artist's work is featured prominently on their site. Millennium's Music House artists are all in the running for inclusion in an annual review by its industry A&R board. The ten winners receive a write-up in *Musician* magazine. The key is to get the most mileage you can out of your site.

4. Finally, seek ways to maximize your online presence. Once you're residing on a chosen site (or a number of sites—this is possible too), use your new Internet address on all your mailers, flyers, album and tape covers, photos and business cards. Send out a special press release to everyone on your media, fan and industry mailing list letting them know you've gone online. Remember, one of the Net's key features is interactivity. Contests, polls, trivia questions and other devices get browsers involved and interested. Use you imagination and work with your IPP to design these elements for your page.

HOW TO CHOOSE AN INTERNET ACCESS PROVIDER

Request information from various providers and then ask the following questions:

- What's the total cost? The true cost of Internet service is made up of several elements: a monthly charge, which may include a fixed or unlimited number of hours online; a fixed hourly charge for additional time; and a charge for the connection itself, which may require long-distance telephone calls or access through a data network such as Sprintnet.
- Can you connect easily? The lowest cost is not always the best choice. If you spend more time listening to busy signals than you do online, it's time to cancel your account. System downtime also holds up connections. It's true that modems, servers, and routers sometimes fail, but if you suffer frequent and prolonged stretches of time when the system does not answer, you need a different service provider.
- Is support available? Is it useful? Sooner or later, you'll need some kind of hand-holding. You might want to configure a new modem, or a program that has worked flawlessly for months might mysteriously die. What happens when you call for help? Calls to tech support tend to come in bunches, especially when some part of the service provider's setup crashes. If you can't get an immediate answer, will someone return your call within a couple of hours?
- What kind of extra services do you get? Many service providers offer a plain connection and nothing more, but if you look around, you might find some extras. For example, some accounts include space on a Web server or an

FTP server. Other providers offer their own conferences or newsgroups, or a toll-free telephone number for access from out of town. Especially in competitive markets like Seattle and Boston, it's worth asking about extras. And don't ignore the commercial online services. Some hard-core Internet heads may sneer at @aol.com or @prodigy.com e-mail addresses, but these services are relatively easy to use, and their prices can be competitive with those of other Internet access providers.

NATIONAL INTERNET ACCESS PROVIDERS

HOLONET—(510) 704-0160
INTERNET EXPRESS—(800) 592-1240
PERFORMANCE SYSTEMS INTERNATIONAL (PSI)—(800) 827-7482
NETCOM—(800) 501-8649; e-mail: info@netcom.com

There may be local Internet access providers in your area. Check with your local computer user groups and/or computer stores to get information.

INTERNET RESOURCES

Each listing below is followed by its URL (Uniform Resource Locator). This is the company's World Wide Web address. "HTTP" stands for HyperText Transfer Protocol and it allows World Wide Web pages to be transferred over the Net. With a Netscape browser (downloadable at the Netscape site http://www.netscape.com) you don't have to type the "http://" prefix anymore; Netscape automatically resolves it. Mosaic and other browsers still require it. URLs, phone numbers and addresses are current as of this writing, however, they are subject to change.

Music Web Sites Sampler
(Note: Additional Internet resources can be found in the resource directory at the back of this book.)
One of the most comprehensive lists of music-related Internet sites can be found at
http://www.music.indiana.edu/misc.music_resources.html

Indie Record Labels
Mammoth Records—http://www.nando.net/mammoth/mammoth.html
Higher Octave—http://www.smartworld.com/hioctave/
Rykodisc—http://www.rykodisc.com
Curve of the Earth—http://www.mw3.com/curve/
Q-Records—http://www.shore.net/~qdiv/qrec.htm

Major Record Labels
SONY—http://www.music.sony.com
Warner Bros. Records—http://www.iuma.com/warner/
MCA—http://www.mca.com
Polygram—http://polygram.com

Musician Sites Mentioned in Chapter
IUMA (Internet Underground Music Archive), 303 Potrero, #7A, Santa Cruz CA 95060.
(408) 426-IUMA. http://www.iuma.com
E-mail: info@iuma.com

The Music House (Millennium Productions), 41 Second St., Ste. 333, Cambridge MA
02142. (617) 577-8585. http://www.arts-online.com
E-mail: music@arts-online.com

Kaleidospace, PO Box 341556, Los Angeles CA 90034. (310) 399-4349.
http://kspace.com
E-mail: pete@kspace.com

Sonicnet, 67 Vestry St., New York NY 10013. (212) 941-5912. http://www.sonicnet.com
E-mail: info@sonicnet.com

MUSIC UNIONS

by James A. Sedivy and Gregory T. Victoroff

Union members have greater negotiating strength than do individuals. A labor union is a group of people that have joined together to demand better pay and working conditions. A music union is a labor union whose membership is comprised of musicians. This chapter discusses many of the rules and benefits of the two major U.S. music unions, the American Federation of Musicians (AFM) and the American Federation of Television and Radio Artists (AFTRA). The American Guild of Musical Artists (AGMA)represents vocalists in the fields of opera, classical music and ballet. The Screen Actors Guild (SAG) represents vocalists that sing in theatrical motion pictures. These unions will not be reviewed in this chapter, however, if you need to contact them, their addresses and phone numbers are included in the resource directory at the back of this book.

American Federation of Musicians of the United States and Canada, AFL-CIO, CLC

The AFM is one of the largest unions of performing artists, with over 400 Locals and more than 150,000 members.

AFM members are instrumentalists, leaders, contractors, orchestrators, copyists, music librarians, arrangers and proofreaders. They work in all mediums of music including, live performance, television, movies, etc.

American Federation of Television and Radio Artists, AFL-CIO

AFTRA members are singers, sound effects artists, actors, announcers and narrators, working in radio, television and phonograph recording.

Locals

The AFM and AFTRA are comprised of local unions and governing organizations known as the International Executive Board (AFM) and the National Board (AFTRA). They grant charters to "locals" in certain geographic areas, like Los Angeles, Detroit or Nashville. AFTRA locals are usually referred to by the name of the community, whereas AFM locals are given numbers. Each local is basically autonomous and independent from other locals and the International Board or National Board, so some pay rates, such as live performance rates, and benefits vary from local to local.

SIGNATORY COMPANIES

Every two to five years, music employers, such as record companies and television and movie producers, negotiate contracts (agreements) with the AFM, AFTRA and SAG.

A music employer who signs an agreement promises to hire only union members and provide at least the minimum pay and working conditions set forth in the agreement. The employer signing the agreement is called a signatory company. If you are employed by a nonsignatory company, such as a small record label or nonunion bar or restaurant, you may be violating union rules and receiving less than union approved pay or scale. In so doing, you may also be undermining the bargaining strength of the union and its members. Union locals can tell you whether or not your employer is a signatory company.

Membership Benefits

No union can promise professional success, especially in the highly competitive music industry, which is subject to ever changing tastes and trends. Nevertheless, union membership does offer certain opportunities for career advancement and some very real benefits. The most important of which is your eligibility for employment by signatory companies.

The benefits you get by joining a union depend on the strength of the particular union and local. For example, AFM Local 47 in Los Angeles provides job referrals for professional bands and musicians; death benefit group insurance; legal counsel and representation in grievance and arbitration proceedings; credit union membership; notary public service and business discounts; scholarship and awards programs; listings and information on agents, managers, record companies, casual leaders, nightclubs, studio contractors and community orchestras; club memberships, social activities and monthly membership meetings; a disabled musicians' fund; subscription to Local 47's monthly newspaper and *International Musician,* the AFM newspaper; a 24-hour telephone assistance line; contract preparation and consultation in areas concerning your musical career; free help wanted and audition notices; rehearsal space; and low-cost instrument insurance. If a person fails to pay you for your services, the union will attempt to collect your money without any cost to you. Also, through the Booking Agent Agreement, commissions charged by booking agents are limited to 15% to 20%.

Recording Contracts

Another good reason to join a music union is a common provision in recording contracts between musicians and record companies that are signatories to AFM or AFTRA Agreements:

"Artist represents that during the term of this recording agreement, Artist is and will remain or will promptly become and remain a member in good standing of any applicable guild and/or union to the extent that Company may legally require such membership. All applicable provisions of the collective bargaining Agreement to which Company is a party shall be deemed a part of this Agreement and shall be incorporated herein by reference."

This provision obligates a signatory record company to pay you at least minimum union pay or scale for recording sessions (as well as providing other benefits), after you become a union member.

AGREEMENTS

The following sections discuss most of the major AFM and AFTRA agreements that control phonograph recordings, movies, television, commercials and live performance. In calculating your minimum scale be sure to refer to the correct and current agreement.

Also, the different payments for recording, production, sideline musicians, contractors, leaders, instrumentalists and vocalists are found in each agreement. Although these scales change periodically, many of the "terms of art" have the same meaning from one agreement to another. When an agreement expires and is not extended, the expired terms and conditions are usually followed until a new agreement can be negotiated and signed.

Funds

In addition to pay scales, some union agreements also require employers to pay money to various funds. Depending on the particular fund, the money is used for pension, welfare and retirement benefits, payments to recording members, to members that perform in videos, and to members that perform free live concerts in parks, veterans' hospitals, schools and other public places.

TERMS OF ART

As with all professions, union musicians share certain terms of art: ordinary words that have special meanings, which derive from the various union agreements discussed in this chapter. Common terms of art used throughout the AFM Agreements follow:

Contractor

A contractor's duties are to locate and hire musicians for particular jobs. The contractor will prepare the contracts and make sure that they are filed with the union. A contractor need not be a musician, but must attend the engagement. Contractors may also be responsible for rehearsals.

Leader

When a musical group is hired one of the members is designated as the leader. The leader is responsible for the group and is the person who deals directly with the employer. The leader must file the contracts with the union and collect payment from the employer. If the leader fails to collect payment and fails to report the uncollected payment to the union, the leader may be personally liable to the other union members for the uncollected amount.

Arranging

This is the art of preparing and adjusting an already written composition for presentation in other than its original form. This includes reharmonization, paraphrasing and/or development of a composition so as to fully present its melodic, harmonic and rhythmic structure.

Orchestrating

The orchestrator is the person who writes the musical score (a written musical composition that indicates the part to be performed by each voice and instrument) of an arrangement without changing or adding to the melodies, counter-melodies, harmonies and rhythms.

AFM SCALE: RECORDINGS

One of the fundamental things a union does is establish minimum pay rates for its members. Remember that these rates are minimum and you are free to negotiate higher pay.

Called "scales," "rates," "union fees," or "minimums," they all mean money paid to you (the member), at a variable minimum rate established in the applicable agreement. For the sake of consistency, throughout this article, these minimum payments will be called scales. Examples of the various scales appearing throughout this article are current only as of this writing and are included for illustrative purposes only and should not be relied upon. Always consult your local for current scale.

The AFM Phonograph Record Labor Agreement sets scale for instrumentalists, leaders, contractors, arrangers, orchestrators and copyists working in the phonograph recording industry. Vocalists are paid according to scales set by AFTRA.

Session Scales

For instrumentalists, leaders and contractors the AFM sets basic scale and overtime scale for regular sessions (three hours) and special sessions (one and one-half hours). You can also get premium scale for work done during specified holidays, at odd hours (between midnight and 8:00 a.m.), and after 1:00 p.m. on Saturdays and Sundays. The rates are different for symphonic and nonsymphonic work. As of this writing, the basic regular session scale is $263.81. Leaders and contractors get double scale.

Doubling, Cartage and Electronic Instruments

Additional payments may be paid if you play more than one instrument during a session. This is called doubling. If you play an electronic device to simulate sounds of instruments in addition to the normal sound of the instrument to which the electronic device is attached or applied, such use is treated as a double. For the first double you get an additional 20% of the applicable session scale, and 15% more for each additional double. You may also be entitled to compensation for cartage (hauling) if an employer requires you to bring a heavy instrument to a session. If you bring a large or heavy piece of equipment, such as a harp, you are entitled to an additional $30. If you bring a string bass, tuba, drum set or amplifier you are entitled to an additional $6.

Orchestrators, Etc.

Arrangers', orchestrators' and copyists' scales are set according to a detailed pay schedule based on the extent of the work done, per page or per line, or sometimes hourly. For example, page rates for orchestrators depend on what you do: For transcribing a melody from voice, instrument or mechanical device, including chords, symbols and lyrics (one staff) you get $37.13 for the first page (up to 32 bars) and $26.52 for each additional page. Arrangers usually negotiate their own rates, based in part on orchestrators' rates. Copyists get paid at least $17.68 per hour, or per page, according to certain detailed criteria set forth in the agreement.

Dubbing

The AFM discourages dubbing (using recordings not originally released in phonograph records [such as a film soundtrack] in a phonograph recording or using a recording made at an earlier time in a present recording). These rules relate to recordings that contain performances by persons covered by any AFM Phonograph Record Labor Agreement since January 1954. Dubbing is allowed where the record company notifies the union and pays the current scale to the artist who made the original recording that is being used.

Royalty Artists

When it comes to overdubbing, tracking, sweetening or playing multiple parts there are special provisions for "royalty artists." The AFM considers you a royalty artist if you record pursuant to a recording contract, which pays you royalties of at least 3% of the suggested retail price of records sold or, you are a member of a self-contained group of two or more, performing together in fields other than phonograph records under a group name (like a band or orchestra that performs live) and the group is under a recording agreement, which provides for a royalty payment of at least 3% of the suggested retail price of records sold. As a royalty artist, you receive the basic session rate per song for the first session at which you perform in respect to each song. This applies whether or not you play multiple parts, double, overdub or sweeten.

Personal Services Contract

The AFM bylaws do not allow you to enter into any personal service contract (such as a recording contract) for any period of more than five years without the approval of the AFM. This is true even in states such as California, where the maximum length of a personal service contract is allowed, by law, to be longer.

Recoupable Payments

Most recording agreements allow record companies to recoup recording costs from artists' royalties. A record company may seek to include all payments made to the AFM as recoupable recording costs. However, payments made by the record company under the Phonographic Record Trust Agreement and Phonograph Record Manufacturers Special Fund Agreement, which are based on record sales, are not properly recoupable as recording costs.

Music Performance Trust Fund

The Phonographic Record Trust Agreement requires signatory record companies to pay the trustee of the agreement .20475% of the suggested retail price of records and tapes (to a maximum suggested retail price of $8.98) for each sold; (or in the case of compact discs, a maximum retail price of $10.98). This money is used for the presentation of free live concerts in parks, veterans' hospitals, schools and other public places. During a recent fiscal year, the Music Performance Trust Fund paid union musicians over $13 million to perform these concerts, making the AFM the largest employer of musicians in the world.

Phonographic Record Manufacturers Special Payments Fund Agreement (February 1987) (PRMSP Fund)

This agreement requires record companies to pay a small percentage of the price of each record sold (about 5 cents for a top priced LP) to the PRMSP Fund. The money in this fund is paid annually, to members, in amounts determined by the number of union recording sessions each has played during the year. For example, during a recent fiscal year the Special Payments Fund distributed more than $9 million among approximately 26,000 recording musicians.

Video Promo Supplement

The Phonograph Record Labor Agreement also provides that musicians, which appear in music videos, be compensated when the video incorporates a recording produced by a signatory record company.

Musicians other than royalty artists that perform on camera are paid $188.04 per day.

If the record company receives money from the licensing, sale, or leasing of the video, the company pays the AFM 1% of revenues received after the company has recouped $75,000. This is distributed among all the musicians involved in producing the recording used in the video.

If the record company sells the video as a videodisc or videocassette in the consumer market, it must pay $500 to the AFM after the company has received $5,000 in revenues from sales. The $500 is considered an advance against the 1% payment revenue required after $75,000 is recouped.

AFM SCALE: MOVIES

The AFM Theatrical Motion Picture Agreement defines and sets different scales for recording, production, and sideline musician members.

Recording Scale

If you play on the recording of a movie soundtrack, you are entitled to receive recording scale. The scale depends on the number of musicians employed, with the highest rate being for a group of 23 musicians or less. There are separate rates for single sessions (three hours or less) and double sessions (six hours or less) with overtime rates as well. You are also entitled to additional pay if you are asked to double. If there are 23 or fewer musicians employed, you get $230.90 for a single session and $461.79 for a double session.

Production Scale

Musicians are paid production scale when they perform at rehearsals for a movie. These musicians do not record on the soundtrack or appear on camera and are paid either single session or double session scale. Scales are quoted in the agreement for longer rehearsal periods of 30 or 40 hours per week. For a single session, $121.80; for a double session, $219.28. For a 30-hour week $974.45; for a 40-hour week, $1,169.33.

Sideline Scale

Sideline musicians appear on camera but do not record. The basic scale is $142.76 for a minimum of eight hours. You are also paid extra for time spent in costume fittings, interviews, wardrobe and makeup.

Orchestrators, etc.

Scale for orchestrators, copyists, proofreaders and music librarians, per page, hourly and weekly, are set forth in the Theatrical Motion Picture Agreement. An orchestrator who writes a score page of not more than 13 lines is paid $20.82 per page.

Music Sound Consultant

If you are not a conductor, leader or contractor and are assigned by a producer to advise on the sound quality of the music being recorded you are entitled to $46.98 per hour.

Overscale Employees

By individual negotiations between you and a producer, it can be agreed that any payment you receive, which is in excess of the minimum scale, be applied to any of the minimum payments, premiums, allowance, doubling, penalties, overtime or other minimum requirements of the agreement.

Theatrical Motion Picture Special Payments Fund

This agreement requires a signatory movie producer to make residual payments to the AFM on behalf of musicians who perform on the film soundtrack. One to 1-2/3% of the producer's accountable receipts from the exhibition of the motion picture on free television and supplemental markets (i.e., videocassettes, pay-type CATV, pay television) must be paid to the Theatrical Motion Picture Special Payments Fund. The administrator of the fund then pays you a percentage of these receipts based on a detailed formula set forth in the agreement.

AFM SCALE: TELEVISION

The AFM Television, Videotape Agreement sets scale for network and syndicated television, both live and taped.

Types of Programs

In this agreement, the AFM sets rates according to the type and length of the television program. Signatory producers of 30-, 60- or 90-minute television programs, classified as variety programs, strip variety programs, nonprime-time children's variety shows, and other types, pay different rates to AFM members.

Recording Scale

You are entitled to recording scale if you actually play on the recording of the television program soundtrack. Scale is set according to the length of the program and session. For a 90-minute variety program, not a strip show (i.e., not a daily program like The Tonight Show), such as a Bob Hope Special, the scale is $473.25.

Production Scale

If you play for rehearsals only and do not record on the program's soundtrack and do not appear on camera, you are entitled to production scale. The hourly rate, for a minimum session of two hours is $55.15.

Orchestrators, etc.

If you render services as an orchestrator or copyist, you are entitled to the per page or hourly scale set forth in the agreement. An orchestrator who writes a score page of not more than 10 lines is paid $21.15 per page.

Reuse Fees

The AFM Videotape Agreement also requires employers to pay reuse fees for reruns of programs. If a program is rerun in the United States or Canada, the instrumentalists, leader, contractor and music sound consultant receive 75% of the original scale payment for the second and third run; 50% for the fourth, fifth and sixth runs; 10% for the seventh run and 5% for each additional run. There are separate schedules covering payments for foreign broadcasts.

AFM SCALE: MOVIES MADE FOR TELEVISION

The AFM Television Film Labor Agreement sets rates for movies made for TV, situation comedies and dramatic series (e.g., *NYPD Blue*). These programs are shot on film or tape and are broadcast on free commercial television first. As with the Basic Theatrical Motion Picture and Television Videotape Agreements, the TV Film Labor Agreement has separate wage scales for recording, production and sideline musicians, orchestrators, copyists and music librarians.

Recording Scale

If you play on the soundtrack recording of a program covered by this agreement, you are entitled to recording scale. For a single session of three hours, scale is $200.77. For a double session, $401.52.

Production Scale

If you play at rehearsals but are not recorded and do not appear on camera, you are entitled to receive nonrecording production scale. Scale for a single session (up to three hours) is $121.80. A double session (up to six hours) is $219.28.

Sideline Scale

If you appear on camera, but are not recorded, you are a sideline musician and are entitled to $142.76 for a minimum eight-hour session.

Orchestrators, etc.

If you render services as an orchestrator, arranger, copyist, music librarian or proofreader on a TV movie, situation comedy or dramatic series you are entitled to minimum rates set forth in the agreement. An orchestrator who writes a score page of not more than 13 lines is paid $20.82 per page.

Television Film Producers Special Payments Fund

Residuals of 1% of producers' accountable receipts from the distributors of TV movies in supplemental markets (i.e., cassettes, pay-type CATV and pay television) are paid by producers to the Motion Picture and Television Producers Special Payments Fund, which is distributed to you according to the formula set forth in the fund agreement.

AFM NONSTANDARD TELEVISION (PAY TELEVISION) AGREEMENT

This agreement covers cable TV, pay or subscription TV, pay cable TV and closed-circuit TV. It provides rates for recording and production musicians, orchestrators, arrangers, copyists and music librarians, which are calculated in the same manner as the Television and Videotape Agreement. For example, for a one-hour variety program, other than a strip program, for a minimum eight-hour session, the recording scale is $369.55. The rehearsal scale is $64.50 per hour, with a two-hour minimum.

AFM NATIONAL PUBLIC TELEVISION AGREEMENT

This agreement sets minimum rates for the services of instrumentalists, leaders, contractors (varying as to the length of the program) and arrangers, orchestrators, copyists and librarians. An instrumentalist performing in one one-hour program is entitled to $133.50.

Supplemental Market Fees

This agreement calls for supplemental market fees (i.e., cassettes, pay-type CATV, pay television and in-flight [commercial airlines, trains, ships and busses] exhibitions).

Reuse Fees

Reuse payments must be made by signatory producers, to the AFM, for subsequent broadcast cycles. If a producer elects to pay the instrumentalist under the higher of two wage scales, the program may be exhibited for a longer initial release period. Following the initial release, the producer must pay reuse fees, to the AFM, on behalf of the musicians. The exact amounts are calculated according to a formula set forth in the agreement.

AFM SCALE: COMMERCIALS

The AFM Television and Radio Commercial Announcements Agreement sets scales, which are usually paid by the signatory advertising agency making the commercial.

Session Scale

The Commercials Agreement calls for a minimum session for instrumentalists, leaders and contractors of one hour, during which three different commercial announcements may be recorded, the total length of which may not exceed three minutes. The maximum rate varies as to the number of musicians at the session. For example, for the minimum session, for one musician, you are entitled to $172, and if there are two to four musicians, $86.

Synthesizers Prohibited

This agreement (like the Theatrical Motion Picture Agreement) provides that electronic synthesizers and similar devices cannot replace performances by instrumentalists.

Reuse Fees

The initial scale payment allows the commercial's producer to broadcast the commercial by television or radio, but not both, during a period of 13 weeks from the date of first broadcast. Thereafter, you should be paid reuse fees for each additional 13-week cycle. The reuse fee for an instrumentalist who does not double, playing in a combo of two or more musicians, for a national broadcast, is $64.50.

Orchestrators, etc.

You are entitled to specific scale payments set forth in the agreement if you render services as an arranger, orchestrator, copyist or music librarian. An orchestrator who writes a score page of not more than 10 lines is paid $14.91 per page.

AFM SCALE: LIVE PERFORMANCE

The AFM represents instrumentalists and vocalists when they perform live concerts. The individual locals set minimum wage scales and working conditions for nightclubs, hotels and other venues where live music is performed.

Booking Agents Agreement

The AFM Booking Agents Agreement sets limits on the commissions agents may charge members for securing live performance engagements. Approved agent commissions range from 15% to 20% depending on the duration of the employment secured by the agent, provided your net pay, after deducting the agent's commission, is never below scale.

Union Form Contracts

Members are required to use union approved form contracts for their live performances. One advantage of using the union form contracts is the union contract provision requiring the concert promoter or venue owner to pay you interest and attorneys' fees in addition to other damages if you are not paid for your services or the contract is otherwise violated. In California, if you bring an action against a promoter for a breach of the contract and you lose, you will have to pay the promoter's attorneys' fees.

Recording or Broadcasting Prohibited

You are entitled to additional payments if your live performance is recorded (either on audio or video or both), or transmitted on television or radio. For this reason, no live performances may be recorded, reproduced or transmitted without making prior arrangements with the AFM.

Casuals

Casual engagements are one- or two-night performances. The locals negotiate minimum scale for rehearsals and various types of shows including, dance only; dance with an incidental act; show and dance; cocktail hour, tea dance, fashion shows; show with accompanying act; casual concert where admission is charged; and park concerts.

The scale is based on the number of musicians and length of show and includes payment by the employer to the union pension and welfare funds.

Continuous/Extended Engagements

The locals negotiate scale for musicians that are hired for extended live performances. There are separate scales for hotel nightclubs, freestanding nightclubs, and beer and wine establishments. Within each of these scale structures the pay is based upon the number of days per week you perform, the length of each performance and the number of musicians.

Arbitration

The union form contract provides that if any dispute or claim arises out of the engagement covered by the contract, the parties shall submit the matter to either the local's trial board or to an arbitrator who is picked by the parties. In a California lawsuit between Bill Graham, a concert promoter, and Leon Russell, a performer, the court ruled that union arbitration provisions must provide the parties with an opportunity to obtain an unbiased and neutral arbitrator.

AFM DUES
Membership

If you play a musical instrument of any kind or are a vocalist or render musical services for pay, you are classified as a professional musician and you are eligible for membership in the AFM. You may apply for membership in any local in the area where you live.

Initiation Fees

You must pay initiation fees to both the AFM local and to the International Federation. Each local sets its own initiation fee and the International Federation's fee varies according to the amount of the local's fee. You pay the total initiation fees to the local.

Indoctrination

When you apply for AFM membership you must participate in an indoctrination procedure administered by the local. This will introduce you to the rules and benefits of the AFM. The local also holds an examination meeting in which the applicant will be asked for further information about his or her musical education and proficiency. No auditions are required.

Dues—Periodic

You are required to pay annual or semiannual dues to the local and the Federation. For Local 47 the rates are $136 per year or $69 semiannually. These payments include AFM dues. The dues for Local 47 include death benefit group insurance.

Work Dues

You must pay work dues based on your total earnings for all musical services performed. Upon joining the AFM, you must authorize all employers to deduct from your pay the work dues owed, and to remit that amount to your local.

Work dues for Local 47 are 2-1/2% of scale wages for live performances. If services are rendered for any of the various recording sessions (i.e., phonorecord, television, motion picture) the work dues are 4% of scale wages.

If the musician is a traveling member (member of another local), the work dues are paid to the AFM, not to the local where the work took place.

Health and Welfare Funds

Locals use Health and Welfare Funds to provide health insurance benefits for members. To be eligible for these benefits, a total of $400 must be contributed to the Fund by your employers every six months.

Employers Pension and Welfare Fund, Strike Fund

Members can also participate in a Employers Pension and Welfare Fund. Should it be necessary for the union to call a strike, the AFM also maintains a strike fund for its members.

Fines, Defaulters List

Members are not allowed to render services for an employer on the AFM's Defaulters List. It is also improper for members to record or perform for a company which is not a signatory to the AFM Agreement. The union feels that musicians that play for defaulters condone unfair practices and undermine the bargaining power of the union and its members. Also, an AFM member is not permitted to render musical services outside of Canada or the United States, or their territories or possessions, without the approval of the union.

AFTRA SCALE: RECORDINGS

AFTRA Code of Fair Practice for Phonograph Records sets the following scales for the recording industry.

Hourly and Side Scale

Scale under this agreement is determined per hour or per side, whichever is greater. A side is defined as one song or a bona fide medley on a single record not exceeding three and one-half minutes, and for each 60-second portion thereof over three and one-half minutes playing time, an additional 50% of the applicable per side unit is paid. For soloists and duos, the minimum scale is $132.50 per person per hour or side, whichever is greater.

Solo and Group Scale

The individual scale is the same for soloists and duos but is lower for groups of three or more singers. If, however, as a singer in a group of three or more vocalists, you step out and sing 16 or more cumulative bars on a particular side, you are paid at the soloist and duo scale. There are separate scales for vocalists that make classical recordings or original cast show albums.

Dubbing

Under AFTRA rules dubbing is allowed when the record company notifies AFTRA and pays scale to the artists that were involved in making the original recording. The company must also obtain the written consent of any star, featured or overscale artist.

Royalty Artists

The minimum rates mandated by AFTRA are payable even if you are a royalty artist. AFTRA considers you a royalty artist if your recording contract pays you record royalties. As a royalty artist you are not entitled to more than three times the minimum scale per side.

AFTRA SCALE: TELEVISION

AFTRA National Code of Fair Practice for Network Television Broadcasting Agreement sets rates for AFTRA members' services in the television industry.

Solo or Group Scale

The AFTRA Code sets different wage rates for soloists, duos and chorus singers. (An example is in the following paragraph.)

Program Scale

The scale increases for programs with a longer running time. Another variable affecting scale is whether the program is a single performance or multiple performances during a calendar week. The specific scale varies for work that is done on camera, or off camera, and whether or not the program is a dramatic prime time program. For instance, if you sing, on camera, in a group of three to eight singers, in a prime time dramatic program, you are entitled to a program fee of $563.04 per person for a minimum session of three hours.

Replay Fees

For the first and second network replay, you are paid 75% of the applicable minimum program fee plus 20% of the rehearsal and doubling fees for programs originally telecast after November 16, 1976. For all other replays you are paid 75% of the applicable basic minimum program fee for the first and second replay; 50% for the third, fourth and fifth replays, 10% for the sixth replay and 5% for each replay thereafter.

Supplemental Market Fees

Supplemental market fees must be paid by the producer of a program when the program is exhibited on pay television, basic cable or in-flight. The producer pays 2% of the distributor's gross receipts in the supplemental markets. This 2% is paid for the benefit of all performers, except walk-ons and extras. If the program is a network prime time dramatic program produced after July 1, 1983, the producer pays 3.6% of the distributor's gross receipts, rather than 2%. You will receive your portion of these payments directly from the producer or the producer will deposit the fees with AFTRA for distribution to you.

AFTRA SCALE: TELEVISION COMMERCIALS

Signatories to the AFTRA 1994 Television Recorded Commercials Agreement pay the following fees for commercials:

Session Scale

Session scale is based on an eight-hour day. Scale varies for soloists and duos and groups of different sizes when you work on camera. If you work off camera, the minimum session scale is for two hours. For a solo or duo, the off camera scale for a single two-hour session is currently $333.30.

Use Scale

Scale for use of program commercials is divided into classes, according to the number of cities in which it is telecast, (class C is one to five cities, class B is six to 20 cities, class A is over 20 cities.) New York, Chicago and Los Angeles each count as 11 cities.

Principals, Group Rates

Use payments for each class have separate scales for principal performers and group performers and within each of those scales are different rates for on camera and off camera performances, each time the commercial is used. For example, if you are an off camera solo vocalist, your session fee may include payment for the first class A use. For the second class A use, you get an additional $96. For the third through the 13th uses you receive $76.35 each, thereafter you are entitled to $34.65 for each additional use.

AFTRA SCALE: RADIO COMMERCIALS

Signatories to the AFTRA Radio Recorded Commercials Agreement pay for sessions of 90 minutes in duration. Reuse fees under this agreement are affected by many variables, including special scale for wild spots, dealer commercials, network program commercials, regional and network program commercials, single market commercials and foreign uses. Scales are determined according to complex formulas set forth in the agreement.

AFTRA MEMBERSHIP DUES

You are eligible for AFTRA membership if you have performed or intend to perform as a singer in the fields of radio, television or phonograph recording. AFTRA does not regulate the musical services of its members outside the United States.

Initiation Fees

AFTRA's Los Angeles Local imposes an initiation fee of $800, however, this need not be paid when you first work. You have 30 days from your first engagement before the initiation fee and dues are payable.

Dues

Dues are payable semiannually and are based on the performer's gross earnings under AFTRA's jurisdiction for the previous year. They range from $75 to $1,585.

Other AFTRA Benefits

Benefits of the AFTRA Welfare Fund are available if you have $1,000 in earnings within AFTRA's jurisdiction, during any one of four consecutive 12-month earning periods. This fund includes life insurance, accidental death insurance and medical insurance.

The AFTRA Pension Fund provides benefits determined by the number of years you are active with AFTRA and your earnings during those years.

A Dental Assistance Plan is available if you have earnings of $2,500 within AFTRA's jurisdiction, during any one of four consecutive 12-month earning periods. A credit union is also available to AFTRA members.

Discipline

As an AFTRA member, if you violate union rules, you may be disciplined by means of fine, suspension or expulsion from the union.

NEW TECHNOLOGIES

In keeping pace with ever changing technology, AFTRA has recently negotiated an agreement relating to services rendered in the production of interactive programs, the 1994 AFTRA Interactive Media Agreement.

Although the AFM has not yet formulated an interactive agreement, it does negotiate session fees and scales on a project by project basis.

CONCLUSION

For a union to be successful, its members must respect its rules. By reporting unfair practices and conscientiously participating in union activities and elections you help protect other union members and, to an extent, you exercise a degree of control over how the union represents you and protects your interests. The complex array of union scales and payments for royalties, reuses and supplemental markets, were not guaranteed to musicians by employers out of friendship. Unions organized and fought for these payments. As long as enthusiastic and ethical professionals are involved in unions, they will help to ensure fair treatment for all musicians.

MERCHANDISING AGREEMENTS

by Lawrence J. Blake

Merchandising companies regularly pay in excess of $100,000 for the right to sell T-shirts at the concerts of artists that have just released their first record on a major label and may spend millions of dollars to secure that right with respect to superstars.

Merchandising agreements are big business. Superstars can earn royalties on merchandise in excess of $4 per attendee at concerts. Artists of this caliber include U2, Pearl Jam, Michael Jackson, The Rolling Stones, Bruce Springsteen, Guns N' Roses, Metallica, Madonna, etc., and new artists can make lucrative agreements as well.

In my practice we have a nonstop flow of merchandising agreements being drafted and negotiated. Very often these are for artists that have just made their first record album or are about to tour the United States for the first time. Merchandising agreements commonly provide the money for the start-up expenses of an artist's tour. In most instances the artist's recording fund or advance is entirely depleted by the time the album has been delivered. Often, the album is over budget and the record company has been advancing, on a noncontractual basis, the band's living expenses while waiting for the record to be released. Once the album is released, the artist needs to tour extensively and often needs money for new equipment and other expenses to get that tour going. All too often, however, the record company is so far unrecouped that it is unwilling to provide advances for tour support.

FUNDING SOURCES

Generally speaking, the two most likely sources for additional funding are a publishing agreement and/or a merchandising agreement. There is absolutely no doubt that a merchandising agreement should be the artist's first choice. With a customary exclusive songwriting and copublishing agreement, there are substantial and long-term downsides (e.g., the giving up of a substantial portion of publishing income and long-term appreciation in the value of the publishing catalog) in merchandising agreements there typically are no such downsides. The deals are relatively short-term and essentially risk free.

Of course, it is possible, at least for new artists, to sell their own T-shirts at concerts without the intervention of a third party and many artists have done this. In these cases, artists make a greater per shirt profit than if a merchandising company sells the shirts. However, it is not practicable for artists to sell T-shirts and other merchandise in larger venues, and the burdens of manufacturing, shipping, and selling the shirts militate toward making a deal with an established merchandising company.

WHO TO MAKE A MERCHANDISING DEAL WITH

Only a handful of companies control the merchandising business for musical artists in the United States, and since the first edition of this book, their ownership has been consolidated in the hands of the major record companies or their parent companies. The largest such company is Winterland Productions, founded by Bill Graham, operating out of San Francisco and now owned by MCA. Its main competitor in the 1980s and early 1990s has been the Brockum Company of Toronto, Canada, which is owned and operated by the BCL Entertainment Group, which is also very active in concert promotion. Recently, however, Brockum has had financial difficulties and its future is uncertain. The other major companies are Giant Merchandising (owned by Warner Bros.), Sony Signatures (owned by Sony), Nice Man Merchandising (a joint venture between the original owners and BMG), and Great Entertainment Merchandising (owned by Polygram). Generally, a given deal is shopped to most of the major companies and, although there are numerous instances when the decision is based on personal rapport or personal relationships between the artist and the representatives of a particular company, in most cases, artists go with what is the best deal on paper.

GRANTING MERCHANDISING RIGHTS

Certain companies, as part of their standard recording contract, require that the artist grant them exclusive or nonexclusive merchandising rights. While a grant of nonexclusive merchandising rights is less problematic than a grant of exclusive merchandising rights, it is not in the artist's best interest to grant merchandising rights to any company pursuant to an unrelated contract such as a recording contract.

This is especially true if the company is not a major merchandising company or does not have a substantial merchandising company as a related division, because it will have to license the rights it obtains from the artists to a third party merchandising company and then take a share of the monies which the real merchandising company would have been willing to pay directly to the artists.

Second, the merchandising royalties earned by the artist pursuant to the clause in that recording contract would normally be cross-collateralized with the artist's record royalty account, meaning that royalties otherwise payable to the artist from the sale of merchandise would be subject to being applied toward any unrecouped balance of recording costs and other advances in the artist's account. This is extremely disadvantageous.

Unfortunately, since the ownership of merchandising companies has been consolidated nearly exclusively in the hands of the major record companies or their affiliates, these companies may choose to impose requirements that new artists grant merchandising rights to the record company as a condition of the record contract. There are, however, serious concerns that such activity on the part of record companies would constitute an illegal tie-in in violation of applicable antitrust laws, but a detailed discussion of that issue is beyond the scope of this chapter. Suffice it to say that the artist should never give up merchandising rights other than to a real merchandising company unless it is unavoidable.

TOUR AND RETAIL MERCHANDISING AGREEMENTS

Merchandising agreements are basically divided between tour merchandising agreements and so-called retail merchandising agreements. Tour merchandising agreements are strictly limited to the right to sell merchandise at the artist's concerts, except for sell-off rights, which detail the products that may be sold through retail channels after the term of the agreement has expired. Retail merchandising agreements encompass retail sales (i.e., sales at wholesale to department stores, record shops, T-shirt shops and other retail outlets), mail-order sales, so-called bounce-backs placed in record albums, and licensing by the merchandising company to third party licensees of rights to produce specific items that the primary company does not customarily manufacture and sell through its own channels, e.g., calendars, tapestries, key chains, towels, lunch boxes, drinking glasses, etc. Reprinted in this book is a copy of a tour merchandising agreement which is used by one of the major merchandising companies. We have not reprinted that company's standard retail merchandising agreement, since most of the clauses are duplicative and the royalty provisions are already contained in the sell-off provisions of the tour merchandising agreement.

Most of the major companies now use one contract to acquire all these rights (tour, retail, and licensing), and it is becoming unusual for one artist to be contracted with one company for tour merchandising and another for retail and licensing. However, even in these consolidated agreements, the key business and legal issues are primarily those of tour merchandising, so the following focuses primarily on that.

KEY CONTRACT CLAUSES OF A
TOUR MERCHANDISING DEAL
Term (Including Options, Matching Rights, Buyout Rights, etc.)

From the lawyer's perspective, the term of the merchandising agreement requires the most careful attention. Often, merchandising agreements are made in principle by managers on behalf of their artists. Managers, particularly those of new artists, are sometimes not aware of the intricacies of structuring the term, options, matching rights and buyout rights and it is important to have a lawyer experienced with these types of agreements negotiate these points so that artists retain as much freedom as possible to renegotiate agreements when they achieve greater success or to change merchandising companies should that become necessary or desirable.

The term of nearly all tour merchandising agreements made today is the longer of some specified period of time or until recoupment of all advances paid to the artist. Most typically this time component is one "album tour cycle" or a fixed period of time which approximates a typical album tour cycle, e.g., one year or 18 months. An album tour cycle is the period of time from the release of one album to the release of the next album, including all touring in connection with the first album. The reason for using the album tour cycle is that each time artists release new albums in today's market, they need, almost without exception, to tour in support of those albums to increase sales. Specific lines of merchandise are developed to be sold in conjunction with particular tours. They utilize album cover artwork and graphics which specifically identify the particular tour. As the release of each album marks a new stage in the artist's development, it makes good business sense for the contract to be structured along the lines of album tour cycles, so that the parties can reevaluate their relationship at the designated milestones and decide whether to pick up options or to buy out of one agreement and try to make an agreement with a competitor, and so on. It is very awkward to accomplish a changeover from one merchandising company to another in the middle of a tour cycle, which is another reason for the term to be keyed to the beginning and ending of album tour cycles.

For superstars, the merchandising business is an artist's market. Companies aggressively compete with each other to sign artists and artists are able to negotiate the highest advances the market will bear. The companies pay relatively high royalty rates which leave relatively low profit margins compared to the profit margins left to the record companies under a recording contract for the same artist. However, the balance of power is beginning to shift, at least for artists of less than superstar stature, as the merchandising companies are beginning to abandon cutthroat competition in favor of cooperating to joint venture big deals in order to spread risk and as they are becoming less flexible in negotiations for deals with less established artists.

The relationship between the merchandising company and the artist is somewhat closer to the relationship between a bank and a borrower than it is to the relationship between a record company and an artist. Unless the artist dies, retires from touring, or, in the case of a group, breaks up, the merchandising company will eventually recoup its advance. However, the cost of money is a very important consideration to merchandising companies, and the time within they expect to recoup or be repaid advances is always taken into consideration in determining the size of the advances and under what circumstances they become repayable. Moreover, in recent contracts, if the artist dies, retires from touring, or in the case of a group, breaks up, the entire unrecouped advance generally must be repaid.

Until recently, many tour merchandising agreements were limited to the longer of either a single album tour cycle or recoupment. Thus, if at the end of the album tour cycle, the artist was recouped, a new deal could be negotiated with a competitor of the original merchandising company, upon the release of the artist's next album. Companies began to cut back on the free agent, artist's market mentality of these deal structures by insisting on so-called matching rights to the artist's next album tour cycle. Such rights are also commonly referred to as "rights of last refusal" or sometimes, although less accurately, as "rights of first refusal." Although these rights can be written in somewhat different ways, the fundamental principle is that the artist is not free to make a new deal with a different merchandising company unless the current merchandising company is offered the right to match whatever deal the artist was willing to accept from a third party. If the original merchandising company agrees to match that deal, the artist must re-sign with that company.

This matching rights mechanism is, generally speaking, more favorable to the artist than a structure whereby the merchandising company has one or more options to acquire the rights for subsequent album tour cycles, since the rights to the particular tour cycle are negotiated at the time that the tour cycle is about to happen, which makes the artist in effect a free agent able to negotiate his fair market value, rather than allowing the merchandising company to acquire the rights pursuant to terms set at the time the original deal was made when, generally speaking, the artist would have had less bargaining power.

However, the consolidation of the business into the hands of only a handful of merchandising companies, the relatively low profit margins and the frustration and embarrassment of having an artist who has been supported by a merchandising company switch allegiances to that company's rival at the time the artist breaks into stardom, are contributing toward a new trend for merchandising companies to demand longer terms on their contracts, with built in options. It is my expectation that the term of a typical merchandising agreement will grow ever closer to the term of a typical recording contract.

Because merchandising contracts are structured so that they continue until recoupment of advances, the artist's attorney typically negotiates for buyout rights. This basically means that when a tour cycle comes to an end, if the artist's royalty account is unrecouped, the artist has the right to pay the unrecouped balance to the merchandising company and thereby terminate the contract. In some instances, the payment price may include interest on the unrecouped balance or may include a payment for unsold inventory. The reasons for this are that the merchandising company does not want merely to be made "whole" (not suffer a loss), but wants to make a positive return on its investment.

Buyout rights, if agreed to by the merchandising company, are generally made subject to the company's matching rights, so that the artist can buyout only if the merchandising company has declined to match a third party's offer. Generally the buyout payment is made by or through the merchandising company which has outbid the original merchandiser.

For the reasons discussed above, merchandising companies are often reluctant to grant buyout rights, particularly when the amount of the unrecouped balance is a substantial percentage of the advances made by them. So, for example, the company might allow the artist to buyout only if the artist had recouped at least 75% of the advances paid to the artist or might require the buyout price to be more than 100% (e.g., 110%) of the unrecouped balance.

Territory

The territory covered by a typical tour merchandising agreement entered into in the United States is usually the world, although superstars can often negotiate separate deals for each leg (e.g., North American, European, Australasian), of a worldwide tour. At this time all of the major merchandising companies have worldwide operations, so it is not a concern as to whether one will be able to perform adequately in foreign territories. The only major territory that should be withheld from the merchandising agreement made in the United States is Japan, because Japanese promoters often insist on acquiring the merchandising rights themselves and are often prepared to pay large advances for those rights because in certain cases the per capita gross sales for a superstar touring in Japan may well exceed their per capita sales in the United States or elsewhere.

Advances

In most merchandising deals the amount of the initial advance is the single most important element and is the one that determines which merchandising company acquires the rights. In comparing offers from different companies, it is important to analyze the timing of when advances are payable, because deals are often structured such that a portion of the total advance, usually one-quarter to one-half, is payable upon signing of the contract, a similar portion is payable upon commencement of a tour, and the balance is payable only after the artist has played a certain number of shows or played before a certain number of attendees or when a certain level of gross sales has been achieved.

Wherever advances are deferred until the performance of a certain number of shows, the attainment of a certain number of attendees or the receipt of a certain amount of gross dollars, the use of the term "advance" is misleading. For example, if a $25,000 advance installment is payable when $100,000 in gross receipts have been generated, then, assuming the artist has a 30% royalty rate, it is misleading to call that $25,000 an advance, as the artist earns $30,000 in royalties in respect of that $100,000 in gross receipts. In almost all cases, even without a specific contractual requirement, the merchandising company will advance the artist royalties that have already been earned but which are technically not yet payable (due to customary allowances for time needed to process accounting statements). Therefore, the real issue is how far ahead is the merchandising company willing to put the artist or how far unrecouped is the merchandising company willing to put itself.

Is the biggest advance always the best? Generally it is, but since the issue of whether the artist is obligated to the merchandising company for the future often turns on the point of whether or not the artist's account is unrecouped, an argument can be made that the artist should not accept an advance which he cannot reasonably expect to recoup by the end of the current tour cycle, if so doing will obligate him to the merchandising company for the next tour cycle without the ability to buy out of the contract.

A few questions are indirectly raised by an advance which is too large to be recouped from the sales likely to be made during the current tour cycle. First, does the artist's manager receive a commission on the entire advance if it is received during the current tour cycle even if the manager is no longer the manager during the next tour cycle in which some portion of the advance is still being recouped? Second, if a portion of the advance must be repaid is the manager obligated to repay his commission on that portion? Third, what if one of the band members were to leave the group prior to the advance having been fully recouped? Is there an agreement, e.g., a partnership agreement, among the band members which provides that the leaving member must repay his share of the unearned advance remaining as of the time such individual becomes a leaving member?

Royalty Rates: Tour Merchandise

Generally this is the second most important deal point, although if the artist expects to recoup the advance and can afford to take a longer perspective, e.g., where there is little or no need for a quick influx of cash to mount a tour, this could be the most important point. Royalties on merchandise sold at the artist's concerts are paid on gross sales at the venue less, in most cases, only sales taxes, credit card fees, and customs duties, if applicable. Royalties for new artists for sales at concerts in the United States, stated as a percentage of gross less taxes, are generally in the range of the high 20s to the low 30s. Royalties for superstars in the merchandising field can be significantly higher and often involve more sophisticated calculations. A T-shirt selling for $25 with a royalty of 30%, yields a royalty of $7.50. By comparison an artist would probably have to sell five records at full price to earn the same in record royalties.

Royalty rates for sales outside the United States are generally lower due to lower sales volume, higher taxes and customs duties, which combine to reduce the gross profit margins to the merchandising company.

Royalties for sales of tour merchandise are generally the same for all items except for high-priced items, such as designer tour jackets, and tour programs. Due to the high start-up cost of producing a tour program (designer fees, photographer and related fees, clearance costs, etc.), the major companies have begun to shift from paying a royalty in gross sales to paying a percentage of the company's net profits, generally 70% to 75%.

Royalty Rates: Retail Merchandise

Royalties from retail sales of merchandise (i.e., sales through T-shirt shops, record stores, department stores, etc.), are generally stated as a percentage of wholesale, that is the price at which the merchandising company sells the shirts to its own customers, namely the retail stores or, in some cases, subdistributors who in turn sell to the retail stores. These royalty rates are much lower. Customarily, retail royalties on T-shirts run from 10% to 15% of wholesale in the United States. This is true even for superstar artists. Accordingly, the royalty which an artist makes from the sale of one T-shirt at a department store is only a small fraction of what the artist would receive if that T-shirt had been sold at his concert. Most commonly, the royalty on a T-shirt selling for $25 in a department store is 95 cents to $1.25. The primary reason for this is the large markup taken by department stores and other retail outlets. However, this is not to say that a great deal of royalties cannot be earned from the retail merchandising market. Artists as diverse as Guns N' Roses and New Kids On The Block have earned millions of dollars from the sale of retail merchandise. While these artists are certainly exceptions, they have had the effect of broadening the market for music-related merchandise to include the mass merchandisers, which could have a significant trickle-down effect to a wide range of other artists.

A much greater variety of merchandise is sold through retail channels than is sold on tour. Generally, tour merchandise is limited to a few categories of top selling items, namely T-shirts, sweatshirts, hats, tour programs and buttons. In the retail market, however, all kinds of merchandise may be offered for sale. Many of these items are sold only through sublicensees that specialize in those particular types of products. A major merchandising company may have a number of different sublicensees to whom it licenses the rights to the various types of products. Generally, the merchandising company will pay the artist a large percentage of its receipts from the sublicensee. This essentially amounts to the merchandising company taking a licensing fee, generally 20% to 30% of the gross receipts, and remitting the balance to the artist.

Royalties from retail merchandising sales are usually cross-collateralized with tour merchandising royalties. Since the artist is tied to the merchandising company until all advances have been recouped it is in the artist's interest to allow the company to recoup them from any royalties.

Performance Guarantee

In nearly all merchandising contracts, the artist must guarantee the merchandising company either that the artist will perform to a certain minimum number of people within a certain period of time after the execution of the contract or, alternatively, will perform at least a specified number of concerts in a specified territory or territories within a certain period of time. The merchandising company calculates the advance it is willing to pay primarily on the basis of the tour itinerary the artist provides in the contract negotiations.

The merchandising company will take a very close look at the proposed tour, including the geographic locations, the venues to be played, the other acts on the bill, and the artist's past history of merchandise sales on concert tours, if any, in order to determine how large of an advance to offer. The company then requires that the artist warrant to perform to at least the number of people indicated on the tour itinerary or perform at least the number of concerts indicated in venues of a certain minimum size. A deadline is usually specified for the performance of this minimum guarantee.

The consequences of the artist's failure to perform this minimum guarantee are that the merchandising company may elect to require a repayment of either the entire unrecouped balance or, if the artist's attorney has successfully negotiated this point, the lesser of that number or a pro rata portion of the total advances, based upon the shortfall in the number of attendees or the number of concerts played, as the case may be. Often however, the merchandising companies are willing to let the unrecouped balance ride—and not demand immediate repayment—if the artist has not completely met the performance guarantee, unless the company believes that the artist is not likely to recoup in the foreseeable future. But they will insist on charging interest on the unrecouped balance, generally starting as of the missed deadline for the performance guarantee.

Creative Matters/Approvals

Artists are almost always given strong rights of approval in connection with their merchandise. Provided the artist is responsive to the company's requests for approval, the merchandising company will not sell any product unless the artist has specifically approved it and its design. Most merchandising companies are also willing to allow the artist to submit designs and concepts rather than just select from those the merchandising company's own designers create. This allows the artist to have a great deal of control, fun and satisfaction in the creative process.

LEGAL ELEMENTS

Aside from contract law, the legal foundations upon which merchandising agreements rest are the trademark laws, laws with respect to right of publicity and the copyright laws.

Artist's Name

The most important element requiring legal protection in order to exploit merchandising rights is the artist's name. In the case of a solo artist who uses his own legal name, this generally does not present any problems. For all artists who use fictional names, however, it is quite important to choose a name which is sufficiently distinctive to avoid lawsuits and threatened lawsuits from companies or other artists with similar names. It is generally a good idea to conduct a trademark search, which costs a few hundred dollars, before selecting a fictitious name, and, once a suitable name is found and is begun to be used, to file for state and federal trademark registration, and, once the artist or the artist's records enter the international market, foreign trademark registrations in the major foreign territories. If the artist believes that he or she will be successful, it is worth the money to take the necessary steps to protect his or her rights in the fictitious name.

Ownership of Artwork

Another important consideration is the ownership of the artwork which will be used on the merchandise. Merchandising contracts require the artist to provide a reasonable selection of photographs or other artwork from which the merchandising company can prepare designs for the products. Sometimes the artwork consists of the artist's album cover and related publicity shots that are owned by the record company. In that case, the artist must be sure that he may use those photographs or designs without the need for separate approval by the record company. Record companies often agree to allow artists to use this artwork for merchandising, but only upon payment of all or a portion of its costs of producing the applicable artwork. If the artwork comes from some other source, the artist must be sure to have a written agreement with the creator of the artwork which specifically allows the artist to reproduce that artwork on merchandise. In such event, the creator of the artwork may negotiate for a royalty or a flat fee payment. Except in rare instances, the artist will have to pay any such fees or royalties out of their own royalties. The most important thing is to be sure that there is an agreement in writing for each piece of artwork used. Otherwise the artist may wind up on the wrong end of a very expensive lawsuit.

Rights and Obligations of Individual Group Members

An important legal issue is how, if at all, the contract deals with the rights and obligations of the various members in the case of a group. Usually the agreement will provide that all members of the group are jointly and severally liable for any sums which the group is obligated to pay back to the merchandising company. This creates a problem if the group disbands with an unrecouped balance or a member leaves and is replaced by a new member at a time when there is an unrecouped balance. This is an issue for the group's lawyer to handle.

Rights of Solo Artists

Another issue is whether the merchandising company has any rights with respect to the individual members apart from the group. In most instances, the merchandising company will not and should not have these rights, but in some cases the merchandising company may feel that in order to protect its investment in the group, it must have rights to sell merchandise pertaining to an individual or individuals as solo artists. If so, this should be limited to cases where the group breaks up at a time when it has an unrecouped balance.

If the artist and the merchandising company intend for the merchandising company to sell items which feature the individual group members apart from the group, some provision will have to be made as to how to take that into account in computing the group members' individual shares of the total merchandising royalties, particularly if advances have already been paid in equal shares, but have not yet been totally recouped. This would normally require an internal accounting among the group members which might result in one or more of them paying royalties to one or more of the others so that the royalties are shared in proportion to the actual earnings. These problems are not addressed in the merchandising agreement, but in a partnership or similar agreement among the group members.

Commercial Tie-ins

Another area which must be carefully scrutinized is the possible conflict between merchandising agreements and commercial tie-ins or endorsements. As artists become stars, they are often presented with opportunities for commercial tie-ins and endorsements, all or some of which will involve the sale or promotional distribution of merchandise with the artist's name and/or likeness on it. Although merchandising contracts generally contain broad language which addresses this issue, they do not for the most part, adequately cover the variety of situations which can occur. Accordingly, the artist's lawyer should carefully try to negotiate these provisions up front to be sure that they will give the artist maximum flexibility in making commercial tie-ins and endorsements. However, whenever an artist has a merchandising agreement and is subsequently approached to do some kind of commercial tie-in or endorsement, the artist's attorney must be certain to review the merchandising agreement to be sure that the activities proposed do not conflict with the rights of the merchandising company. If they do, it is best to advise the merchandising company of this at the deal making stage to avoid any misunderstandings or breaches of contract and the relationship between the artist and the merchandising company can be maintained as a mutually beneficial and amicable one.

TOUR MERCHANDISING AGREEMENT

(Please note, the Tour Merchandising Agreement and Exhibit B, Addendum to Merchandising Contract Royalties contain references to the following documents that have not been included here: Merchandising Agreement [standard retail merchandising agreement]; Exhibit "A" [list of preapproved merchandise]; Exhibit "C" [copyright and/or trademark notice designated by Licensor]; Exhibit "D" [prices of licensed products]; and Exhibit "E" [schedule with respect to any other licenses for the Licensed Products and/or heat transfers and/or any other retail merchandising or mail order licenses].)

Gentlepersons:

The following will confirm the understanding between _____ (hereinafter "Licensor"), and _____ (hereinafter "Licensee"):

1. Licensor hereby grants Licensee the exclusive right to utilize the name, symbols, emblems, designs, likenesses, visual representations, service marks, copyrights in graphic designs, and/or trademarks of the musical group and all of the individual members thereof, both as members of and, subject to the provisions of subparagraph 1(c) below, as individual artists and its individual members hereinafter referred to as "Artist" (such name, symbols, etc. hereinafter referred to as the "Licensed Property") in connection with the manufacture, advertisement, distribution, and sale by Licensee of any products utilizing the Licensed Property (hereinafter "Licensed Products"), including but not limited to the preapproved merchandise listed as Exhibit "A" attached hereto, in and about the premises and environs of and at any and all live concerts given by Artist throughout the world (such premises and environs hereinafter referred to as the "Licensed Area"). Notwithstanding anything to the contrary, the grant hereunder shall include the exclusive right to sell all nonfood and nonbeverage items at Artist's concerts in the Licensed Area for a period beginning with the congregation of the audience outside Artist's concert sites and ending with the dispersement of the audience after Artist's concerts. No other licenses exist which would permit the distribution and/or sale of Licensed Products during the Licensed Term in the Licensed Area, and Licensor warrants that it has not entered into and will not enter into any other license agreements which would permit the sale of products bearing the Licensed Property during the Licensed Term in the Licensed Area without Licensee's written consent. All rights and interests with respect to the Licensed Property not specifically granted to Licensee herein shall be and are specifically reserved to Licensor and/or its licensees without limitation during the term hereof.

(a) Notwithstanding anything to the contrary contained herein, Licensee shall be entitled during the Licensed Term to sell the following merchandise through Licensee's retail distribution network at the royalty rates set out in paragraph 6(a) of the merchandising agreement of even date herewith (hereinafter "Merchandising Agreement"):

(i) Licensed Products no longer offered for sale at Artist's concerts; and

(ii) all Licensed Products (if Artist does not perform at a live concert in the Licensed Area for a period of thirty (30) consecutive days at any time during the Licensed Term).

(b) Notwithstanding anything to the contrary contained in this agreement, in addition to having the exclusive right to utilize the Licensed Property with respect to the members of Artist as members of _____, Licensee shall have the exclusive right to utilize the names, symbols, emblems, designs, likenesses, visual representations, service marks, and/or trademarks of each of the individual members of Artist other than as members of _____ (e.g., as solo artists, members of other musical groups, etc.) until recoupment of all advances payable hereunder.

2. For the license granted herein, Licensee will pay Licensor the advances, deposits, and royalties set out in Exhibit "B" attached hereto.

(a) Licensor's representative shall have the right to be present at all load-ins and load-outs of Licensed Products at Artist's concert sites and during all settlements with halls. The night after each concert, Licensee shall furnish Licensor with complete and accurate statements showing the following with respect to Licensed Products sold by Licensee during the previous concert: quantity and gross selling price of each of the Licensed Products, as well as the hall fees, vendor fees, and sales taxes paid by Licensee with respect to its sale of the Licensed Products in connection with such concert.

(b) The night after each concert, Licensor shall furnish Licensee with complete and accurate attendance counts for the previous concert, specifying both the number of paying and nonpaying attendees for such concert.

(c) Every two (2) weeks, Licensee shall furnish Licensor with summary statements for such two-week period based upon the information provided in the nightly statements furnished pursuant to subparagraph 2(b) above.

(d) Within thirty (30) days after the later of:

(i) the last date of the Licensed Term; or

(ii) Licensee's receipt of a statement of bona fide, paid attendees (as defined in Exhibit "B" and in accordance therewith) or other attendance which may affect bona fide, paid attendees for all live concerts given by Artist for which a statement is due;

Licensee shall furnish Licensor with a royalty statement setting forth in reasonable detail the following with respect to Licensed Products sold on the tour for which royalties are paid as a percentage of gross sales: quantity and gross selling price of all such Licensed Products; hall fees, vendor fees, and sales taxes paid by Licensee with respect to its sale of the Licensed Products in connection with such tour. Such statement shall be accompanied by payment of royalties earned hereunder and due Licensor, less any advances paid hereunder.

(e) Within sixty (60) days after the later of:

(i) the last date of each leg of a Tour; or

(ii) Licensee's receipt of a statement of bona fide, paid attendees or other attendance which may affect bona fide, paid attendees for all live concerts given by Artist for which a statement is due; and again within sixty (60) days after the later of:

(A) the last date of the Licensed Term; or

(B) Licensee's receipt of a statement of bona fide, paid attendees or other attendance which may affect bona fide, paid attendees for all live concerts given by Artist for which a statement is due;

Licensee shall furnish Licensor with a royalty statement setting forth in reasonable detail the following with respect to Licensed Products sold during the Licensed Term for which royalties are paid as a percentage of net profits; quantity and royalties paid as a percentage of net profits; quantity and gross selling price of all Licensed Products, hall and vendor fees, freight and trucking expenses (equipment and personnel), insurance on goods shipped outside the United States, customs duties, mutually approved costs of production, mutually approved bootleg security and direct legal costs incurred with respect to same, road staff expenses (including without limitation salaries, per diems, and travel directly related to services hereunder), a mutually agreeable royalty payable with respect to designer garments (i.e., garments which sell for more than $35), and other mutually approved expenses. Such statement shall be accompanied by royalties earned hereunder and due Licensor, less any unrecouped advances paid hereunder. Within forty-five (45) days after the last date of the Licensed Term, Licensee shall furnish Licensor with payment representing a good faith estimate of such royalties due, with reasonable reserves withheld for charges incurred but not yet paid.

(f) Licensee will compute any royalties due Licensor relative to sales hereunder in the currency of the country earned, and:

(i) with respect to earnings in Europe, same shall be converted to pounds sterling when the monies are transferred to the United Kingdom. Such transfer shall be effected as quickly as practicably possible, but in any event, within fourteen (14) days of Licensee's receipt thereof unless governmental instrumentalities prevent such transfer, in which case, said monies shall be converted at the rate in effect at the actual time of transfer;

(ii) any earnings in Europe so converted to pounds sterling, as well as earnings in the United Kingdom, shall be converted to United States dollars as of the day such earnings are received or deemed received in the United Kingdom;

(iii) with respect to earnings in the remainder of the Licensed Area, monies shall be converted to United States dollars at the exchange rate received by Licensee when such funds are transferred from the country in which earned to the United States. Licensee shall use its reasonable efforts to have such monies remitted to the United States as soon as practicably possible, it being understood that Licensee shall not be held responsible for delays in such remittance due to reasons beyond Licensee's control.

If Licensee is required by a foreign governmental instrumentality, to deduct taxes based on Licensee's receipts from merchandise sales hereunder, Licensee may deduct a proportionate amount of such taxes (based on Licensor's royalty rates hereunder) from Licensor's accrued earnings with respect to such sales only; if such governmental instrumentality requires deduction of any other taxes on Artist or Licensor's behalf due to Artist or Licensor's liability in such territory, payment to such instrumentality shall be from Licensor's accrued earnings. Licensee shall provide tax certificates in Artist or Licensor's name with respect to such deductions. If any law or governmental ruling of any country places a maximum limit on the amount Licensee may pay Licensor, Licensee shall pay Licensor the lesser of (aa) such maximum; or (bb) the amount earned hereunder. If the amount earned hereunder is greater than such maximum, Licensee shall, if permissible, deposit the difference between such amounts in an account in Licensor's name in the country of such law or ruling. For accounting purposes, such deposit shall constitute royalty payment hereunder. Licensee shall notify Licensor immediately of any such governmental intervention relative to payment of monies to Licensor. If Licensee is unable to remove Licensor's royalties earned hereunder from the country in which earned and Licensor's account is in a fully recouped position, Licensee shall notify Licensor of such inability, then at Licensor's request and expense and if Licensee is able to do so, Licensee shall deposit such earnings in Licensor's name in a foreign depository selected by Licensor in the country in which such royalties were earned and in the currency thereof. For accounting purposes, such deposit shall constitute royalty payments to Licensor.

3. During the Licensed Term, Licensor shall supply Licensee with a list of Artist's proposed live concerts setting out the date, city, venue, and hall capacity (as scaled for each such live concert) of any and all such concerts by facsimile (FAX) to FAX number _____ (or such other FAX number as Licensee may direct), attention: tour department, by the earliest of the following:

(a) the date any such live concerts have been booked and confirmed through a booking agent and concert promoter; or

(b) the date tickets for such live concerts have been placed on sale; or

(c) the date fourteen (14) days prior to such live concerts.

Licensor shall notify Licensee within twenty-four (24) hours of the cancellation or postponement of any live concerts of which Licensee has previously been notified.

4. The term of this agreement (hereinafter "Licensed Term") shall consist of an Initial Term, as set out in subparagraph 4(a) below, and an Option Term (if exercised by Licensee), as set out in subparagraph 4(b) below.

(a) The Initial Term shall commence upon execution and continue until the later of:

(i) one (1) year after Artist's first Performance (as defined in Exhibit "B" attached hereto) in the Licensed Area; or

(ii) recoupment of all advances payable hereunder.

(b) Licensee shall have the option to extend the Licensed Term (hereinafter "Option"), exercisable only by notice in writing given to Licensor by the earlier of:

(i) fourteen (14) days after Licensor's notice of the United States commercial release of Artist's second as-yet unrecorded, unreleased studio album following the date hereof (hereinafter "Option Term Album"); or

(ii) thirty (30) days after the end of the Initial Term; or for an additional period (hereinafter "Option Term") commencing on Licensee's exercise of the Option and terminating the latest of:

(A) one (1) year after Artist's first Performance in the Licensed Area in support of the Option Term Album; or

(B) completion of all touring by Artist in support of the Option Term Album; or

(C) recoupment of the Option Term Advances (including the unrecouped balance of advances previously paid).

As used herein, "album" shall specifically exclude record albums consisting of re-released or "live" material. If, for any reason, Licensor fails to provide Licensee with such notice, Licensee may exercise the Option at any time.

(c) Notwithstanding the foregoing, if:

(i) recoupment of all advances payable hereunder occurs while a tour by Artist is in progress in the Licensed Area; and

(ii) the Licensed Term would otherwise expire on such recoupment; the Licensed Term shall automatically be extended upon such recoupment until completion of such tour.

(d) In the event that Licensee elects not to exercise the Option, Licensor shall have the option to terminate the Licensed Term by repaying to Licensee the full amount of all unrecouped advances theretofore paid and purchasing Licensee's inventory of Licensed Products remaining and on hand, calculated at Licensee's cost (up to a cost of _____). Such option to terminate the Licensed Term must be exercised in writing by Licensor no later than the earlier of:

(i) the date seventy-four (74) days after the United States commercial release of the Option Term Album; or

(ii) the date of execution of a tour merchandising agreement with respect to Artist's tour in support of the Option Term Album between Licensor and a third party.

Upon such payment and purchase by Licensor, this agreement shall terminate.

(e) Notwithstanding the foregoing, if the advances paid hereunder are unrecouped by the later of the dates set out in subparagraph 2(e)(ii)(A) or 2(e)(ii)(B) above, Licensor shall have the option to terminate the Licensed Term by repaying to Licensee the full amount of all unrecouped advances theretofore paid and purchasing Licensee's inventory of Licensed Products remaining and on hand, calculated at Licensee's cost (up to a cost of _____). Such option to terminate the Licensed Term must be exercised in writing by Licensor no later than ninety (90) days after the date set out in subparagraph 2(e)(ii)(A) or 2(e)(ii)(B) above, as the case may be. Upon such repayment and purchase by Licensor, this agreement shall terminate.

5. During the Licensed Term and for a period of two (2) years thereafter, Licensee will keep and maintain at its principal place of business true and accurate records of all transactions which relate to or affect this agreement or any provision thereof, which books and records, together with supporting vouchers, shall be open for inspection by Licensor or its representative during regular business hours upon seventy-two (72) hours' written notice, but no more than once with respect to any period to be examined. At such time, copying of books and records relating directly to monies due Licensor hereunder will be allowed.

6. At its sole cost and expense, Licensor shall supply Licensee with artwork embodying the Licensed Property as reasonably requested by Licensee, including but not limited to a sufficient number of suitable photographs for a complete tour program and for other reasonable artwork needs. Licensor shall use its best efforts to grant Licensee the rights to artwork from Artist's most recent EP, and if Licensor is so able, it shall provide same to Licensee at Licensor's sole cost and expense no later than thirty (30) days after execution hereof. Licensor shall use its best efforts to grant Licensee the rights to artwork from any of Artist's albums subsequently released during the Licensed Term, and if Licensor is so able, it shall provide same to Licensee at Licensor's sole cost and expense no later than thirty (30) days after such release.

(a) All artwork and products shall be mutually agreed upon prior to the manufacture, and Licensee shall furnish samples of each of the Licensed Products, as well as the packaging therefor, to Licensor for its approval as to quality, style, and cost (which approval shall not be unreasonably withheld). Licensor shall use its best efforts to provide such approval or disapproval within seven (7) days of receipt of such samples. In the event that Licensor does not provide written approval of any of same in whole or in part within seven (7) days after receipt thereof, such failure shall automatically constitute disapproval by Licensor.

(b) Notwithstanding the above, Licensee shall be obligated only to use its best efforts to obtain mutually agreed upon unprinted T-shirts, and in the event it is unable to secure adequate quantities of same as a result of limited supply and the special nature of the shirts, Licensor and Licensee shall mutually agree on alternate unprinted T-shirts.

(c) Promptly after initial shipment of the Licensed Products, Licensee will so notify Licensor and supply Licensor with twenty (20) samples of each such Licensed Product, at no cost to Licensor. Licensor may purchase reasonable additional quantities of Licensed Products at the prices set out on Exhibit "D" attached hereto, but such merchandise shall not be offered for resale.

7. During the Licensed Term, Licensor shall not, by itself or through third parties, engage in any premiums, giveaways, or promotional tie-ins of merchandise utilizing the Licensed Property, including but not limited to souvenirs, booklets, T-shirts, wearing apparel, posters, stickers, programs, visors, and shorts, which are specifically related to Artist's concert appearances (e.g., radio station and tour-sponsor promotions) and which would result in the advertisement or distribution of the above described merchandise at any concert site or other location within twenty (20) miles of such concert and less than forty-eight (48) hours prior thereto, nor shall Licensor, by itself or through third parties, engage in any other distribution or sale of such merchandise within two (2) miles of such concert and less than forty-eight (48) hours prior thereto. Notwithstanding the foregoing, nothing herein shall preclude standard, record industry promotion by _____(name of record company) or its distributors in support of album releases by Artist.

8. Licensee represents and warrants that the Licensed Products will be of high standard in style, appearance, and quality, and that no liability will attach to Licensor for merchandise manufactured or sold by Licensee.

(a) Licensee recognizes the value of the publicity and goodwill associated with the Licensed Property, and with respect thereto, acknowledges that, as between Licensor and Licensee, such goodwill belongs exclusively to Licensor. In addition, Licensee acknowledges that the Licensed Property has a secondary meaning in the mind of the purchasing public.

9. Licensee shall print, stamp, or mold the copyright and/or trademark notice designated by Licensor as Exhibit "C" attached hereto on all Licensed Products and on each package or container used in connection therewith, and shall print such notice on each label, advertisement, and promotional release concerning the Licensed Products, all in accordance with instructions from Licensor, including but not limited to instructions with respect to position and letter size.

(a) (i) If Licensee fails to affix proper copyright and/or trademark notice on all Licensed Products and such failure does not result from:

(A) Licensor's failure to provide proper copyright and/or trademark notice; or

(B) Licensor changing the copyright and/or trademark notice during the Licensed Term or Sell-Off Period (as defined in paragraph 15 below); and (ii) If such failure results in any Licensed Product being adjudicated as having fallen into the public domain; Licensor shall have the right to terminate this agreement within fifteen (15) days of such adjudication upon thirty (30) days' written notice to Licensee.

10. Licensor agrees to assist Licensee to the extent necessary in the procurement of any protection or to protect any of Licensee's rights to the Licensed Property, and if it so desires, Licensee may, at its own expense and with Licensor's prior approval, commence or prosecute any claims or suits in its own name or in the name of Licensor, or it may join Licensor as a party thereto (but all such actions undertaken by Licensee shall be at Licensee's sole expense). Each party shall provide the other with written notice of any infringements or limitations by others of the Licensed Property on articles similar to those covered by this agreement which may come to its attention. In the event any sums are recovered as a result of any judgment or settlement from prosecution of any claim or suit, Licensor shall receive _____ percent (___%) of the net amount recovered, after deduction from gross amounts recovered of all related legal fees (from litigation only) incurred by Licensee, subject to other arrangements on a suit-by-suit basis. With Licensor's approval and after submission of a budget therefor, Licensee shall obtain seizure orders at various concert sites during a tour to combat bootleggers during such tour. Licensee may treat as a recoupable advance _____ percent (___%) of the cost of each such seizure order, including legal fees and court costs (which costs shall be allocated on a reasonable basis among Licensor and all other artists who are the subject of such seizure order), and ____ percent (___%) of the cost of security actually paid by Licensee and may recoup same from Licensor's accrued royalties. The preceding sentence applies only if Licensor's royalties are calculated on the basis of gross sales. Licensee shall allocate legal costs between programs (if applicable) and all other Licensed Products, and shall not take double deductions for such costs.

11. Licensor warrants and represents that it is free to enter into and fully perform this agreement, and that use of the Licensed Property hereunder will not infringe upon or violate any third party's rights of any nature whatsoever. Licensor will at all times indemnify and hold Licensee and those with whom Licensee has contractual arrangements with respect to the Licensed Property harmless from and against any and all claims, damages, loss of profits, liabilities, costs, and expenses, including reasonable attorneys' fees, arising out of any breach by Licensor herein. The above indemnification shall apply only to final judgments entered by a court of competent jurisdiction thereof or settlements entered into with Licensor's written consent, which shall not be unreasonably withheld.

12. Licensor represents and warrants that it is the sole owner of the professional name "_____" (hereinafter "Name") and that to the best of Licensor's knowledge, no other musical artist or entertainer has or will have the right to use the Name or permit the Name to be used in connection with phonograph records, entertainment services, or clothing. Licensor has the authority to grant Licensee the right to use the Name as provided herein and warrants that Licensee's use of the Name will not infringe upon the rights of any third parties.

(a) Licensor agrees that Licensee may cause a search to be instituted at Licensee's expense to determine whether there have been any third party uses of the Name in connection with phonograph records and/or entertainment and/or clothing and other merchandise.

(b) Licensor warrants and represents that it has made an application for United States registration of the Name in Licensor's name for phonograph records, entertainment services, and clothing, or that it shall file such an application within thirty (30) days of execution of this agreement and promptly provide Licensee with a copy of such application. Licensor further agrees that if Licensee has not received a copy of such application within sixty (60) days of execution of this agreement, Licensee may cause such application to be made in Licensor's name for phonograph record purposes, entertainment services, and clothing. Licensor agrees that any amounts expended by Licensee pursuant to this paragraph shall be deemed to be advances against and recoupable by Licensee from royalties otherwise payable to Licensor hereunder. Nothing contained in this paragraph shall release Licensor and/or Artist from their indemnification of Licensee with respect to Licensee's use of Artist's name as specified herein.

13. Licensor hereby acknowledges and agrees that it and each member of Artist have fully complied with all necessary laws, statutes, or regulations and have taken any action required to exempt Licensee from reporting, withholding, or paying so-called "withholding" taxes, which include the following without limitation: federal and state income taxes, federal social security tax, and California unemployment insurance tax (hereinafter "Withholding Taxes").

(a) Licensor warrants that all members of Artist are United States citizens. If, at any time during the Licensed Term, a non-United States citizen is a member of Artist, Licensor shall promptly notify Licensee thereof, and Licensor acknowledges and agrees that in any such case, it shall fully comply with all necessary laws, statutes, or regulations, and shall take any action required to exempt Licensee from reporting, withholding, or paying Withholding Taxes and any federal withholding taxes on nonresident aliens. Notwithstanding the foregoing, in such case, Licensee shall withhold the appropriate amount from payments to nonresident aliens (whether individuals or corporations) as required by Sections 1441 and 1442 of the Internal Revenue Code unless Licensor provides Licensee with appropriate documentation relieving Licensee of such responsibility.

14. Subject to paragraph 11 above, Licensee will at all times indemnify and hold Licensor harmless from and against any and all claims arising out of the use or possession of any Licensed Products manufactured, advertised, distributed, or sold. At its own expense, Licensee will maintain throughout the Licensed Term an insurance policy for products liability in a form acceptable to Licensor, naming Licensor and Artist (as well as their employees, agents, and representatives, if the insurance company so permits) as additional insureds. Such policy shall have the following minimum limits:

(a) basic coverage in the amount of $_____ per occurrence; and

(b) umbrella coverage in the amount of $_____.

15. Upon expiration of this agreement, all rights granted to Licensee herein shall forthwith revert to Licensor, with the following consequences:

(a) Licensor shall thereafter by free to use and license others to use the Licensed Property in connection with the manufacture, advertisement, distribution, and sale of items identical or similar to the Licensed Products.

(b) Licensee shall not thereafter manufacture, advertise, distribute, or sell Licensed Products in any place whatsoever. However:

(i) for a period of one hundred twenty (120) days (hereinafter "Sell-Off Period") and in accordance with all the terms and conditions contained in this agreement, Licensee may continue to sell any Licensed Products previously manufactured and on hand on a nonexclusive basis; and

(ii) in connection with the Sell-Off Period, Licensee may manufacture during the Sell-Off Period sufficient quantities of Licensed Products which come in different sizes to restore the ratio of Licensee's inventory to the following ratio per dozen: 1 small, 3 medium, 5 large, 3 extra-large. The quantities of Licensed Products so manufactured during the Sell-Off Period shall not exceed _____ percent (___%) of quantities previously manufactured pursuant to this agreement.

(c) The royalties payable with respect to Licensed Products sold through wholesale distribution during the Sell-Off Period shall be at the rates set out in paragraph 6(a) of the Merchandising Agreement. Notwithstanding the foregoing, no royalties shall be payable to Licensor for Licensed Products sold during the Sell-Off Period at a price less than _____ percent (___%) of Licensee's listed wholesale price for quantities of eighteen (18) dozen or less of such items (fifteen [15] dozen for sales of jerseys only).

(d) Licensee shall notify Licensor of the quantity of unsold Licensed Products remaining at expiration of the Licensed Term, and Licensor shall have the right to purchase all such unsold merchandise from Licensee at its cost in lieu of permitting Licensee to exercise its "sell-off" or manufacturing rights granted under this paragraph.

(e) If:

(i) for any reason, fifteen (15) or more concerts about which Licensee has been notified are canceled and not made up during the Licensed Term; and

(ii) Licensee has manufactured Licensed Products in anticipation of the occurrence of such concerts; and

(iii) Licensee has not, subsequent to notification of such cancellation, manufactured any Licensed Products which are overstocked because of such cancellation; the Sell-Off Period shall be one hundred eighty (180) days instead of one hundred twenty (120) days.

16. In the last one hundred twenty (120) days of the Licensed Term, Licensee shall not manufacture, in anticipation of the Sell-Off Period, quantities of Licensed Products greater than those necessary to meet reasonably anticipated demand therefor during the remainder of the Licensed Term.

17. Nothing contained herein shall be construed to constitute a partnership or joint venture between the parties hereto, and neither Licensee nor Licensor shall become bound by any representation, act, or omission of the other.

18. This agreement and all matters or issues collateral thereto shall be governed by the laws of the State of California applicable to contracts performed entirely therein.

(a) Any controversy or claim arising out of or relating to this agreement or the making, performance, or interpretation hereof shall be settled in accordance with the rules of the American Arbitration Association in Los Angeles, California, but the choice of an arbitrator shall be subject to agreement of the parties hereto, not the rules of said Association, and judgment upon the arbitration award may be entered in any court having jurisdiction over the subject matter of the controversy. The prevailing party in any such arbitration or litigation related to such controversy or claim shall be entitled to its reasonable attorneys' fees and court costs in addition to any award received.

19. The entire understanding between the parties hereto relating to the subject matter hereof is contained herein, and no warranties, representations, or undertakings are made by the parties hereto except as are expressly provided herein.

(a) This agreement cannot be modified or amended except by a written instrument executed by the parties hereto, and any prior or contemporaneous agreement of the parties hereto, whether oral or in writing, pertaining to the subject matter hereof, shall be deemed merged herewith.

(b) Neither party shall be deemed to have waived any of its rights hereunder except by a written instrument executed by such waiving party.

20. Licensor agrees to the terms of, and shall propose in all its contracts with promoters for concerts at which Artist is the major headliner, a provision in substantially the following form, and Licensor shall use its best efforts to insure inclusion of such provision in the final version of all such contracts:

Promoter agrees that artist's designee _____(name of merchandiser) shall have the sole and exclusive right to sell all nonfood and nonbeverage items, including but not limited to souvenir books, phonograph recordings, wearing apparel, posters, stickers, programs, and other items of merchandise, at or about the venue on the day of artist's concert and prior to, during and after each concert, whether or not such items bear artist's name and/or likeness.

Promoter shall provide adequate space for artist's designee to vend such material, and promoter agrees that artist's designee shall, as it may require, have access to any hall facilities and any and all areas adjacent to the venue.

Promoter further agrees to use its best efforts to prevent and stop the sale or distribution of any merchandise sold by any person other than artist's designee at artist's concerts, whether inside or outside the venue. It is understood that no person or entity other than artist's designee shall have the right to sell or distribute any nonfood and nonbeverage items at the engagement without the express written consent of _____(name of merchandiser).

Promoter further agrees to use its best efforts to obtain the lowest possible hall and vendor fees payable to the venue for the sale of artist's merchandise hereunder, and promoter represents and warrants that it will receive no interest or fee, either directly or indirectly, from the proceeds of sales of artist's merchandise.

21. Licensee may assign or sublicense this agreement or any portion hereof to a subsidiary or affiliated company or to any person, firm, company, or entity owning or acquiring a substantial potion of Licensee's stock or assets, provided that Licensee remains primarily responsible for its obligations hereunder. Notwithstanding the

foregoing, Licensee may assign or sublicense this agreement, any part hereof, or any rights hereunder, other than those relating to the United States, to any person or entity who is or may be a parent, subsidiary, or affiliate. "Affiliate" shall mean any person or entity with whom Licensee enters into an agreement with respect to rights hereunder or with respect to any other merchandising agreement outside the United States. Licensor may assign this agreement to any party, provided that Licensor remains primarily liable for its obligations hereunder. Any other attempted or purported assignment or other transfer, sublicense, mortgage, or other encumbrance of this agreement by either party without prior approval of the other shall be void and have no effect.

22. All notices required to be given hereunder shall be in writing and shall be delivered personally, by facsimile (FAX), or by certified or registered mail, return receipt requested, postage prepaid, as follows:

(a) if to Licensor, at

_____,

ADDRESS

with a courtesy copy to

_____;

(b) if to Licensee, at

_____,

ADDRESS

with a courtesy copy to

_____.

    Any notice so given shall be deemed effective upon receipt by any party to whom it is addressed. Either party may change the address to which notice is to be sent by giving written notice of such change of address to the other party as provided herein. Notwithstanding the foregoing, either party's failure to send a courtesy copy of notices pursuant to subparagraph 22(a) or 22(b) above, as the case may be, shall not be deemed a material breach of this agreement.

23. If Licensor believes Licensee to be in default, Licensor shall provide Licensee with written notice thereof as provided in paragraph 22 above and Licensee shall have fifteen (15) days within which to cure said default before Licensor may pursue other remedies.

24. Concurrently with execution hereof, Licensor shall attach a schedule hereto as Exhibit "E" with respect to any other licenses for the Licensed Products and/or heat transfers and/or any other retail merchandising or mail order licenses, which schedule shall include the following with respect to each license: licensor; licensee; duration of licensed term; licensed products; and licensed area. In addition, Licensor shall submit a sample of any item licensed pursuant to any license set out above concurrently with attachment of Exhibit "E."

25. This agreement has been the result of negotiations between the parties. Each party and its counsel have reviewed this agreement. Accordingly, the rule of construction

embodied in California Civil Code §1654 (or in the laws of any other jurisdiction), to the effect that uncertainty in a contract is to be resolved against the drafting party, shall not be employed in the interpretation of this agreement.

26. This agreement may be executed in any number of counterparts, each of which shall be deemed to be an original and all of which together shall be deemed to be one and the same agreement.

AGREED TO AND ACCEPTED:

_____   _____
(LICENSOR)   (LICENSEE)

_____   _____
ADDRESS   ADDRESS

_____   _____
FEDERAL I.D. / SS#   FEDERAL I.D. / SS#

_____
DATE

EXHIBIT B
ADDENDUM TO MERCHANDISING CONTRACT ROYALTIES

For the license granted herein, Licensee shall pay Licensor the following and Licensor shall make the warranties set out herein to secure such payment:

1. ADVANCES/DEPOSITS

(a) *Initial Term*: Licensee shall pay Licensor the following Initial Term Advances and Initial Term Deposits:

(i) an Initial Term Advance of _____ plus an additional sum of _____ to buy out Licensor's outstanding merchandising deal, within five (5) business days after execution of this agreement;

(ii) an Initial Term Advance of _____ within five (5) business days after gross sales hereunder exceed _____.

(iii) after recoupment of the prior advances, Licensee shall pay Licensor an Initial Term Deposit equal to _____ percent (___%) of Licensor's projected earnings for the remainder of the Initial Term (but in no event more than _____) if, in Licensee's good faith business judgment, it is anticipated said sum will be earned hereunder, which earnings shall be calculated by Licensee on the basis of merchandise sales up to the date of such recoupment, anticipated attendance for the remainder of the Initial Term, the venues to be played and venue location, and geographic sales patterns, and Licensee shall pay Licensor a deposit equal to _____ percent (___%) of Licensor's projected earnings each time the prior deposit is recouped if calculations of projected earnings as set out above so warrant in Licensee's good faith business judgment. The initial deposit hereunder shall be paid within five (5) days after recoupment of the prior deposit. If, by expiration of the Initial Term, any portion of said deposits has not been recouped by Licensee from Licensor's accrued royalties, Licensor shall repay Licensee the full unrecouped amount thereof within five (5) business days of said expiration or when otherwise subject to repayment under this Exhibit "B";

(iv) notwithstanding anything to the contrary contained herein, if Artist fails by August 1, 19__ (hereinafter "Initial Term Scheduled Commencement Date"), to commence a tour of the United States and Canada consisting of at least thirty (30) Performances scheduled during the Initial Term within a period of approximately eight (8) weeks (such tour hereinafter referred to as an "Initial Term U.S. Tour"), Licensor shall be charged an amount equal to _____ per annum on the unrecouped balance of advances theretofore paid (such charge of ___ per annum hereinafter referred to as a "Delayed Performance Fee"), which shall be charged between the Initial Term Scheduled Commencement Date and the actual commencement of an Initial Term U.S. Tour and shall be treated as an additional Initial Term Advance paid hereunder.

(b) *Option Term*: Licensee shall pay Licensor the following Option Term Advances and Option Term Deposits:

(i) an Option Term Advance equal to the greater of:

(A) _____; or

(B) an amount equal to _____ percent (___%) of Licensor's earnings during the Initial Term, less the unrecouped balance of advances and deposits theretofore paid (but in no event more than _____), payable as follows:

(I) _____ (___) on Licensee's exercise of the Option;

(II) _____ (___) on the first Performance of a tour by Artist of the United States and Canada consisting of a series of at least thirty (30) Performances scheduled within a period of approximately eight (8) weeks (such tour herein after referred to as an "Option Term U.S. Tour");

(III) _____ (___) when gross sales during the Option Term exceed _____;

(ii) after recoupment of the prior advances and deposits, Licensee shall pay Licensor an Option Term Deposit equal to _____ percent (___%) of Licensor's projected earnings for the remainder of the Option Term (but in no event more than _____) if, in Licensee's good faith business judgment, it is anticipated said sum will be earned hereunder, which earnings shall be calculated by Licensee on the basis of merchandise sales up to the date of such recoupment, anticipated attendance for the remainder of the Option Term, the venues to be played and venue location, and geographic sales patterns, and Licensee shall pay Licensor a deposit equal to _____ percent (___%) of Licensor's projected earnings each time the prior deposit is recouped if calculations of projected earnings as set out above so warrant in Licensee's good faith business judgment. The initial deposit hereunder shall be paid within five (5) days after recoupment of the prior advances and deposits, and each subsequent deposit shall be paid within five (5) days after recoupment of the prior deposit. If, by expiration of the Option Term, any portion of said deposits has not been recouped by Licensee from Licensor's accrued royalties, Licensor shall repay Licensee the full unrecouped amount thereof within five (5) business days of said expiration or when otherwise subject to repayment under this Exhibit "B";

(iii) notwithstanding anything to the contrary contained herein, if Artist fails to commence an Option Term U.S. Tour by the date four (4) months after the United States commercial release of the Option Term Album (hereinafter "Option Term Scheduled Commencement Date"), Licensor shall be charged a Delayed Performance Fee, which shall be charged between the Option Term Scheduled Commencement Date and the actual commencement of an Option Term U.S. Tour and shall be treated as an additional Option Term Advance paid hereunder.

(c) The advances and deposits payable pursuant to this agreement shall be recoupable from the royalties payable pursuant to paragraph 15(c) of the main body of this agreement, paragraph 2 below, and from royalties earned pursuant to paragraph 6(a) of the Merchandising Agreement.

(d) Licensee shall have the right to deduct from any payment of monies due Licensor hereunder the amounts shown to be due all of Licensee's outstanding invoices, if any, to or on behalf of Licensor or any member of Artist.

2. ROYALTIES PAYABLE

The advances and deposits shall be recouped and/or royalties paid as follows:

(a) on sales of Licensed Products (other than tour programs and specialty items, in the event Licensor and Licensee mutually agree to market same hereunder) in the United States:

(i) at concerts where Artist performs as a sole headliner before at least 1,500 bona fide, paid attendees, _____ percent (___%) of gross sales on gross sales from _____ to _____, and _____ percent (___%) of gross sales on gross sales in excess of _____;

(ii) at concerts where Artist performs in all other capacities:

(A) before at least 1,500 bona fide, paid attendees, _____ percent (___%) of gross sales on gross sales from _____ to _____, _____ percent (___%) of gross sales on gross sales from _____ to _____ and _____ percent (___%) of gross sales on gross sales in excess of _____.

For the purpose of all calculations in this agreement, "gross sales" shall exclude sales tax, value-added tax, or any equivalent taxes;

(b) on sales of Licensed Products (other than tour programs and specialty items, in the event Licensor and Licensee mutually agree to market same hereunder) in the United Kingdom and Germany, _____ percent (___%) of gross sales;

(c) on sales of Licensed Products (other than tour programs and specialty items, in the event Licensor and Licensee mutually agree to market same hereunder) in the remainder of the Licensed Area, _____ percent (___%) of gross sales;

(d) on sales of tour programs, in the event Licensor and Licensee mutually agree to market same hereunder, throughout the entire Licensed Area, of net profits; as used in this subparagraph 2(d), "net profits" shall mean gross sales of programs hereunder less mutually approved costs of production, other mutually approved expenses, and a pro rata share of the following expenses attributable to programs: value-added tax or its equivalent, freight and trucking expenses (equipment and personnel), hall and vendor fees, insurance on goods shipped outside the United States, customs duties, mutually approved bootleg security and direct legal costs incurred with respect to same, road staff expenses (including without limitation salaries, per diems, and travel directly related to services hereunder);

(e) on sales of specialty items, including designer garments (i.e., garments which sell for more than ____), _____ percent (___%) of net profits; as used in this subparagraph 2(e), "net profits" shall mean gross sales of specialty items hereunder, less mutually approved costs of production, other mutually approved expenses, a mutually agreeable royalty payable with respect to specialty items and a pro rata share of the following expenses attributable to specialty items: hall and vendor fees, freight and trucking expenses (equipment and personnel), insurance on goods shipped outside the United States, customs duties, mutually approved bootleg security and direct legal costs incurred with respect to same, and road staff expenses (including without limitation salaries, per diems, and travel directly related to services hereunder).

(f) Notwithstanding the foregoing, on sales of tour programs and specialty items, in the event Licensor and Licensee mutually agree to market same hereunder, in Japan and Australia, the royalty rate set forth in subparagraph 2(c) above shall apply.

(g) Royalties on sales of Licensed Products in Northern Ireland and the Republic of Ireland shall be payable at the rate for Europe, rather than the rate for the United Kingdom.

(h) The royalties set out above only apply to Licensee's standard blank stock for and style and design of the Licensed Products listed on Exhibit "A."

(i) Notwithstanding anything to the contrary contained herein, if Licensee is required by a foreign governmental instrumentality to deduct taxes based on

Licensee's receipts (due to Licensor or Artist's liability in such territory, not to Licensee's income tax liability, if any) and/or Licensor's earnings from merchandise sales hereunder or if such governmental instrumentality requires deduction of any other taxes on Licensor or Artist's behalf due to Licensor or Artist's liability in such territory, Licensee may:

(A) deduct the full amount of any such taxes actually paid or estimated to be required for payment to such instrumentality; and/or

(B) in the event the advances paid hereunder by Licensee to Licensor are unrecouped, Licensor shall pay Licensee the amount of such taxes paid by Licensee to such instrumentality on presentation of appropriate proof of payment by Licensee.

Notwithstanding anything contained in this subparagraph 2(i), Licensee shall notify Licensor as soon as reasonably possible after having been contacted by any governmental instrumentality with respect to the taxes described above. If Licensor or Artist itself makes the payments of any such taxes, Licensee may not avail itself of the remedies set out in subparagraphs 2(i)(A) and 2(i)(B) above, provided that the governmental instrumentality involved has recognized such payment by Artist or Licensor and has provided Licensee, prior to the time its payment to the governmental instrumentality is due, with its appropriate governmental notification that it need not make the payment with respect to Licensor or Artist's taxes. Licensee shall provide Licensor with suitable confirmation of any such taxes paid by Licensee.

3. PERFORMANCE MINIMUM

(a) Initial Term:

(i) In order to induce Licensee to pay the Initial Term advances, deposits, and royalties set out above, Licensor warrants that between the date of this agreement and August 1, 19__ (hereinafter "Initial Term Performance Minimum Period"), Artist shall perform live musical concerts at shows:

(A) held in the United States;

(B) where Artist is the sole headliner or second-billed act supporting an artist for which Licensee is the tour merchandiser;

(C) before at least 500 bona fide, paid attendees; and

(D) not given in conjunction with another nonmusical public performance, air, or amusement event, unless a separate admission price is charged for Artist's concert.

Concerts satisfying the above criteria hereinafter referred to as a "Performance(s)." A "bona fide, paid attendee" shall mean a person who has paid the full ticket price for admission to a Performance (with the exception of Stadium Shows, for which the number of bona fide, paid attendees shall be counted pursuant to subparagraph 3(a)(ii) below) and actually attended such Performance and whose attendance is verified by facility drop counts supplied to Licensee. Licensor and Licensee agree that in the event Artist plays before bona fide, paid attendees during the Initial Term Performance Minimum Period in excess of the Initial Term Performance Minimum, the Initial Term shall include the dates at which Artist performs before such excess number of bona fide, paid attendees. Licensor also warrants that when Artist performs as a headliner, there will be at least one (1) intermission and one (1) opening act at each Performance.

(ii) Notwithstanding the foregoing, with respect to concerts during the Initial Term Performance Minimum Period at venues with capacities in excess of

22,000 people at which three (3) or more musical artists perform (hereinafter "Stadium Shows"), the number of bona fide, paid attendees to be counted for purposes of fulfilling the Initial Term Performance Minimum shall be the following:

(Licensor's gross sales of Licensed Products at Stadium Shows) DIVIDED BY (Licensor's average gross sales of Licensed Products [determined at the end of the tour] per bona fide, paid attendee at Performances [other than Stadium Shows] during Initial Term Performance Minimum Period) EQUALS Number of bona fide, paid attendees to be counted for such Stadium Show (but the number to be inserted shall not exceed the actual number of full-paying attendees at such Stadium Show).

(iii) Notwithstanding anything to the contrary contained herein, in the event that Artist fails at any Performance during the Initial Term Performance Minimum Period to substantially perform, the number of bona fide, paid attendees to be counted at such Performance toward fulfillment of the Initial Term Performance Minimum shall be calculated as follows:

(Licensor's gross sales of Licensed Products for such Performance) DIVIDED BY (Licensor's average per-head gross sales of Licensed Products at Performances during Initial Term Performance Minimum Period at which Artist does substantially perform) EQUALS Number of bona fide, paid attendees to be counted (but the number to be inserted shall not exceed the actual number of bona fide, paid attendees at such Performance) As used herein, to "substantially perform" shall mean to play at least sixty (60) minutes of live music when Artist is a headliner and thirty (30) minutes of live music when Artist is not a headliner.

(iv) If the Initial Term Performance minimum is not met and the advances and deposits then paid have not been recouped by Licensee from Licensor's accrued royalties, Licensor shall pay Licensee the lesser of I or II within five (5) business days of Licensee's request therefore:

I. 66,000 MINUS (bona fide, paid attendees) DIVIDED BY 66,000 MULTIPLIED BY (Advances paid by Licensee) EQUALS Sum due Licensee; OR

II. (Advances paid by Licensee) MINUS (Licensor's accrued royalties when repayment requested) EQUALS Sum due Licensee

(v) If Artist fails to commence an Initial Term U.S. Tour by September 1, 19__, or there is a gap of at least thirty (30) days between Performances during the Initial Term, Licensee may invoke the terms of subparagraph 3(a)(iv) above by letter, in which event, the repayment shall be due within five (5) business days of Licensor's receipt of such notice.

(b) Option Term:

(i) in order to induce Licensee to pay the Option Term advances, deposits, and royalties set out above, Licensor warrants that during the period of one (1) year after Licensee's exercise of the Option (hereinafter "Option Term Performance Minimum Period"), Artist shall give Performances before a minimum number of bona fide, paid attendees equal to the following (hereinafter "Option Term Performance Minimum"):

(Option Term Advance) DIVIDED BY (Average Per-Head Gross Sales) MULTIPLIED BY (Option Term Royalty Rate)

Where "Average Per-Head Gross Sales" means Licensor's aggregate gross sales of Licensed Products during the Initial Term divided by the aggregate number of bona fide, paid attendees at Artist's concerts in the Licensed Area during the Initial Term, and "Option Term Royalty Rate" means the royalty rate payable during the Option Term at Performances during the Option Term Performance Minimum Period.

Solely by way of example, if the Option Term Advance is _____, Average Per-Head Gross Sales are _____, and the Option Term Royalty Rate is _____, the Option Term Performance Minimum will be _____ bona fide, paid attendees, calculated as follows: Licensor and Licensee agree that in the event Artist plays before bona fide, paid attendees during the Option Term Performance Minimum Period in excess of the Option Term Performance Minimum, the Option Term Performance Minimum shall include the dates at which Artist performs before such excess number of bona fide, paid attendees. Licensor also warrants that when Artist is a headliner, there will be at least one (1) intermission and one (1) opening act at each Performance during the Option Term;

(ii) Notwithstanding the foregoing, with respect to Stadium Shows during the Option Term Performance Minimum Period, the number of bona fide, paid attendees to be counted for purposes of fulfilling the Option Term Performance Minimum shall be the following:

(Licensor's gross sales of Licensed Products for individual Stadium Show) DIVIDED BY (Licensor's average gross sales of Licensed Products per bona fide, paid attendee at Performances [other than Stadium Shows] during Option Term Performance Minimum Period) EQUALS Number of bona fide, paid attendees to be counted for such Stadium Show (but the number to be inserted shall not exceed the actual number of full-paying attendees at such Stadium Show).

(iii) Notwithstanding anything to the contrary contained herein, in the event that Artist fails at any Performance during the Option Term Performance Minimum Period to substantially perform, the number of bona fide, paid attendees to be counted at such Performance toward fulfillment of the Option Term Performance Minimum shall be calculated as follows:

(Licensor's gross sales of Licensed Products for such Performance) DIVIDED BY (Licensor's average per-head gross sales of Licensed Products at Performances during Option Term Performance Minimum Period at which Artist does substantially perform) EQUALS Number of bona fide, paid attendees to be counted (but the number to be inserted shall not exceed the actual number of bona fide, paid attendees at such Performance).

As used herein, to "substantially perform" shall mean to play at least sixty (60) minutes of live music when Artist is a headliner and thirty (30) minutes of live music when Artist is not a headliner.

(iv) If the Option Term Performance Minimum is not met and the advances and deposits then paid have not been recouped by Licensee from Licensor's accrued royalties, Licensor shall pay Licensee the lesser of I or II within five (5) business days of Licensee's request therefore:

I. (Option Term Performance Minimum) MINUS (bona fide, paid attendees) DIVIDED BY (Option Term Performance Minimum) MULTIPLIED BY (Advances paid by Licensee) EQUALS Sum due Licensee; OR

II. (Advances paid by Licensee) MINUS (Licensor's accrued royalties when repayment requested) EQUALS Sum due Licensee.

(v) If Artist fails to commence an Option Term U.S. Tour within four (4) months after the release of the Option Term Album or there is a gap of at least thirty (30) days between Performances during the Option Term, Licensee may invoke the terms of subparagraph 3(b)(iv) above by letter, in which event, the repayment shall be due within five (5) business days of Licensor's receipt of such notice.

(c) If any lawsuit is filed to collect the amount set out in subparagraph 3(a)(iv), 3(a)(v) and 3(b)(v) above, the prevailing party shall be entitled to full court costs and attorneys' fees incurred in connection with such effort.

(d) Any sum due Licensee pursuant to subparagraph 3(a)(iv), 3(a)(v), 3(b)(iv), or 3(b)(v) above, if not timely paid, shall accrue interest from the date due at the rate of ten percent (10%) per annum.

(e) If a fee is charged by another entertainer for Licensee's right to sell merchandise, Licensor, rather than Licensee, shall pay such fee.

(f) Licensor hereby warrants that at each of Artist's concerts during the Licensed Term, including but not limited to support dates with _____, Licensee will be permitted to sell Artist's merchandise.

(g) Notwithstanding anything contained in this agreement, the Licensed Term shall continue until the repayment due, if any, plus interest thereon, pursuant to subparagraph 3(a)(iv), 3(a)(v), 3(b)(iv), or 3(b)(v) above is received by Licensee. Repayment of all sums owed by Licensor to Licensee pursuant to the terms of subparagraph 3(a)(iv), 3(a)(v), 3(b)(iv), or 3(b)(v) above shall result in termination of this agreement upon the date of such repayment.

Your signature, together with ours, shall constitute this a binding agreement between us.

AGREED TO AND ACCEPTED:

_____   _____
(LICENSOR)   (LICENSEE)

_____   _____
ADDRESS   ADDRESS

_____   _____
FEDERAL I.D. / SS#   FEDERAL I.D. / SS#

_____
DATE

MANAGERS AND AGENTS

What A Manager Does

**Analysis Of A Personal
Management Agreement**

Talent Agencies

Business Managers

WHAT A MANAGER DOES

by Alfred Schlesinger

Let's say you are an artist who says to a prospective manager, "OK, I'm a talent, here I am, here's what I look like, here's what I do. Are you interested?" And the manager says "Yes!"

First off, your manager will probably say to you, "Look, approximately one hundred percent of our energies have to go toward getting a record contract. Anything else we do is more or less avoiding the main issue. You are not going to make it, you are not going to become a star, you won't make good money and nothing monumental will happen to you as a musical performer without a record. Let's get a record contract!"

I shall presume that the manager, whether an individual or a company, has honesty and integrity, knowledge and capability. If any one of these attributes is missing, the manager will not be effective.

WHAT TO LOOK FOR IN A MANAGER

Your manager represents, advises and works for you. This person or organization handles all of your day-to-day business while you create and for that, receives a percentage of your earnings. If you make money, your manager makes money. If not, your manager will have spent an awful lot of time and effort for nothing.

When considering managers, check out their reputations. People have reputations because they have earned them. Nobody can be liked by everybody, but if a person is spoken of as being genuine and honest, you can assume this is probably true.

However, a good reputation means nothing unless there is a trust and good feeling between artist and manager. I don't see how anyone can have a personal manager they don't like.

The manager's enthusiasm and belief in you are essential for a successful relationship. A manager cannot and should not represent you if he or she doesn't understand your motives, priorities, beliefs, way of life and what's important to you.

The personality of the manager must be considered. Some managers can break down doors (literally and figuratively), scream, holler, demand and be very effective. Some artists like that, others might want someone more laid back. The object is to enable the artist to write, rehearse and perform; to create with a free, clear mind. The idea is not, however, to remove artists from business entirely, but rather to free them from the nitty-gritty work-a-day affairs. Artists should know what is going on with their careers and be familiar with the agent, record company personnel, business manager, attorney, public relations people and whoever else has a hand in their success or failure. Managing an artist is a tremendous job; artists choosing to do it alone will have great difficulty finding time to create music and run their business.

THE MANAGER'S ROLE

A manager provides knowledge, judgment and objectivity in the following key areas:

Record Companies

It's a manager's job to know the record companies. Certain record companies are better for certain types of music. Some record companies are stronger on the West Coast than on the East. Certain companies have political problems, and you don't want to get into the midst of a political situation. Some record companies are losers and can't give their records away; others are hot. Some own their own branch distribution centers while others depend on several independent distributors.

It's up to the manager to know which companies are in trouble, financially or politically. Some of the rather well-known and respected record companies are in financial straits, and though the vast majority of record companies are honest, there are some that are very shy about paying royalties.

The artist usually doesn't know these things. He or she usually goes to the manager and says, "You know, I like the way that company promotes their records. I like their covers, their roster, the way they handle this and that." The artist's opinions along these lines are very important, and most managers will want to know what the artist fancies and why. It's a happy situation when the manager agrees with the artist and it all sounds good. But, like the artist, the record company has an image to maintain, and sometimes that's all the artist will see. The manager has to know the truth behind the company's image and if the record company is the right one for a particular artist.

Scheduling

It's important for a manager to help schedule an artist's life by structuring recording and performing contracts appropriately. Some performers schedule sixteen months of activity into a year. There is no way that can be done. A manager has to help the artist plan ahead, sometimes a year or more at a time. Time should be set aside for creative activity, vacation, recording and for touring. To help do that, the manager has to be very sensitive to the artist's habits and needs. For example, if the artist is a songwriter, the manager must realize that songs take a certain amount of time to produce. It's difficult for some artists to write songs while recording, while on the road or on vacation. It's important to set aside enough time out of the year for this kind of creativity.

Recording Habits

A manager must understand the artist's recording habits and should know how long a recording is likely to take. Some artists can spend two days at a recording studio and come out with ten tracks for a flawless, marvelous album. Others will take up to eighteen months in the studio. One of the most devastating things that can happen to a recording artist is having a manager get a very heavy commitment from a record company to release a certain number of albums each year when the artist can't handle that many albums or that kind of pressure. That contract can wind up being, virtually, a contract for life.

For example, you are committed to delivering two albums a year for five years, but in the first year only one album is made. In the second year three albums must be delivered. If only one is done that year, the next year four are due, etc. It's possible under some circumstances and in some jurisdictions for you to be recording for a company for ten years, or longer, if less than one album is produced per year.

Recording Package

The manager should help put together a recording package. Instrumentation, musicians, singers, a producer and engineer must be selected. (The role of the engineer has long been overlooked, but is very significant in the recording process today.) Presumably, the manager knows the top people and studios and can help select a package appropriate for the artist.

Selecting the best songs to record is another part of the manager's function. If the artist is a writer, he or she may have a great wealth of material. Which songs put on a demo or subsequent album will best represent the artist's talent?

All of these are critical decisions that should be made before the process of getting a contract is started. The manager then seeks out the record company that can combine all the elements of the recording package the manager has put together on the artist's behalf.

Objectivity

The manager provides objectivity. One reason artists need help in all these areas is that they often lack objectivity. Is the artist capable of stepping back and saying, "This is great; this is bad; this is OK?" Sometimes yes, but more often than not, no.

Most of the people in the business are reasonably sensitive, even the strictly business people. They will never tell an artist, "I hated your last album, it stunk." A record company executive may sugarcoat his remarks to the artist, but he will level with the manager. Then it is the job of the manager, who one hopes is also a sensitive person, to get the story across to the artist.

The artist who deals directly with this sort of feedback is making a serious error. Moreover, show business is an image business. A great deal of time, effort and money is spent to create an image. It can be very damaging to an artist's image to get in there and do battle. The artist should always be the hero, the good guy. The manager should always be the fall guy. If, as sometimes happens, bad feeling is created, the artist should never suffer by it.

THE RECORDING TEAM

The manager's role in helping to successfully negotiate a recording contract is only the beginning. With the signing of the contract, the manager becomes the captain of an incredibly varied team of people, both inside and outside of the record company. Managers work with these people on behalf of artists.

Record Company

The most important of all the relationships an artist maintains (after his or her personal manager) is with the record company. It can be the artist's best friend or worst enemy. If the record company is not with the artist all the way, the artist's career is definitely going to suffer delays and setbacks.

A manager has to have a lot of insight concerning the people within the record company that he or she is dealing with. Keeping them friendly and committed to furthering the artist's career is important.

If the president of the record company is behind a record, that album has a much greater chance of "happening." A manager must have access to the top people and be able to intelligently discuss situations and gain their support.

Artist Relations

The artist relations person, a creative, very important member of the team, takes the artist's part and stands up for the artist in the company (even though the A&R person is employed by the company). The artist relations person introduces the artist and manager to all the other employees in the record company, acting as a general communications liaison and information resource.

Promotion Representative

The national promotion representative does all the long-distance calling to the key top forty radio markets and has a feel for what's happening in the field. Remember, airplay is absolutely essential for success.

Sales and Marketing

The head of sales and marketing helps choose the sales tools that supplement live performances and airplay. These tools range from store displays and merchandising accessories to ads in Sunday supplements, co-op deals with leading record dealers, radio time, etc.

Relationships should be maintained with local sales and promotion representatives who can help get that important extra push.

At the appropriate time, the manager will want to work with the person in charge of international sales and promotion to help set up foreign tours and release the record in other countries.

ALBUM RELEASE AND TOURING

The best time for a record to be released is when it's going to get the most attention and when a tour has been set up to support that release.

Arguments can be made for bringing out an album alone, and for coming out with a group of albums by various artists on the same label. For example, if the label has a release of 10 albums, the company is likely to spend a lot more promotional money and do a lot more for that 10 album package. But bringing out an album alone will give it more individual attention, even if less money is spent.

Some managers believe there are times during the year when you shouldn't release an album. Generally, those times are November, December, June and July. Disc jockeys rarely add records to their play lists during the last part of the year. They're playing Christmas records and the top 100 of the year or the top 400 of the century, and new records, particularly those by new artists, don't get much attention. Also, record dealers are busy selling; they're not going to take the time to order a new record unless it's moving at a tremendous clip. Albums just released in November or December aren't going to be in that position yet. In June and July, kids are getting out of school, finishing their exams, going away on vacations. It's just not the time when anything is going to get the best possible push. On the other hand, a June-July release might mean that a record will be released alone and the record company can put its full strength behind it.

Tour Timing

Anywhere between three and four weeks after an album is released is considered a good time for an artist to start a tour. After an album is released, it takes a few weeks for it to go through all the channels of distribution for reviews to start happening and a couple more weeks before the radio stations get it, give it a listen, and, with luck, start to play it.

It's very important for a manager to know when the album will be released, so that a tour can be planned and booked. For example, if you go into the recording studio in the beginning of January, figure maybe it's going to be a May release. Your manager should know by February whether that release date will be met. If it is, the booking agent is asked to begin the tour in June. On the other hand, if February comes around and you have only one track down, your manager knows to forget the May release, stay on the safe side and look for the album sometime in August. Around March or April the manager will contact the booking agent and plan a tour for the fall.

Sometimes a tour is not necessary until after a few records have been released. The first single, the second single, maybe the first or even the second album may sell without the buying public knowing that you are a working, touring act. But after these first few albums, it's important for the public to see your face and equate the sounds they hear on the record with a live human being.

Your manager should also know what you can handle as far as touring is concerned. Some artists are "touring fools" who go out 300 to 325 days a year. An average act will tour at least 50 to 100 days a year; 300 days might show dedication, but I feel it's absolutely devastating.

Clout

Whether a manager's opinions about when to start a tour or when to have a record released carry any weight depends on whether or not the record company is enthusiastic about the album. If everybody at the record company is excited beyond belief, your manager's opinion is going to carry some muscle. But if the attitude of the company is, "Look, it's not bad for a first album; we'll put it out and see what happens," then the manager has hardly any influence at all.

Nevertheless, if the manager can go in with a good working plan for coordinating a tour with an album release, then he or she will have a shot at being heard. The management at many record companies is extremely astute, intelligent and willing to listen. They recognize that they are dealing with as many as forty or fifty acts and that a manager focuses on only a few. As in many other areas of business, managers can perform extremely important functions by doing some of the record companies' homework for them.

MANAGEMENT ORGANIZATIONS

There are one-person firms and small and large organizations. A one-person organization has its limitations because the manager can't always be supported by one talent and probably will manage other clients. But a good manager will not take on more clients than can be served effectively.

Some management companies consist of more than one person with others working for them. Selecting a large company like this can be a mistake for a young performer. An artist might think, "John/Jane Doe who runs this organization is the heaviest manager in the business and I'm going to get Doe's personal attention." Usually this doesn't happen.

Probably they will get the services of someone working for the firm instead of those of the top person. This is not necessarily bad if the right relationship is established with this person, and the muscle of a large organization is behind the artist.

But if you sign a contract thinking that Ms. A will be representing you, only to find after six months or so that you're dealing with Mr. B, you should be able to terminate the contract.

Again, it depends on feelings. Many performers enter the offices of a large organization and immediately turn and walk out. They don't feel comfortable and don't want to get involved with a machine, no matter how well oiled.

MANAGEMENT CONTRACTS

If something is important to you, get it in the contract. If a manager will not put a provision in writing, then the manager probably has no intention of living up to it.

The Term of the Contract

Management contracts vary in term from one to five years. What's important here is for the artist to decide what goals should be reached and in what time. Some contracts state that if the artist doesn't have a recording contract in six months, he or she can terminate; another might require two network variety performances in the first year. If the manager agrees, those terms should be put into the contract.

The artist should understand, however, that a manager needs a fair length of time to help an artist towards success. It sometimes takes two years or more before an artist starts to make any real money. It would be unfair for a hardworking, honest and reasonably effective manager to be terminated at the end of a year after laying the groundwork and not be around to collect the rewards. Artists must be realistic about the time in which they can expect to reach their goals.

Unfortunately, there are rarely outs in contracts for someone who no longer loves their manager. The personal relationship is so important and quite hard to define on paper. It's very difficult to frame a contract saying, "Notwithstanding the fact that we have a five-year contract, if at any time during that contract I don't like you, I can terminate."

POWER OF ATTORNEY

In standard management contracts, managers are given a blanket power of attorney, meaning that they can sign and approve anything regarding the artist's career without the consent or knowledge of the artist. Certainly, artists should work to limit that power if they are available to sign; or at least specify the circumstances under which the manager has that power, e.g., not being able to sign for engagements longer than a certain period of time or for a certain amount of money. At the very least, artists can have clauses requiring consultation and approval, if only verbal, before the manager signs anything on their behalf.

Normally, a manager makes day-to-day decisions, but leaves major ones open for discussion and consultation. But artist and manager should develop a modus operandi, an understanding of what can be done without consultation.

Percentages and Expenses

Manager percentages usually fall between 15% and 20%, although there are exceptions. For instance, a manager investing large sums of money in an artist, at a risk, might receive 25%.

In standard contracts, the manager is not specifically obligated to advance or lend money, but many artists expect it. If a manager does advance money, the artist must repay it.

Sometimes a manager is excluded from receiving percentage commissions on publishing, songwriting or monies from ASCAP, BMI or recording, etc. My feeling is that managers promote all their artists' causes and, if you limit their income, you may find it detrimental in the long run—if only as an erosion of feeling between you.

Costs incurred on behalf of the artist by the manager (other than normal overhead) should be paid by the artist. This includes travel, phone calls, publicity photographs, etc.

Many artists include clauses in their management contracts limiting the circumstances and amounts that a manager can spend without their consent.

CONCLUSION

The results of a manager's efforts are not realized in days or weeks, they accumulate over a period of years.

The manager's job is multifaceted: administrator, friend, salesperson, employer, negotiator, advisor. In any one day the manager may need to effectively communicate with a record company president, bartender, road manager, lead guitarist's girlfriend, lawyer, journalist, disc jockey, record producer, food caterer, etc.

Finding a competent, knowledgeable manager at the beginning of a band's career, when he or she is most needed, is extremely difficult. Many professional managers are reluctant to sign a band until it has achieved some success in the marketplace, such as a large draw in a major city or a contract with an independent record label. Therefore many new bands must manage themselves, sharing the tasks, until they can attract a professional manager.

ANALYSIS OF A PERSONAL MANAGEMENT AGREEMENT

by Neville L. Johnson

It is often necessary, yet difficult, for a musician to find a good personal manager. Personal managers are the supervisors and coordinators of the business and career activities of professional entertainers. They are the liaison to those who do business with the artist. Depending on the needs of the client, personal managers must at times motivate, direct, market, make demands, and advise. Managers are involved in such issues as which employment to seek and accept, the artist's public mystique or image, and the marketing and promotion of the artist's career. In most instances, communications with agents, attorneys, business managers, publicists, record companies and music publishers are routed through the personal manager.

Many artists are unwilling, or unable to devote the time necessary to supervise and coordinate the many services required from those who build and maintain their careers. Virtually all successful recording artists have personal managers, as do some record producers.

Some personal managers invest money, in addition to time, into the acts they represent. Their profession is risky and often costly.

Fledgling or unsigned acts have difficulty obtaining qualified personal managers because those that are desirable are busy with successful acts and do not have the time or interest to focus on a developing talent. Being a personal manager is often a thankless job, sometimes lucrative, and always difficult.

Personal managers, are in effect, employees of the acts they represent and operate in a fiduciary capacity to the artist. Thus, the artist is always boss—but has usually engaged the manager because of their superior knowledge of and capabilities in the business arena. A fiduciary is one in whom a special trust is placed and who, consequently, owes special duties to the client. Like attorneys and accountants, personal managers must subordinate their own interests to those of their clients. The client's best interests always come first: There must at all times be complete disclosure of all material information and no "side-dealing" of any nature, and no "secret profits."

A personal manager is the eyes and ears of the artist and must disclose completely all business dealings involving said artist. The personal manager must never obtain an unfair economic advantage with respect to the client, must exercise no undue influence over the client's affairs, and must always operate with the highest standards of good faith and fair dealing. Personal managers must always use their best efforts to see that the client has independent advice when necessary, as in, for example, a conflict of interest situation where the manager seeks to be an employer or partner with the client and thus may be biased when giving advice to the artist.

A personal manager relationship is the business equivalent of a marriage. It must be entered into with sobriety, intelligence and forethought. The successful artist will understand, appreciate and supervise the myriad duties of the personal manager. Similarly, artists should understand and fulfill their obligations regarding their personal managers. They need each other so that they can make money by contributing their respective services and abilities to the mutual enterprise of advancing the artist's career.

MANAGERS AT PERIL

Although the personal manager is the chief executive responsible for the promotion and marketing of the artist, procuring of labor for a musician can be a difficult and treacherous area for all personal managers that operate in California. (The only other state where procurement of labor may be a problem is New York.) California's Labor Code, in a section called the Talent Agencies Act, regulates the offer, promise, procurement or attempted procurement of employment for entertainers. There has been much controversy about this law over the years. Except with respect to the procurement of recording agreements, personal managers are not allowed to so act without a state license giving them permission to operate as a talent agency. Most personal managers have failed to obtain such licenses because of various state rules and union regulations. For example, anyone with a talent agency license must operate in an office, not a residence.

The AFM, AFTRA and SAG allow union members to terminate agency agreements if work is not secured within a specified period of time. Many managers cannot operate within these strictures. There have been attempts to produce a workable arrangement that is satisfactory to all parties but the matter has yet to be resolved. For example, a personal manager may not solicit a live engagement for an entertainer unless he or she possess a talent agency license. Most talent agencies (and most established personal managers) are not interested in musical acts that do not have record agreements with major labels. Thus, personal managers representing talent in that position are effectively required to seek such employment, or at least deal with offers that come in, but may violate state law if they do so. (If the manager takes no commission, his conduct is probably lawful.) The Talent Agencies Act has been used by many musicians over the years as a legal maneuver to terminate management agreements.

In 1993, the California Court of Appeals, in the landmark decision of *Wachs v. Curry*, ruled that a personal manager's contract would not be voided unless the personal manager was predominantly in the business of securing labor. Personal managers, thus, can breathe easier, but the coast is by no means clear for them to secure or promise to secure employment.

PERSONAL MANAGEMENT AGREEMENT

1. TERM

Manager is hereby engaged as Artist's exclusive personal manager and advisor. The agreement shall continue for three (3) years (hereinafter the "initial term") from the date thereof, and shall be renewed for one (l) year periods (hereinafter "renewal period(s)") automatically unless either party shall give written notice of termination to the other not later than thirty (30) days prior to the expiration of the initial term or the then current renewal period, as applicable, subject to the terms and conditions hereof.

Most personal management agreements have a three-year term, although some can last up to five years, at the manager's discretion. Artists sometimes insert provisions that provide for a minimum of earnings which the artist must earn during the period before any option period may be exercised. Most personal management agreements with newer acts provide that if a recording agreement is not secured within a period of up to eighteen months, after commencement of the term, then the management agreement may be terminated by either party.

2. SERVICES

(a) Manager agrees during the term thereof, to advise, counsel and assist Artist in connection with all matters relating to Artist's career in all branches of the music industry, including, without limitation, the following:

(i) in the selection of literary, artistic and musical material;

(ii) with respect to matters pertaining to publicity, promotion, public relations and advertising;

(iii) with respect to the adoption of proper formats for the presentation of Artist's artistic talents and in determination of the proper style, mood, setting, business and characterization in keeping with Artist's talents;

(iv) in the selection of artistic talent to assist, accompany or embellish Artist's artistic presentation, with regard to general practices in the entertainment industries;

(v) with respect to such matters as Manager may have knowledge concerning compensation and privileges extended for similar artistic values;

(vi) with respect to agreements, documents and contracts for Artist's services, talents, and/or artistic, literary and musical materials, or otherwise;

(vii) with respect to the selection, supervision and coordination of those persons, firms and corporations that may counsel, advise, procure employment, or otherwise render services to or on behalf of Artist, such as accountants, attorneys, business managers, publicists and talent agents; and

(b) Manager shall be required only to render reasonable services which are called for by this Agreement as and when reasonably requested by Artist. Manager shall not be required to travel or meet with Artist at any particular place or places, except in Manager's discretion and following arrangements for cost and expenses of such travel, such arrangements to be mutually agreed upon by Artist and Manager.

The foregoing details what managers do. Travel requirements should be negotiated on a case by case basis. An artist might resist paying for travel and long-distance phone charges when the manager chooses to live in a location remote from the residence of the artist. Travel should be necessary and the cost reasonable. An artist may also require an allocation of costs if the manager, when traveling, does other business unrelated to the artist.

As far as "advising and counseling"—although it is a vague job description, this is as far as most agreements go. Further, it is difficult to articulate the efforts that may be required.

Some artists find it frustrating that the manager's obligations are so vaguely defined. There is no reason why an artist cannot require the manager to specify in further detail the services required. For example, artists could require their managers not to represent more than three other acts, and require their manager to meet with them bi-weekly, or monthly, to create or present strategies and goals for the artist. An artist should require that all material information about his or her business be provided as soon as it is obtained or learned.

There should be a specific provision where the manager acknowledges that a fiduciary relationship (one of special trust) exists. An artist should never agree that no such relationship exists.

Further, what are the obligations of the manager after the term of the agreement? For example, one of our current cases involves a manager who claims to own music publishing rights of the artist. We had to sue him to get him to turn over all documents relating to the same. Thus, artists should try and insert a provision requiring the manager to keep the artist informed at all times of all activities of the manager and rights in which the manager claims an interest, and certainly upon request of the artist, or the artist's representative.

3. AUTHORITY OF MANAGER

Manager is hereby appointed Artist's exclusive, true and lawful attorney-in-fact, to do any or all of the following, for or on behalf of Artist, during the term of this Agreement:

(a) approve and authorize any and all publicity and advertising, subject to Artist's previous approval;

(b) approve and authorize the use of Artist's name, photograph, likeness, voice, sound effects, caricatures, and literary, artistic and musical materials for the purpose of advertising any and all products and services, subject to Artist's previous approval;

(c) execute in Artist's name, American Federation of Musicians contracts for Artist's personal appearances as a live entertainer, subject to Artist's previous consent to the material terms thereof; and

(d) without in any way limiting the foregoing, generally do, execute and perform any other act, deed, matter or thing whatsoever, that ought to be done on behalf of the Artist by a personal manager.

The key words "subject to Artist's approval" should be inserted at the end of subparagraph 3(d). An artist will usually want to delete any last clause which gives the manager the right to execute agreements on behalf of the artist. The intelligent artist always supervises and understands his contractual relations. Too much control—and the possibility of abuse—reside in any manager that has unchecked freedom to bind the artist. Managers should only be appointed to execute AFM agreements as noted in subparagraph 3(c) and when the artist is reasonably not available to do so, which will be rare, given the existence of courier services and fax machines.

4. COMMISSIONS

(a) Since the nature and extent of the success or failure of Artist's career cannot be predetermined, it is the desire of the parties hereto that Manager's compensation shall be determined in such a manner as will permit Manager to accept the risk of failure as well as the benefit of Artist's success. Therefore, as compensation for Manager's services, Artist shall pay Manager, throughout the full term hereof, as when received by Artist, the following percentages of Artist's gross earnings (hereinafter referred to as the "Commission"):

(i) Fifteen percent (15%) of Artist's gross earnings received in connection with Artist providing their services as a recording artist for the recording of master recordings to be manufactured and marketed as phonograph records and tapes during the term hereof. Manager shall receive said Commission in perpetuity on the sale of those master recordings recorded during the term hereof. In no event shall the term "gross earnings" be deemed to include payments to third parties (which are not owned or controlled substantially or entirely by Artist), in connection with the recordings of master recordings prior to or during the term hereof;

Managers in the music business usually take a 15% or 20% commission of an artist's earnings.

(ii) Fifteen percent (15%) of the Artist's gross earnings from live performances;

The artist should seek to, and generally does, limit the manager's compensation on live engagements to the artist's "net" derived from such engagements: i.e., after the deductions of travel, lights, and other out-of-pocket payments that an artist makes to third parties, including agents and musicians.

(iii) Fifteen percent (15%) of the Artist's gross earnings derived from any and all of Artist's activities in connection with music publishing, or the licensing or assignment of any compositions composed by Artist alone or in collaboration with others (it being understood that no commissions shall be taken with respect to any compositions that are the subject of any separate music publishing agreement between Artist and Manager).

Some managers seek to administer the compositions of their artists and/or take a higher percentage from music publishing royalties. Although nothing is inherently wrong with such practices, the personal manager will be subjected to extra scrutiny as to the fairness of the agreements if the artist has no independent advice or unless the circumstances otherwise dictate that the arrangement is fair. See discussion after paragraph 12.

(b) The term "gross earnings" as used herein shall mean and include any and all gross monies or other consideration which Artist may receive, acquire, become entitled to, or which may be payable to Artist, directly or indirectly (without any exclusion or deduction) as a result of Artist's activities in the music industry, whether as a performer, writer, singer, musician, composer, publisher, or artist.

Note that virtually all aspects of entertainment are covered. Artists can and do limit the authority of a manager and his or her compensation in certain areas. This must be decided on a case by case basis. For example, if an artist has a thriving jingle or sound-track business, or is an established actor, then the artist may desire to exclude these areas from the manager's commission.

(c) Manager shall be entitled to receive his full commission as provided herein in perpetuity on Artist's gross earnings derived from any agreements entered into during the term of this agreement, notwithstanding the prior termination of this agreement for any reason. Artist also agrees to pay Manager the commission following the term hereof upon and with respect to all of Artist's gross earnings received after the expiration of the term hereof but derived from any and all employments, engagements, contracts, agreements and activities, negotiated, entered into, commenced or performed during the term hereof relating to any of the foregoing, and upon any and all extensions, renewals and substitutions thereof and therefore, and upon any resumptions of such employments, engagements, contracts, agreements and activities which may have been discontinued during the term hereof and resumed within one (1) year thereafter;

This is a tricky area. In the music business, many personal managers are limited to a commission derived from activities performed during the term of the agreement, and not with respect to activities performed after the personal management agreement but pursuant to agreements that were entered into during the term of the management agreement. For example, should the manager get a commission on records recorded after the management term pursuant to a record deal entered into during the term? There are two views. The manager will argue that if he or she is responsible for building up the career of the artist, the fruits of the manager's labor should be enjoyed for as long as that "contractual tree" bears fruit and it would not be fair to build up an artist's career over a five album period, so that the artist was about to "break" on a major scale, only to be excised from the deal on the next album when the artist achieves major success. The artist will attempt to limit the compensation to only employment activity by the artist rendered to third parties during the term of the management agreement. Artists will argue that they will be forced to pay two commissions: one to the previous manager and one to a new manager, which would be unduly onerous. Moreover, what if the failure to achieve success theretofore was in some part the manager's fault? Possible compromises are a reduced percentage for the manager, an "override" that extends for a limited period, or that the parties will negotiate a fee or override at the end of the term, and if they cannot agree, a third party can decide a fair buyout.

There was major litigation and a trial in 1994 over the relationship between the personal manager of blues-great Willie Dixon and his Estate. The personal manager helped Dixon obtain reversions of various copyrights and was paid up to a third of the revenue stream earned from various compositions, all written before the commencement of the personal management agreement. Such work is generally outside the traditional artist-manager relationship, but if the contract is not specific enough, the personal manager might be entitled to share in such revenues.

Some managers are so "heavy," they operate without written agreements. We foresee trouble, and recommend against any oral agreements. As Samuel Goldwyn, the movie producer, once said, "A verbal contract isn't worth the paper it's written on." It's just very tough to establish and prove an oral contract in a court of law.

"Negotiated" could use more definition, and most times the parties will agree that this include that the material (basic) terms have been agreed upon and the final contract is executed within 90 days after the expiration of the term of the management agreement.

(d) Manager is hereby authorized to receive, on Artist's behalf, all "gross monies and other considerations" and to deposit all such funds into a separate trust account in a bank or savings and loan association. Manager shall have the right to withdraw from such account all expenses and commissions to which Manager is entitled hereunder and shall remit the balance to Artist or as Artist shall direct. Notwithstanding the foregoing, Artist may, at any time, require all "gross monies or other considerations" to be paid to a third party, provided that such party shall irrevocably be directed in writing to pay Manager all expenses and commissions due hereunder.

This is a subject near and dear to both parties. The manager wants to be assured of getting paid; the artist needs to be sure of a fair count. In the early days of a career, when there is little to be made, most managers collect and disburse revenue. Any artist who becomes successful should have an accountant or business manager who supervises the financial activities of the artist. The artist must have the absolute right to audit the books of the manager at reasonable intervals.

It is also a good idea to have the manager acknowledge that he is a fiduciary to the artist, particularly with respect to the financial aspects of the relationship. (The penalties are much stronger for one who violates a fiduciary relationship, as opposed to a mere contractual relationship. If a fiduciary breaches a relationship, punitive or exemplary damages may be claimed—they may not in an ordinary breach of contract situation. Most managers would balk at placing such a provision in the agreement, even though that is the true nature of the agreement).

(e) The term "gross monies or other considerations" as used herein shall include, without limitation, salaries, earnings, fees, royalties, gifts, bonuses, share of profit and other participations, shares of stock, partnership interests, percentages music related income, earned or received directly or indirectly by Artist or Artist's heirs, executors, administrators or assigns, or by any other person, firm or corporation on Artist's behalf. Should Artist be required to make any payment for such interest, Manager will pay Manager's percentage share of such payment, unless Manager elects not to acquire Manager's percentage thereof.

Sometimes artists are offered deals which, for example, would include a stock purchase at a reduced price in return for services. The manager may want to—and should have the right to—get in on the deal.

5. LOANS AND ADVANCES

Manager will make loans or advances to Artist or for Artist's account and incur some expenses on Artist's behalf for the furtherance of Artist's career in amounts to be determined solely by Manager in Manager's best business judgment. Artist hereby authorizes Manager to recoup and retain the amount of any such loans, advances and/or expenses, including, without limitation, transportation and living expenses while traveling, promotion and publicity expenses, and all other reasonable and necessary expenses, from any sums Manager may receive on behalf of Artist. Artist shall reimburse Manager for any expenses incurred by Manager on behalf of Artist, including, without limitation, long-distance calls, travel expenses, messenger services, and postage and delivery costs. Notwithstanding the foregoing, no travel expenses and no single expense in excess of fifty dollars ($50.00) shall be incurred by Manager without the prior approval of Artist. Manager shall provide Artist with monthly statements of all expenses incurred hereunder and Manager shall be reimbursed by Artist within fourteen (14) days of receipt by Artist of any such statement. Notwithstanding the foregoing, any loans, advances or payment of expenses by Manager hereunder shall not be recoupable by Manager hereunder until Artist has earned revenue in the entertainment industry and there is sufficient such revenue to so recoup, repay and compensate Manager without causing Artist hardship or leaving insufficient funds for Artist to pursue his career.

This is another area of controversy. The artist must be careful to see that they are not being sent to the poor house by the manager. A cap on expenses, such as $50.00 per transaction as aforesaid is the best type of insurance. It does cost money to promote and further the career of an artist, however, so it makes sense that managers should be reimbursed for their out-of-pocket expenses occurred on behalf of an artist. Most publicists, attorneys, accountants and business managers charge and obtain reimbursement for out-of-pocket expenses.

6. NONEXCLUSIVITY

Manager's services hereunder are not exclusive. Manager shall at all times be free to perform the same or similar services for others, as well as to engage in any and all other business activities.

The artist may wish to insert a clause guaranteeing that the manager will have sufficient time to devote to the career of the artist or a "key man" clause guaranteeing that the manager, not some employee, will be primarily rendering services to and on behalf of the artist may be inserted instead.

7. ARTIST'S CAREER

Artist agrees at all times to pursue Artist's career in a manner consistent with Artist's values, goals, philosophy and disposition and to do all things necessary and desirable to promote such career and earnings therefrom. Artist shall at all times utilize proper theatrical and other employment agencies to obtain engagements and employment for Artist. Artist shall consult with Manager regarding all offers of employment inquiries concerning Artist's services. Artist shall not, without Manager's prior written approval, engage any other person, firm or corporation to render any services of the kind required of Manager hereunder or which Manager is permitted to perform hereunder.

The manager/artist relationship is built on trust and mutual agreement. All major decisions should be mutually agreed upon, especially concerning those who will work closely with the manager and artist.

8. ADVERTISING

During the term hereof, Manager shall have the exclusive right to advertise and publicize Manager as Artist's personal manager and representative with respect to the music industry.

Managers have businesses too, which may benefit from promotion. The artist might want to approve any advertising or publicity in which his name is used.

9. AGENT

Artist understands that Manager is not licensed as a "talent agency" and that this agreement shall remain, in full force and effect subject to any applicable regulations established by the Labor Commissioner of California, and Artist agrees to modify this agreement to the extent necessary to comply with any such laws.

See the sidebar "Managers at Peril" regarding this subject.

10. ENTIRE AGREEMENT

This constitutes the entire agreement between Artist and Manager relating to the subject matter hereof. This agreement shall be subject to and construed in accordance with the laws of the State of California applicable to agreements entered into and fully performed therein. A waiver by either party hereto or a breach of any provision herein shall not be deemed a waiver of any subsequent breach, nor a permanent modification of such provision. Each party acknowledges that no statement, promise or inducement has been made to such party, except as expressly provided for herein. This agreement may not be changed or modified, or any covenant or provision hereof waived, except by an agreement in writing, signed by the party against whom enforcement of the change, modification or waiver is sought. As used in this agreement, the word "Artist" shall include any corporation owned (partially or wholly) or controlled (directly or indirectly) by Artist and Artist agrees to cause any such corporation to enter into an agreement with Manager of the same terms and conditions contained herein.

11. LEGALITY

Nothing contained in this agreement shall be construed to require the commission of any act contrary to law. Whenever there is any conflict between any provision of this agreement and any material law, contrary to which the parties have no legal right to contract, the latter shall prevail, but in such event the provisions of this agreement affected shall be curtailed and restricted only to the extent necessary to bring them within such legal requirements, and only during the time such conflict exists.

12. CONFLICTING INTERESTS

From time to time during the term of this agreement, acting alone or in association with others, Manager may package an entertainment program in which the Artist is employed as an artist, or Manager may act as the entrepreneur or promoter of an entertainment program in which Artist is employed by Manager or Manager may employ Artist in connection with the production of phonograph records, or as a songwriter, composer or arranger. Such activity on Manager's part shall not be deemed to be a breach of this agreement or of Manager's obligations and duties to Artist. However, Manager shall not be entitled to the commission in connection with any gross earnings derived by Artist from any employment or agreement whereunder Artist is employed by Manager, or by the firm, person or corporation represented by Manager as the package agent for the entertainment program in which Artist is so employed; and Manager shall not be entitled to the commission in connection with any gross earnings derived by Artist from the sale, license or grant of any literary rights to Manager or any person, firm or corporation owned or controlled by Manager. Nothing in this agreement shall be construed to excuse Artist from the payment of the commission upon gross earnings derived by Artist from Artist's employment or sale, license or grant of rights in connections with any entertainment program, phonograph record, or other matter, merely because Manager is also employed in connections therewith as a producer, director, conductor or in some other management or supervisory capacity, but not as Artist's employer, grantee or licensee.

> *Many managers also act as producers or packagers of television shows, live concerts or operate production companies, record companies or music publishing companies. For this reason, a manager might find himself in a partnership with a client, or as the employer of a client. There is nothing inherently wrong with this, but because the manager may have control in excess of that ordinarily granted to them in the management agreement, or greater compensations than ordinarily would be paid in his or her capacity as manager, it is incumbent upon the manager to insure that the artist is provided for fairly. First, the manager should not obtain "double commissions"; that is, a fee and percentage as a producer or employer, in addition to a management commission from the artist from the same activity which the manager is compensated as an employer or partner. Second, the artist's participation should be negotiated by an independent third party. Sometimes, the artist and manager will have the same attorney. This is the kind of situation where artists should hire their own attorney. It's wise for the artist to have an attorney who does not also represent the manager.*
>
> *It is generally foolish for a manager to try and act as the employer and manager of the act, as an inherent conflict of interest is created. For example, a manager who signs an artist to his own production company and music publishing company is going to have a hard time arguing that as the artist's manager he/she fought hard for the artist against his or her own interests. Clint Black was in a very expensive and unpleasant litigation in the mid–1990s over this very issue.*
>
> *In the last few years, we have been embroiled in several lawsuits concerning managers who claim to represent a "group" and take positions adverse to a member of that group, including even to terminate the musician or a partner/member. From an artist's perspective, this is very troubling—any artist should demand that any personal manager and any lawyer for the group not be allowed to take sides should such problems develop.*

13. SCOPE

This agreement shall not be construed to create a partnership between the parties. Each party is acting hereunder as an independent contractor. Manager may appoint or engage any other persons, firms or corporations, throughout the world, in Manager's discretion, to perform any of the services which Manager has agreed to perform hereunder except that Manager may delegate all of his duties only with Artist's written consent. Manager's services hereunder are not exclusive to Artist and Manager shall at all times be free to perform the same or similar services for others as well as to engage in any and all other business activities. Manager shall only be required to render reasonable services which are provided for herein as and when reasonably requested by Artist. Manager shall not be deemed to be in breach of this agreement unless and until Artist shall first have given Manager written notice describing the exact service which Artist requires on Manager's part and then only if Manager is in fact required to render such services hereunder, and if Manager shall thereafter have failed for a period of thirty (30) consecutive days to commence the rendition of the particular service required.

An independent contractor may also be a type of employee. As noted above, the personal manager effectively works for the artist (and hopefully is effective).

14. ASSIGNMENT

Manager shall have the right to assign this agreement to any and all of Manager's rights hereunder, or delegate any and all of Manager's duties to any individual, firm or corporation with the written approval of Artist, and this agreement shall inure to the benefit of Manager's successors and assigns, provided that Manager shall always be primarily responsible for rendering of managerial services, and may not delegate all of his duties without Artist's written consent. This agreement is personal to Artist, and Artist shall not assign this agreement or any portion thereof, and any such purported assignment shall be void.

The artist will want the manager to be always personally responsible and liable, notwithstanding any assignment or delegation of any rights and duties, and as noted previously, this responsibility can and should be provided.

15. NOTICES

All notices to be given to any of the parties hereto shall be addressed to the respective party at the applicable address as follows:
("Artist")   and   ("Manager")
All notices shall be in writing and shall be served by mail or telegraph, all charges prepaid. The date of mailing or of deposit in a telegraphy office, whichever shall be first, shall be deemed the date such notice is effective.

16. ARTIST'S WARRANTIES

Artist is over the age of eighteen, free to enter into this agreement, and has not heretofore made and will not hereafter enter into or accept any engagement, commitment or agreement with any person, firm or corporation which will, can or may interfere with the full and faithful performance by Artist of the covenants, terms and conditions of this agreement to be performed by Artist or interfere with Manager's full enjoyment of Manager's rights and privileges hereunder. Artist warrants that Artist has, as of the date hereof, no commitment, engagement or agreement requiring Artist to render services or preventing Artist from rendering services (including, but not limited to, restrictions on specific musical compositions) or respecting the disposition of any rights which Artist has or may hereafter acquire in any musical composition or creation, and acknowledges that Artist's talents and abilities are exceptional, extraordinary and unique, the loss of which cannot be compensated for by money.

17. ARBITRATION

In the event of any dispute under or relating to the terms of this agreement or any breach thereof, it is agreed that the same shall be submitted to arbitration by the American Arbitration Association in Los Angeles, California in accordance with the rule promulgated by said association and judgment upon any award rendered by be entered in any court having jurisdiction thereof. Any arbitration shall be held in Los Angeles County, California. In the event of arbitration arising from or out of this agreement or the relationship of the parties created hereby, the trier thereof may award to any party any reasonable attorneys' fees and other costs incurred in connection therewith. Any litigation by Manager or Artist arising from or out of this agreement shall be brought in Los Angeles, County, California.

An alternative is the "Rent a Judge" program, a type of arbitration which provides that controversies be heard by retired judges. Litigation via the courts is expensive and time consuming. A typical case in the Superior Court of California may take two to three years and cost hundreds of thousands of dollars. Arbitration or "Rent a Judge" is private, swift, and less expensive than our court trial system, but many people do not like these programs because they believe that the best form of justice is that meted out in the court system, and there is no right to appeal an arbitration. Notwithstanding any arbitration clause, the Labor Commissioner will have exclusive jurisdiction over any dispute where the Talent Agencies Act is alleged to have been violated.

IN WITNESS WHEREOF, the parties hereto have signed this agreement as of the date hereinabove set forth.

_____   _____
("ARTIST")   ("MANAGER")

TALENT AGENCIES

By Steven H. Gardner and Brad Gelfond

Talent agents, in today's music industry, are highly specialized employment procurers. As agents (persons authorized by others to act for them), they are restricted in their relationship with their clients by law and by provisions in various trade union collective bargaining agreements. Leaving the day-to-day rigors of career planning to the personal manager, the talent agent's main task is to obtain and negotiate contracts of employment, including bookings, for their clients. California and New York have, historically, been the center of the entertainment industry, and this discussion focuses on them. The first part of the chapter will explore the legal reins that define the role of the talent agent (hereafter "agent"), while the second portion discusses the considerations in choosing an agent.

THE LEGAL REINS

Every state has a system for the licensing and regulating of talent/employment agencies. Some license talent agencies under general employment agency laws while others have statutes tailored to the entertainment field. For instance, when the California legislature began its regulation of employment agencies in 1913, the first distinction between "general agencies" and "theatrical employment agencies" was made. Until 1967, there were four categories of talent agents licensed by California: employment agent; theatrical employment agent; motion picture employment agent; and artist's manager.

California's Talent Agencies Act (first passed in 1978) attempts to provide the talent agent with the exclusive right to procure, offer, promise, or attempt to procure employment for an artist. In addition, talent agents (like personal managers) may counsel or direct artists in the development of their professional careers.

In affording this exclusive status, California has set up a variety of agent licensing regulations, including requirements for the filing of detailed applications, posting of a $10,000 bond, logging of fingerprint cards, and, most importantly, acquiring the Labor Commissioner's prior approval of all form contracts between the agent and the client. This prior approval must appear on the contract itself—look for it. Moreover, agents must post, in their offices, a schedule of fees, and a description of what to do if a dispute arises. In any event, if a problem occurs between an agent and client that cannot be worked out informally (or through an alternative dispute resolution forum as provided in the contract as discussed below), the office of the Labor Commissioner should be the artist's next stop.

However, under California Labor Code §1700.45, the contract between the artist and the talent agent may contain a provision that refers disputes to a system of arbitration *other* than one conducted by the Labor Commissioner. California has numerous alternative dispute resolution forums, staffed by skilled attorneys, retired judges, and trained mediators. While sometimes expensive, they often prove to be more effective than the arbitrations conducted by the Labor Commissioner. Under the statute, notice of such arbitration must be given to the Labor Commissioner, and the Labor Commissioner (or his/her representative) has the right to attend the arbitration proceedings. Arbitration is a dispute-resolution forum outside the court system, but it may end up as a court judgment and preclude further court action. Many states, including California, are experiencing a clogged judicial system that severely delays the decision-making process (sometimes up to five years). Arbitration avoids such delays by limiting pre-hearing discovery, quickly setting hearings, and making binding decisions. Also, rules of evidence, which are guidelines to the court system as to what may and may not be said in court, are generally not applicable to arbitrations, unless agreed to by all sides. Therefore, while *informal* in structure, arbitration has a *formal* result.

Fees and Commissions

Talent agents located in the state of New York are governed by New York's general business law. Classified as "theatrical employment agencies," the agents are subject to a statutory fee ceiling, which does not have a California counterpart. In New York, for any single theatrical engagement (including employment as an actor, performer, or entertainer), the agent may take no more than 10% of the gross compensation payable to the client, except that for engagements in the orchestral, operatic or concert field, the agent's commission may go as high as 20%.

California sets no maximum on fees that agents may charge for services. Fee ceilings are imposed, however, by the various entertainment guilds (i.e. AFM, AFTRA) in the form of constitutions and bylaws. Agents are "franchised" (recognized) by these guilds and agree to abide by the rules set forth by the guilds. Artist members of the craft guilds are required to utilize only franchised agents, or face disciplinary action in the form of suspension or fines.

The union franchise stringently regulates at least two major areas: the term (length) of the agent's employment agreement with the client, and the maximum compensation payable to the agent. The franchise is essentially an agreement between the agent and the guild that commits the agent to abide by particular regulations as to the representation of their members.

For example, the American Federation of Musicians (AFM) franchise rules allow variable lengths of contract terms dependent upon the services rendered by an agent. A booking agent (one who primarily arranges such personal appearances as clubs, tours, Las Vegas shows) is restricted to a term of three or five years, while a general agent (one who represents a client for film, television, recording, personal appearance, commercials, writing, etc.) can sign a client for up to seven years. Regardless of the franchise or the services rendered this is the longest period allowable for a personal service contract in California. However, the artist may always renew the contract after the seven years are up, if the artist so desires. (It is at this point that the artist's negotiation opportunity may be at its height.)

Fees are also governed by guild franchises. Although the norm is a 10% maximum on general services, increased fees can be obtained by the agent. For instance, the AFM uses a variable fee scale related to the length of the booked engagement. These scales escalate from 10% up to 20% for a one-day engagement, but in no event can the commission reduce the artist's net income below that specified as scale by the particular guild. These fee specifications represent the amount of money available to the artist, and other representatives (personal and business managers) may be entitled to other chunks of the gross compensation earned on a performance date. Agents should not charge commissions on BMI or ASCAP performance income received by an artist.

The incentive to become a licensed talent agent is the almost monopolistic status bestowed upon them to procure employment for artists in the entertainment field. California, however, has carved out a niche for unlicensed persons in the area of recording agreements. California Labor Code §1700.4 provides that the activities of producing, offering or promising to procure recording contracts for an artist does not, of itself, require licensing under the act. This was an experiment in the law to allow traditionally unlicensed personal managers, who normally perform the duties involved in the procurement of recording contracts, to operate free from the fear of retribution by the Labor Commissioner.

New York law permits a personal manager whose business "only incidentally involves the seeking of employment" to remain unlicensed. For the unlicensed individual in California who acts in the procurement of employment, one of the severest sanctions is the power of the Labor Commissioner to order the return of all commissions obtained while the representative was unlicensed. This result was first and most dramatically presented by the Jefferson Airplane case of *Buchwald v. Katz* where the personal manager was ordered by the Labor Commissioner to return $40,000 in commissions that he had received while managing the group, and he was also denied reimbursement for all moneys advanced by him to the group. A new trial was ordered in this particular case, however, and certain portions of the management agreement were upheld while other publishing agreements (i.e., music publishing agreements where the manager is in effect the publisher) were voided. This was also recently the case where Arsenio Hall sought return of all of his former manager's commissions for "procuring employment" during a period when the manager was unlicensed as a talent agent *(Wachs v. Curry)*. These cases are important in two respects: first, they ratify the powerful role of the Labor Commissioner in settling controversies in the talent agent arena; and second they begin to provide guidelines to define "unlicensed procurement activity" in California. As more of these cases are decided and reported, the line between the sanctioned activities of licensed agents and unlicensed managers will become less hazy.

SEEKING PERSONAL APPEARANCE TALENT AGENCY REPRESENTATION

An agent is a valuable member of the artist's "career team," and it is worthwhile to spend some time examining the elements involved in the agency selection process. As you begin seeking personal appearance representation by a talent agency, you will discover that there are many of them, all seemingly providing the same services. A closer look will reveal that each agency has its own areas of expertise and services it can offer an artist. Because the selection can be a difficult decision, the following should be considered.

Research Information About Agencies

The best way to do research on the various agencies is to obtain copies of the client lists of the various companies. There is a publication called *Pollstar* (phone number (800) 344-7383 or, in California, (209) 224-2631; fax (209) 224-2674) that publishes a listing of every agency, their client lists and the various agents who work for the companies. It is highly advisable to get a copy of the most recent edition and to spend some time reviewing it. Pay attention to the number of clients the various agencies have. Note the agencies that have clients in your genre of music, the number of agents there, etc. You might also ask your musician friends who represents them, and how to get in contact with their agency.

Compatibility

First and foremost, it is important to be represented by people who are excited about the kind of music (or art) you perform. Agents that are passionate about their clients and their art are always more formidable representatives than those that are not. Even the best agency is useless unless the artist finds agents there he or she can communicate with and trust.

Many people compare selecting an agent to selecting a spouse. It is important that you have a good feeling about the person who is about to become your agent. You must be able to communicate artistic ideas and business strategy with this person. Since your agent represents you in business deals, make sure it is someone you trust to act in your best interest, even when you are absent. Also, be sure that your agent will project an attitude and demeanor that you want to be associated with.

If you find a particular person whom you like (and you sign with their agency), make sure that this person becomes your responsible agent. The responsible agent is the artist's conduit to the agency. It is through this agent (or team of agents in some cases) that the artist will communicate with the entire agency. The responsible agent's ability to motivate the other agents determines in large part whether the agency will succeed on behalf of the artist. You should be certain that your responsible agent is not spread so thin by overwhelming client responsibilities so as to be unable to pay attention to your needs. Sign with someone who has time to devote to you and with whom you expect to spend many years. While it is important to insure you have the best responsible agent possible, it is also important to consider your relationship with all the agents. When you sign with an agency, you are not just signing with one agent, but with the entire agency. You should evaluate the company from the top executives to the newest agent. An agency should encourage personnel stability, as it is important to insure continuity in your personal appearance career. Even the largest agencies with the most impressive client lists can become ineffectual if their personnel changes too dramatically.

Developing Acts

Check an agency's client list, it can yield valuable information. A new artist should be compatible with at least some of the artists on the agency's list. For example, it might be a mistake to be a country artist in an agency dominated by heavy metal clients. But there are exceptions to this rule, especially if an agency is making concerted forays into new areas.

It is also important to examine what successes the agency has had. If you are a new act, just about to begin your personal appearance career, it wouldn't be wise to sign with an agency that only booked arena headliners. It is important for an agent to know the proper places for you to play while you develop your personal appearance career. There are some clubs that are better for metal acts, others better for alternative acts, etc. If you play ethnic music, there are some venues where your performance will be more successful. Your agent must know this information.

Maximizing the Relationship

The best way to establish the relationship with your agent is to spend time together. You both need to learn what makes each of you tick. Your manager, if you have one, should be involved here, too. Have your agent come see you perform as often as possible.

Obviously, it is to your advantage to give your new agent as much information about yourself as possible. Provide a history of the shows and tours you have done, along with copies of all your recordings. You might want to give your agent a copy of the demos for your next album, or an advance copy of the album. After the album comes out, it is a good idea to supply the following tools that are available from your record company. *Radio Tracking* sheets list the radio stations playing your record and *BDS* (Broadcast Data Systems) information lists the number of times each station plays your record and when. *SoundScan* information lists the number of albums sold in each of the major markets in the country. It is helpful to provide foreign sales information if your record is released internationally. Press clippings and video (MTV, VH-1 or regional) airplay are also valuable information to an agent. The more information you provide, the better you will be represented.

In addition, make sure that your agent knows your show requirements, both technical and otherwise. Any special staging or technical information will help your agent make sure your needs are taken care of when you arrive to perform. If you have specific show, advertising, or dressing room requirements, make sure your agent knows what they are before making any deals on your behalf. Let your agent know as much as possible in advance to make sure there are no misunderstandings.

Packaging

Packaging generally refers to the practice of placing a support act(s) on a headliner's tour. This can happen in clubs, theaters, arenas, and stadiums. In the past, agents wielded tremendous influence in placing opening acts on key tours. While agents still maintain some control over packaging, today the headliner makes the final decision on the selection of supporting acts. However, agents have great input on this decision along with the inside track on upcoming support slots. But, it is foolish for a developing band to sign with an agency because they are interested in doing a tour with one of the agency's headliners as these things are never guaranteed. You should listen to the prospective agent's ideas on how he or she feels you would be best packaged, and with which acts. Check also to see what success the agency has had packaging their clients with other agencies, as both support and headliners.

Venue Deals

If you are a headline act, you should check to see if the agency has experience making building (venue) deals. Agents are now involved in negotiating venue expenses like rent, ticket commissions, and merchandising deals for their clients. Favorable deals can yield you additional tour revenue.

Clout

Clout is a product of the special relationship between agencies and major music business "players." Large agencies make repeated deals with buyers, enabling buyers many opportunities to make money. This creates a solid business relationship. An agent who delivers several money-making concerts to a talent buyer has more leverage to command maximum guarantees, more favorable deals, and to create career opportunities for the agent's developing acts. Concert promoters attempt to protect their relationships with the major agencies. They often worry that the agency will do business with a different promoter, and they won't get the opportunity to play some of the agency's acts. By playing an agency's developing acts, promoters hope to be benefited in two ways.

First, if they help develop an act by playing it in its early stages, they will develop a relationship with it and be given the opportunity to play the act in the future. Second, they hope to develop good will with the agency by helping in the development process. It is possible for small agencies to develop relationships like those mentioned above with promoters, but this generally doesn't happen to the same degree as with large agencies.

Small Agencies

Small agencies do have their advantages. In a small agency, the artist/agent ratio tends to be lower (there are exceptions at large agencies). This allows each agent the opportunity to spend more time booking and working for each client. The work load of agents in a small agency allows them to initiate special projects, and to spend as much time as is needed for any given client.

Coverage

Coverage refers to the number of buyers that any given agent will be responsible for servicing. In an agency the "buyer pie" (concert promoters, club owners, college buyers, etc.) is divided up among all the agents. In a large agency, each agent will have fewer buyers to deal with and can become more specialized. Typically, the buyers are divided up geographically and/or by type (contemporary buyers, middle of the road buyers, country buyers, etc.) and by size of venue (concert, club, college). Large agencies do more business, so they tend to have a thorough awareness of the concert business and of individual markets.

Specialized vs. Full-service Agencies

There are certain structural differences between agencies that an artist should consider. The differences relate to the scope of representation that the agencies offer. A specialized agency offers representation in one area; personal appearance representation is one example. Full-service agencies, on the other hand, offer a broad range of services, representing television, film, and commercial actors, producers, directors, writers, editors, and other "below-the-line" personnel, as well as personal appearance clients (musicians, bands, singers). Full-service agencies offer representation to their clients in whichever areas they choose. This is especially useful for musicians who want to explore acting or film scoring.

Data Management

Whether large or small, full service or specialized, another consideration of an agency is its ability to manage data and efficiently communicate that data to its clients and their representatives. In order to maximize efficiency, innovative agencies have turned to computer technology to help them assimilate data. This technology has created the opportunity for thorough and efficient inter office data sharing as well as new methods for sharing information with clients.

CONCLUSION

It is important to consider as many variables as possible. You should research prospective agencies with some current clients and their managers and with talent buyers, record company executives and attorneys. You should find out how the agency you are considering is regarded by the rest of the music business. Ask for a copy of the agency's client list. The best recommendation for an agency is a history of long associations with successful clients. Good luck.

AFM EXCLUSIVE AGENT-MUSICIAN AGREEMENT
FOR USE IN THE STATE OF CALIFORNIA ONLY*

Name of Agent: _____

Legal Name of Musician: _____

Address of Agent: _____

Professional Name of Musician: _____

Name of Musician's Group or Orchestra: _____

AFM Booking Agent Number: _____

Musician's AFM Locals: _____

This Agreement Begins on _____19___ and Ends on _____ 19___.

1. SCOPE OF AGREEMENT

Musician hereby employs Agent and Agent hereby accepts employment as Musician's exclusive artist manager throughout the world with respect to musician's services, appearances and endeavors as a musician. As used in this Agreement "Musician" refers to the undersigned musician and to musicians performing with any orchestra or group that Musician leads or conducts and whom Musician shall make subject to the terms of this agreement; "AFM" refers to the American Federation of Musicians of the United States and Canada. Also, as used in this agreement, the word "Agent" shall refer to "Artists' Manager" as that term is defined in Section 1700.4 of the Labor Code of the State of California.

Note that this is an exclusive agreement. The musician may not enter into other agreements covering the specific area of concern (music); however, it would not prohibit the musician from hiring an agent for commercials, broadcasting, etc.

2. DUTIES OF AGENT

(a) Agent agrees to use reasonable efforts in the performance of the following duties: assist Musician in obtaining offers of, and negotiating, engagements for Musician; advise, aid, counsel and guide Musician with respect to Musician's professional career; promote and publicize Musician's name and talents; carry on business correspondence on Musician's behalf relating to Musician's professional career; cooperate with duly constituted and authorized representatives of Musician in the performance of such duties.

(b) Agent will maintain office, staff and facilities reasonably adequate for the rendition of such services.

(c) Agent will not accept any engagements for Musician without Musician's prior approval which shall not be unreasonably withheld.

(d) Agent shall fully comply with all applicable laws, rules and regulations of governmental authorities and secure such licenses as may be required for the rendition of services hereunder.

These are renditions of the classic duties of the talent agent. Reasonable efforts (rather than the stricter "best efforts" found in some contracts), however, are required of the

---

* This can be a three-year or five-year agreement in California.

agent. Note also that although the contract provides that the duties of the agent are to "advise, aid, counsel and guide Musician" with respect to his professional career, this is an area usually left to the personal manager.

3. RIGHTS OF AGENT

(a) Agent may render similar services to others and may engage in other businesses and ventures, subject, however, to the limitations imposed by paragraph 8 below.

Note the nonexclusivity of the agent to your professional career—the agent can take on as many clients as he or she can handle (but see below).

(b) Musician will promptly refer to Agent all communications, written or oral, received by or on behalf of Musician relating to the services and appearances by Musician.

(c) Without Agent's written consent, Musician will not engage any other person, firm or corporation to perform the services to be performed by Agent hereunder nor will Musician perform or appear professionally or offer so to do except through Agent.

(b) & (c) Everything concerning music employment must go through the agent—to accept a freelance job may be in breach of the agreement (and your agent will get his or her commission anyway). It is in the artist's best interests to refer job queries to the agent because the agent can often negotiate more favorable terms. However, stay on top of the negotiations in the event the agent is unable to close the deal.

(d) Agent may publicize the fact that Agent is the exclusive agent for Musician.

(e) Agent shall have the right to use or to permit others to use Musician's name and likeness in advertising or publicity relating to Musician's services and appearances but without cost or expense to Musician unless Musician shall otherwise specifically agree in writing.

You may find an awful picture of yourself in a brochure or on a poster. Negotiate for the right to approve all publicity releases whenever possible.

(f) In the event of Musician's breach of this agreement, Agent's sole right and remedy for such breach shall be the receipt from Musician of the commissions specified in this agreement, but only if, as, and when, Musician receives monies or other consideration on which such commissions are payable hereunder.

If you violate the contract, the agency may not enjoin (i.e., get a court order to stop) your performance—the agency is limited to the remedy of damages determined by the amount of commissions due it.

4. COMPENSATION OF AGENT

(a) In consideration of the services to be rendered by Agent hereunder, Musician agrees to pay to Agent commissions equal to the percentages set forth below of the gross monies received by Musician, directly or indirectly, for each engagement on which commissions are payable hereunder:

(i) Ten percent (10%)

(ii) In no event, however, shall the payment of any such commissions result in the retention by Musician for any engagement of net monies or other consideration in an amount less than the applicable minimum scale of the AFM or of any local thereof having jurisdiction over such engagement.

(iii) In no event shall the payment of any such commissions result in the receipt by Agent for any engagement of commissions, fees or other consideration, directly or indirectly, from any person or persons, including the Musician, which in aggregate exceed the commissions provided for in this agreement. Any commission, fee, or other consideration received by Agent from any source other than Musician, directly or indirectly, on account of, as a result of, or in connection with supplying the services of Musician shall be reported to Musician and the amount thereof shall be deducted from the commissions payable by the Musician hereunder.

The commission percentages are fairly clear, (ii) makes sure that you will always earn at least scale. This, however, does not take into consideration amounts that you may be obligated to pay to personal managers, business managers and the like. The AFM has little control over these.

(b) Commissions shall become due and payable to Agent immediately following the receipt thereof by Musician or by anyone else on Musician's behalf.

Normally, the check will be sent to the agency prior to the engagement, after which monies (less commission) will be paid to you.

(c) No commissions shall be payable on any engagement if Musician is not paid for such engagement irrespective of the reasons for such nonpayment to Musician, including but not limited to nonpayment by reason of the fault of Musician. This shall not preclude the awarding of damages by the International Executive Board to an agent to compensate him for actual expenses incurred as the direct result of the cancellation of an engagement when said cancellation was the fault of the member.

If you are not paid, your agent isn't paid. But note, if you are the cause of the cancellation, you may be liable for the actual expenses (i.e., air fare or booking expenses) incurred by the agent that result from the cancellation.

(d) Agent's commissions shall be payable on all monies or other considerations received by Musician pursuant to contracts for engagements negotiated or entered into during the term of this agreement; if specifically agreed to by Musician by initialing the margin hereof, to contracts for engagements in existence at the commencement of the term hereof (excluding, however, any engagements as to which Musician is under prior obligation to pay commissions to another agent); and to any modifications, extensions and renewals thereof or substitutions therefor regardless of when Musician shall receive such monies or other considerations. However, to be entitled to continue to receive commissions on the aforementioned contracts after the termination of this agreement, agent shall remain obligated to serve Musician and to perform obligations with respect to said employment contracts or to extensions or renewals of said contracts or to any employment requiring musician's services on which such commissions are based.

The agent is entitled to commissions on engagements negotiated during the term of this agreement, even if the monies are actually received at a later time. You can exclude commissions to the agent on current engagements by not initialing the margin.

(e) As used in this paragraph and elsewhere in this agreement, the term "gross earnings" shall mean the gross amounts received by Musician for each engagement less costs and expenses incurred in collecting amounts due for any engagement, including costs of arbitration, litigation and attorneys' fees.

(f) If specifically agreed to by Musician by initialing the margin hereof, the following shall apply:

(i) Musician shall advance to Agent against Agent's final commissions an amount not exceeding the following percentages of the gross amounts received for each engagement, 15% on engagements of three (3) days or less; 10% on all other engagements.

(ii) If Musician shall so request and shall simultaneously furnish Agent with the data relating to deductions, the Agent within forty-five (45) days following the end of each twelve (12) month period during the term of this agreement and within forty-five (45) days following the termination of this Agreement, shall account to and furnish Musician with a detailed statement itemizing the gross amounts received for all engagements during the period to which such accounting relates, the monies or other considerations upon which Agent's commissions are based, and the amount of Agent's commissions resulting from such computations. Upon request, a copy of such statement shall be furnished promptly to the Office of the President of the AFM.

(iii) Any balances owed by or to the parties shall be paid as follows: by the Agent at the time of rendering such statement; by the Musician within thirty (30) days after receipt of such statement.

If you initial this clause, you agree to pay to your agent monies against commissions to be earned. (i) This is usually not to your advantage. The trade-off, however, is the detailed itemization of account which you can demand of the agent (ii).

5. DURATION AND TERMINATION OF AGREEMENT

(a) The term of this agreement shall be as stated in the opening heading hereof, subject to termination as provided in paragraphs 5(b), 6 and 10 below.

(b) In addition to termination pursuant to other provisions of this agreement, this agreement may be terminated by either party, by notice as provided below, if Musician

(i) is unemployed for four (4) consecutive weeks at any time during the term hereof; or

(ii) does not obtain employment for at least twenty (20) cumulative weeks of engagements to be performed during each of the first and second six (6) month periods during the term hereof; or

(iii) does not obtain employment for at least forty (40) cumulative weeks of engagements to be performed during each subsequent year of the term hereof.

(c) Notice of such termination shall be given by certified mail addressed to the addressee at their last known address and a copy thereof shall be sent to the AFM. Such termination shall be effective as of the date of mailing of such notice. Such notice shall be mailed no later than two (2) weeks following the occurrence of any event described in (i) above; two (2) weeks following a period in excess of thirteen (13) of the cumulative weeks of unemployment specified in (ii) above; and two (2) weeks following a period in excess of twenty-six (26) of the cumulative weeks of unemployment specified in (iii) above. Failure to give notice as aforesaid shall constitute a waiver of the right to terminate based upon the happening of such prior events.

(d) Musician's disability resulting in failure to perform engagements and Musician's unreasonable refusal to accept and perform engagements shall not be themselves either deprive Agent of its right to or give Musician the right to terminate (as provided in (b) above).

(e) As used in this agreement, a "week" shall commence on Sunday and terminate on Saturday. A "week of engagements" shall mean any one of the following:

(i) a week during which Musician is to perform on at least four (4) days; or

(ii) a week during which Musician's gross earnings equals or exceeds the lowest such gross earnings obtained by Musician for performances rendered during any one of the immediately preceding six (6) weeks; or

(iii) a week during which Musician is to perform engagements on commercial television or radio or in concert for compensation equal at least to three (3) times the minimum scales of the AFM or of any local thereof having jurisdiction applicable to such engagements.

Although the agreement is for three years, you can call it quits if any of the circumstances contained in this clause occur. You must give timely notice, however, and strictly follow the method outlined in (c). Note the various definitions of "week." Odds are you signed with the particular agency because of a personal relationship or reputation of a particular person with whom you expect to work. You may also want to negotiate a term that if that particular agent leaves the agency, you can terminate all your agreements with the agency. This so-called key-man clause insures that you will not be "passed around" from agent to agent within the shop.

6. AGENT'S MAINTENANCE OF AFM BOOKING AGENT AGREEMENT

Agent represents that Agent is presently a party to an AFM Booking Agent Agreement, which is in full force and effect. If such AFM Booking Agent Agreement shall terminate, the rights of the parties hereunder shall be governed by the terms and conditions of said Booking Agent Agreement relating to the effect of termination of such agreements which are incorporated herein by reference.

7. NO OTHER AGREEMENTS

This is the only and the complete agreement between the parties relating to all or any part of the subject matter covered by this agreement. There is no other agreement, arrangement or participation between the parties, nor do the parties stand in any relationship to each other that is not created by this agreement, whereby the terms and conditions of this agreement are avoided or evaded, directly or indirectly, such as, by way of example but not limitation, contracts, arrangements, relationships or participations relating to publicity services, business management, music publishing, or instruction.

Any oral representations of the agent to "puff" the contract may not be binding due to this warranty. "Puffing" is representing more than what is written in the contract. Typical representations such as "Don't worry, we never enforce that provision" should be disregarded. Specifically, certain relationships are directly prohibited by way of example.

8. INCORPORATION OF AFM CONSTITUTION, BY-LAWS, ETC.

There are incorporated into and made part of this agreement, as though fully set forth herein, the present and future provisions of the Constitution, By-laws, Rules, Regulations and Resolutions of the AFM and those of its locals, which do not conflict therewith. The parties acknowledge their responsibility to be fully acquainted, now and for the duration of this agreement, with the contents thereof.

The AFM constitution, bylaws, rules, regulations, and resolutions run numerous pages. They are, however, controlling as to the terms of this document.

9. SUBMISSION AND DETERMINATION OF DISPUTES

(a) Every claim, dispute, controversy or difference arising out of, dealing with, relating to, or affecting the interpretation or application of this agreement, or the violation or breach, or the threatened violation or breach thereof shall be submitted, heard and determined by the International Executive Board of the AFM in accordance with the rules of such Board (regardless of the termination or purported termination of this agreement or of the Agent's AFM Booking Agent Agreement), and such determination shall be conclusive, final and binding on the parties.

(b) This provision is inserted herein by AFM, a bona fide labor union, in connection with the regulation of the relations of its members to Musician's agents and managers. Under this agreement, Agent undertakes to endeavor to secure employment for the Musician. Reasonable written notice shall be given to the Labor Commissioner of the State of California of the time and place of any arbitration hearing hereunder. The said Labor Commissioner or his authorized representative has the right to attend all arbitration hearings. The provisions of this agreement relating to said Labor Commissioner shall not be applicable to cases not falling under the provisions of Section 1700.45 of the Labor Code of the State of California. Nothing in this agreement nor in the AFM Constitution, Bylaws, Rules, Regulations, and Resolutions shall be construed so as to abridge or limit any rights, powers or duties of said Labor Commissioner.

You may not get to court immediately when a dispute occurs. A grievance procedure is outlined and adhered to, and you and the agent are bound to abide by it. Legal representation is not prohibited, and if you think you need it, get legal counsel early in the dispute.

10. NO ASSIGNMENT OF THIS AGREEMENT

This agreement shall be personal to the parties and shall not be transferable or assignable by operation of law or otherwise without the prior consent of the Musician and of the AFM. The obligations imposed by this agreement shall be binding upon the parties. The Musician may terminate this agreement at any time within ninety (90) days after the transfer of a controlling interest in the Agent.

> *You cannot assign (i.e., transfer) this agreement to your piano player, and the agent cannot pawn you off to "Skylab Booking Agency." Also, if the controlling interest (and this can be less than 51%) in the agency is transferred, you can get out.*

11. NEGOTIATION FOR RENEWAL

Neither party shall enter into negotiations for or agree to the renewal or extension of this agreement prior to the beginning of the final year of the term hereof.

12. APPROVAL BY AFM

This agreement shall not become effective unless, within thirty (30) days following its execution, an executed copy thereof is filed with and is thereafter approved in writing by the AFM.

IN WITNESS WHEREOF,
The parties hereto have executed this agreement the _____ day of _____ 19__.

_____	_____
AGENT	MUSICIAN
_____	_____
BY	RESIDENCE ADDRESS
_____	_____
NAME AND TITLE	CITY/STATE/ZIP

STANDARD AFTRA EXCLUSIVE AGENCY CONTRACT UNDER RULE 12-B

THIS AGREEMENT, made and entered at _____by and between
_____, hereinafter called the "AGENT" and
_____, hereinafter called the "ARTIST."

1. SCOPE OF AGREEMENT

The Artist employs the Agent as his sole and exclusive Agent in the transcription, radio broadcasting and television industries (hereinafter referred to as the "broadcasting industries") within the scope of the regulations (Rule 12-B) of the American Federation of Television and Radio Artists (hereinafter called AFTRA), and agrees not to employ any other person or persons to act for him in like capacity during the term hereof, and the Agent accepts such employment. This contract is limited to the broadcasting industries and to contracts of the Artist as an artist in such fields and any reference hereinafter to contracts or employment whereby the Artist renders his services, refers to contracts or employment in the broadcasting industries, except as otherwise provided herein.

> *This clause limits the scope of the representation to broadcasting engagements within the purview of the guild.*

2. MEMBERSHIP

The Artist agrees that prior to any engagement or employment in the broadcasting industries, he will become a member of AFTRA in good standing and remain such a member for the duration of such engagement or employment. The Artist warrants that he has the right to make this contract and that he is not under any other agency contract in the broadcasting fields. The Agent warrants that he is and will remain a duly franchised agent of AFTRA for the duration of this contract. This paragraph is for the benefit of AFTRA and AFTRA members as well as for the benefit of the parties to this agreement.

> *You must maintain your membership in good standing in AFTRA.*

3. TERM

The term of this contract shall be for a period of _____ commencing on the _____ day of _____, 19__.
NOTE—The term may not be in excess of three years.

4. AGENT COMPENSATION

(a) The Artist agrees to pay to the Agent a sum equal to _____ per cent (not more than 10%) of all moneys or other consideration received by the Artist, directly or indirectly, under contracts of employment entered into during the term specified herein as provided in the Regulations. Commissions shall be payable when as such moneys or other consideration are received by the Artist or by anyone else for or on the Artist's behalf.

(b) Any moneys or other consideration received by the Artist or by anyone for or on his behalf, in connection with any termination of any contract of the Artist on which the Agent would otherwise be entitled to receive commission, or in connection with the settlement of any such contract, or any litigation arising out of such contract, shall also be moneys in connection with which the Agent is entitled to the aforesaid commissions; provided, however, that in such event the Artist shall be entitled to deduct arbitration fees, attorneys' fees, expenses and court costs before computing the amount upon which the Agent is entitled to his commissions.

(c) Such commissions shall be payable by the Artist to the Agent, as aforesaid, during the term of this contract and thereafter only where specifically provided herein.

(d) The agent shall be entitled to the aforesaid commissions after the expiration of the term specified herein, for so long a period thereafter as the Artist continues to receive moneys or other consideration under or upon employment contracts entered into by the Artist during the term specified herein, including moneys or other consideration received by the Artist under the extended term of such employment contracts, resulting from the exercise of an option or options given an employer under such employment contracts, extending the term of such employment contracts, whether such options be exercised prior to or after the expiration of the terms specified herein.

(e) If after the expiration of the term of this agreement and during the period the Agent is entitled to commissions, a contract of employment of the Artist be terminated before the expiration thereof, as said contract may have been extended by the exercise of options therein contained, by joint action of the Artist and employer, or by the action of either of them, other than on account of an Act of God, illness or the like and the Artist enters into a new contract of employment with said employer within a period of sixty (60) days, such new contract shall be deemed to be in substitution of the contract terminated as aforesaid. In computing the said sixty (60) day period, each day between June 15th and September 15th shall be counted as three-fifths (3/5) of a day only. No contract entered into after said sixty (60) day period shall be deemed to be in substitution of the contract terminated as aforesaid. Contracts of substitution have the same effect as contracts for which they were substituted; provided however, that any increase or additional salary, bonus or other compensation payable to the Artist (either under such contract of substitution or otherwise) over and above the amounts payable under the contract of employment entered into prior to the expiration of the term of this agreement shall be deemed an adjustment and unless the Agent shall have a valid Agency contract in effect at the time of such adjustment the Agent shall not be entitled to any commissions on any such adjustment. In no event may a contract of substitution with an employer entered into after the expiration of the term of this agreement, extend the period of time during which the Agent is entitled to commission beyond the period that the Agent would have been entitled to commission had no substitution taken place except to the extent, if necessary, for the Agent to receive the same total amount of commission he would have received had no such substitution taken place; provided, however, that in no event shall the Agent receive more than the above percentages as commissions on the Artist's adjusted compensation under the contract of substitution. A change in form of an employer for the purpose of evading this provision, or a change in the corporate form of an employer resulting from reorganization or like, shall not exclude the application of these provisions.

(f) So long as the Agent receives commissions from the Artist, the Agent shall be obligated to service the Artist and perform the obligations of this contract with respect to the services of the Artist on which such commissions are based, subject to AFTRA's Regulations Governing Agents.

(g) The Agent has no right to receive money unless the Artist receives the same, or unless the same is received for or on his behalf, and then only proportionate in the above percentages when and as received. Money paid pursuant to legal process to the Artist's creditors, or by virtue of assignment or direction of the Artist, and deductions from the Artist's compensation made pursuant to law in the nature of a collection or tax at the source, such as Social Security or Old Age Pension taxes, or income taxes withheld at the source, shall be treated as compensation received for or on the Artist's behalf.

Both the length of this contract and the commission payable under it are negotiable up to the maximums specified. The agreement can be for as little as a day or up to three years. An artist in a strong bargaining position could possibly negotiate less than the maximum 10% commission, but this will be rare.

5. EMPLOYMENT OFFERS

Should the Agent, during the term or terms specified herein negotiate a contract of employment for the Artist and secure for the Artist bona fide offer of employment, which offer is communicated by the Agent to the Artist in reasonable detail and writing, which offer the Artist declines, and if, after the expiration of the term of this agreement and within ninety (90) days after the date upon which the Agent gives such written information to the Artist, the Artist accepts said offer of employment on substantially the same terms, then the Artist shall be required to pay commissions to the Agent upon such contract of employment. If an Agent previously employed under a prior agency contract is entitled to collect commissions under the foregoing circumstances, the Agent with whom the present contract is executed waives his commission to the extent that the prior agent is entitled to collect the same.

6. DURATION AND TERMINATION

(a) If during any period of ninety-one (91) days immediately preceding the giving of the notice of termination hereinafter mentioned in this paragraph, the Artist fails to be employed and receive, or be entitled to receive, compensation for fifteen (15) days' employment, whether such employment is from fields under AFTRA's jurisdiction or any other branch of the entertainment industry in which the Agent may be authorized by written contract to represent the Artist, then either the Artist or the Agent may terminate the employment of the Agent hereunder by written notice to the other party. (1) For purposes of computing fifteen (15) days' employment required hereunder, each separate original radio broadcast, whether live or recorded, and each transcribed program, shall be considered a day's employment, but a rebroadcast, whether recorded or live, or an off-the-line recording, or a prior recording or time spent in rehearsal for any employment in the radio broadcasting or transcription industry, shall not be considered such employment. (2) During the months of June, July and August, each day's employment in the radio broadcasting industry, shall, for purposes of computing fifteen (15) days' employment under this subparagraph "(a)" and for no other purpose, be deemed one and one-half (1-1/2) days' employment. (3) For the purposes of computing the fifteen (15) days' employment required hereunder, each separate television broadcast (including rehearsal time) shall be considered two and one-half (2-1/2) days' employment. However, any days spent in rehearsal over three days inclusive of the day of the telecast, and any days of exclusivity over three days inclusive of the day of telecast, will automatically extend the ninety-one (91) day period by such coverage. (4) During the months of June, July and August, each day's employment in the television broadcasting field shall, for the purpose of computing fifteen (15) days' employment under this subparagraph "(a)" and for no other purpose, be deemed three and three-quarters (3-3/4) days' employment. (5) Each master phonograph record recorded by the Artist shall be one (1) day's employment.

(b) The ninety-one (91) day period, which is the basis of termination, shall be suspended during any period of time which the artist has declared himself to be unavailable or has so notified the agent in writing or has confirmed in writing a written communication from the agent to such effect. The said ninety-one (91) day period, which is the basis of termination, shall also be suspended (1) during the period of time in which the artist is unable to respond to a call for his services by reason of physical or mental incapacity or (2) for such days as the artist may be employed in a field in which the artist is not represented by the agent.

(c) In the event that the Agent has given the Artist notice in writing of a bona fide offer of employment as an Artist in the entertainment industry and at or near the Artist's usual places of employment at a salary and from an employer commensurate with the Artist's prestige (and there is in fact such an offer), which notice sets forth the terms of the proposed employment in detail and the Artist refuses or negligently fails to accept such proffered employment, then the period of guaranteed employment specified in said offer, and the compensation which would have been received thereunder shall be deemed as time worked or compensation received by the Artist in computing the money earned or time worked with reference to the right of the Artist to terminate under the provisions of this paragraph.

(d) No termination under paragraph 6 shall deprive the Agent of the right to receive commissions or compensation on moneys earned or received by the Artist prior to the date of termination, or earned or received by the Artist after the date of termination and during the term or terms specified herein, or commission or compensation to which the Agent is entitled pursuant to paragraphs 4(e) and 5 hereof.

(e) The Artist may not exercise the right of termination if at the time he attempts to do so, either:

   (i) the Artist is actually working under written contract or contracts, which guarantee the Artist employment in the broadcasting industries for at least one program each week for a period of not less than thirteen (13) consecutive weeks. For the purposes of this subparagraph a "program" shall be either (1) a regional network program of one-half (1/2) hour length or more; (2) a national network program of one-quarter (1/4) hour length or more; or (3) a program or programs the aggregate weekly compensation for which equals or exceeds the Artist's customary compensation for either (1) or (2), or

   (ii) the Artist is under such written contract, as described in the preceding subparagraph (i) or in subparagraph (v) below, and such contract begins within forty-five (45) days after the time the Artist attempts to exercise the right of termination, or

(iii) where the Artist attempts to exercise the right of termination during the months of August or September, and the Artist is under such written contract as described in the preceding subparagraph (i) or in subparagraph (v) below and such contract begins not later than the following October 15th, or (iv) if during any period of ninety-one (91) days immediately preceding the giving of notice of termination herein referred to, the Artist has received, or has been entitled to receive, compensation in an amount equal to not less than thirteen (13) times his past customary compensation for a national network program of one-half (1/2) hour's length, whether such employment or compensation is from the broadcasting industries or any other branch of the entertainment industry in which the agent may be authorized by written contract to represent the Artist.

(v) The Artist is actually working under written contract or contracts which guarantee the Artist either (a) employment in the television broadcasting field for at least one (1) program every other week in a cycle of thirteen (13) consecutive weeks where the program is telecast on an alternative week basis, or (b) employment for at least eight (8) programs in a cycle of thirty-nine (39) consecutive weeks, where the program is telecast on a monthly basis or once every four (4) weeks.

In the cases referred to in subparagraphs (i), (ii), (iii) and (v) above, the ninety-one (91) day period begins upon the termination of the contract referred to in such subparagraphs; and for the purpose of such subparagraphs any local program, which, under any applicable AFTRA collective bargaining agreement, is the equivalent of a regional or national network program, shall be considered a regional or national network program as the case may be.

(f) Where the Artist is under a contract or contracts for the rendition of his services in the entertainment industry in any field in which the agent is authorized to act for the artist, during the succeeding period of one hundred and eighty-two (182) days after the expiration of the ninety-one (91) day period in question, at a guaranteed compensation for such services of twenty-five thousand ($25,000) dollars or more, or where the Artist is under a contract or contracts for the rendition of his services during said 182 day period in the radio phonograph recording and/or television fields at a guaranteed compensation for such services of twenty thousand dollars ($20,000) or more, then the artist may not exercise the right of termination.

(g) Periods of layoff or leave of absence under a term contract shall not be deemed to be periods of unemployment hereunder, unless under said contract the Artist has the right during such period to do other work in the radio or television field or in any other branch of the entertainment industry in which the Agent may be authorized by written contract to represent the Artist. A "term contract" as used herein means a contract under which the Artist is guaranteed employment in the broadcasting industries for at least one program each week for a period of not less than thirteen (13) consecutive weeks, and also includes any "term contract" as defined in the Regulations of the Screen Actors Guild, Inc. in respect to the motion picture industry, under which the Artist is working. Also, a "term contract" as used herein relating to the television field means a contract under which the Artist is guaranteed employment in the television field as set forth in subparagraph (e)(v) above.

(h) Where the Artist has a contract of employment in the broadcasting industries and either the said contract of employment, or any engagement or engagements thereunder, are canceled by the employer pursuant to any provision of said contract which does not violate any rule or regulation of AFTRA, the Artist shall be deemed to have been employed and to have received compensation for the purposes of paragraph 6(a) for any such canceled broadcasts, with the following limitation—where a contract providing for more than one program has been so canceled, the Artist shall not be deemed to have been employed or to have received compensation under such contract, with respect to more than one such program on and after the effective date of cancellation of such contract.

(i) For the purposes of this paragraph 6, where the Artist does not perform a broadcast for which he has been employed but nevertheless is compensated therefor, the same shall be considered employment hereunder.

(j) If at any time during the original or extended term of this contract, broadcasting over a majority of both the radio stations as well as a majority of the television broadcasting stations shall be suspended, the ninety-one (91) days period mentioned in this paragraph 6 shall be extended for the period of such suspension.

Generally, the artist must be ready, willing and able to accept employment of at least 15 days duration, every 90 days. The exact provisions and exceptions pertaining hereto are complicated, but the guild will help you sort out the time requirements if you are really interested in terminating the contract.

7. AGENT REPRESENTATION

The Agent may represent other persons. The Agent shall not be required to devote his entire time and attention to the business of the Artist. The Agent may make known the fact that he is the sole and exclusive representative of the Artist in the broadcasting industries. In the event of a termination of this contract, even by the fault of the Artist, the Agent has no rights or remedies under the preceding sentence.

8. ARTIST'S AGENCY REPRESENTATIVES

The Agent agrees that the following persons, and the following persons only, namely (HERE INSERT NO MORE THAN FOUR NAMES) shall personally supervise the Artist's business during the term of this contract. One of such persons shall be available at all reasonable times for consultation with the Artist at the city or cities named herein. The Agent, upon request of the Artist, shall assign any one of such persons who may be available (and at least one of them always shall be available upon reasonable notice from the Artist), to engage in efforts or handle any negotiations for the Artist at such city or its environs and such person shall do so. Employees of the Agent who have signed the AFTRA covenant and who are not named herein may handle agency matters for the Artist or may aid any of the named persons in handling agency matters for the Artist.

9. AGENCY CONTINUITY

In order to provide continuity of management, the name or names of not more than four (4) persons connected with the Agent must be written in the following space, and this contract is not valid unless this is done:

(HERE INSERT NOT MORE THAN FOUR NAMES)

In the event three (3) or four (4) persons are so named, at least two (2) of such persons must remain active in the Agency throughout the term of this contract. In the event only one (1) or two (2) persons are so named, at least one (1) such person must remain active in the Agency throughout the term of this contract. If the required number of persons does not remain active with the Agency, the Artist may terminate this contract in accordance with Section XXIII of AFTRA's Regulations Governing Agents.

This clause insures continuity of representation within the agency, which many of the other agency agreements do not provide for. (The persons named in clause 8, Artist's Agency Representatives, do not have to be the same as those named in clause 9. Also see "key-man" discussion under AFM Agreement paragraph 5.)

10. USE OF ARTIST'S NAME

The Artist hereby grants to the Agent the right to use the name, portraits and pictures of the Artist to advertise and publicize the Artist in connection with Agent's representation of the Artist hereunder.

Any portraits and pictures used by the agency should be approved by the artist.

11. AGENT WARRANTIES

The Agent agrees:

(a) To make no deductions whatsoever from any applicable minimums established by AFTRA under any collective bargaining agreement.

(b) At the request of the Artist, to counsel and advise him in matters which concern the professional interests of the Artist in the broadcasting industries.

(c) The Agent will be truthful in his statements to the Artist.

(d) The Agent will not make any binding engagement or other commitment on behalf of the Artist, without the approval of the Artist, and without first informing the Artist of the terms and conditions (including compensation) of such engagement.

(e) The Agent's relationship to the Artist shall be that of a fiduciary. The Agent, when instructed in writing by the Artist not to give out information with reference to the Artist's affairs, will not disclose such information.

(f) That the Agent is equipped, and will continue to be equipped, to represent the interests of the Artist ably and diligently in the broadcasting industry throughout the term of this contract, and that he will so represent the Artist.

(g) To use all reasonable efforts to assist the Artist in procuring employment for the services of the Artist in the broadcasting industries.

(h) The Agent agrees that the Agent will maintain an office and telephone open during all reasonable business hours (emergencies such as sudden illness or death excepted) within the city of _____ or its environs, throughout the term of this agreement, and that some representative of the Agent will be present at such office during such business hours. This contract is void unless the blank in the paragraph is filled in with the name of a city at which the Agent does maintain an office for the radio broadcasting and television agency business.

(i) At the written request of the Artist, given to the Agent not oftener than once every four (4) weeks, the Agent shall give the Artist information in writing, stating what efforts the Agent has rendered on behalf of the Artist within a reasonable time preceding the date of such request.

(j) The Agent will not charge or collect any commissions on compensation received by the Artist for services rendered by the Artist in a package show in which the Agent is interested, where prohibited by Section VIII of AFTRA's Regulations.

12. SUBMISSION AND DETERMINATION OF DISPUTES

This contract is subject to AFTRA's Regulations Governing Agents (Rule 12-B). Any controversy under this contract, or under any contract executed in renewal or extension hereof or in substitution herefor or alleged to have been so executed, or as to the existence, execution or validity hereof or thereof, or the right of either party to avoid this or any such contract or alleged contract on any grounds, or the construction, performance, nonperformance, operation, breach, continuance or termination of this or any such contract, shall be submitted to arbitration in accordance with the arbitration provisions in the regulations regardless of whether either party has terminated or purported to terminate this or any such contract or alleged contract. Under this contract the Agent undertakes to endeavor to secure employment for the Artist.

(FOR CALIFORNIA ONLY)

This provision is inserted in this contract pursuant to a rule of AFTRA, a bona fide labor union, which Rule regulates the relations of its members to agencies or artists managers. Reasonable written notice shall be given to the Labor Commissioner of the State of California of the time and place of any arbitration hearing hereunder. The Labor Commissioner of the State of California, or his authorized representative, has the right to attend all arbitration hearings. The clauses relating to the Labor Commissioner of the State of California shall not be applicable to cases not falling under the provisions of Section 1647.5 and/or Section 1700.45 of the Labor Code of the State of California.

Nothing in this contract nor in AFTRA's Regulations Governing Agents (Rule 12-B) shall be construed so as to abridge or limit any rights, powers or duties of the Labor Commissioner of the State of California.

Whether or not the agent is the actor's agent at the time this agency contract is executed, it is understood that in executing this contract each party has independent access to the regulations and has relied and will rely exclusively upon his own knowledge thereof.

IN WITNESS WHEREOF, the parties hereto have executed this agreement the _____day of _____, 19__.

_____	_____
AGENT	ARTIST
_____	_____
ADDRESS	ADDRESS
_____	_____
CITY/STATE/ZIP	CITY/STATE/ZIP

GENERAL SERVICES AGREEMENT

1. SCOPE OF AGREEMENT

I hereby employ you as my sole and exclusive representative, talent agency and agent in the entertainment, literary and related fields throughout the world for a period of _____ years from the date hereof. You accept said employment and agree to counsel and advise me, during normal business hours at your office, in the advancement of my professional career and to use reasonable efforts to negotiate employment and other contracts providing for the rendition of my services in those branches of the entertainment, literary, music, and related fields throughout the world, in which I am now or hereafter shall be willing and qualified to render services, including without any limitation, motion pictures, television and radio, publishing, audio and video recordings, personal appearances, concerts, theater, merchandising, testimonials and commercial tie-ins, whether or not using my name, voice or likeness.

This is a general services agreement that goes beyond areas traditionally covered by union contracts. It authorizes representation in all areas of the entertainment industry, but you can exclude areas where you feel the agent may not be particularly helpful or needed (i.e., music publishing, where you may already have another established relationship). It is also exclusive (i.e., you cannot have general services representation by more than one agency).

2. WARRANTIES

I have the right to enter into this agreement. I have not entered into and will not hereafter enter into any agreement that will conflict with the terms and provisions hereof. I agree that you may have interests of any kind either in your own or in the activities of others as well as the right to render your services for others during the term hereof either in the capacity in which you are employed by me hereunder or otherwise, whether similar to or competitive with the interests and activities for which you are employed to represent me hereunder, including without limitation, on behalf of the owners of package programs or other productions in which my services are used. Such representation shall not constitute a violation of your fiduciary or other obligations hereunder. With respect to the rendition of my services outside of the continental United States, you shall have the right to designate without my consent any one or more persons, firms or corporations to carry out or do any or all acts or things hereunder otherwise to be performed by you. No breach of this agreement by you or failure to perform the terms hereof shall be deemed a material breach of this agreement unless within thirty (30) days after I learn of such breach I serve written notice upon you of such breach and you do not remedy such breach within fifteen (15) days, exclusive of Saturdays, Sundays and holidays, after receipt by you of such written notice; provided, however, that the provisions of this sentence shall not be applicable to the provisions of Paragraph 6 of this agreement.

Packaging is allowed by the agent, as is the representation of other (possibly competing) clients. Ask for a list of the agent's other clients. Note the warranty that you are free to enter into this agreement (meaning that you have not signed with another agent for representation in the same areas).

3. COMPENSATION

I agree to pay you 10%, as and when received by me or by any person, firm or corporation on my behalf, directly or indirectly, or by any person, firm or corporation owned or controlled by me, directly or indirectly, or in which I now have or hereafter during the term hereof acquire any right, title, or interest, directly or indirectly, or by my successors and assigns, of the gross compensation paid or payable to me or for my account, during or after the term hereof, pursuant to or as a result of or in connection with (a) any employment or contract now in existence or negotiated or entered into during the term hereof (or within six months after the term hereof, if any such employment or contract is on terms similar or reasonably comparable to any offer made to me during the term hereof and is with the same offeror thereof or any person, firm or corporation directly or indirectly connected with such offeror) whether procured by you, me or any third party; and (b) all modifications, extensions, renewals, replacements, supplements or substitutes for such employment or contract or pertaining thereto whether procured by you, me or any third party; however, it is expressly understood that to be entitled to continue to receive the payment of compensation on the aforementioned contracts during or after the termination of this agreement you shall remain obligated to serve and to perform obligations with respect to said employment contracts and to extensions or renewals of said contracts and to any employment requiring my services on which such compensation is based. Commissions on considerations other than money shall be payable, at your election, either in money based on the fair market value of such other considerations, or in pro rata share in kind of such other considerations.

> *The commission amount can vary, depending upon a maximum established in union-regulated areas or that negotiated by the client. At the time of signing a series of agreements, the artist may want to negotiate an "across the board commission," applicable to all areas of representation—AFM, AFTRA, general services, etc. Also, commissions may be figured either on gross receipts (all amounts paid to or on behalf of the artist) or net receipts (gross receipts less the deduction of certain expenses, such as travel, weekly guarantees to artist, or such artificial amount as 10% on monies earned after the first $50,000). And, if the agent receives a "packaging fee" from the buyer for your services coupled with that of other agency clients, no additional commission on your earnings should be allowed—no "double-dipping!" Finally, try to restrict commissions on renewed contracts after termination to those renewals actually negotiated by the agent before termination of the agent.*

4. OTHER ARTIST BUSINESSES

If any firm, corporation, partnership, joint venture or other form of business entity now or hereafter owned or controlled by me in which I now or hereafter have any right, title or interest has or hereafter during the term hereof acquires directly or indirectly any right to my services in the entertainment, literary, music and related fields, then said firm, corporation, etc., shall be deemed to have engaged you as its sole and exclusive agent and shall confirm such engagement by executing an agency agreement in the same form as this agreement or your then standard form pertaining to such activity. Regardless of whether such business entity executes any such agreement with you, such agency agreement shall be deemed executed and shall be of full force and effect, and I shall remain primarily liable, jointly and severally, with such third party, to pay commission to you as provided in paragraph 3 above, based upon the gross compensation paid and/or payable to such third party, directly or indirectly, for furnishing my services, as fully and effectively as if such gross compensation were paid and/or payable to me. For the purposes of Paragraph 3 above, the term "gross compensation" shall be deemed to include such gross compensation paid and/or payable to such third party. If such third party does not, for whatever reason, execute such agreement with you, you shall nevertheless remain my exclusive agent to represent me in connection with my services on the terms and conditions as herein contained and I shall remain liable to pay commissions to you as provided in this contract and in the preceding sentence hereof.

> *This clause attempts to cover the situation where artists form other business entities, usually for tax purposes, which "loan-out" the services of the artist. Due to the legal fiction that separates the identities of a corporation from that of its shareholders, this paragraph insures that not only the artist but also his loan-out corporation is firmly bound to the representation agreement.*

5. COMPENSATION DEFINITION

As used herein, "gross compensation" means all monies, properties, considerations and other things of value of every kind and character whatsoever including but not limited to salaries, earnings, fees, royalties, rents, bonuses, gifts, proceeds, rerun fees and stock (without deductions of any kind) and shall likewise include, without limitations, any gross compensation paid and/or payable to me or for my account on a so-called pay-or-play basis, as a guarantee or otherwise in lieu of the rendition of my services; "services" shall include any and all of my services in any capacity whatsoever, whether as an employee, independent contractor or otherwise; "employment" and "contract" shall include any and all employment or contracts (including contracts to refrain from services or activities) of every kind whatsoever whether written or oral, in any way pertaining to services, materials or interests in any branch of the entertainment, literary, music and related fields.

6. DURATION AND TERMINATION

If I do not obtain a bona fide offer of employment from a responsible employer during a period in excess of four (4) consecutive months, during all of which time I have been ready, willing, able and available to accept employment, either party hereto shall have the right to terminate this contract by notice in writing to that effect sent to the other party by registered mail, provided no such bona fide offer has been obtained subsequent to the expiration of said four (4) month period and before the giving of said notice. The exercise of my right to terminate under this paragraph shall not affect your rights under Paragraph 3 hereof with respect to employment or contracts in existence or negotiated for prior to the effective date of such termination.

> *This is your "out"—if no bona fide offer of employment is received by you during at least four consecutive months during the term of the contract, you can fire the agency and they can cancel you. You may also negotiate here for a minimal annual sum to be booked by the agent in order to keep the agreement in force— i.e., if the agent fails to procure employment earning you at least "$X" per year,*

or 10% over the previous year's earnings, you have the option of terminating all the agency's agreements with you.

7. ASSIGNMENT OF REPRESENTATION

You shall have the right to assign this agreement or any part thereof to any persons, firms or corporations ("companies") now or hereafter controlling, controlled by or under common control with you, any companies resulting from a merger or consolidation with you, any companies succeeding to a substantial part of your assets, or any parent, affiliated or subsidiary companies.

> *This clause allows the agency to assign your representation to another affiliated company. This should be looked at carefully, especially when you are signing because of the lure of one particular agent. The artist should include a "key-man" clause specifying that if a particular agent leaves the agency, the artist can follow the agent. (See "key-man" clause discussion under AFM Agreement paragraph 5.)*

8. DISPUTES

Controversies arising between us under the provisions of the California Labor Code relating to Talent Agencies and under the rules and regulations for the enforcement thereof, shall be referred to the Labor Commissioner of the State of California, as provided in Section 1700.44 of said Code.

> *The Labor Code permits controversies to be submitted to either the Labor Commissioner or arbitration. This clause opts for the Labor Commissioner.*

9. SIGNEES

In the event this agreement is signed by more than one person, firm, corporation, or other entity, it shall apply to the undersigned jointly and severally, and to the activities, interests and contracts of each of the undersigned individually. If any one of the undersigned is a corporation or other entity, the pronouns "I," "me" or "my" as used in this agreement shall refer to the undersigned corporation or other entity, and the undersigned corporation or other entity agrees that it will be bound by the provisions hereof in the same manner and to the same extent as it would, had its name been inserted in the place of the pronouns.

10. ORAL PROMISES AND EXTENSIONS OF TERM

This instrument constitutes the entire agreement between us and no statement, promises or inducements made by any party hereto, which is not contained herein, shall be binding or valid and this contract may not be enlarged, modified or altered except in writing, signed by both parties hereto. The term of this agreement stated in Paragraph 1 hereof shall be automatically extended for one (1) year, unless I shall give you written notice to the contrary no later than thirty (30) days prior to the end of such term. The termination of any other agency agreement between us for any reason shall not affect this agreement in any respect.

> *This is an all-inclusive clause disavowing any oral promises made. Moreover, all changes in the agreement must be made in writing. Note the automatic extension for one year of the term of the contract unless the artist gives notice 30 days before the term ends.*

Very truly yours,

_____

AGREED TO AND ACCEPTED:

_____	_____
AGENT	ARTIST
_____	_____
BY	BY
_____	_____
NAME AND TITLE (AN AUTHORIZED SIGNATORY)	NAME AND TITLE (AN AUTHORIZED SIGNATORY)
_____	_____
FEDERAL I.D. / SS#	FEDERAL I.D. / SS#

PROVISIONS THAT SHOULD BE CONSIDERED WITH ALL AGENCY AGREEMENTS

Agent will represent no more than two clients: The agent may make the representation that he will handle you and one other client, exclusively. The trade-off is that the agent gets a larger cut, subject, of course, to your getting at least scale.

Other provisions, which can be negotiated in connection with this agreement and other agency contracts include the following:

1. The simultaneous ending of all agreements with the agency when any one (i.e., a group member who signed the agreements) is terminated or any agreement expires. This is important to a group.
2. The exclusion of commissions for performances already set, or in the areas of recording agreements, music publishing, literary fields, etc.
3. No double commissions on employment arising under different agreements, or when agent receives a commission from a buyer of talent, (i.e., packaging).
4. No commissions on residuals or repeats of TV programs or films.
5. Specific maximum commissions as to all agency contracts.
6. Commission computation on net receipts rather than gross receipts.
7. Agreements are terminated if agent hasn't procured employment resulting in offers exceeding a specific dollar amount in a certain amount of time.

BUSINESS MANAGERS

by Todd Gelfand and Margaret Robley

Business managers oversee the financial aspects of their clients' lives. The business manager takes an active role in the collection of income; prepares budgets and monitors expenditures; actively participates in the client's investment decisions; oversees insurance coverage; initiates and participates in estate planning; and constantly monitors the tax consequences of all transactions. While accounting is universal for all businesses, business management as described herein is unique to the entertainment industry.

There are no credential, licensing or educational requirements to become a business manager. However, in order to offer investment advice, the business manager must be licensed as an investment advisor. Since the problems business managers deal with are very complex, most are certified public accountants (CPAs), attorneys, or business people with varied financial backgrounds.

Business management started in Los Angeles in the 1930s in response to the vast amount of money being earned in the movie industry. Over the next 50 years, the business management field grew rapidly and spread to New York, Nashville and San Francisco due to the expansion of the television and music industries in these cities. Seattle and Atlanta are currently becoming major music centers and, consequently, may become business management centers also. Business management did not develop very rapidly outside the United States and is in its infancy in most overseas markets. The London market has developed more rapidly than the others, however, and has several business management firms.

SELECTING A BUSINESS MANAGER

An artist usually does not engage a business manager until after he/she has had some success in the music industry, such as a gold album. Until that time, artists can engage accountants, on an hourly basis, to prepare tax returns and advise them on tax and business matters.

Once the artist has decided that a business manager is needed, he/she should interview several firms before making a decision. The artist should meet everyone within the organization that will be working on his/her account.

When searching for a business manager, the artist should ask colleagues and advisors for referrals and check out the firm before setting up an appointment. It is very important for the business manager to have experience in dealing with music clients and the expertise to handle any specific problems or situations that the artist may have. The artist should be prepared with questions for the business manager to answer during their initial meeting, and should check references to make sure that the business manager and firm are responsive to their clients' needs.

Artists should consider interviewing small local companies and international accounting firms, which have a worldwide network of services available, before deciding which is best for their specific needs. Whether the artist chooses a large firm or small one, he/she should feel comfortable and have a good rapport with their individual business manager. It is very important that the artist be able to communicate openly and easily with the business management team. Normally, there is no contract between the artist and the business manager; a good personal relationship is very important and it is imperative that they both feel free to leave at any time.

The business manager is the last member added to the management team and the artist should consult with the other members of the team before engaging one as it is crucial that they all work together cohesively.

DUTIES OF THE BUSINESS MANAGER

Business managers perform many functions in overseeing the financial affairs of their clients. A synopsis of some of these functions follows.

Bookkeeping and Collection of Income

In a business management firm the bookkeepers and account managers, under the supervision of the managers and partners, are responsible for reviewing invoices; verifying their validity and processing them for payment; preparing payroll checks for clients' employees; preparing incoming checks for deposit; and monitoring bank accounts to make sure there are sufficient funds to cover checks and clients' withdrawals from ATM machines. Any excess funds, which will be needed in the near future, are transferred to short term investments to earn interest income.

Many artists have one or more contracts: recording, merchandising, publishing, various foreign subpublishing, etc., which the business manager is responsible for monitoring to ensure that all contractual amounts are received. The business manager has a monitoring system that keeps track of the various types of income due and the projected due dates. All receipts are verified to ensure that all income is received in a timely manner. If moneys are not received when due, the business manager pursues collecting the delinquent amounts. The business manager also monitors sales and advances to make sure that income is properly reported and paid and determines if record royalties are being escalated properly and whether any cross-collateralization is contractually allowed.

If the client controls his/her own publishing, the process of monitoring income becomes more difficult as there may be many subpublishing deals and synchronization licenses to account for. The business manager maintains a continuous income schedule to monitor the publishing and subpublishing royalties earned and keeps in close contact with the music publishing administrators to make sure that moneys are received for all synchronization and mechanical licenses granted.

Financial Reporting

Most business management firms use a computerized system for bookkeeping that generates statements showing all cash receipts and disbursements, cash balances, and financial statements reflecting monthly and cumulative year-to-date income and expense figures. These monthly financial statements are reviewed by the staff accountants that use them to prepare tax projections, budgets, annual meeting packages and special reports requested by the client.

Based on projected income and conversations with the client, the business manager prepares a budget that reflects projected expenditures for the period. The budget includes capital items (which may be a large portion of the client's spending) and the client's personal discretionary spending—an area that is hard to control due to the ease of using credit cards. The business manager can prepare a budget for personal expenditures, but it is the client who makes the decision either to stay within the budget and maintain long-term financial security, or not. Periodically, budget to actual comparisons are prepared to show the client any discrepancies.

Tax Services and Estate Planning

Tax planning for clients is a constant process for business managers. This entails determining which type of entity (sole proprietorship, partnership, corporation, S-corporation) is best; whether a pension plan or medical reimbursement plan is desirable; whether to buy or lease an automobile; which investment strategies to pursue; etc.

The business manager is responsible for tax compliance and prepares payroll tax, sales tax, gift tax, and income tax returns for filing with the appropriate authorities. In addition, the business manager represents all clients in examinations by tax agencies, including the Internal Revenue Service. With the recent establishment of the Entertainment Task Force by the IRS, we will be seeing more examinations of entertainers' tax returns.

Business managers interact with attorneys and other advisors in preparing estate and retirement plans for clients. They compile information on current assets and liabilities and assemble information on future goals with an emphasis on financial security for their clients and their clients' beneficiaries. Once the life insurance trusts, living trusts, wills, and other estate planning vehicles are in place, the business manager contracts for life insurance to pay any projected estate taxes.

Touring Services

Before a client agrees to go on a U.S. or foreign tour, the business manager works with the personal manager to project income and expenses for the tour. Today, in most cases, touring is an effective method of promoting an artist's current album. Even though tour support is recoupable by the record company, a tour usually generates sufficient album sales to pay any excess costs and still give the artist a profit. Once the tour is confirmed, the business manager monitors income and expenditures; ensures that adequate insurance (including cancellation insurance, if applicable) is in place; ensures compliance with multi-state taxing authorities; prepares budgets; negotiates to minimize tax withholding in various states and overseas; reviews all third party contracts; obtains social security clearances for applicable foreign countries; monitors the budget-to-actual income and expenses and resolves discrepancies; and prepares tax returns for all necessary jurisdictions.

The business management staff reviews tour settlements and, when necessary, a staff member or partner may accompany the client to assist in box office settlements with promoters and venues.

Insurance, Investments and Asset Administration

To protect the client's long range security, adequate insurance coverage is a must. The business manager is responsible for ensuring that the client has sufficient insurance coverage for his/her employees, businesses, autos and real estate. The client also needs insurance to protect his/her assets in case of a lawsuit, to cover medical bills, and to furnish income in case of disability.

Due to the Federal Deposit Insurance Corporation regulations, a minimum amount of money should be kept in bank accounts. All excess cash should be invested.

Artists should choose business managers whose investment strategy corresponds to their desires. The artist and the business manager should develop an investment policy that is comfortable for the artist. A conservative approach, which preserves capital and avoids risk, could be investing in U.S. Treasury securities and insured municipal bonds from the state of residence. A slightly aggressive profile would be investment in blue chip stocks; and if the client wants an opportunity for even more growth potential with higher risk, investment can be made in more volatile securities.

Depending on the age of the client, any funds in an Individual Retirement Account (IRA) or pension plan may be invested in growth rather than preservation funds. The growth funds are best for clients who still have several years before they reach retirement age.

The business manager advises and assists the client in the acquisition, sale and improvement of residences or other real estate to assure that costs are minimized. This assistance includes working with loan brokers and direct lenders to acquire financing or refinancing of mortgages that take advantage of the most favorable plans and rates. Business managers also deal with the purchases and sales of other assets (such as automobiles) and are instrumental in obtaining asset appraisals to ensure that adequate insurance coverage is in place.

Royalty Examination

A few business management firms have separate royalty examination departments that perform examinations of U.S. record and publishing companies and their foreign distributors to determine if there have been underpayments of royalty income. These examinations may be conducted for individual artists, writers, and licensors of rights. The royalty examination department may also perform examinations on merchandisers and other licensees and on the distribution records of television shows and motion pictures for profit participation clients. Due diligence/rights valuations can also be performed for clients interested in purchasing a copyright or other investment. In firms where business management and royalty examination departments fall under the same roof, the client has the advantage of constant monitoring of royalties, which can result in substantially more income.

Music Publishing Administration

Some business managers have the capability to copyright, license and administer songwriter clients' musical compositions. Music publishing administration consists of analyzing domestic, foreign and performing rights societies royalty statements and issuing royalty statements to other writers and publishers; issuing synchronization licenses; issuing mechanical licenses; and issuing print/reprint licenses. Some business management firms also assist in structuring and administering foreign sub-publishing deals throughout the world and can perform computations to establish catalog valuation.

Most artist/songwriters will need to secure the services of a music publishing administrator due to the complexity of the agreements, the substantial amount of time necessary to administer the various licenses, and the potential for royalties to slip through the cracks. Once again, if the music publishing administrator is a division of the business management firm, it is of benefit to the artist.

THE BUSINESS MANAGER AS PART OF
THE MANAGEMENT TEAM

An artist has talents and skills that must be marketed to make him/her successful. It is the responsibility of the management team to do that marketing.

The business manager accounts for the client's money once it has been earned and thus is an important part of the management team, which also consists of the personal manager, who is the controller of the artist's life including the recording contract, touring activities, public relations profile and the entire plan for his/her career; the talent agent, whose primary job is to work with promoters to book and promote live performances, or to negotiate roles on television shows or in movies; and the lawyer, who is involved in structuring deals and shaping the artist's career in addition to providing routine legal advice.

These four people work together to help further their client's career and maintain his/her financial stability. The management team makes recommendations, but it is the client who has the final say in all aspects of his/her life or career.

Each advisor has a role in the client's life and by working together, yet separately, they maintain a cohesive whole. Although their total fees may range from 25% to 30% of gross income, the financial stability provided by the team is worth the cost.

STRUCTURE OF THE CLIENT'S BUSINESS ENTITIES

An artist must be viewed as a business that is capable of generating several million dollars per year. For most creative artists, however, taking care of business is not the most effective use of their time. For that reason it is important to choose a business manager who has specialized knowledge of taxes, royalty examination, investments, and touring to handle these technical and complex matters.

In the business management firm, the bookkeepers and account managers function as the client's bookkeeping and accounting department. The staff accountants act as assistant controllers; the supervisors or managers act as treasurers or controllers; and the partner acts as the vice president or chief financial officer of the client's business. The client's personal manager acts as the general manager or chief operating officer; and the client acts as the president or chairman of the board and is the final decision maker.

Since the careers of most artists are of limited life, as compared to the 45-year work span of most people, artists need to put their yearly income in perspective and spend accordingly. When an artist is successful and money is pouring in, overspending is not noticed. When income drops, however, this overspending can lead to bankruptcy. If the client controls spending and operates in an efficient manner he/she will generate more after tax dollars and have a brighter future. Musicians' strengths lie in their musical talents and it is the function of a capable business manager to ensure that the artist is prepared for the likelihood of lean years.

BUSINESS MANAGEMENT FEES

Accounting and professional fees are traditionally billed on an hourly basis. In the business management field, however, the general billing rule is a percentage fee (usually 5%) of the client's gross income. In some cases, a maximum and minimum is placed on the total yearly fee. Business managers occasionally charge a monthly retainer fee instead of the hourly or percentage billing.

GENERAL FINANCIAL ADVICE

Once an artist has sold a million records, he/she dreams about how the platinum record will look on the wall and ponders how to spend the money that will soon be received. However, before running out and spending those anticipated royalties, the artist must consider how recording and publishing contracts are structured.

There was a recording budget for the album that had to cover all record production costs with any balance left over going to the artist upon completion. Since the artist ultimately pays all of the costs for the record, it is very important that recording costs be minimized as much as possible. These costs must be recouped by the record company before the artist receives any royalties. Even if the artist's lawyer has negotiated a fantastic royalty rate, the initial royalties must cover the recoupment of recording costs, free goods, packaging, and hold back for reserves, so the first royalty checks will be substantially reduced. After paying the personal manager, talent agent, business manager, and applicable taxes, the artist could end up with a minimal amount of money—or none.

The artist may have also received a publishing advance, which must be recouped before any publishing royalties are payable. The balance of the recording budget and the publishing advance were probably spent on ordinary living expenses before the artist hit the big time and the meager royalties may be quite shocking.

The artist should prepare a budget (with the business manager) and make every effort to stay within its guidelines so as to accumulate a nest egg. Whenever income is received the amount of money that will be necessary to pay income taxes should be segregated, so that it won't be available for personal expenses. The artist should not overextend finances when purchasing real estate, autos, equipment and other assets. If possible, pay cash so there will be no payments due if money gets tight. Adequate insurance coverage should be maintained (including life and medical), to protect against lawsuits and catastrophes. The artist should establish a retirement plan in which investments of after tax dollars will accumulate. And estate planning should be a priority in order to minimize the effect of estate taxes.

Keep in mind that cost cutting measures implemented now will result in more money in the future. To live comfortably, it is necessary for an artist to conserve money in the peak years.

CONCLUSION

By overseeing all financial aspects of their clients' lives, business managers strive to maximize earnings, plan for the future and preserve and expand asset bases. Although it is difficult for some artists to entrust their business and personal finances to someone else, no matter how highly regarded, it is necessary to do so in order to focus on furthering their careers. Once this happens, artists can build for the future, secure in the feeling that their finances are being handled properly.

Because of the trust that is placed in them by their clients, business managers must have integrity and be able to make sound decisions. Since most business management clients are not experienced business people, business managers must be able to explain transactions, situations, and laws in language that their clients' can understand. Business managers will deal closely with their clients' personal managers, attorneys, agents, and personal assistants; however, their loyalty is to their clients and they must, therefore, protect their clients in all matters.

RECORDING

**Practical Aspects Of
Securing Major Label Agreements**

Analysis Of A Recording Contract

**How To Read And Evaluate
Your Artist Royalty Statements**

Analysis Of A Record Producer Agreement

**Recording And Distribution Contracts
With Independent Labels**

**Contracts And Relationships
Between Independent And Major Labels**

PRACTICAL ASPECTS OF SECURING MAJOR LABEL AGREEMENTS

by Neville L. Johnson

alent alone will not guarantee a record deal, and seeking one can be a discouraging and fruitless crusade. There are only a few hundred deals available each year and many of them are snatched by artists moving from one label to another.

There is no standard method for obtaining a recording agreement with a major record company, but here are some guidelines. Approach record companies with a "physical package," utilize a "human package" as an integral element of the presentation, and be familiar with the business practices and marketing philosophy of the record company to which presentation is made. After discussing the components of a physical package and a human package, I will analyze the best method of presenting a "total package" to a record company, and discuss the important factors to be considered in selecting a company.

TODAY'S REALITY

After 20 years as a music attorney, I am more frustrated than ever about shopping bands to major labels. My law office hired a person to specialize in this area, and in 1993 and 1994, every major label passed on the band on which we most concentrated. That band is now a top selling act, but it had to return to its hometown in the South, and release its own record (which sold 20,000 units), before a major label showed interest.

The reality today is that most acts are signed after being released on their own or on a small independent label. Since the advent of "Sound-Scan," which via bar-coding, measures over half the sales of recorded music in the United States, it is now possible for a record company to realize when a local act is hot, or when a "regional breakout" is occurring.

THE PHYSICAL PACKAGE

The physical package consists of the artist, the act, a demonstration tape, and additional materials such as lyric sheets, pictures, reviews, biographical information, letters, and invitations.

A demonstration tape (demo) is necessary for most acts that have not had a record deal prior to the time of the presentation. A demo, most importantly, must contain music that is unique, creative, and commercial. The majors want music that can sell in large quantities. These days, it's rock and roll, pop, triple A or "AAA," country, R&B, rap, jazz and classical, with the latter two categories being particularly difficult to break into because their market share is so limited. Most executives want to get a million seller. An A & R (Artists and Repertoire) executive who doesn't deliver hot acts that get on the radio will not have a job for long. An important function of A & R executives is talent acquisition, but most are primarily busy with, and responsible for, the talent that is already signed to their label.

The artist should keep in mind that the ultimate sale will be to the public, not to a record company. Music executives evaluate music, in large part, on the basis of its sales potential. Record companies are not philanthropic organizations: they are in business to make money, and can only do so with records that have commercial appeal.

Besides great music, a demo should have the following characteristics:

Cassette Tape or CD

Cassette tapes work. Today, many artists press and send their own CDs.

Good Tape Quality

The tape should be the best available. Good quality tape will allow the listener to hear the performances clearly. Never send the master tape. Although most demo tapes are eventually returned, delays are common and some are simply lost or forgotten.

Good Performance

Artists must sound as though they are ready to cut tapes of master quality. Although high quality production is not a decisive factor to record companies, the quality of demo tapes has improved measurably, especially with the "MIDI" (Musical Instrument Digital Interface) revolution. Today many acts are recording demos in home studios, which are equipped to simulate the sound quality of commercial 16- and 24-track studios.

Four Song Maximum

Record company personnel that listen to demos are very busy and listen to many in a day's work. Unless it's a CD, don't discourage them with one that has too many selections.

Song Names and Order Listed on Container

The name of each selection and the order of performance should be clearly written or typed on the demo box. Make it easy for listeners to name the songs they like. Include whether Dolby noise reduction is used; and the person to contact about the demo (personal manager, attorney or band leader).

The other components of the physical package, listed below, can significantly enhance the listener's evaluation, and should accompany the demo.

Lyric Sheets

Lyric sheets involve the listener in the music. While the ears follow the sounds, the eyes follow the words.

Photographs/Videotape

If an artist has a look or image, the record company should know about it. A professional and attractive appearance is a valuable asset in today's music industry. Record companies are increasingly interested in an artist's visual impact due to the MTV (and related channels) and videotape markets, and the growing interrelationship between motion pictures, television, and records. Some recording acts have been signed on the strength of a videotape of a live performance sent in lieu of or in addition to a demo. For an act with significant visual appeal, a videotape, if economically feasible, should be considered.

Biographical Information

A succinct, factual statement of an artist's credentials and background helps to explain the music to the listener and to distinguish the artist from others. The bio is analogous to a resume in other professions: it informs the reader of the qualifications of the applicant.

Reviews and/or Itinerary

Favorable reviews tell the reader that the artist has stage experience and is enjoyable to hear. If the artist can excite an audience or has a following, the record company will want to know about it because live performance is an important method of promoting records. If a number of impressive gigs have been played, or if the artist is regularly working, an itinerary should be enclosed to communicate that the talent is stage-wise and has a source of income.

By paying attention to the details of the physical package, an aura of professionalism can be projected to the record company by the artist, the music, and people that advise and work with him or her. A clever, enticing physical package will merit special attention by its recipient. With so many contenders vying for a deal, an effort to create an appealing physical package is warranted.

THE HUMAN PACKAGE

Most successful artists are members of a team. A critical issue in a record company's decision whether to sign an act is who will carry the ball after a record is released. If an act has inexperienced, incompetent or no personnel to support and direct it, the record company's job of selling records will be difficult and hampered. An artist will substantially improve the chance of securing a recording agreement if he or she is part of a functioning, well-organized business machine that can work with the record company towards the common goal of generating income.

The Personal Manager

The personal manager is the most important member of the human package. If the would-be recording artist is able to arrive at the doorstep of a record company arm-in-arm with a highly regarded manager, the record company will be more easily swayed to invest its monies. Record company executives feel secure when an artist's career, recording duties, public performance, songwriting, and other professional activities are being coordinated on a day-to-day basis by a professional.

The artist must be extremely selective in choosing a personal manager. Some managers are persona non grata because of their pushy and demanding demeanor, unsavory reputation, or incompetence. If a would-be recording artist associates with such a personal manager, it may result in a case of guilt (and rejection) by association. Also, most established personal managers are not interested in unsigned acts.

Talent Agent

The human package can include a talent agent who is successfully booking the artist in live engagements. The artist with a talent agent offers the record company an added inducement for making a deal because it will be able to rely upon a skilled professional to book the artist into live engagements before, during and after the release of the artist's album. This will promote record sales.

Attorney

The attorney can be an important member of the human package because of their contacts at record companies and elsewhere in the industry through the clients they represent. It is predominantly lawyers, managers, music publishers, and record producers that shop record deals to the major labels, but again, lawyers are notoriously unsuccessful at shopping musical acts. An artist should have the guidance of a professional to assist in any legal needs and in helping to select the other members of the human package. Sound advice: get a lawyer *and* someone else with influence to work for you.

Business Manager

A business manager, or anyone that has a strong relationship with executives at a label can also function as part of the human package.

Record Producer/Production Company

A record producer and/or production company (an entity which finances and shops record deals) is another route to a deal. One caveat must be stated with regard to the artist who approaches the record company already signed to a production deal, or firmly allied with a record producer. The record company may be unimpressed with such producer's talent or track record. If the artist cannot or refuses to work with another producer, this consideration may be a deal-breaker, that ends any chance of a recording agreement with that company.

An artist signed to a production company will, generally, make less money than if signed directly to a label.

Anybody With Influence

The music business is small and insular. Other musicians may be willing to go to bat for you, or even those outside the music industry that have personal relationships with an A & R person. Network, network, and network some more. The word will get out.

WRITE A HIT SONG

That's true—write a hit song for another artist—there's no faster entree into the recording world.

TOTAL PACKAGE

There are two ways of presenting the total package to a record company. The first is to have a representative of the record company see the artist perform live; the second is to present or send a demo to the record company. An artist will usually have to do both in order to clinch a deal. What you want to present are credits and creditability. Write a hit song and the doors are wide open. If the critics love the show, it may be all that is needed.

Showcases and Live Performances

Record companies want to sign artists that perform well on stage. Performing live, by "showcase" (an act performed primarily for representatives of record companies) or other live engagement, can be an effective way of attracting the attention and interest of a record company. If an artist's performance is a knockout it will enhance the prospects of a record deal or a future demo at the company's expense.

It is not easy to induce record executives that are involved with talent acquisition, such as A & R personnel, to attend a gig or showcase. If the artist is performing in, say, Phoenix, Arizona, the chances of getting a record company person to attend are poor. New York City, Los Angeles and Nashville are the main cities where record companies are located, and it is still very tough to get executives to turn out for shows there. Virtually all country acts are signed in Nashville.

Invitations to attend a showcase or gig should be in writing and be delivered or mailed to each invitee. A follow-up telephone call the day before or on the day of the performance is the best reminder. Be certain that the names of all who have been invited are on the guest list.

Demos

The most effective way of presenting a demo is through a personal meeting with the individual to whom it is to be given. If this cannot be arranged, the demo should be accompanied by a concise, clearly typed letter stating the purpose for which it is sent, the level of production (4–, 8–, 16–, or 24–track), whether the songs are original, and who the members of the human package are. The record company will, if it finds the demo worthy of further consideration, usually request an itinerary of live performances by the artist so that it can have a choice of when to attend.

Because of the problems with live engagements and showcases (such as getting record company executives to attend), the artist in search of a deal should seriously consider providing the record company with both a demo and an invitation to a subsequent showcase or gig. As a practical note, demos, as opposed to showcases, are the most common method of approaching a record company.

Occasionally, a record company will request other material or that the artist return with subsequently written material. Some companies will pay for recording sessions to make additional demonstration recordings.

SHOPPING THE PACKAGE

Assuming the total package is ready to be shopped, it must be decided who will perform this function and who will be approached. If an invitation to a showcase is sent by an individual unknown to the record company, it will probably be ignored. If a demo is sent solo to a record company—through the mail with a letter of introduction by the artist, the probable response of the record company will be to reject it and return it to the sender. If the record company accepts the demo, in most cases it will be referred to a listener in the A & R department. This person listens to thousands of demos a year, and most demos get less than two minutes. The listener is a filter for the rest of the A & R department with a mandate to say, "No."

The artist should bypass individuals on the lower rungs of the record company and attempt to get the package presented to the president of the record company, the chairman of the board or the head of the A & R department, persons that have the authority to commit the record company to signing an artist. Many companies work on a committee basis, and most signings occur via the A & R department. Other members of the A & R hierarchy and employees in other departments of the company, such as promotion or marketing, may be approached also. The higher the person approached is in the management of that department, the better the chances are of serious consideration by the head of the A & R department or other executive involved with talent acquisition. Many acts have been signed as a result of recommendations from local or regional promotion people that have noticed an act in a city other than New York or Los Angeles.

There is, in the usual situation, but one avenue of reaching someone at the record company who wields substantial influence or is in a decision-making position to sign an artist—personal contact. An invitation to a showcase/gig will be favorably answered and the demo will get serious consideration only if they are sent or referred by someone who is recognized and respected by the person receiving such invitation or demo. This doesn't mean that the person sending such invitation or demo need be famous within the music industry, he or she simply needs to be credible. The adage that it is not what you know, but who you know, definitely applies to the music business.

A number of personal managers, producers, lawyers and publishers can, because of their success and power, induce the president or chairman of the board of a record company to listen to a demo. Each member of the human package should be called upon to present the package to those at the record company with whom they are acquainted. Because personal contacts are so important in the industry, the artist who wishes to secure a recording agreement should attempt to get to know as many people in the music business as possible. The young promotion man at a record company today may be the head of the A & R department tomorrow. An artist who is friendly with a promoted person may, on the strength of that contact, have both a friend and a business acquaintance who will be helpful in advancing the artist's career.

A number of music attorneys are well connected throughout the industry. Many of these attorneys will "run a demo," doing so for anywhere from a flat fee ($250 to $5,000 or more!) to a percentage (of the initial advance or the entire deal and all music publishing revenues earned from compositions on sound recordings subject to the record deal), to a percentage of the artist's earnings derived from the record deal, should one be secured. I am fairly cynical about the success ratio of attorney-shopped acts—I cannot think of an act that has been signed in the last decade to a major label that was obtained exclusively by an attorney.

The human package must operate at the same level of professionalism as the physical package. Any person presenting the total package must have a good relationship with and be enthusiastic about the artist; know and understand the music; be aware of the long-term career goals of the artist and; most importantly, be able to communicate with and be credible to the record company being approached. Finally, the best method of attacking a record company is the flying wedge approach: a strong manager, attorney, publisher, producer and agent all working for a talented artist will eventually succeed.

Here is the simple truth: the artist and his or her marketing team must be aggressive, but *never* rude, when pushing the artist to those who have influence or signing ability. One must be relentless, patient, cunning and charming to distinguish one's product from others, and make sure it is heard.

CHOOSING A RECORD COMPANY

Of equal importance to the preceding is which record company to contact. Record companies all press, distribute and promote records, but there the similarity ends. The artist must carefully investigate the business structure, the standing in the industry, and the marketing philosophy of any record company being pursued. An artist needs a company that is both committed to the artist and has the organization to support that commitment.

Most artists want a company that is, or is part of, a strong and successful worldwide enterprise. This does not mean that an artist need pursue only the big companies. The artist should look for a capable company that has the organization and financial wherewithal to exploit records successfully throughout the world. At the time this edition is published, the record industry is dominated by the following major distributors: BMG (BMG, RCA, Arista); CEMA (Capitol, EMI, Virgin); Polygram (Polygram, A&M, Island, Motown); Sony (Sony, Columbia, Epic); UNI (MCA, Geffen); and WEA (Warner Brothers, Elektra/Asylum, Atlantic). Know which companies support the music you make. If it is jazz or new age, then approach those companies that specialize in those genres.

READ THE TRADES

Billboard is the industry magazine that charts the events of the music business on a week-to-week basis. Any artist that wants to obtain a record deal in today's competitive music business should read it to become aware of the trends and developments in the industry and to keep track of key executives. I also recommend *Music Connection* for artists that are seeking to get signed by a company with offices in Los Angeles, and *CMJ (College Music Journal)*, for alternative acts.

THE FUTURE

The times are definitely changing, and technology is evening out the playing field. The impediments to entry into the marketplace are the cost of manufacture and the vagaries of independent distribution, where the name of the game often is slow pay or no pay. With fiber optics and computers, the digital transmission of sound recordings is a few years away. The record companies of the future will become primarily *marketing* and *financing* entities, and the record stores of the future will be "downloaders," as opposed to purveyors of preexisting stamped pieces of plastic. This augurs well for musicians. Artists today can release their material and sell it mail order via the Internet. As distribution channels open up (the majors control the flow now), it will become easier and much cheaper to distribute your product. Keep up with the developments in technology and use them to your benefit.

CONCLUSION

The individuals that evaluate music at record companies are asked to make extremely difficult decisions. They must determine what music will be commercially viable. No amount of hype can sell a demo or a performance that doesn't have it "in the grooves," yet no reliable definition of this phrase has ever been articulated.

Moreover, an artist should seek a record deal only if he or she is ready, dedicated, and willing to spend years in the studio and on the road. The effort necessary to launch a career is enormous.

However, with enthusiasm, hard work and perseverance, a talented artist can achieve the goal of a record deal. Sure, rejection is commonplace, but there is only one person who really matters—the executive who says "Yes." That executive wants to find you as much as you want to find him or her. Keep at it!

Have a backup plan. There are labels overseas which may be interested in your music and be more receptive. Consider attending MIDEM, the annual music business convention where music publishers and record executives congregate at the end of each January in Cannes, France. I know of at least 30 U.S. acts that have foreign deals and whose records are imported into the United States. There are other conventions where one can network and make contacts. The biggest and best convention is South by Southwest each May in Austin, Texas, but there are other conventions in other cities which should be considered.

ANALYSIS OF A RECORDING CONTRACT

by Lawrence J. Blake

Obtaining a recording contract is one of the most important goals for a musical artist. In addition to royalties from the sale of records, which can be very substantial, records generate radio play and other media exposure that leads to higher live performance income and other opportunities. Thus, the recording contract may be the most important agreement an artist signs during his or her career.

Before discussing that agreement, however, a few preliminary points should be made. The form of agreement reproduced and discussed here is derived from a first draft contract submitted by one of the major record labels. Since certain clauses may not be identical with that company's standard form, we have chosen to use the fictional name, Label Records, Inc. However, the agreement is representative of the kind of agreement a major label would present an artist as they commence negotiating a first recording contract.

Although the following discussion points to a number of areas where the artist will seek to change the agreement, this form of agreement is not unusually bad or one-sided. The artist should never expect any record company to present a recording agreement which the artist can sign without negotiating changes. It is the artist's and his or her advisers' responsibility to negotiate the agreement until it is satisfactory to them. The degree to which the record company will improve its initial draft depends in large measure on how badly it wants the artist to sign with it. An artist making his or her first record deal will obviously have less leverage than a platinum selling artist. There are many points, however, which record companies are willing to concede if the issues are raised. The artist's representative should ask for all points that he or she feels the record company could reasonably be expected to agree to, and perhaps even a few more. The artist should not fear being branded as difficult simply because he or she thoroughly negotiates the recording contract. If anything, negotiation reflects that the artist is taking the commitment seriously and is handling it in a professional manner. However, the artist and the artist's representatives must not lose sight of the main objective—securing a recording contract.

Since recording contract negotiations can involve heated bargaining over many different points, and since recording contracts have grown more and more complex over the years, particularly due to the advent of videos, it is a practical necessity for the artist to engage an attorney, who generally works with the artist's manager, to handle the actual negotiations. This insulates the artist from any possible personal friction with record company personnel, with whom the artist needs to have a smooth, working rapport. Still, even if the artist is not participating in the head-to-head negotiations, he or she should monitor their progress, be consulted with and kept advised of the outcome of all significant points.

When aspiring recording artists dream of getting a recording contract, they usually envision a deal with a major record label. A major record label is one that is owned by one of the six major record distributors, namely WEA (Warner Bros., Elektra and Atlantic), Sony (Columbia and Epic), Polygram (A&M, Island and Motown), BMG (RCA and Arista), Uni (MCA and Geffen) and CEMA (Capitol, Virgin, and EMI) or a label whose records are distributed by one of the major distributors. Quite often, however, it will not be a major record company which offers the artist a first recording deal. Instead it may be an independent record label or a so-called production company. Accordingly, before analyzing a typical major label recording contract I want to touch briefly on recording contracts with independent labels and somewhat more extensively on recording contracts with production companies.

A record contract with an independent record label is structurally the same as one with a major label, except that it is generally shorter and simpler, in order to make the contract less intimidating to a new artist and to keep legal costs to a minimum. Nonetheless, the recording commitment the artist is being asked to make will generally outlast the career life span of the average recording artist, so once again it is essential that the artist have experienced legal representation, even if the amount of money the label is willing to offer does not seem to allow much room to pay legal fees.

Production companies take a variety of forms—from fly-by-night one-person operations to well-established, well-staffed companies—but they all serve basically the same function. They try to put together a "package" for a record company. This package normally consists of an artist, musical material, and a producer. Some well-established production companies have ongoing deals with record companies to provide a specified number of packages per year. These production companies sometimes have the right to control all of the creative elements of making the album and will simply deliver a completed master tape to the record company, which then is obligated to release and promote the album. Other production companies will be searching for a deal with a record company. In these cases the production company may approach a record company by shopping demos of the artist. It may offer the record company a package including the artist and a producer, or, alternatively, the production company may first produce a finished master tape and then attempt to shop it to a label for release and distribution.

Whether the production company already has a deal or is looking for one, it will usually seek to put the artist under contract as part of its effort to assemble a package for the record company. The form of the recording agreement presented to the artist will be very similar to the one offered by the record label, but the artist will be under contract to the production company, not the label. The production company, in turn, will furnish the artist's services to the label under a separate agreement, generally known as a "production contract."

As far as the recording artist is concerned, the production company is a middleman, standing between the artist and the record company. Undoubtedly it collects more from the record company than it pays the artist. Whether the production company deserves its share depends entirely on how valuable a service it can provide. The question for the artist is, can the production company get a deal that I would be unable to get on my own? Some production companies have a strong enough track record so that they will have little difficulty making a deal for any artist they sign. Entering a contract, of reasonable terms, with a company like that can make a great deal of sense. In other cases an artist may sign an exclusive recording contract with a production company and find the production company is unable to place the artist. The artist then may be trapped—too legally entangled for anyone else to deal with, but still under a binding multiyear contract to a production company that cannot get a record contract. In those circumstances the artist has made his or her position worse by becoming involved with a production company.

The artist's strategy, when negotiating with a production company, must be different from when negotiating directly with a record label. The point to remember is that the production company is only useful to the artist if it can get a deal and even then its usefulness is a function of how good a deal it makes. It is crucial to find out if the production company has a prearranged deal with a record company and what that deal is. If there is a preexisting deal between the production company and a major record label, the artist should ask for a copy of it. The production company may want to redact or white out certain financial provisions, but since the artist's contract must follow the form of the production company's contract with the major label, and since the major label is going to provide the compensation which the production company pays to the artist, it is not unfair or unreasonable for the artist to insist on knowing what the production company is keeping as its "spread." Indeed, if the production company is unwilling to disclose the terms of its agreement with the major label to the artist, the artist should seriously reconsider entrusting his or her career to that production company.

Production companies that do not already have deals with recording labels may try to justify a one-sided recording contract by claiming that they cannot predict what terms they will obtain from the record company, and therefore they cannot make certain concessions to the artist because the record company may not be willing to accept those terms. The result can be an extremely unfair contract. Accordingly, if there is no preexisting agreement between the production company and the major label, the agreement between artist and production company should provide that unless the production company obtains a production contract which meets the artist's specified requirements or which is submitted to and approved by the artist within a certain time period, the artist will be freed from all obligations to the production company.

Please note, the recording agreement below deals only with the artist's services as a *performer* on records. Where an artist writes songs as well as performs, the rights in the songs are properly handled in a separate publishing agreement. It used to be a common practice of record companies to demand that performers grant rights to a publishing company affiliated with the record company. This practice has generally been discontinued by the major record labels, although many production companies will still seek to obtain publishing rights.

EXCLUSIVE ARTIST'S RECORDING AGREEMENT

AGREEMENT made and entered into as of this _____ day of _____, 1995 by and between LABEL RECORDS, INC., Conglomerate Plaza, New York, New York ("Company") and _____ ("Artist") whose address is: _____.

1. Company hereby engages Artist's exclusive personal services as a recording artist in connection with the production of records and Artist hereby accepts such engagement and agrees to render such services exclusively for Company during the term hereof and all extensions and renewals.

   (a) The rights herein granted to Company and the obligations of Artist shall be for the world (the "Territory").

These clauses state very succinctly two key elements of this agreement, first that it is exclusive, and second that it is a worldwide agreement. That exclusivity will be set forth in greater detail later on in the contract, and certain exceptions to exclusivity can sometimes be negotiated, as will be discussed. Nearly every recording agreement made in the United States is made on a worldwide basis. This is true even as to independent record labels, which may have no offices outside the United States and may indeed have no network of licensees to distribute their records in foreign territories. However, the agreement contemplates that the company will have the right, although perhaps not the obligation, to distribute the records throughout the world.

2. The term of this agreement shall be for an initial period commencing on the date hereof and continuing until eight (8) months following the Delivery Date of the last masters required to be delivered ("minimum recording commitment") during said period ("Initial Period"). Artist hereby grants to Company _____ (__) consecutive separate options to extend the term for further periods ("Option Periods") (here-inafter the Initial Period and the Option Periods shall sometimes be referred to generically as "Contract Periods"), each upon the same terms and conditions applicable to the Initial Period, except as otherwise hereinafter set forth. Each Option Period for which Company has exercised its option shall commence upon the expiration of the immediately preceding Contract Period and shall continue until eight (8) months following the Delivery Date of the minimum recording commitment for the applicable Option Period. The Initial Period and every Option Period for which Company has exercised its option are hereinafter sometimes referred to together as the "Term." Each option shall be exercised, if at all, by notice to Artist at any time prior to the later of (1) six (6) months after the initial release date in the United States of the Album (hereinafter defined) that is delivered by Artist for the prior Contract Period or (2) thirty (30) days after Artist's written notice to Company of Artist's request that Company decide whether to exercise such option.

The "term" of a recording agreement means the period of time during which the artist is under contract exclusively to the record company. However, certain rights and obligations of the parties will extend beyond the expiration of the term of the contract, e.g., as you will see, the company retains the perpetual right to sell records containing the recordings made by the artist during the term and must continue to account and pay royalties for the sales of those records.

The term of this contract is not a fixed number of years, but rather is measured from the delivery of the recordings required to be made and delivered by the artist to the company. Therefore it can not be determined how long the term of the contract will run. Instead, it will depend primarily on how quickly the artist records new material.

For many years, the standard new artist recording contract consisted of an initial term of one year followed by four one-year options, with a recording commitment of one album plus an optional "overcall" album in each period, making a maximum of 10 albums. The so-called Olivia Newton-John case (MCA Records, Inc. v. Newton-John, 90 Cal. App. Third 18 [1979]) forced record companies, at least those operating in California, to change the term of their contracts so that it would expire not by the passage of time, but on the delivery of product (e.g., a one album deal with nine additional options for one album each). This is because the court appeared to have ruled that a standard one-year plus four one-year options contract could not be enforced to prevent the artist from recording for a third party after the expiration of five calendar years from its commencement, even though the contract contained the usual standard clause allowing the record company to suspend the running of the term of the contract if Ms. Newton-John failed to fulfill her recording commitment before the end of the applicable year. I say "appeared" because there is still widespread disagreement in the legal community as to the meaning and precedential value of the court's statements on this point.

Under the contract structures now used by nearly every record company, the term does not need to be suspended or extended by reason of the artist's failure to deliver an album; it merely runs until the required number of albums have been delivered. California law limits the enforceability of all personal service contracts to seven years, i.e., after seven years the record company cannot prevent the artist from recording for another record company. However, this same California law gives the record company a right to recover damages in a situation where the artist has not completed his or her recording commitment to the record company by the time the seven years have expired. This provision has never been interpreted in the courts. Although lawsuits have been filed involving certain high-profile artists (Metallica, Don Henley) neither artists nor record companies are particularly anxious to set a precedent in this regard, and the cases have settled.

Generally, in new artist recording contracts, the minimum recording commitment is one album and the number of option periods coincides with the number of additional albums which the company has the right to require the artist to perform. Generally, the maximum number of albums required under a typical new artist recording agreement with a major record company ranges from six to eight. Independent record companies, however, often offer contracts for one album only ("one-off" deals) and most do not go beyond four albums. Generally, a new artist is looking for the independent record label to generate a buzz and plant the seeds for breaking the artist, who would like to be free to sign with a major label if the opportunity should present itself. This requires either a limited recording commitment or a right to buy out of the contract.

Finally, this clause provides a formal mechanism for the company to exercise its option for the next album or other group of recordings. Generally, this requires the record company to keep track of when options will expire. Occasionally a record company has lost a valuable artist by inadvertently allowing an option to lapse. In order to avoid this, some record companies, as in this contract, have inserted into their agreements a fail-safe clause, which provides that the artist must give the record company notice that it is time to exercise an option, which then serves to remind the record company and eliminate the possibility that the artist's services will be lost inadvertently.

3. During the Initial Period and each Option Period for which the Company exercises its option, Artist shall record and deliver to Company masters the equivalent in playing time of one (1) Album ("minimum recording commitment").

Generally, the minimum recording commitment is one album. In the earlier days of the recording industry, the minimum commitment may have been only two sides, i.e., enough to make up the "A" and "B" sides of a single. If the single wasn't a hit, the artist might not get the chance to record any additional material. This practice occurred as recently as the early 1980s, particularly with artists performing Top 40 or dance-oriented material.

Obviously, it is to the artist's advantage to obtain a firm commitment from the record company to record more than one album. This becomes more attainable when there is more than one record label bidding for the services of the artist. A two-album initial commitment is quite common, although a firm commitment by the record company to finance more than two albums is unusual for a new artist.

Conversely, the artist does not want to be committed to the record company for more than the number of albums it is likely to take the artist to break. Once the artist has a proven track record of selling records, his or her bargaining strength will greatly improve. Therefore, it is in the artist's interest to be able to become a free agent in the marketplace as soon as reasonably possible. So, whereas the record company would like the original contract to give them options to as many albums as possible, the artist would like to limit the maximum recording commitment to as few albums as reasonably possible. This becomes particularly important if the artist should desire to renegotiate the terms of the contract based upon having achieved success in the marketplace. If the artist does not then owe the record company more than one, two, or three additional albums, it will be very valuable to the record company to obtain the artist's commitment to another album. On the other hand, if the artist is already committed to the record company to deliver the artist's next five or six albums, the value of an additional album is quite speculative.

(a) The masters recorded hereunder by Artist shall be recorded in a recording studio selected or approved by Company at such times as Company may designate or approve. Each master delivered hereunder shall consist of Artist's newly recorded studio performances of material mutually approved by Artist and Company and not previously recorded by Artist. Each master delivered hereunder shall be commercially satisfactory in Company's opinion. Artist shall deliver to Company a two-track stereo tape for each master. Each master shall be delivered to Company in the form of a completed, fully edited, mixed, leadered and equalized 1630 tape for each configuration (e.g., compact disc, analog cassette), and otherwise in the proper form for the production of the parts necessary for the manufacture of commercial records. Upon the request of Company, Artist shall rerecord any selection until a commercially satisfactory master shall have been obtained. Only masters delivered in full compliance with the provisions of this agreement shall be applied in fulfillment of Artist's recording and delivery obligation and no payments shall be made to Artist in connection with any masters which are not in full compliance. Each master shall be delivered to Company at the address set forth on page 1 hereof or such other place as Company may notify Artist in writing.

This clause deals with the so-called creative elements of the recordings. The first is that the recordings must be made in a recording studio. Generally speaking, live albums are not allowed to be delivered in satisfaction of the recording commitment, since they generally do not sell as well as studio albums, although there are notable exceptions (e.g., MTV's "Unplugged" albums). However, after an artist has achieved enough success to create market demand for a live album, the artist may be able to negotiate for the right to deliver one. Often, however, that album will be in addition to and will not count toward the number of albums required to be delivered under the deal. Generally, the record company will approve any recording studio the artist or the artist's producer wishes to use, so long as it has satisfactory recording equipment and the studio's rates fit within the recording budget.

More importantly, the company seeks to have approval over the songs the artist will record. It is less common today for a record company to insist on the right to designate the songs to record. However, until the artist has established a track record, it is unlikely that the artist will be given the right to decide which songs to record without the record company having a right of approval. As a practical matter, however, there are very few disputes between record companies and artists as to the songs to be recorded.

Perhaps the most important creative element to the company is its right to approve the producer of the masters. This right of approval is set forth later on in the contract, but I will address it here. In certain types of music, e.g., R&B, the producer is often the person who writes much of the material and shapes the overall sound of the recordings. In certain other types of music, e.g, rock and alternative rock, the producer may not be involved with songwriting at all, but may simply be responsible for shaping and capturing the sound of the artist. Most commonly, recording contracts provide that the producer will be mutually designated by the artist and the record company. In practice, the artist or the artist's manager will select the producer or producers and the record company will consult, but will generally defer to the artist's choice unless they have had a negative experience with a particular producer, which is quite rare.

The most troublesome stipulation in this clause is that the masters be "commercially satisfactory" in the company's opinion and that, if they are not, the artist must rerecord a song or songs until they are commercially satisfactory to the company. Obviously, there is no objective standard to determine whether a recording is commercially satisfactory or not. This essentially becomes a question of the company's subjective opinion versus the artist's and producer's subjective opinions. Generally, the artist's representatives will fight for a "technically satisfactory" standard, which simply means that the recordings have been recorded in a professional manner, and does not address the artistic quality or commercial sales potential of the music. Some record companies use the term "satisfactory," rather than "commercially satisfactory." This eliminates the apparent offensiveness of suggesting that the artist's intent should be making records that will sell well, as distinguished from records which are artistically meritorious, but it does not avoid the fundamental problem that the results of the artist's creative efforts are subject to the company's approval.

There is simply no way to eliminate contractually the possibility that the record company will not be excited about the record the artist delivers. What can be resolved are the parties' respective rights and obligations if this should occur. In this contract, the artist must rerecord whatever the company asks to be rerecorded, and there is no additional money required to be provided by the record company to pay for such additional recording sessions. Generally, however, the record company will be prepared to pay the *additional cost of rerecording certain songs or, more commonly, will request the artist to record an additional song or songs approved by the company until the artist has delivered a record which the record company believes it can successfully market. Often in a new artist's deal there will not be sufficient money left in the artist's recording fund to cover much additional recording, so the company will be forced to pay for whatever additional recording it may require. This tends to discourage record companies from exercising this right too frequently. However, major record companies have been known to shelve records by established artists, which the record company felt were not up to the caliber of that artist's prior recordings. In summary, the relative bargaining power of the artist will determine how this clause is ultimately resolved, but contractual language can only go so far and if the record company is not satisfied with the record delivered by the artist, it will take the parties' mutual cooperation to work out a satisfactory solution.*

Finally, this clause gives the record company the right not to pay for records which are not delivered in compliance with the creative approvals process. Accordingly, to the extent that payments are due to be made to the artist upon delivery of the record, if the creative approvals process has not been followed or if the ultimate record is not satisfactory to the record company, the record company could refuse to pay the payments due upon delivery. If the delivery advance is quite large, e.g., $500,000 in the case of an artist whose star has begun to dim, the record company might choose to enforce this clause strictly.

(b) The first Album required to be delivered during the Initial Period or any Option Period shall be delivered to Company within six (6) months following commencement of the applicable Contract Period. The additional masters (if any) required to be delivered during the Initial Period or any Option Period shall be delivered to Company within sixty (60) days following Company's request therefor. It is understood that Artist shall not deliver any Album within six (6) months from the date of delivery of a prior Album.

These time periods are generally quite negotiable. The record company wants to have a steady flow of product. The artist, however, needs to wait until new material has been created and therefore needs to be protected from the record company having the right to terminate the agreement abruptly if the delivery schedule is not met. Generally, the artist is given a longer cure period in the case of the failure to timely deliver recordings than with respect to other breaches of the recording contract.

4. Artist warrants and agrees that:
   (a) During the Term, Artist shall not perform for the purpose of making records for anyone other than Company and shall not authorize the use of Artist's name, likeness, or other identification for the purpose of distributing, selling, advertising or exploiting records for anyone other than Company in the Territory.

This restates the artist's exclusivity to the company in a more specific way. Generally, the artist will want to negotiate certain exceptions from exclusivity. Among the most common are the rights to write and produce material for other artists and to be credited as such on the records, which activities, if the contract is read literally, could be interpreted as breaches of this contract. However, as a practical matter, they are not regarded as such. Another is the so-called sideman exception, which is set forth in subclause 4(d). A contractual provision similar to this may account for the fact that although the various press accounts have described the recent album entitled Mirror Ball as having been recorded by Neil Young and Pearl Jam, the album itself makes no mention of Pearl Jam (although the individual members of Pearl Jam are given credit in their individual names as performers and a courtesy credit is given to their record label, Epic Records).

A more significant exception would be to allow individual members of a group or to allow a solo artist to participate in outside projects on other record labels. This is far less commonly granted, although it is not unprecedented.

Another exception which is sometimes granted is the right to do outside soundtrack album projects. Inclusion in the soundtrack album from a major motion picture can be a big boost to an artist's career. Unless such an exception is provided in the contract, if an offered soundtrack album is to be released on a competing label, the artist will have to negotiate with his or her label for permission at the time, which may involve allowing his or her label to share in the record royalties payable for the artist's services, generally on a fifty-fifty basis.

Please note that the term "records" is a defined term, which has a very broad meaning. See subclause 26(f) of the contract. Any recording, including a home video release of a live concert or a television performance, falls within the definition of a record. Technically, even a motion picture or television program itself, as distinguished from a soundtrack album derived therefrom, falls within the definition of a record. As a practical matter, record companies have not held artists to be in breach of contract for performing music in motion pictures or television programs, but have restricted their concerns to soundtrack albums derived therefrom. However, record companies have been taking the position that video games and multimedia and other computer software programs, which are sold for home use, e.g., on CD-ROM, are records, and the companies are enforcing their rights of exclusivity with respect thereto.

(b) Artist shall not perform any selection recorded hereunder for anyone other than Company for use in the Territory for a period of (1) five (5) years after the initial date of release of the respective record containing such selection or (2) two (2) years after the expiration or other termination of this agreement, whichever is later ("Rerecording Restriction").

(c) Should Artist make any sound recording during the Term for motion pictures, television, electrical transcriptions or any other medium or should Artist after the Term perform for any such purpose any selection recorded hereunder to which the Rerecording Restriction then applies, Artist will do so only pursuant to a written agreement prohibiting the use of such recordings, directly or indirectly, for record purposes in the Territory. Artist shall furnish to Company a copy of the provisions of any such contract relating to the foregoing.

This rerecording restriction is virtually identical to that contained in nearly every major record company contract. It prevents the artist who has left the label from rerecording material for a new label for the specified period of time. This is intended to preserve the value of the original label's recordings by preventing competing releases by the departed artist.

(d) Notwithstanding anything to the contrary contained herein, Artist shall have the right, during the term hereof, to perform as a background sideman, background vocalist or background instrumentalist for the purpose of making phonograph record master recordings which do not embody Artist's performances as a featured artist on the following terms and conditions:

(i) Any such performances by Artist shall be subject to Company's prior written approval in each instance, which approval shall not be unreasonably withheld;

(ii) Artist's such performances shall be only in a background capacity and under no circumstances shall Artist perform as a featured artist or perform any so-called solo or step-out performances;

(iii) Any such performances shall not interrupt, delay or interfere with the rendition of Artist's services hereunder, nor with any professional engagements to which Artist is committed, which such professional engagements are intended to aid in the promotion of the phonograph records embodying the masters hereunder;

(iv) Neither Artist's name, likeness, nor biographical material shall be utilized in any manner in connection with the manufacture, sale or other exploitation of any such phonograph records embodying Artist's performances or in connection with the advertising thereof, except that subject to Company's prior written approval in each instance, Artist's name may be printed on the liner notes of any album embodying Artist's such performances in type no larger or more prominent than that used for any other background sideman, background vocalist or background instrumentalist whose performances are embodied therein; and

(v) In the event Company shall so approve of Artist's name appearing on such liner notes, Artist shall cause Company to be accorded a courtesy credit in the customary manner.

5. All masters recorded by Artist during the Term from the inception of the recording thereof and all reproductions derived therefrom, together with the performances embodied thereon, shall be the property of Company for the Territory free from any claims whatsoever by Artist or any person deriving any rights or interests from Artist. Each such master shall be considered a work made for hire for Company; if any such master is determined not to be a work made for hire it will be deemed transferred to Company by this agreement, together with all rights in it. Without limiting the generality of the foregoing, Company and its designee(s) shall have the exclusive and unlimited right to all the results and proceeds of Artist's recording services rendered during the Term, including, but not limited to, the exclusive, unlimited and perpetual rights throughout the Territory:

(i) To manufacture, advertise, sell, lease, license, distribute or otherwise use or dispose of, in any or all fields of use by any method now or hereafter known, records embodying the masters recorded by Artist during the Term, all upon such terms and conditions as Company may elect, or at its discretion, to refrain therefrom;

(ii) To use, reproduce, print, publish or disseminate in any medium, and to permit others to use, reproduce, print, publish or disseminate in any medium, Artist's name (including any professional name heretofore or hereafter adopted by Artist), photographs, portrait, likeness, and biographical material concerning Artist for advertising and trade purposes in connection with all masters recorded by Artist and all pictures produced during the Term, including, without limitation, in the marketing, sale or other exploitation of records, and as news or other information, in connection with Company's business or otherwise;

(iii) To obtain copyrights and renewals thereof in sound recordings (as distinguished from the musical compositions embodied thereon) recorded by Artist during the Term, in Company's name as owner and employer-for-hire of such sound recordings;

(iv) To release records derived from masters recorded by Artist during the Term under any name, trademark or label which Company or its subsidiaries, affiliates or licensees may from time to time elect;

(v) To perform the records publicly and to permit public performances thereof by means of radio broadcast, television or any other method now or hereafter known.

This is a typical "grant of rights" clause in a recording contract. In nearly every recording contract, the record company owns the copyright in the recordings made under that agreement (i.e., the sound recording copyright, designated by the symbol ℗, as distinguished from the copyright in the underlying song, which is an entirely different matter). Only in the cases of a handful of superstars, e.g., Bruce Springsteen, is the artist able to maintain ownership of the master recordings or to obtain a reversion of ownership at some point in the future. However, this is not something which should be of great concern to the typical artist, since the record company's obligations to pay royalties will continue throughout the term of copyright.

In this contract the company's ownership purportedly extends not only to the masters which are recorded for the company with the company's money, but also to any other masters made during the term. This is intended to give the company ownership of alternate takes and extra songs which did not make the album (outtakes), but, if strictly interpreted, also encompasses other recordings made outside the record company's purview, e.g., live concert recordings or recordings made for television or radio programs. Obviously, if a third party, such as a television or radio broadcaster were to undertake the production of certain live recordings, e.g., the BBC's recordings of the Beatles' early radio performances or MTV's recordings of the "Unplugged" series, there would be a conflict of rights which would need to be worked out before the recordings are released on records.

Whether the recordings made by a recording artist under a typical recording contract such as this are truly works made for hire within the meaning of the United States Copyright Act is not entirely clear. Accordingly, it is important to the company that there be a clause which provides that even if the recordings are not works made for hire, nevertheless, all the rights therein are transferred and assigned to the record company by this agreement. One difference between works made for hire and sound recordings which are not works made for hire is that the term of copyright protection for works made for hire is 75 years from their first publication, whereas the term of copyright for recordings that are not works made for hire is the life of the author plus 50 years. More importantly, the record company's rights as owner of a work made for hire would not be subject to termination at any time, whereas the present copyright act gives a right of termination to authors of works that are not works made for hire, which right is exercisable 35 years after the grant of rights was made.

Subclause 5(i) states some of the company's specific rights, and also points out that the company is not obligated to exercise all of those rights. This illustrates the need to have a commitment from the record company to release and exploit the records.

(a) Company shall only use such photographs, portraits and biographical material concerning Artist in the United States during the term hereof as shall have been submitted or approved by Artist. However, in the event that Artist shall fail to submit sufficient such materials within ten (10) business days after Company's written request therefor, Company shall have the right to utilize such photographs, portraits and biographical material as Company shall select.

(b) Notwithstanding the foregoing:

(i) Company shall not, without Artist's prior consent, release on a midpriced, budget or low-priced record line in the United States any LP embodying solely masters recorded hereunder during the twelve (12) month period following the initial release of such LP in the United States.

(ii) Company shall not, without Artist's prior consent, sell during the term hereof in the United States any record hereunder as a premium or in connection with the sale or promotion of any other product.

(iii) Company shall not release in the United States any EPs containing masters recorded hereunder without Artist's prior consent, which shall not be unreasonably withheld.

This clause sets forth three very commonly granted "marketing restrictions." Normally, these are not contained in a first draft recording contract for a new artist. However, since these are relatively minor concessions, this company has granted them in advance in order to show that it is "artist oriented" and to reduce the need for negotiation. There are a whole host of other marketing restrictions which are commonly requested, the most prevalent of which are restrictions on "coupling" the artist's recordings with recordings by other artists and restrictions on synchronizing the artist's masters in motion pictures, television programs, or commercials without the artist's consent.

6. Artist acknowledges that the sale of records is speculative and agrees that the judgment of Company with regard to any matter affecting the sale, distribution and exploitation of such records shall be binding and conclusive upon Artist. Nothing contained in this agreement shall obligate Company to make, sell, license, or distribute records manufactured from masters subject hereto.

This clause is intended to prevent and defend against lawsuits by an artist alleging that the record company breached the contract by failing to successfully market the record or by not undertaking certain marketing and promotional activities or by failing to spend as much money as on another artist's records. This clause further provides that the company is not obligated to release the albums delivered to it. It is up to the artist's representatives to negotiate specific release commitments and, if they have sufficient bargaining leverage, negotiate particular marketing commitments, such as the release of singles, the production of videos, the spending of specified amounts on independent promotion or independent retail marketing, the hiring of publicists, and providing tour support.

7. Company shall pay to Artist the following sums which shall be advances against and recoupable by Company out of all royalties becoming payable to Artist pursuant to this or any other agreement:

(a) In connection with each Album recorded pursuant to Artist's minimum recording commitment, Company will pay Artist an Advance in the amount by which the applicable sum indicated below ("Recording Fund") exceeds the Recording Costs (including anticipated costs not yet paid or billed) for the Album:

In nearly all record deals with major record companies today, the company's financial commitment to the artist is made by way of an all-inclusive recording fund. This replaces the older approach of allocating a recording budget for each album and agreeing to pay a separate, specified cash advance to the artist for each album. In the recording fund, the budget for recording costs and the artist's advance are combined, which achieves the company's objective of having a fixed production cost for the album. It also gives the artist an incentive to minimize the recording costs, since the unspent portion of the recording fund is paid to the artist as a cash advance. However, the downside for the artist is that if the entire recording fund is spent on recording costs, there will be no cash advance to the artist to cover the artist's expenses during the period of time from the delivery of the album until royalties have begun to be earned, which, even with a successful album, will take anywhere from six months to 15 months from delivery of the album. Even worse, if the recording costs exceed the recording fund, the artist may be required to repay the excess to the company or, in any event, the company will have the right to deduct the excess from other monies, which may include mechanical royalties and future advances as well as artist royalties, which become payable to the artist.

Fundamentally, the entire amount of the recording fund is recoupable from royalties payable to the artist. This is one of the most basic principles of recording contracts and it is rarely varied in any significant way. Accordingly, before the artist receives any royalties from the sale of his or her album, the company repays to itself the entire cost of recording the album, as well as any cash advances it paid to the artist. This recoupment is not achieved by deducting the recording costs off the top, out of the company's gross receipts, as would be the case if the company and the artist split net profits, but is instead accomplished by deducting those recording costs and advances solely from the artist's royalties. This makes it possible for the company to have achieved a profit before the artist has received any royalties beyond the initial advance, if any, actually paid to the artist as the unspent balance of the recording fund. It follows, then, that the higher the artist's royalty rate, the more quickly the artist will recoup the recording costs of his or her album.

(i) The amount of the Recording Fund for the first Album Delivered during the Initial Period ("First Album") will be _____ Dollars ($_____). The amount of the Recording Fund for each Album of Artist's minimum recording commitment (other than the First Album) delivered hereunder will be two-thirds (2/3) of whichever of the following amounts is less (subject to clause 7(a)(ii) below):

(A) The net amount of the royalties credited to Artist's account on Net Sales Through Normal Retail Channels in the United States of the Album made under this agreement released most recently before the delivery of the Album concerned (the "Prior Album"), as determined by Company from its most recent monthly trial balance accounting statement as of the date nine (9) months after the initial United States release of the Prior Album; or

(B) The average of the amounts of such royalties on the two (2) Prior Albums. (ii) No such Recording Fund will be more than the applicable maximum or less than the applicable minimum prescribed below:

	MINIMUM	MAXIMUM
Album Delivered during the first Option Period:	$_____	$_____
Album Delivered during the second Option Period:	$_____	$_____
Album Delivered during the third Option Period:	$_____	$_____

[ETC., AS APPLICABLE TO THE DEAL]

The foregoing is the most common structure for allocating recording funds. The fund for the first album is a fixed amount, and the fund for all subsequent albums is determined by a formula based on the gross amount of royalties earned by the artist from the sales of the prior album or albums. In this "formula advance" or "mini-max" structure, there is always a minimum amount of the fund, which generally escalates modestly from album to album, and a maximum amount, which is approximately twice the minimum amount of the fund. The fund is computed with reference to sales of albums only (not singles) through normal retail channels (i.e., sales through record stores and other retail outlets, as distinguished from record club and other ancillary sales) in the United States, within a specified period of time, generally nine to 12 months after the release of the prior album.

(b) Each Advance will be reduced by the amount of any reasonably anticipated costs of mastering, remastering, remixing and/or "sweetening"; any such anticipated costs which are deducted but not incurred will be remitted promptly to Artist.

(c) The balance of the Advance with respect to the First Album and all other Advances will be made within thirty (30) days after the Delivery to and acceptance by Company of the Album concerned.

Usually, the artist will need or want some portion of the recording fund to be paid upon exercise of the option or commencement of recording sessions for the album in order to cover living expenses during the period of production of the album. If the artist is going to pay the recording costs directly, the normal, up-front advance will be 50% of the entire recording fund, whereas if the record company is going to pay the recording costs directly, the up-front advance will be limited to 10% or 20% of the fund, so that there is less risk that the recording fund will not be sufficient to cover all of the recording costs.

(d) All monies (other than record royalties and mechanical royalties) paid by Company to Artist during the term of this agreement will constitute Advances. Each payment (except such royalties) made by Company during the term to anyone else on behalf of Artist will also constitute an Advance if it is made with the knowledge of Artist, if it is required by law, or if it is made by Company to satisfy an obligation incurred by Artist or in connection with the subject matter of this agreement.

This clause is designed to protect the company when it makes additional payments to the artist which are not required by the contract, so that it will have the right to recoup those amounts of money as advances. This same result can be achieved simply by placing a legend on a check paid to the artist stating that it is a recoupable advance, but the company may forget to do so or the artist may challenge that after the fact. This clause therefore puts the burden on the artist when negotiating for additional payments to be made by the record company to cause the record company to agree that such payments are nonrecoupable, if indeed that is the parties' understanding.

8. Prior to any recording session for any master(s) hereunder, Artist shall submit to Company a written recording budget. Such recording budget shall include the following information: (1) the producer mutually approved by Company and Artist with whom Artist has concluded arrangements and the financial terms of the agreement between Artist and such producer; (2) selection of approved material, including the number of compositions to be recorded (to be mutually approved by Artist and Company; (3) specification of accompaniment, arrangement and copying services, (4) recording fees or arranging fees which will exceed union scale and the proposed recipient thereof, (5) the dates of recording and mixing and studios where recording and mixing are to take place, including the cost of each recording session and (6) an estimate of all costs to be incurred in each and every recording session and all studio time. Upon receipt of Company's written approval of such recording budget, Artist shall commence such session(s).

The insistence upon the submission and approval of written recording budgets prior to the commencement of each recording session is designed to give the company an opportunity to control the recording costs and prevent cost overruns. As a practical matter, however, written recording budgets are not always submitted and recording budgets are often exceeded. It is important for the artist to remember that it is in the artist's interest to keep recording costs down, since they are recoupable dollar-for-dollar from the royalties earned by the artist under the contract. Accordingly, if the artist is successful, the artist ultimately pays 100% of the recording costs. For this reason, artists have the incentive to be well-rehearsed before they go into the studio and to have a definite plan for what they wish to accomplish at each session.

(a) Artist shall be solely responsible for and shall pay all recording costs incurred in the production of masters subject to this agreement and shall provide Company with copies of paid invoices evidencing the payment thereof. In the event Company elects to pay any such recording costs, all such costs paid by Company shall be deducted from any and all monies becoming payable to Artist under this or any other agreement.

It is the structure of this agreement that the record company is providing an all-inclusive recording fund to the artist, out of which the artist is to pay all of the recording costs. In other contracts, the record company will allocate a recording fund, but will pay the studio costs and other recording costs directly and will then pay the artist the difference. It is simply a difference as to who is controlling the money. In either event the entire amount of the recording fund is recoupable from the artist's royalties, as are any additional amounts paid by the record company in excess of the recording fund.

(b) It is of the essence of this agreement that Artist obtain prior to each applicable recording session and deliver to Company within forty-eight (48) hours following each such recording session, a duly completed and executed Form I-9 (or such similar or other form[s] as may be prescribed by the United States

Immigration and Naturalization Service or other government agency regarding citizenship, permanent residency or so-called documented worker status) in respect of each individual employed to render services in the recording of masters hereunder. Artist shall simultaneously obtain and deliver to Company true and complete copies of all evidentiary documents relating to the contents or subject matter of said form(s). In the event Artist fails to comply with any of the foregoing requirements, Company may deduct any resulting penalty payments from any and all monies due under this or any other agreement.

The laws of the United States require that each musician or other performer on phonograph records be either a United States citizen or otherwise permitted to work in the United States. The violation of these laws can result in criminal penalties and fines. The record company passes these obligations on to the recording artist who is in a position to control who is hired and to require documentation of their eligibility to be employed. It is therefore a serious matter for the artist to obtain the completed Form I-9 in respect of each individual rendering services on the project, whether as a musician, vocalist, producer, engineer, or otherwise.

(c) Artist shall be solely responsible for and shall pay all monies becoming payable to all parties rendering services or otherwise in respect of sales of recordings derived from masters subject to this agreement.

This is a somewhat broadly drafted clause. Essentially, the recording funds and royalties agreed to be paid by the record company are intended to constitute its total obligation, and the artist is expected to pay all third parties such as producers and artists out of the monies paid by the record company to the artist.

(d) All recording sessions hereunder shall be held under artist's license and, if required, Artist shall notify the appropriate local of the American Federation of Musicians in advance of each recording session. Artist warrants and represents that Artist is a party to all applicable agreements with all applicable unions and guilds and that said license is and shall remain in full force and effect. At Company's request, Artist shall furnish Company with appropriate documentation confirming the foregoing.

All of the major record companies are signatories to the AFM Phonograph Record Labor Agreement and their related trust fund agreements. These collective bargaining agreements require the signatory record companies to pay musicians at the specified minimum scale rates and to make specified pension, health and welfare payments. In this agreement, since the artist is being given control of the recording fund, the artist is delegated the obligation to comply with the union's requirements. However, although artists may be members of the AFM, they are not likely to become signatories to the AFM Phonograph Record Labor Agreement and therefore licensed employers for purposes of conducting recording sessions. Therefore, where this type of clause is used, my sense is that it is largely ignored by artists. An alternative is for the sessions to be conducted under the record company's license, in which event the record company will generally insist on controlling the payment of the recording costs and will want to limit the amount of the fund which is paid out to the artist prior to delivery of the completed record.

9. Each master delivered hereunder shall be produced by a producer mutually approved by Artist and Company. Artist shall be solely responsible for and shall pay all monies becoming payable to such producer. In the event Company elects to pay any such producer directly, all such sums so paid by Company shall be deducted from any and all monies otherwise payable to Artist under this or any other agreement.

As stated above, the most important creative approval to the company is generally the right to approve the producer of the individual masters. Financially, this contract is structured as an all-in deal, i.e., the payments agreed to be made by the record company are inclusive of all payments due to the record producer and any other third parties that may be entitled to be paid money in connection with the recording of the masters or the sale of records. Normally, producers are paid a fee for their services in producing the masters, which is almost always treated as a fully recoupable advance against their royalties. Their fee is normally paid half upon commencement of their services and half upon completion of the album. This is paid out of the recording fund and is one element of the recording costs of the album. Most commonly, producers are paid a royalty rate of approximately 3% of the royalty base price, assuming it is computed on a retail basis, as is the case in this contract. Generally, producers' royalties are paid "retroactively" to the first record sold after recoupment of the recording costs of the album at the "net artist's rate." This means that if the record is not successful enough to recoup its recording costs, the producer will not be paid any royalties in addition to the fee paid to him, but if it is, the producer will be paid royalties on all records sold. The net artist's rate means the all-in rate payable to the artist, which would be the rate set forth in this agreement, less the producer's rate, e.g., 13% less 3% equals 10%. If the record is successful enough that the recording costs have been recouped at the net artist's rate, then the producer will be credited with royalties on all records sold, not merely those sold after recoupment. Of course, those royalties will be reduced by the producer's fee since it is really an advance of royalties. Ultimately, then, if the record is successful, the producer does not bear any of the recording costs, but rather all such recording costs are borne by payment out of the artist's net royalties.

10. Conditioned upon Artist's full and faithful performance of each and all of the terms hereof, Company shall pay Artist the following royalties in respect of records subject to this agreement:

(a) In respect of retail sales of records in the United States, Artist's royalty shall be at the rates specified in the U.S. Schedule below:

U.S. SCHEDULE

(i)	Record	Royalty Rate
	Required LP 1	13%
	Required LP 2	13%
	Required LP 3	14%
	Required LP 4	14%
	Required LP 5	15%
	Required LP 6	15%
(ii)	All EPs/Singles	10%

The above stated royalty rates are typical of a new artist recording agreement, although they could be somewhat lower or higher. Sometimes the base royalty rate stays the same for all albums under the deal and only escalates based on sales of the particular album. Sales escalations are normally given, on a prospective basis, at "gold" (for sales of more than 500,000 copies) and "platinum" (for sales of over 1,000,000 copies). The base or basic royalty rate in all record negotiations is the rate for sales of albums through normal retail channels in the United States at a top line price. Likewise, escalations are generally limited to those same sales. That basic rate, without regard to escalations based on sales, is the rate upon which virtually all other royalties set forth in the contract are based. In nearly all contracts the rate for sales of singles is substantially less than the rate on albums, since the profit which may be derived by the company from singles is much lower, and companies tend to regard singles primarily as promotional tools.

(b) In respect of retail sales of records in Canada, Artist's royalty shall be eighty-five percent (85%) of the applicable royalty rate payable in respect of United States retail sales.

    (i) In respect of retail sales of records in the European Union, Japan and Australia ("Major Territories"), Artist's royalty shall be two-thirds (2/3) of the applicable royalty rate payable in respect of United States retail sales.

    (ii) In respect of retail sales of records through normal distribution channels in countries other than the United States, Canada and the Major Territories ("Minor Territories"), Artist's royalty shall be fifty percent (50%) of the applicable royalty rate payable in respect of United States retail sales.

The royalty rates in subclauses 10(b) through 10(b)(ii) are fairly typical reductions which reflect the fact that the company receives less income and arguably has a lesser profit margin on sales in foreign territories than on U.S. sales. The countries to which the higher rates are applicable are those in which U.S. originated product sells well.

    (iii) Notwithstanding anything to the contrary contained herein, with respect to records sold in Brazil, Greece, Portugal, India, Kenya, Zambia, Zimbabwe, Nigeria and any other territory in which governmental or other authorities place limits on the royalty rates permissible for remittances to the United States in respect of records sold in such territory(ies), the royalty rate payable to Artist hereunder in respect of sales of records in such territory(ies) shall equal the lesser of (1) the royalty rate otherwise payable hereunder, or (2) the effective royalty rate permitted by such governmental or other authority for remittances to the United States less a royalty equivalent to three percent (3%) of the retail list price and such monies as Company or its licensees shall be required to pay to all applicable union funds in respect of said sales.

    (A) Royalties in respect of sales of records outside the United States shall be computed in the same national currency as Company is accounted to by its licensees and shall be paid to Artist at the same rate of exchange as Company is paid. It is understood that such royalties will not be due and payable until payment thereof is received by Company in the United States of America. In the event Company is unable to receive payment in United States dollars in the United States due to governmental regulations, royalties therefor shall not be credited to Artist's account during the continuance of such inability except that (1) if any accounting rendered to Artist hereunder during the continuance of such inability shows Artist's account to be in a credit position, Company will, after Artist's request and at Artist's expense, if Company is able to do so, deposit such royalties to Artist's credit in the applicable foreign currency in a foreign depository designated by Artist, or (2) if the royalties not credited to Artist's account exceed the amount, if any, by which Artist's account is in a debit position, then Company will, after Artist's request and at Artist's expense, and if Company is able to do so, deposit such excess royalties to Artist's credit in the applicable foreign currency in a foreign depository designated by Artist. Deposit as aforesaid shall fulfill Company's obligations under this agreement as to record sales to which such royalty payments are applicable.

Subclauses 10(b)(iii) and 10(b)(iii)(A) are quite technical and do not generally have much economic impact and, therefore, are not highly negotiated.

(c) With respect to records sold (1) through any direct mail or mail order distribution method or any direct to consumer method, including, without limitation, record club distribution, whether or not such record club is affiliated with Company; (2) by distribution through retail outlets in conjunction with special advertisements on radio or television; (3) outside of the United States in conjunction with a television advertising campaign, during the calendar semi-annual period in which that campaign begins and the next two (2) such periods; or (4) by any combination of the methods set forth above, the royalty payable in connection therewith shall be one-half (1/2) of Company's net earned royalty receipts in respect of reported sales through such channels. No royalties shall be payable with respect to records given away as "bonus" or "free" records as a result of joining a record club or plan or of purchasing a required number of records or with respect to records received by members of any such club operation either in an introductory offer in connection with joining such club or upon recommending that another join such club operation.

The payment of a one-half royalty rate on record club sales is one of the fixtures of the business, which even superstars must accept. The provision also applies to any other direct-to-consumer method, which could include "records" sold by direct digital transmissions. In this contract there is a specific provision addressing such sales (subclause 10(h) below), but in other contracts this more general clause would apply, with its much lower royalty rate.

(d) With respect to mid-priced records, the royalty rate shall be two-thirds (2/3) of the applicable royalty rate payable in respect of full-priced records in the same configuration or format.
(e) With respect to budget records and multiple sets, the royalty rate shall be one-half (1/2) of the applicable royalty rate payable in respect of full-priced records in the same configuration or format.

It is typical for the recording contract to provide a royalty rate reduction for sales of mid-priced records and a further royalty rate reduction for sales of budget or low-priced records, although the amount of the specific reduction is negotiable if the artist has bargaining leverage. This gives the company in effect a double reduction, e.g., if the price of a mid-priced record is 75% of the price of a top-line record and if the company pays the artist two-thirds of his basic royalty rate, the royalty which the artist would receive in pennies (sometimes referred to as the "penny rate") would be one-half of the number of pennies the artist would have received on the sale of that record at the top-line price.

(f) Notwithstanding anything to the contrary contained in this agreement, in the event that Company (or its licensee[s]) shall in any country(ies) of the Territory adopt a policy applicable to the majority of Albums in Company's (or its licensee[s]') then current catalogue pursuant to which the retail list price of an Album is reduced subsequent to its initial release, then the royalty rates otherwise payable to Artist under this agreement shall be reduced in the proportion that such reduced retail list price of the applicable Album bears to the retail list price of such Album as initially released in the applicable country.

(g) Notwithstanding anything contained herein:

(i) With respect to records in compact disc form, the royalty rate payable shall be one hundred percent (100%) of the otherwise applicable royalty rate, if such compact discs are sold at Company's then current top suggested retail list price ("SRLP") for standard compact discs (the "Top SRLP"). Currently, Company's Top SRLP for standard compact discs sold in the United States is $15.98. For compact discs that are sold at an SRLP that is less than the Top SRLP, the royalty rate will be the otherwise applicable royalty rate multiplied by a fraction, the numerator of which is the actual SRLP of said compact discs and the denominator of which is the Top SRLP.

The various major record companies have different policies with respect to the payment of royalties on compact discs. When CDs were first introduced, the manufacturing costs were very high and, of course, CD sales accounted for only a very small percentage of all record sales. Accordingly, the record companies developed policies whereby for an introductory period of three years or so, artists were paid the same number of pennies for a sale of a CD as they were paid for a sale of a record in vinyl disc form, even though the CDs had a much higher suggested retail list price. This policy was made nonnegotiable. After the introductory period elapsed and manufacturing costs had decreased and market share had grown somewhat, each record company evolved its own policies to limit royalties on CDs. Every major record company in the United States has adopted a 25% "packaging deduction" for sales of compact discs. Some have adopted a reduced royalty rate of 80% or 85% of the artist's normal rate. Others base the royalty rate on a so-called constructed retail price that is determined by utilizing the wholesale price of the record multiplied by an "uplift," generally 130%. This contract is one of the few in which the royalty on CDs will be calculated at the artist's full royalty rate based upon the full suggested retail list price, so long as the CD is sold at $15.98 or more. If the CD is by a new artist, the company could choose to release it at a lower price, e.g., $13.98, in which event the artist would be paid 87.5% of the artist's normal royalty rate on the $13.98 price.

(ii) With respect to records in digital compact cassette form and records in minidisc form, the royalty rate payable shall be eighty percent (80%) of the otherwise applicable royalty rate.

(iii) With respect to records in digital audiotape form, the royalty rate payable shall be seventy-five percent (75%) of the otherwise applicable royalty rate.

(iv) With respect to records in any form, configuration, format or technology not herein described, which is now known but not widely distributed or which hereafter becomes known ("New Technology Configurations"), the royalty rate payable shall be seventy-five percent (75%) of the otherwise applicable royalty rate.

Subclauses 10(g)(ii) through 10(g)(iv) illustrate the range of reduced rates generally offered for sales of records in new configurations, which have little or no market share.

(h) In the event that Company shall sell or license third parties to sell "records" via telephone, satellite, cable or other direct transmission to the consumer over wire or through the air ("Satellite Sales"), Artist shall be paid royalties with respect thereto at the otherwise applicable royalty rate, but with respect to any such sales in the United States royalties shall only be paid with respect to eighty-five percent (85%) of such sales. For purposes of calculating royalties payable in connection with such sales, the retail list price of such "records" shall be deemed to be the then-current retail list price of analog tape copies of such records.

For these direct transmission sales a royalty is paid on 85% of sales in the United States. This is the same as for records sold through normal retail channels, after deducting the "free goods" allowance (which will be discussed later). The suggested retail list price is deemed to be that of a corresponding analog cassette tape in order to minimize royalties, since that is the least expensive format.

(i) The royalty rate payable for records sold to the United States Government, its subdivisions, departments and agencies, and to educational institutions and libraries shall be one-half (1/2) of the otherwise applicable basic U.S. rate and shall be based upon the retail list price (Post Exchange list price where applicable) of such records.

(j) The royalty rate payable for records sold as "premiums" shall be one-half (1/2) of the otherwise applicable royalty rate, and the retail list price for such records shall be deemed to be Company's actual sales price. It is understood that Company shall not use Artist's name or likeness in connection with any such "premium" record as an endorsement of any product or service.

(k) Company shall have the right to license the masters to third parties for record use and/or all other types of use on a flat-fee or royalty basis. With respect to masters licensed on a flat-fee basis, Company shall credit Artist's royalty account with fifty percent (50%) of the net amount received by Company under each such license. With respect to masters licensed on a royalty basis, Company shall credit Artist's royalty account with the lesser of (1) fifty percent (50%) of Company's net earned royalty receipts under each such license or (2) one-half (1/2) of the otherwise applicable royalty rate.

This clause applies to licenses of the masters for use in motion picture soundtracks and compilation albums released by third parties, such as soundtrack albums or tribute albums. The fifty-fifty split is universally accepted.

(l) As to records not consisting entirely of masters recorded and delivered hereunder, the royalty rate otherwise payable to Artist hereunder with respect to sales of any such record shall be prorated by multiplying such royalty rate by a fraction, the numerator of which is the number of masters recorded and delivered hereunder embodied on such record and the denominator of which is the total number of royalty-bearing masters embodied thereon.

This is a typical proration clause, which would apply, for example, if the company released a compilation or sampler of its own artists' recordings on its own label.

(m) As to masters embodying performances of Artist together with the performances of another artist or artists, the royalty rate otherwise payable hereunder with respect to sales of any record derived from any such master and the recording costs and/or advances otherwise payable by Company hereunder with respect to any such master shall be prorated by multiplying such royalty rate or recording costs and/or advances by a fraction, the numerator of which is one and the denominator of which is the total number of artists whose performances are embodied on such master.

This is another type of proration clause in which the royalty on the particular master is itself to be divided among the royalty participants, e.g., where the artist records a duet with another artist on the same label.

(n) Company shall have the right to include or to license others to include any one or more of the masters in promotional records on which such masters and other recordings are included, which promotional records are designed for sale at a substantially lower price than the regular price of Company's Albums. No royalties shall be payable on sales of such promotional records.

(o) No royalties shall be payable in respect of: (1) records given away or furnished on a "no-charge" basis to "one-stops," rack jobbers, distributors or dealers, whether or not affiliated with Company; (2) records given away or sold at below stated wholesale prices for promotional purposes to disc jockeys, record reviewers, radio and television stations and networks, motion picture companies, music publishers, Company's employees, Artist or other customary recipients of promotional records or for use on transportation facilities; (3) records sold as scrap, salvage, overstock or "cut-outs"; (4) records sold below cost; and (5) "sampler" records intended for free distribution to automobile purchasers and containing not more than two (2) masters delivered hereunder.

This clause addresses a variety of distributions of nonroyalty bearing records. These fall into three principal categories: (1) Truly promotional records, which are given away to customary recipients, e.g., radio stations, record reviewers, etc.; (2) records sold at drastically reduced prices, i.e., cut-outs, which are records marked with a hole punched or cut in the packaging so that they cannot be returned to the record company for credit at full price; and (3) free goods, records which are given away as sales incentives or are sold at a discount to stimulate sales.

(i) For convenience, those records sold at a discount in lieu of or in addition to records furnished on a so-called no-charge basis and records furnished on such a so-called no charge basis are collectively sometimes referred to herein as "Free Goods." References in this agreement to "records for which no royalties are payable hereunder," or words of similar connotation, shall include, without limitation, all Free Goods. Free Goods embodying albums or EPs hereunder are sometimes referred to herein as "Album Free Goods," and Free Goods embodying Single Records hereunder are sometimes referred to herein as "Single Free Goods." It is acknowledged and agreed that, pursuant to Company's current policy, fifteen percent (15%) of the aggregate units of all albums and EPs distributed by Company hereunder shall be Album Free Goods ("Standard Album Free Goods"), and twenty-three percent (23%) of the aggregate units of all such Single Records distributed by Company hereunder shall be Single Free Goods ("Standard Single Free Goods"). Standard Album Free Goods and Standard Single Free Goods are sometimes herein collectively referred to as "Standard Free Goods."

This clause defines the percentages of records sold which will be deemed to be nonroyalty bearing free goods. This clause corresponds to the policy of the label's distributor, which is a standard policy applied to all of that distributor's sales in the United States. All of the major labels have this same 15% standard free goods allowance, although some labels accomplish that result differently, namely by calculating the royalty rate on 85% of records sold. This clause is generally not applicable outside the United States, although this contract does not specifically limit its applicability to the United States.

In addition to the so-called standard or policy free goods, there are also special free goods, special sales incentive or discount programs which are offered from time to time for limited periods, generally on a seasonal basis, e.g., in the fall as an incentive to retailers to stock up on product in anticipation of the Christmas season. Sometimes the amount of special free goods which may be given by the company is limited in the contract, e.g., to an additional 10% of records shipped. If such a limit were violated, the company would be obligated to pay royalties on the records distributed as free goods in excess of the specified limits.

(p) As to records sold at a discount to "one-stops," rack jobbers, distributors or dealers, whether or not affiliated with Company, in lieu of the records given away or furnished on a "no-charge" basis as provided in subparagraph 10(o) above, the applicable royalty rate otherwise payable hereunder with respect to such records shall be reduced in the proportion that said discount wholesale price bears to the usual stated wholesale price.

The payment of a proportionately reduced royalty on records sold at a discount is the functional equivalent of giving away as free goods the percentage of the total records shipped that equals the percentage of the discount granted. For example, if 100 records are shipped by the company to its customer, paying royalties on 85 of the records and treating the remaining 15 records as free goods is the same as paying the artist 85% of the regular royalty rate on all 100 records shipped to the customer at a 15% discount.

(q) The royalty rates provided for in this paragraph 10 shall be applied against the retail list price (less Company's container deductions, excise taxes, duties and other applicable taxes) for records sold which are paid for and not returned. The term "retail list price" as used in this agreement shall mean (1) for records sold in the United States, the manufacturer's suggested retail price in the United States and (2) for records sold outside the United States, the manufacturer's suggested retail price in the country of manufacture or sale, as Company is paid. To the extent that in computing royalties payable to Company the retail list price utilized by Company's licensee in the country concerned is based upon the dealer price with an "uplift" to yield a suggested retail list price, Company shall use the same dealer price plus "uplift" to compute royalties payable for that territory pursuant to this paragraph 10. To the extent that Company's licensee in the country concerned computes royalties payable to Company on a dealer price, then Company shall apply the then generally accepted "uplift" in the country concerned, to yield a deemed suggested retail list price to compute royalties payable for that territory pursuant to this paragraph 10. Notwithstanding the foregoing, the retail list price for a "Maxi-single" shall be deemed to be the retail list price for a Single. In computing sales, Company shall have the right to deduct all returns made at any time and for any reason. Records distributed in the United States by any of Company's affiliated branch wholesalers shall be deemed sold for the purposes of this agreement only if sold by any such affiliated branch wholesaler to one of its independent third-party customers.

This clause, together with clause 10(r) below, establishes the base upon which the royalty rate is applied. In this contract the royalties are based on the retail list price. In the United States, this is generally the price suggested by the manufacturer. For each such retail list price there is a corresponding wholesale price at which the company sells the records to its customers; a record having a higher suggested retail list price will always have a higher wholesale price. Sony computes its U.S. royalties on a wholesale price basis. Because of this, the percentage royalty rates payable in Sony's contracts are much higher than the royalty rates payable under a retail contract, such as this. The rule of thumb is that the royalty rate on a wholesale price basis is twice as high as the percentage royalty rate on a retail price basis, for sales in the United States, although this is not exactly accurate, since wholesale prices are generally more than 50% of the suggested retail list price. It certainly would not be accurate outside the United States, where in many territories the relationship between wholesale and retail (uplift), is approximated to be 130%.

(r) Company's container deductions shall be a sum equal to (1) twelve and one-half percent (12.5%) of the retail list price for Singles in vinyl disc form, (2) twenty percent (20%) of the retail list price for (A) records in vinyl disc form (other than Singles) and (B) records in analog prerecorded tape form, and (3) twenty-five percent (25%) of the retail list price for (A) records in digital compact cassette form; (B) records in mini-disc form; (C) records in compact-disc form; (D) records in digital audiotape form; (E) records in analog prerecorded tape form of more than sixty minutes of playing time; (F) records in vinyl disc form in "double-fold" jackets or covers or in jackets which contain an insert or any other special elements; (G) Satellite Sales; (H) New Technology Configurations; and (I) any other prerecorded tape and cartridge boxes or containers and any other form of package, container or box other than as described herein.

So-called container or packaging deductions are another fixture of computing royalties in the record business. The amounts of these deductions have much more to do with the history and customs of the industry than they do with actual cost structures. For example, the 20% packaging deduction for tape configurations became an unwavering standard and remains so even after the costs of manufacturing cassettes, originally much higher than manufacturing vinyl discs, dropped to approximately the same level. Likewise, the 25% deduction for compact discs has become the universal standard, despite the fact that manufacturing costs have dropped drastically and are significantly less than 10% of the suggested retail list price of a typical newly released compact disc. Accordingly, these packaging deductions are generally not negotiable. Instead, the basic royalty rate itself is what is negotiated.

(s) The monies payable to Artist hereunder shall be inclusive of all monies, if any, required to be paid to the AFM Music Performance Trust Fund, Phonograph Record Manufacturers Special Payments Fund, AFTRA Pension and Welfare Fund and all other union funds with respect to the manufacture, distribution and sale of records hereunder. In the event that any monies shall become due to any such union funds, Company shall deduct such monies from any and all monies payable to Artist under this or any other agreement and shall pay same directly to such union funds.

This is a decidedly untypical clause. Generally, the company is responsible for the AFM trust fund payments, which amount to slightly more than 1% of the retail base price. This contract puts the burden on the artist because the contract specifies that the artist will be the signatory to the union agreements. However, in such event the artist's representatives must be sure that the artist's net royalty, after any trust fund payments, is what the artist is truly worth in the marketplace.

11. Statements as to royalties payable hereunder shall be sent by Company to Artist within sixty (60) days after the expiration of each calendar quarter for the preceding quarterly period ending February 28, May 31, August 31 or November 30. Notwithstanding the foregoing, Company may, if Company elects, change the aforesaid time and dates, provided, however, in the event of such change, statements shall be rendered to Artist no less frequently than semi-annually. Concurrently with the rendition of each statement, Company shall pay Artist all royalties shown to be due by such statement, after deducting all recording costs paid by Company, all payments made on behalf of Artist, all other permitted charges and all advances made to Artist prior to the rendition of the statement. No statements need be rendered by Company for any such quarterly period after the expiration of the Term hereof for which there are no sales of records derived from masters hereunder. All payments shall be made to the order of Artist and shall be sent to Artist at Artist's address first above written.

Company shall be entitled to maintain a single account with respect to all recordings subject to this or any other agreement. Company shall have the right to retain as a reserve against charges, credits or returns, such portion of payable royalties as shall be reasonable in Company's business judgment; provided, however, that said reserves shall in no event exceed thirty percent (30%). Company further agrees that a base reserve established in a particular accounting period shall be liquidated by the end of the fourth semiannual accounting period after such reserve has been established. If Company makes an overpayment of royalties in respect of the sale of records derived from masters hereunder, Artist will reimburse Company for same, failing which Company may recoup any such overpayment from any monies becoming payable to Artist pursuant to this or any other agreement. Royalty payments on records subsequently returned are considered overpayments. Artist shall be deemed to have consented to all accountings rendered by Company hereunder; said accountings shall be binding upon Artist, shall constitute an account stated, and shall not be subject to any objection by Artist for any reason unless specific objection, in writing, stating the basis thereof, is given to Company within two (2) years after the date rendered, and after such written objection, unless suit is instituted within one (1) year after the date upon which Company notifies Artist that it denies the validity of the objection.

In this contract the company accounts for royalties on a quarterly basis, which is more favorable to the artist than the more typical policy of accounting on a semiannual basis. However, the frequency of accountings is not negotiable as a rule, since the preparation of royalty statements requires elaborate systems and is very time consuming and to vary the standard procedures would be difficult and would increase the risk that errors would be made.

This contract allows the company to deduct charges and advances made after the close of the accounting period for which the statement is rendered, but prior to the rendition of the statement. This is often a hotly negotiated point, since it can have the effect of eliminating advances, i.e., the artist could wind up paying his next album's advance out of his last album's royalties.

This contract is typical in that all recordings made under this agreement are treated as part of a single, consolidated account. For example, if the artist's first album is quite successful, but the artist's second album is costly and unsuccessful, the recording costs and advances attributable to the second album will offset the royalties earned from sales of the first album, on a dollar-for-dollar basis, so that there may be no net payment due to the artist. This concept of consolidating the recoupable advances and charges and the earned royalties associated with one project with the recoupable advances and charges and the earned royalties associated with another project is known as "cross-collateralization." Cross-collateralization limited to the recordings made under a single agreement is almost universally accepted. However, this agreement goes beyond that to cross-collateralize any other agreement to which the artist may be a party with the company, e.g., a prior or subsequent recording agreement. This is always a point to be negotiated. It becomes particularly contentious when the company requires cross-collateralization with mechanical royalty payments or with a publishing agreement with the company's affiliate.

It is typical for the recording contract to allow the company to maintain reserves against anticipated returns of records. Very often there is no limit on the amount of reserves which a company can maintain, except that they will be "reasonable." Such a provision makes it very difficult for the artist to do anything if the company is maintaining levels of reserves which the artist believes to be unreasonable in view of the company's actual returns experience with respect to the artist's records. In this contract a specific maximum limitation is established. Where such limitations are stated, they are generally in the range of 20% to 30%. In the United States records are generally sold with a 100% privilege of return and without any limit on the time period during which the records can be returned by the stores to the company. Accordingly, it is quite important for the company to be able to maintain a royalty reserve. Generally the company will agree to liquidate the reserve within three or four semiannual periods, i.e., 18 to 24 months, after it has been established. This means that the reserve will either be used up by applying returns against it or it will be paid out in the form of royalties to the artist if it is not used up. However, in this contract the company further protects itself by providing that if it did not hold sufficient reserves, i.e., returns exceed reserves, the artist must reimburse the company.

12. Artist shall have the right at Artist's sole cost and expense to appoint a Certified Public Accountant who is not then currently engaged in an outstanding audit of Company to examine Company's books and records as same pertain to sales of records subject hereto as to which royalties are payable hereunder, provided that any such examination shall be for a reasonable duration and shall take place at Company's offices during normal business hours on reasonable prior written notice and shall not occur more than once in any calendar year. Artist may examine Company's books and records with respect to a particular statement only once. Artist shall not be entitled to examine any manufacturing records or any other records that do not specifically report sales of records on which royalties are payable to Artist or gratis distributions of records.

Recording contracts typically place specified time limits upon the artist's right to audit the company's books and records. These time periods are generally shorter than the time periods which are otherwise allowable under state law. The company justifies such limitations because of the tremendous amount of record keeping involved and the cost associated therewith. Generally the company tries to limit the audit and objection period to one year, whereas the artist's representatives will seek to make it as long as possible, but two years is a fairly typical compromise.

13. All notices to Artist may be served upon Artist personally, by prepaid telegram, or by depositing the same, postage prepaid, in any mail box, chute, or other receptacle authorized by the United States Postal Service for mail, addressed to Artist at Artist's address first above written.

    (a) All notices to Company shall be in writing and shall be sent postage prepaid by registered or certified mail, return receipt requested, addressed to Company's address first above written.

14. All musical compositions or material recorded pursuant to this agreement which are written or composed, in whole or in part by Artist or any individual member of Artist or any producer of the masters subject hereto, or which are owned or controlled, directly or indirectly, in whole or in part, by Artist or any individual member of Artist or any producer of the masters subject hereto (herein called "Controlled Compositions") shall be and are hereby licensed to Company:

This section of the contract addresses in a typical way the royalties payable to the own-ers (known as music publishers) of the musical compositions recorded by the artist, known as mechanical royalties. Even if the artist does not write his or her own mater-ial, this section is nonetheless important, because its main purpose is to limit the amount of mechanical royalties the company will be required to pay for any record it releases and to hold the artist responsible for exceeding the specified limits.

These clauses typically distinguish between controlled compositions and noncon-trolled compositions, although the definitions may differ somewhat from contract to contract. Generally the company seeks to obtain a lower mechanical royalty rate and more favorable payment terms on controlled compositions than on noncontrolled compo-sitions. The definition of a controlled composition is important. Generally, the entire composition is treated as a controlled composition even if the artist is merely a cowriter of the composition and even if the artist has already transferred his or her publishing rights to an unrelated music publisher. Moreover, the definition, as herein, often applies to compositions written or cowritten by the producer, which has the effect of requiring the artist to obtain the same rates and terms from the producer in the artist's agreement with the producer. These points are often hotly negotiated.

> (i) For the United States, at a royalty per selection equal to seventy-five per-cent (75%) of the minimum statutory per selection rate (without regard to playing time) effective on the date on which the applicable LP or master is delivered or required to be delivered to Company. The aforesaid seventy-five percent (75%) per selection rate shall hereinafter sometimes be referred to as the "U.S. Per Selection Rate"; and

A 3/4 rate is customarily required by the company in its agreements with new artists. This is based upon the minimum statutory rate, so that the company would pay the same rate for a 10-minute song as for a two-minute song. More importantly, it fixes the rate at the time the master is delivered or required to be delivered to the company. The minimum statutory rate for records made and distributed as of January 1, 1994 is 6.6 cents. The statutory rate is the greater of that or 1.25 cents per minute of playing time or portion thereof. When the current copyright act became effective on January 1, 1978 the minimum statutory rate was 2.75 cents. As you can see, it has risen quite dramatically and it is anticipated that it will continue to rise in the future. However, under this provision the mechanical royalty rate on a master delivered in 1995 will never increase regardless of increases in the statutory rate.

> (ii) For Canada, at a royalty per selection equal to seventy-five percent (75%) of the statutory per selection rate (without regard to playing time) effective on the date on which the applicable LP or master is delivered or required to be delivered to Company, or, if there is no statutory rate in Canada on such date, seventy-five percent (75%) of the per selection rate (without regard to playing time) generally utilized by major record companies in Canada on such date. The applicable aforesaid per selection rate shall hereinafter some-times be referred to as the "Canadian Per Selection Rate."

Canada has its own copyright laws which operate independently of U.S. Copyright Law. However, CMRRA, the Canadian record industry's mechanical rights organization, generally follows the U.S. trend, so that in a typical recording contract mechanical royalty rates for Canadian sales are generally the same number of Canadian pennies as U.S. pennies.

(a) Notwithstanding the foregoing, the maximum aggregate mechanical royalty rate which Company shall be required to pay for any record shall be the applicable U.S. Per Selection Rate or Canadian Per Selection Rate, respectively, multiplied by two (2) for any Single or Maxi-single, multiplied by five (5) for any EP or mini LP, and multiplied by ten (10) for any Album, regardless of the total number of compositions contained therein.

This is the most important clause in paragraph 14 since it affects every artist, even those who do not write their own material. Obviously, if the artist's album contains more than 10 compositions, the maximum is going to be exceeded, and as you will see, the artist is held responsible for that excess. CDs have become the dominant configuration and it is more common now than it used to be for albums to contain more than 10 selections; there are single-disc CDs that contain more than 20 selections. Obviously, negotiating these "caps" on mechanical royalties is critical.

(b) It is specifically understood that in the event that any Single, Maxi-single, EP or Album contains other compositions in addition to the Controlled Compositions and the aggregate mechanical royalty rate for said Single, Maxi-single, EP or Album shall exceed the applicable rate provided in this paragraph 14, the aggregate rate for the Controlled Compositions contained thereon shall be reduced by the aforesaid excess over said applicable rate. Additionally, Company shall have the right with respect to any Single, Maxi-single, EP or Album, the aggregate mechanical royalty rate for which exceeds the applicable rate provided in this paragraph 14 to deduct such excess payable thereon from any and all monies payable to Artist pursuant to this or any other agreement. All mechanical royalties payable hereunder shall be paid on the basis of net records sold hereunder for which royalties are payable to Artist pursuant to this agreement. Company may maintain reserves with respect to payment of mechanical royalties. If Company makes an overpayment of mechanical royalties in respect of compositions recorded under this agreement, Artist will reimburse Company for same, failing which Company may recoup any such overpayment from any monies becoming payable to Artist pursuant to this or any other agreement. Mechanical royalty payments on records subsequently returned are considered overpayments. Notwithstanding anything to the contrary contained herein, mechanical royalties payable in respect of Controlled Compositions for sales of records for any use other than as described in subparagraphs 10(a), (b) and (g) hereof shall be seventy-five percent (75%) of the otherwise applicable U.S. Per Selection Rate or Canadian Per Selection Rate, as the case may be. Controlled Compositions which are arranged versions of any musical compositions in the public domain, when furnished by Artist for recording hereunder, shall be free of copyright royalties. Any assignment of the ownership or administration of copyright in any Controlled Composition shall be made subject to the provisions hereof and any inconsistencies between the terms of this agreement and mechanical licenses issued to and accepted by Company shall be determined by the terms of this agreement. If any Single, Maxi-single, EP or Album contains other compositions in addition to the Controlled Compositions, Artist will obtain for Company's benefit mechanical licenses covering such composition on the same terms and conditions applicable to Controlled Compositions pursuant to this paragraph 14.

This clause addresses several different issues. First, it holds the artist responsible for excess mechanical royalties. The company's first option to recover such excess is to reduce the amount paid for controlled compositions. As stated before, mechanical royalties on controlled compositions are generally, but not always, payable to the artist; they may be payable to a producer or third-party music publisher, which can result in disputes between them and the artist if the company reduces the amounts payable to them. As a second option, the company can deduct the excess from other monies payable to the artist, which could include the artist's next album advance or royalties payable under a prior or subsequent recording agreement with the company. A last resort is to require the artist to reimburse company for the overpayment.

A second point of concern is that the mechanical royalties are payable on only those records for which record royalties are payable, whereas under the compulsory mechanical license provisions of the copyright act mechanical royalties are required to be paid on all records "made and distributed" by the company, subject to certain allowances for reserves and returns as specified in the regulations promulgated thereunder and subject to industry customs which have been developed in negotiations between the record companies and The Harry Fox Agency, Inc., which represents a large number of music publishers for the collection of mechanical royalties. Artists can often successfully negotiate to be paid mechanical royalties on all or a percentage of the records distributed as free goods.

Another issue is the payment of a further reduced mechanical rate, i.e., 75% of 75% of the minimum statutory rate, on sales of records other than through normal retail channels, which include mid-priced sales, budget record sales, record club sales, etc. Record clubs have succeeded in obtaining reduced royalty rates from all licensors, in large part as a result of the efforts of the major record companies which own the clubs.

Finally, this particular contract requires the artist to obtain mechanical licenses for noncontrolled compositions on the same terms and conditions as for controlled compositions, which is simply not attainable as a practical matter, since an unrelated music publisher will insist on being paid the statutory rate on terms and conditions customarily accepted by The Harry Fox Agency, Inc., known as "Fox terms."

(c) In respect of all Controlled Compositions performed in Videos, Company is hereby granted an irrevocable perpetual worldwide license to record and reproduce such Compositions in such Videos and to distribute and perform such Videos including, but not limited to, all A-V Devices thereof, and to authorize others to do so. Company will not be required to make any payment in connection with those uses, and that license shall apply whether or not Company receives any payment in connection with those Videos. Simultaneously with Artist's submission to Company of the information required pursuant to subparagraph 20(c)(1) hereof, Artist shall furnish Company with a written acknowledgment from the person(s) or entity(ies) controlling the copyright in each Noncontrolled Composition to be embodied on any Video confirming the terms upon which said person(s) or entity(ies) shall issue licenses in respect thereof. Upon Company's request therefor, Artist shall cause said person(s) or entity(ies) to forthwith issue to Company (and its designees) licenses containing said terms and such other terms and conditions as Company (or its designees) may require. Royalties in connection with licenses for the use of Noncontrolled Compositions pertaining to Videos and A-V Devices are included in the royalties set forth in subparagraph 20(g)(i) hereof. If the copyright in any Controlled Composition is owned or controlled by anyone else, Artist will cause that person, firm or corporation to grant Company the same rights described in this paragraph 14, on the same terms.

This provision calls for a free synchronization license, which is a license to "fix" or synchronize the musical composition with visual images, in each video. Publishers ordinarily do not object to this, since it is generally considered to be a promotional use for which the publisher will reap the rewards by increased air play of the composition, which generates public performance royalties to the publisher.

However, this also provides that, unlike records, the per-unit payment for the reproduction of the composition in A-V devices such as videocassettes and videodiscs (which technically is not a mechanical royalty since under the copyright act audiovisual devices are not phonorecords and are not subject to the compulsory mechanical license, but which are nevertheless sometimes referred to as "video mechanicals") is not paid separately to the publishers as mechanical royalties are paid, but is included within the all-in royalty payable to the artist for sales of those A-V devices. Since, as you will see later, those all-in artist royalties are not paid until recoupment of all production costs of all videos, the artist would be required to pay out of his or her own pocket the per-unit equivalent of mechanical royalties payable to the publishers of compositions reproduced in those A-V devices.

(e) Notwithstanding anything in the foregoing provisions of this paragraph 14 to the contrary, if a particular selection recorded hereunder is embodied more than once on a particular record, Company shall pay mechanical royalties in connection therewith at the applicable rate for such composition as though the selection were embodied thereon only once.

This clause is a recent addition to record contract forms which has come as a result of the popularity of 12-inch singles or their equivalent in other configurations, where the "A" side of the single is often reproduced in three or four versions or edits. The problem is that publishers of noncontrolled compositions are not obligated to accept payment on only one version, but may require payment in full on all versions or, if all versions are treated as one, payment at the "long song rate," i.e., based on the cumulative playing time of all such versions, which amounts to as much or nearly as much money.

15. In the event that Artist for any reason fails to timely deliver the minimum recording commitment hereunder in accordance with all of the terms and conditions of this agreement, then, in addition to any other rights or remedies which Company may have, Company shall have the right, upon written notice to Artist at any time prior to the expiration of the then current Contract Period, (1) to terminate this agreement without further obligation to Artist as to unrecorded or undelivered masters or (2) to reduce the minimum recording commitment for the then current Contract Period to the number which have been timely recorded and delivered during such Contract

Period. It is specifically understood that Company may exercise any or all of its rights pursuant to paragraph 15 hereof at any time(s) prior to the date the Term would otherwise expire. In addition, Company's obligations hereunder shall be suspended for the duration of any such default in Artist's production and delivery commitments.

This clause gives the company the right to terminate the agreement for late delivery. Normally the artist will negotiate for a notice and cure period of longer duration than for other alleged breaches of contract, e.g., so that the company could not terminate the contract until they had sent the artist written notice and the artist failed to complete the recordings and deliver them within 60 or 90 days thereafter. In some contracts the company also takes the right to demand repayment of any advances which have been paid to the artist for recordings which were required to be delivered but were not delivered prior to termination.

(a) Nothing herein contained shall obligate Company to permit Artist to record the minimum number of masters specified herein to be recorded during the Term hereof, it being understood that Company's sole obligation to Artist as to each unrecorded required master shall be to pay Artist an amount equal to the minimum union scale payment which Company would have been required to pay to Artist had Artist in fact recorded such unrecorded master.

This is a so-called pay or play clause which has the effect of undoing the company's commitment to the artist. This is a clause the artist's representatives should always try to delete. In a contract, such as this, where the company's commitment is one album at a time, such a clause is usually deleted if the artist so requests, because once the company has exercised its option there is little reason why it should be allowed to change its mind shortly thereafter. However, if the deal is for a firm commitment of two or more albums, the company will usually nevertheless insist on having a buyout right as to each album of the firm commitment beyond the first. Usually the negotiated amount is based upon the difference between the total amount of the recording fund the company would have been obligated to pay for the committed album or albums and the projected recording cost of such album or albums, which is generally deemed to be the amount of recording costs of the prior album. This is intended to give the artist approximately the same amount the advance would have been for the canceled album or albums.

The artist's representative should also request a provision that upon exercise by the company of any such pay or play option, the contract is terminated. Although this would seem to follow and will almost always be conceded without much argument, the recording agreement, as here, often does not so state, which could result in needless dispute later on.

(b) Company reserves the right, at its election, to suspend the operation of this agreement for the duration of any of the following contingencies, if by reason of any such contingency, it is materially hampered in the performance of its obligations under this agreement or its normal business operations are delayed or become impossible or commercially impracticable: Act of God, fire, catastrophe, labor disagreement, acts of government, its agencies or officers, any order, regulation, ruling or action of any labor union or association of artists, musicians, composers or employees affecting Company or the industry in which it is engaged, delays in the delivery of materials and supplies, or any other cause beyond Company's control. Any such suspension due to a labor controversy which involves only Company shall be limited to a period of six (6) months.

This is a typical force majeure clause, which absolves the company from performance of its obligations if performance is prevented by an act of God or similar occurrence. Typically the artist's representative seeks to limit the duration of any suspension period due to a cause which only affects the particular company and also seeks to clarify that accounting statements will be rendered and royalty payments will be made except to the extent that the company is rendered unable to do so.

(c) If Artist's voice or Artist's ability to perform as an instrumentalist should be materially or permanently impaired, then in addition to any other rights or remedies which Company may have, Company shall have the right, upon written notice to Artist, to terminate this agreement and shall thereby be relieved of any liability in connection with unrecorded masters.

The artist's representative should attempt to clarify that impairment must be determined by artist's own physician or a competent, independent physician. Also, if the artist is strictly a vocalist, obviously artist's ability to perform as an instrumentalist is irrelevant, and vice-versa.

16. Artist expressly acknowledges that Artist's services hereunder are of a special, unique and intellectual character which gives them peculiar value, and that in the event of a breach or threatened breach by Artist of any term, condition or covenant hereof, Company will be caused immediate irreparable injury. Artist expressly agrees that Company shall be entitled to injunctive and other equitable relief, as permitted by law, to prevent a breach or threatened breach of this agreement, or any portion thereof, by Artist, which relief shall be in addition to any other rights or remedies, for damages or otherwise, available to Company.

This is a standard clause, which states that the artist's services are unique. The purpose of this clause is to establish the company's entitlement to obtain an injunction against the artist should the artist attempt to breach the agreement by recording for another record company. However, this alone is not enough to entitle the company to obtain an injunction. The company will still be required to prove its entitlement according to the standards which have been developed in the case law. Additionally, for contracts governed by California law, which may include not only those which specifically state that California law is applicable but may also include those which the artist signed before becoming a resident of California, there are specific guarantees which must be made by the company in order to entitle it to injunctive relief. These will be discussed in clause 22(b)and the accompanying commentary.

17. Artist warrants and represents that Artist is under no disability, restriction or prohibition, whether contractual or otherwise, with respect to Artist's right to execute this agreement and perform its terms and conditions. Without limiting the foregoing, Artist specifically warrants and represents that no prior obligations, contracts or agreements of any kind undertaken or entered into by Artist will interfere in any manner

with the complete performance of this agreement by Artist or with Artist's right to record any and all selections hereunder. Artist warrants and represents that there are now in existence no prior unreleased masters embodying Artist's performances. Artist further warrants and represents that Company shall not be required to make any payments of any nature for, or in connection with, the rendition of Artist's services or the acquisition, exercise or exploitation of rights by Company pursuant to this agreement, except as specifically provided hereinabove. Artist warrants and represents that each member of Artist is a United States citizen and at least twenty-one (21) years of age.

In every recording contract the Artist is required to make "warranties and representations." These are statements of fact upon which the Company is entitled to rely. If they should turn out to be untrue, or if a third party should claim that they are not true, the indemnification provisions of the agreement will be triggered. The warranties and representations that the artist is free to enter into the contract and is not a party to any conflicting contract are fundamental. The representation and warranty that each member is a U.S. citizen and at least 21 years old is not critical. That is, even if the artist is not a U.S. citizen or is under 21 years old, the company is still entitled to sign the artist. However, if the artist is not a U.S. citizen, the company will want proof that the artist has the appropriate visa if the artist is going to record in the United States. Since employing an undocumented alien can subject the company to civil and criminal penalties, the company must be sure that the appropriate visas are obtained. If the artist is under the age of majority, which varies from state to state, the company will need to take steps so that the artist cannot disaffirm the contract by reason of age. For example, in California anyone who makes a contract when a minor, i.e., anyone under 18 years old at the time of execution of the contract, has the right to disaffirm (cancel), a contract even after performance under it has begun, unless the company gets the contract approved by a court. This is true whether or not the company knew that the artist was under 18 years old. This could prove disastrous to the company, so the purpose of this clause is to require the artist to advise the company prior to execution if the artist is in fact not a U.S. citizen or is not at least 21 years old, so that the company can take appropriate measures.

(a) Artist warrants and represents that no materials, or any use thereof, will violate any law or infringe upon or violate the rights of any third party. "Materials," as used in this subparagraph 17(a) shall include: (1) all musical compositions and other material contained on masters subject hereto, (2) each name used by Artist, in connection with masters recorded hereunder, and (3) all other materials, ideas, other intellectual properties or elements furnished or selected by Artist and contained in or used in connection with any masters recorded hereunder or the packaging, sale, distribution, advertising, publicizing or other exploitation thereof.

These warranties and representations are also fundamental and are contained in all recording contracts. The basic thrust is that the artist is solely responsible for the content of the records and any other material or elements furnished by the artist which is used in the packaging or advertising thereof, e.g., album cover artwork. However, it is somewhat broadly drafted in favor of the company in that it makes the artist responsible for musical compositions even if they are not written or controlled by the artist and because it is silent as to the company's obligation for materials, ideas, and elements furnished or selected by the company.

(b) Artist hereby agrees to defend, hold harmless and indemnify Company from any and all damages, liabilities, costs, losses and expenses (including legal costs and attorneys' fees) arising out of or connected with any claim, demand or action (collectively referred to below as a "Claim") by a third party which is (1) inconsistent with any of the warranties, representations or covenants made by Artist in this contract and (2) reduced to a final judgment or settled with Artist's consent, which consent Artist shall not unreasonably withhold. Artist agrees to reimburse Company, on demand, for any payment made by Company at any time with respect to any such damage, liability, cost, loss or expense to which the foregoing indemnity applies. In the event Artist shall fail to do so, Company shall have the right to recoup such payment from any monies payable to Artist hereunder. Company shall notify Artist of any such Claim promptly after Company has been formally advised thereof. Pending the determination of any such Claim, Company shall have the right, at Company's election, to withhold payment of any monies otherwise payable to Artist hereunder in an amount reasonably related to the amount of Company's attorneys' fees and costs in connection therewith and, if Company shall determine that such Claim has merit and/or is not spurious, the amount of such Claim. Artist shall have the right to post a bond in form, amount and duration and with a bonding company satisfactory to Company, and in the event Artist shall so post such a bond, Company shall no longer withhold any monies hereunder in connection with the Claim in respect of which such bond shall be posted.

This is a typical indemnification clause which has been improved from the normal first draft by incorporating points usually requested by artists' representatives. The way this clause works is as follows. If a claim is made that the company considers to be inconsistent with the artist's warranties and representations, e.g., a claim by a third party that a song on the artist's album which the artist claims to have written infringes the third party's copyright in another song or incorporates an unauthorized sample, the company would notify the artist of the claim and the artist would hire an attorney to defend it. The company would have the right to withhold payment of any monies, i.e., not only artist royalties, but mechanical royalties and album advances as well, in an amount reasonably related to the claim (which ordinarily will be a huge sum), unless the artist posts a bond to cover the potential judgment, which is difficult for virtually any artist to do. However, this clause extends the company's right of indemnification only to those claims which are either reduced to a final judgment or settled with the artist's consent. If the artist does not consent, the company is not given the right to reimburse itself for the amount of the settlement, should it decide to settle the claim without the artist's consent, nor for its attorneys' fees in defending it. In other contracts the company insists on the right to settle such claims if the artist does not post a bond, thereby eliminating the risk that a large judgment will be entered against the company. The reason for this is that in most instances the artist does not have the financial resources to fulfill its obligation to indemnify the company should a judgment be entered. On the other hand, artists are not comfortable giving companies the rights to settle claims the artists may consider to be meritless and to charge the amount of the settlement and the attorneys' fees against the artists.

18. Wherever in this agreement Artist's approval or consent is required, such approval or consent shall not be unreasonably withheld. Company may require Artist

to formally give or withhold such approval or consent by giving Artist written notice requesting same and by furnishing Artist with the information or material in respect of which such approval or consent is sought. Artist shall give Company written notice of approval or disapproval within five (5) days after such notice. Artist shall not hinder nor delay the scheduled release of any record hereunder. In the event of disapproval or no consent, the reasons therefor shall be stated. Failure to give such notice to Company as aforesaid shall be deemed to be consent or approval.

Record companies like to have a free hand in marketing the artist's masters and records as they see fit. When they do agree to give the artist rights of approval over creative and/or marketing matters, they want to be sure that the artist will exercise that right of approval promptly. Accordingly, this type of clause whereby the artist's approval is deemed given if the artist does not expressly disapprove the company's proposal within a specified period of time, has been adopted by most record companies.

19. During the Term, Artist shall become and remain a member in good standing of any labor unions with which Company may at any time have agreements lawfully requiring such union membership, including, but not limited to, the American Federation of Musicians and the American Federation of Television and Radio Artists. All masters subject hereto shall be produced in accordance with the rules and regulations of all unions having jurisdiction.

This type of clause is required whenever the company is a signatory to the AFM and AFTRA agreements. All of the majors are signatories, whereas most independent record companies are not.

20. Artist shall, upon Company's request, appear on dates and at film studios or other locations designated by Company upon reasonable notice to Artist for the filming, taping or other permanent fixation of audiovisual reproductions of Artist's performances embodied in any masters hereunder (each such audiovisual reproduction or recording shall be referred to herein as a "Video"). Company shall have the right to produce and utilize each Video subject to the terms and conditions set forth below:

As you will see, there are many provisions relating to the production and exploitation of videos, which are different from the corresponding provisions relating to the production and exploitation of audio masters. This section gives the company the right to require the artist to perform for videos on dates designated by the company. Some artists may not want to be obligated to perform for videos at all. Most commonly, however, companies can obligate them to perform, but on mutually agreeable dates and times.

(a) Company shall be responsible for and shall pay the production costs (including, without limitation, all direct, out of pocket expenses incurred in connection with the development, creation and production) for each Video, pursuant to a production budget to be established in advance by Company. Notwithstanding the foregoing, in the event that Company shall pay any excess production costs which are caused solely by Artist's failure to perform Artist's obligations in connection with such Video in a timely fashion, Company shall, without limiting Company's other rights and remedies in such event, have the right to deduct an amount equal to such excess costs from any monies payable by Company to Artist hereunder. Company shall have the right to recoup such production costs from royalties payable to Artist hereunder; provided, however, Company agrees that not more than fifty percent (50%) of such production costs shall be recoupable from record royalties payable by Company to Artist hereunder.

Generally the company designates the video production budget, but sometimes will agree that the budget will be not less than a specified minimum amount designed to ensure that customary production values can be achieved. Video production costs are customarily recoupable in the manner provided in this contract, i.e., they are fully recoupable, but no more than 50% can be recouped from record royalties. The remainder can be recouped from video royalties, but since very few artists ever sell a significant quantity of home videos (A-V devices), the other 50% may never be recouped. This has led people to somewhat loosely characterize video production costs as being only 50% recoupable. In many contracts, however, if the production budget is exceeded, the entire excess may be recouped from the artist's record royalties.

(b) As between Artist and Company, Company shall be the sole and exclusive owner in perpetuity of any such Video, and shall have the right to utilize or exploit any such Video in any manner which Company may deem appropriate.

It is standard for the company to own all rights to the video, but many artists insist on the right to approve any commercial exploitation, particularly on A-V devices.

(c) Artist shall issue (or shall cause the music publishing companies who have the right to do so to issue) (1) worldwide, perpetual licenses to Company for the use of all Controlled Compositions in Videos, and (2) perpetual licenses for public performance in the United States (to the extent that ASCAP and BMI are unable to issue same) of all Controlled Compositions in Videos, each such license to be issued to Company at no cost, effective as of the commencement of production of the applicable Video (and Artist's execution of this agreement shall constitute the issuance of such licenses by any music publishing company which is owned or controlled by Artist or by any entity owned or controlled by Artist). In the event that Artist shall fail to cause any such music publishing company to issue any such license to Company, and if Company shall thereupon pay any fee to such music publishing company in order to obtain any such license, then Company shall have the right to deduct the amount of such license fee from any monies payable to Artist hereunder.

(d) Company shall have the right to use and publish, and to permit others to use and publish, Artist's name and likeness and biographical material concerning Artist in each Video and for advertising and purposes of trade in connection with the Video, subject to paragraph 5(a) hereof.

(e) Company shall consult with Artist with respect to the selection of the producer, director and all other production personnel in the production of each Video, but Company's decision shall be final. The determination and/or selection of the concept and the script of each Video shall be subject to approval by Artist and Company. Artist shall fully cooperate with the producer, director and all other production personnel in the production of each

Video, and to the extent required, Artist shall provide Artist's services as a visual performer in connection with each Video.

Companies often insist on having the final say on the creative elements of videos, but many are willing to give artists mutual approval over all creative elements, and some are willing to give artists free rein subject to not violating broadcast standards.

(f) In the event that, at any time from and after the date when Company schedules the commencement of production of a particular Video, but prior to the completion of Artist's services with respect to such Video, Artist is prevented from commencing or continuing such services, as set forth herein, by reason of injury or sickness, Artist shall (1) immediately notify Company of such circumstances, (2) immediately procure the attention of a duly qualified physician, (3) obtain and provide to Company such physician's certificate detailing fully the nature of Artist's such incapacity and the circumstances in which such incapacity arises, (4) submit to such examinations with respect to such incapacity as shall be required by Company's insurance carrier, and (5) cooperate with Company, and Company's insurance carrier with respect to any insurance claim in connection with such incapacity; provided, however, that Artist shall not be required to fulfill any obligations under this paragraph in excess of those required by Company's insurance carrier. Notwithstanding the provisions of paragraph 20(a) above, if and to the extent that Company recovers from any production costs for a particular Video in excess of the production budget therefor, for which excess costs Artist is responsible pursuant to paragraph 20(a) above, and which have been previously charged against Artist's account hereunder, Company shall, upon such recovery, recredit Artist's account in the amount of such recovery.

Companies often seek to exercise more control over the conduct of video production sessions than they do over audio recording sessions because the daily production costs are much greater.

(g) With respect to any commercial exploitation of Videos by Company's third party licensees (other than as specified in subparagraph 20(g)(i) below), Company shall credit to Artist's account hereunder an amount equal to one-half (1/2) of Company's Net Video Receipts. As used herein, the term "Our Net Video Receipts" shall mean any and all sums paid to Company by any third party in connection with Company's licensee's exploitation or use of any Video produced and owned by Company less all production costs, distribution costs and all other direct out-of-pocket costs or expenses incurred or paid by Company in connection with such Video or the exploitation or distribution thereof.

This clause would apply to uses of the video in A-V devices manufactured and sold by unrelated licensees, e.g., in another label's home video compilation. The split between company and artist is the same as for a third party license of an audio master, except that, as you will see in subclause 20(g)(ii) below, the artist's share includes any payment for the musical composition embodied in the video, whereas in a third party license of an audio master, the fee payable in respect of the musical composition is either the subject of a separate license or, if included, is deducted off the top before arriving at the net receipts to be split by the company and the artist.

(i) With respect to any so-called "home video devices" (e.g., audiovisual discs or tapes intended primarily for home use) embodying one or more Videos ("A-V Devices" herein), Company shall pay to Artist the following royalties: (A) with respect to net sales of A-V Devices manufactured and distributed by Company and sold in the United States, a royalty equal to (1) ten percent (10%) of Company's Video Royalty Base Price (hereinafter defined) with respect to A-V Devices with a suggested retail list price of Twenty Dollars ($20) or less; and (2) fifteen percent (15%) with respect to A-V Devices with a suggested retail list price in excess of Twenty Dollars ($20); and (B) with respect to net sales of A-V Devices manufactured and distributed by Company or Company's foreign licensees and sold outside the United States, a royalty equal to ten percent (10%) of Net Foreign A-V Receipts (as hereinafter defined). As used herein: the "Video Royalty Base Price" shall mean (a) with respect to A-V Devices sold by Company through normal retail channels, the wholesale receipts from Company's distributor (or subdistributors) of such A-V Devices less an amount equal to twenty percent (20%) thereof and (b) with respect to A-V Devices sold by Company (as opposed to Company's licensees) through mail order and other direct-to-consumer operations: if sold directly by Company and not through a distributor, a price equal to the average Video Royalty Base Price applicable to sales by Company through normal retail channels of the applicable A-V Device during the accounting period during which such mail order or other direct-to-consumer sales occurred, or, if sold through a distributor, an amount equal to the price at which Company sells such A-V Devices to such distributor less twenty percent (20%) thereof; and "Net Foreign A-V Receipts" shall mean one hundred percent (100%) of the wholesale receipts actually received by Company or Company's foreign licensees from the exploitation of A-V Devices outside of the United States less ten percent (10%) thereof. Notwithstanding the foregoing, Artist's royalty under this paragraph 20(g)(i) shall be reduced for returns, refunds, credits, settlements, allowances, rebates, discounts and other similar adjustments and there shall be deducted from each Video Royalty Base Price and Net Foreign A-V Receipts (prior to calculating Artist's royalty percentage thereof) sales, foreign withholding, excise, use and value added or similar taxes included in such price or wholesale receipts, including, without limitation, in connection with the exploitation or distribution of such A-V Devices outside of the United States. Without limiting the generality of any of the foregoing, any A-V Device manufactured and distributed for Company or on Company's behalf pursuant to an agreement whereby the distributor thereof deducts a percentage of its receipts as its distribution fee and pays Company the balance of such receipts (rather than whereby the distributor finances the costs of production and/or manufacture of such devices [and/or the Videos embodied therein] and pays Company on a stated royalty basis) shall be deemed to be "manufactured and distributed by Company" for the purposes of this paragraph 20(g)(i).

The royalty payable for the sale of home A-V devices sold by the company differs from the royalty payable on records in the following principal ways: (1) It is based on a wholesale price rather than the retail list price; (2) it is generally inclusive of payments to music publishers in addition to payments to producers, directors, and other artists participating therein (see subclause 20(g)(ii) below); and (3) the royalty percentage rates are often less than the artist's percentage royalty rates for album sales. In this contract the wholesale price is further reduced by 20% for sales in the United States and 10% for sales outside the United States.

(ii) The royalties payable in accordance with this paragraph 20(g) are inclusive of all royalties that may be payable to all third parties including, without limitation, producers of any masters embodied in any Video, producers and directors of the visual portion of any Video and publishers of both Controlled Compositions and Noncontrolled Compositions. If Company make any payments to third parties with respect to such A-V Devices, then Company shall have the right to deduct such payments from royalties otherwise payable to Artist under this paragraph 20(g).

As discussed above, this makes the artist's video royalties inclusive of payments to publishers of both controlled compositions and noncontrolled compositions. This clause is problematic for the artist, since the artist is obligated to go out-of-pocket to pay royalties on sales of the A-V devices prior to recoupment of the artist's overall video account, which is likely to be substantially unrecouped at the time any A-V device is released.

(iii) If Company couples Videos hereunder with videos or other audiovisual recordings which are not Videos hereunder, then the amounts otherwise payable to Artist hereunder with respect to such coupled Videos shall be multiplied by a fraction, the numerator of which is the number of Videos involved and the denominator of which is the aggregate number of videos or other audiovisual recordings (including the Videos hereunder) involved and each selection embodied in each Video or other video (or other audiovisual recording) shall count as one (1) Video or video song for such purposes.

(iv) The provisions of paragraph 11 above shall apply with respect to Company's obligations to render accountings to Artist and pay royalties with respect to Videos pursuant to this paragraph 20(g).

(v) Notwithstanding any of the foregoing, any and all monies payable by Company to the American Federation of Musicians ("AFM") on Artist's behalf or in respect of services rendered by Artist in connection with any Video in respect of any exploitation of any Video hereunder shall be recoupable from any and all monies payable to Artist under this paragraph 20(g) or, at Company's election, Company may reduce the amount payable by Company to the AFM by the amount paid to Artist under this paragraph 20(g).

Again, this contract is atypical in that it requires the artist to pay the AFM per-unit royalties on sales of home videos as it did with respect to sales of phonorecords. The rationale for this seems to be that the recordings are being done under the artist's licenses. However, the video royalty rates have not been adjusted upward to cover these payments.

21. Subject to Artist's reasonable availability, Company shall consult with Artist with respect to the form and content of the proposed album cover artwork for each Album, and such artwork shall be made available at Company's offices for Artist's inspection and approval in accordance with the terms hereof.

(a) In no event shall Company be required to incur any costs in excess of Company's then-current standard costs of producing such artwork and/or manufacturing Album jackets, compact disc booklets, inner sleeves and other packaging elements. In the event Company incurs any such excess costs due to Artist's request, Artist shall pay Company, upon Company's request, an amount equal to the amount of any such excess production and/or manufacturing costs.

(b) If Artist shall not promptly pay all such applicable costs to Company, Company shall have the right to deduct from any and all monies payable to Artist under this or any other agreement an amount equal to such costs as set forth in subparagraph 21(a) hereof.

Generally the company's in-house department prepares album cover artwork for the artist's approval. However, in some instances the artist will be given a budget to hire artists of his or her own choice to create the album artwork, in which event the company will insist on the right to approve it, at least to ensure that it is not offensive or objectionable, and to ensure that the costs of manufacturing album covers, CD booklets, etc. will not be excessive. If they are the company will usually insist that the artist pay these costs out of the artist's own pocket, rather than advancing the costs and hoping to recoup them.

22. Company agrees to make annual payments of compensation ("Annual Payments") to Artist during each of the first seven (7) "Contract Years" (as hereinafter defined), as follows:

First Contract Year: Nine Thousand Dollars ($9,000), less all "Artist Payments" (as hereinafter defined);
Second Contract Year: Twelve Thousand Dollars ($12,000), less all Artist Payments; Third through Seventh Contract Years, inclusive: Fifteen Thousand Dollars ($15,000) per Contract Year, less all Artist Payments.

(a) Each Annual Payment shall be due on or before the last business day of the Contract Year to which applicable; provided that if this agreement expires or terminates prior to the end of a particular Contract Year, Company shall pay the applicable amount of the Annual Payment reduced prorata or such greater amount, if any, as is required pursuant to California Civil Code §3423.

(b) If, during the term hereof, Company desires to seek injunctive relief hereunder, Company shall have the right to make the applicable of the "aggregate additional compensation payments" (as such term is used in California Civil Code §3423), if any, required to be paid pursuant to California Civil Code §3423(e)(2)(A)(ii); any such additional compensation payment is referred to herein as an "Optional Payment." Each such Optional Payment, if any, shall be deemed compensation to Artist for the purpose of satisfying the requirements of California Civil Code §3423. If Company actually makes any such Optional Payment and thereafter elects not to seek the injunction in connection with which such payment was made, such payment shall constitute an Artist Payment hereunder.

(i) If Company seeks injunctive relief hereunder and Company is obligated to make an Optional Payment as a prerequisite to doing so in accordance with

California Civil Code §3423(e)(2)(A)(ii), each Artist Payment not applied to the Annual Payments theretofore due to Artist will be credited toward satisfying Company's such obligation.

(c) As used in this agreement, the term "Artist Payments" means all compensation (other than mechanical copyright royalties) theretofore paid to Artist (or to Artist's designee as compensation to Artist) during: (1) the Contract Year in question or (2) during any preceding Contract Year to the extent such monies paid during any such preceding Contract Year exceeded the Annual Payment prescribed for such Contract Year.

(d) As used in this agreement, the term "Contract Year" means each consecutive twelve (12) month period during which this agreement is in effect, commencing with the date hereof.

(e) All Annual Payments and Optional Payments (if any) made or credited shall be credits against and deductible from any and all advances otherwise payable to Artist by Company and shall be recoupable by Company from all royalties (other than mechanical copyright royalties) becoming otherwise payable to Artist by Company hereunder.

(i) Notwithstanding anything to the contrary contained herein, wherever in this agreement Company has the right to deduct excess expenditures (including, without limitation, excess recording costs, mechanical copyright royalties and artwork manufacturing costs) from any and all monies otherwise payable by Company hereunder, Company's such right shall not extend to deducting such excess expenditures from any Annual Payments or Optional Payments.

For many years California Civil Code §3423 provided that in order for a company to obtain an injunction preventing an artist from breaching a contract for unique personal services, the company was required to have guaranteed payment to the individual of at least $6,000 per year. In 1993 it was amended without any legislative debate to $50,000 per year. The record companies learned of this to their horror and mounted a lobbying effort which resulted in the law being amended as of January 1, 1994 to require minimum annual payments starting at $9,000 and escalating as outlined in this paragraph 22. The statute is quite a bit more complicated than it used to be and has yet to be interpreted in a judicial decision. Since the minimum payment applies to each member of a group, the company may be put to a difficult choice as to whether it should guarantee the minimum compensation to all members of a group which is newly signed to a label and therefore has no track record of sales, or perhaps only to the key member or members, or whether it should forego entirely the possibility of injunctive relief. In this regard it is important for the artist to realize that even if the company is not entitled to injunctive relief to prevent the artist from recording for a new label in breach of the artist's recording contract, the company would be entitled to recover damages, which could be greater than the entire amount of royalties the artist will be paid by the new record company.

23. This agreement is intended to bind the individuals listed on the first page hereof jointly and severally. Accordingly, whenever the word "Artist" is used in this agreement, it shall mean, except as is expressly otherwise provided for herein, said individuals jointly and individually, except that all payments to Artist shall be made to Artist jointly.

(a) The individuals comprising Artist agree that, for so long as this agreement shall be in effect, they will perform together as a group (the "Group") for Company. If any individual comprising Artist refuses, neglects or fails to perform together with the other individuals comprising Artist in fulfillment of the obligations agreed to be performed under this agreement or leaves the Group, Artist shall give Company prompt written notice thereof. Said individual shall remain bound by this agreement, including, but not limited to, the provisions of subparagraph 23(b) hereof or Company may, by notice in writing, (1) terminate this agreement with respect to such individual or (2) terminate this agreement in its entirety without any obligation as to unrecorded or undelivered masters. The individual whose engagement is so terminated or who refuses, neglects or fails to perform with the Group or who leaves the Group may not perform for others for the purpose of recording any selection as to which the applicable restrictive period specified in paragraph 4 of this agreement has not expired. Any member of the Group who refuses, neglects or fails to perform with the Group or who leaves the Group shall not thereafter use the professional name of the Group in any commercial or artistic endeavor; said professional name shall remain the property of those members of the Group who continue to perform their obligations hereunder and whose engagements are not terminated. The person, if any, engaged to replace the individual whose engagement is terminated shall be mutually agreed upon by Company and the remaining individuals comprising Artist. Neither party shall unreasonably withhold agreement with regard thereto; and, if agreement cannot be reached, Company may terminate this agreement by notice in writing. In the event that an individual engagement is terminated by notice from Company, or by mutual consent, (1) each party shall be relieved and discharged from liability for masters unrecorded at the time of such notice or mutual consent and (2) Artist will be solely responsible for and shall pay all monies required to be paid to any individual whose engagement is so terminated in connection with all masters theretofore or thereafter recorded under this agreement and Artist will hold Company harmless with respect thereto. Each person added to Artist, as a replacement or otherwise, shall become a party to this agreement as a condition precedent to being so added.

An important part of any recording agreement for a group artist is the section dealing with changes in the group membership, the so-called leaving member provisions. In the typical first draft agreement, if any member leaves the group, the company has the right to terminate the agreement. This could be disastrous and unfair to the group, particularly if the member is not a key member. Accordingly, artist's representatives will sometimes negotiate to restrict this clause to situations where a specified key member has left the group. Of course, this is a tricky subject for the artist's representative to address, since merely discussing who is key and who is not key can cause strains in relationships among group members and in relationships with their representatives.

Another primary function of these provisions is to provide that the individual who leaves the group is still bound by the agreement in certain respects. For example, the leaving member is bound by the rerecording restrictions and is prohibited from using the group name in connection with his own activities thereafter. This section also provides that the remaining group members are solely responsible for making any payments due to the leaving member. Where a member has been thrown out of the group by the rest of the members, there is a likelihood of protracted litigation over the right of that leaving member to share not only in income derived by the group from the member's activities with the group, e.g., albums on which the departed member performed, but also on future income of the group. Courts have found there is "goodwill" in the group name, for which the remaining members must pay the departing member his or her allocable share of the value thereof at the time the departed member left the group. In the case of a superstar group, this can be an enormous sum of money. In this contract the company is stating that this is the group's problem, not the company's. This issue, and many of the other issues touched on by this section, are best addressed in a written partnership agreement among the group members. Ideally, a written partnership agreement should exist for every group and should be created as soon as the group is able to afford it, preferably at the same time they make their first recording agreement. However, as stated above, the various issues relating to how the group members share in money, who makes the decisions for the group, and what happens if a member voluntarily leaves the group or if the other members want to force a member out of the group are extremely emotional and sensitive issues which many groups simply do not wish to confront, preferring instead to work out their own informal rules. The downside of this approach is that if the group becomes successful and these issues have not been addressed in a written agreement, the consequence can be years of litigation costing tremendous amounts of time, money, and emotional distress.

Finally, the company takes the right to approve replacement members and requires that they become a party to this agreement. In most instances the company does not take an active role in the process of selecting a replacement member, although in certain situations, e.g., the replacement of the lead singer of a superstar act, the company will exercise this right if it has it. Also, if an original member of a superstar act leaves the group for any reason, it is common not to make the replacement an "equity" member of the group, but merely a paid employee of the rest of the members or their affiliated corporation, in which event that replacement member would not have all of the rights of the original members and would not be a party to the recording agreement, although the company might insist on having the member sign an "inducement letter" whereby the member would give the company certain rights and agree to some or all of the same restrictions placed on the equity members, e.g., rerecording restrictions.

(b) In addition to the rights provided in subparagraph 23(a) hereinabove, Company shall have, and each individual comprising Artist hereby grants to Company, an irrevocable option for the individual and exclusive services of each of the individual(s) comprising Artist for the purpose of making phonograph records. Said option with respect to such individual(s) may be exercised by Company giving such individual(s) notice in writing within three (3) months after Company receives the notice provided for in subparagraph 23(a) to the effect that such individual(s) has refused, neglected or failed to perform with the other individuals comprising Artist or that such individual(s) has left the Group or that the Group has disbanded. In the event of Company's exercise of such option, such individual(s) shall be deemed to have entered into a new and separate agreement with Company with respect to such individual(s)' exclusive recording services upon all the terms and conditions of this agreement except that: (1) such individual shall record and deliver to Company four (4) demonstration recordings ("Demos") pursuant to a recording budget approved by Company therefor; (2) within ninety (90) days following Company's receipt of said notice, but not sooner than sixty (60) days following Company's receipt of the Demos, Company shall have the option by written notice to require such individual to record and deliver to Company masters sufficient to comprise one

(1) Album ("minimum recording commitment") and Company shall thereafter have the right to increase the minimum recording commitment and the right to extend the term for option periods so that Company shall have the right under such agreement to the same number of Albums as Company then has rights or options for under this agreement, provided that Company shall have the right to request not less than six (6) Albums under such agreement; (3) Company shall advance all recording costs in respect of masters to be recorded by such individual up to the amount of the budget approved by Company therefor; (4) Company's royalty obligation to such individual in respect of such recordings shall be the payment to such individual of the royalties computed as set forth in this agreement except that the Basic U.S. Singles Rate shall be _____ percent (___%) and the Basic U.S. Album Rate shall be _____ percent (___%) with royalties for all other uses (foreign sales, clubs, licensing, etc.), reduced proportionately; (5) Company shall maintain separate accounts with respect to recordings subject to this agreement and recordings subject to such agreement in respect of such individual(s); and (6) recordings by such individual shall not be applied in diminution of Artist's minimum recording commitment as set forth in this agreement.

Perhaps the most important consequence of a member leaving the group or the group disbanding is that the company has the option to retain the services of the leaving member or, if the group disbands, of any individual member(s). However, the company is usually not content to obtain the services of the leaving member(s) on the same terms as would have been applicable had the group stayed together. Instead the contract often requires the leaving member(s), in effect, to go back to square one, i.e., be compensated on the same basis as for the first album of the contract. Sometimes the terms are even less favorable than that. For example, in this contract, the leaving member is obligated to record four demos and there is no recording fund or advance payable in connection with albums by the leaving member. Instead the company merely allocates a recording budget. Here the royalty rates are left blank, but generally they are a couple of points lower than the group's royalty rate would have been for its next album. Moreover, in some contracts the company is allowed to cross-collateralize all or at least a prorata portion of the unrecouped balance, if any, of the group's royalty account against the leaving member's royalty account, and is allowed to use a pro-rata portion of the group's account to recoup recording costs and charges under the leaving member's agreement. Accordingly, although a group breakup may be the furthest thing from the members' minds at the time they are being signed to a recording contract, it is important that they be aware of these provisions and negotiate the best possible terms.

(c) No changes in the individuals comprising Artist may be made without Company's prior written consent. Artist shall not have the right, so long as this agreement is in effect, to assign Artist's professional name as mentioned on page 1 hereof (or any other name(s) utilized by Artist in connection with recordings subject hereto) or to permit the use of said name(s) by any other individual or group of individuals without Company's prior written consent, and any attempt to do so shall be null and void and shall convey no right or title. The individuals comprising Artist jointly and severally represent and warrant that they are and shall be the sole owners of all such professional name(s), and that no other person, firm or corporation has the right to use said name(s) or to permit said name(s) to be used in connection with phonograph records, and that the individuals comprising

Artist have the authority to grant Company the exclusive right to use said name(s) in the Territory. Company shall have the exclusive right to use said name(s) in accordance with all of the terms and conditions of this agreement.

The warranties and representations regarding the Artist's ownership of the group name are quite important. If there are concerns at the time of signing the agreement that the Artist's group name may infringe upon someone else's name, a resolution of the competing claims ought to be worked out quickly, or the Artist ought to pick a new name, before the stakes escalate, which will happen if the Artist has a hit record.

(d) In addition to its rights pursuant to subparagraphs 23(a) and (b), Company shall have the right to record the performances of any one or more of the individuals comprising Artist without the other individuals comprising Artist upon all of the terms and conditions herein contained; provided, however, that should Company elect to do so, the provisions set forth in subparagraph 23(b) hereof shall be applied with respect to such individual or individuals whose performances are actually so recorded. In the event that any individual member of Artist wishes to record performances of any of the individual(s) comprising Artist, which such individual(s) remains a member of Artist and continues to perform their obligations hereunder, Artist shall give Company prompt notice thereof. Company shall thereafter have the irrevocable option to acquire such recordings, and if exercised, such recordings shall be acquired upon the terms set forth in subparagraph 23(b). If Company shall decline to acquire any such recordings, then Artist hereby warrants, represents and agrees that such recordings shall not be made or if made, that no use, including, but not limited to, any commercial release thereof, shall be made by Artist or anyone deriving any rights therefrom.

This paragraph allows for the possibility that a member of the group will want to record solo albums while still maintaining membership in the group.

24. Company, in its sole discretion, shall have the right to expend monies in connection with the independent promotion of any record(s) embodying master recordings hereunder. Fifty percent (50%) of all such expenditures shall be advances against and recoupable by Company out of any and all royalties becoming payable to Artist under this or any other agreement.

Independent promotion is the practice of using individuals outside the company to obtain radio airplay of the company's singles. The practice has been much criticized and has been the subject of investigations into payola, the crime of paying to obtain the broadcast of records. However, independent promotion remains a key ingredient to the success of a hit single. When record companies spend money for independent promotion, it is usually either 100% or 50% recoupable, depending on the contract. When a major record company hires independent promotion people, it is in addition to the promotional efforts of the company's own in-house promotion department. However, if the artist is contracting with a small company which does not have its own promotion staff, it is difficult to justify 100% recoupability of independent promotion, since one of the primary functions of the record company is to market and promote the records and therefore some portion of its promotion expense ought to be nonrecoupable.

25. If, during the term of this agreement, Artist desires to grant to a third party the exclusive right to Artist's songwriting services or the right to own or administer any interest in or to one (1) or more Controlled Compositions (whether written prior to or during the term hereof) (such rights being herein referred to as "Publishing Rights"), then prior to commencing negotiations with any such third party with respect to any such Publishing Rights, Artist shall notify Company thereof and Artist and Company shall promptly begin good faith negotiations regarding the material terms and conditions of an agreement between Artist and Company's publishing company designee relating to such Publishing Rights ("Publishing Agreement"). If, after such good faith negotiations, Artist and Company are unable to agree on the material terms of such Publishing Agreement, then Artist shall have the right to offer such Publishing Rights to third parties and to enter into a Publishing Agreement with any person with respect thereof ("Third Party Publishing Agreement"), subject, however, to the following conditions:

(a) In no event shall Artist have the right to offer such Publishing Rights to any third party prior to the date occurring sixty (60) days after the commencement of negotiations regarding the terms of a Publishing Agreement between Artist and Company; and

(b) In the event Artist shall receive a proposal for a Third Party Publishing Agreement ("Third Party Proposal"), Artist shall first:

(i) notify Company in writing ("Your Notice") of the Third Party Proposal;

(ii) furnish Company with complete copies of all of the instruments constituting the Third Party Proposal; and

(iii) offer to enter into an agreement with Company on the same material terms as are contained in the Third Party Proposal. If Company does not accept that offer within thirty (30) days after Company's receipt of Artist's Notice ("Offer Period"), Artist may then enter into the agreement set forth in the Third Party Proposal, provided that agreement is consummated within thirty (30) days after the end of the Offer Period upon the same terms and in the same form set forth in the Third Party Proposal. If that agreement is not so consummated within the latter thirty (30) day period, the right of pre-emption granted to Company in this paragraph will be revived and no party other than Company will be authorized to enter into any agreement concerning the Publishing Rights unless Artist first notify Company and offer to enter into an agreement with Company as provided in this paragraph.

This is not a clause typically found in a major record label contract, but clauses of this type are often found in contracts with smaller record companies. This is essentially a compromise between having no provision regarding ownership of the artist's music publishing interests and one which automatically grants to the record company an ownership interest (usually 50%) in the artist's publishing. This is a combination right of first negotiation and right of last refusal, which is designed to give the company the right to match any offer which the artist would otherwise be willing to accept. The justification for these types of clauses is that the company is the entity primarily responsible for creating the value of the artist's songs and therefore ought to have an edge in acquiring the publishing rights. This type of clause gives the artist the freedom not to make a publishing deal if the artist so chooses and gives the artist the benefit of being able to obtain the fair market value for his or her compositions. The only downside for the artist is that it may be more difficult to obtain an offer for the fair market value of his or her musical compositions if the third party which would otherwise be willing to make an offer knows that the company has a matching right, in which event the third party may believe that it is simply being used as a stalking horse to raise the price without having a realistic prospect of getting the deal.

26. For the purposes of this agreement, the following definitions shall apply:
    (a) "Master"—the equivalent of a seven (7") inch 45 rpm single-sided recording of not less than 3-1/2 minutes of playing time intended for use in the manufacture and sale of records.

    This is a somewhat strange definition. What if a recording is less than 3-1/2 minutes of playing time? If it is not a master, then what is it?

    (b) "Single"—A record embodying thereon two (2) masters.
    (c) "Maxi-single"—A record embodying thereon not more than four (4) masters.
    (d) "EP"—A record embodying thereon either five (5) masters or six (6) masters, provided, however, that in the event that more than one (1) of such masters embody the same musical composition, such record shall be deemed to be a Maxi-single for the purposes of this agreement.
    (e) "Album"—A record of not less than 35 minutes of playing time. A "multiple set" consists of more than one (1) Album intended to be released, packaged and sold together for a single overall price. Multiple sets shall be deemed to be the equivalent of one (1) Album for the purposes of this agreement, but shall not be recorded or delivered hereunder without Company's prior written consent.

    What if the record consists of more than 6 masters but is less than 35 minutes in playing time? Is it an album or an EP or something different? As a practical matter, if the Artist was required to deliver an album and if the Company accepts it and releases it, it will be treated as an album.

    (f) "Records," "phonograph records," "recordings" and "sound recordings"—All forms of recording and reproduction by which sound may be recorded now known or which may hereafter become known, manufactured or sold primarily for home use, juke box use, or use on or in means of transportation, including, without limiting the foregoing, magnetic recording tape, film, electronic video recordings and any other medium or device for the production of artistic performances manufactured or sold primarily for home use, juke box use or use on or in means of transportation, whether embodying (1) sound alone or (2) sound synchronized with visual images, e.g. "sight and sound" devices.

    This is likely the definition which a person reading a recording contract for the first time would find most surprising, but it has long been established as common practice in the record industry to treat audiovisual recordings sold for home use as records. This is fundamental to the understanding of the rights and obligations prescribed by the recording contract.

    (g) "Delivery," "deliver" or "delivered"—The actual receipt by Company of completed, fully edited, mixed, leadered and equalized 1630 tapes for each configuration (e.g., compact disc, analog cassette) of all the masters comprising the applicable minimum recording commitment, commercially satisfactory in Company's opinion and ready for Company's manufacture of records, together with all materials, consents, approvals, licenses and permissions.

This is another uncommon definition, since it encompasses not only physical delivery, but also the delivery of all consents, approvals, licenses, and permissions necessary for the release of the record. This is intended to give the company remedies in the event that any such consent, etc. is never delivered, as well as to defer company's payment obligations until all such consents, etc. are delivered. This particular clause also adds the requirement that the masters be "commercially satisfactory." This is rather sneaky. It would be more straightforward for the company to state that recordings must be delivered to the company and accepted by the company. This is simply a way of hiding the requirement of acceptance. This is one example of why definitions must always be carefully read and negotiated.

(h) "Delivery Date"—The earlier of (1) the date of completion of the lacquer, copper or equivalent master to be used in the manufacture of records derived from the masters comprising the applicable minimum recording commitment, or (2) the date thirty (30) days after Company's receipt of notice from Artist that Artist has delivered the applicable masters.

This is designed to produce a certain date on which both parties can agree and rely, since the date of delivery sets the date by which the company must do certain important things, e.g., release the album and exercise its next option.

(i) "Recording Costs"—Wages, fees, advances and payments of any nature to or in respect of all musicians, vocalists, conductors, arrangers, orchestrators, engineers, producers, copyists, etc.; payments to a trustee or fund based on wages to the extent required by any agreement between Company and any labor organization or trustee; all studio, tape, editing, mixing, remixing, mastering and engineering costs; all costs of travel, per diems, rehearsal halls, nonstudio facilities and equipment, dubdown, rental and transportation of instruments; all costs occasioned by the cancellation of any scheduled recording session; and all other costs and expenses incurred in producing the master recordings hereunder which are then customarily recognized as recording costs in the recording industry.

This is a rather typical definition of recording costs, although it could be argued that mastering costs are manufacturing costs and therefore should be borne entirely by the company.

(j) "Mid-priced record"—A record which is sold by Company or its licensee(s) at a price which is below Company's or the applicable licensee's then prevailing top-line suggested retail list price, which price is consistently applied by Company to such records and which records are sold by Company or its licensee(s) as mid-priced records.

(k) "Budget record"—A record which is sold by Company or its licensee(s) at a price which is below Company's or the applicable licensee's then prevailing top-line suggested retail list price, which price is consistently applied by Company to such records and which records are sold by Company or its licensee(s) as budget records.

These definitions of "mid-priced record" and "budget record" are obviously quite vague. It is more customary to find definitions which set the price of a mid-priced record as a percentage range below the company's top-line price and of budget records as a percentage range just below mid-price. However, stating specified percentages obviously locks the company in to price points which may not work for all configurations and all territories, particularly as prices change. This approach is intended to give the company more flexibility, but could wind up leading to more frequent audit claims.

(l) "Or any other agreement"—any other agreement between Artist (or any entity furnishing the services or recordings of Artist) and Company relating to the services or recordings of Artist.

(m) References to a payment or royalty "received by Company" shall mean any such payment or royalty which is received by Company or credited (in lieu of receipt by Company) to Company's account against a previously received advance.

(n) "United States" shall mean the United States of America, its territories, possessions, and military installations wherever located.

27. Company shall have the right, at its election, to assign this agreement, and any or all of its rights and obligations hereunder, in whole or in part, to any subsidiary, affiliated, or related company or to any entity that owns or acquires a substantial portion of Company's stock or assets. Any such assignee shall likewise have the right to assign this agreement. Company shall have the unlimited right to sublicense any of its rights hereunder.

28. Provided Artist has fulfilled all of Artist's material obligations hereunder, Company hereby commit to release in the United States each Album. Company shall so release such Album during the Release Period (hereinafter defined) for such Album. In the event that Company shall not, during such Release Period, release such Album in the United States, Artist's sole remedy shall be to notify Company in writing, by certified or registered mail, return receipt requested, of such failure within sixty (60) days after the end of such Release Period, and of Artist's desire that this contract be terminated if Company does not, within sixty (60) days after Company's receipt of such notice from Artist, release such Album in the United States. In the event Company shall effect such release within such sixty (60) day period, Company shall be deemed to have released such Album during the applicable Release Period. In the event Company shall fail to effect such release within such sixty (60) day period, Company shall have no liability whatsoever to Artist in connection therewith, and this contract shall terminate as of the end of such sixty (60) day period. As used herein, the "Release Period" for a particular Album shall mean six (6) months after Artist shall deliver to Company such Album; provided, however, that in the event that the last day of such six (6) month period (such last day is sometimes referred to herein as the "Last Release Date") shall occur during the period between November 1st and December 31st of any particular year, then in no event shall Company be obligated to release any such Album prior to the third week of the following January.

This is a very typical release commitment for a new artist. It is limited to albums only; it does not provide a guaranteed release of any singles. The rationale for this is that the company has all the necessary incentive to release singles and will release them when it believes it is going to be helpful to promote the artist. Additionally, it is difficult to craft a remedy for the failure to release a single which would be fair and appropriate. On the other hand, if the company fails to release any album of the artist's recording commitment in the United States, and fails to cure that after written notice, the customary remedy is that the artist has the right to terminate the contract.

In other contracts the company will also commit to release the artist's albums in certain specified foreign countries. However, the remedy for failure to do so is not to allow the artist to terminate the agreement, but generally is to allow the artist to find a willing licensee to release the record, in which event the licensee will pay the advances and royalties to the company, which will then apply half to the artist's account. In some instances the company's failure to obtain the release of an album or albums in a particular foreign release territory will result in the loss of that territory, with the artist being able thereafter to grant the rights for that territory to a third party without the company sharing in the income therefrom.

29. This agreement sets forth the entire agreement between the parties with respect to the subject matter hereof. No modification, amendment, waiver, termination or discharge of this agreement shall be binding upon Company unless confirmed by a written instrument signed by an officer of Company. A waiver by Company of any term or condition of this agreement in any instance shall not be deemed or construed as a waiver of such term or condition for the future, or of any subsequent breach thereof. All of Company's rights, options and remedies in this agreement shall be cumulative and none of them shall be in limitation of any other remedy, option or right available to Company. Should any provision of this agreement be adjudicated by a court of competent jurisdiction as void, invalid or inoperative, such decision shall not affect any other provision hereof, and the remainder of this agreement shall be effective as though such void, invalid or inoperative provision had not been contained herein. It is agreed that all accountings and payments required herein, and all grants made herein, shall survive and continue beyond the expiration or earlier termination of this agreement. A party hereto (the "Breaching Party") shall not be in breach of any of its material obligations hereunder unless and until the other party shall have given the Breaching Party specific written notice by certified or registered mail, return receipt requested, of the nature of such breach and the Breaching Party shall have failed to cure such breach within thirty (30) days after the Breaching Party's receipt of such written notice. Notwithstanding the foregoing, nothing herein shall prevent Company from immediately seeking equitable relief to prevent Artist from breaching any provision hereof.

This paragraph encompasses a number of standard boilerplate provisions, most important of which is the cure provision. It is important that any cure provision operate reciprocally and not merely in the company's favor.

30. This agreement shall be deemed to have been made in the State of California and its validity, construction, performance and breach shall be governed by the laws of the state of California applicable to agreements made and to be wholly performed therein. Artist agrees to submit to the jurisdiction of the federal or state courts located in Los Angeles, California in any action which may arise out of this agreement and said courts shall have exclusive jurisdiction over all disputes between Company and Artist pertaining to this agreement and all matters related thereto. In this regard, any process in any action or proceeding commenced in the courts of the state of California arising out of any claim, dispute, or disagreement under this agreement may, among other

methods, be served upon Artist by delivering or mailing the same, via Registered or Certified Mail, addressed to Artist at the address provided herein for notices to Artist; any such delivery or mail service shall be deemed to have the same force and effect as personal service within the state of California. Nothing contained in this paragraph 30 shall preclude Company from joining Artist in an action brought by a third party against Company in any jurisdiction, although Company's failure to join Artist in any such action in one instance shall not constitute a waiver of any of Company's rights with respect thereto, or with respect to any subsequent action brought by a third party against Company. Nothing contained herein shall constitute a waiver of any other remedies available to Company.

This clause specifies that California law will govern the contract. Generally a record company will choose the law of a jurisdiction other than California if there is a sufficient nexus with such other jurisdiction. For example, if the company is located in New York and California, it will always choose New York law to govern its contracts, since California law has certain provisions, e.g., the guaranteed compensation requirement and the seven-year limit on personal services contracts, which are more favorable to the artist than the laws of other jurisdictions such as New York.

This clause also contains an exclusive jurisdiction and venue clause, which is designed to ensure that all legal proceedings are conducted in the company's home state. Again, where the company has offices outside California, this is generally insisted on by the company in order to avoid the prospect of the artist bringing suit in California, which is viewed as pro-artist and unpredictable.

31. This agreement shall not become effective until it is executed by all parties.
IN WITNESS WHEREOF, the parties hereto have executed this agreement on the day and year first above written.

AGREED TO AND ACCEPTED:

_____   _____
(ARTIST)   (LABEL RECORDS, INC.)

_____   _____
ADDRESS   ADDRESS

_____   _____
FEDERAL I.D. / SS#   FEDERAL I.D. / SS#

How To Read and Evaluate Your Artist Royalty Statements

by John R. Phillips

Suppose you are a newly successful artist with a hit album on your hands. In August, *Billboard* shows your album has gone "gold," which means "…sales of 500,000 units or more." In early October you receive your first royalty statement, which, when you finally distinguish between the album and the single with the same name, seems to add up to only about 100,000 units. Have you been taken? Probably not.

EXAMPLE OF GOLD ALBUM VS. REPORTABLE UNITS

Release Date	January 15, 199X
Certification Date	September 15, 199X
Certified Units	500,200
Record Club Distribution	(99,950)
Record Company Distribution	400,250
Standard Free Goods – 15%	(60,038)
Special Program Free Goods – 10%	(34,021)
90% Unit Base Adjustment	(30,619)
30% Reserve Adjustment	(82,672)
Units Distributed After June 30	(89,250)
Units Reported On June 30, 199X Statement	103,650

DISCREPANCIES? DON'T PANIC

First of all, the 500,000 unit criterion probably includes sales plan and special program free goods that can range from 15% to 25% of the units counted for certification, although royalties by agreement are not normally paid on them. Additionally, gold album criteria include record club sales, bonus and free units (if the album has been out long enough), which may be communicated from the club to the record company for certification purposes well before the record club remits the money due on the sales. Even then, all or at least a portion of the club bonus and free units are usually royalty free by your negotiated contract. Also by agreement, your royalties may only be payable on a percentage of net sales, say 85% or 90%. Usually these "royalty reducers" are offset by a royalty rate higher than a record company would pay in their absence. Your contract may also allow a reserve for returns in calculating royalties, which can amount to 25% or more. You will eventually receive royalties on units in reserve to the extent returns do not deplete them. Lastly, don't forget, some of the 500,000 units could be from the period between your royalty statement period end, for example June 30th, and the *Billboard* edition in September.

Don't fret. Now that you are a star, you can command a better deal in the future—if you keep working hard!

Similar situations can occur with the reporting of royalties on your foreign sales. Suppose a friend from London has told you what a megahit your album is there, only for you to find zero royalties for the United Kingdom. The problem is probably a matter of time lag. The English affiliate or licensee record company has a normal accounting period to accumulate, process and report the sales and royalties to your record company in the U.S., which should report them on your next statement.

ARTIST ROYALTY STATEMENT FORMAT

Not only are each record company's royalty statements different, but the royalty statements of the individual labels of a record company group, may differ. Often, preceding the details may be a summary of the various types of earnings, including domestic, which may or may not include Canada, domestic licensee sales such as record clubs, and foreign licensee sales, (who may actually be affiliates). Additionally, the summary will often give the previous statement balance and payment, if any, reserves currently held and prior reserves released, recording costs and advances deducted, charges, including session costs, video costs, producer royalty deductions, miscellaneous adjustments and an ending balance.

DOMESTIC ROYALTIES

The common thread among record companies in reporting domestic royalties is the presentation of at least selections, units, royalty rates and amounts. The selections, or titles, are usually identified by a number and the title. Presently, the two primary configurations of an album, i.e., compact disc (CD) and cassette tape (often abbreviated to TC, CT, CA or MC—we will use TC for our example record company), are usually identified by the addition of a prefix or suffix letter or number, for example 2 = CD, and 4 = TC. Seven-inch 45 RPM singles may be identified by a 7 prefix. Or, a "CFG," configuration code, may be given, for example, S3 for a CD three-inch single. Generally you can tell the difference between the product by the royalty cent rate. For example, the CD might have the highest rate to correspond with the highest price. 45s generally have the lowest rate. To confuse things, however, there may be 12-inch vinyl singles, CD singles and cassette singles, in between. Ultimately, your record company may have to be consulted to identify some or all of the selections, particularly if titles are not given.

As mentioned previously, the record companies differ widely in their representation of data. Some, for example, Record Company X (RCX) disclose all the elements used to calculate royalties for normal domestic sales, i.e., catalog number, title description, configuration code, royalty percentage rate, packaging deduction percentage, the suggested retail list price (SRLP), royalty cent rate, quantity base (if other than 100%), quantity of royalty units, royalty amount for each configuration and a total for the catalog number. Since it would be beyond the intended scope of this article to cover all the variations between record companies, we will utilize RCX as an example for further discussion. To calculate your royalty in this case, you multiply the SRLP, e.g., $10.98 by the reciprocal of the packaging percentage, i.e., $1.05408 which would be rounded to $1.0541. This cent rate multiplied by the number of units gives the royalty amount.

Simple? Not exactly, as you will see.

Prices

RCX, our example record company, negotiates contractually to pay royalties on the suggested retail list price basis. Other companies may use a wholesale basis, or variation thereof.

In the early part of 1995, for new releases by superstars, RCX's prices (SRLPs) for full priced normal retail channel sales were $16.98 for CDs and $10.98 for TCs. For newer artists, special genre, and some catalog releases the price might be $15.98 and $9.98 for CDs and TCs respectively. Twelve-inch singles usually are priced at $4.98, CD singles at $4.98, cassette singles at $3.49 and 45s at $1.99. Most albums are currently being released only on TC and CD. However, vinyl discs, DCCs, mini discs and CD ROM versions may be released depending on market strategy. For new product configurations the contract may provide that your royalties are based on the cassette price. If you have some older releases you may see them at mid price, such as $11.98 for CDs and $6.98 or $7.98 for TCs.

Military sales through post exchanges (PXs) and ship's stores, etc., have lower list prices, generally $11.95 for CDs and $7.95 for TCs.

Price changes should be properly reflected in your royalties. Suppose, unlike RCX which retains a "dollar" reserve for returns, a record company has held a "unit" reserve on your first album. Two years, and two albums later, the first album is reduced to mid price. Any reserves still held on the first album relating to sales at the higher price should be reported at the higher royalty than the current mid price sales. For another illustration, assume all TCs go from $9.98 to $10.98, or from $10.98 to an $11.98 price. To the extent that there are any returns after the price increase that relate to sales at the old price they should be segregated and charged back at the old, lower royalty rate.

Packaging Deductions

Packaging allowances are customarily deducted to arrive at a royalty base price on which your royalty percentage rate is applied. Generally, they are 20% for TCs and 25% for CDs. Your agreement may allow a 10% packaging deduction for seven-inch and 12-inch vinyl singles in four color sleeves, 20% for cassette singles and 25% for CD singles. You may, as has been common, have agreed to be paid royalties for CDs or other new formats on a black vinyl disc LP or equivalent TC basis for a certain time period. In that case, usually the 25% CD packaging is superseded by a provision for the same cent rate to be paid as for the LP or TC.

Royalty Percentage

Typically, for the progressive albums of your commitment there are higher rates. There may also be increases of royalty percentage rates, or "escalations," for reaching plateaus of sales levels. Suppose your album came out and within the first six month royalty statement period 600,000 units were reported. Assume an escalation from 12% to 13% was required by your contract at 500,000 units. Suppose further that the sales were equally distributed between TCs and CDs, i.e., 300,000 of each. So, in our example, 50,000 units of each should receive 1% more, i.e.,

$$\text{CDs: } \$15.98 \times 75\% \times 1\% = \$.1199 \times 50{,}000 = \$5{,}995$$
$$\text{TCs: } \$8.98 \times 80\% \times 1\% = \$.0718 \times \underline{50{,}000} = \underline{3{,}590}$$
$$100{,}000 \qquad \$9{,}585$$

However, record companies often claim that their systems are not capable of pro-rating unit sales between the different configurations. Therefore, one configuration is counted first and only the last one would fall over the plateau and get the entire escalation. For example:

TCs: $.0718 x 100,000 = $7,180

If this was the case, since TCs have a lower base price, you would have been underpaid by $2,405.

Your agreements may also allow the record company royalty relief for albums sold at mid prices. For example, by contract you may receive 75% of your normal royalty rate for albums sold at SRLPs between 66.6% and 80% of the normal full price. Obviously, $7.98 divided by $9.98 equals 79.96% and therefore qualifies. However, if your contract defines mid price as between 66.6% and 75%, it would not qualify. In that case you should have received your full royalty percentage rate.

Your agreement may also state that your approval must be obtained for mid pricing, or that a certain amount of time must have passed since the initial full priced release.

PX sales are often paid at a reduced royalty percentage rate, as are singles, record club and foreign sales. You need to summarize the differing percentages from your contract and compare them to what is shown on the statement. For record companies where just a cent rate is presented, it is more difficult to check. In this case knowing your contractual royalty percentage rate and packaging percentage, you can check if the price is reasonable. For example, your agreement specifies a 12% rate and 20% packaging for the TC version of your album. Your royalty statement simply shows a royalty cent rate of $1.0541. However, $1.0541 divided by 12%, divided by 80% (100% less the 20% packaging allowance) equals $10.98 and seems reasonable. If it does not work out, you question why. Perhaps the producer's royalty is being paid directly from the record company and deducted from yours.

Quantity

Since only net units payable are usually shown on the statements, not much can be done to check the quantities reported without access to the record company's internal records. Primarily, you can check reasonableness and make inquiries about an omission of product you know is out in the market. Considering all possible reasons, if quantities still appear too low, you may want to consider a royalty examination by professionals.

Record Club and Other Domestic Licensees

Our example record company, RCX, gives details of the U.S. Record Club reportings amongst its foreign detail. Often artists receive one-half of receipts from the club as their share of royalties. Sometimes you might notice a record club name, i.e., BMG, followed by F/G. This is most likely your one-half share of the record club's reporting of excess bonus and free units distributed, usually made at the end of a contract period, often three years or more. If you do not have a percentage of receipts club provision you should check if your agreement allows club royalties to be paid on less than 100% of net sales. Often clubs pay on a reduced unit basis, for example 85%.

A special product licensing arrangement may also have occurred for which you are receiving a 50% of receipts royalty. These are compilation albums, which usually have an intense media advertising campaign and a short life. Normally the royalties are prorated among the tracks included based on their share of the total number of tracks. If artist approval was required by your contract you have a means of checking for unreported product. However, the approval may have been obtained and then the track may not have been included or the product never released. Royalty examination groups, like the one the author leads, subscribe to *Phonolog* to be able to tell what product is out in the market. However, most large record stores have copies you can look at.

FOREIGN ROYALTIES

Record companies vary widely in their presentation of foreign royalties. While some simply report an amount due you for each territory, our example record company, RCX, gives a substantial amount of detail. However, even RCX shows only a U.S. dollar equivalent base price i.e., the local currency suggested retail list price or constructed price if there is no SRLP, has already been reduced by taxes and packaging allowances and a conversion rate has been applied. The conversion rate may have been adjusted for withholding taxes in the territory. All these actions are probably permitted by your contract. However, you cannot tell if they have been done correctly. For example, to "construct" the retail price, the foreign dealer price may have been incorrectly marked up or not marked up at all. The local territory's copyright royalty collection organization, upon whose requirements the constructed price may be based, has probably long ago negotiated for a mechanical royalty based directly on the dealer price, called the PPD (published price to dealers). The taxes deducted may also be incorrect. Suppose you received a royalty based on wholesale (dealer) prices and the foreign tax was calculated applying the correct percentage incorrectly to a price including taxes. The packaging deductions made may also have been conformed to the local copyright society's allowances, which may differ from your agreement.

Unfortunately, it would require prohibitively detailed statements to give all the necessary information to check all of these concerns. Once again, however, you can check for reasonableness and inquire about what looks really odd. For example, if you are now supposed to be paid on the SRLP for CDs you should see the premium CD price being reflected in foreign territories as well, unless you agreed otherwise. Prices generally are higher in foreign territories, so you should not normally see a significant number of your albums being sold at an equivalent U.S. price that is notably lower than on your domestic sales. However, it could be a territory that has runaway inflation. It may also be your older album(s) being mid or budget priced, if allowable. To test for reasonableness you should see if the older album(s), if any, which is being reported at the contractually reduced mid-price rate fits the price criterion required. It should not be reported, for example, at a price that is 90% of the full priced latest album.

You can also check that the rates specified in your contract are being correctly utilized in reporting. If you are to receive 75% of your normal 12% domestic rate for major foreign territories you would expect to see 9% for the U.K., Germany, etc., as major is defined in your agreement. Also, if your recordings are generally successful overseas, you might want to inquire into significant missing territories for any of your selections.

PREVIOUS STATEMENT BALANCE

Surprisingly, sometimes the amount labeled "Previous Balance Forward" on your current statement does not agree with the balance on the previous statement. Perhaps an undetailed adjustment has been made, which should be queried.

Payment dates for the statement balance are usually contractually specified, usually within 60 or 90 days of the royalty statement period end. If you are receiving payment directly, no doubt you will notice a delinquency. If payment goes to your business manager, and you expect it to be substantial, there is no harm in checking if it has been received. Usually the large record companies are quite reliable in getting their statements and payments out.

RESERVES

A record company can withhold the normally allowed reserve for returns and credits in two ways—in units or in dollars. In the former instance you may or may not see the reserve quantities on your royalty statement. If not, you should request and your record company should easily supply this information, at least for domestic sales.

Sometimes record companies may withhold a percentage of "royalties otherwise payable…" as a reserve. This will usually be shown on the royalty statement. Your contract may limit the percentage of allowable reserves and specify a time schedule for release. With the necessary information at hand, you can readily see if the limits are being exceeded, or that the release schedule is not being adhered to.

Many contracts permit the record company to hold "reasonable" reserves in their best business judgment. If you are a new artist and they have pushed your product out into the stores, you can expect a high reserve percentage. About all you can do is reason with them for a reduction. Perhaps you're about to deliver another album. Also, if you have several releases that are cross-collateralized, i.e., negative royalties from net returns on one are offset against positive royalties otherwise payable on another, there is a good deal less justification for a high reserve percentage. High reserves on foreign royalties are a possibly objectionable area as well. Returns are not as readily accepted overseas. Normally, 5% to 10% is the maximum actually accepted. If reserves have been held in a foreign territory, the domestic record company has no reason to hold reserves on the same income.

ARTIST ROYALTY STATEMENT
EXAMPLE OF A SUMMARY

Period 07/01/9X to 12/31/9X

Balance Forward	$467,246.00
Royalty Payments	(467,246.00)
Prior Reserves Held	116,812.00
Beginning Balance	**$116,812.00**

Earnings

Domestic Sales	$1,302,298.44
Military Sales	49,306.20
Licensee Sales	478,969.62
Licensee Club Sales	7,043.74
Licensee Miscellaneous Sales	1,250.00
Total Earnings	**$1,838,868.00**

Charges

Advances	($300,000.00)
Session Charges	(348,790.18)
Miscellaneous Charges	(94,512.88)
Total Charges	**($743,303.06)**
Reserves	(487,430.72)
Balance Payable	$724,946.22
Producer Deduction (Album #2)	(289,366.00)
Ending Balance Payable	**$435,580.22**

CHARGES AGAINST ROYALTIES

Session charges, other recording costs and advances are usually the largest charges on your royalty statements, at least on your initial royalty statement. Combined with producer fees and advances and some miscellaneous charges, these elements usually make up a recording fund as defined in your agreement.

It is important to remember that typically, record companies desire to foster artists' good will by cooperating and providing explanations and reasonable support for any significant charges you have questions about. The amount of details involved with sessions will prohibit total disclosure in your royalty statement. If any detail is given on sessions, it is likely to be invoice dates, descriptions, maybe just the vendor name and amounts. Presuming you have been in the studio recently, about all you can do with this information is to look for familiar company and individual names.

The record company is normally contractually allowed to charge all recording costs up to the point where the recording is ready for manufacture. Thus, sometimes you will note remix costs for example, for a 12-inch single, or remastering costs, for an old album being readied for release on CD. When you see these types of charges, you should expect to see some new product released soon after the date charged.

Also you may notice miscellaneous charges for hotels and per diems, limos, gold record copies, etc. Despite the erroneous assumption that sometimes these items are being given free, it is normal for them to be charged against your royalties. Normally, you can only prevail on something that was not in your control, unless your contract specifically states otherwise.

The recording fund for your album may, after the first album, be based on the results of your previous album. For example, your agreement may say that the current recording fund will amount to 66.6% of the net royalties earned on the last album. Producer fees and advances, along with the recording costs and your advances, will normally equal the current fund, i.e., the delivery advance will be adjusted to make it so.

Videos, because of their high cost and modest independent earning power in the past, have developed their own customary treatment. Typically, 50% of the cost is chargeable against your royalties from audio recordings. You should be aware of the budget and check that no more than 50% is charged to your royalty account, unless contractually permitted.

Currently, even with commercially exploited video for home viewing, it is not unusual for the video earnings to be less than production costs. However, you might check if your contract allows your record company to apply 100% of earnings to the 50% share of costs not charged to you. In other words, the earnings, however modest, should be shared fifty-fifty from the first dollar unless the contract allows the record company to first recoup their share. Additionally, as MTV, VH1, etc., revenues increase, you may question how the record company distributes the earnings between the videos submitted. For example, some record companies may receive large catalog guarantee advances periodically, with no identification of the airplay of individual videos. Therefore, they may simply apportion a share equally to all videos submitted, which would be detrimental to you if your's received a great deal of airplay.

Producer Royalty Deductions

Producer royalty deductions are shown on your statement in one of three ways: (1) the producer's royalty cent rate may be deducted from yours and just a net rate shown; (2)

the producer deduction is shown by a repetition of a line showing the unit sales, etc., but using the negative producer cent rate to calculate the amount to be deducted; or (3) the total producer royalties payable could be deducted in a lump sum on the summary page. In the last case, you should request a copy of the producer's statement, which gives the details of the calculation. You will want to check that the producer is not being paid a higher rate than appropriate.

Also there is the concern as to when the producer royalty starts to be payable. You need to consult your agreement as to whether the producer royalty should commence only when your account is recouped and whether the costs and advances should be recouped at rates inclusive or exclusive of the producer's rate. Also, check whether the producer is then paid from record one, or just after recoupment. In addition, if the producer has received an advance charged to you, then you should not see any producer deductions until his advance is recouped from his royalties. At that point, only royalties in excess of his advance, should be deducted from yours.

Miscellaneous Adjustments

After receiving more than one royalty statement, you may notice adjustments on the current statement correcting errors made by the record company on previous statements rendered. If, for example, a rate is being corrected, you should be able to see that the applicable quantities adjusted agree with those on your previous statement. Analyzing your rate, as discussed previously, should reveal if the correction is appropriate.

Another adjustment you may notice, if you write songs as well, may be for the deduction of "excess mechanicals." Your recording agreement may provide in a "controlled composition" clause that, for example, your artist royalties may be charged for the excess of mechanical royalties the record company must pay over ten times 75% of the minimum statutory rate at time of release of the album. In other words, if you have cowritten one or more songs with individuals not in your recording group, and you have ten songs on the album, you are likely to be charged "excess mechanicals." This is because it is likely that the outsider will have to be paid at the full statutory rate. This calculation can be complicated by multiple cowritten songs, statutory rate changes, and escalations of the maximum based on reaching sales levels. It may be best to simply request the record company to provide support for their calculation.

There may also be charges for costs of special packaging or artwork, which exceed contractually allowed amounts.

Royalty Examinations

If you have applied all of the procedures discussed herein, you have gained some satisfying comfort that your royalty statements contain no glaring improprieties, or you are contemplating a royalty examination. If an examination appears warranted, and routine periodic examinations are usually warranted after several releases/royalty statements, you should consult your contract concerning any limitation on the time period to object to your statements. Record companies normally put a great deal of effort into making timely and accurate royalty accountings. However, errors do occur and contracts often contain language that can be interpreted in various ways.

When we review artist royalty statements on behalf of clients, we ask ourselves the same questions and apply the same procedures heretofore described. However, we often find that the royalty statements do not supply enough information. To get satisfied, we need to actually see the details available only at the record company and we try to impress upon them the urgency of our information requests.

Royalty examinations, if preceded by the thorough analysis suggested, usually have cash benefits that exceed the cost. They just make good business sense. Otherwise you may never know the record company has, for example, exceeded the contractual limit of nonroyalty bearing free goods, has not reported a share of income received from a licensee, or has not correctly applied a value-added tax in calculating royalties on foreign sales.

ARTIST ROYALTY STATEMENT
EXAMPLE OF DETAIL OF DOMESTIC EARNINGS

Period 07/01/9X to 12/31/9X

LABEL	CATALOG NUMBER	DESCRIPTION	CFG	ROY%	PACK%	SRLP	$RATE	QUANTITY	AMOUNT	NET PAYABLE
RCX	010001	Single #1	SS	12.0000		$1.99	0.2388	2,421	$578.13	
RCX	010001	Single #1 - Producer	SS	-3.0000		1.99	-0.0597	2,421	(144.53)	
RCX	010001	Single #1	S3	12.0000	25.00	4.98	0.4482	3,631	1,627.41	
RCX	010001	Single #1 - Producer	S3	-3.0000	25.00	4.98	-0.1121	3,631	(406.85)	
RCX	010001	Single #1	TC	12.0000	20.00	3.49	0.3350	12,106	4,055.99	
RCX	010001	Single #1 - Producer	TC	-3.0000	20.00	3.49	-0.0838	12,106	(1,014.00)	$4,696.15
RCX	010002	Single #2	SS	12.0000		1.99	0.2388	37,573	8,972.43	
RCX	010002	Single #2	S3	12.0000	25.00	4.98	0.4482	56,374	25,266.83	
RCX	010002	Single #2	TC	12.0000	20.00	3.49	0.3350	187,921	62,961.05	97,200.31
RCX	020001	Album #1	AQ	12.0000	25.00	15.98	1.4382	12,106	17,410.85	
RCX	020001	Album #1 - Producer	AQ	-3.0000	25.00	15.98	-0.3596	12,106	(4,352.71)	
RCX	020001	Album #1	TC	12.0000	20.00	10.98	1.0541	6,052	6,379.29	
RCX	020001	Album #1 - Producer	TC	-3.0000	20.00	10.98	-0.2635	6,052	(1,594.82)	17,842.61
RCX	020002	Album #2	AQ	12.0000	25.00	16.98	1.5282	515,884	788,373.93	
RCX	020002	Album #2	TC	12.0000	25.00	16.98	1.5282	257,941	394,185.44	1,182,559.37

| | | | | | | | | TOTAL DOMESTIC SALES | | $1,302,298.44 |

ANALYSIS OF A RECORD PRODUCER AGREEMENT

by Linda A. Newmark

The record producer is one of the most important individuals involved in creating recordings. Certain producers are sought out by recording artists because they believe that the producer can assist them in creating the sound that will help them achieve record sales at platinum or multiplatinum levels.

This article focuses upon the situation in which the producer is engaged to produce a master recording for use on an album by an artist who already has a recording agreement with a record company.

PRODUCER COMPENSATION

The producer of master recordings, for an artist with a record deal, generally receives an advance that is recoupable from future royalties. Generally, the artist's recording agreement with the record company will provide that the artist receives an "all-in" royalty on net sales of the artist's records. However, in certain genres, such as country music, the recording agreement may provide for the artist to receive a net artist royalty, with no payment obligations to the producer. An all-in royalty means that the artist must pay the producer out of the artist's royalty. In most cases, the record company will agree to pay the producer directly, after receiving a "letter of direction" from the artist requesting it to do so. Thus, if the artist's all-in royalty rate is 12% of the retail selling price (after deduction of a packaging charge) on net sales of records sold through normal retail channels in the United States, and the producer's royalty rate on such sales is 3% of the retail price (with appropriate reductions), the royalty rate that the artist is really entitled to is 9% of the retail price. However, the artist and the producer must both bear in mind that they will not receive royalties from the moment the first record is shipped from the record company to the record store (or other purchaser). The record company only pays royalties on "net sales," which are some portion of the records that are sold and not returned, with no royalties payable on "free goods." (See the chapter "Analysis of a Recording Contract" for an explanation of free goods.) Furthermore, the artist and the producer will not receive royalties until they have recouped recording costs and advances from the royalties earned in connection with the sales of records embodying the relevant master recordings. The artist and the producer will have to recoup different sums at different royalty rates. The concept of recoupment for record producers is discussed below in paragraph 6 of the sample "Producer Agreement."

WHO CHOOSES THE PRODUCER?

Generally, when an artist receives an all-in royalty, the recording agreement will specify that the artist is responsible for engaging the producer; however, the record company usually retains the ultimate control over determining which producer will be engaged. The artist's attorney should always attempt to obtain the right for the artist to approve the producer. Nevertheless, recording agreements for new artists generally provide that the record company and the artist will mutually approve the producer and if the record company and the artist disagree, the record company's decision will prevail. As the artist becomes more successful, the record company will probably allow the artist to have more control over creative decisions, including the selection of a producer.

In some cases, a producer who is on the staff of the record company will produce the album. Many recording agreements contain provisions relating to the minimum compensation (usually $1,500 per master or $15,000 per album and a 3% of retail royalty) that would be payable if the record company's staff producer produces any master recordings for the artist. The artist's attorney should require that a provision be included in the recording agreement stating that a staff producer can only be engaged with the artist's consent and that the advances and royalties that are payable to the staff producer will be prorated if there are coproducers on the master recordings or if there are other master recordings on the album that are produced by someone else.

When the producer is not an employee of the record company and is not the artist, a producer agreement is prepared, either by the artist's attorney or by the record company. The producer agreement provided below was prepared by an attorney for a record company. With slight modifications, it could easily be an agreement between an artist and a producer.

Since most producer agreements favor the artist or the record company, I will review the provisions of the following agreement from the perspective of the attorney who is negotiating on behalf of the producer.

PRODUCER AGREEMENT

The subject matter of this Agreement is your services to us as the producer of _____ (insert #) master recording(s) ("Master(s)") embodying performances by _____ ("Artist"). You and we agree as follows:

1. The term of this Agreement ("Term") shall commence as of the date hereof and shall continue until the Master(s) are completed to our satisfaction and delivered to us or until we terminate the Term upon written notice to you. During the Term, you shall render your services as the producer of the Master(s) in cooperation with us and Artist, at times and places designated or approved in writing by us. You shall produce the Master(s), and you shall deliver the Master(s) to us or our designee promptly after the Master(s) are completed. All elements for the creation and production of the Master(s), including, without limitation, the compositions to be recorded in the Master(s) and other individuals rendering services in connection with the production of the Master(s), shall be designated or approved by us in writing. We shall pay or cause to be paid all costs to produce and record the Master(s) in an amount not to exceed a recording budget therefor, which is designated or approved by us in writing. If the costs to produce and record the Master(s) exceed the recording budget for reasons within your control or which you could have avoided, then you shall, upon our demand, pay to us the amount of those excess costs, and we may, at our election, deduct the amount of those costs from any royalties or other monies payable to you under this Agreement.

> *The agreement should contain a more definite completion standard than "completed to our satisfaction." The producer's attorney should attempt to obtain a "technically satisfactory" delivery standard (i.e., the masters must be of suitable sound quality from a sound engineer's perspective); however, if (as most current recording agreements provide) the artist's recording agreement contains a "technically and commercially satisfactory" delivery standard, the artist's or record company's attorney should not provide a more favorable provision to the producer than "until the completion of technically and commercially satisfactory Masters as determined by the record company."*
>
> *Generally, the artist and/or record company will retain a right of approval over the elements for the creation and production of the masters. If the producer intends to use his or her own studio, a statement that the studio is approved for recording the masters should be included in the agreement to avoid any doubt about what studio will be used. The titles of the musical compositions to be recorded, if known, should be included as well.*
>
> *This agreement provides that the record company will pay the recording costs. (In some instances the producer's agreement provides that the producer will receive an all-in advance, which is a lump sum that may be paid in two or three installments during the recording of the masters, which includes the money to pay the recording costs and the producer's advance.)*
>
> *The producer should be certain to find out the amount available to record the masters before agreeing to take on the project. If the recording costs for the masters exceed the amount of the authorized budget, those excess costs may be charged against monies payable to the producer and; accordingly, the producer could lose part of the advance or be delayed or prevented from receiving royalties.*

Many agreements provide that any excess recording costs will constitute a direct debt from the producer to the artist or record company, which must be repaid on demand. The producer's attorney should attempt to delete the record company's and artist's right to direct repayment from the producer and should limit the rights of recovery to the excess costs caused only by situations that were within the producer's control. And those excess costs should be recoverable from any royalties or advances payable to the producer under the specific agreement. In any event, the producer should know at the beginning of the project how much money is available to record the masters and should bear that figure in mind while working. Although the record company may pay excess recording costs, the producer should make every effort to complete the masters within the originally approved budget.

2. From the inception of the recording of the Master(s), we shall own the entire worldwide right, title and interest, including, without limitation, the copyright, in and to the Master(s), the performances embodied therein and the results and proceeds of your services hereunder, as our employee for hire for all purposes of the applicable copyright laws, free of any claims by you or any person, firm or corporation. Alternatively, you grant to us the entire worldwide right, title and interest derived from you, including, without limitation, the copyright, in and to the Master(s).

This language is very standard in producer agreements and would not be subject to negotiation by the producer's attorney. The artist and record company want the masters created by the producer to be works made for hire as defined in the United States Copyright Act of 1976. The benefit to the artist and record company of this is the creator of a work made for hire has no right to terminate the transfer of the work and reacquire the copyright at a later date. Nevertheless, since there is some question as to whether the masters that are created as the result of the producer's services qualify as works made for hire, the agreement also contains language stating that the producer grants all rights in the masters to the artist or record company. To protect the artist's or record company's interests better, this agreement should state that the last sentence of paragraph 2 would apply only if the masters were determined not to be works made for hire.

If the producer wrote all or part of any of the compositions embodied in the masters, they should be excluded from the provisions of paragraph 2.

3. You hereby grant to us and our designees the worldwide right in perpetuity to use and to permit others to use, at no cost, your name, likeness and biographical material concerning you in connection with any and all phonograph records and other reproductions made from the Master(s), the advertising in connection therewith and institutional advertising. We shall accord you appropriate production credit on the jackets, labels or liner notes of all records embodying the Master(s), which you agree may be in substantially the following form: "Produced by _____." Any failure to comply with the provisions of this paragraph shall not be a breach of this Agreement. Your sole right and remedy in that event shall be to notify us of that failure, after which we shall use reasonable efforts to accord that production credit to you on records manufactured after the date we receive that notice.

The producer should have a right of approval over all photographs, likenesses and biographical material concerning him or her that is used under this paragraph.

"Institutional advertising" should be limited to the record company's institutional advertising. Producer credit should be placed on all record labels and on jackets or liner notes on all records in all configurations (including compact disc and tape packaging). The producer should receive credit in all one-half page or larger trade and consumer advertisements featuring a master produced by the producer. The producer's attorney should attempt to obtain a provision relating to credit so that the producer's credit will be of similar size and placement as any other producer's credit on the album and will appear in advertising relating to the album if another producer is credited (unless the advertisement features a master that is produced by another producer). The agreement should state that the credit will be in the following form: "_____," not "may be in substantially the following form."

The failure to provide the credit should not be a material breach of the agreement provided that the record company and/or artist uses its best efforts to cure the failure on records (in all configurations) manufactured after receipt of the notice of the failure from the producer and in advertisements authorized after the receipt of such notice.

4. In full consideration for your entering into and executing this Agreement and your fulfilling all of your obligations hereunder, you shall be paid _____ Dollars ($_____), payable one-half (1/2) promptly after the later of the execution of this Agreement or the commencement of recording sessions for the Master(s) and one-half (1/2) promptly after the later of the completion and delivery to us of all Master(s) or our determination of the aggregate costs to record the Master(s). Those monies payable to you shall be an advance recoupable from royalties earned by you hereunder.

The producer's attorney may wish to delete the word "full" in the first sentence since the possibility of the producer receiving royalties under the agreement is also consideration to the producer. ("Consideration" is a legal concept that requires that in order for a contract to be binding upon the parties, one party must give or do something of value in exchange for receiving something of value from the other party.) Additionally, the word "material" should be added before the word "obligations" because the producer should still receive his or her advance even if there is some kind of failure to fulfill a minor, nonmaterial obligation under the agreement. The agreement should specify that the advance is nonreturnable once it is paid.

The amount of the advance is based upon the experience and reputation of the producer. The advance for a single master is, generally, not less than $1,000, and is more commonly about $3,000. An advance of $5,000 to $7,500 is a good advance for an established producer. Of course, there are always exceptions, with a few superstar producers receiving $10,000, $15,000 or more (depending on their status and the status of the artist). As mentioned previously, this agreement presents the situation where the record company pays the recording costs and pays a separate advance to the producer. In the all-in advance situation, the producer would receive a sum of money from which the recording costs would be paid and any remaining monies would be retained by the producer. This works best for a producer who has his or her own studio and can keep recording costs down. But, in this case, the producer may have a real need to obtain the advance monies more quickly than as set forth in this agreement.

One method of payment of the all-in advance could be one-half upon the commencement of recording, one-fourth upon the producer's delivery of a rough mix of the *master, and one-fourth upon delivery of the completed master. A typical all-in advance for producing a master for a new pop artist on a major label is $12,000 to $15,000 (or more). A more established producer producing an established artist might receive an all-in advance of $20,000 to $25,000 (or more).*

The producer's attorney should try to limit the time that the artist or the record company has to determine the aggregate costs to record the masters to no more than 30 days after delivery. I am aware of at least one situation where a record was released and on the charts for several months and the record company's attorney still claimed that the recording costs had not yet been determined, notwithstanding the fact that all recording was conducted in the artist's own studio.

5. Conditioned upon your full and faithful performance of all the terms hereof, you shall be paid a royalty on reproductions and exploitations of the Master(s) at the following rates in accordance with the following terms:

The word "material" should be inserted before the word "terms" in the first sentence of this paragraph. The producer should request to be paid directly from the record company rather than from the artist. The artist should sign a letter of direction to that effect, which would be attached to the agreement as an exhibit.

(a) (i) On sales of full-priced, top-line long-playing phonograph records embodying solely Master(s) (in the form of conventional vinyl-discs and cassette tapes), which are sold through normal retail distribution channels in the United States ("Base Rate") of _____ percent (___%) of the suggested retail list price ("SRLP") of those Base Rate Records (or the equivalent). Your Base Rate on Base Rate Records shall be prorated, calculated, adjusted and paid on the same percentage of net sales of Base Rate Records as Artist's royalty rate on sales of Base Rate Records is prorated, calculated, adjusted and paid under the recording agreement between us and Artist ("Artist Agreement"). On sales in and outside of the United States of all records other than Base Rate Records, you shall be paid a royalty at a rate equal to the Base Rate but which is prorated, calculated, proportionately reduced, adjusted and paid on the same percentage of net sales as Artist's base royalty rate on sales of Base Rate Records is prorated, calculated, proportionately reduced, adjusted and paid under the Artist Agreement; and

A producer royalty rate generally ranges between 2% and 4% of the suggested retail list price of Base Rate Records (as defined in the producer agreement), with a few top producers receiving 5%. A typical royalty rate to a producer is 3% of the retail price of records. If two producers coproduce a master they might each receive a royalty at the rate of 1-1/2% or 2% of the retail price of records embodying the master. If the artist's royalty is computed on the basis of the wholesale price of records, rather than the retail price, then the producer's royalty would be computed based on the wholesale price of records. In that event, the producer's royalty rate would be approximately double (e.g., approximately 6% of wholesale rather than 3% of retail). Many producers receive increased royalties if the record they produce sells a certain number of units. A typical royalty rate structure is a 3% of retail royalty rate escalating to 3-1/2% on all sales in excess of 500,000 units and escalating to 4% on all sales in excess of 1,000,000 units.

The producer's royalty is generally paid on the same basis as the artist's. In the situation where the artist has a recording agreement with a production company and the production company has an agreement with the record company whereby it agrees to provide the artist's services to the record company, the producer's attorney should attempt to have the producer's royalty paid on the same basis as the production company's. Note that this agreement states that the producer's royalty is to be prorated on the same basis as the artist's royalty—this is not technically correct: the producer's royalty is prorated based on the number of masters produced by the producer that are on the particular record, and the artist's royalty is prorated based upon the number of masters recorded by the artist on the record. For example, if the producer produced five of 10 masters on Artist A's most recent album and the producer's basic royalty rate was 3% of the retail price of records comprised entirely of masters produced by the producer, the producer's royalty on Artist A's album would be reduced from 3% to 1-1/2% because the producer only produced half of the masters. The artist's royalty rate would not be reduced in this fashion since the entire album was comprised of masters embodying the artist's performance.

Many established producers obtain a special exception to one of the proration provisions in their producer agreements. This is known as "A-side protection" and it applies only to singles where the A-side is produced by one producer and the B-side is produced by another. When a producer who does not have A-side protection produces only the A-side of a single, that producer's royalty rate is cut in half. The producer with A-side protection does not receive this royalty rate reduction on singles where that producer's master appears on only the A-side, because the vast majority of people who buy a single do so because of the A-side. Since few people buy a single for the B-side, the theory is that the royalty of the producer of the A-side should not be reduced because of the B-side. In most instances, the producer of the B-side of a single would still be entitled to a prorated royalty on the B-side of the single, even if the producer of the A-side of the single has A-side protection.

(ii) On exploitations of the Master(s) for which Artist is paid a percentage of our net royalty or net flat fees under the Artist Agreement, you shall be paid a royalty equal to _____ percent (_____%) of our net flat fees or net royalties on such exploitations. On exploitations of the Master(s) embodied in audiovisual devices (such as videodiscs and videocassettes), however, you shall be paid a royalty equal to _____ percent (_____%) of our net flat fees or net royalties on those exploitations;

When the artist is paid based on a percentage of the record company's net royalty or net flat fee, then the producer should be paid a percentage of the amount received by the artist computed by dividing the producer's basic royalty rate (without regard to escalations) by the artist's basic all-in royalty rate (without regard to escalations). For example, if the producer's basic royalty rate is 3% of retail and the artist's basic all-in royalty rate is 12% of retail, the producer would receive 25% of any monies that the artist received as a percentage of the record company's net royalties or net flat fees. On net receipts from the exploitation of audiovisual devices, the producer would generally receive one-half of the otherwise applicable net receipts royalty.

Thus, in the foregoing example, the producer would receive 12-1/2% (rather than 25%) of the monies the artist received from the record company for the exploitation of audiovisual devices. Again, if the artist is signed to a production company instead of directly to the record company, the producer's attorney should attempt to have the producer's royalty calculated based upon the royalties payable by the record company to the production company rather than on the royalties payable from the production company to the artist; however, the producer's attorney should be aware that this may be a difficult concession to obtain.

In any event, subparagraphs 5(a)(i) and 5(a)(ii) make it clear that in order to know what royalties may be payable on a particular project, the producer must know the royalty provisions of the artist's recording agreement. Accordingly, a copy of the royalty provisions relating to the applicable album and the definitions provisions of the artist's (or, if applicable, the production company's) recording agreement should be attached, as an exhibit, to the producer agreement.

(b) Your royalty rate on records and other devices embodying Master(s) and other master recording shall be the otherwise applicable royalty rate multiplied by a fraction, the numerator of which is the number of Master(s) embodied in that record or other device and the denominator of which is the total number of master recordings (including Master[s]) embodied in the record or other device;

This paragraph sets forth the appropriate proration of the producer's royalty. The words "royalty-bearing" should be inserted after the words "total number of" towards the end of the sentence.

(c) Your royalty rates hereunder shall not be increased due to increases in Artist's royalty rates under the Artist Agreement based on record sales; and

The producer does not generally share in sales escalations received by the artist; however, as discussed in subparagraph 5(a)(i), the producer or the producer's attorney can sometimes negotiate for escalations based on sales, which would be separate from the sales escalations received by the artist.

(d) Your royalties hereunder shall be reduced by the royalties payable by us for the services of any other person to produce or complete the production of the Master(s) until they are satisfactory to us.

The producer's attorney should request that the producer be accorded the first opportunity to do any mixing, remixing, editing or other material altering of the masters produced by the producer. If any other person performs these services, the producer should have the right, at the producer's sole discretion, to remove his or her name from the master. Also, if another person is engaged to perform production work on the master, the producer's royalty should not be reduced unless the producer is in material breach of the agreement. The producer's attorney should require that if a mixer is engaged to mix the masters, any royalties payable to the mixer should be borne one-third by the record company, one-third by the artist and one-third by the producer. If the record company refuses to bear any of the royalties payable to the mixer (usually 1% of retail), they should be borne one-half by the artist and one-half by the producer.

6. No royalties shall be credited to your account hereunder unless and until the aggregate of recording costs of the Master(s) and advances and fees payable to you for the Master(s) are recouped from royalties on reproductions and exploitations of the Master(s) at the "Net Artist Royalty Rate." The term Net Artist Royalty Rate shall mean the aggregate royalty rate payable to Artist and the producers on reproductions of the Master(s), less the aggregate royalty rate payable to the producers on reproductions and exploitations of the Master(s). After that recoupment, your royalty account shall be credited with royalties earned by your hereunder on all exploitations of the Master(s) retroactive to the first record sold. We shall account for and pay royalties earned by you hereunder within ninety (90) days after the end of each of our then-current six-month accounting periods, currently ending on June 30 and December 31. Accountings and statements for royalties earned by you on reproductions and exploitations of the Master(s) shall be based upon our receipt in the United States of an accounting and payment or final credit for the actual reproductions and exploitations of the Master(s) in the accounting period for which a statement is rendered. We shall have no obligation to account for or pay to you any royalties unless and until we receive in the United States an accounting for and payment of or final credit for royalties on actual reproductions and other exploitations of the Master(s). All statements and accountings rendered to you shall be binding and not subject to any examination, audit or objection for any reason unless you shall notify us in writing of your specific objection thereto within one (1) year after the date the statement is rendered or was to be rendered. No action, suit or proceeding regarding any royalty statement or accounting rendered to you may be maintained by or on behalf of you unless commenced in court within one (1) year after the date the statement is rendered or was to be rendered. We may deduct from any amounts payable to you hereunder that portion hereof required to be deducted under any statute, regulation, treaty or other law, or under any union or guild agreement.

> *The first three sentences of this paragraph deal with recoupment of the recording costs and the producer advance and/or fees. The producer will not receive royalties until the recording costs incurred by the record company and/or the artist and all advances and fees paid to the producer in connection with the masters produced by that producer are recouped from royalties earned at the Net Artist Royalty Rate (i.e., the artist's royalty rate minus the producer's royalty rate) from sales of records embodying the masters produced by the producer. The producer's attorney should attempt to exclude any advances or fees to the artist from the recording costs for the purposes of determining recoupment by the producer. Furthermore, the advances to the producer should be excluded as well since paragraph 4 states that the advance to the producer will be recouped from royalties payable to the producer. A failure to exclude the producer advance from this provision may result in double recoupment of the producer advance and, accordingly, may delay (or prevent) the producer's receipt of royalties.*
>
> *Once the appropriate costs are recouped at the Net Artist Royalty Rate, the producer's royalty account is credited with all royalties earned from the first record that was sold. These royalties will be paid to the producer after deduction of the producer's advance. This provision is favorable to the producer. The artist receives royalties "prospectively" after recoupment of all recording costs for the album at the artist's all-in rate. This means that if the appropriate costs are recouped after sales of 200,000 units, the artist will receive royalties for the 200,001st unit and future units sold, as long as the artist's*

royalty account remains in a recouped position; however, the artist will not receive any royalties on the first 200,000 units sold prior to recoupment.

If the producer is entitled to receive royalties "retroactively from the first record sold" and the costs chargeable against the producer's account are recouped after sales of 100,000 units, the producer's account would be credited with the producer's royalty on units one through 100,000 and these royalties would be paid to the producer after deduction of the advance previously paid to the producer. The producer would then be paid royalties on all sales in excess of 100,000 units. In some cases the producer is only to be paid prospectively after recoupment of the recording costs. In that event, the producer's attorney should request that the producer be paid retroactively from the first record sold after recoupment of the appropriate costs at the Net Artist Royalty Rate. This is an important deal point that should not be overlooked in any producer agreement.

The producer should be paid directly from the record company. Accounting statements and payments (if any) should be sent to the producer at the same time they are sent to the artist. If the record company fails or refuses to send accounting statements directly to the producer, the artist should be required to send such statements and payments (if any) within 30 days after the artist receives them. The producer should have a minimum of two years after the date a statement is rendered (delete "or was to be rendered") to audit the artist and/or record company and to object to that statement, and two and one-half years from the date the statement was rendered in which to file a lawsuit based on that statement.

7. You warrant, represent, covenant and agree as follows:
   (a) You have the right and power to enter into this agreement, to grant the rights granted by you to us hereunder and to perform all the terms hereof; and
   (b) No materials, ideas or other properties furnished or designated by you and used in connection with the Master(s) will violate or infringe upon the rights of any person, firm or corporation.

This is a standard provision in producer agreements. Subparagraph 7(b) should be limited to elements "furnished" by the producer, not "designated" by the producer. The producer's attorney should require a warranty from the artist or record company be included in the agreement similar to subparagraph 7(b) stating that all elements not furnished by the producer will not violate or infringe on the rights of others.

8. You hereby indemnify, save and hold us and any person, firm or corporation deriving rights from us harmless from any and all damages, liability and costs (including legal costs and attorneys' fees) arising out of or in connection with any claim, demand or action by us or by any third party that is inconsistent with any of the warranties, representations, covenants or agreements made by you in this Agreement. You shall reimburse us, on demand, for any loss, cost, expense or damage to which the foregoing indemnity applies. Pending the disposition of any claim, demand or action to which the foregoing indemnity applies, we shall have the right to withhold payment of any monies payable to you hereunder and under any other agreement between you and us or our affiliates.

This paragraph is called an indemnity provision. If the artist or record company is sued (or sues the producer) based on any facts (or purported facts) that are inconsistent with any of the promises made by the producer in the producer agreement, the record company and/or artist could look to the producer to pay all costs incurred in connection with that lawsuit or claim.

The producer's attorney should limit the producer's indemnity of the artist and/or record company to claims reduced to final judgment by a court of competent jurisdiction or to settlements with the producer's consent. The word "reasonable" should be inserted before the words "attorneys' fees" in the first sentence of this paragraph. This provision should also state that monies will not be withheld in an amount exceeding the producer's probable liability under the producer agreement, would be held in an interest bearing account, and would be released if no action was taken on the claim during a one-year period. The following phrase at the end of the paragraph should be deleted: "and under any other agreement between you and us or our affiliates." The artist or record company should indemnify the producer with respect to materials not furnished by the producer to the same extent that the producer indemnifies the artist or record company pursuant to this paragraph.

9. The respective addresses of you and us for all purposes hereunder are set forth on page 1 hereof, unless and until notice of a different address is received by the party notified of that different address. All notices shall be in writing and shall either be served by certified mail return receipt requested or by telex, in each case with all charges prepaid. Notices shall be deemed effective when mailed or sent by telex, all charges prepaid, except for notices of a change of address, which shall be effective only when received by the party notified. A copy of each notice to us shall be sent to: _____ (Attorney's name and address).

This is a standard provision. If the producer is represented by an attorney, the attorney should receive a copy of any notice sent to the producer so that the attorney can advise the producer whether any action needs to be taken on any notices received by the producer.

10. We may, at our election, assign this Agreement or any of our rights hereunder or delegate any of our obligations hereunder, in whole or in part, to any person, firm or corporation. You may not delegate any of your obligations hereunder.

The record company's right to assign its rights and/or obligations under the producer agreement should be limited to a person, firm or corporation that acquires all or substantially all of its stock and/or assets. If the agreement is with the artist, the artist's right to assign his or her rights under the agreement should be limited to assigning it to a record company. Any assignment by the artist or record company should not relieve them of liability for their obligations to the producer under the producer agreement.

11. During the Term and for three (3) years thereafter, you shall not produce or coproduce any recording for any person, firm or corporation other than us embodying, in whole or in part, the musical selections recorded in the Master(s).

This provision is called a rerecording restriction. The restriction period should be reduced from three years to two.

12. You acknowledge and agree that your services hereunder are of a special, unique, intellectual and extraordinary character which gives them peculiar value, and that if

you breach any term hereof, we will be caused irreparable injury which cannot adequately be compensated by money damages.

> *This language assists the artist and/or record company in obtaining an injunction against the producer should the producer engage in activities that violate the terms of the producer agreement. An injunction is a court order that demands that an individual or firm stop doing something. An injunction could prevent the producer from working for someone else. Since issuing an injunction is such a drastic action, a court will not issue an injunction in the situation where a person is rendering personal services unless there is a showing that the person's services are unique and that the injured party would not be made whole by the payment of money. The language contained in paragraph 12 is almost always found in the artist's recording agreement, but is not as common in a producer agreement. The producer's attorney should attempt to delete the paragraph or, at a minimum, insert the word "material" before the word "term" and substitute the word "may" for "will" and the words "may not" for the word "cannot."*

13 (a) This document sets forth the entire agreement between you and us with respect to the subject matter hereof and may not be modified except by a written agreement signed by the party sought to be bound. Except as expressly provided herein to the contrary, you are performing your obligations hereunder as an independent contractor;

(b) In the event of any action, suit or proceeding arising from or based upon this Agreement brought by either party hereto against the other, the prevailing party shall be entitled to recover from the other its attorneys' fees in connection therewith in addition to the costs of that action, suit or proceeding;

(c) The validity, construction, interpretation and legal effect of this Agreement shall be governed by the laws of the State of California;

(d) Nothing contained in this Agreement or otherwise shall obligate us or any other person, firm or corporation to reproduce or exploit the Master(s) in any manner or media;

> *These provisions are all very standard. In subparagraph 13(b), the word "reasonable" should be inserted before the words "attorneys' fees."*

(e) We may terminate the Term for any reason, with or without cause, on the date of our notice to you terminating the Term;

> *This subparagraph should be deleted. If the subparagraph is not deleted it should be limited to the situation in which the producer is in material breach of the producer agreement and has failed to cure that breach within 30 days after the artist or record company provides written notice to the producer of that breach. In any event, the producer should receive the advances and royalties that he or she is otherwise entitled to under the agreement.*

(f) We shall not be in breach of any of our obligations under this Agreement unless and until you notify us in writing in detail of our breach or alleged breach and we fail to cure that breach or alleged breach within thirty (30) days after our receipt of that notice from you; and

This subparagraph should be made mutual (i.e., the artist or record company should have to provide notice and a 30-day cure period to the producer prior to the producer being placed in breach of the agreement). The cure period for the artist or record company should be reduced to 15 days if the artist or record company fails to pay any monies owing to the producer.

(g) You have been represented by independent counsel or have had the unrestricted opportunity to be represented by independent counsel of your choice for purposes of advising you in connection with the negotiation and execution of this Agreement. If you have not been represented by independent legal counsel of your choice in connection with this Agreement, you acknowledge and agree that your failure to be represented by independent legal counsel in connection with this Agreement was determined solely by you.

This paragraph is a standard provision in producer agreements. Due to the complexity of the issues involved in the negotiation of a producer agreement, the producer is advised to seek an attorney's advice in the negotiation and execution of any agreement.

If the foregoing sets forth your understanding and agreement with us, please so indicate by signing in the space provided below.

Very truly yours,

AGREED TO AND ACCEPTED

_____	_____
BY	BY
_____	_____
FEDERAL I.D. / SS#	FEDERAL I.D. / SS#

The foregoing covers most of the issues in producer agreements. If the producer wrote all or part of any of the musical compositions embodied in the masters, the agreement would contain a provision that required the producer to grant a reduced rate mechanical license, giving the record company the right to reproduce the compositions on records (in all configurations) in exchange for payment to the producer/songwriter of mechanical royalties at 75% of the minimum statutory rate on a specified date (usually either the date of the commencement of recording or the date of delivery of the master to the record company—the later the date the better for the producer). The producer's attorney should attempt to revise this provision to provide for payment of 100% of the minimum statutory rate (as of January 1, 1994 that rate in the United States is 6.6 cents for each record sold that embodies one use of a composition that is five minutes or less in length); however, many record companies refuse to negotiate on this issue unless the producer has some clout. The provision relating to the licensing of musical compositions may also contain a requirement that the producer/songwriter issue a free "synchronization license" to the record company. A synchronization license is an agreement that grants the right to synchronize, or use a musical composition in the soundtrack of an audiovisual work (e.g., a music video or television program). The producer should only be required to grant a free synchronization license for MTV type free promotional videos. The terms relating to the licensing of musical compositions, written by a producer, can be very complex. They should be reviewed very carefully by the producer and his or her attorney.

RECORDING AND DISTRIBUTION CONTRACTS WITH INDEPENDENT LABELS

by Edward R. Hearn

An alternative to seeking a major recording contract or raising funds to produce your own recording is to approach independent record companies. Within the last decade, independent record labels specializing in particular styles of music have become very successful in reaching and developing niche markets. By researching these labels, you may find one that successfully markets music that fits your style and is interested in producing, manufacturing and/or distributing your record. Some of these independent labels have been very successful and have become subsidiaries to major recording labels, such as GRP (MCA), Narada (MCA), Tommy Boy (Warner Bros.) and Private Music (BMG), or have developed strong relationships or affiliations with major label branch distribution, such as Windham Hill.

In 1994 and 1995, combined sales through all of the independents collectively, were greater than each of the major label distributors, except for the WEA (Warner Bros. Records, Elektra, and Atlantic) distributed companies and their associated labels.

SMALL LABEL ADVANTAGES

The chief advantages of releasing your album with independent record labels are similar to the reasons for signing with major labels. They generally have a distribution mechanism in place. They are organized to handle the time and costs of financing and administering the production, manufacture, marketing and distribution of records. They can better absorb the financial risks and have more leverage in collecting money from the wholesalers and retailers of records. In addition, the company may have developed a reputation in the music community for a certain style of music and can move a great volume of records in a wide geographical territory.

Bear in mind, however, that if a small label invests time and money in your career and is successful in generating a reasonable level of income for you, you should carefully weigh the benefits of signing with a major label if asked (where you probably will be one of many)—against staying with the smaller one (where you may be the star!) Far too often, the benefits of a smaller label are discovered only after an unhappy relationship with a major recording label occurs. Much depends on the style of music involved, for example, pop and rock may get more attention from a major label than a style of music aimed at more narrow and focused audiences, such as jazz, new age, children's music, or Yiddish folk songs. Both small and large labels have demonstrated effectiveness at heavy metal, dance and rap music.

CONTRACTS

Although contracts with independent labels can be very similar to those negotiated with major labels, smaller independent companies sometimes work out arrangements that do not mirror these standards. For example, these companies may be willing to step away from obtuse and confusing language to create a contract in plain English that is balanced between the interests of the record company and those of the artist, namely, to more equitably share the economic benefits realized from the skills and talents of the artist and the business expertise and mechanisms of the recording company. With increasing frequency, however, the smaller labels are reflecting the contractual style and approach of the major labels, perhaps because of the investment costs and financial risks incurred in developing an artist and the desire to be secure that the contract with the artist is sufficiently strong so that a larger label will not be in a position to tempt the artist to switch labels without the smaller label participating in the benefits of that switch. Many smaller labels also insist on participating in some or all of the music publishing of the artist. That is an issue that needs to be carefully examined, and if it occurs should be the subject of a separate deal.

Here are some options not usually available to musicians signing with major labels:

Distribution Deals

In this type of deal, you deliver an agreed amount of fully manufactured and packaged records, cassettes or compact discs to a record company. Some labels may only distribute product, while you do the marketing and promotion; others may do everything.

In a distribution only deal, the record label will either contract directly with stores or deal with networks of independent distributors or both, selling to them at wholesale prices.

If the company only distributes your record, you will receive a sum equivalent to the wholesale price, minus a fee of 20% to 30% and other direct expenses that you authorize the company to spend, but you pay for all the manufacturing costs and all associated marketing and promotion costs. A standard contractual agreement is that you will receive money only on records actually sold and paid for.

These types of deals often result after bands release recordings for a regional audience, find themselves with growing popularity, and use the added leverage to make a deal that will broaden their audiences.

Unlike major recording labels, independent labels sometimes encourage the sale of records, cassettes or compact discs at performances or to fan mailing lists. In this case, a clause can be added to the standard recording contract that will state that the musician can buy product at a low wholesale price. This inventory may be provided as an "advance" against the royalties or other fees that will be owing. This practice is actively discouraged by most major recording labels.

Pressing and Distribution Deals (P&D Deals)

In P&D deals, you deliver a fully mixed recording master and artwork to the record label, which then assumes the responsibility of manufacturing and distributing your records, cassettes or compact discs. If the label advances the manufacturing costs, it will reimburse itself out of the sales proceeds of your phonorecords, plus, perhaps, some value for the use of its money, in addition to the distribution fee.

If the record label also picks up promotion, publicity and marketing, then the deal is usually structured as a royalty deal that will leave the record label with a sufficient margin to cover all of its costs and make a reasonable profit. The royalty is sometimes higher than in standard recording contracts because you have already invested the costs of recording and producing. That is not always the case, however. When negotiating this type of deal, ask that any royalty percentages be specified as net cents per unit for each configuration.

As an alternative, if marketing and promotional duties are involved, these expenses could be deducted as direct costs also, along with the distribution fee and manufacturing costs, with the balance paid to you, but more likely the deal will be structured on a royalty basis, with a royalty of anywhere from 10% to 18% of retail, plus mechanical royalties on the music.

Production Deals

In this type of deal, you sign as an artist with a production company. The company is responsible for recording your music and for obtaining distribution through independent distributors or a record company. In many cases, contracts for these deals are structured similarly to record contracts because the production company will typically make a pressing and distribution deal with a record label that also includes marketing and promotion and then contract with you for a percentage of the royalty paid to it by the record company.

For example, a production company may have a deal with a record company that pays 14% to 18% of the retail selling price on records sold, depending in part on whether the recording costs are paid by the production company or advanced by the record company. The production company might then have contracted with the artist to pay a royalty from between 6% and 10% of the retail selling price or 50% to 60% of the royalty paid to the production company by the record company.

CONTRACTS AND RELATIONSHIPS BETWEEN INDEPENDENT AND MAJOR LABELS

by Christopher Knab and Bartley F. Day

Since the 1950s, major labels have presented almost all of the pop icons that have helped to define our culture. They have also secured a place in history for many of the giants of jazz, blues, and classical music. The role of independent labels, on the other hand, has been to discover new sounds, and preserve select musical traditions.

The major labels have historically concentrated on selling music to a wide audience through their own systems of distribution, while the independent labels have traditionally specialized in niche market music and have sold product through separate networks of distributors and stores.

In the late 1970s, a new generation of musicians was causing a stir and independent labels were at the forefront of a new music revolution. Not wanting to miss out on an opportunity, the majors rushed in and signed some highly visible acts to capitalize on the new sounds. By the early 1980s, the major labels' lack of understanding of the market for the new music had led to disappointing sales. As the decade progressed, independent labels garnered the reputation as being reliable sources of discovery for new talent. That tradition continues in the 1990s. Today, any indie label that carefully budgets, organizes, and implements promotion, marketing, and distribution plans, sells its artists' music at all live performances, and takes advantage of new opportunities, can increase its odds of getting the attention of major labels (*if* that is what the independent label wants).

This chapter summarizes the main types of legal relationships which exist today between independent and major labels. A knowledge of the various possible relationships with major labels, and the advantages and disadvantages of each alternative, can help a new label determine the best strategy for attaining its long-term objectives. For those independents presently being courted by one or more major labels, an understanding of the ramifications of the various types of relationships can enable you to negotiate more effectively.

REASONS FOR MAJOR LABEL AFFILIATION

Independent labels affiliate with majors to increase their artists' exposure in commercial media and to expand their distribution networks by increasing their access to major retail record chain stores and rack jobbers.

Major label affiliation may also provide the independent label with a substantial cash infusion, which eliminates the need to continually focus on day-to-day survival issues and allows more effective operation. The major label may also take on such responsibilities as manufacturing and promotion. These factors may in turn permit the independent label to expand and/or upgrade its artist roster, or enter a mainstream genre where developmental and promotional costs are much higher than for niche market music.

In addition, affiliating with a major label can maximize the likelihood of the independent getting *paid* for records sold. Independent labels, using the traditional independent distribution system, have always faced the risk that an independent distributor will go bankrupt and not pay them. This risk is drastically reduced (if not eliminated) when an independent label distributes through a major label distribution system. These distributors have the financial backing of their multinational parent companies and are able to weather the financial storms of the music industry. They also have more clout than independent distributors to collect from retail and wholesale accounts and are better able to implement strict controls over how many records those retail and wholesale accounts are allowed to buy on credit.

ISSUES TO CONSIDER

When an independent label is considering an affiliation with a major label, there are many issues to consider. Here are some specific questions that will help to focus research and analysis: What are the independent label's present sales volumes and what are they likely to be in the next few years (i.e., with major label affiliation versus without major label affiliation)? Will the major label distribute to the mom-and-pop stores, which formerly carried the independent label? Will the major label be responsive to regional demands and the demands of niche markets? What kind of reputation and support does the independent label have among its fans? Will a major label affiliation jeopardize this? Will the independent label's core fans be best served by the major label's distribution system?

There are other issues to consider as well. For example, will an affiliation with a major label create an unhealthy pressure on the independent label to sell more records than it can comfortably or realistically sell? What is the present financial status of the independent label and what is its access to additional resources without major label affiliation? Assuming affiliation, what will the cash infusion (if any) be used for? How can the independent label's existing staff—promotion, marketing and administrative—be best utilized after affiliation? How will the long-term business objectives of the independent label be served by affiliating with a major label? Do the owners of the independent label really want the responsibilities and financial burdens of operating a fully-staffed record company and overseeing the promotion and marketing of records? Or are they only interested in the creative process of signing artists and producing records? What is the personal style of the independent label's owner(s)? Do they place a high value on being able to operate independently? Are they willing to take input and direction from a large corporate entity? What is the major label's real motivation for entering into the relationship? Is it to use the independent label as an "indie front," or to take over the label's strongest artists? Or does it view the relationship as a mutually beneficial long-term strategic alliance? What is the corporate style of the major label's management? Is there sound long-term vision? Is there good personal chemistry between the management of the major label and the independent label?

TYPES OF DEALS

There are numerous types of deals between independent and major labels, the most common of which are as follows: (1) Pressing and distribution (P&D) deals; (2) distribution only deals; (3) fulfillment deals; (4) production deals; (5) joint ventures; (6) equity deals; (7) the licensing of records to major labels; (8) the licensing of records from major labels; and (9) rights buyouts.

Due to the complexity of these types of contracts, it is not possible to discuss each comprehensively. However, their essential features are addressed later in this chapter.

As a practical matter, the type of contract offered by a major label, its specific terms, and the degree of flexibility in the major label's bargaining position, will all be dictated by the extent to which the independent label has strong artists, a healthy and ever-improving sales record, and the confidence of the major label in the independent's key personnel. There are a number of independent labels—Sub Pop Records, for example—which resisted the repeated entreaties of major labels until they achieved sufficient bargaining power to obtain acceptable terms.

Before entering into a contract with a major, it must first be determined whether such arrangements are permissible under the terms of the independent label's existing recording contracts with its artists. Do the contracts limit or prohibit assignment of artists' rights to the major? Are there clauses requiring that artists be able to review, and/or reject, any affiliation?

Even if there is no contractual limitation on the assignment of rights, the independent label will want to find out how its artists feel about major label affiliation. Some artists perceive it as a wonderful windfall, while others view it as an abandonment of principles. Such considerations should be addressed prior to entering into any contracts.

The independent should also examine its existing royalty and other obligations to its artists, to determine whether the terms offered by the major label make economic sense.

The independent label should pay close attention to the allocation of tasks and decision-making authority between it and the major label. To the extent practicable, the parties' respective rights and obligations should be clearly defined in their contract. For example, how will the number of records to be manufactured be determined? What will happen if there are disagreements on promotion or marketing strategies and/or budgets? Or, if the major label is not fully meeting its obligations, will the independent label have the right to terminate the relationship? And if so, on what terms?

With regard to recording content and costs, how much freedom will the independent label retain? Will the contract give the major label the right to *reject* a record recorded by one of the independent label's artists? And will the contract contain a right of first refusal, that gives the major label the rights to a new artist that an independent label has signed or wants to sign. (This is sometimes referred to as a "first look" clause).

Pressing and Distribution (P&D) Deals

In the typical P&D deal, the independent label signs recording artists to recording contracts, produces the recordings and the graphics and delivers the master to the major label. The independent label is financially responsible for these tasks.

The major label then presses the records and distributes them through its distribution system. After records are sold, the major label deducts its pressing costs and a distribution fee from the monies it receives from its distributors and pays the balance to the independent label. The independent label is responsible for handling (and paying for) all advertising, promotion and publicity, including exposure in commercial and noncommercial media.

P&D deals used to be the most common kind of deal between independent and major labels. However, major labels often found themselves involved with numerous independents, each one selling only small numbers of records.

As a result, major labels concluded that it was not worth clogging their distribution pipelines with low-selling records merely to receive a distribution fee. Therefore, P&D deals are now less common than they were. Today the relationship is more likely to involve a joint venture or equity deal, or the licensing of the independent label's records, because these types of deals are potentially more profitable for the majors. They also give the major labels a broader role in artist development, marketing and promotion.

Even so, an independent label in strong financial condition with high sales volumes will often have the leverage to negotiate a P&D deal.

Artistic Control

The independent label usually retains control over the content of songs, the design and copy of artwork, and the content of promotional and advertising materials. However, the major label may require a right to screen content for any extreme language or references to sexual or political topics, since certain genres of music (rap and alternative rock, for example) have the potential for causing adverse publicity.

Ownership of Masters

Typically, the independent label retains ownership of master recordings. However, the major label will have the right to use those masters as collateral for the financial obligations of the independent to the major label. The major label is entitled to be reimbursed its manufacturing costs from the income generated by its sales of the independent label's records. But sometimes those records do not sell in sufficient quantities to do this. In anticipation of this possibility, P&D contracts generally grant a security interest in the independent's masters, and in the records manufactured, to the major label.

Bonds and Letters of Credit

As an additional means of assuring that they will be fully paid for their manufacturing costs, major labels often require that the independent provide a bond or letter of credit from a financial institution. This depends on various factors, including the track record of the independent label and the personal financial circumstances of its owners. If a bond or letter of credit is required, the face amount will generally be from $50,000 to $1 million.

Bonds and letters of credit should, if at all possible, be avoided by independent labels, due to the cost of obtaining them.

Exclusivity

Most P&D agreements require that the independent label's records be distributed only through the major label's normal distribution system (or through an ostensibly "independent" distributor owned by the major label) for sale to retail record stores, chains, and rack jobbers.

However, the following exceptions may be granted:

(1) A major label may allow an independent label to sell a limited number of

records through its independent distributors to retail outlets other than those directly serviced by the major label—for example, health food stores, specialty book and record stores, nonprofit organizations, etc.

(2) A major label may allow an independent label to sell records at gigs and by mail order to their bands' fan lists.

In either case, these special sales channels will be specified in the contract and the number of records that the independent label is allowed to sell may be limited. In most cases, the independent will be entitled to buy product from the major at a price determined by a formula specified in the contract. (The price is often one or a variation of the following: the actual manufacturing cost [calculated on a per record basis], the manufacturing cost per record plus a certain additional monetary amount per record, or the regular wholesale price.)

Sometimes the major label will require a "hold back" clause that forbids sales by the independent label until six months to a year after the major label's initial commercial release of the record.

Term

Typically, a P&D deal will be for an initial term of one to three years (most often two), with the major label having the unilateral right to extend the term of the agreement for an additional three to four years after the initial term. (Usually, these options are exercisable on a year-to-year basis by the major label.)

Distribution Fees and Pressing Costs

The most significant fees and costs deducted by the major label are as follows:

(1) The manufacturing costs (i.e., for the pressing of the records, printing of artwork, etc.). The manufacturing prices are often itemized in a price schedule attached to the P&D contract.

(2) A distribution fee, which in most P&D contracts is defined as being a percentage of the wholesale price (usually 17% to 25%).

(3) Sometimes the major label will be providing the services of its in-house promotion and marketing staffs. If so, it will receive an additional fee (usually 10%) on top of the distribution fee. The contract may also provide that the major label will be reimbursed for its out-of-pocket costs (e.g., the costs of hiring independent promotion companies to promote records to radio programmers), sometimes up to a certain specific dollar limit per record. The contract should provide that the independent label will have the right to approve (or at least the right to be consulted about) the marketing and promotion strategies involved and the way in which monies will be spent.

The major label will deduct these fees and costs from the monies it receives from record buyers (chain stores, rack jobbers, etc.), then pay the balance to the independent label. In some P&D deals, these fees and costs are subtracted from the full wholesale price, in others from a percentage (for example, 90%) of the wholesale price. (But note: The royalties paid by record labels to *recording artists* are, in the typical recording contract, computed as a percentage of the *retail* price of records.)

Reserves for Returns

P&D agreements often include a "reserve" clause that allows the major label to temporarily withhold a percentage (usually 20% to 35%) of the sums that may be otherwise owing to the independent label. This reserve is to avoid overpayments that might result from returns of unsold records. (In the United States, most of the large retail record chain stores are granted a 100% return privilege by the major labels on certain titles, with restrictions as to time limits and, in most cases, only for new product. It is also common practice to offer the 100% return policy to smaller chain stores and select independent retail record stores, but only on certain titles.

The reserves are generally released to the independent label within 12 to 24 months after each reserve period. (As established in the contract.)

The independent label should seek the lowest possible reserve percentage. A low reserve percentage is especially warranted now because of the new SoundScan technology which allows distributors to efficiently monitor sales patterns and reduce the oversupply of records in the marketplace. As a result, the actual percentage of records being returned today is much lower than previously.

In any event, vague terminology, such as "reasonable reserves," should be avoided, since it gives the major label considerable leeway about what percentage of sale proceeds can be reserved. The independent should also try to avoid provisions that require an additional letter of credit or bond against reserves.

Free Goods

The major label may wish to provide its wholesale and retail accounts with free goods. (The term "free goods," as used here, refers to any and all CDs or cassettes given away by a label as an incentive for a retail store to purchase an artist's product. For example, a distributor might give a store 15 records as free goods for every 100 records purchased.)

The independent label should seek a clause that specifies what percentage of manufactured records can be distributed as free goods.

Key Person Clause

Contracts may include a "key person" clause, which gives the major label the right to terminate the agreement if one of the principals of the independent label dies, becomes incapacitated, or ceases to be actively involved.

Advances

The amount of money (if any) to be advanced by the major label will depend on the leverage and negotiating ability of the independent label. The major label will be entitled to recoup any such advances from future monies owed by the major label to the independent.

Distribution Only Deals and Fulfillment Deals

There are two other types of contracts—distribution only deals and fulfillment deals—which are similar to P&D deals, but are distinguishable in certain important respects.

Distribution Only Deals

The independent label manufactures the records and delivers them to the major label, which is then responsible for distribution through its system. In almost all other respects, a distribution only contract will be identical to a P&D contract.

Fulfillment Deals

The major label will press the independent label's records and distribute those records through the traditional independent distribution system.

A fulfillment deal is very similar to a P&D deal, except that the major label presses the records and ships them to the independent label's usual independent distributors, rather than to the major label's own distribution system (as is the case with a P&D deal). The major label will collect from the independent distributors, deduct the manufacturing costs and a distribution fee, then pay the balance to the independent label. The deal may also include the collection of previous monies owed to the independent label.

One benefit of a fulfillment deal is that major labels generally have more leverage than independents to collect from independent distributors. Another benefit is that the independent label is saved the trouble of overseeing the manufacturing and distribution of its records.

When sales warrant, the parties to a fulfillment deal may agree to use the major label's own distribution system.

Piggyback Deals

Independent labels which do not have sufficient leverage to obtain a deal with a major label can try to piggyback onto another independent label's existing deal.

In a piggyback deal, the independent label with the existing relationship will deduct a separate and additional distribution fee for itself, then pay the balance to the piggybacked label. For example, the major label may first deduct an 18% distribution fee from the wholesale proceeds, and pay the balance to the independent label with which it has a relationship. That independent label may deduct another 7% as its own distribution fee, before paying the piggybacked label the balance of the monies. The piggybacked label is, in effect, being charged a total combined distribution fee of 25%.

Typically, the piggybacking label will depend on accountings and payments from the independent label. Therefore, before entering into this type of deal it should fully understand the exact terms of the relationship between the other independent label and the major.

Production Deals

Production companies find and sign talent and produce records. Many are owned by producers that have reputations for turning out commercial hits. Others are vanity labels, owned by successful recording artists that have been rewarded by their labels with production deals.

The production company delivers master recordings to the major label, which presses, distributes, markets and promotes the records directly or through its subsidiaries.

The production company signs artists to a recording contract and agrees to pay royalties at a specified rate. The production company also signs, separately, a production agreement with the major label. (This almost always provides for a significantly higher royalty rate to be paid by the major label to the independent, than the royalty rate which the independent label has agreed to pay to the artist.) The production company's profit is based on the difference between the rate it receives from the major label and the rate which it is obligated to pay to its artists.

Term

A production deal will typically have an initial term of two or three years, with the major label having options for an additional one to three (or more) years.

Signing of Artists

These contracts typically limit the total number of artists the production company may sign over the entire term of the agreement and/or for each year during the term. The more established and successful the production company is, the more artists it will be entitled to sign.

The contract will specify the total number of albums the production company will be required to supply for each artist. The production company (and its artists) will be obligated to ultimately deliver that number of albums even if the term of the production agreement expires before that happens.

Ordinarily the major label will not be obligated to commercially release all albums delivered by the production company. For example, the major label might reject an album or artist which the major label considers to lack significant commercial potential. As a result, the production agreement should allow the production company the right to offer any rejected artists or masters to another major label.

Royalties

Production deals provide for the major label to pay royalties to the production company, based on a percentage of the retail price. The typical range is 14% to 18%, less the same packaging and other deductions that are standard in most recording agreements. (For more information see the chapter, "Analysis of a Recording Contract.")

Advances

The major label may advance monies for administration costs and other overhead costs not necessarily attributed to any specific recording project; and/or it may advance the recording costs for each album produced. It will have the right to recoup those costs before it pays any royalties. Recording budgets for each album project are specified in detail in the contract.

From a production company's perspective, recording costs should be recouped only on an artist-by-artist basis; the production company should avoid any cross-collateralization clause that allows the major label's recoupment of recording costs for all artists from the total amount of royalties owing for all artists. Otherwise, the lack of sales of one artist will drastically reduce the payment of royalties to a successful one.

Ownership of Masters

Typically, the major label, not the production company, owns the masters of any recordings released and sold. Although some production companies have been successful in negotiating for a reversion of that ownership to occur sometime after the end of the term of the agreement (typically seven to 10 years).

Joint Ventures

In a joint venture contract, the major label fronts all operating costs, and the independent label and the major label then share the net profits of the joint venture. To compute the net, the major label typically deducts a fee of 10% of the joint venture's gross income for overhead; an additional 15% to 25% for distribution; and the actual out-of-pocket costs incurred by the major label. After the major label deducts all of these costs and fees from the joint venture's gross income, the parties divide the profits, often equally.

Normally the joint venture agreement will provide that a certain number of artists will be signed each year, with the major label often having the right to make the final decision about which artists are signed.

Depending on the independent label's bargaining power, it may be able to obtain the right to direct all marketing and promotion decisions, and perhaps the right to spend up to a certain specified amount each year for that marketing and promotion. However, since the major label holds the purse strings, the independent label will have little practical recourse if the major label later decides to spend more (or less) money than agreed, unless the independent had been able to insert favorable remedy clauses regarding such a scenario into the agreement.

The agreement may also include a clause stating that after an artist sells a specified amount of records on the joint venture's label, the major label will have the option to release any new recordings by that artist under the name of only the major label.

The agreement will provide that the joint venture will last for a certain period of time (typically three to seven years) and will also contain buy-sell provisions, stating that at the end of the joint venture, each party will have the right to buy out the other's rights, but specifying which party has the first right and priority to do so.

Equity Deals

In an equity deal, the major label will either buy an independent label outright, or buy a part-interest in it. In this situation, the major label actually owns stock in the independent company itself, rather than merely receiving rights to sell its records.

Sometimes the major label's buyout rights will have been originally negotiated between the parties as part of a P&D or joint venture deal, whereby the major label receives, as a part of the overall deal, an option to buy part or all of the independent label at some future time. Sometimes the major label will exercise its buyout rights incrementally.

When a major label is purchasing the independent outright, the price is, of course, heavily negotiated. A rule of thumb is that an independent label will sell for approximately six to ten times its annual net earnings or two and one-half times its annual gross revenues.

When a major label is buying only a partial interest in the independent label, there are other issues which will be as heavily negotiated as the price. For example, the major label will often be agreeing to pay all of the label's operational costs, and the parties must resolve the specific terms on which future income will be allocated.

Also, there must be contractual arrangements for determining how the label's operations will be shared. Normally the major label will want the original owners to remain active, since they had the vision to make the independent label a success in the first place. But how much autonomy (if any) will the original owners have with regard to the signing of new artists? Who will have the direct relationship with the artists? How will marketing and promotion strategies, and other operating decisions (such as pricing strategies) be made? Will the original owners be primarily responsible for promotion and marketing activities on a day-to-day basis? If not, how will that responsibility be shared? Who can make the decisions about spending money? Will the major label make commitments to spend at least a certain amount of money per year on marketing, promotion, tour support, etc.? Will the independent label's original owners have a clear contractual right to terminate the relationship if the major label does not meet its commitments?

There is no standard answer to any of these questions. The terms of equity deals are customized to fit the specific needs of the parties involved. Even so, these issues must be considered if the independent label is to make a wise decision.

Licensing Records to Major Labels

The independent label may license recordings of one or more of its artists to a major label, generally in exchange for a specified royalty. The independent label might license only certain existing records, or agree to license certain future records.

The royalty is usually 15% to 20% of the retail price of records sold. But from this 15% to 20%, the independent label must pay artist/producer royalties of usually 10% to 14%.

Independent labels are sometimes not interested in licensing only certain artists to a major label, particularly when it involves a major label's "cherry picking" of the independent label's best artists.

Rights Buyouts

Sometimes, when an artist's career is breaking faster than the independent label's financial and promotional capacities can handle, a major label and an independent label will enter into a separate one-artist agreement, whereby the independent label will assign to the major all of the independent's rights in the artist. In return, the major label will pay the independent a substantial "recoupable but nonrefundable" cash advance against future "override" royalties on some or all of the artist's future recordings.

The term "override royalties," in this context, means royalties paid by the major label directly to the independent label; these royalties are separate from the artist royalties paid by the major label to the recording artist. Typically the override royalty rate is from 1% to 3% (or more) of the retail price of records sold, and such royalties are customarily paid by the major label at the same intervals as artist royalties are paid (usually semi-annually).

Sometimes an independent label will have an artist who is the subject of a major label bidding war. In that situation, the independent label may have the bargaining power to demand that part of the cash payment from the major label will not be considered recoupable (deductible) from the future override royalties payable to the independent label.

Licensing of Records from Major Labels

Sometimes an independent label will license particular recordings from a major label. The recordings may be either new or previously-released recordings.

New Recordings

New artists are sometimes licensed to an independent label when that label has credibility and marketing strength in a specific genre of music and will help build a fan base for the artist. The major label will usually provide marketing and promotion funds to enable the independent label to effectively promote the artist's records. This type of deal resembles a joint venture in some respects, since the parties often agree to split the net profits after all costs have been paid.

They may agree that the major label will have the right to take back the artist once his/her records reach a certain sales level. When that happens, the independent label's financial participation may change—for example, from a share of profits to a royalty structure (which may be substantially less rewarding).

Previously Released Recordings

Licensing by a major label can also occur in connection with an independent label's reissue of records that are no longer available to the public.

In order to acquire reissue rights, the owner of the master recordings must be identified. Generally, it will be the label which had previously handled the product. However, in some situations, the ownership of the masters may have been sold, or the rights may have reverted to the artist. It is essential that before finalizing the contract and reissuing such recordings, the independent label clearly determines the ownership rights. In addition, it should be sure that the contract contains all appropriate ownership warranties, as well as a "hold harmless" clause.

CONCLUSION

An artist's relationship with his or her label may be substantially impacted by changes in record company personnel, a new affiliation between the artist's independent label and a major label, or the independent label's assignment of the artist's contract to another label (major or independent). Therefore, artists should address these possible changes in their contracts.

Artists can seek clauses prohibiting their independent label from assigning their recording contract to another label without prior written consent, to avoid the possibility that they could become associated with an unacceptable label.

A "key person" clause should be inserted that permits the artist to terminate the contract if certain personnel leave the label (the key personnel being those particular individuals whose presence has caused the artist to have confidence in the independent label).

If such clauses are obtained and the independent label later undertakes to establish a relationship with another label, it is important that the artist review the "nonassignment" and "key person" clauses in his or her contract, to be sure that they take all necessary and required procedural steps to preserve their rights under the recording contract.

Artists should also, if possible, avoid "leaving member" clauses which give labels the rights to the future recordings of group members that branch out with recordings of their own.

An artist who signs a contract with an independent label, which already has a relationship with a major label, should clearly understand how that relationship works and how responsibilities are allocated between the two labels. Artists should meet with various key personnel at the major label to determine whether the major label has a sincere commitment to promoting their records. By so doing, they can determine whether the proposed relationship will be a boost or a hindrance to their careers. This evaluation process is, of course, particularly relevant when an artist has contract offers from more than one label.

A clear understanding of the possible relationships between independent and major labels will help you to take the best advantage of any such opportunities that come your way.

RESOURCES, SERVICES AND BIBLIOGRAPHY

CONSUMER AND TRADE PUBLICATIONS

Alternative Press
6516 Detroit Avenue
Suite 5
Cleveland, OH 44102
(216) 631-1212

Axcess
4502 Cass Street
Suite 205
San Diego, CA 92019
(619) 270-2054

Bam
3470 Buskirk Avenue
Pleasant Hill, CA 94523
(510) 934-3700

Bass Player
411 Borel Avenue
Suite 100
San Mateo, CA 94402
(415) 358-9500

Billboard
1515 Broadway
39th Floor
New York, NY 10036
(212) 764-7300

Blues Revue
Route 2, Box 118
West Union, WV 26456
(304) 782-1971

Cash Box
6464 Sunset Boulevard
Suite 605
Hollywood, CA 90028
(213) 464-8241

CD Review
86 Elm Street
Peterborough, NH 03458
(603) 924-7271

Circus
6 West 18th Street
2nd Floor
New York, NY 10011
(212) 242-4902

Communications Week
CMP Publications Inc.
600 Community Drive
Manhasset, NY 11030
(516) 562-5000

Country America
1716 Locust Street
Des Moines, IA 50309
(515) 284-3000

Country Music Magazine
329 Riverside Avenue
Suite 1
Westport, CT 06880
(203) 221-4950

Daily Variety
5700 Wilshire Boulevard
Suite 120
Los Angeles, CA 90036
(213) 857-6600

Dirty Linen
PO Box 66600
Baltimore, MD 21239
(410) 583-7973

Down Beat
102 North Haven
Elmhurst, IL 60126
(708) 941-2030

Entertainment Law and Finance
345 Park Avenue South
8th Floor
New York, NY 10010
(800) 888-8300

Entertainment Law Reporter
2118 Wilshire Boulevard
Suite 311
Santa Monica, CA 90403
(310) 829-9335

The Entertainment and Sports Lawyer
American Bar Association
750 North Lake Shore Drive
Chicago, IL 60611
(312) 988-5000

EQ
939 Port Washington Boulevard
Port Washington, NY 11050
(516) 944-5940

Folk Alliance Newsletter
PO Box 5010
Chapel Hill, NC 27514
(919) 542-3997

Guitar Player
411 Borel Avenue
Suite 100
San Mateo, CA 94402
(415) 358-9500

Hollywood Reporter
5055 Wilshire Boulevard
6th Floor
Los Angeles, CA 90036
(213) 525-2000

Interactivity
411 Borel Avenue
Suite 100
San Mateo, CA 94402
(415) 358-9500

Internet Business Report
Jupiter Communications
627 Broadway
2nd Floor
New York, NY 10012
(800) 488-4345 or
(212) 780-6060

Internet World
Mecklermedia Corporation
20 Ketchum Street
Westport, CT 06880
(203) 226-6967

Jazziz
3620 NW 43rd Street
Suite D
Gainesville, FL 32606
(904) 375-3705

JazzTimes
7961 Eastern Avenue
Suite 303
Silver Springs, MD 20910
(301) 588-4114

Keyboard
411 Borel Avenue
Suite 100
San Mateo, CA 94402
(415) 358-9500

Melody Maker
26th Floor
King's Reach Tower
Stamford Street
London SE1 9LS
England

Mix Magazine
6400 Hollis Street
Suite 12
Emeryville, CA 94608
(510) 653-3307

Modern Drummer
12 Old Bridge Road
Cedar Grove, NJ 07009
(201) 239-4140

Music Connection
6640 Sunset Boulevard
Suite 201
Los Angeles, CA 90028
(213) 462-5772

Musician
1515 Broadway
11th Floor
New York, NY 10036
(212) 536-5208

New Music Express
25th Floor
King's Reach Tower
Stamford Street
London SE1 9LS
England

Offbeat
333 St. Charles Avenue
Suite 614
New Orleans, LA 70130
(504) 522-5533

P.A.I.N. Independent Music
18758-6 Bryant Street
Northridge, CA 91324
(818) 772-6589

Performance
1101 University
Suite 108
Fort Worth, TX 76107
(817) 338-9444

Pollstar
4333 North West Avenue
Fresno, CA 93705
(800) 344-7383

Pulse!
2500 Del Monte Street
West Sacramento, CA 95691
(916) 373-2450

Radio and Records
10100 Santa Monica Boulevard
5th Floor
Los Angeles, CA 90067
(310) 553-4330

Recording
7318 Topanga Canyon
Boulevard
Suite 200
Canoga Park, CA 91303
(818) 346-3404

Rolling Stone
1290 Avenue of the Americas
2nd Floor
New York, NY 10104
(212) 484-1616

Sing Out!
PO Box 5253
Bethlehem, PA 18015
(610) 865-5366

Songtalk
6381 Hollywood Boulevard
Suite 780
Hollywood, CA 90028
(213) 463-7178

The Source
594 Broadway
Suite 510
New York, NY 10012
(212) 274-0464

Spin
6 West 18th Street
New York, NY 10011
(212) 633-8200

Street Sound
333 W. 52nd Street
New York, NY 10019
(212) 397-6203

URB Magazine
1680 Vine Street
Suite 1012
Hollywood, CA 90028
(213) 993-0291

Variety
5700 Wilshire Boulevard
Suite 120
Los Angeles, CA 90036
(213) 857-6600

Vibe
205 Lexington Avenue
3rd Floor
New York, NY 10016
(212) 522-7092

Victory Review
PO Box 7515
Bonney Lake, WA 98390
(206) 863-6617

DIRECTORIES AND REFERENCE MATERIALS

The Album Network's Yellow Pages of Rock
The Album Network, Inc.
120 North Victory Boulevard
3rd Floor
Burbank, CA 91502
(800) 222-4382

Billboard Directories
PO Box 2015
Lakewood, NJ 08701
(800) 223-7524 or
(212) 536-5174

International Talent and Touring Directory

International Buyer's Guide

Record Retailing Directory

International Tape/Disc Directory

Nashville 615/Country Music Sourcebook

International Recording Equipment & Studio Directory

Fall Edition—The Power Book Directory of Music Radio & Record Promotion

International Latin Music Buyer's Guide

Performance Guide Series
1101 University
Suite 108
Fort Worth, TX 76107
(817) 338-9444

Facilities

Talent/Personal Managers

Manufacturers/Production Personnel

Promoters/Clubs

Booking Agencies

The Black Book (An industry-wide phone and fax directory)

International Markets

Country Talent/Variety

Concert Production

Transportation/Accommodations

Phonolog
Attn: Editorial
10996 Torreyana Road
San Diego, CA 92121
(619) 457-5920

The Recording Industry Sourcebook
Cardinal Music
Entertainment Group
6400 Hollis Street
Suite 12
Emeryville, CA 94608
(510) 653-3307

LEGAL PUBLICATIONS
American Bar Association
750 North Lake Shore Drive
Chicago, IL 60611
(312) 988-5000
Call for a complete
publications list.

Entertainment And Sports Law Bibliography, 1992.

Researching The Right Of Publicity Bibliography, 1994.

Beverly Hills Bar Association
300 South Beverly Drive
Suite 201
Beverly Hills, CA 90212
(310) 553-6644
Call for a complete
publications list.

*That's Interactive! An Introduction
To Legal Issues In The Emerging
Area Of Interactive Media*

*It Happened Last Year—Annual
Update On Entertainment Law*

*The Big Picture—Negotiating
Motion Picture Development And
Production Agreements In The '90s*

California Lawyers for the Arts
Fort Mason Center
Building C, Room 255
San Francisco, CA 94123
(415) 775-7200
Call for a complete
publications list.

Seminar Handbooks
(Published in conjunction
with CLA seminars.)

Multimedia Seminar

Music Business Seminar

Nashville Songwriters
Association International
15 Music Square West
Nashville, TN 37203

*The Essential Songwriter's
Contract Handbook*

Practising Law Institute
810 Seventh Avenue
New York, NY 10019
(800) 260-4754 or
(212) 824-5700
Call for a complete
publications list.

*Counseling Clients In The Enter-
tainment Industry 1995: Sound
Recordings; Music Publishing;
Ethics And Entertainment Law
Practice; Film*

GUILDS, ORGANIZA-
TIONS AND TRADE
ASSOCIATIONS

Academy of Country Music
6255 Sunset Boulevard
Suite 923
Hollywood, CA 90028
(213) 462-2351

American Federation of
Musicians (AFM)

AFM–New York
1501 Broadway
Suite 600
New York, NY 10036
(212) 869-1330

AFM–Hollywood
1777 Vine Street
Suite 500
Hollywood, CA 90028
(213) 461-3441

AFM–Local 47
817 Vine Street
Hollywood, CA 90028
(213) 462-2161

American Federation of
Television and Radio Artists
(AFTRA)

AFTRA–New York
260 Madison Avenue
New York, NY 10016
(212) 532-0800

AFTRA–Hollywood
6922 Hollywood Boulevard
8th Floor
Hollywood, CA 90028
(213) 461-8111

American Guild of Musical
Artists
1727 Broadway
New York, NY 10019
(212) 265-3687

American Society of
Composers, Authors, and
Publishers (ASCAP)

ASCAP–New York
One Lincoln Plaza
New York, NY 10023
(212) 595-3050

ASCAP–Los Angeles
7920 Sunset Boulevard
Suite 300
Los Angeles, CA 90028
(213) 883-1000

ASCAP–Nashville
2 Music Square West
Nashville, TN 37203
(615) 742-5000

Association of Independent
Music Publishers
PO Box 1561
Burbank, CA 91507
(818) 842-6257

Beverly Hills Bar Association
300 South Beverly Drive
Suite 201
Beverly Hills, CA 90212
(310) 553-6644

Broadcast Music Incorporated
(BMI)

BMI–New York
320 West 57th Street
New York, NY 10019
(212) 586-2000

BMI–Los Angeles
8730 Sunset Boulevard
3rd Floor West
Hollywood, CA 90069
(310) 659-9109

BMI–Nashville
10 Music Square East
Nashville, TN 37203
(615) 401-2000

California Lawyers for the Arts
(CLA)

CLA–Southern California
1549 11th Street
Suite 200
Santa Monica, CA 90401
(310) 395-8893

CLA–Northern California
Fort Mason Center
Building C, Room 255
San Francisco, CA 94123
(415) 775-7200

Copyright Arbitration Royalty
Panel (CARP)
PO Box 70977
Southwest Station
Washington, DC 20024
(202) 707-8380

Copyright Data Management
405 Riverside Drive
Burbank, CA 91506
(818) 558-3480

Country Music Association
(CMA)
1 Music Circle South
Nashville, TN 37203
(615) 244-2840

Country Music Society
of America
One Country Music Road
PO Box 2000
Marion, OH 43306
(800) 669-1002

Electronic Industries
Association (EIA)
2500 Wilson Boulevard
Arlington, VA 22201
(703) 907-7500

Gospel Music Association
1205 Division Street
Nashville, TN 37203
(615) 242-0303

The Harry Fox Agency
711 Third Avenue
8th Floor
New York, NY 10017
(212) 370-5330

Los Angeles Songwriter's
Showcase (LASS)
PO Box 93759
Hollywood, CA 90093
(213) 467-7823

Los Angeles Women In Music
PO Box 1817
Burbank, CA 91507
(213) 243-6440

Mix Bookshelf
Information Resources for
Music Professionals
c/o Whitehurst and Clark
Raritan Industrial Park
100 Newfield Avenue
Edison, NJ 08837
(908) 417-9575 or
(800) 233-9604

Music and Entertainment
Industry Educators Association
(MEIEA)
Dr. Scott Fredrickson,
President
College of Fine Arts
University of Massachusetts
Lowell
Lowell, MA 01854
(508) 934-3882

Musician's Contact Service
PO Box 788
Woodland Hills, CA 91365
(818) 374-8888

Musician's Referral Service
1655 McCadden Place
Hollywood, CA 90028
(213) 462-1384

National Academy of
Recording Arts and Sciences
(NARAS)

NARAS–Atlanta
999 Peachtree Street NE
Suite 110
Atlanta, GA 30309
(404) 249-8881

NARAS–Austin
747 Bee Cave Road
Suite 209
Austin, TX 78746
(512) 328-7997

NARAS–Chicago
410 Michigan Avenue
Suite 921
Chicago, IL 60605
(312) 786-1121, Ext. 1125

NARAS–Los Angeles
3402 Pico Boulevard
Santa Monica, CA 90405
(310) 392-3777

NARAS–Memphis
168 Beale Street
2nd Floor
Memphis, TN 38103
(615) 525-1340

NARAS–Nashville
1017 16th Avenue South
Nashville, TN 37212
(615) 327-8030

NARAS–New York
157 West 57th Street
Suite 902
New York, NY 10019
(212) 245-5440

NARAS–Philadelphia
250 South Broad Street
Suite 609
Philadelphia, PA 19102
(215) 731-9515

NARAS–San Francisco
1702 Union Street
San Francisco, CA 94123
(415) 749-0779

National Academy of
Songwriters (NAS)
6381 Hollywood Boulevard
Suite 780
Hollywood, CA 90028
(213) 463-7178

National Association of
Independent Record
Distributors and Manufacturers
(NAIRD)
PO Box 988
Whitesburg, KY 41858
(606) 633-0946

National Association of Record
Merchandisers (NARM)
9 Eaves Drive
Suite 120
Marlton, NJ 08053
(609) 596-2221

National Music Publishers
Association
711 Third Avenue
8th Floor
New York, NY 10017
(212) 370-5330

Recording Industry Association
of America, Inc. (RIAA)
1020 19th Street NW
Suite 200
Washington, DC 20036
(202) 775-0101

Screen Actors Guild (SAG)

SAG–New York
1515 Broadway
44th Floor
New York, NY 10036
(212) 944-1030

SAG–Los Angeles
5757 Wilshire Boulevard
Los Angeles, CA 90036
(213) 954-1600

SESAC

SESAC, Inc.–New York
421 West 54th Street
4th Floor
New York, NY 10019
(212) 586-3450

SESAC Inc.–Nashville
55 Music Square East
Nashville, TN 37203
(615) 320-0055

Society of Composers, Authors
and Music Publishers of Canada
(SOCAN)
41 Valley Brook Drive
Don Mills, Ontario M3B 2S6
Canada
(416) 445-8700

The Songwriter's Guild of
America (SGA)

SGA–East
1500 Harbor Boulevard
Weehawkan, NJ 07087
(201) 867-7603

SGA–West
6430 Sunset Boulevard
Los Angeles, CA 90028
(213) 462-1108

Trademark Register of the
United States
National Press Building
Suite 1297
Washington, DC 20045
(800) 888-8062

United States Copyright Office
Library Of Congress
Washington, DC 20559
(202) 707-3000
(202) 707-9100 (To order
forms, if you know the specific
form you want.)

INTERNET RESOURCES
Business & Marketing On The Net
(Information and resources to help bring you up to speed on commercial use of the net.)

Cyberpreneurs Guide to the Internet
http://asa.ugl.lib.umich.edu/ chdocs/cyberpreneur/ Cyber.html

The Internet Business Center
http://www.tig.com/IBC/ index.html

Techniques for Internet Acceptable Marketing & Advertising
http://arganet.tenagra.com/net -acceptable.html

General Internet Information
General Net Information and Terms Explained
http://www.nww.com/netref/ technobabble.html

How Big Is the Internet and Who Uses It?
http://arganet.tenagra.com/how big.html

Indie Record Labels
Curve of the Earth
http://www.mw3.com/curve/

Higher Octave
http://www.smartworld.com/ hioctave/

Mammoth Records
http://www.nando.net/ mammoth/mammoth.html

Q-Records
http://www.shore.net/~qdiv/ qrec.htm

Rykodisc
http://www.shore.net/ ~rykodisc

Major Record Labels
MCA
http://www.mca.com

Polygram
http://polygram.com

SONY
http://www.music.sony.com

Warner Bros. Records
http://www.iuma.com/warner/

Music Web Sites Sampler
One of the most comprehensive lists of music-related Internet sites can be found at http://www.music.indiana.edu/ misc.music_resources.html

Musician Sites
IUMA (Internet Underground Music Archive)
303 Potrero, #7A
Santa Cruz CA 95060
(408) 426-IUMA.
http://www.iuma.com
E-mail: info@iuma.com

Kaleidospace
PO Box 341556
Los Angeles CA 90034
(310) 399-4349
http://kspace.com
E-mail: pete@kspace.com

The Music House
(Millennium Productions)
41 Second Street
Suite 333
Cambridge MA 02142
(617) 577-8585
http://www.arts-online.com
E-mail: music@arts-online.com

Sonicnet
67 Vestry Street
New York NY 10013
(212) 941-5912
http://www.sonicnet.com
E-mail: info@sonicnet.com

National Internet Access Providers
Holonet
(510) 704-0160

Internet Express
(800) 592-1240

Netcom
(800) 501-8649
E-mail: info@netcom.com

Performance Systems International (PSI)
(800) 827-7482

Other Music Sites
Harmony Central
http://harmony- central.mit.edu/

Newbury Comics Interactive
http://www.newbury.com

On-Site Entertainment
http://www.ose.com/ose

Tower Records
http://www.singnet.com.sg/ ~skyeo/tower.html

Virtual Radio
http://www.microserve.net/ vradio/vr.html

Web Wide World of Music
http://american.recordings. com/wwwofmusic/

Performing Rights Societies
ASCAP—
http://www.ascap.com

BMI—http://bmi.com

SESAC—http://online.music- city.com/sesac.html

SELECTED BIBLIOGRAPHY

Alexander, Peter L. *How To Be Successful In Music Without Overpaying Your Dues.* Newbury Park, California: Alexander Publishing, 1987.

Anderton, Craig. *MIDI for Musicians.* New York: Music Sales Corp., 1987.

Ashburne, Michael, Esq. *Sampling In The Record Industry.* Oakland, California: Law Offices of Michael Ashburne, 1994.

Bagehot, Richard. *Music Business Agreements.* New York: Pergamon Press, 1989.

Baker, Bob. *One-hundred One Ways To Make Money Right Now In The Music Business.* San Diego, California: Rockpress Publishing Co., 1993.

Bartlett, Bruce. *Practical Recording Techniques.* Indianapolis, Indiana: Howard W. Sams and Co., 1992.

Baskerville, David, Ph.D. *Music Business Handbook And Career Guide,* (6th Ed.). Thousand Oaks, California: Sage Publications, Inc., 1995.

Biederman, Donald, and Berry, Pierson, Silfer and Glasser. *Law and Business Of The Entertainment Industries,* (2nd Ed.). Westport, Connecticut: Praeger Publishers, 1991.

Bjorneberg, Paul, Ed. *Exploring Careers In Music.* Reston, Virginia: Music Educators National Conference, 1990.

Blake, Andrew. *The Music Business.* North Pomfret, Vermont: Trafalgar Square, 1993.

Brabec, Jeffrey and Brabec, Todd. *Music, Money and Success: The Insider's Guide To The Music Industry.* New York: Schirmer Books, 1994.

Braheny, John. *The Craft And Business Of Songwriting.* Cincinnati, Ohio: Writer's Digest Books, 1995.

Buttwinick, Marty. *How To Make A Living As A Musician: So You Never Have To Have A Day Job Again!* Glendale, California: Sonata Publishing, 1994.

Carter, Walter. *The Songwriter's Guide To Collaboration.* Cincinnati, Ohio: Writer's Digest Books, 1988.

Chapple, Steve and Garofalo, Reebee. *Rock 'N' Roll Is Here To Pay (The History And Politics Of The Music Industry).* Chicago: Nelson-Hall, 1978.

Chickering, Robert B., and Hartman, Susan. *How To Register A Copyright And Protect Your Creative Work.* New York: Charles Scribner's Sons, 1987.

Citron, Stephen. *Songwriting: A Complete Guide To The Craft.* New York: Limelight Editions, 1990.

Clevo, Jim. *Networking In The Music Industry: Making The Contacts You Need To Succeed In The Music Business.* San Diego, California: Rockpress Publishing Co., 1993.

Dannen, Fredric. *Hit Men: Power Brokers & Fast Money Inside The Music Business.* New York: Vintage Books, 1991.

Davis, Sheila. *The Craft Of Lyric Writing.* Cincinnati, Ohio: Writer's Digest Books, 1985.

Davis, Sheila. *Songwriter's Idea Book.* Cincinnati, Ohio: Writer's Digest Books, 1992.

Davis, Sheila. *Successful Lyric Writing.* Cincinnati, Ohio: Writer's Digest Books, 1988.

Dearing, James. *Making Money Making Music,* (Rev. Ed.). Cincinnati, Ohio: Writer's Digest Books, 1990.

Dorf, Michael and Appel, Robert. *Gigging: The Musician's Underground Touring Directory.* Cincinnati, Ohio: Writer's Digest Books, 1989.

Drews, Mark. *New Ears: The Audio Career & Education Handbook,* (2nd Rev. Ed.). Syracuse, New York: New Ears Productions, 1993.

Erickson, J. Gunnar, Hearn, Edward R. and Halloran, Mark. *Musician's Guide To Copyright.* New York: Charles Scribner's Sons, 1983.

Faulkner, Robert R. *Music On Demand: Composers And Careers In The Hollywood Film Industry.* New Brunswick, New Jersey: Transaction Publications, 1982.

Fink, Michael. *Inside the Music Business: Music In Contemporary Life.* New York: Schirmer Books, 1989.

Frascogna, Xavier M. and Hetherington, H. Lee. *Successful Artist Management.* New York: Billboard Books/Watson-Guptill Publications, 1990.

Garvey, Mark, Ed. by Cindy Laufenberg. *Songwriter's Market.* Cincinnati, Ohio: Writer's Digest Books, updated annually.

Gibson, James. *Playing For Pay: How To Be A Working Musician*. Cincinnati, Ohio: Writer's Digest Books, 1990.

Goldfield, Paul, Ed. by Peter L. Alexander. *Recording, Syncing And Synths*. Newbury Park, California: Alexander Publishing, 1988.

Hall, Tom T. *The Songwriter's Handbook,* (Rev. Ed.). Nashville, Tennessee: Rutledge Hill Press, 1987.

Huber, David Miles and Runstein, Robert E., Ed. *Modern Recording Techniques,* (4th Ed.). Indianapolis, Indiana: Sams Publishing, 1995.

Hustwit, Gary. *Releasing An Independent Record,* (5th Ed.). San Diego, California: Rockpress Publishing Co., 1995.

Hustwit, Gary. *Getting Radio Airplay,* (2nd Ed.). San Diego, California: Rockpress Publishing Co., 1993.

Janal, Daniel S. *The Online Marketing Handbook*. NewYork: Van Nostrand Reinhold, 1995.

Kimpel, Dan. *Networking In The Music Business*. Cincinnati, Ohio: Writer's Digest Books, 1993.

Kohn, Al and Kohn, Bob. *The Art Of Music Licensing*. Englewood Cliffs, New Jersey: Prentice-Hall Law & Business, 1992.

Krasilovsky, William M. and Shemel, Sidney. *This Business Of Music,* (7th Ed.). New York: Billboard Books/Watson-Guptill Publications, 1995.

Krasilovsky, William M. and Shemel, Sidney. *More About This Business Of Music* (5th Ed.). New York: Billboard Books/Watson-Guptill Publications, 1995.

Liggett, Mark and Liggett, Cathy. *The Complete Handbook Of Songwriting: An Insider's Guide To Making It In The Music Industry,* (2nd Ed.). New York: NAL/Dutton, 1993.

Linderman, Hank. *Hot Tips For The Home Recording Studio*. Cincinnati, Ohio: Writer's Digest Books, 1994.

Luboff, Pat and Luboff, Pete. *88 Songwriting Wrongs & How To Right Them*. Cincinnati, Ohio: Writer's Digest Books, 1992.

Mandell, Jim. *The Studio Business Book*. Emeryville, California: Cardinal Business Media, 1994.

Martin, George, ed. *Making Music: The Guide To Writing, Performing And Recording*. New York: W.M. Morrow & Co., 1983.

Muench, Teri, and Pomerantz, Susan. *ATTN: A&R: A Step-By-Step Guide Into The Recording Industry*. Los Angeles: Alfred Publishing, 1988.

Murray, Lyn. *Musician: Hollywood Journal Of Wives, Women, Writers, Lawyers, Directors, Producers And Music*. Secaucus, New Jersey: L. Stuart, 1987.

Newquist, Harvey. *Music And Technology*. New York: Billboard Books/Watson-Guptill Publications, 1989.

Newsam, Barbara and Newsam, David. *Making Money Teaching Music*. Cincinnati, Ohio: Writer's Digest Books, 1995.

Nimmer, Melville B. and Nimmer, David. *Nimmer On Copyright*. New York: Matthew Bender & Co., 1992.

Oland, Pamela P. *You Can Write Great Lyrics*. Cincinnati, Ohio: Writer's Digest Books, 1989.

Passman, Donald. *All You Need To Know About The Music Business,* (2nd Ed.). New York: Simon & Schuster Trade, 1994.

Pettigrew, James, Jr. *The Billboard Guide to Music Publicity*. New York: Billboard Books/Watson-Guptill Publications, 1989.

Pincus, Lee. *The Songwriter's Success Manual,* (2nd Ed.). New York: Music Press, 1978.

Pinskey, Raleigh. *You Can Hype Anything: Creative Tactics & Advice For Anyone With A Product, Business Or Talent To Promote*. New York: Carol Publishing Group, 1995.

Pinskey, Raleigh. *The Zen Of Hype: An Insider's Guide To The Publicity Game*. New York: Carol Publishing Group, 1991.

Poe, Randy. *Music Publishing: A Songwriter's Guide*. Cincinnati, Ohio: Writer's Digest Books, 1990.

Pohlmann, Ken. *Advanced Digital Audio*. New York: McGraw-Hill, 1991.

Pohlmann, Ken. *Principles of Digital Audio,* (3rd Ed.). New York: McGraw-Hill, 1995.

Rachlin, Harvey, Ed. *The Songwriter's Workshop*. Cincinnati, Ohio: Writer's Digest Books, 1991.

Rapaport, Diane Sward. *How To Make & Sell Your Own Recording: A Guide For The Nineties,* (Rev. 4th Ed.). Upper Saddle River, New Jersey: Prentice-Hall, Inc., 1992.

Resnick, Rosalind and Taylor, Dave. *The Internet Business Guide,* (2nd Ed.). Indianapolis, Indiana: Sams Publishing, 1995.

Rudolph, Thomas E. *Music And The Apple II: Applications For Music Education, Composition And Performance*. Philadelphia, Pennsylvania: Unsinn Publications, 1984.

Schreiber, Norman. *The Ultimate Guide To Independent Record Labels And Artists*. New York: Pharos Books, 1992.

Shoemaker, Joanie, Ed. *Note By Note: A Guide To Concert Production,* Oakland, California: Redwood Cultural Work, 1989.

Siegel, Alan H. *Breakin' Into The Music Business*. Rochester, New York: Cherrylane Books, 1993.

Siegel, Howard, Esq., Ed.-In-Chief. *Entertainment Law*. Albany, New York: New York State Bar Association, 1990.

Stone, Al. *Jingles: How To Write, Produce & Sell Commercial Music*. Cincinnati, Ohio: Writer's Digest Books, 1990.

Strangelove, Michael. *How To Advertise On The Internet*. Strangelove Press, 1994.

Strong, William S. *The Copyright Book: A Practical Guide,* (4th Ed.). Cambridge, Massachusetts: MIT Press, 1992.

Strong, William S. *The Copyright Book: Supplemental Copy,* (4th Ed.). Cambridge, Massachusetts: MIT Press, 1993.

Taylor, Barbara. *National Directory Of Record Labels & Music Publishers*. Atlanta, Georgia: Rising Star Music Pubs., 1993.

Wadhams, Wayne. *Sound Advice: The Musician's Guide To The Record Industry*. New York: Schirmer Books, 1990.

Wadhams, Wayne. *Sound Advice: The Musician's Guide To The Recording Studio*. New York: Schirmer Books, 1990.

Warner, Jay. *How To Have Your Hit Song Published,* (Rev. Ed.). Milwaukee, Wisconsin: Hal Leonard Publishing Corp., 1988.

Weissman, Dick. *Creating Melodies*. Cincinnati, Ohio: Writer's Digest Books, 1994.

Weissman, Dick. *Making A Living In Your Local Music Market: How To Survive And Prosper*. Milwaukee, Wisconsin: Hal Leonard Publishing Corporation, 1989.

Weissman, Dick. *Music Business*. New York: Crown Publishers, 1990.

Whitburn, Joel. *Music And Video Yearbook*. Menomonee Falls, Wisconsin: Record Research, Inc., updated annually.

Williams, George J. III., Ed. by Bill Dalton. *The Songwriter's Demo Manual and Success Guide,* (2nd Rev. Ed.). Dayton, Nevada: Tree by the River Publishing/Music Business Books, 1994.

Woram, John. *Sound Recording Handbook*. Indiana: Howard W. Sams and Co., 1989.

Woram, John and Kefauver, Alan P. *The New Recording Studio Handbook,* (Rev. Ed.). Commack, New York: Elar Publishing Co. Inc., 1989.

Yudkin, Marcia. *Marketing Online*. New York: Penguin, 1995.

Zollo, Paul. *Beginning Songwriter's Answer Book,* (Rev. Ed.). Cincinnati, Ohio: Writer's Digest Books, 1993.

CONTRIBUTORS

STEPHEN BIGGER, a graduate of Yale Law School, is a partner in the New York law firm of Weiss, Dawid, Fross, Zelnick & Lehrman. He authors the "International Notes" column in *The Trademark Reporter,* the official publication of the International Trademark Association.

LAWRENCE J. BLAKE is a 1976 graduate of Harvard Law School. He now practices law as a partner with the Los Angeles firm of Manatt, Phelps & Phillips, which has one of the largest music practices in the United States. They represent a broad and diverse clientele of established and emerging artists, major record labels and independents, songwriters and music publishers, record distribution companies and merchandising companies. Mr. Blake represents clients in connection with all of their activities in the music business. His practice consists of structuring, negotiating, drafting, and reviewing the entire gamut of contracts pertaining to the music industry and related areas, such as merchandising. He advises clients with respect to related intellectual property matters, such as copyright, trademark, and rights of publicity, and entertainment related litigation matters. Mr. Blake has written various articles pertaining to the music business and has testified as an expert witness in connection with music industry matters. He has also taught a course for industry professionals and aspiring industry professionals at the UCLA Extension entitled "Understanding Contracts in the Music Industry."

JOHN BRAHENY is cofounder/director of the Los Angeles Songwriters Showcase (LASS), a national nonprofit service organization founded in 1971, executive vice president of Wynnward Music Enterprises, a music publishing/production company and past president of the California Copyright Conference. He is the author of *The Craft and Business of Songwriting* (revised second edition, Writers Digest Books, 1995) and has produced the annual Songwriters' Expo since 1976. He has worked as a musician, folksinger, recording artist, commercial jingle writer/producer, and film music composer. He publishes the *Songwriters Musepaper,* a monthly magazine with a circulation of 20,000.

ROBERT M. DUDNIK is a partner in the law firm of Paul, Hastings, Janofsky & Walker, which has offices throughout the United States and in Tokyo. Mr. Dudnik, whose office is in Santa Monica, cochairs the firm's Entertainment Practice Group, which functions on a nationwide basis and handles both litigation and transactional matters covering all aspects of the entertainment and related industries. This includes theatrical motion pictures, television, recorded music and broadcasting. Their litigation practice deals with intellectual property and business related disputes of all types, and handles matters in various state and federal courts, as well as a broad range of arbitrations. Mr. Dudnik is a graduate of Cornell University and the Yale Law School, where he was a member of the Order of the Coif and graduated cum laude.

Mr. Dudnik practiced and taught law in Cleveland, Ohio from 1964 to 1969. Since moving to Los Angeles in 1969, his practice has been primarily related to the handling of entertainment litigation matters and providing prelitigation counseling to clients in all areas of the entertainment industry.

STEVEN GARDNER is a partner in the Century City (Los Angeles), California law firm of Cohon and Gardner, P.C., where he practices entertainment law and litigation. He is a founding member of the Committee for the Arts, a past president of the Committee for the Arts, Beverly Hills Bar Association Barristers and Beverly Hills Bar Association Foundation, and a former member of the Beverly Hills Bar Association board of governors.

TODD E. GELFAND, CPA is a partner of the international business management firm of Gelfand, Rennert & Feldman (a division of Coopers & Lybrand), one of the largest and renown of firms specializing in this area. He is a graduate of the University of California at Berkeley.

BRAD GELFOND began his career at Regency Artists, a small specialized agency. He moved with the company when it merged with a literary agency and a motion picture and television talent agency to become Triad Artists. Triad, a full service agency, ultimately merged with the William Morris Agency after eight years and Mr. Gelfond became Vice President and West Coast Head of the Contemporary Music Department. He retired from his career as an agent in December, 1994.

Some of the artists Mr. Gelfond represented during his career are Lou Reed, Paul Simon, David Byrne, Bjork, Laurie Anderson, Kate Bush, Paul Westerberg, Rickie Lee Jones, Nanci Griffith, The Pet Shop Boys, Johnny Clegg, Dead Can Dance, Electronic, New Order, Cyndi Lauper, The Posies, Kirsty MacColl, Love & Rockets, The Cocteau Twins, Alison Moyet, The Ocean Blue, Lush, Ian McCulloch, Jellyfish, Eddi Reader, Heidi Berry, Charles & Eddie, Deborah Harry, X, The Sugarcubes, Mike Oldfield, Southside Johnny, Ofra Haza, and Ladysmith Black Mambazo.

RONALD H. GERTZ is president of Copyright Data Management, a management and consulting organization that represents songwriters, composers and other creators and owners of intellectual property rights. CDM helps its clients to maximize collection of royalties and fully exploit licensing opportunities throughout the world. CDM offers a number of services to songwriters and music publishers including direct representation and collection of performing rights royalties in foreign territories.

Mr. Gertz is also president and CEO of Media Reports, Inc. (MRI), a joint venture with the television broadcast industry. MRI provides the broadcast industry with statistical data regarding the amount, type and frequency of music that is broadcast on television and radio. He was trained as a classical vocalist and guitarist, and has performed professionally in many rock tours. He received his bachelor's degree in finance from California State University, Northridge, and his law degree from the University of San Fernando Valley College of Law. Mr. Gertz's legal practice began with the representation of clients in the television, publishing and recording fields. He eventually joined EMI Videograms, Inc. as general counsel, concentrating on the production and acquisition of home video product.

A frequent speaker at colleges, law schools and seminars throughout the country, Mr. Gertz has written articles for the *Los Angeles Daily Journal, Billboard Magazine,* the *Century City Bar Association Journal,* the *Beverly Hills Bar Association Journal, The Entertainment Law Journal, Entertainment Publishing and the Arts,* and *Soldier of Fortune.*

Currently, Mr. Gertz is on the board of directors of the Intellectual Property Section of the Los Angeles County Bar Association and the Academy of Interactive Arts and Sciences. He is a member of the Interactive Multimedia Association's Intellectual Property Task Force and is a past president of the California Copyright Conference.

MARK HALLORAN, a graduate of UCLA and Hastings College of Law, is one of the founding partners of Alexander, Halloran, Nau & Rose. Previously, he was vice president of Feature Business Affairs, at Universal Pictures. Prior to Universal, Mark was business affairs counsel at Orion Pictures where he negotiated deals for The Woman In Red soundtrack (Stevie Wonder), The Falcon and the Snowman (Pat Metheny/David Bowie) and Orion's overall music publishing deal with CBS Songs

(Sony Music). Mark specializes in entertainment financing, production, distribution deals and music law. He has coauthored two nationally distributed books about the music business, *Musician's Guide to Copyright,* and the current *The Musician's Business and Legal Guide,* and has written numerous articles on entertainment business and legal issues.

EDWARD (NED) R. HEARN is in private law practice. He has offices in San Jose, Menlo Park and San Francisco. Mr. Hearn's practice concentrates on entertainment and computer software businesses. His clients include record companies that are affiliated with major label branch distribution, independently distributed labels, recording artists that record for major record labels and independent record labels, music publishers, songwriters affiliated with major and independent music publishers, personal managers, producers, video production companies, and computer and multimedia software developers and publishers. He is director of the California Lawyers for the Arts, an organization that provides legal assistance to musicians and other artists, board president of the Northern California Songwriter's Association and coauthor of *The Musician's Guide to Copyright.* Mr Hearn also lectures on music business and legal issues.

NEVILLE L. JOHNSON is an attorney with Neville L. Johnson and Associates, in West Los Angeles. He is a Phi Beta Kappa graduate of UC Berkeley, where he was the music critic for *The Daily Californian.* He obtained his law degree from Southwestern University School of Law, graduating near the top of his class. Mr. Johnson has practiced as a music industry attorney since 1975, representing such clients as Yoko Ono Lennon and the estate of John Lennon, the Academy of Country Music, Parliament\Funkadelic, Bug Music, and numerous independent labels, publishers and managers. He has extensive litigation experience in music industry related matters and is a specialist at collecting unpaid royalties, in which regard he has represented the heirs of Gram Parsons and Kid Ory, Mitch Ryder and the Detroit Wheels, The Mothers of Invention and others. In 1995, Mr. Johnson won the first case in America (against ABC News) where substantial compensatory and punitive damages were awarded for invasion of privacy because of the utilization of a hidden camera on a news magazine show. He is the author of a definitive law review article on California law applicable to personal managers and talent agencies. For fun, he writes songs and plays pretty good guitar.

EVANNE L. LEVIN graduated with honors from UCLA and Loyola Law School in her native Los Angeles. Since 1974 she has specialized in the music and entertainment law fields. She currently maintains her own law practice in Sherman Oaks. Ms. Levin has been associated with the law firm of Mason & Sloane, where she represented clients such as Motley Crue, Olivia Newton-John, Kenny Rogers, and Sammy Hagar, and with Ervin, Cohen & Jessup as attorney to the California Jam II which attracted 300,000 concert-goers. Her in-house legal and business affairs experience includes MTM Productions, Zodiac Entertainment, Twentieth Century Fox, Orion Pictures, Paramount and ABC. Ms. Levin was a founding member and cochair of the Beverly Hills Bar Association Committee for the Arts, and has served on the board of directors of numerous industry organizations including the Hollywood Women's Coalition and Los Angeles Women in Music. She has taught courses in personal management, music publishing and television at institutions including UCLA and contributed articles to numerous music and entertainment publications. She is listed in *Who's Who in American Law* and *World Who's Who of Women.*

LINDA A. NEWMARK is vice president, Business Affairs for Polygram Music Publishing Group. Linda handles the negotiation and drafting of music publishing agreements, oversees acquisitions and promotes the general business development of the company. Prior to this position, Linda was director of International Acquisitions for Polygram and obtained opportunities for Polygram Music Publishing companies throughout the world to enter into subpublishing agreements, administration agreements and acquisition agreements for a variety of music publishing catalogues. Previously, Linda was a music attorney with the law firm of Cooper, Epstein & Hurewitz in Beverly Hills. Linda received her Bachelor of Arts degree in Communications Studies from UCLA and her Juris Doctorate degree from Stanford Law School.

PETER T. PATERNO, a 1976 graduate of UCLA Law School, formerly practiced law as a partner with Manatt, Phelps, Rothenberg, Tunney & Phillips in Los Angeles, specializing in music law. He was president of Hollywood Records until 1993 when he left to return to private practice. He is now with the firm of King, Purtich and Holmes.

JOHN R. "JACK" PHILLIPS is the partner-in-charge of royalty and participation examinations at the Los Angeles headquarters office of Gelfand, Rennert & Feldman (a division of Coopers & Lybrand L.L.P.). Jack received a BBA and MBA from Iona College and Graduate School in New York. Since 1979 he and his staff have performed royalty examinations in all of the major territories around the world.

DIANE SWARD RAPAPORT was an artist manager with Bill Graham Productions and a pioneer in the field of music business pedagogy. She is president of Jerome Headlands Press, Inc. a publishing and public relations firm in Northern Arizona. Ms. Rapaport is the author of *How To Make and Sell Your Own Recording,* a widely respected guide to independent recording.

MARGARET ROBLEY, E.A. is an associate in the international business management firm of Gelfand, Rennert & Feldman (a division of Coopers & Lybrand). Margaret has an MBA from Chapman College and an MST from California State University Northridge.

ALFRED SCHLESINGER has been a music business attorney for the past thirty years. Prior to becoming an attorney, he had his own record and music publishing companies. His entire practice is now, and has been, in the field of music, representing record companies, music publishing companies, recording artists, record producers, songwriters, personal managers, talent agents and disc jockeys.

In addition to his activities as an attorney, he was the personal manager of the recording and performing group Bread, from its inception in 1968 to its dissolution in 1978.

Alfred Schlesinger has written articles for the *Beverly Hills Bar Association Journal,* the National Academy of Songwriters (of which he is a founding member), the Association of International Entertainment Attorneys (of which he is a charter member) and various educational institutions throughout the United States. He has also taught courses on the music business and has been a guest lecturer and panelist for many educational institutions and music oriented organizations. He currently teaches a yearly intensive ten-day, eighty-hour music business course at Full Sail Center for the Recording Arts in Winter Park, Florida.

Mr. Schlesinger is a past president of the California Copyright Conference, a past president of the Los Angeles Chapter of the National Academy of Recording Arts and Sciences (NARAS) and past two-term national chairman of the board of said academy. He is also a past recipient of *Billboard Magazine's* award as Entertainment Attorney of the Year.

JAMES A. SEDIVY is an attorney practicing primarily in the fields of entertainment law, civil and business litigation and intellectual property. He is a past cochairman of the Committee for the Arts of the Beverly Hills Bar Association Barristers, as well as past president of the Beverly Hills Bar Association Barristers. He is a graduate of Syracuse University and Gonzaga University School of Law.

MADELEINE E. SELTZER, formerly a practicing attorney, is a partner in Seltzer Fontaine Beckwith, a legal search firm based in Los Angeles. She received her JD from the University of Southern California Law School in 1975. She is a volunteer mediator for Arts Arbitration and Mediation Services, a program of California Lawyers for the Arts and an advisory board member for Sojourn Services for Battered Women and Their Children.

PETER SPELLMAN is Career Development Coordinator at Berklee College of Music, Boston MA and director of The Music House, an online Internet service for musicians and music businesses at Millennium Productions, Cambridge MA. He is a frequent speaker on topics related to music career development, the music business and advanced technology resources for artists. Peter is also a member of the music group Friend Planet which collaborates with scientists and physicians on interdisciplinary multimedia projects. His latest project is writing the score for a video game designed for instructing chronically ill children on self-care. Peter has written for *Motif, Epiphany, The New Oxford Review, New England Performer, Berklee Today* and many other publications.

GREGORY T. VICTOROFF has been an entertainment litigation attorney since 1979, representing clients in the music, film and fine art businesses in Los Angeles. He is cochairman of the Committee for the Arts of the Beverly Hills Bar Association and is a frequent author and lecturer on copyright and art law. As an orchestral musician, he has backed such artists as Huey Lewis and the News, Santana and Bobby McFerrin.

THOMAS A. WHITE is a consultant in the record and music publishing industries. He is based in Beverly Hills, California and is the author of "The Crisis of A&R Competence and Record Industry Economics" and other analytical articles. Mr. White headed the Artist Development Department at CBS Records (Epic, Portrait and the CBS Associated Labels), West Coast, and was president of the European label CBO Records Inc., and president of Harmony Gold Music Inc.

INDEX

ABOUT JEROME HEADLANDS PRESS, INC.

Jerome Headlands Press, Inc., based in Jerome, Arizona, designs and produces business books for musicians, visual artists and professionals working in entertainment and the arts.

I feel strongly that artists should have access to business information and training to help them make a living and avoid costly mistakes. Until artists learn to treat their art as a business, they will sign bad contracts and be prey to people that will exploit their talents without fair compensation.
—Diane Rapaport, President and founder, Jerome Headlands Press, Inc.

How to Make and Sell Your Own Recording (revised fourth edition), by Diane Sward Rapaport, was published in the fall of 1992. The book has been a friend and guide to more than 125,000 musicians, producers, engineers and owners of small recording labels. It has helped revolutionize the recording industry by providing information about setting up new recording labels independent of major label networks.

This is the bible for musicians…anyone about to embark on a first release can profit from the information, even if they already have a major label contract.
—Jon Sievert, Guitar Player.

The Visual Artist's Business and Legal Guide (a presentation of the Beverly Hills Bar Association Committee for the Arts), compiled and edited by Gregory T. Victoroff, Esq., was published in the fall of 1994. Written by prominent art lawyers, professionals and business experts, this comprehensive resource can improve artists' chances for success by providing valuable legal and business information.

This book will tell you how to protect your work, your integrity, your character and your right to enjoy the returns of your own labor. The annotated analyses of actual legal agreements include such hard to control areas as public art and institutions that are notorious for avoiding legal agreements with artists. This work covers important issues for a variety of visual artists and gives artists' advocates a call to arms and provides educators, managers and artists with some important tools to help avoid getting ripped off.
—Joan Jeffri, Director, Research Center for Arts Culture, Columbia University and Coordinator, Program in Arts Administration, Teachers College, Columbia University.

Performing and Recording Unplugged, by Mike Sokol, scheduled for publication in 1996, will help acoustic musicians set up appropriate sound reinforcement systems at their performances and make high quality live recordings.

Jerome Headlands Press books are designed and produced by Julie Sullivan, Sullivan Scully Design Group, in Flagstaff, Arizona.

Jerome Headlands Press, Inc.
PO Box N
Jerome, Arizona 86331